c.1

D0507295

THE EXCEPTIONAL CHILD
INCLUSION IN EARLY CHILDHOOD EDUCATION
Third Edition

Delmar Publishers' Online Services
To access Delmar on the World Wide Web, point your browser to:
http://www.delmar.com/delmar.html
To access through Gopher: gopher://gopher.delmar.com
(Delmar Online is part of "thomson.com", and Internet site with information on
more than 30 publishers of the International Thomson Publishing organization.)
For more information on our products and services:
email: info@delmar.com
or call 800-347-7707

THE EXCEPTIONAL CHILD
INCLUSION IN EARLY CHILDHOOD EDUCATION

Third Edition

K. EILEEN ALLEN
and
ILENE S. SCHWARTZ

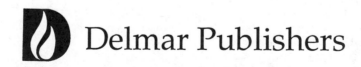

Delmar Publishers

I(T)P™ An International Thomson Publishing Company

Albany • Bonn • Boston • Cincinnati • Detroit • London • Madrid • Melbourne
Mexico City • New York • Pacific Grove • Paris • San Francisco • Singapore • Tokyo
Toronto • Washington

NOTICE TO THE READER

Cover design: Eva Ruutopôld

Delmar Staff

Sponsoring Editor: Jay Whitney
Associate Editor: Erin J. O'Connor

Publisher: Diane L. McOscar
Production Coordinator: James Zayicek
Art and Design Coordinator: Timothy J. Conners

COPYRIGHT © 1996
By Delmar Publishers
a division of International Thomson Publishing Inc.
The ITP logo is a Trademark under license
Printed in the United States of America

For more information, contact:

Delmar Publishers
3 Columbia Circle, Box 15015
Albany, New York 12212-5015

International Thomson Publishing Europe
Berkshire House 168 - 173
High Holborn
London WC1V7AA
England

Thomas Nelson Australia
102 Dodds Street
South Melbourne, 3205
Victoria, Australia

Nelson Canada
1120 Birchmount Road
Scarborough, Ontario
Canada M1K 5G4

International Thomson Editores
Campos Eliseos 385, Piso 7
Col Polanco
11560 Mexico D F Mexico

International Thomson Publishing GmbH
Königswinterer Strasse 418
53227 Bonn
Germany

International Thomson Publishing Asia
221 Henderson Road
#05 - 10 Henderson Building
Singapore 0315

International Thomson Publishing - Japan
Hirakawacho Kyowa Building, 3F
2-2-1 Hirakawacho
Chiyoda-ku, Tokyo 102
Japan

1 2 3 4 5 6 7 8 9 10 XXX 01 00 99 98 97 96 95
Library of Congress Cataloging-in-Publication Data

Allen, K. Eileen, 1918–
    The exceptional child : inclusion in early childhood education /
K. Eileen Allen and Ilene S. Schwartz. — 3rd ed.
        p.   cm.
    Includes bibliographical references (p.   ) and index.
    ISBN 0-8273-6698-1
    1. Handicapped children—Education (Preschool)—United States.
2. Early childhood education—United States.   3. Mainstreaming in
education—United States.   4. Handicapped children—United States—
Development.   5. Special education—United States.   I. Schwartz,
Ilene S.   I. Title.
LC4019.2.A43   1996
371.9'0472—dc20   95-19167

Contents

Preface

Revising a textbook in early childhood education and early intervention is an ongoing process. What defines best practice continues to change as we attempt to integrate traditionally sound developmental truths with what we learn from children and families and the current research literature. In this third edition, the most obvious change is in the title—the word *inclusion* replacing the word *mainstreaming*. A one-word change may seem a small thing, yet the implications are enormous in terms of the substance of this text. Inclusion, as we will see, goes far beyond mainstreaming as a concept. It means that children with special needs attend preschool, child care, and recreational programs with children who are developing typically. Inclusion, however, is not about a place, or a teaching strategy, or a curriculum. Inclusion is about belonging, being valued, having choices; about accepting and respecting human diversity; about providing the kind of support that allows all children and their families to participate in the programs of their choice. The foregoing statements are taken from the opening paragraph of the third edition of this early intervention textbook; they represent its philosophical essence.

The authorship of the third edition has been expanded to include a second author also named Ilene (but not spelled Eileen). Ilene Schwartz and Eileen Allen were first associated at the University of Kansas at Lawrence in the 1980s. Within a year or so of Allen's retirement and return to Seattle, Schwartz joined the early childhood special education faculty at the University of Washington. A part of her job is to direct the teacher training program and the laboratory preschools in the Experimental Education Unit—the very programs and classrooms that Allen had supervised for so many years before going to the University of Kansas. As will be seen in notes on the authors, Schwartz is also a major figure in the current inclusion movement and so makes a unique contribution to this third edition.

There also has been a major reorganization of the text. The new format introduces the inclusion of children with special needs immediately, in the opening section. The next section focuses on specific developmental disabilities and is followed by a section on family and community involvement. These two sections, formerly the last two in the earlier editions, now set the tone and provide context for the final section on implementing inclusive early childhood programs. Following is a brief sketch of the overall format:

Section One, Units 1, 2, and 3, explores the concept of inclusion in early education by first describing types of programs and program implementation. Then comes a review of the legislative and public policy activities that have moved us from segregation to inclusion in the early education of children with special needs. A focus feature by Vickie Louden, the mother of a young child with Down syndrome, concludes the section. Louden gives us firsthand insights into what inclusion means to her child and her family.

Section Two, Units 4 through 8, deals with likenesses and differences among children. As in the earlier editions, the jumping off point is normal growth and development. It cannot be overemphasized that genuine understanding of both atypical development and appropriate early education practices depends upon a thorough knowledge and frequent review of normal growth and development. The remainder of Section Two deals with causes and classifications of developmental disabilities and provides overviews of specific disabilities. The unit on behavior and learning disorders has been added to this section.

Section Three, Units 9 through 12, focuses on planning for inclusion. Partnership with families is the cornerstone of this section, with the material on families updated and expanded. Following the family unit are units that examine the early identification of developmental problems, the IEP process, and current information on program-to-program transitions by Susan Fowler and Robin Hazel. The concluding unit in this section concentrates on preparing teachers to teach in inclusive programs. Emphasis is on the overarching significance of their role: that to effectively support and encourage every child's development, teachers must be aware of the character and quality of their own responsiveness as they plan for and interact with each and every child. A special feature by Wendie Bramwell follows the teacher preparation unit. Bramwell deals with the often-avoided topic of death and dying and suggests ways that teachers of young children can deal with such issues when they arise in the classroom.

Section Four, Units 12 through 19, is the *how-to* section—how to arrange the learning environment through a developmental-behavioral approach; how to facilitate social development, speech and language skills, preacademic skills and cognitive development, and self-help and independence skills. As in the earlier editions, special attention is given to the management of behavior problems in that such problems are of universal concern in early childhood programs and occur among all young children, both the typically developing and those with special needs.

The final special feature, Unit 20, by Mary McEvoy and Christina Sheran offers a look ahead. These two authors, also foremost in inclusion research and policy making, discuss the directions that inclusion of children with special needs is likely to take.

In addition to these major changes, there are updated appendices on testing and screening instruments and on sources of information and support for teachers and families. There also is new material and expanded coverage of key issues throughout the text. Examples include updated and more extensive discussions of:

- developmentally appropriate practices (DAP) as related to inclusion and the needs of both special children and typically developing children.
- the tragic toll of increasing poverty among our nation's children and the factors that put infants and young children at ever greater risk for every type of developmental problem.

- cultural diversity, nontraditional families, and alternative family life styles with suggestions for establishing connections with these parents and their children.
- putting the focus on the child first, not the disability; what is now referred to as *people first* language.
- ADHD, its history and treatment with a discussion of rulings by the American Psychiatric Association related to diagnosis and intervention.
- autism as a medical or biological condition rather than a strictly behavioral manifestation.
- Fragile X syndrome as perhaps the leading cause of learning problems, especially among males.
- augmentative communication with emphasis on nonverbal and nonvocal systems and various signing systems.
- gifted and talented children with discussions related to *kinds* of giftedness as well as the early identification of gifted children among those with special needs.

This textbook, as it goes to press, represents the most current information on inclusive early childhood programs and the teaching of all young children—those who are developing typically as well as those with special needs. It must be remembered, though, that we are part of a lively and dynamic profession. Students and teachers, therefore, are urged to keep abreast of new information as it becomes available from the organizations and journals listed in Appendix C. Making inclusion work well is an ongoing endeavor that requires us to work with families, other professionals, and community members to create and support caring and safe environments for all children.

K. Eileen Allen
Professor Emeritus
University of Kansas

Ilene S. Schwartz
Assistant Professor
University of Washington

About the Authors

K. Eileen Allen—When one of my sons was not quite three-years-old, I enrolled the two of us in what was then a new and exciting adult education movement, the parent cooperative preschool. That son (who just turned 50!) eventually graduated from preschool; I never did. With no credentialing other than that of once-a-week participating parent, I somehow became the come-every-morning co-op "teacher." The very first thing I learned was how much I didn't know. I began taking a course, every quarter or so, close to home, at the University of Washington. Many courses and many years later, I found myself on the faculty there, teaching in the Developmental Psychology Laboratory Preschool and publishing research about early learning and the adult–child relationship.

Extensive work with children with developmental disabilities began when I accepted a position as coordinator of the early childhood research and education program in the University's new Child Development and Mental Retardation Center. What followed were several years of ongoing inter-disciplinary team involvement; working with parents as participating partners in their children's learning; and a revamping of teacher-training strategies to enable student teachers to work effectively with both normal and atypical children. Our integrated classrooms, it might be noted, became nationwide demonstration models, even though mainstreaming was not yet popular or mandated and inclusion was yet to be introduced as an educational concept.

When invited to join the faculty of the Department of Human Development at the University of Kansas in Lawrence, I hesitated only briefly—Kansas might be new, but I would still be in preschool! There, for more than a dozen years, I continued to teach, conduct widely disseminated research related to children, parents, and teachers, and to write articles and early childhood college textbooks.

Upon retiring from the University of Kansas my husband and I returned to our home in Seattle. And now it is nine years later and I'm still in preschool, at least vicariously. I continue to interact with (and advocate for) children and teachers and parents, to write, to consult, and to work on a variety of professional projects in both the private and public sectors. One of my most exciting jobs to date has been consulting at Microsoft on developmentally sound computer programs for children, ages two to six.

But my days are not all work and no play. I take time to travel, garden, write for fun (the kinds of things I never had time for before) and to walk my lovely remote beach, hour upon treasured hour.

Ilene Schwartz—My first experience with inclusive early childhood education came when I was working at a school for children with autism and we shared an elementary school building with other community groups, including the local Head Start program. After sharing some recesses and doing some preliminary planning, the Head Start teacher and I worked together to include a four-year-old boy with autism in the Head Start classroom. It was a wonderful experience for everyone involved. The young child with autism made some new friends and learned how to participate in a group of his peers; the other children in the class learned about supporting a friend who may look and behave a little differently; the Head Start teacher and I learned that children can teach each other lessons that adults are unable to teach and that these lessons about play, friendship, and caring are some of the most important lessons learned during early childhood.

Shortly after this experience I decided to return to graduate school to study child development and developmental psychology. I first met Eileen Allen at the University of Kansas where I was attending graduate school. We became reacquainted when I moved to Seattle, after completing my Ph.D., to join the faculty of the University of Washington in the area of early childhood special education. At the University of

Washington I am the faculty advisor for integrated early childhood programs at the Experimental Education Unit serving children from birth to age six. I am also involved in research that evaluates the effects of preschool inclusion and looks at what components of existing systems facilitate or act as barriers to the full inclusion of preschool children with disabilities. I am also very involved in preparing personnel, at both the preservice and the inservice levels, to teach in inclusive early childhood settings.

In addition to my research and teaching activities, I am involved in local and national organizations that advocate for young children including the National Association for the Education of Young Children (NAEYC) and the Division of Early Childhood (DEC) of the Council for Exceptional Children.

Acknowledgments

Our first acknowledgment is to the many children, families, and teachers who gave us the insights on early intervention and inclusive programs that we write about and picture throughout the text. Many people and schools are responsible for supplying the actual photographs. These include:

The Experimental Education Unit, Child Development and Mental Retardation Center, University of Washington, Seattle and the principal of the school, Jennifer Annable and the photographers, Jennifer Anders and Mary Levin. Thanks go also to Marie Hanak of the Center's media services.

Raintree Montessori School in Lawrence, Kansas, and its founder and director, Lleanna Reynolds; also Barbara Thompson, Research Associate at the University of Kansas and Donna Wickam for their contributions to the Raintree photography.

Wing Lake and Fox Hill schools in the Bloomfield Hills School District, Michigan and Mel Kozek, the administrator who took so much time to make the photographing possible.

The Child Development Laboratory Preschools of the Department of Human Development and Family Life at the University of Kansas, Lawrence and to Alita Cooper and Lynn Marotz in particular.

Lynn Marotz receives our special thanks for bringing us up-to-date on health issues as did Pam Richardson on issues related to physical and orthopedic disabilities.

Another important set of acknowledgments is to the several contributors to the text itself, listed in the order in which they appear in the text:

Vickie Louden and the focus piece on her family's experience with inclusion and their child with Down syndrome.

Ann Atkinson Witte for providing the material on creating an enabling environment for infants; we thank her, too, for the photographs that she supplied.

Wendie Bramwell and her reflections on the teacher's role in helping young children understand and deal with death and dying.

Susan Fowler and Robin Hazel for updating their program-to-program transition unit.

Mary McEvoy and Christina Sheran for the closing unit on looking to the future of inclusion.

Finally, we want to acknowledge the help of the several reviewers listed below who provided useful input during the revision process.

Alice Beyrent, MEd
Hessner College
Manchester, NH

Mary Henthorne
Western Wisconsin Technical College
La Crosse, WI

Ann Higgins Hains, PhD
University of Wisconsin
Milwaukee, WI

Deanna Lederer
St. Cloud Technical College
St. Cloud, MN

Patti Zaske
Modesto Junior College
Modesto, CA

SECTION I

Early Intervention and Public Policy

An Inclusive Approach to Early Education

OBJECTIVES

After studying this unit the student will be able to

- trace society's changing attitudes toward children with disabilities.
- define inclusion.
- discuss inclusion in terms of early development, critical learning periods, and teachable moments.
- list the benefits of inclusive environments for children with and without disabilities.
- discuss the challenges associated with implementing inclusive early education programs.

This book is about inclusion in the lives of young children. Inclusion means that children with special needs attend preschool, child care, and recreational programs with their typically developing peers. But inclusion is not about a place, or an instructional strategy, or a curriculum; inclusion is about belonging, being valued, and having choices. Inclusion is about accepting and valuing human diversity, and providing the necessary support so that all children and their families can participate in the programs of their choice.

A major change in public educational policy came about with the Education for All Handicapped Children Act (PL 94-142) in 1975. (This law was renamed the Individuals with Disabilities Education Act [IDEA] when it was reauthorized in 1990 as PL 101-476.) This law entitles everyone with a disability, ages 3 to 21 to a "free and appropriate public education." Additionally, it requires every child with a disability to be educated in the *least restrictive environment*. This means that to the fullest extent possible, the school environment for children with disabilities must be the same as, or similar to, that for typically developing children.

For at least the past 25 years parents and professionals have been working to provide free and appropriate education for all children in the least restrictive environment. The first attempt at implementing this vision was called *mainstreaming*. The term *integration* also has been used to describe the inclusion of children with disabilities in programs for normally developing children. Some educators argue that there are clear-cut differences between integration and mainstreaming; others use the terms interchangeably. Both terms refer to children with disabilities being placed full- or part-time in programs designed for typically developing children. You may also encounter the terms *reverse mainstreaming* or *integrated special education*. These terms are used to describe special

1

education classes that also include some typically developing children. In a reverse mainstreaming or integrated special education class, the majority of the children have identified special needs, and only one-quarter to one-third of the children are normally developing.

The difference between mainstreaming and inclusion is more than semantic. In mainstreaming, children with disabilities had to "be ready" to be integrated into the mainstream. The emphasis was placed on helping the child with disabilities meet the existing expectations of the classroom. Often the child with disabilities was regarded as a visitor in the classroom and was actually assigned (according to school records) to a special education class (Schorr 1990). In inclusive education, children with disabilities are full-time members of the general education classroom. The emphasis in inclusive education is providing the support necessary so that the children can participate in a meaningful way in the ongoing classroom activities. Support may include adaptation of the curriculum, materials, or instructional practices. Support may also include additional staff, consultation, or specialized training for the existing staff. Support services, such as speech therapy and physical therapy, are conducted in natural places in the school environment, including the classroom, gym, and playground.

This unit focuses on current perspectives on inclusive education for young children. A brief overview of effective practices will be given; the specifics of what to do are reserved for the remaining units of the text. The outcomes of inclusive education, the benefits of inclusion, and some of the barriers to inclusion also will be discussed.

INCLUSION DEFINED

"Inclusion is a right, not a privilege for a select few" (*Oberti v. Board of Education in Clementon School District* 1993). The call for inclusion is coming from families, professional organizations, and advocacy groups. Inclusion means

> providing all students within the mainstream appropriate educational programs that are challenging yet geared to their capabilities and needs as well as any

support and assistance they and/or their teachers may need to be successful in the mainstream. But an inclusive school also goes beyond this. An inclusive school is a place where everyone belongs, is accepted, supports, and is supported by his or her peers and other members of the school community in the course of having his or her educational needs met. (Stainback and Stainback 1990, p. 3)

Inclusion is not a set of strategies or a placement issue. Inclusion is about belonging to a community—a group of friends, a school community, or a neighborhood. Ehlers (1993) describes three ways to view inclusion: through beliefs and values, through experiences, and through outcomes. We should consider all three views when planning for and implementing inclusive early education programs.

The *beliefs and values* that every family brings to inclusion reflect the unique history, cultural influences, and relationship of that family (Hanson and Lynch 1992; Luera 1993). Family choices must drive the inclusion process. The family identifies the community to which it belongs and in which the child is to be included. The concept of "goodness of fit" (Thomas and Chess 1977) is essential when developing inclusive programs. An inclusive program must consider the uniqueness of every child and family and how it can address the child's strengths and needs as well as family priorities.

The beliefs and values that influence inclusion occur at the levels of the family, the community, and society (Peck 1993). A family's belief system will have direct impact on their views about inclusion. The sociopolitical context in which children and families live and work also impacts inclusion. This includes how our society views high quality early childhood care and education for all children. In other words, if providing high quality child care for typically developing children is not a societal priority, providing high quality child care for children with disabilities will not be a priority either.

The *experience* of inclusion varies from child to child and from family to family. The goal is to create a match between the program and the child and family. Inclusive classrooms are caring communities that support the ongoing development of participants (Salisbury, Palombaro, and Hollowood 1993). Inclusion requires planning, teamwork, and support. Our values and beliefs will help define our experience with inclusion; in turn, our experience will shape future values and beliefs.

The *outcomes* observed and reported by the parents and teachers of children in inclusive educational programs are broad-based and **holistic**. The outcomes include some of the developmental changes observed in segregated special education programs (e.g., improved communication skills, improved motor skills). They also include important changes in social behavior and a general sense of belonging. Many parents of children in inclusive educational programs report that their child received his or her first invitation to a birthday party or to play at a friend's house after being involved in inclusive education. Some parents report that they feel more included in the community because their child is attending a "regular" school.

Schwartz, Peck, Staub, and Gallucci (1994) propose a three-domain conceptualization of the outcomes of inclusive education. These three interlocking domains are membership, relationships, and development. The membership domain includes the child's interactions with groups. This includes being a member of a class, being a member of a small group within a class, and being a member of non–school related groups (e.g., children's choir at church). The defining criterion of this domain is that other members of the group are willing to make accommodations for the child with disabilities to support inclusion and membership. The relationships domain describes peer relationships, that is, relationships with playmates and classmates. This domain looks at the different roles that the child plays in her or his relationships with peers. For example, in the majority of interactions with peers is the child with disabilities receiving help? Does the child with disabilities have opportunities to be in a role of helping other children? Are there reciprocal or play and companionship types of interaction? Looking at relationships this way allows us to provide rich descriptions of the peers in the child's social network and the many different roles each peer plays.

The development domain looks at more traditional types of early childhood special education outcomes: changes in participation in classroom routine and ritu-

als, changes in social-communicative behavior, changes in functional skills, changes in preacademic skills, and other goals that are included on a child's Individualized Education Plan (IEP) or Individualized Family Service Plan (IFSP). Together these three domains provide a tool for teachers and families to use to describe the unique outcomes found in inclusive educational settings. This outcome framework also can be used to guide the development of goals and objectives for inclusive educational programs. (See the discussion of IFSP and IEP development in Unit 10.)

The Division of Early Childhood (DEC) of the Council for Exceptional Children has developed and adopted a position statement on inclusion. This position statement is found in Figure 1–1.

INCLUSION IN PERSPECTIVE

Early Attitudes.   The number of children with disabilities in the educational mainstream has increased steadily over the past 20 years. This is in marked contrast to the way children with disabilities were viewed in the past. Caldwell (1973) gives the following description of the stages our society has gone through in its treatment of people with disabilities.

Forget and hide.   Until the middle of the twentieth century, families, communities, and society in general seemed to try to deny the existence of the disabled. As much as possible, the children were kept out of sight. Families often were advised to immediately institutionalize an infant with an obvious disability.

In 1950 the National Association of Retarded Children (now the National Association for Retarded Citizens) was founded. Efforts were put into motion to identify children with mental retardation and other disabilities and to bring them out of attics and backrooms. Members of President John F. Kennedy's family also were influential through their public acceptance of their own mentally retarded family member. The Kennedys' acceptance went a long way in breaking down the social stigma attached to a family that allowed a child with a disability (especially a child with mental retardation) to be seen in public.

DEC Position Statement on Inclusion

Adopted: April 1993

Inclusion as a value supports the right of all children regardless of their diverse abilities to participate actively in natural settings within their communities. A natural setting is one in which the child would spend time if he or she had not had a disability. Such settings include but are not limited to home and family play groups, child care, nursery schools, Head Start programs, kindergartens, and neighborhood school classrooms.

DEC believes in and supports full and successful access to health, social service education, and other supports and services for young children and their families that promote full participation in community life. DEC values the diversity of families and supports a family guided process for determining services that are based on the needs and preferences of individual families and children.

To implement inclusive practices DEC supports: (a) the continued development, evaluation, and dissemination of full inclusion support services and systems; (b) the development of preservice and inservice training programs that prepare families, administrators, and service providers to develop and work within inclusive settings; (c) collaboration among all key stakeholders to implement flexible fiscal and administrative procedures in support of inclusion; (d) research that contributes to our knowledge of state-of-the-art services; and (e) the restructuring and unification of social, education, health, and intervention supports and services to make them more responsive to the needs of all children and families.

FIGURE 1–1

Screen and segregate.   About the same time, special education came into being in public school systems. Caldwell describes her personal experiences during this period:

My first experience in lobbying was in Jefferson City, Missouri, where we were trying to get classes for the

educable and trainable mentally retarded. The children would be tested, labeled, segregated into a special facility, and virtually isolated again. These special facilities would keep them out of everybody's hair . . . and [avoid] the irritation of not only the parents but also the teachers. . . . It would also get them out of the way of other children who would supposedly be held back by them. (p. 5)

Identify and help.   The *screen and segregate* period lasted for 20 years or more at which point the constitutional rights of the disabled began to be recognized. The *identify and help* period came about during the 1960s because of political and social activities. Caldwell summed up this period: "We have not abandoned concern with screening, with trying to find children who need help. . . . We now try to make the search earlier in hopes of affording early remediation or more accurately, **secondary prevention.**" (p. 5).

Include and support.   This stage is our addition to Caldwell's stages. It describes our current view of people with disabilities. The beginning of the period of include and support was signaled by the passage of the Americans with Disabilities Act in 1990, and the rulings in both the Holland and Oberti court cases (*Oberti v. Board of Education of Clementon School District* 1993; *Sacramento School District v. Holland* 1992). These two court cases resulted in rulings that demonstrated clear support for inclusive educational programs.

Children with disabilities are no longer hidden away.

Further support comes from the National Association of State Boards of Education in the document *Winner's All* (1992), which calls for inclusive education for all students. The underlying assumption of the *include and support* period is that people with disabilities should be included as full members of society and that they should be provided appropriate supports such as education and accessible environments to ensure their inclusion and meaningful participation.

RATIONALE FOR INCLUSIVE EARLY EDUCATION

Early childhood education has gained widespread acceptance in our society during the past quarter of a century. The integration of young children with and without disabilities into these programs is relatively new to the early education scene. The rationale for inclusive early childhood programs will be discussed in terms of ethical issues, socialization concerns, developmental considerations, and the always pressing issue of cost effectiveness.

The Ethical Issue.   The rights of children with disabilities to as full a life as possible has been a major ethical

The inclusion of young children with developmental problems runs parallel with multicultural activities. Photo credit: Mary Levin

force among mainstreaming advocates. It was Dunn (1968) who first brought the unfairness of segregated education for children with disabilities into public consciousness. He asserted that special classes, for the most part, provided inadequate education for developmentally disabled children. The integration of children with disabilities runs parallel to the multicultural approach to early education. According to Derman-Sparks (1988–1989), the mutual goal is to gain acceptance in our educational system for children with noticeably different cultural, intellectual, or physical characteristics. Until this is accomplished, ethical issues related to any kind of segregation in our schools remain unresolved.

The Socialization Issue.   Including young children with disabilities in the educational mainstream implies equal social status with children who are developing normally. Inclusion promotes awareness. Members of the community become more accustomed to children with developmental disabilities; this leads to greater acceptance. It cannot be overemphasized that young children with developmental disabilities are entitled to the same kinds of enriching early experiences as normally developing children. As Haring and McCormick (1990) point out, "separating young children with handicaps from normal experiences creates distance, misunderstanding, and rejection. . . . Moreover, separating these youngsters from the *real world* means that there must be reentry. Reentry problems can be avoided by not removing the child from normal settings" (p. 102). Young children with disabilities who play and interact only with other children with disabilities will not learn normal social skills. Play with normally developing children must be an integral part of any program designed to promote healthy development in a young child with a disability (Thurman and Widerstrom 1990).

Normally developing preschool children need to get to know children who are disabled, especially children whose disabilities are obvious—children who are blind, deaf, physically disabled, or less able mentally. During their very early years, nondisabled children, unless otherwise influenced, seldom have trouble accepting children who are developmentally different. In fact, the disability may not even figure in a child's efforts to describe a classmate with a handicap. One parent tells the following story:

Andrea came back from preschool saying she wanted to invite Katie home for lunch the next day. I could not figure out who Katie was. Andrea tried to describe Katie's hair, then her new jacket, then her paintings. I still couldn't place her. Finally Andrea said, "Katie's the one who comes with shiny ribbons in her hair," and I knew immediately who Katie was. She was the child in the wheelchair who always had big colorful bows at the ends of her braids! Apparently, being confined to a wheelchair was not one of Katie's outstanding characteristics for my child.

Developmental Issues.   The significance of the early years in laying the foundations for lifelong learning is all but indisputable. During these early years children acquire a broad range of basic skills in all areas of development:

- They learn to move about, to get from one place to another independently, to explore and experiment.
- They become skilled at grasping, holding onto, releasing, and manipulating ever more complex objects.
- They become increasingly able to take care of their personal needs—toileting, dressing, eating.
- They acquire their native language and use it in a variety of ways to get what they need (and prefer) from others in their environment.

Young children seldom have problems accepting children who are developmentally different.

- They develop the ability to think, get ideas, solve problems, make judgments, and influence others.
- They respond with increasingly sophisticated words and gestures when others speak to them or attempt to influence them.
- They discover ways of getting along with and interacting with others—those who are like themselves and those who are different.

A quality early childhood program can assist all children in acquiring the developmental skills just mentioned. The experience is of special benefit to children with developmental disabilities or children-at-risk for developmental problems. For these children, it is like opening a door to both the present and the future. The integrated early childhood program may be their *only* access to appropriate early learning experiences. Each day they will encounter a variety of challenging materials, equipment, and activities, planned and unplanned. There will be interactions with all kinds of other children who serve as models to imitate and to play with, children who will help and who will need help. There will be teachers who understand the regularities and irregularities of development and will assist each child (with or without a developmental problem) in taking advantage of sensitive learning periods and teachable moments.

Sensitive periods.   The majority of young children will acquire basic developmental skills on their own. Some of these learnings, however, seem to come about more readily at particular points in time, known as developmentally *sensitive* or *critical periods.* During these periods, the child appears to be especially responsive and able to learn from specific kinds of stimulation. The same stimulation at other times seems to have little impact on development. It is important that all children be in an enriched and responsive learning environment during these periods. For children with developmental problems, it may be even more essential, as we will see in a moment.

A developmental disability or delay often prevents a child from reacting in ordinary ways during a sensitive period. Parents, especially if they are inexperienced, may not recognize signals from their child that a critical learning period is at hand. By contrast, teachers in an inclusive classroom, where there is such a range of developmental differences among children, tend to pick up on all kinds of subtle behavioral variations.

Critical learning periods that are not recognized and not utilized are common among visually or hearing impaired infants and children. Think of the learning experiences so readily available to nondisabled children: hearing the difference between the doorbell and the telephone; puzzling over a bird call, a flash of lightning, or an angry face. The normally developing child turns automatically, dozens of times a day, to look and listen and learn specific things at specific moments. These same cues, quite literally, are *not there* for the child with a sensory deficit. Without special assistance and opportunities to follow the lead of other children who are responding to what is going on, the child with a sensory impairment is isolated every waking moment from everyday events.

Language acquisition appears to be especially tuned to a sensitive period in development. A hearing impaired child may never acquire truly adequate language if the hearing loss is not treated prior to what is thought to be the critical period for language development. On the other hand, a child whose hearing problem is identified early may experience many fewer problems in language development. A combination of appropriate treatment and a special deaf education program or an inclusive preschool (or a combination, depending on the child's age and severity of loss) allows for building on critical learning periods as they occur.

Children who are physically disabled also are denied critical learning opportunities, but for different reasons. Many cannot move around. They cannot explore their environment. They may not be able to open doors, get into cupboards, run to the window, or learn by simply getting into mischief. Contrast this with physically able children who are on the move from morning to night. They are touching, reaching, running, tumbling, climbing, getting into this and that. They try adults' patience at times, especially during critical learning periods when they seem to be in constant motion as in the following example:

The infant who is learning to walk is forever on the go. Once walking is mastered, a great cognitive

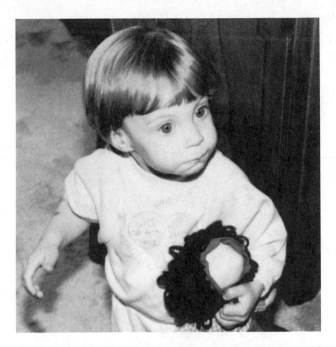

The normally developing child turns to look—and learn—dozens of times each day.

advance seems to take place. Then comes another surge of motor development. The child learns to run, jump, and climb, practicing these skills relentlessly, all day long. On the other hand, children who do not walk until late childhood may have continuing problems. They may never get good at activities that involve sustained running, jumping, and climbing. Even more serious, they may have missed other critical aspects of early learning during the sensorimotor stage when cognitive development and motor activity are so interdependent.

Teachable moments.   For teachers in an inclusive setting, another concept of developmental significance is that of *teachable moments*. These are points in time (perhaps associated with critical periods) when a child is highly motivated and better able to learn particular skills such as walking, riding a tricycle, or learning to count. All children, including those who are severely disabled, have many such teachable moments every day. They occur any time during daily routines and activities. It is important that teachers recognize these opportunities and make sure they lead to develop-

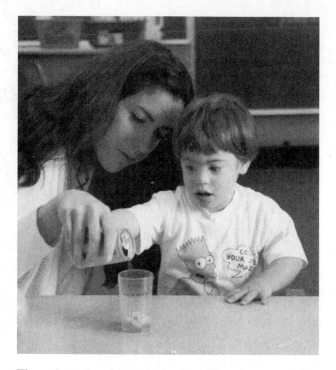

Throughout the program day, all children have teachable moments.

mentally appropriate learning experiences. Teachers also can help parents understand the significance of teachable moments and guide parents in recognizing them and finding ways of responding. The inclusive classroom is an especially suitable place for parents to observe teachers and try out various ways of working with their child.

The infant who is blind and getting ready to learn to walk is a good illustration of teachable moments. First, though, think about developmental sequences and the sighted infant. Walking usually is preceded by a period of just standing, then holding onto furniture, and finally cruising about. Most infants do this spontaneously; no teaching is necessary and no special arrangements are needed.

On its own, the baby who cannot see may barely progress beyond the standing stage. The baby seems to sense that it is too risky to step out into an unseen void. What is needed is someone who recognizes *pulling-to-stand* as a teachable moment and helps the

baby build on it. Experienced parents usually recognize the sign; inexperienced parents may not. The teacher in an infant center is geared to such moments and ready to provide encouragement. Once standing is mastered, the baby's hands may be moved along the table top to teach the fundamentals of cruising. (Usually the baby's feet follow almost automatically.) Teachers also make sure the environment is safe by keeping things off the floor so the baby does not have frightening falls that may discourage further cruising.

As an infant becomes skilled at cruising, another teachable moment occurs—lifting one hand and one foot as if ready to try a step with less support from the furniture. Again, the infant who cannot see will need special encouragement and a safe environment. Pieces of equipment and furniture, for example, should be left in the same place. It is frightening to reach for the support of a familiar table or chair to find it is no longer there. The infant also needs someone to describe what he or she is doing and promote more of it: "You walked to *Delia's* chair. Can you *walk* back to the piano?"; "You have your *hand* on the *rocking* chair. Let's go find the *rocking* boat." Simple games such as "Find Maryanne" (from the direction of the teacher's voice) also build on teachable moments and keep the baby moving.

The more the visually impaired infant (or any other disabled or normal infant) moves about, the more the infant learns in every area of development. In fact, a major reason for utilizing teachable moments as often as possible is to keep the child involved in the process of learning. Hanson and Lynch (1989) put it this way:

> The child learns to be motivated and engaged in the environment and to seek interactions both with the social aspects of the environment—people—and with the nonsocial or physical aspects of the environment of toys, materials, and household items. (p. 210)

Imitation.   Another important rationale for inclusion is that young children with disabilities will observe and imitate more advanced skills modeled by normally developing children (Goldstein 1993). The logic is sound. Imitating others is a major avenue of learning for everyone, old and young alike.

Young children learn by doing. If children with developmental problems are to learn to play appro-

Imitating others is a major avenue for learning. Photo credit: Mary Levin

priately, they must have children to imitate and play with who play appropriately. If children with behavior problems are to learn to share and take turns, they must have opportunities to imitate and interact with children who know how to share and take turns. If a young hearing impaired child is to learn appropriate speech, the child must have interactions with children who model good speech. In a segregated classroom where there are only children with autism, it is unlikely that children will do much talking or modeling of appropriate language skills for each other; thus a powerful argument for inclusive education.

The Cost Issue.   The cost of providing inclusive early education services is an issue of concern to parents, program providers, administrators, and other program consumers. Although the economic aspect of early childhood special education programs is important in viewing early education, "it is not the only, or even preeminent perspective that one might wish to use" (Barnett and Escobar 1990, p. 560). The existing data on cost analysis of inclusive education programs suggest that these programs can be an economical alternative because they take advantage of existing program structures rather than creating parallel and often duplicate structures (Salisbury and Chambers 1994). The cost of providing appropriate educational services for young children with special needs can be reduced by capitalizing on existing programs in the community. This savings is a related benefit of inclusion, but should not be the primary reason driving the agenda of inclusive education in a school district.

Another aspect of the cost issue is the large numbers of typically developing children, as well as young children with developmental disabilities, who continue to go unserved. Simply put, there are not enough early childhood programs to go around. Investing public money in segregated rather than inclusive facilities should be seen as a setback—philosophically and financially—in meeting the developmental needs of all children.

SUPPORTING INCLUSION: IMPLICATIONS FOR TEACHERS

The mere act of placing children with and without disabilities together in a classroom does not ensure inclusion. Teachers must take that responsibility. Particular skills are needed. Many of these stem from knowledge of child development as discussed in Unit 4; the other skills are discussed in detail in Unit 13 and under various headings throughout the text. Effective inclusion requires specific planning and implementation by teachers whose responsibilities include:

- Individualizing programs and activities to meet each child's specific needs and abilities (Unit 10).
- Recognizing there are no well-defined markers distinguishing normal, at-risk, and developmentally disabled children.
- Avoiding the possibility of limiting children's learning by labeling.
- Recognizing the value of play as an avenue of learning for children with disabilities as well as for normally developing children; at the same time recognizing that play skills often have to be taught to children with disabilities, many of whom neither play spontaneously nor know how to play.
- Arranging a balance of large and small group experiences, both vigorous and quiet, so that all

children, at their own levels, can be active and interactive participants.

- Structuring a learning environment in which children without and without disabilities are helped to participate *together* in a variety of activities related to all areas of development.
- Supporting the development of all children by creating a learning and playing environment that includes a range of materials and activities such that the lowest functioning children can be independent and the highest functioning children are challenged.

Structuring Child–Child Interaction.   The effectiveness of inclusion depends on ongoing interactions between children with and without disabilities. Such interactions do not necessarily come about spontaneously. Guralnick (1990) and his colleagues continue to conduct research on this issue. One of their early efforts (Devoney et al. 1974), indicated that disabled and nondisabled children played together *when the teacher structured the environment to promote such interaction.* (Units 13 and 14 discuss ways for teachers to accomplish this structure.) An interesting sidelight in the Devoney study was that children with disabilities, playing with nondisabled children, played in a more

Teachers structure the learning environment so that children with a disability and those without can learn together. Photo credit: Mary Levin

organized and mature way than had been characteristic of their earlier play.

Another classic study focused on imitation and the teacher's role. It was found that children with developmental disabilities were more likely to imitate nondisabled children *if* they were trained to do so and reinforced for it (Peck, Apolloni, Cooke and Raver 1978). From these and many other research studies, it is apparent that the teacher's structuring of play activities is essential. Curriculum planning for an inclusive early childhood program must focus on activities that lead to children with and without disabilities working and playing together.

Planning classroom activities.   Curriculum planning for inclusive classrooms also requires teachers to integrate the goals and activities on the children's IFSP/IEPs into ongoing classroom activities. Using an **activity-based approach** to planning inclusive classrooms draws from the strong traditions of early childhood education and special education to best meet the unique learning needs of young children with disabilities (Bricker and Cripe 1992). This approach allows teachers to use traditional early childhood activities such as dramatic play, art, nature walks, and water play to address specific goals and objectives across the developmental domains (e.g., cognitive, social, communication, motor, self-care) for children with special needs.

Professional Collaboration.   In addition to classroom practices, integrating children requires integrating professional efforts. Administrators, teachers, aides, volunteers, and members of the interdisciplinary team need to work together. Professional growth comes with collaboratively searching for ways to provide for developmentally disabled children in the inclusive setting. Part of the search has to do with looking for paths that lead to a genuine partnership with parents. As will be discussed in Unit 9, this means listening to parents, consulting with them, learning from them. In fact, everyone—children, parents, teachers, classroom staff, and clinicians—can learn from each other in an integrated early childhood program. Early childhood teachers, however, receive a special bonus. In learning to meet the special needs of children with disabilities they become more skilled at meeting the special needs of *all* children. By learning to build on the capabilities of special children, they become better attuned to the special capabilities of *all* children.

BENEFITS OF INCLUSION

Benefits for children with disabilities.   In addition to the philosophical and legal issues discussed earlier, there are many clear benefits for educating young children with special needs in inclusive programs. In a review of the research of developmental outcomes for young children with disabilities in inclusive early childhood settings, Lamorey and Bricker (1993) noted that generally, children made significantly better gains in the areas of social competence and social play, and similar gains in the other developmental domains. The improved benefits in the social domain may be due to an emphasis on social development by programs that have implemented inclusive educational programming.

Children with developmental problems are likely to benefit from a good inclusive preschool experience because it provides:

More stimulating, varied, and responsive experiences than special classrooms composed of children with limited skills.

Developmental scaffolding for curriculum activities rather than a **deficit model curriculum** where major emphasis is on the pathological aspects of development.

Opportunities to observe, interact with, and imitate children who have acquired higher-level motor, social, language, and cognitive skills.

Implicit motivation to "try a little harder," in that children with disabilities often expect and encourage improved behaviors on the part of less skilled children—as Peterson (1987) puts it: "A more demanding environment may push the child ahead to develop more appropriate behavior repertoires" (p. 359).

Opportunities to learn directly from other children; it appears that certain skills are learned more easily from another child; the explanations and demon-

strations often are closer to the developmentally disabled child's capabilities than are the adults' explanations and demonstrations.

Benefits for typically developing children.   Normally developing children may have greater access to early childhood programs when there is full implementation of the preschool component of PL 99-457. As noted in the *costs issue*, many normally developing children who would profit from an early education program are not being served. As inclusive programs become common, many more enrollments for both normally developing children and children with developmental disabilities should become available.

Developmental progress.   Normally developing children make normal developmental progress in inclusive settings. Summarizing a number of studies, Thurman and Widerstrom (1990) suggest that children without disabilities benefit from integrated programs, "at least to the same degree and sometimes to a greater degree than would have been expected if they had attended nonintegrated preschools" (p. 39). There is *no evidence* of negative effects on normally developing children (Odom and McEvoy 1988). Similar levels of achievement occur whether children are enrolled with children who are disabled or with children who are not (this holds true even in preschool settings where children with disabilities outnumber nondisabled children). Another safe conclusion to be drawn from the current research, according to the above authors, is that the *developmental outcome for children in inclusive programs depends on the quality of teaching, rather than integration.*

Peer tutoring.   A well-documented benefit of inclusion for normally developing children is *peer tutoring*—one child instructing another. It appears that both the child being tutored and the child doing the tutoring receive significant benefits from the experience. The common sense of this is readily apparent; most of us have discovered that given an unpressured opportunity to teach someone else something we know (or are learning), our own skill and understanding are increased. The same is true of children. As pointed out by Spodek et al. (1984), voluntary peer tutoring

Normally developing children make normal developmental gains (or greater) in inclusive settings.

among young children of all developmental levels can promote

social interactions among disabled and nondisabled children
acceptable play behaviors
appropriate and enhanced use of materials

In fact, peer tutoring tends to be of special value for gifted children. It provides and exciting and challenging stretch for their own creativity and ingenuity. Though not directly related to peer tutoring, a study by Strain et al. (1985) provided an interesting slant on inclusion and giftedness. A follow-up on 10 children who had been the normal models in one inclusive preschool indicated they were all enrolled in regular kindergartens. Of the 10, four were in programs for gifted children.

Benefits for families.   In general, parents' attitudes about inclusion were influenced by their experiences with inclusion (Lamorey and Bricker 1993). Parents of children with disabilities were most often positive in their responses, although they did identify some concerns (see below). Attitudes of parents of typically developing children improved as experience with inclusion increased. In a study involving 125 parents of nondisabled children who attended inclusive preschool programs, Peck, Carlson, and Helmstetter (1992) found that parents perceived their children's experience as generally positive and were supporters of inclusive education. Additionally, Peck and his colleagues found that parents reported that their children were more accepting of human difference and had less discomfort with people with disabilities and people who looked or behaved differently than they did.

Benefits for society.   Not only does inclusion have positive effects on all types of children; it appears to be of long-term benefit to society. Nondisabled children who grow up with opportunities to interact with children with disabilities are likely to be more tolerant in later years. They tend to mature into adults with greater understanding and respect for those less able in our society (Bricker and Sandall 1979). Many teachers report that most young children, unless influenced by inappropriate adult attitudes, have a natural acceptance of individual differences. They are unlikely to make negative judgments and comparisons about children who are developmentally disabled. When they do comment or ask questions, it is because they need to learn about whatever it is that is unfamiliar about the child with a disability.

CONCERNS AND CHALLENGES OF INCLUSION

It is not appropriate to frame the discussion of inclusion around questions like "Does inclusion work?" or "Is inclusion right for our program?" Inclusion is the law. All early childhood programs that receive federal funds must include children with special needs. With passage of the Americans with Disabilities Act, it is also against the law for private early childhood programs to refuse to serve a child because of an identified disability. It is important, however, to discuss the concerns that parents and professionals have about inclusion, and to work together to overcome challenges that may interfere with providing quality inclusive programs for all young children. The discussion that follows identifies the most common concerns and provides brief glimpses of research findings that address those issues.

Will special needs be served?   Parents and teachers have expressed concern that the special needs of children with disabilities may not be met adequately in inclusive early childhood programs. They feel that teachers many not have the time or the skills. They also are concerned that children will not receive specialized support services, such as occupational therapy, physical therapy, and speech therapy. The opposite is also of concern: If a program is meeting the special needs of children with disabilities, then what about the normally developing children? Are they going to be shortchanged?

These concerns have been addressed in a number of research studies. By and large, the data indicate

that parents believe their children (with and without disabilities) benefit from integrated programs. These findings are based on well-structured programs with knowledgeable teachers. Little parental satisfaction is found in poor-quality programs, integrated or otherwise. In a review of a number of research studies, Lamorey and Bricker (1993) state that in general the needs of the children were met in inclusive programming. Some parents were concerned about the quality of training received by teachers in inclusive programs. This indicates that there is a need for different types of training in early childhood education. Professionals need to work on adapting preservice training for teachers in early childhood, early childhood special education, and related therapy fields to prepare professionals to work together to deliver quality services to children with special needs in inclusive programs (Odom and McEvoy 1990; Washington, Schwartz, and Swinth 1994).

Many researchers have documented that parents of normally developing children report that their children are learning important social and academic lessons from their experiences in inclusive classrooms (e.g., Guralnick 1994). A similar reaction is found among parents of children with disabilities. They also felt the program helped their children worked harder. Bailey and Winton (1987) reported the following:

Parents of handicapped children felt that the important components—real-world exposure and community acceptance of the handicapped—were being promoted. . . . For parents of nonhandicapped children, prior concerns related to teachers and resources were not realized. (p. 86)

In general, teachers' attitudes are favorable toward integration, once they have actually worked with children with disabilities in an inclusive setting. In the many studies they reviewed, Odom and McEvoy (1988) conclude:

It appears that teacher attitudes toward including children with handicaps in mainstreamed settings were generally positive. In most situations, teachers have the skills for integrating children. However, to integrate children with certain handicaps, additional training and support for the teacher is needed. (p. 262) (This issue is discussed in Unit 12).

Thurman and Widerstrom (1990) offer the following summary statement: There does not appear to be any basis for this fear [children being slighted] as an examination of successful programs at the preschool level demonstrates. The authors then go on to talk about their personal experiences: "Individualized programming for the children with disabilities often spilled over into better practices with the nonhandicapped children. Teachers who thought mainly in terms of group activities learned, through their work with special children, to plan for individual differences among all children more effectively" (p. 40).

Concerns about inappropriate behaviors. Another frequently expressed concern is that normally developing children will learn immature or inappropriate behaviors from classmates with disabilities. Again, this is an unfounded fear. This is not to imply that normally developing children do not imitate other children. They do. They should. Imitation is an important avenue for learning. But normally developing children imitate each other. Rarely (and then only briefly) do they imitate the atypical behaviors of another child. The exceptions are those children who get undue attention from teachers and parents for imitating inappropriate behaviors. Data collected by a group of researchers working with autistic children and reported by Odom and McEvoy (1988) indicate that "normally developing children did not imitate the unusual and stereotypic behavior of children with autism" (p. 259).

SUMMARY

Including young children with developmental disabilities in regular early childhood programs is the law. The reasons for inclusion are based on ethical, social, developmental, and cost considerations. No longer is it acceptable, or legal, to keep children with disabilities out of the social and educational mainstream.

For children with and without developmental problems, the early years are critical. A variety of learnings seem to be *programmed* in at particular times as a part of the developmental plan. These learnings may never again be acquired as readily or as well. An abundance of *teachable moments* occur during infancy and the preschool period. These are best utilized in an inclusive setting with teachers who are trained to recognize such developmental opportunities. An integrated early childhood program also provides opportunities for children with developmental problems to imitate normally developing children. At the same time, normally developing children are provided significant learning experiences in helping less able children acquire a variety of skills—motor, social, and intellectual. However, children with developmental problems and normally developing children do not necessarily work and play together of their own accord. Teachers must structure the program so that interactions can occur and be reinforced.

A number of concerns about inclusion continue to be voiced. A common one, expressed by parents and teachers, is that the special needs of children with disabilities may not be adequately met in an integrated program. Another is that normally developing children will receive less than their share of attention if children with disabilities are properly served. Then there is the concern that normally developing children will learn inappropriate and bizarre behaviors from atypical children. Numerous research studies conducted over the past 10 years demonstrate that these anxieties are largely unfounded. In fact, the opposite is true: The advantages of inclusion for both nondisabled young children and children with developmental disabilities are numerous and well documented.

STUDENT ACTIVITIES

1. Put together a panel discussion on the pros and cons of inclusion.
2. Observe in an inclusion early childhood program. Try to identify children with developmental problems. Describe both their problems and their strengths.
3. Talk with a teacher in an infant center or early childhood center. Ask about the types and numbers of children with disabilities in the program. If there are no children with disabilities, try to find out why.
4. Observe an early childhood setting. Record any episodes of a child learning through observing, imitation, or peer tutoring.
5. Set up a simulated parent conference with three other students, two playing the child's parents and two of the child's teachers. The parents' concern is that their normally developing 3-year-old may not get enough attention because a child who is blind is scheduled to be included into the program. Role-play a discussion of the situation.

REVIEW QUESTIONS

A. *Short answer.*
   1. Define inclusion.
   2. What are some possible outcomes of inclusion?
   3. Name and briefly describe the four stages that we talked about in reference to children with disabilities.
   4. What do inclusion and cultural antibias curriculum have in common?
   5. Define teachable moments; give an example.
   6. If a child seems not to know how to play, what does the teacher do?
   7. What is peer tutoring?
   8. Of what benefit to society is inclusion?

B. *True or False. Choose the best answer regarding what inclusion and integration infer.*
   T F 1. There should be ongoing opportunities for disabled and nondisabled children to work and play together.
   T F 2. Children with developmental problems should be labeled and have their own separate large and small group programs.
   T F 3. Teachers must make sure that children do not imitate or copy each other.
   T F 4. Normally developing children and children with disabilities should be allowed to play together only twice a week.

   T F 5. There is no gain for normally developing children in playing with children with developmental problems.
   T F 6. Delayed children in segregated programs may have less opportunity to learn a wide range of developmental skills than in integrated programs.
   T F 7. Play activities are of little value in teaching developmental skills to young children with disabilities.
   T F 8. Play activity must be allowed to develop spontaneously in all children, regardless of their developmental problems.
   T F 9. Teachers should never interfere in children's play by attempting to promote social interactions between disabled and nondisabled children.
   T F 10. Most parents of nondisabled children find inclusion good for their children.

C. *Lists.*
   1. List five responsibilities of the teacher in an inclusive preschool.
   2. List three major concerns that parents and teachers have about inclusion.
   3. List five arguments in favor of inclusion for young children with developmental problems.

REFERENCES

Bailey, D.B., and Winton, P.J. (1987). Stability and change in parents' expectations about mainstreaming. *Topics in Early Childhood Special Education, 7:1,* 73–88.

Barnett, W.S., and Escobar, C.M. (1990). Economic costs and benefits of early intervention. In S.J. Meisels and J.P. Shonkoff (Eds.), *Handbook of early intervention* (pp. 560–582). New York: Cambridge University Press.

Board of Education, Sacramento City Unified School District v. Holland, 7867, Supp. 874 (E. D. Cal 1992).

Bredekamp, S. (Ed.). (1987). *Developmentally appropriate practice in early childhood programs serving children birth through 8.* Washington, DC: National Association for the Education of Young Children.

Bricker, D., and Cripe, J. (1992). *An activity-based approach to early intervention.* Baltimore: Brookes.

Bricker, D., and Sandall, S. (1979). The integration of handicapped and nonhandicapped preschoolers. Why and how to do it. *Education Unlimited, 1,* 25–29.

Caldwell, B.M. (1973). The importance of beginning early. In J.B. Jordan and R.F. Dailey (Eds.), *Not all little wagons are red: The exceptional child's early years.* Reston, VA: Council for Exceptional Children.

Derman-Sparks, L., and the A.B.C. Task Force. (1988– 1989). *Anti-bias curriculum.* Washington, DC: The National Association for the Education of Young Children.

Devoney, C., Guralnick, M.J., and Rubin, H. (1974). Integrating handicapped and nonhandicapped preschool children: Effects on social play. *Childhood Education, 50,* 360–364.

Dunn, L.M. (1968). Special education for the mildly retarded—Is much of it justified? *Exceptional Children, 35,* 5–22.

Ehlers, L. (1993). Inclusion in the lives of young children with disabilities. In S.M. Rehberg (Ed.), *Starting Point: A series of definition papers* (pp. 33–43). Olympia, WA: Office of the Superintendent of Public Instruction.

Goldstein, H. (1993). Structuring environmental input to facilitate generalized language learning by children with mental retardation. In A.P. Kaiser and D.B. Gray (Eds.), *Enhancing children's communication: Research foundations for intervention.* Baltimore: Brookes.

Guralnick, M.J. (1990). Social competence and early intervention. *Journal of Early Intervention* 14(1), 3–14.

Guralnick, M.J. (1994). Mothers' perceptions of the benefits and drawbacks of early childhood mainstreaming. *Journal of Early Intervention, 12,* 168–183.

Hanson, M.J., and Lynch, E.W. (1989). *Early intervention.* Austin, TX: PRO-ED.

Hanson, M.J., and Lynch, E.W. (1992). *Developing cross-cultural competence: A guide for working with young children and their families.* Baltimore: Brookes.

Haring, N.G., and McCormick, L. (1990). *Exceptional children and youth.* Columbus: Merrill.

Lamorey, S. and Bricker, D. (1993). Integrated programs: Effects on young children and their programs. In C.A. Peck, S.L. Odom, and D.D. Bricker (Eds.), *Integrating young children with disabilities into community programs* (pp. 249–270). Baltimore: Brookes.

Luera, M. (1993). Honoring family uniqueness. In S.M. Rehberg (Ed.), *Starting point: A series of definition papers* (pp. 1–9). Olympia, WA: Office of the Superintendent of Public Instruction.

National Association of State Boards of Education. (1992). *Winner's all: A call for inclusive schools.* Alexandria, VA: Author.

Oberti v. Borough of Clementon School District. WL 178480 (3rd Cir. N.J. 1993).

Odom, S.L., and McEvoy, M.A. (1988). Integration of young children with handicaps and normally developing children. In S.L. Odom and M.B. Karnes (Eds.), *Early intervention for infants and children with handicaps.* Baltimore: Brookes.

Odom, S.L. and McEvoy, M.A. (1990). Mainstreaming at the preschool level. *Topics in Early Childhood Special Education,* 10(2), 48–61.

Peck, C.A. (1993). Ecological perspectives on the implementation of integrated early childhood programs. In C.A. Peck, S.L. Odom, and D.D. Bricker (Eds.), *Integrating young children with disabilities into community programs* (pp. 3–15). Baltimore: Brookes.

Peck, C.A., Apolloni, T., Cooke, T.P., and Raver, S. (1978). Teaching retarded preschoolers to imitate the free-play behaviors of non-retarded classmates: Trained and generalized effects. *Journal of Special Education, 12,* 195–207.

Peck, C.A., Carlson, P., and Helmstetter, E. (1992). Parent and teacher perceptions of outcomes for typically developing children enrolled in integrated early childhood programs. A statewide survey. *Journal of Early Intervention,* 16, 53–63.

Peterson, N.L. (1987). *Early intervention for handicapped and at-risk children.* Denver: Love.

Salisbury, C.L., and Chambers, A. (1994). Instructional costs of inclusive schooling. *Journal of the Association for Persons with Severe Handicaps, 19,* 215–222.

Salisbury, C.L., Palombaro, M.M., and Hollowood, T.M. (1993). On the nature and change of an inclusive elementary school. *Journal of the Association for Persons with Severe Handicaps, 18,* 75–84.

Schorr, R. (1990). Peter, he comes and goes. *Journal of the Association for Persons with Severe Handicaps, 19,* 215–222.

Schwartz, I.S., Peck, C.A., Staub, D., and Gallucci, C. (1994, October). Membership, relationships, and development: Facilitating meaningful outcomes in inclusive preschool programs. Paper presented at the Division of Early Childhood Conference, St. Louis, MO.

Spodek, B., Saracho, O.N., and Lee, R.C. (1984). *Main-streaming young children.* Belmont, CA: Wadsworth.

Stainback, W., and Stainback, S. (1990). *Support networks for inclusive schooling: Interdependent integrated education.* Baltimore: Brookes.

Strain, P.S., Hoyson, M., and Jamieson, B. (1985). Normally developing preschoolers as intervention agents for autistic-like children: Effects on class deportment and social interaction. *Journal of the Division of Early Childhood, 9,* 105–115.

Thomas, A. and Chess, S. (1977). *Temperment and development.* New York: Bruner/Mazel.

Thurman, K.S., and Widerstrom, A.H. (1990). *Infants and young children with special needs.* Baltimore: Brookes.

Washington, K., Schwartz, I.S., and Swinth, Y. (1994). Physical and Occupational therapists in naturalistic early childhood settings: Challenges and strategies for training. *Topics in early childhood special education,* 14(3), 333–349.

SPECIAL FOCUS:
Coming Home to Regular Life

VICKIE LOUDEN*

Seven years ago when my son was a few hours old, I left behind the world I was familiar with and entered a strange new one. With the diagnosis of Down syndrome came a separate and different language. Instead of having a baby, I had a "client." Instead of infancy, I had "early intervention." Instead of natural play, we had "infant stimulation." I am absolutely grateful for the excellent services we received and the incredible people who helped us immeasurably. But not until this year when I had the chance to walk with my son to the neighborhood bus stop, watch him get on the bus with all the other kids in the neighborhood, and go off to kindergarten at our neighborhood school, did I realize how separate I'd been or how deeply I yearned to be back home, to be part of the simple everyday fabric of regular life.

Inclusion—educating my son in the neighborhood school, in regular classrooms with sisters, brothers, friends, and neighbors—is an idea that struck me as impossible and frightening in the beginning. It seemed that my son needed protection, special care, and assistance that would make separate learning essential. But there was something irresistible about the idea of inclusion, and over time I read everything I could get my hands on about it. As I read, my vision gradually shifted until finally it became impossible to imagine my son excluded and separate. What crime had he committed that earned him banishment?

I listened to parents of kids with developmental disabilities graduating from high school and the picture was grim. Despite success at school nothing at all lay ahead after graduation. Again and again I heard that what is more crucial than anything else is social appropriateness, the ability to interact with the rest of the world. I wanted to prepare my son for life. I could see that in high school

he would need to learn job and community living skills, begin to work in the community, and prepare for the transition beyond school. But what about now? What good could skills learned in isolation, dependent on a controlled, segregated environment, do to promote my son's future life in the community?

I was extremely fortunate. I have a great principal. I found open and caring individuals willing to take a risk and go the extra mile. I found administrators who wouldn't stand in the way. And together we built a kindergarten experience for my son. Challenging, yes. Terrifying and depressing at times, yes. But also exhilarating, heartwarming, inspiring, and satisfying.

Inclusion is not mainstreaming and it is not dumping. It is not just keeping our kids separate most of the time and letting them out into the mainstream a little at recess. And it is not pretending our kids don't have extra needs and just throwing them in over their heads. They do have needs, but they also have gifts—real tangible benefits to offer to other children, teachers, and classrooms. With the vision to recognize those gifts and appropriate support systems, everybody wins. When my son comes home full of tales of pilgrims, and Indians, Dr. Science, and Zachary and AJ, I know he wins. And when Carly hears that he missed her while she was out sick as he welcomes her back, and Zach yells, "Hey, Matt, here's your stuff. Come and get it," and all of them learn to see beneath surface differences, I know they win. And when I read about kids in Minnesota, California, and Colorado, learning the same lessons, I know we all can win. Schools aren't working well for too many kids today. Our country is looking closely at major educational reform. As we restructure our schools to suit today and the future, it is imperative that we build them for *all* kids.

My son has come home. And so my family has come home. Regular life. Don't ever take such a sweet, precious gift for granted. And don't deny it to us any longer. Support inclusive schooling and let all of us come home to work together for quality.

---

*Vickie Louden is the mother of two children. She is an inclusion activist and the co-coordinator of SAFE (Schools Are For Everyone) in Washington State.

Inclusive Programs for Young Children

OBJECTIVES

After studying this unit the student will be able to

- list five features of quality child care programs.
- describe three types of programs where inclusive early childhood services may be provided.
- describe essential elements of an inclusive program for children from birth to age 2.
- describe essential elements of an inclusive program for children 3 to 5 years of age.
- describe essential elements of an inclusive program for children 6 to 8 years of age.

It has long been known that the first years of life are crucial for later development, and recent scientific findings provide a basis for these observations. We can now say, with greater confidence than ever before, that the quality of young children's environment and social experience has a decisive, long-lasting impact on their well-being and ability to learn.

(Carnegie Task Force on Meeting the Needs of Young Children 1994, p. xiii)

Young children (birth through 8 years of age) may spend time in different environments throughout the day. In addition to time spent at home, many are enrolled in child care, preschool, or community recreation programs. Although these programs vary in size, location, programming philosophy, and religious affiliation, they have elements in common simply because they are providing care to young children. Another element they have in common is that they may all be inclusive programs. That is, any of the early childhood programs described in this unit may be appropriate placements for young children with disabilities, given adequate planning and support.

The National Association for the Education of Young Children (NAEYC) has developed guidelines for high quality early childhood programs. The dominant principle is that programs for young children should be developmentally appropriate. Developmental appropriateness includes two significant dimensions: age appropriateness and individual appropriateness. The concept of developmental appropriateness for programs serving infants and toddlers, preschoolers, and children in the primary grades will be discussed in this unit.

WHERE ARE INCLUSIVE EARLY CHILDHOOD PROGRAMS?

Early childhood programs exist in most communities. Some programs are large; others are small. Some are licensed by the state and are housed in buildings specially designed for that purpose; others are unregulated and are housed in the care-provider's home. Some are government-funded; others are privately funded. Some are designed to provide all-day care for children while their parents are at work or school; others are short in duration or specific in focus (for example, community recreation programs may meet for one hour a week and provide only gymnastics instruction). All of these programs are potentially inclusive early childhood programs. Whatever the purpose or location, these programs should share a common goal—providing quality learning environments for young children.

In a recent study of child care arrangements (Galinsky, Howes, Kontos, and Shinn 1994), working mothers of all social and ethnic backgrounds, were consistent in ranking the same five features of early childhood settings as most important. The most necessary features of quality child care, according to these mothers, are:

- attention to the children's safety
- provider's communication with parents about their children
- cleanliness
- attention children receive
- provider's warmth toward children.

These features should be found in all programs, regardless of other features such as length, setting,

and size. Brief descriptions of common early childhood program arrangements are provided below.

Child Care.   In general, early childhood programs are called child care programs when they provide the primary caretaking for the child while the parents are at work or school. Most child care facilities provide all-day care, and many children are in child care for more than eight hours every day. Although the majority of child care facilities are designed to accommodate parents who work during the day, Monday through Friday, some centers are beginning to accommodate families with other schedules. For example, in Seattle there is a program called Swing Shift that provides child care for people who work evenings and nights. The majority of out-of-home child care arrangements fall into the following categories.

Family child care.   Child care in the provider's home is called family child care. Family child care programs usually consist of one provider taking care of a small number of children, usually six or fewer; however, regulations regarding the number of children vary across states. The provider may or may not be related to the child. Family child care often is preferred by families with children who are 2 years old and under. Thirty-three percent of the families participating in the study conducted by Galinsky and her colleagues (1994) used a family child care provider. Child care homes can be regulated by states; however, many children are in unregulated family child care homes.

Center child care.   Programs that employ multiple staff members and care for larger numbers of children are called child care centers. These programs range in size from one classroom to more than 10 classrooms. Staff–child ratios are determined by state regulation, but a typical ratio is approximately one staff per 10 children. Additional staff are required for infant and toddler care. Galinsky et al. (1994) reported that 43 percent of the families with children who were 3 years old and above chose center-based child care.

Corporate child care.   Corporate child care centers are run by businesses for their employees. Children of employees are eligible to enroll in these centers,

Infants and toddlers need continuous supervision.

which usually are located on-site. Working parents are encouraged to visit their child during the day for lunch, snack, or a quick hello. Often, corporations contract with **proprietary** providers to provide the actual child care services. Research has shown that employees with children in on-site child care programs have better attendance, are more satisfied with their jobs, and are more productive.

Preschools.   Preschool programs are usually part-time programs designed for children between the ages of 3 and 5. Some preschool programs have an academic focus, though current **best practices** support a more child-directed, play-based curriculum (Bredekamp 1987). A major distinction between child care and preschool programs is the amount and type of planned activities. Although the actual programming in many child care and preschool programs may be similar, these types of programs may be viewed differently by parents and regulatory agencies. Preschool programs can be run by public or private agencies. Common types of preschool programs are described in the following paragraphs.

Observing and participating in every day experiences is critical to early learning.

Public schools.   Public school programs are usually housed in elementary school buildings or in school district early childhood centers. Most public school preschools were designed initially as special education or **compensatory education** programs. Some states, however, are expanding early childhood services to provide at least one year of preschool experience for all children.

Community groups.   Many community centers offer preschool programs. They often rely heavily on parent participation, and are sometimes called parent cooperative (co-op) programs. Co-ops require parents to work a specified number of hours in the program, or to provide an equal amount of support in other ways. Parent co-op programs often are associated with community colleges and provide a valuable source of parent education and support.

Religious organizations.   Many children attend preschool programs at churches, temples, and religious community centers. In addition to the benefits provided by all quality early childhood programs, these programs provide religious and cultural activities.

Head Start.   Head Start originally was funded in 1965 under the Elementary and Secondary Education Act. It was developed as a compensatory education program for young disadvantaged children as part of the War on Poverty (see Schorr 1988 for an interesting account of the history of Head Start). Head Start programs now serve over 500,000 children and their families every year. Although most programs are half-day preschools for 3- and 4-year-olds, Head Start is beginning to expand its services to provide all-day child care and programs for younger children.

Recreation Programs.   Recreation programs for young children are increasing in popularity. Many preschoolers participate in organized dance, gymnastics, or swim programs. As children enter elementary school many also become involved in organized sports (e.g., soccer, t-ball) and various scouting activities. These programs are excellent opportunities for inclusive experiences for young children.

RECOMMENDED PRACTICES FOR INCLUSIVE EARLY CHILDHOOD PROGRAMS

The *DEC* Recommended Practices: Indicators of Quality Programs for Infants and Young Children with Special Needs and Their Families* (DEC Task Force on Recommended Practices 1993) puts forth six general principles. These should be used to identify the **best practices** for meeting the needs of young children with special needs in early childhood programs. The principles are equally useful when discussing quality early childhood education programs for **all** children. To be considered a recommended practice, strategies have to reflect or be compatible with the following principles: research-based or value-based, family-centered, multicultural in emphasis, cross-disciplinary, developmentally/chronologically age-appropriate, and normalized. A brief description of each of these principles follows.

The caregiver encourages and supports child-initiated activities.

Research-based or value-based.   Accountability must be a cornerstone practice for teachers working with young children with and without disabilities and their families. Practices, strategies, and techniques used in early childhood education (ECE) and early childhood special education (ECSE) must be supported by **empirical** research. In some instances (e.g., the inclusion movement) practices are pushed by personal and societal values rather than empirical research. In these cases it is necessary to work toward gathering the empirical evidence necessary to evaluate those practices.

Family-centered.   In family-centered or family-focused intervention, practices are designed with, rather than for, the child and family. This view of intervention acknowledges that the child is part of a dynamic family system and that any change in the system (e.g., intervention or change in programs) affects all parts of the system.

Multicultural emphasis.   Recommended practices embrace a multicultural perspective and celebrate the concept of family uniqueness. **Family uniqueness** encompasses ethnic and racial differences as well as the unique history and traditions of individual families. This is especially important as our society becomes more pluralistic and families are more commonly unique blends of backgrounds. This multicultural perspective recognizes and respects different needs and value systems of the children and families. This respect must be translated into practice by developing programs that are **culturally sensitive** and supportive of differences.

Cross-disciplinary participation.   Early childhood and early childhood special education programs should involve professionals from different disciplines working as a team, on behalf of young children and their families. Disciplines, in addition to education and special education, that often are represented on early childhood teams include **speech pathology, audiology, occupational therapy, physical therapy, nursing, medicine, nutrition, psychology**, and **social work**. Team

---

*DEC refers to the Division of Early Childhood, one of the affiliated groups of the Council of Exceptional Children (CEC).

members develop expertise in their own discipline as well as expertise in working cooperatively with other professionals. (Unit 10 provides additional information about interdisciplinary teams.)

Developmentally/chronologically age-appropriate. The concept of developmentally appropriate practice can be equated with "the problem of the match" (Hunt 1961) or "the goodness of the fit" (Thomas and Chess 1977) between a child and an intervention technique. With children with developmental disabilities the issue of chronologically age-appropriate practices is crucial (Brown et al., 1979). This principle challenges researchers and practitioners to consider the unique learning needs of an individual child; at the same time they must develop an intervention program that is appropriate within the context of an environment and learning experiences that are chronologically age-appropriate. In other words, a 5-year-old with severe disabilities should be using materials and exploring environments that are typical for all 5-year-olds, regardless of his or her developmental age.

Normalized. Normalization refers to opportunities for individuals with disabilities to go to school and participate in education experiences as do other children and youth. For young children these experiences may include preschool, child care, swimming lessons, play groups, going to the movies, religious training, and dance lessons. A family with a child with disabilities should have the same range of activities and services available to them as any other family (Bailey and McWilliam 1990).

Although these principles were proposed for programs designed to meet the needs of young children with disabilities, they also can be applied to programs for typically developing children and inclusive programs that serve children with a wide range of abilities. These principles are appropriate for all programs across the early childhood period, from infants and toddler to children in the early primary grades. Although there are many cross-age similarities in quality programming, there also are practices that are age-specific. The rest of this unit will discuss age-specific elements of inclusive programs. The information in these sections is based primarily on the recommenda-

tions of the National Association for the Education of Young Children (NAEYC) (Bredekamp 1987) and the Division of Early Childhood (DEC Task Force 1993).

ESSENTIAL ELEMENTS OF INCLUSIVE PROGRAMS SERVING CHILDREN BIRTH TO 2[1]

Programs for infants and toddlers pose unique challenges for early childhood educators. Very young children require more individual attention and caregiver's time if their physical and nutritional needs are to be met adequately. Providing appropriate experiences is rooted in a caregiver's knowledge of typical development and what constitutes a safe and healthy day-by-day environment for infants and toddlers.

Interactions among adults and children. One goal of the infant caregiver, whether at home or in out-of-home settings, is the healthy development of the infant. The role of the infant caregiver becomes even more of a challenge with infants who are developmentally delayed. A caregiver must believe in the ableness of the infant, and in the caregiver's ability to be responsive to the infant's ableness at whatever level it exists. The caregiver helps the infant "make things work," thereby increasing the infant's ability to act on the environment. For the caregiver of an infant or toddler the focus is on providing a setting in which daily routines, play activities, caregiver's responsiveness, and intervention procedures are geared to the infant's responsiveness and skill levels. Such an environment is not only developmentally appropriate; it is also an **enabling environment** because:

- It encourages the infant to respond and adapt to environmental experiences by helping the baby regulate biological rhythms (sleeping, eating, eliminating) and psychological state (soothability, excitability, responsiveness).

[1] The material in this section is adapted from A. Witte (1992). The infant caregiver/teacher/interventionist. In K. E. Allen, *The exceptional child: Mainstreaming in early childhood education* (pp. 337–360). Albany, NY: Delmar.

- It helps the infant learn to maintain a balance between avoiding environmental events that deter development and approaching events that support healthy attachment and **intentional communication**. Infants accomplish this best when caregivers help them learn to respond in mutually satisfying ways to people and activities.
- It promotes the infant's emerging abilities to select and practice simple, more specific responses out of global, **undifferentiated responses**. The interactions between the caregiver and the child foster the child's sense of control and use of various senses to experience the environment in selective ways.
- It facilitates the infant's efforts to initiate new responses to people, objects, and events. The foundation for new responses is provided by the interaction between the caregiver and the infant's efforts to initiate activities in ways that lead to more complex behavioral and emotional patterns.

Environment. First and foremost, an appropriate developmental environment for infants and toddlers is a safe and healthy environment. It offers protection for children and their undertakings, wherever care is provided—in the child's home, in a family child care home, or in a center-based child care center. An appropriate environment for very young children is also a **responsive environment.** A responsive environ-ment actively engages and reacts to the child. It supports infants and young children when they interact with adults and other children. It supports them when they are using materials and equipment. It supports them when they are alone, engaged in calming or entertaining themselves. By its very nature, a responsive environment encourages and supports active exploration by providing individual infants and toddlers with opportunities and options for:

- Freely accessing what is happening in the environment
- Making choices that respond to the child's overtures and also reflect expressed intentions
- Engaging in experiences that evolve from simple to more complex
- Causing things to happen

Equipment. The extent to which infants are supported in initiating their own activities is largely determined by the space that is provided and how it is divided, how materials are stored and presented, and the actual materials that are available. When arranging toys and accessories (e.g., mobiles), teachers must consider how items will be viewed and accessed from the infants' and toddlers' perspective. Caregivers also must choose play materials that are visually appealing and invite handling and manipulation. Safety considerations always come first when selecting materials. All objects must be large and smooth enough to be mouthed because infants and toddlers suck, bite, or chew just about everything they come in contact with. To prevent objects from becoming lodged in the throat, mouth, ears, or nose a general *rule of fist* should be used: A child under 3 should not have access to objects smaller than his or her own fist. Appropriate toys for very young children include:

- Bells
- Busy boxes
- Balls
- Vinyl-covered pillows to climb on
- Childproof mirrors
- Nesting toys
- Large beads that snap together
- Small blocks

Infants thrive on being held and cuddled.

- Washable squares of cloth (24 x 24 in.) of different colors and textures
- Shape sorters
- Squeeze toys that squeak or rattle
- Rattles, spoons, and teethers
- Dolls
- Picture books
- Pull toys
- Music boxes and other musical toys
- Small wagons
- Various types of containers (and things to put in them)

Health, safety, and nutrition.   Promoting health and safety are priorities in planning a program for very young children. Teachers must be sure that the environment is well prepared before children arrive and that procedures are in place to maintain health and safety measures. Gonzalez-Mena and Eyer (1989) point out that caregivers must rehearse fire and disaster plans for getting children to safety. In addition, the

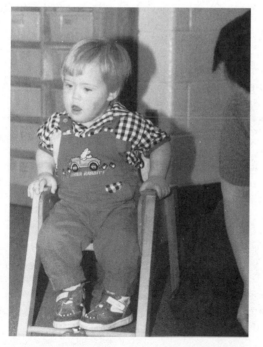

A chair with arms provides this toddler with security and support.

authors emphasize the need for emergency numbers posted by the telephone and a quickly accessible file indicating what parents want done if they cannot be reached in an emergency. Guidelines for a safe and healthy environment for very young children include the following:

- Toys are safe, washable, and too large for young children to swallow. Mouthed toys are replaced with clean ones so that the mouthed toys can be disinfected with a bleach solution (one-quarter cup bleach to a gallon of water or one tablespoon bleach to a quart of water).
- Electrical outlets are covered; extension cords are not exposed; hazardous substances are kept out of children's reach.
- Each infant has his or her own bedding, diapers, clothing, pacifiers, and special comforting objects. Personal items are labeled with the child's name.
- Diaper-changing areas are easily and routinely sanitized after each change of each child.
- Staff are healthy and take precautions not to spread illness.
- Caregivers wash their hands before and after every diaper change and the feeding of each infant.
- Adults are aware of the symptoms of common childhood illnesses and diseases, of children's allergies to food and other sources, and of potential hazards in the environment.
- Infants always are held with their bodies at an appropriate angle ("head above the heart") when being fed from a bottle.
- Children who can sit up are fed with one or two other infants and a caregiver to provide assistance.
- Safe finger foods are encouraged. Only healthy foods are offered. Eating is considered a sociable, happy time.

Staff–parent interactions.   Maintaining positive and honest interactions among parents and staff members is important. Staff must remember that parents are the primary source of affection and care in the child's life. Positive interaction between staff and parents can help parents feel more confident in their roles and with the child care choice they have made. Guidelines for positive staff interactions with parents include:

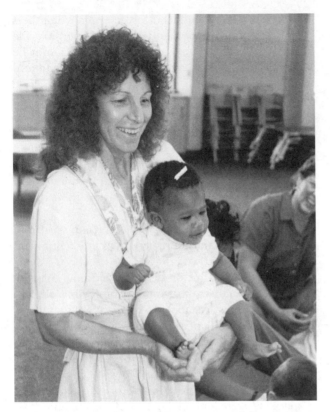

From the security of the caregiver's arms, an infant learns to respond to new people and activities.

- Interact with parents to share important information about the child
- Demonstrate respect for a family's culture and life choices
- Have appropriate information to be able to answer questions about child development and available community resources
- Respond to parents' questions, comments, and concerns

ESSENTIAL ELEMENTS OF INCLUSIVE PROGRAMS SERVING CHILDREN 3–5[2]

Programs for 3- to 5-year-old children are often a child's and a family's first experience with a center-based program. For many children, it is their first time with a large group of children. A key to children's adjustments is that teachers not expect too much or too little from the children or their parents. Clear and consistent expectations along with a well-planned learning environment results in a positive experience for young children and their families.

Curriculum goals. Young children learn by doing; therefore, curriculum goals should incorporate child-initiated, teacher-supported exploration and discovery activities. Play is the medium through which children learn best, and should be a primary consideration in setting up curriculum goals and classroom activities. Curriculum goals should be developed using an integrated model of child development that acknowledges the interdependence of development across domains. Individual diversity is planned for, and each child's unique pattern of growth and development is supported by the classroom curriculum.

Teaching strategies. Appropriate teaching strategies provide opportunities for young children to learn skills and acquire information in meaningful contexts. Teaching strategies must be both age- and individually appropriate, so teachers will have to use a variety of strategies to meet the needs of all the children in the classroom. An important component of teaching young children is preparing environments that invite and support learning. In inclusive classrooms, teachers need to design learning environments that provide carefully matched opportunities and contexts for children with diverse abilities. Teachers also must be able to use incidental teaching strategies (see Units 12 and 16) to take advantage of teachable moments that occur throughout the day. Teaching strategies also must support children's independence and self-determination. Children must be given the opportunity and guidance when needed, to make and carry out choices. Additionally, teachers must recognize that there is more than one right answer or one right way to solve a problem, tell a story, or build a tower of blocks. Appropriate environments for preschool children support self-directed problem solving and experimentation.

Guidance of social-emotional development. Developing social skills and peer relationships is a major skill

---

[2] Section 4 of this text provides detailed descriptions of how to implement programs for preschool children. Therefore, detailed lists of strategies are not provided in this section.

young children must learn. Early childhood educators can play an important role in supporting young children as they learn to play together, cooperate, give and receive help, negotiate, and solve interpersonal problems. Social-emotional development can be facilitated by teachers who model self-control, encourage appropriate behaviors, use positive statements and other social forms of praise, and set clear limits. Social norms vary across cultures; the social skills taught in preschool must not conflict with a child's culture. The guidance for social-emotional development provided at preschool should supplement, not contradict, what is taught at home. At the same time, many children need explicit instruction and intensive support to develop appropriate social skills and peer-directed play skills. (Facilitating the development of these skills is described in Unit 15.)

Language and literacy development.   Functional use of language and support of children's emerging literacy are essential during the preschool years. Although most typically developing children will have functional communication skills when they enter preschool, many children with disabilities may still be developing rudimentary conversational skills. Functional communication skills enable children to control their envi-

Caregivers promote development by responding positively.

ronment by using speech or signs to get what they need and want. (Unit 16 focuses on facilitating communication skills in the classroom.) Literacy development is also an important goal. Though formalized instruction in reading and writing is not considered appropriate in preschool curricula, nevertheless, preschool classrooms must provide a rich literacy environment with many experiences that help children learn to read. There must be opportunities for children to see books, hear and tell stories, engage in word games (e.g., rhyming songs or recitations), play with sandpaper and magnetic letters, write, and draw. In her book, *Beginning to Read: Thinking and Learning about Print*, Marilyn Adams (1990) states that the most important activity for building the skills that characterize a good reader is reading aloud to children. (This and other literacy activities are an important part of an appropriate preschool curriculum and are discussed further in Unit 17.)

Physical development.   Children need daily opportunities to engage in **gross motor** and **fine motor** activities. They are growing fast and need to move and use their bodies throughout the day. Gross motor activities offer children opportunities to use large muscles through jumping, balancing, and running. Activities should be fun, challenging, noncompetitive, and take place every day, preferably outdoors. Fine motor activities are often referred to as manipulative or table-top activities. Included are writing, drawing, painting, cutting, pegboards, puzzles, and parquetry blocks. Children should be provided with opportunity and support to explore these and many other materials and develop skills through participating regularly in these activities.

Aesthetic development.   Experience in art and music should be available every day in preschool classrooms. Emphasis is on exploration, spontaneity, self-expression, and appreciation rather than on completing a specific product or learning a particular tune. Art and music activities should represent the cultures of the children and staff in the classroom.

Parent–teacher relations.   Parents and teachers must work together to provide consistency for young children. Teachers may see some parents every day when they drop off and pick up their children; other parents are at the school less often. Teachers need to establish regular communication with all parents. This allows teachers and parents to discuss the child's behavior on a regular basis, so that if a problem occurs, teachers and parents already have a relationship established that will facilitate their addressing the problem in an efficient and productive manner. Many preschools use newsletters or weekly schedule notes to keep parents connected with classroom activities. (Communicating with parents is discussed in detail in Unit 9.)

ESSENTIAL ELEMENTS OF INCLUSIVE PROGRAMS SERVING CHILDREN 6–8

Although these programs are part of elementary school, the recommended practices for early childhood education continue to be appropriate. The primary grades are an amazing time for children, academically and socially. They learn to read and write and understand simple mathematics, and they learn to function as a part of a large and complex social institution. A developmentally appropriate primary classroom plays an important role in helping the child and family establish a positive relationship with the school.

Curriculum goals.   In the primary grades, an appropriate curriculum is broad-based; it includes physical, social, emotional, and intellectual goals. Children will progress at different rates; thus, individualized planning and instruction are important parts of a developmentally appropriate primary curriculum. As children enter kindergarten and the early grades, they are usually just beginning their relationship with the public school system. Therefore one goal of the primary curriculum should be to establish a foundation for lifelong learning and to create a positive school experience for the child and family. Activities that promote self-esteem and help children increase their confidence and competence as students also are important curricular goals.

Teaching strategies.   "The relevant principle of instruction is that teachers of young children must always be cognizant of the whole child" (Bredekamp 1987, p.

63). Therefore teaching strategies in the primary grades reflect the interdependence of developmental domains and the importance of learning in contexts that are meaningful to the student (Dewey 1938). Teachers in the primary grades create environments that support student exploration and child-directed inquiry; they also offer explicit instruction to provide children with the academic tools they need. There must be time for spontaneous play, too, because children continue to learn through unstructured activities. Although children in the primary grades can sit still for longer periods of time than preschoolers, they still need to be active to ensure learning. Children continue to be dependent on firsthand experience to learn new concepts: "Therefore, an important principle for primary-age children is that they should be engaged in active, rather than passive, activities" (Bredekamp 1987, p. 63).

Integrated curriculum.   "Children's learning, like development, is integrated during the early years" (Bredekamp 1987, p. 63). **Integrated curricula**, therefore, meet the developmental needs of children in the primary grades. An integrated curriculum teaches around themes, experiences, and projects that include skills from many curricular areas; it resists establishing artificial boundaries between academic areas. For example, if children are working on the life cycle of salmon, an integrated approach could include literacy skills (reading, writing, spelling), math and science skills, social studies, geography, and art. An integrated curriculum provides children an opportunity to learn and teachers an opportunity to teach academic skills in a meaningful context. Rather than discrete worksheets and abbreviated individual assignments, students work in cooperative groups. A collaborative project for the life cycle of the salmon theme could include a story for the class newspaper, a map of where salmon live during different parts of their life cycle, charts depicting changes in the salmon population, and drawings of different types of salmon. Field trips related to the theme would be an important component of an integrated curriculum. Appropriate field trips for the salmon project could include trips to a hatchery, fish ladder, or aquarium.

Guidance of social-emotional development.   The role of peer relationships continues to be important as children enter elementary school. Friendships play an essential role in personal identity development and social adjustment. Children who do not make friends are more likely to experience both academic and mental health problems as adolescents and adults (Walker, Colvin, and Ramsey 1995). "The relevant principle of practice is that teachers recognize the importance of developing positive peer group relationships and provide opportunities and support for cooperative small group projects that not only develop cognitive ability but promote peer interaction" (Bredekamp 1987, p. 64). Emphasis in the primary grades is on teaching young children self-control, self-assessment, and problem-solving techniques as an integrated part of the curriculum, rather than being addressed only when a problem occurs. Primary grade children often are taught in multiage groups (Bailey, Burchinal, and McWilliam 1993). Such grouping adds to the diversity of the classroom and provides natural opportunities for children to learn helping and nurturing roles. More competent children in the classroom should have experiences with older students, so that they too receive as well as provide assistance.

Parent–teacher relations.   A challenge for teachers in the primary grades is to develop good working relationships with parents, given the limited amount of naturally occurring contact. Teachers should be in regular contact with parents either through visits, phone calls, or notes. Parents should be welcomed in the classroom at any time, and strategies to facilitate their comfortable participation in classroom activities should be developed. For example, parents can be invited to share their talents, expertise, interests, and cultural backgrounds with the class.

Evaluation.   The evaluation of children's work in the primary grades needs to be **contextually based** and **formative**. Rather than viewing mistakes as indicators of what children do not know, teachers should evaluate mistakes as a way of learning about children's understanding of concepts. Further instruction then can be based on this error analysis. Letter grades should not be used; rather, teachers should use narra-

The potential for positive developmental progress is there in every child.

tive progress reports. The use of standardized testing with young children has been widely criticized as invalid and of limited utility (NAEYC 1988). More appropriate strategies for student assessment include classroom-based procedures such as direct observation, collection of work samples, and portfolios (Keefe 1995).

SUMMARY

There are many types of inclusive early childhood programs found in child care, preschool, Head Start, community recreation programs, and elementary schools. Despite the different structures and purposes of these programs, they share certain elements such as program planning and implementation that enable teachers to meet the needs of young children with diverse abilities. Inclusive programs also must be culturally sensitive and responsive to differences in language, social values, and educational background of the children and their families.

Although inclusive early childhood programs may look very different, they share elements that define high quality. The features that working mothers identified as indicators of quality child care programs were attention to the children's safety, provider's communication with parents about their children, cleanliness, attention children receive, and provider's warmth toward children.

The principle of developmental appropriateness is important for programs serving all children birth through age 8. Developmental appropriateness has two dimensions: chronological age appropriateness and individual appropriateness. The dimension of chronological age appropriateness is especially important when working with children with developmental disabilities. This dimension also indicates that programs for young children of different ages will be different in focus and implementation.

Quality programs for infants and toddlers provide a safe, healthy, well-supervised environment, filled with developmentally appropriate play materials, and responsive caregivers. Experiences are not imposed on infants and toddlers; instead, caregivers patiently work to engage the infants' active participation as initiators as well as responders. Only by observing what a very young child is doing and how the child responds to overtures from others, can caregivers decide how best to respond to individual abilities and needs.

For children from 3 to 5 years of age, a quality program provides many opportunities to learn by doing. Children acquire knowledge of the world through play. Good programs provide well-planned learning environments across developmental domains including language, literacy, science, social development, and the arts.

As children enter kindergarten and the primary grades, they still need programs that adhere to the principle of developmental appropriateness. Quality primary programs provide integrated learning opportunities. Child-directed and teacher-supported active learning is the key to quality programs for children this age.

STUDENT ACTIVITIES

1. Visit at least two different early childhood programs— family child care, center-based child care, preschool, kindergarten or primary grade classrooms, community recreation programs. List features that these programs share and ways in which they differ.
2. Find out what agency in your state regulates child care programs. Write to that agency and inquire about the child care regulations in your state. How do they relate to the best practices described in this unit?
3. Think about a caregiving routine for infants or toddlers—diapering, feeding, bathing—and list the kinds of learning experiences that a caregiver can weave into the routine.
4. Observe an inclusive program for children 3 to 5. Observe one child with disabilities and one typically developing child. Describe the similarities and differences in their experiences during your observation.
5. Observe a kindergarten, first-grade, or second-grade classroom. Describe the elements of developmentally appropriate practice you saw demonstrated during your visit.

REVIEW QUESTIONS

A. *Lists*

1. List the five features most frequently identified by mothers to indicate quality child care programs.
2. List at least four types of early childhood programs that could potentially be inclusive early childhood programs.
3. List the six general principles that DEC used to evaluate recommended practices in early childhood special education.
4. List the essential elements for quality early childhood programs serving children ages 0 to 2.
5. List the essential elements for quality early childhood education programs serving children ages 3 to 5.
6. List the essential elements for quality early childhood education programs serving children ages 6 to 8.

B. *True or False. Choose the best answer.*

T F   1. Inclusive early childhood programs must be located in public school buildings.

T F   2. Head Start serves children with disabilities.

T F   3. A gymnastics class can be a quality inclusive early childhood program.

T F   4. An enabling learning environment encourages and supports an infant's efforts.

T F   5. Chronological age does not play a role in evaluating the developmental appropriateness of an early childhood program.

T F   6. A responsive learning environment is based on formal lesson plans to be presented at scheduled times during the day.

T F   7. A developmentally appropriate preschool program never has teacher-planned activities.

T F   8. Literacy development is not an important concern until children enter first grade.

T F   9. An integrated curriculum may teach reading, math, and writing in a lesson based on a single theme.

T F   10. Evaluating the effects of an early childhood education program is not an important concern for teachers.

REFERENCES

Adams, M. (1990). *Beginning to read: Thinking and learning about print.* Champaign, IL: Center for the Study of Reading.

Bailey, D.B., Burchinal, M.R., and McWilliam, R.A. (1993). Age of peers and early child development. *Child Development, 64,* 848–862.

Bailey, D.B., and McWilliam, R.A. (1990). Normalizing early intervention. *Topics in Early Childhood Special Education, 10:2,* 33–47.

Bredekamp, S. (1987). *Developmentally appropriate practice in early childhood programs serving young children from birth through 8.* Washington, DC: NAEYC.

Brown, L., Branston, M.B., Hamre-Nietupski, S., Pumpian, I., Certo, N., and Gruenewald, L. (1979). A strategy for developing chronological age appropriate and functional curricular content for severely handicapped adolescents and young adults. *Journal of Special Education, 13,* 81–90.

Carnegie Task Force on Meeting the Needs of Young Children. (1994). *Starting points: Meeting the needs of our youngest children.* New York: Carnegie Foundation.

DEC Task Force on Recommended Practices. (1993). *DEC recommended practices: Indicators of quality in programs for infants and young children with special needs and their families.* Reston, VA: Council for Exceptional Children.

Dewey, J. (1938). *Experience and education.* New York: Collier Books.

Galinsky, E., Howes, C., Kontos, S., and Shinn, M. (1994). *The study of children in family child care and relative care.* New York: Families and Work Institute.

Gonzalez-Mena, J., and Eyer, D.W. (1989). *Infants, toddlers, and caregivers.* Mountain View, CA: Mayfield.

Hills, T.W. (1993). Assessment in context—Teachers and children at work. *Young Children 48:5,* 20–28.

Hunt, J. McV. (1961). *Intelligence and experience.* New York: Ronald Press.

Keefe, C.H. (1995). Portfolios: Mirrors of learning. *Teaching Exceptional Children, 27:2,* 66–67.

Meisels, S.J. (1993). Remaking classroom assessment with the work sampling system. *Young Children, 48:5,* 34–40.

National Association for the Education of Young Children (1988). Position statement on standardized testing of young children 3 through 8 years of age. *Young Children, 43,* 3.

Schorr, L. (1988). *Within our reach: Breaking the cycle of disadvantage.* New York: Anchor Books.

Thomas, A., and Chess, S. (1977). *Temperament and development.* New York: Bruner/Mazel.

Federal Legislation: Early Intervention and Prevention

OBJECTIVES

After studying this unit the student will be able to

- specify social and political forces that helped bring about federal legislation on behalf of exceptional children, including the gifted.
- list five rulings of PL 94-142 that affect programs for young children; list additional rulings in PL 99-457 that are of benefit to infants, toddlers, and their families.
- discuss PL 99-457 in terms of its impact on the early childhood profession.
- explain secondary disabilities and the importance of their prevention in a child with a major disability.
- describe three pieces of legislation designed to prevent developmental disabilities in children.

Public policy on behalf of infants and children with developmental disabilities (or at-risk for acquiring disabilities during the developmental years) has been expanding steadily over the past several decades. Beginning in the 1960s Congress passed a number of laws that support early identification, prevention, and treatment of developmental problems. Treatment often is spelled out as comprehensive health care and adequate nutrition coupled with early educational intervention (these serve as preventive measures also, as we will see). The most recent legislation emphasizes family support, thereby recognizing that infants and young children are best served in the context of a strong and healthy family. The undergirding support for inclusion of children with disabilities in general education programs is also contained in this legislation. This support has been strengthened in the past 10 years by court decisions that promote children's rights to be educated alongside their peers in community-based programs. These court cases (also called **case law**) will be described briefly in this unit.

The three principles of early identification, intervention, and prevention of developmental problems are traditional values among child developmentalists and early childhood educators. The laws that support these concepts and the impact of the legislation on children, families, and early childhood teachers are the focus of this unit.

THE EARLY INTERVENTION MOVEMENT

Early intervention has become a popular social-educational movement. Where did it begin? How did it unfold? Where are we now?

Environment and Experience. The importance of early intervention began to be recognized with a reevaluation of evidence about institutionalized infants and young children. It appeared that the majority of these children need not grow up retarded if provided appropriate stimulation very early in life (Skeels and Dye 1936; Skeels 1966). Then came research that intelligence was not *fixed* at the time of birth, not determined solely by genetics. Instead, intelligence was greatly influenced by environment and experience (Hunt 1961; Bloom 1964). (Prior to that, genetic predeterminism—heredity—was believed to be the deciding factor in the distribution of intelligence among individuals.)

During this same era, Kirk (1958) began an experimental preschool for young children considered to be mentally retarded. For several years he provided groups of children with enriched preschool experiences. His data suggested strongly that an inadequate learning environment might well be the cause of so-called mental retardation in many young children. The combined findings of these and other researchers gave convincing evidence that children's intelligence develops most rapidly during the early years. The findings also demonstrated that the development of sound intelligence is dependent on appropriate stimulation from the environment.

The next move was up to public policy makers. Before long, they, too, were convinced of the need for providing enriched learning environments for young children. The outcome was the widely publicized early intervention and compensatory education program known as Head Start. Since then, innumerable studies demonstrate that early intervention has improved both the learning capabilities and the quality of life for millions of young low-income children and their families (Zigler and Muenchow 1992).

At the end of 1990 the 101st Congress came out unequivocally on behalf of programs for young children, thus earning itself the title of "The Children's Congress." Head Start was reauthorized at its highest funding level ever. The Child Care and Development Block Grant was authorized in order to provide families with affordable child care, improved program quality, and increased availability of child development services. The block grant also offered unprecedented provisions for improvement in pay for early childhood teachers and care providers, both full- and part-time. Additional funding was authorized, too, to expand and improve staff training. The Americans with Disabilities Act was approved, extending full civil rights protection to all people with disabilities, and the National Commission on Children was formed "to serve as a forum on behalf of children of the nation" (PL 100-203). Such vigorous legislative activity adds up to federal recognition of the benefits of providing early education and intervention services for young children. It also points up the need for greatly expanded numbers of early childhood personnel trained to provide the services that have been authorized.

Civil Rights.   Awareness of the impact of environment and experience on early development ran parallel to an emerging awareness of the potentials and rights of individuals with disabilities. The civil rights movement had exposed grossly unequal, even inhumane, schooling conditions for minority children. This led to a searching of the public conscience about overall differences in educational opportunities. Civil rights advocates worked tirelessly to assure that the constitutional rights of *all* citizens were upheld. The right to a free and equal education received particular attention. Special interest groups, recognizing that individuals with disabilities also represented an unequally treated minority, began speaking out. One of the earliest and most influential of the special interest groups was the National Association for Retarded Children (NARC). Later renamed the Association for Retarded Citizens (ARC), the ARC continues to be a powerful **advocacy group**. Other organizations, both professional and citizens' groups, also became active on behalf of individuals with developmental disabilities. Among them are:

Council for Exceptional Children (CEC)
Division for Early Childhood (DEC) (an affiliation of CEC)
American Speech, Language, and Hearing Association
American Association on Mental Retardation (AAMR)
The Association for Persons with Severe Handicaps (TASH)

The efforts of these and other organizations helped produce a number of important laws referred to as **landmark legislation**. Never before had there been such significant federal rulings on behalf of people with disabilities. What follows is a brief review of the laws that provide specifically for young children with developmental problems and their families. First, however, a note on the lack of legislation on behalf of gifted children.

PUBLIC POLICY AND THE GIFTED

Concern for the gifted has not been a major focus on public policy in this country. Information on preschool intervention with gifted children is limited

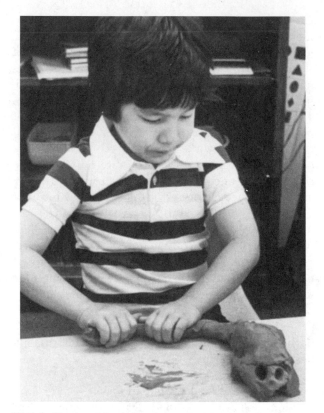

Well-defined public policy is needed on behalf of young children who show signs of giftedness.

in scope, provides few examples of model programs, and suffers from lack of controlled research studies (Stiles and Kitano 1991). True, there have been short episodes of interest as when the famous Terman study on high IQ individuals was published in the mid-1950s. In the late 1950s came another bit of interest due to the Russian spacecraft (Sputnik) scare. The result of that was seeking out gifted math and science students and putting them into enriched academic programs. With the civil rights movement, total concentration was on underserved minorities, low-income children, and children with disabilities. In 1972 the U.S. Commissioner of Education reported that more than two million gifted children in our nation were receiving no special programming. He described these children as the nation's most neglected yet most potentially productive. Out of that report came the Office of Gifted and Talented within the federal Department of Education. The office was abolished in 1981 and funding for gifted programs was greatly reduced.

Over the years various advocacy groups such as the Council of Exceptional Children (CEC) and the Gifted Advocacy Information Network (GAIN) have worked to obtain adequate funds for the education of the gifted. In addition, a number of states have local parent and professional groups working toward support of gifted programs in their communities. Some states now require the development of the same formal IEP for the gifted as is mandated for children with disabilities (Wolf 1994). In 1988 the Jacob K. Javits Gifted and Talented Student Education Act was funded. The federal monies are to be used for:

- Identifying and serving gifted and talented students
- Training and providing professional development programs for teachers of the gifted
- Creating a National Center for the Education of the Gifted

No legislation has focused exclusively on giftedness in the very young child. Yet attention should be directed toward these children and early childhood programs; it is during these earliest years that "attitudes toward learning are solidified and rampant curiosity becomes either encouraged or discouraged" (Gallagher 1988, p. 110). According to Renzulli and Reis (1991), support for demonstration programs for gifted children should be a part of our national agenda. Perhaps that will become the next target of early childhood advocates.

LANDMARK LEGISLATION AND PEOPLE WITH DISABILITIES

Beginning in the early 1960s a number of laws have been passed to try to provide services for (and decent treatment of) individuals with developmental disabilities. These enactments have taken many forms and have effected change for a wide range of individuals. This unit will focus only on those mandates having direct bearing on young children and their families.

University Affiliated Facilities (PL 88-164). This 1963 law provided federal funds to establish University

Affiliated Facilities (UAF for the Mentally Retarded). These centers were (and are) staffed by teams of professionals from various disciplines. Their goal is to promote exemplary professional team practices related to the **interdisciplinary** aspects of early intervention so as to better serve infants and children with developmental problems. The UAFs (some renamed University Affiliated Programs, UAPs) are located across the country, approximately one per state. Their main purposes are:

- To create, demonstrate, and evaluate intervention and educational programs for children and youth
- To provide professional trainees with interdisciplinary training
- To conduct research related to human development and developmental problems

Over the years, the UAF legislation has been updated, expanded, and assigned new names including the term *developmental disabilities*. Expansion of services came about mainly through the efforts of various special interest groups. The major changes are:

- Inclusion of individuals with epilepsy, cerebral palsy, and other neurological impairments as well as disorders such as autism and dyslexia
- Establishment of Regional Resource Centers to develop educational strategies for working with infants and children with developmental problems
- Special centers and services for children born deaf and blind because of an earlier measles (rubella) epidemic

Handicapped Children's Early Education Assistance Act (PL 90-538).   In 1968 came a law focused on the very young: the Handicapped Children's Early Education Program. Most often referred to as HCEEP, the major purpose of this legislation is to improve early intervention services for children with disabilities, children who are at-risk for disabilities, and their families. Federal funds supported experimental centers known as the *First Chance Network* and model demonstration projects. These projects develop, validate, and disseminate new and better approaches to early educational practices for children with develop-

mental problems. They also focus on parent involvement activities and program evaluation systems. In the 1980s emphasis shifted somewhat to include funding for several major research institutes and outreach projects. Outreach allows other programs throughout the country the opportunity to learn from the demonstration projects. In 1994, for example, 20 projects were funded for regional and national outreach. This program was renamed in 1992 to reflect the Department of Education's use of "**people-first**" terminology. The new name is Early Education Project for Children with Disabilities (EEPCD).

Head Start Amendments (PL 92-424).   Amendments related to children with disabilities were attached to Head Start legislation in 1972. Head Start's tradition had always been an "open door" policy—*all* children who met the economic requirement, regardless of their developmental status, were to be included in Head Start programs. The new law, however, mandated (required) that 10 percent of Head Start's enrollment be reserved for children with developmental disabilities. In 1974 the regulations were changed to ensure that children with more severe disabilities, who also met the economic requirements, were being served by Head Start. According to the new definition

Head Start welcomes all children.

of disability, the 10 percent was to be made up of young children who were diagnosed as having:

mental retardation
deafness or serious hard-of-hearing
serious speech impairments
serious visual impairment
crippling orthopedic impairments
chronic health disabilities
learning disabilities

The above definition, of course, does not exclude children with milder disabilities. It simply means that they are not to be counted as part of the 10 percent requirement. Nor does it mean that all children who have severe disabilities are best served in a Head Start program. The law states: "Severely handicapped children are enrolled in Head Start only when the professional diagnostic resource recommends that placement in the program is in the child's best interest and when the parents concur."

Head Start has been a pioneer in the field of including young children with severe disabilities in community-based programs. The newest Head Start regulations continue to stress this aspect of the program and to encourage local programs to work with other local agencies (such as public schools and universities) to provide appropriate inclusive programs to young children with disabilities.

Head Start continues to grow. By 1990 Head Start was serving 575,802 children between the ages of 3 and 5. Although this is an impressive number and Head Start was receiving more funding than any time in its history, still only 30 percent of the children and families who met the economic requirements for Head Start were receiving services (National Commission of Children 1991).

Parent–Child centers. Since 1967 Parent–Child Centers (PCC), serving infants, toddlers, and their families, have existed as a part of the Head Start program. In 1990 there were 35 PCCs throughout the country, serving about 4,500 children (Pizzo 1990). The centers provide comprehensive services for promoting overall development in children from birth up until age 3, as well as support services for their

Parent–Child Centers (PCC) were introduced in 1967.

families. There is growing demand for increase in these services among policy makers and leaders within the field of early childhood development and education. As noted pediatrician T. Berry Brazelton (1990) argued in his testimony before the Congressional Committee on Education and Labor: "I would strongly recommend that the Head Start authorization be increased sufficiently so that more resources can be devoted to eligible children between birth and age three" (quoted in Pizzo 1990, p. 31).

Regional Access Projects. In 1972 another part of the Head Start legislation called for the establishment of Regional Access Projects (RAPs). Their purpose is to help Head Start programs more effectively serve children with developmental disabilities. Located throughout the country, RAPs provide information, personnel training, services, and equipment in collaboration with various agencies. The agencies include community health departments and mental health centers, speech and hearing clinics, developmental disabilities programs in colleges and universities, and a number of private facilities.

Developmental Disabilities Act (DDA) (PL 93-112). Another set of rulings related to handicapping conditions was authorized in the Rehabilitation Act of 1973. Section 504 focused on reducing discrimination against individuals with disabilities. The law required that everyone with a disability be given access to jobs, education, housing, and public buildings. The popular name for part of this law was the *wheelchair requirement*. This law also ruled that states offering preschool services to nondisabled children must offer comparable services to those with disabilities. This act was reauthorized in 1992 to change its language to reflect the people-first terminology adopted by the U.S. government and to make it easier for people with severe disabilities to access vocational rehabilitation services.

Education for All Handicapped Children Act (PL 94-142).   This legislation was signed into law in 1975. Its popular title is *The Bill of Rights for Handicapped Children*. Advocacy groups hailed the legislation as a major step in upholding the constitutional rights of citizens with disabilities. It guaranteed (for the first time in our country's history) all children and youth, regardless of the severity of their disability, the right to a free and appropriate public education. Among other things, the law gives specific support to early education programs for children under 5 years of age. Special funds, called *incentive monies*, are authorized to encourage states to locate and serve preschool children in need of early intervention services. *Child Find* is the title put on this federally supported process of finding and identifying such children.

In addition to the early intervention component, PL 94-142 has a number of rulings that apply to all children with developmental disabilities. These are summarized as follows:

Zero reject.   Local school systems must provide all children, regardless of the severity of their disability, with a free education appropriate to each child's unique needs.

Nondiscriminatory evaluation.   No child may be placed in a special education program without full individual testing. The tests must be nondiscriminatory; that is, appropriate to the child's *language and cultural background*. Assessment is to be based on several types of evaluation and is to include cognitive, **adaptive**, and social performance.

Appropriate education.   Local school districts must provide educational services that are appropriate to each individual child. The specifics of the educational program are described in a child's Individualized Education Plan (IEP). (Unit 10 will describe the IEP process in detail.)

Least restrictive environment: inclusion.   To the greatest extent possible, children with disabilities must be educated alongside students who do not have disabilities. It is important to remember that the least restrictive environment clause assumes that children with disabilities in the general education environment will be receiving the specialized support necessary to optimize their development. Including children with disabilities without adequate support does not meet the letter or the spirit of this law. (The principle of inclusion was discussed in detail in Unit 1 and will be addressed throughout the text.)

Due process.   Parents must legally be able to call a special hearing when they do not agree with the school's educational plans for their child. Due process further ensures that a child cannot be removed from a classroom simply because of annoying or inconvenient behavior. In brief, due process gives parents the right to:

- Examine all records that pertain to their child
- Be consulted about their child's educational program before it is put into effect
- Receive written notice of any proposed changes in their child's educational classification or placement
- Demand legal representation if disagreements between themselves and school personnel cannot be resolved

Parent participation.   PL 94-142 recognized the importance of parents' contributions to their child's progress. Amendments to this law, described below, further emphasize parents' participation.

Education of the Handicapped Amendments (PL 99-457).   In 1986 Congress passed the most comprehensive legislation ever enacted on behalf of infants and

PL 99-457 emphasizes family involvement.

young children, the amendments to PL 94-142, discussed above. The new law has far-reaching implications for young children and their families. It also has far-reaching implications for everyone who provides services for young children—child care staff, preschool teachers, and health care providers. The continued need for a tremendously increased number of early childhood teachers and related staff is obvious. It is reflected in the long-range planning of many two- and four-year teacher-training programs. Projected increases in staff is reflected also in programs that train the trainers of teachers and early childhood administrators. Greatly increased numbers of health care providers also will be needed. Many of these professionals, from various disciplines, will be trained to work in early childhood centers. They will work with teachers, in the classroom, implementing programs for individual children.

PL 99-457 has several parts or Titles; only those that focus on the very young, Titles I and II, will be discussed here.

Title I Infants and toddlers with disabilities.   Often referred to as Part H, this part of the law is known as **discretionary legislation**. This means that a state may serve children from birth through 2 years of age if it chooses, but it is *not* required by law to do so. (*Exception:* Any state serving nondisabled infants and toddlers must serve infants and toddlers with disabilities.)

Legislators explained the reasoning behind Title I:

Congress finds an urgent and substantial need to enhance the development of handicapped infants and toddlers and minimize their potential for developmental delay; reduce the education costs to society, including our schools; minimize the likelihood of institutionalization; and enhance the capacity to provide quality early intervention services and expand and improve existing services.

It is therefore the policy of the United States to provide financial assistance to states to develop and implement a statewide, comprehensive, coordinated, interdisciplinary program of early intervention services for handicapped infants and toddlers and their families. (Federal Register 1986)

Following is a brief summary of the Title I part of PL 99-457:

- *Individuals to be served:* Infants and toddlers who are experiencing developmental delays, or are at-risk of having substantial delays unless they receive early intervention services.
- *Labeling no longer required:* Very young children no longer need to be labeled as having a particular kind of disability. As discussed in Unit 5, they do not have to be put into a category such as mentally retarded or emotionally disturbed.
- *Individualized Family Service Plan (IFSP):* Each infant and toddler and his or her family must receive a **multidisciplinary**, written assessment of their needs and of the services prescribed. This service will be provided by a team of qualified personnel that includes special educators, speech and language pathologists and audiologists, occupational and physical therapists, social workers, nutritionists, and other professionals as deemed necessary. Services will be coordinated by a service coordinator assigned specifically to each family. One purpose of the service coordinator is to make sure the family has a part in planning the child's IFSP; another is to help the family obtain and coordinate services that ensure identified needs are being met. (The IFSP and its requirements will be discussed in detail in Unit 9.)

Title II Children with disabilities—ages 3 to 5.   Services for 3-, 4- and 5-year-olds remain much as they were under PL 94-142, except for two important changes.

One was substantial increases in funding. The second was a five-year time schedule for channeling the additional money to the states. This change in the legislation provided the necessary impetus to make universal early childhood special education services a reality. Beginning in the 1990–1991 school year every state and territory in the United States provided preschool services to young children (ages 3–5) with developmental disabilities.

As noted earlier, most of the requirements of PL 94-142 are retained in the PL 99-457 amendments. The mandate that children with disabilities be educated in the least restrictive environment (the inclusion concept) is still in effect. *Due process*, *Child Find*, and *individualized education plans* (IEPs) also are continuing requirements. Title II of PL 99-457 is *not* discretionary. States receiving federal funds for early intervention programs *must* serve young children with developmental disabilities according to the same formula and requirements as before. Furthermore, parent support services are allowable as "related services."

The combination of PL 94-142 and PL 99-457 fulfills goals for young children that the early childhood profession long has advocated. Furthermore, the laws indicate that Congress is willing to accede fully to popular opinion that early identification and intervention is important. The laws also indicate a "quality-of-life" recognition: that early intervention is the best way to improve the well-being of developmentally disabled young children and their families.

Americans with Disabilities Act (PL 101-336).   In 1990 the Americans with Disabilities Act (ADA) was passed into law. Patterned after Section 504 of the Rehabilitation Act, ADA gives civil rights protection to individuals in private employment, all public services and accommodations, transportation, and telecommunications. For early childhood education, some of the most significant implications are in the area of access to child care and community recreation programs. (This is discussed in Unit 2.)

Individuals with Disabilities Education Act (PL 101-476).   The Individuals with Disabilities Education Act (IDEA) amended and changed the name of the EHA in 1990. This amendment also changed the emphasis of the program from providing segregated programs for specific conditions to providing support to individuals with disabilities in community settings.

INCLUSION AND CASE LAW

Case laws are clarifications of existing laws that are drawn from judicial decisions. Once a law is enacted, questions concerning interpretations and applications of that law often are determined in court. These interpretations affect how the law actually impacts the lives of the people the law was meant to benefit. Case law has played an important role in school reform and in advancing the rights of students with disabilities in the public school system beginning in 1954 with *Brown v. Board of Education* ruling, where the court found that segregated schools violated the Fourteenth Amendment of the Constitution. Although this case involved race, and not ability, it is often noted as a landmark case for the inclusion of all children. It is beyond the scope of this chapter to review all the case law relevant to inclusion or early childhood special education (see Haring, McCormick, and Haring 1994 for a summary). Rather, we will present brief summaries of two recent cases that have been heralded as landmark cases supporting the inclusion of *all* children in general education classes.

Sacramento Unified School District v. Holland (1992). This case involved a 9-year old girl with Down syndrome. The district court ruled that she must be fully included in a general education classroom and provided a four-part test that must be used to evaluate the feasibility of inclusion. The test asks:

1. What educational benefits are available to the child with disabilities when supplemented by the appropriate supports?
2. What are the nonacademic (e.g., social) benefits of placement in a general education classroom?
3. What is the effect on nondisabled children?
4. What is the cost?

Oberti v. Board of Education of Clementon School District (1993). This case was similar to *Holland*, except that the child involved had severe disabilities. The judge ruled strongly in favor of the child's right to receive inclusive education and said, "Inclusion is a right, not a privilege for a select few."

These cases, along with the work of parents and advocates, have been extremely important in advancing inclusive education. These decisions have helped support the interpretation of the least restrictive environment being the general education classroom.

PREVENTION AND RELATED LEGISLATION

In many instances, intervention services might never have been needed had prevention been available. In the unit on causes of handicapping conditions (Unit 5), it is noted, for example, that the incidence of developmental problems could be drastically reduced if every family's most basic needs were met. The issue of prevention and its relationship to federal legislation will be addressed in this section.

The Timing of Prevention.   Just as disabling conditions can be a threat at any point in development, so preventive measures can be called into action at any point. Prevention should begin before conception with the good health of the mother and father and continue throughout the developmental years. For all children, prevention should be an ongoing process.

Children who participate in early education are less likely to be in special education in later years.

Prevention before conception.   As noted in Unit 5, one source of developmental problems is the genetic makeup of each infant. Chromosomal mishaps account for only a small percentage of such problems; even so, most are preventable. Many parents seek genetic counseling and chromosomal analysis if they have reason to suspect their child may inherit a problem. When results are favorable, they can proceed with a pregnancy with a fair degree of confidence. In the case of negative results, a difficult choice may be the only option. One choice is to forego having children; another is to adopt them. Another choice might be to proceed with pregnancy and then have a prenatal diagnosis to see if the unborn infant has a genetically related disease or disabling syndrome. Information of this kind can be obtained through **amniocentesis** or **chorionic villus sampling (CVS)**. Should the results of either test indicate abnormality, parents then have another difficult choice related to continuing or terminating the pregnancy. Usually the decision is based on their moral and religious beliefs. Many couples have strong feelings that it is immoral to bring an infant with severe disabilities into the world. Others have equally strong feelings about the immorality of abortion. There are no easy answers in these situations.

Prevention during pregnancy.   Ensuring the good health of a mother during pregnancy is a major preventive measure in reducing developmental disabilities. Good health and adequate prenatal care go hand in hand with appropriate medical services. As noted in Unit 5, most diseases in the mother are preventable with immunization or appropriate medical treatment. Damage to the unborn child also can be prevented by foregoing the use of nicotine, alcohol, cocaine, and other chemical substances. These are known to have harmful effects on the infant **in utero**. What is not known is *how much* of any of these substances is harmful. Each woman has a different biochemical makeup that governs how much is too much for the baby she is carrying. In some instances, even relatively small amounts of a substance can have damaging effects.

Another damaging but preventable factor is malnourishment. Infants born to mothers whose diets were seriously deficient in protein and other necessary nutrients almost surely will be of low birth weight.

A low-birth-weight infant is at-risk for a variety of problems that can persist throughout the developmental years (Children's Defense Fund 1991). All of these problems, commonplace to mothers subsisting at or below the poverty level, will be discussed further in the section on legislation and prevention.

Prevention during and following birth.   Appropriate medical services, before and during birth, can prevent many developmental problems. A doctor or nurse midwife, who has provided care throughout a pregnancy, knows what to expect and how to handle individual problems that might arise. In this age of modern medicine, few infants need suffer any kind of damage at the time of birth.

The first minutes and hours following birth is a crucial time for identifying potential problems. Routine screening of newborns is an important aspect of prevention. The Apgar rating scale (to be discussed in Unit 11) is in widespread use for this purpose. A low score indicates the infant is likely to be at serious developmental risk and in need of immediate and constant attention. With intensive and highly specialized medical care, crippling disabilities often are prevented.

Potential problems, not so visible, also can be detected during the newborn period. Most states in this country require a blood test taken on the third or fourth day after birth (no earlier, as adverse biochemical reactions do not show up during the first few days of life). Analysis of the blood will reveal certain metabolic disorders, if present. The most widely known of these is PKU. As mentioned in Unit 5, mental retardation can be prevented if the infant is placed immediately on the prescribed diet. It should be stressed that even a few weeks' delay can result in serious brain damage—hence the need for preventive screening of all newborns.

Not all problems can be identified so readily. Many have symptoms so subtle or so unalarming they are not recognized. Others may be recognized but appear harmless enough at the moment. This situation may result in *wait-and-see* advice that allows a problem to progress from preventable to developmentally disastrous (as in the case in a serious hearing loss). Other problems, present at birth, may not show up until later childhood. Sexually transmitted diseases such as syphilis, passed on to the child prenatally, is one such example. By the time the symptoms show up in middle childhood, considerable developmental damage, preventable and unnecessary, already may have taken place.

Prevention of Secondary Disabilities.   When a handicapping condition does occur—before, during, or following birth—prevention continues to be the watchword. Now it becomes prevention of secondary disabilities. These are developmental problems that come about because of the primary disability. A hearing impaired child, for example, may never develop language or adequate cognitive skills unless preventive measures to overcome the language and cognitive deficits are undertaken early in the child's life. Secondary conditions can become even more disabling than the original problem.

A child may also become more disabled than need be because of the **cumulative effects** of a handicapping condition. Untreated problems tend to snowball: The farther the child gets behind in any area of development, the more damaging it is. For example, a 4-year-old who talks like a 3-year-old is not necessarily disabled. It is a different story if that child is still talking like a much younger child at age 12. It is likely the child's problems (in several areas of development) have increased out of all proportion to those created by the initial language delay. In such cases, preventive measures might well have reduced the cumulative deficit in the child's language skills and lessened the secondary problems.

Preventive measures also are needed to keep some disabilities from becoming worse, even irreversible. For example, early identification and treatment of an infant's eye problems may prevent total and irreversible loss of vision; residual vision often can be saved and strengthened. Another example might be the permanently crippling (and painful) joint contractures in a child with severe spasticity. These are likely to have had a good chance of being prevented if an appropriate positioning and exercising program had been ongoing.

Prevention and Federal Legislation.   In recent years, much of the legislation on behalf of young children has been directed toward the prevention of developmental problems. Inadequate nutrition and lack of medical services all too often result in developmental damage. Low-income families have the greatest numbers of children with developmental problems. At the same time, these are the families least able to provide themselves and their children with the kind of nutrition and health care that helps prevent developmental problems. What follows are examples of legislative acts designed to prevent developmental problems while benefiting children and families. Society itself benefits from this legislation on at least two levels: (1) reduction of health care costs for preventable disabilities; and (2) improvement in our reputation as a nation that, presumably, cares about its children and families.

Early and periodic screening, diagnosis and treatment—EPSDT (PL 90-248).   The major focus of EPSDT is the prevention of developmental problems. The intent of the law is that low-income children be screened regularly during infancy and the preschool years to prevent (and treat) health problems that could interfere with development. At the time the law was passed (1967) it reflected two major concerns of congress. One had to do with the extreme variations among states in the number of children receiving treatment for developmental problems. Some states did a good job of caring for these children; others did not. The second was the issue of children with serious but unserved health problems. There were many such children in every state with problems so severe that the outcome often was irreversible developmental damage. Since the enactment of EPSDT, millions of children have received the health care necessary for preventing disabling problems. The Children's Defense Fund (1991) points out that children who receive comprehensive preventive health services have fewer health problems and developmental disabilities, which represents 10 percent lower health care costs for taxpayers.

Childhood immunization.   The Childhood Immunization Program, administered by the Centers for Disease Control (CDC), helps establish and maintain immunization centers. The purpose is to prevent childhood diseases such as rubella, mumps, measles,

diphtheria, tetanus, and **pertussis**. This program improves the lives of millions of young children while being cost effective in its own right. According to testimony before Congress:

> For every dollar spent on the Childhood Immunization Program, the government saves $10 in medical costs. . . . Centers for Disease Control studies indicate that the millions of dollars spent over several years on a measles vaccination program saved $1.3 billion in medical and long-term care by reducing hearing impairments, retardation, and other developmental problems. (Staff Report of the Select Committee on Children, Youth and Families, 1989, p. 19.)

Supplemental food program for women, infants, and children. Commonly referred to as WIC, this federal program has an excellent record in the prevention of developmental problems. Established in 1972, the law allocates nutrition money to state agencies and to certain Indian tribes. The funds are to be used to provide healthy foods for low-income pregnant and nursing mothers and for infants and young children at-risk for medical problems. The program also provides nutritional counseling and education. Evaluations of WIC show that the program is of great benefit to those who participate; however, less than half of the eligible women and children are served (Children's Defense Fund 1991). For those families who have received the supplements, major benefits are documented as follows:

Reduced infant mortality—fewer infant deaths at the time of birth or during the first few months of life
Increase in the birth weight of many infants; and reduction in number of low-birth-weight infants
Reduction in number of premature infants

Each of these benefits leads to fewer health problems in both mothers and their infants. Furthermore, medical research demonstrates that full-term infants of adequate birth weight are less likely to become developmentally delayed or disabled during the early childhood years. All of this adds up to a program that improves the quality of children's lives while demonstrating its cost effectiveness: "Each $1 spent to provide nutrition help to a pregnant woman under

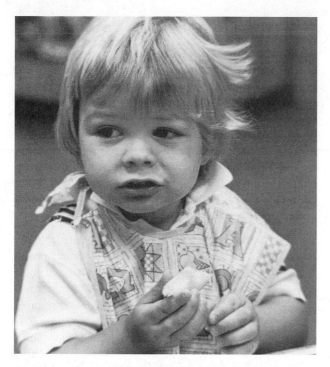

Good nourishment and good health go hand-in-hand.

the WIC program saves more than $3 in a child's infancy alone by reducing rates of prematurity and low birthweight" (Children's Defense Fund 1991, p. 6).

Medicaid.   Medicaid is a jointly funded federal and state program. It provides medical assistance to low-income families and children with disabilities. For large numbers of pregnant women it is their only access to health care before and during the birth of their infants. It also is the only health care available to even larger numbers of children. While millions of women and children receive no medical services, study after study reports the cost effectiveness of preventive health care: Every dollar spent can save thousands of dollars over a child's lifetime.

Although the amount of resources allocated to prenatal care has increased, the crisis in availability of care continues:

> Recent increase in federal and state funding for maternal and child health services have helped make prenatal care available to many pregnant women, yet fragmented, narrowly defined policies and programs often create financial, administrative, and geographical barriers to early and regular care. The result is a disjointed tangle of services that reach some but not all of those who need them. As in other areas of human services, it is typically the women who need prenatal care the most who are least likely to receive it. Unfortunately, these are also the women who are most likely to have frail, unhealthy babies, who, in turn, will bear the long-term consequences of poor or inadequate care. (National Commission on Children 1991, p. 124)

SUMMARY

Intervention in the form of remedial and compensatory early childhood programs has become a popular approach to reducing both the number and the severity of developmental problems. The importance of early intervention came to be recognized with research related to the role of experience in determining developmental outcome. Out of the findings of this research came Head Start and then early intervention programs for young children with handicaps. Both the civil rights movement and the efforts of various advocacy groups helped advance programs for individuals with disabilities. Legislation on behalf of gifted children, especially young gifted children, has been less widespread.

Significant and ground-breaking laws have been passed on behalf of young children classified as disabled or at-risk for developmental problems. These included authorization for university-based interdisciplinary training programs (UAPs) for clinicians, development of innovative early intervention programs (HCEEP/EEPCD), and the long-awaited Education for All Handicapped Children Act (PL 94-142). More recently, another piece of landmark legislation (PL 99-457) requires that states provide all 3- to 5-year old children with developmental disabilities (and their families) with individualized programs. This law also allows, but does not require, states to provide intervention services for children in the birth-to-3 age range who have (or are at risk for) developmental problems. Most states are providing such services. The demand for early childhood personnel—teachers, clinicians, administrators—will be enormous as birth-to-6 programs come into full implementation.

Case law has played an important role in promoting inclusive education for students with disabilities. Recent cases have supported every child's right to attend school in the mainstream, and reinforce the intent of the original legislation to provide free and appropriate education to all children with disabilities.

Prevention of developmental disabilities has become a major focus of both children's advocacy groups and Congress. The majority of developmental problems are preventable. Prevention of developmental disabilities can occur all along the lifespan (and even starting with conception). More than 50 percent of disabling conditions and crippling health problems in this nation are linked directly to poverty-related factors: substandard medical care, nutrition, and housing, as well as inadequate education about the care of infants and young children. Laws have been enacted that provide programs for the early identification of medical needs, immunization of children against the serious childhood diseases, supplemental nutrition for pregnant women and their infants, and pre- and postnatal care. All of these programs have proven worthwhile on two scores: improving the quality of children's lives and saving vast amounts of taxpayers' dollars. Nevertheless, large numbers of needy infants, children, and pregnant women go unserved for lack of adequate funding.

STUDENT ACTIVITIES

1. Write to your State Department of Education and ask for information regarding early education programs for exceptional children in your state. Ask for programs for gifted children in particular.

2. Locate the offices of a local advocacy group and arrange for a speaker to talk to your class about their work on behalf of young children with disabilities.

3. Contact your local DSHS (Department of Social and Health Services), or comparable agency, and get details of the implementation of the WIC program in your community.

4. Write to one of your members of Congress and ask for an update on federal legislation related to young children with disabilities and their families.

5. Form into several small groups. Each group select one of the pieces of legislation described in the unit. "Advocate" for that law—that is, convince the rest of the class why they should have voted for that law.

REVIEW QUESTIONS

A. *Define each of the following terms and give an example of each.*
1. Landmark legislation
2. Advocacy group
3. Nondiscriminatory testing
4. Zero reject
5. Due process
6. Discretionary legislation
7. Cumulative deficit
8. Secondary disability
9. Supplemental nutrition program

B. *True or False. Choose the best answer.*

T F 1. Working toward improved legislation is a major task of many advocacy groups.

T F 2. Head Start is not required to serve a child with a disability unless parents demand such service.

T F 3. The "wheelchair requirement" is related to the accessibility of public places for the disabled.

T F 4. Parent involvement is a major part of both PL 94-142 and PL 99-457.

T F 5. PL 99-457 provides funding based on the categorical labeling of young children.

T F 6. Identification and prevention of developmental disabilities is a major purpose of EPSDT.

T F 7. By WIC reports, low-birth-weight newborns are at risk for developmental problems.

T F 8. Case management provides assistance to families in procuring prescribed services.

T F 9. Federally funded child care programs are not required to serve 3-, 4-, and 5-year olds with disabilities.

T F 10. All states are required to serve developmentally disabled children in the birth-to-3 age range.

C. *Mix and Match.* Select the one *best* match from the items in Column II and place that letter in the appropriate space in Column I.

I	II
____ 1. ADA	A. Section 504 (DDA)
____ 2. Division for Early Childhood	B. supplemental food
	C. Americans with Disabilities Act
____ 3. CVS	D. individualized education
____ 4. HCEEP	E. newborn screening
____ 5. wheelchair requirement	F. First Chance Network
____ 6. IEP	G. early screening, diagnosis, and treatment
____ 7. PL 94-142	H. affiliate of CEC
____ 8. WIC	I. zero reject
____ 9. EPSDT	J. prenatal screening
____ 10. APGAR	

REFERENCES

Bloom, B. (1964). *Stability and change in human characteristics.* New York: John Wiley and Sons.

Brazelton, T. Berry. (1990). Committee on Education and Labor, U.S. House of Representatives. *Human Services Reauthorization Act of 1990.* Report # 101–480.

Children's Defense Fund. (1991). *A vision for America's future.* Washington, DC.

Gallagher, J.J. (1988). National agenda for educating gifted students: Statement of priorities. *Exceptional Children, 55:2,* 107–114.

Haring, N.G., McCormick, L., and Haring, T.G. (1994). *Exceptional children and youth.* 6th ed. New York: Merrill.

Hunt, J.McV. (1961). *Intelligence and experience.* New York: Ronald Press.

Kirk, S.A. (1958). *Early education of the mentally retarded: An experimental study.* Urbana: University of Illinois Press.

National Commission of Children. (1991). *Beyond rhetoric: A new American agenda of children and families.* Washington, DC: Author.

Pizzo, P.D. (1990). Family-centered Head Start for infants and toddlers. *Young Children, 45:6,* 30–35.

Renzulli, J.S., and Reis, S.M. (1991). Building advocacy through program design, student productivity, and public relations. *Gifted Child Quarterly, 35,* 182–187.

Skeels, H.M. (1966). Adult status of children with contrasting early life experiences. *Monographs of the Society for Research in Child Development.*

Skeels, H.M., and Dye, H.B. (1939). A study of the effects of differential stimulation on mentally retarded children. *Proceedings and Addresses of the American Association on Mental Deficiency, 44,* 495–507.

Staff Report of the Select Committee on Children, Youth, and Families. (1989). *Opportunities for success: Cost-effective programs for children.* Washington, DC: U.S. Government Printing Office.

Stiles, S., and Kitano, M. (1991). Preschool-age gifted children. *DEC Communicator, 17,* 3–4.

Wolf, J.S. (1994). The gifted and talented. In N.G. Haring, L. McCormick, and T.G. Haring (Eds.), *Exceptional children and youth* (pp. 456–500). New York: Merrill.

Zigler, E., and Muenchow, S. (1992). *Head Start: The inside story of America's most successful educational experiment.* New York: Basic Books.

SECTION II
Likenesses and Differences Among Children

Unit 4

Normal and Exceptional Development

OBJECTIVES

After studying this unit the student will be able to

- describe types of children referred to as being *normal, atypical, developmentally delayed, at-risk,* and *gifted.*
- provide three reasons to justify this statement: To work effectively with children with developmental problems and with gifted children, teachers need to have thorough knowledge of normal growth and development.
- distinguish between developmental sequences and developmental milestones; give examples of each in motor, cognitive, and language development.
- discuss developmental disabilities in terms of range and variations as well as factors that determine if a disability will seriously interfere with a child's development.
- define giftedness in young children and explain the factors that contribute to giftedness.

Young children are much alike in many ways. They also are different in just as many ways. Too often, the ways an exceptional child is like other children are overlooked, never put to good use; the focus is on remediation of their delays or disabilities. These points need to be kept in mind when working with children with special needs:

A child is first of all a child, regardless of how smart or delayed or troubled that child may be.
Every child is unique, different, and therefore exceptional in one or more ways.

In small, closely knit societies, the fact that some children are different is not an issue. This seldom holds true in complex societies such as ours. Setting these children apart, even excluding them from society seems to have been built into our system almost from the start. As we have seen, however, change is coming about. Inclusive educational programs are a major step in the right direction as is federal legislation calling for noncategorical funding of services for young children.

Even so, the underlying issue of classification is still with us. Having to distinguish between those children said to be developing normally and those who are developing atypically continues to plague us. The problem, as always, is that developmentalists, teachers, administrators, and policy makers put different interpretations on the concepts.

The child with a developmental disability may or may not be easy to recognize.

Definitions of normalcy and exceptionality vary also among physicians, psychologists, and every other professional associated with the growth and development of young children. The variations come from each professional's training, clinical practice, and tradition. Lawyers, for example, use their own specific guidelines to identify the legally blind; educators use different guidelines. (See Unit 5.) There is little consensus as to who are to be referred to as developmentally disabled, who are the gifted and talented, who are the truly normal. The result is confusion for everyone, especially for students and newcomers to the field. This confusion can be increased by attempting to use words in our everyday vocabularies in a technical way. A number of professionals argue that *typical* is a more communicative word than *normal.* In this text, the words will be used interchangeably.

This unit will provide practical definitions of normal development and exceptional development. Normal development will be discussed first, as background. The rationale is obvious: To work effectively with infants and children with developmental problems, teachers must have a thorough knowledge of normal growth and development. All early intervention programs should have as a main goal the improvement of each child's overall development. A parallel goal is the prevention or lessening of developmental problems. Thurman and Widerstrom (1990) add yet another dimension: "To improve the develop-

ment of children with special needs we must understand normal development, including the problems that may occur in normal developmental patterns" (p. 11).

WHAT IS NORMAL OR TYPICAL DEVELOPMENT?

As noted above, there is little general agreement about the meaning of various terms used to describe the developing child. One of the most common and frequently used, *normal development,* has long been the subject of dispute. What is normal for one child may be quite abnormal for another. For example, most early childhood teachers expect children to make eye contact when spoken to. Teachers tend to be concerned if a child fails to do so. In certain other cultures, such as some Native American groups, children are considered disrespectful if they look directly at the adult who is speaking to them.

In addition to culturally defined differences in what is considered normal, there are individual differences among children. No two children grow and develop at the same rate, even within the same culture. Some children walk at eight months; others do not walk until 18 months. Most children begin walking somewhere in between. All children within this range, and even a bit

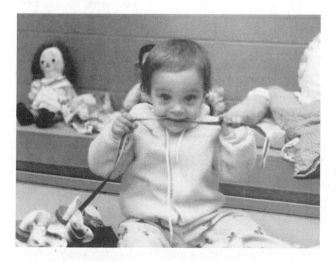

Individual differences begin to show up early.

on either side of it, are normal with respect to walking. The same is true for every other area of development. Typical development, therefore, shows great variation and significant differences among children.

Developmental Sequences.   In spite of the variations in normal development, certain principles serve as guidelines. One is that the sequences of normal development are predictable. The predictions are based on well-documented developmental norms derived from detailed observations of hundreds of children at various age levels. Well-trained early childhood teachers (and experienced parents) know that each typically developing child can be expected to move step-by-step toward mastery of each developmental skill, in every area of development. In so doing, individual differences begin to show up. Each child will accomplish the specific steps but will do so at his or her own rate. Furthermore, no matter how quickly or slowly a child is developing, each preceding step must be mastered

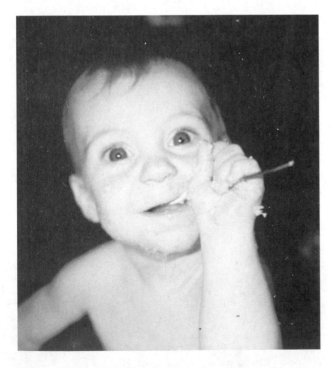

Major milestone: Getting the spoon into the mouth—never mind that the applesauce is smeared every where else!

before practice on the next can begin. A child must roll over before learning to sit, must sit before standing, must stand before walking.

Exceptions are common, even to this basic principle of developmental sequence. For example, most infants crawl before they walk, but some do not. A few infants move about by sitting up and hitching forward with one foot. Others lie flat on their back and push with both feet. Such self-propelling methods of getting about are quite appropriate, even though atypical.

It must be remembered, too, that no two children grow uniformly and at the same rate. Nor do they move forward in all developmental areas at the same time. Rarely is developmental progress smooth and flowing; irregularities and slowdowns are common. Progress in one skill may actually stop when the child is attempting to learn a new skill in a different area of development. A frequent occurence is the infant who talked early and then quit talking for a time, while learning to walk. Some children even regress, that is, slide backward, under certain conditions (the 3-year-old who temporarily loses bladder control with the arrival of the new baby).

Developmental Milestones.   Regardless of the many variations, certain behaviors or skill sequences can be seen in a fairly predictable order in almost every typically developing child. These significant points or events often are referred to as developmental milestones. A child who does not reach, or is seriously delayed in reaching one or more of these milestones, needs attention. It could be a warning signal that something may be amiss in the child's development. Thus, everyone working with the very young needs to have a thorough knowledge of developmental milestones and sequences in each area of development.

A brief overview of common milestones follows. More detailed profiles are given in the units on physical, cognitive, language, and social development. For a comprehensive account of developmental areas see Allen and Marotz (1994).

Infancy.   At one time it was thought that eating and sleeping was about all the newborn could do. More recent research reveals a quite different picture. We know now that within the first days (even hours) of life, infants react to many things in the environment. They follow a moving object with their eyes. They turn their heads in response to a loud noise. They make a face if they taste something unpleasant. They synchronize their body movements with changes in the voice of the person speaking to them. When the voice speeds up, the baby's arms and legs flail about rapidly; when the voice slows, the baby's movements also slow. From earliest infancy, the human face (especially that of the mother or major caregiver) is of great interest to the baby. Very young infants will attempt to imitate facial expressions: sticking out its tongue, pursing its lips, opening its eyes wider when the caregiver makes such faces (Meltzoff and Moore 1983).

Between 4 and 10 weeks babies begin social or responsive smiling. The social smile is a major developmental milestone. Lack of social smiling in a 12- to 14-week-old may signal a potentially serious developmental problem.

Somewhere around 2 or 3 months of age the infant begins to make social kinds of sounds. These sounds, mostly cooing and gurgling, are labeled social for two reasons:

1. They are made in response to the voice of the person talking to the baby.
2. When initiated by the infant, the sounds capture and hold the attention of a nearby adult who usually responds vocally. Thus, the almost totally helpless infant learns that he or she can make things happen, can get people to respond.

Such reciprocity or "give and take" is essential to the **attachment process**. It also is a first major step toward language and social development. Furthermore the *give and take* demonstrates the basic needs of all infants to have responsive caregivers if they are to develop well. Given a responsive environment, the infant soon is smiling readily at people and discovers, with delight, that most people smile back. Infants 3- and 4-months-old also are smiling at objects and even at their own noises and actions. They reach for an object that attracts them and sometimes manage, usually accidentally, to latch onto it. Reaching behaviors are significant signals that eye—hand coordination is beginning to develop.

By 5 or 6 months of age, most infants show trunk control and some rolling over. At 7 months many are sitting, some with support, others without. At 9 months a few infants are walking, many more are crawling or showing readiness to crawl. Cruising— holding onto a low table or other piece of furniture— comes next. Then comes walking! Walking begins at about 12 months though there are great differences between infants. Anywhere between 8 and 18 or 20 months is considered typical.

The baby's cognitive development is closely interwoven with motor development. In fact, all areas of development are interdependent throughout the formative years. It is true that most child development textbooks present cognitive, social, and language development separately. Necessary as this may be for discussion purposes, such separation is artificial. In real life, all developmental areas are closely interrelated. Early

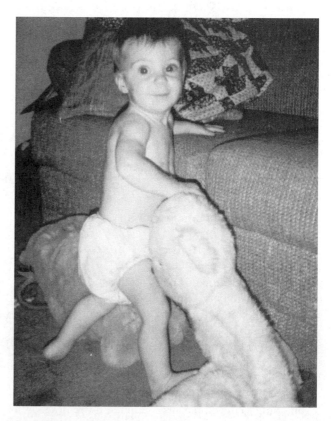

Cruising precedes first steps alone.

language, cognitive, and social skills are intertwined and mutually supportive. Furthermore, all three depend on sound motor skills.

The importance of good motor skills to overall healthy development cannot be overemphasized. Piaget began to analyze this relationship more than 50 years ago. He described the first 24 months of life as the **sensorimotor** stage of development. During these early months the infant learns by poking, patting, touching, banging, and tasting whatever comes to hand. The older infant is on the move every waking moment, crawling and toddling about, experiencing the environment. This early exploring provides the essential foundation for sound cognitive development and intellectual functioning.

Toddlers.   Between 2 and 3 years of age most children are moving about freely. In fact, they seem to move about almost too freely, or so it seems to parents and caregivers as they try to keep up with a toddler. Developmental progress is evident in a number of other ways, too. Most toddlers are able to:

manipulate small toys and a variety of objects
understand much of what is said to them
speak in simple sentences
imitate the behavior of others (a skill needed in all
    learning)
give signs of readiness for toilet training (some are
    using the toilet with variable reliability)
feed themselves (usually somewhat messily)
take off and put on some articles of clothing
play alone and sometimes with other children

The preschool years.   Between 3 and 6 years of age, basic motor skills are perfected. The typical child learns to run, jump, and climb with assurance. Skill in manipulating objects and tools such as paint brushes and pencils and crayons grows day-by-day. Creativity and imagination color everything from role playing to telling tall tales. Vocabulary and concept development expands rapidly. The result is a dramatic increase in the ability to express ideas, make judgments, solve problems, and plan ahead. During these years, children come to develop a strong belief in the *rightness* of their own opinions. At the same time, they are begin-

ning to be aware of the needs of others and to exercise some control of their own behavior in relationship to others needs. All of this combines to allow the child increasing breadth of movement and thought. This, in turn, leads to increasing independence. At the same time, preschool children tend to frequently touch base with important adults. It is as if they need to know there is someone readily available who will give assistance, comfort, and come to the rescue if need be.

During the preschool years the child's physical growth is slower. Consequently, the amount of food needed to support growth is greatly reduced. Too many parents and caregivers are not aware of this biological shift. They think the child is not well or has become a "picky" eater. Unwittingly, they may try to force the child to eat more than he or she needs. Serious conflict can result, creating an unhappy effect on the parent–child or caregiver–child relationship.

Language skills are developing rapidly during the preschool years. It is not unusual, however, for children who were talking well to become a bit less fluent for awhile. That is, they may go through a period of stammering or stuttering which is a perfectly normal or typical developmental irregularity. Usually, this early **dysfluency** disappears unless there is adult pressure to "slow down" or "say it right." Generally speaking, children are talking freely and spontaneously by 6 years of age. In fact, many 6- and 7-year-olds seem to talk all the time, or so it seems to family members and teachers. At this age, a vocabulary of 2500 words is not uncommon with the child using most of the grammatical forms of the native language.

The preschool years are a time of extensive social and emotional development. The child is beginning to understand that he or she is a separate person, with a separate identity from everyone else, and especially from parents. This growing independence, this sense of self-directing individuality is the essence of **autonomy**. Toward the end of the preschool years most children are sharing and taking turns, at least some of the time. Children who have been in group child care much of their lives may demonstrate these particular social skills considerably earlier. Older preschool children usually are beginning to show empathy, that is, an understanding of how another person feels. The notion of "best friends" is taking hold, too.

If all goes well, the developing child passes milestone after milestone in every area of development. Nevertheless, the question posed at the start: *What is normal?* has not been given a truly complete answer. What about a child who is developing normally in some areas but has a delay or disability in another area? What about children with physical problems, for example, who cannot walk, let alone run and jump and climb as normal children do? Many children with such problems are developing normally otherwise, may even be gifted in language, intellectual, or artistic development. The opposite also may be true—children who are delayed in language or cognitive development may have outstanding motor skills.

WHO ARE THE EXCEPTIONAL CHILDREN?

Efforts to decide which children are exceptional have been going on for decades. At times, the term has been all-inclusive. It has covered children with the mildest of speech differences to those who were outstandingly brilliant (but *different*) as in the case of the so-called savants.

Individuals who were noticeably different, either physically or mentally were referred to as crippled or retarded. Society provided "homes for crippled children" and "institutions for the feeble minded" (a common term in those days for individuals who were judged to be of lesser mental abilities). For decades, these were the only public special services available. Then, in 1817, the first residential educational institution, for the deaf, was built in Connecticut. A few years later (1832), came the first facility for those with severe vision impairments—The Perkins Institute for the Blind in Boston.

CHANGING TERMINOLOGY

Long years later, terms that covered a broader but more individualized range of disabilities came into use. At the time, apparently, the language seemed less demeaning. *Behavior disordered, learning disabled, mentally deficient*, along with *handicapped, deviant*, and so on, were commonly used to describe both children and adults. Individual identities were locked into their differences; *He's Down syndrome*; *She's autistic*; *These boys*

are the mentally deficient. Now we vigorously question the appropriateness of such terms, especially when describing a given individual. Statements such as *She is a learning disabled child* highlights the problem, rather than the child; whereas, *This child has a learning disability* puts focus on the child. The new word order and terminology is referred to as *people first language.* Incidentally, the **people first** approach highlights a fundamental assumption of inclusion—that all children are children and our practices should reflect that reality (Wolery and Wilber 1994).

The term handicapped is becoming less acceptable, especially when referring to children and youth. *Children with special needs* or *Children who have special needs* provides a better perspective. The language makes it clear that children who are different from children who have no disabilities are different only because "they need environments that are specifically organized and adjusted to minimize the effects of their disabilities and to promote learning of a broad range of skills." (Wolery, Strain and Bailey 1992, p. 95)

Developmental Disabilities and Delays. Early childhood teachers were among the first to argue against the word handicapped in referring to young children. The term was virtually written out of the early intervention part of PL 99-457. In its stead the law uses words like *developmental delay* and sometimes *developmental disability*. However, even these terms can be variously interpreted and so each state is allowed to construct their own definition. The change in terminology is a positive step. It promotes the concept that young children with atypical characteristics resemble normally developing children in terms of their potential for growth and development. It also emphasizes that many young children who are atypical in one way or another resemble normally developing children more than they differ from them. With the exception of children with severe impairments, both types of children go through the same sequences of development, though at different rates. The fact that a child is different in some ways should never interfere with noting how typical that child is in other ways.

Many infants and young children start out with serious problems they are able to overcome if they receive appropriate early intervention services. Premature

A child may be different in some ways, but typical in other ways.

infants are a good example. Often they are delayed in acquiring early developmental skills. Yet by age 2 or 3, many of these children, with adequate care and nutrition, are catching up. By age 5, most are looking like and performing like all other 5-year-olds.

Some impairments, even though serious, may never interfere with developmental progress if the child receives appropriate intervention services. The condition may continue but the child and family find ways to compensate and to function normally in spite of it.

> Example: Bret was a child born with one short arm and malformed hand. The family, from the start, had referred to this as his "little hand." At preschool, there was nothing Bret could not do as well as any other child: puzzles, form boards, or block building. In kindergarten, he was among the first to learn to tie shoes. By seventh grade he was a champion soccer player.

Developmental Delays. The diagnosis of developmental delay varies from profession to profession. Delay, as used in this text, is said to exist when *a child is*

performing like a typically developing child of a much younger age. A 5-year-old with the social skills of a 3 1/2-year old may be described as having a delay in social development. The 3-year-old who toddles about like a 15-month-old is likely to be thought of as having a delay in motor development. Some children have delays in two or three areas or in only one area as in the following example:

> Josh is a 3-year-old just beginning to put together two-word sentences. He has moved steadily through each earlier milestone in language development. It is evident that this 3-year-old is experiencing a language delay; normal language will come, though later than for other children his age. By the age of 8 or 10, it is unlikely there will be any hint of Josh's earlier delay.

AT-RISK POPULATIONS

Many infants and young children are said to be *at-risk* or *at high-risk*. This means there is reason to believe serious problems are likely to develop. For example, mothers who were heavy drinkers or drug users during pregnancy often bear children who are at-risk developmentally. Their newborns may or may not show immediate problems. Infants that are born both addicted and at a very low-birth-weight are likely to be considered at *high-risk*; they are in grave developmental danger. In the coming months and years children of both risk types, if they survive to school age, are more likely to exhibit disabling learning problems, emotional disorders, and **attentional deficits**. Another less dramatic, but all too frequent example of high-risk children are those born into serious poverty. *Developmental risk is almost certain in cases of malnutrition, inadequate shelter, and poor health care.*

The high incidence of children living in poverty, often at-risk for both short- and long-term problems, will be discussed in some detail in Unit 5. Here, however, while talking about developmental risk, a significant point needs to be emphasized: Many infants and children who are at-risk for developmental problems *have the potential for healthy development.* Many, many of these children have a good chance of overcoming the initial setbacks. What is required is early and comprehensive intervention services: medical treatment, ample nurturance, and in many cases family support

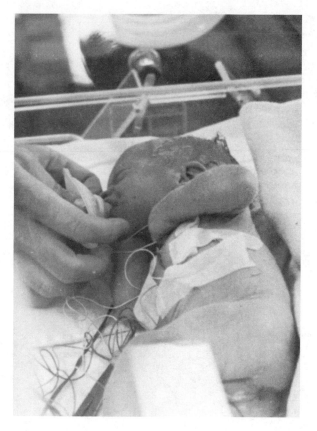

Infants may be at high-risk at time of birth.

Other biological risk factors include genetic and **chromosomal disorders** such as Down syndrome. Heart defects are present in about one third of the infants born with Down syndrome. Without correction, many of these children will die of **cardiac problems** during infancy or early childhood. A further discussion of biological risk factors can be found in Unit 5.

Environmental risk.   Poverty is the greatest single factor associated with environmental risk. As will become evident in Unit 5, the effects of poverty produce many kinds of risk conditions. However, poverty is not the only environmental situation that puts infants and young children at risk. Other causes include:

• Child abuse
• Unfit living conditions due to addicted or diseased family members

services. Risk factors, including those already mentioned can be grouped into two major categories: *biological* and *environmental.*

Biological risk.   This term refers to infants and children whose systems have undergone some kind of *biological insult* such as an accident, injury, or severe stress. The incident may have occurred before birth, at the time of birth, or following birth. Consider these examples:

> A newborn with **respiratory distress syndrome (RDS)** is at-risk—in serious trouble medically—but likely to recover if given immediate and appropriate treatment.
>   Premature birth or low-birth-weight ($5^{1}/_{2}$ pounds or 2500 grams or less) are risk factors that require immediate, intensive intervention. Without it many of these infants will suffer **irreversible developmental damage**.

Chromosomal disorders include Down syndrome.

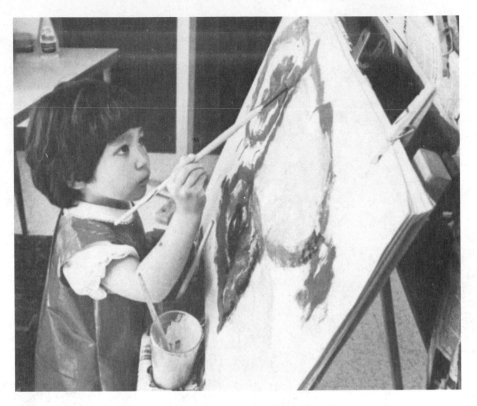

Precocious children tend to demonstrate outstanding talents.

- Religious beliefs that prohibit urgently needed medication, medical treatment, or surgery
- Inaccessible medical care as when families live in remote mountain or rural areas. Services for these families are increasing, but even so, many continue to go unserved.

Children with Special Gifts and Talents.   At the opposite end of the **developmental continuum** are those children who do exceptionally well, who seem to be advanced in one or more areas of development. Furthermore, they tend to maintain this advanced state throughout their developmental years. These children often are a good fit with Gardner's concept of *multiple intelligences.* Gardner (1983) theorizes six types of intelligence: linguistic, logical-mathematical, musical, spatial, bodily-**kinesthetic**, and personal-social. He argues that we have paid little attention to anything but language and logical/mathematics as

sources of intelligence and giftedness. Why? Because that is all that our traditional IQ tests measure. Whatever the explanation, in the truly gifted child, the accomplishments seem to appear spontaneously, as a part of the child's own unique developmental process. It is unlikely that these early and outstanding abilities emerge because of special training or parent pressure. In fact, parents of especially bright or talented children often are surprised when told of their child's remarkable abilities (Robinson 1981).

Origins of giftedness.   What is the source of giftedness, especially when it takes the form of high IQ and general intellectual competence? The child's environment seems to be the major factor. Exceptionally bright children are more likely to come from advantaged, middle-class families than from lower-class or poverty families. This is not to discount genetic influences in all children. Nevertheless, more affluent parents, in general, are better educated as well as better off financially. They can provide the daily, taken-for-granted enrichment that is a key element in their children's performance. Given two children with equally good genetic background, the child in the enriched environment almost surely would come out "brighter" than a poorly nourished child raised in an unstimulating environment. In other words, giftedness, most likely, is a combination of a sound genetic makeup *and* a stimulating environment (Freeman, 1981).

Characteristics of young gifted children. In general, the characteristics that identify young potentially gifted children appear to be a combination of advanced verbal skills, high levels of curiosity, and the ability to concentrate and remember. Many gifted children also seem to learn rapidly and enjoy problem solving. The following list of specific clues to potential giftedness in a young child is adapted from Roedell et al. (1980). The child

> Has a large vocabulary that he or she uses appropriately, has an interest in words, enjoys practicing new words
>
> Uses language to give suggestions, express ideas, pass on information, ask *content* questions: "How did the fox know the baby rabbit was there?
>
> Makes up songs and stories; invents rhymes; plays with the sound and rhythm of words.

The gifted young child appears to understand abstract concepts.

> Modifies his or her language to meet the understanding level of younger children.
>
> Uses language to handle conflicts and aggression in play situations.
>
> Appears to understand abstract concepts such as time, family relationships (that father can be both a husband and a brother), cause and effect (why the ice melted), connections between past and present experiences.
>
> Shows absorption in particular topics, such as dinosaurs—pours over books and pictures about dinosaurs, memorizes their names and characteristics, learns to pronounce the difficult names.
>
> Demonstrates complex classification and discrimination skills—spontaneously groups items such as toy cars, boats, airplanes, and trucks; arranges objects according to size *and* color.
>
> Skilled in putting together new and difficult puzzles; appears to examine puzzle pieces first and then put them in place, rather than depending on trial and error.
>
> Seems to have good orientation skills and sense of spatial relationships—has some idea of how to get back to school when on a walk; maneuvers wheel toys so as to avoid obstacles; keeps to *own space* during dance and rhythmic activities.
>
> Notices what is new and different in the environment such as rearrangement of equipment, a teacher's new hairstyle or new dress, a new drying rack for paintings.
>
> Shows a sense of humor (tells about the new kitten falling in the fruit bowl), makes up "jokes" and riddles.
>
> Indicates awareness of the feelings of others, both children and adults; may comment when a teacher is not feeling well or another child appears withdrawn or especially happy.

The original list of clues to early giftedness was published in its entirety in *Young Children*, (March 1989). Obviously, no one child is likely to show all of the traits; many, however, will show two, three, or more, in various combinations.

Gifted minority children. More than half the clues in the above list are related to high-level language skills. Bright children from minority cultures and different ethnic backgrounds often are not recognized because they lack these middle-class language skills. Never should this difference be viewed as the child having lesser potential; instead, it is usually fewer opportunities to acquire sophisticated language. Other influences also work against the identification of gifted

Giftedness must be defined in ways that reflect the child's culture.

minority preschoolers. In reviewing the work of a number of researchers, Karnes and Johnson (1989) note common factors within our social–educational system:

The *attitude* that giftedness does not exist among children from low-income backgrounds

Defining giftedness in ways that reflect only the majority culture's values

Using identification procedures that are unfavorable to low-income and minority children (discussed further in Unit 10)

Providing few environmental opportunities for enhancing intellectual or artistic achievement in young and bright minority children (No one can excel at anything without the opportunity to try!)

Clearly, there are gifted children in every ethnic and racial group at all socioeconomic levels. Thus,

early identification and appropriate preschool education for children without economic advantages is critical as a means of identifying and nurturing those with special gifts and talents (Stile et al. 1991).

Children with developmental disabilities who are gifted. Often overlooked is the fact that a child with a disability may be a gifted child. A child with a learning disability may have superior intelligence or outstanding artistic or mechanical talents. The same is true of children with hearing impairments, cerebral palsy, or almost any other kind of developmental disability. The potential for intellectual or artistic giftedness in these children seldom receives much attention. Educational emphasis and energy tends to be narrowly focused on helping children overcome physical or sensory deficits. As Gallagher (1988) points out, rarely do we even search for potential giftedness in special populations.

Identifying the gifted among children with developmental problems may be difficult. Conventional assessments often fail to pick up on their strengths, let alone their giftedness. Wolfle (1989) suggests direct observation in a natural setting as a valuable way of discovering the special talents that an exceptional child may have. The importance of this recommendation is borne out by the following story told by a teacher of 4-year-olds in an inclusion preschool:

Benjamin, blind since birth, had developed a number of unusual and repetitive behaviors that sometimes are seen in young children who cannot see. His preschool teachers observed, however, that the strange behaviors stopped whenever there was music in the classroom. Benjamin appeared to listed intently and always asked for more. One teacher began sitting down with Benjamin with musical instruments. One time it was a ukelele, then an autoharp, another time a recorder. After a brief period of experimentation, Benjamin would "find" tunes he could play on any one of the instruments. Next the teacher took him to a classroom that had a piano. Again, with only limited exploration of the instrument, Benjamin began to improvise recognizable tunes. The teacher shared these experiences with Benjamin's parents who were able to buy a piano. Benjamin spent hours at the piano and became an eager piano student. By age 16 he was regarded as a gifted young pianist.

Many young children with impairments have high potential for both intellectual and creative achievement. Attention needs to be directed toward these children in early childhood programs so their curiosity and eagerness to learn is encouraged rather than allowed to wither. Karnes and Johnson (1987) argue that it is important for our nation to fund early intervention demonstration programs that focus on all young and gifted children. These programs could provide training in identifying and nurturing the young gifted from every socioeconomic level. With early intervention and appropriate learning opportunities, children from minorities and children with all kinds of impairments, like all other gifted children, could be helped to realize their potential (Kirk and Gallagher 1986). A pioneer among such programs is the RAPYHT (Retrieval and Acceleration of Promising Young Handicapped and Talented) Project at the University of Illinois. In addition to its curriculum, RAPYHT has developed a *Preschool Talent Checklist* and a *Preschool Talent Assessment Guide*. The materials are in use in many centers around the country. Follow-up studies show that children who had been enrolled in RAPYHT continue high level performance in later school settings. (Karnes, Schwedel and Lewis 1983).

SUMMARY

Decisions as to who are the normally developing children and who are the exceptional children vary among communities, school districts, and professions. Normal development is difficult to define to everyone's satisfaction because it is so complex a process and includes such a range of developmental skills. Certain guidelines are available, however. These include knowledge of developmental sequences, developmental milestones, and the interrelatedness of developmental areas. A thorough knowledge of normal growth and development is necessary to understanding and working with exceptional children.

Arriving at decisions as to who are the exceptional children is as difficult as deciding who are the normally developing. Because young children are in a constant state of developmental change it is preferable to think of them as having a developmental delay, not a handicap. Other shifts in terminology are coming about. One is the movement toward *people first* language—giving the individual precedence over his or her disability: Amy is a 4-year-old with special needs.

Children at developmental risk are those who are likely to develop disabling problems if they do not receive special services as early as possible. Risk factors, either biological or environmental (or both), may occur prenatally, at the time of birth, or during the early developmental years.

Gifted and talented young children are those with exceptionally advanced skills in one or more areas of development. Potentially gifted children from cultural minorities and low income families often are not identified because of restricted learning opportunities and socially biased identification procedures. Many children with developmental disabilities also are gifted but their potential too, often is not identified, the educational focus is on remediation rather than discovery of the child's strengths.

STUDENT ACTIVITIES

1. Talk with your parents about your first two years. Ask them to pinpoint as nearly as they are able, when you passed the major developmental milestones. Try to determine if they remembered you as advanced, normal, or delayed. (If you have older children of your own, think back on your children instead.)
2. Think about exceptional individuals you have known or read about and discuss to what degree their differences did or did not handicap them.
3. Observe a group of preschool children. List any instances of what you feel may be atypical development or behavior.
4. Write to whatever agency is responsible for administering PL 99-457 in your state and ask for your state's definition of developmental disabilities.
5. Have you or any one of your brothers or sisters or friends been described as gifted or talented? Or any of your own children, if you are a parent? Describe the exceptional characteristics that lead to such a label.

REVIEW QUESTIONS

A. *Define and give an example.*
1. Developmental milestone
2. Developmental continuum
3. Handicapped
4. Developmental impairment
5. Atypical development
6. Biological risk
7. People first language
8. Nurturance
9. Irreversible developmental problem
10. Gifted child

B. *Multiple Choice.* Choose the one best phrase to complete each statement.
1. Normal development means
   a. beginning to walk between 8 and 22 months of age.
   b. beginning to walk between 6 and 8 months of age.
   c. beginning to walk after 26 months of age.
2. By 3 years of age all normally developing children
   a. are toilet trained.
   b. understand much of what is said to them.
   c. can be expected to share toys and books.
3. If a child's appetite decreases during the early preschool years parent and caregivers should
   a. realize that this is developmentally normal.
   b. coax or bribe the child to eat more.
   c. punish or at least scold the child for being a picky eater.
4. The *least* acceptable language:
   a. She is a child with special needs.
   b. She is a child who has special needs.
   c. She is a special needs child.
5. Infants and children at high risk for developmental problems
   a. are most frequently found among families living in poverty.
   b. have no potential for normal development.
   c. usually outgrow their problems as they get a little older.
6. Developmental delay means the child
   a. is behind in all areas of development.
   b. can never catch up to children of the same age.
   c. is performing like a much younger normally developing child.

7. A young child with a hearing impairment who can run and jump as well as other children of the same age
   a. does not need special services.
   b. may be gifted in some areas.
   c. should be enrolled in a school exclusively for children who are deaf.
8. Labeling a young child as handicapped
   a. is necessary if the child is to receive special services under PL 99-457.
   b. is inappropriate according to early childhood educators and developmentalists.
   c. is important to the child's overall adjustment.
9. According to the theory of multiple intelligence
   a. the only legitimate assessments of intelligence are the traditional IQ tests.
   b. high scores on language and math tests are the most valid measures of giftedness.
   c. exceptionally good personal and social skills may be a sign of intelligence.
10. A potentially gifted child's abilities
   a. are likely to be genetic in origin and independent of environmental influence.
   b. can never be realized if the child has a developmental disability.
   c. may never be recognized in minority children because of low expectations.

C. *Mix and Match.* Select the one *best* match from the items in column II and place that letter in the appropriate space in column I.

I	II
___ 1. developmental sequence	A. stammering
___ 2. reciprocity	B. cardiac problem
___ 3. atypical	C. different
___ 4. chromosomal disorder	D. typical
___ 5. attention deficit	E. stand, walk, run
___ 6. dysfluency	F. talented
___ 7. normal	G. Down syndrome
___ 8. heart defect	H. give and take
___ 9. high-risk newborn	I. short attention span
___ 10. gifted	J. drug addicted at birth

REFERENCES

Allen, K.E., and Marotz, L. (1994). *Developmental profiles: Birth to six.* Albany: Delmar.

Bee, H. (1992). *The Developing Child.* New York: Harper & Row.

Freeman, J. (1981). The intellectually gifted. *New Directions for Gifted Children,* 7, 75–86.

Gallagher, J.J. (1988). National agenda for educating gifted students: Statement of priorities. *Exceptional Children,* 55 (2), 107–114.

Gardner, H. (1983). *Frames of mind: The theory of multiple intelligence.* New York: Basic Books.

Karnes, M.B., Schwedel, A.M., & Lewis, G.F. (1983). Longterm effects of early programming for the gifted/talented handicapped. *Journal for the Education of the Gifted.* 6, 266–278.

Karnes, M., and Johnson, L. (1989). An imperative: Programming for the young gifted/talented. *Journal for the Education of the Gifted.* 10 (3), 195–214.

Kirk, S.A., and Gallagher, J.J. (1986). *Educating Exceptional Children.* Boston: Houghton Mifflin.

Meltzoff, A.N., and Moore, M.K. (1983). Newborn infants imitate adult facial gestures. *Child Development,* 54, 702–709.

Robinson, N.M., and Robinson, H.B. (1986). *The Mentally Retarded Child.* New York: McGraw-Hill.

Robinson, H.B. (1981). The uncommonly bright child. In M. Lewis and L.A. Rosenblum (Eds.), *The Uncommon Child.* New York: Plenum.

Roedell, W.C., Jackson, N.E., and Robinson, H.B. (1980). *Gifted Young Children.* New York: Teachers College Press.

Stile, S., and Kitano, M. (1991). Preschool-age gifted children. *DEC Communicator,* 17–3, 4.

Thurman, S.K., and Widerstrom, A.H. (1990). *Infants and young children with special needs.* Baltimore: Brookes.

Wolfle, J. (1989). The gifted preschooler: Developmentally different but still 3 or 4 year olds. *Young Children,* 44 (3), 41–48.

Wolery, M., and Wilbers, J.S. (1994). *Including children with special needs in early early childhood programs.* Washington, DC: National Association for the Education of Young Children.

Wolery, M., Strain, P.S., and Bailey, D.B. (1992). Reaching potentials of young children with special needs. In S. Bradekamp and T. Rosegrant, (Eds.), *Reaching potentials: Appropriate curriculum and assessment for young children.* Washington DC: National Association for the Education of Young Children.

Developmental Disabilities: Causes and Classifications

OBJECTIVES

After studying this unit the student will be able to

- specify causes of developmental problems and give examples.
- discuss the correlation between poverty and developmental disabilities in young children.
- argue both for and against labeling young children as having a particular disability; support each argument with examples.
- explain why it is especially inappropriate to use terms like mentally retarded, emotionally disturbed, or learning disabled in reference to young children.
- list at least seven of the major categories of disabling conditions, in order, from the most to the least number of children and youth being served.

What causes developmental problems?

Should we classify children with developmental problems?

These two questions, of significant concern to everyone working with young exceptional children, have no agreed upon answers. Despite years of research and discussion, lack of agreement continues because of the varying professional and legal viewpoints mentioned in Unit 4. These include individual differences in children, differences in knowledge base among professionals, and differences in public policy. Confusion exists, regardless of the type of child under consideration, whether severely impaired, moderately involved, even exceptionally bright. In attempting to assign cause, consider the following examples:

Two 3-year-olds with hearing impairments, both boys: one is talking well, the other not talking at all. Why? Do they have different kinds of hearing losses? Has one child had more frequent or more severe ear infections? Is one child in a better deaf education program? Do cultural and family differences account for the developmental differences?

What about exceptionally bright young children? Are they programmed that way genetically? Have they had earlier and better preschool experiences? Have their parents been reading to them and taking them to the library regularly and frequently? What accounts for performance differences among school-age children with high IQ scores? Most of these children do well in school, some do poorly. Why?

Questions such as these are common among child developmentalists, clinicians, and educators. There are no ready answers. The best response is that the causes of developmental differences appear to be a combination of interacting events: heredity, biology (physical makeup), temperament (personality style), and a long list of environmental factors, especially factors associated with poverty.

To assign a developmentally appropriate category of exceptionality to a young child also is difficult. As noted in Unit 4, the range of both normalcy and individual differences is broad. Furthermore, most young children experience one or more developmental irregularities that may or may not require special attention. One thing is certain: More harm than good comes from prematurely classifying or labeling a child. Predicting developmental outcome based on early behaviors is poor, except in extreme cases (McCall 1979).

What accounts for performance differences among children?

CAUSES OF DEVELOPMENTAL DIFFERENCES

Whatever the cause of a developmental disability, the damage can occur at any stage of development: before the child is born, during the birth process, or any time following birth. A condition present at the time of birth is referred to as *congenital.* Congenital problems may or may not be genetically related. Deafness in one child, for example, may have been caused by an infection the mother had during early pregnancy. In another child it may be genetically linked to deafness in the child's parents. Some disabilities can be recognized at birth; others may not be detected *or* do not become apparent until much later. Generally speaking, the more severe the disability, the earlier it is recognized. Exceptions are many, however. A serious hearing loss may not be discovered until the child starts school.

Biology and environment act together to produce both atypical and normal development. It is nearly impossible to isolate one or the other as the single cause of a developmental problem. In every instance, environmental factors act on a child's biological foundation to determine developmental outcome. Furthermore, children themselves exert influence on the environment. A healthy infant literally *hooks* parents into responding. Strong, early bonding is the usual result. A sick, low-birth-weight infant may not be able to

interact, or may respond inconsistently, and the outcome is often less than positive. Such interactions and transactions, with the infant or child as the pivot point, need to be kept in mind in the discussions that follow.

Biological Factors.   Biology plays a major role in determining both healthy and less-than-healthy development. *Biological insult* is a term that describes interference with or damage to an individual's physical structure or functioning. The insult may occur at the time of conception, with resulting genetic disorders. It may occur during pregnancy, often within the first trimester (initial 12 weeks of pregnancy). The insult also can happen at the time of birth or any time following birth. It may be due to health problems in the mother, complications during the birth process, or malnutrition following birth.

Chromosomal disorders.   The genetic makeup of every individual is determined at the moment of conception. Each parent contributes 23 chromosomes on which there are thousands of genes. In a process called **mitosis** (and **meiosis**), the chromosomes from each parent divide and recombine. This results in enormous numbers of chromosomal combinations—as much as 70 trillion! Physical charactcristics such as size, body build, eye and skin color, sex, even shape of the nose are determined at that moment as are genetically determined abnormalities.

The various syndromes are a major class of genetic abnormalities or anomolies, the preferred term. Syndrome refers to a grouping of characteristics, sometimes called **stigmata**. These stigmata, several of them occurring together, can be seen in all individuals with a similar chromosomal error. In most cases, children with a given syndrome look more like each other than they look like their own brothers and sisters or other family members.

Down syndrome.   The most readily recognized chromosomal anomaly is Down syndrome, also called Trisomy 21. It occurs in approximately one of every 700 births with the risk higher among young teenage mothers and women over 45. The cause (oversimplified) is an abnormal addition to the twenty-first chromosome pair (hence the term Trisomy 21). In about one-third of the cases, the problem originates in the sperm of the father (Bee 1992). Children with Down syndrome are easily identified because they have many of the same physical characteristics. The stigmata include:

- Small, round head and somewhat flattened face
- Protruding tongue due to poor muscle tone
- Short fingers and toes with little fingers and little toes curving inward
- *Simian crease*, a single, almost straight line across the upper part of one or both palms, instead of the usual pair of parallel lines
- Curving folds of skin at the inner corners of the eyes which give an almond shape to the eyes.*

About 50 percent of the children with Down syndrome have heart and intestinal defects. Hearing impairments and severe cases of ear infections such as otitis media also are common as is some degree of cognitive delay, ranging from mild to severe.

Metabolic disorders.   In addition to the many syndromes, other genetically associated disorders have been identified. Frequently these are problems of metabolism, that is, interference in one or more of the complex physical and chemical activities that both create and destroy living cells.

PKU (*phenylketonuria*) is a prime example. It occurs in infants born without liver **enzymes** needed to digest the **amino acid** known as *phenylalanine*. As a result, toxic materials build up, leading to irreversible brain damage. Today, newborns are screened routinely for this disorder through blood tests, three or four days after birth. If placed immediately on a highly restricted diet, the child usually is saved from serious mental retardation. The diet, low in phenylalanine (milk and many other common foods are forbidden) must be continued during most of the child's developmental years (Crain 1984). This condition, occurring approx-

imately once in 8000 births, demonstrates the intertwining of genetic and environmental influences.

Sex-linked anomalies.   A number of diseases are due to sex-linked genetic factors. These include both metabolic disorders and blood composition misfits such as:

- *Tay-Sachs disease*—a rapid degeneration of the nervous system from birth on with death occurring around 3 or 4 years of age. The cause seems to be ineffective metabolism of fats, leading to fatty accumulations in the brain that interfere with critical neurological processes. The disease is most common among children of eastern European Jewish descent.
- *Cystic Fibrosis*—a damaging build up of mucus in the lungs and digestive system. It is a fatal disease, though children who receive adequate medical care and pulmonary therapy often live into their thirties.
- *Sickle-cell anemia*—a disease of the blood that can result in death. The symptoms are severe anemia, painful joints, leg ulcers, and heightened susceptibility to infection. The disease is found mostly among black Americans.
- *Muscular Dystrophy*—a fatal disease found almost entirely in boys in which the muscles literally waste away. The most common type is Duchenne's.

Other sex-linked conditions are associated with one particular pair of chromosomes called the X and Y or *sex chromosomes*. The typical female has an XX pattern on the 23rd pair of chromosomes while the typical male has an XY pattern. The way in which these chromosomes divide and rearrange themselves determines the sex of the child. Improper division can result in a variety of syndromes. Examples:

- *Klinefelter's syndrome*—only boys are affected. They may have unusually long legs, faulty motor coordination, poorly developed testes (testicles), and mild to severe learning disabilities.
- *Turner's syndrome*—only girls are affected; they tend to be unusually short in stature, have thick, webbed necks, and poor spatial abilities; the girls often excel in verbal skills.

---

* It was this characteristic that led, at one time, to these children being called Mongoloid. This is a demeaning term that should *never* be used in describing individuals with Down syndrome. Point of interest: the characteristic folds of skin at the corners of the eyes are typical of one stage of prenatal development in all children, regardless of race.

- *Fragile X syndrome*—both boys and girls can have Fragile X syndrome, but boys are likely to be more seriously impaired physically, mentally, and behaviorally. An estimated 5 to 7 per cent of mental retardation among males may be due to Fragile X syndrome (Zigler and Hodapp 1991); Ho, Glahn and Ho (1988) suggest it is the second leading genetic cause of retardation, with Down syndrome first.

Prenatal Infections and Intoxicants.   Most developmental abnormalities, especially those that occur prenatally, cannot be explained by genetics. It may be that 3 percent or less of all birth defects are purely genetic in origin. Diseases that have a negative effect on a mother's health during pregnancy are responsible for 25 percent or more of all developmental deviations. These include:

- *Rubella* (*German or three-day measles*) can have a devastating effect on the unborn infant. If contracted during the first trimester, Rubella can lead to severe and lifelong disabilities.
- *CMV virus* (*cytomegalic inclusion disease*), contracted by the mother, is a frequent cause of severe damage to the infant. Often the pregnant woman has no symptoms. Ninety percent of CMV infants are *asymptomatic* at birth; that is, they show no problems. It is only later that mental retardation, deafness, diseases of the eyes, and other disabilities begin to show up.
- *Herpes Simplex* is an incurable disease. Even in **remission**, a woman can pass it on to her unborn infant. Results can be devastating, even fatal as in cases of inflammation of the infant's brain and spinal cord. Less damaging results include periodic attacks of genital sores.
- *AIDS* (*acquired immune deficiency syndrome*) interferes with the body's ability to ward off diseases such as respiratory disorders and certain types of cancer. Transmission of AIDS is through sexual contact, shared hypodermic needles, and blood transfusions. It can be passed on to the infant.
- *Diabetes* in the mother puts the infant at high risk for serious developmental problems, even death. True, today's diabetic woman has a better chance

of bearing a healthy baby because of medical advances. Nevertheless, maternal diabetes must be monitored throughout pregnancy.
- *Toxemia* is a frequent complication of pregnancy. It produces a variety of symptoms: swelling of the mother's arms and legs, poorly functioning kidneys, and high blood pressure. Women with toxemia often deliver premature or low-birth-weight babies who are at medical risk.

Alcohol and other drugs.   Maternal use of any chemical substance during pregnancy, for medicinal or "recreational" purposes, can damage the unborn infant. Alcohol consumption, even moderate amounts, has been linked to a variety of developmental problems now grouped under two headings: *Fetal Alcohol Syndrome* (FAS) and *Fetal Alcohol Effect* (FAE). Years of research by Streissguth and her colleagues (1990) indicate that the potential for subnormal IQ is three times greater among children whose mothers drank during pregnancy. These researchers report that even occasional "binge" drinking can be extremely damaging to the fetus. It is not yet known if there is a "safe" amount of maternal alcohol consumption. In light of such incomplete knowledge about alcohol and fetal damage, the only safe course is to refrain from drinking during pregnancy.

A number of drugs used by pregnant women for medicinal purposes also can cause serious birth defects. *Pregnant women should take no medication without consulting a physician.* This is particularly important in terms of over-the-counter drugs. As for illegal drugs—cocaine, for example, and its many variations—used during pregnancy, can put the unborn infant at high risk for both short-term and long-range developmental problems. Many such infants are born prematurely, are very low birth weight, or are stillborn; others die of "crib death" during their first year. Many more suffer neurological damage that may not show up until years later as a serious learning disability (Keith 1989). Again, it is not known how much drug use is too much. It is known, however, that "even a single hit can have a devastating effect at any time during pregnancy. In some cases, it appears to cause a stroke in the fetus resulting in partial paralysis" (Bee 1992, p. 73). As with alcohol, the best thing a woman can do for her baby is to completely abstain from drug use.

Maternal malnutrition and protein deficiency often results in premature and seriously low-birth-weight babies. These infants are at high risk for a number of developmental problems including limited brain cell development. (Note: Poor nutrition is not the only condition responsible for premature and low-birth-weight infants. It is, however, a frequent cause and often is associated with poverty as we will see in a later section.)

Birth Complications.   Birth itself can result in trauma—that is, injury or shock. An infant, perfectly healthy until the moment of birth, can experience damage during the birth process. For example, *anoxia*, lack of oxygen to the brain cells, can occur because of labor complications. Brain damage or severe neurological problems such as cerebral palsy

may result. When damage does occur, it may *not* come from a newborn's inability to breathe immediately. Instead, the failure to start breathing may have been caused by *earlier*, perhaps unsuspected, damage in utero. (This is one example of how difficult it is to be certain about the cause of a developmental problem.)

Premature infants, especially, are subject to another kind of trauma: hemorrhaging or bleeding into the brain. These immature newborns also are at higher risk for breathing problems, heart failure, and infections. Even less severe problems at birth can result in trouble later. It is now thought that school-age learning disabilities may be associated with low-birth-weight or seemingly minor disturbances at the time of birth (Hittleman et al. 1987).

Complications Following Birth.   Once the baby is born, other events can lead to developmental problems. Among these are:

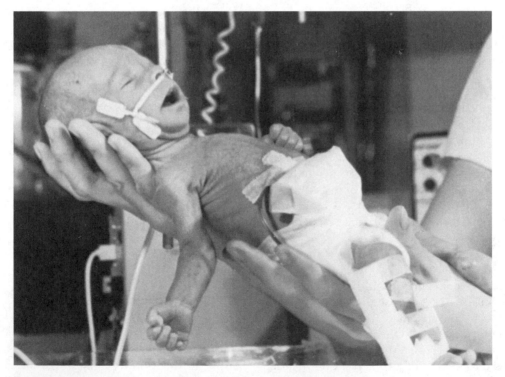

Premature and low birth weight infants usually are in need of intensive care.

Meningitis.   This is a virus or bacterial infection that causes inflammation of the protective covering of the brain and the spinal column. In newborns, when meningitis related death is most likely, the cause usually is organisms found in the intestine or birth canal of the mother (Wolraich 1983). The results of meningitis are unpredictable. Some children show no serious effects; others experience major neurological damage.

Encephalitis.   Encephalitis attacks the brain itself. The symptoms are so many and so varied that the infection often is not diagnosed correctly. A range of after-effects is possible, from no damage to identifiable neurological damage and later learning problems.

Lead poisoning.   Poisoning from lead can cause grave damage to young children whose bodies and nervous systems are still developing. Little children put everything in their mouth so lead-based paint for indoor use and on children's toys has been outlawed. Nevertheless, it is estimated that at least 10 percent of the young children in this country are absorbing excessive

No longer can play equipment be painted with lead based paint.

amounts of lead. Often, it is those children living in old, dilapidated housing. Recent research indicates that even low levels of lead in a newborn's blood (levels classified as *safe* by federal guidelines) can be damaging. As these children grow up they appear to have lower IQ scores when compared with children with lower lead levels at birth (Bellinger 1987).

Poor nutrition.   Inadequate protein intake (milk, cheese, grains, eggs, fish, chicken, and meat) can result in low birth weight, illness and higher risk of death during the baby's first year. Stunted growth throughout childhood often is another consequence. The effects of a poor diet are particularly damaging during the last trimester of pregnancy when significant maturing of the brain and nervous system is taking place. It now is recommended that a pregnant woman gain 25 to 30 pounds during pregnancy, more is she is underweight to begin with.

Recognizing that substandard nutrition often is associated with poverty, *WIC, The Special Supplemental Food Program for Women, Infants, and Children* was established in the early 1970s. It provides nutritious food for women who are pregnant or breastfeeding and to their children up to age 5. It also links food distribution to other health services including prenatal care. Participation in WIC is estimated to reduce up to 25 percent the chance that a high-risk pregnant woman will deliver a premature or low-birth-weight baby. The average cost of WIC services throughout a pregnancy is $250; the cost of sustaining a low-birth-weight baby in neonatal intensive care for even one day is many times that amount (Carnegie Report 1994). Yet WIC has never been fully funded—it serves little more than half of those who are eligible.

POVERTY

Many developmental problems, regardless of when they occur—before, during, or after the birth of the baby—can be directly or indirectly related to poverty. Families living in poverty experience the highest rates of infant death, failure to thrive, and birth defects. The same holds true for subsequent developmental problems: mental retardation, learning disabilities, social and emotional deviations. The estimates are

Infants need a variety of structured and unstructured developmental activities.

appalling: *one quarter of all children under the age of six live in poverty in this nation of ours!* It is equally appalling that more and more children are being born into poverty each year. *While the number of children under age 6 increased by less than 10 per cent between 1971 and 1991, the number of poor children under age 6 increased by 60 per cent.* (Carnegie Report 1994).

Not every child living in poverty will have developmental problems. Many, many parents find ways to cope, to raise bright and healthy children in spite of severely challenging circumstances. The reverse also is true: adequate living conditions do not ensure children a good life. Many families, with seemingly adequate resources, abuse and neglect their children or fail to provide necessary stimulation. Nevertheless, the devastating link between poverty and developmental problems cannot be denied. Poverty undermines development in the several significant ways described as follows.

Inadequate health care and education.   A major preventive measure for developmental problems is adequate health care: for the pregnant woman from the very start of pregnancy; for mother and infant following delivery; for the child throughout the developmental years. According to the Carnegie Report (1994) about one-fourth of pregnant women do not receive adequate prenatal care. Even more disturbing, the percentage of women who receive virtually no care is increasing steadily. Pregnant women who are young, poor, unmarried, relatively uneducated, uninsured, or living in inner cities or rural areas are the least likely to have even minimal medical care. For those able to obtain public health services, the program's financing is often insufficient. Sometimes it does not cover delivery; often it fails to provide follow up care for new mothers who are most in need of support and education in the care of infants and young children.

Homelessness and substandard housing.   Many American children living in poverty also are homeless. It is estimated that there are in excess of 100,000 children without a home on any given night; half of the children are less than 6 years old. Even with a place to call home, thousands upon thousands of children are in serious developmental jeopardy because of overcrowded housing, unsafe buildings, and violent neighborhoods, what have been called "inner-city war zones" (Earls 1991).

Single parent families.   While single parent families and mother-only families occur at all social-economic levels, they are overly represented among our poorest families, especially those headed by teenage girls. The fathers, 50 per cent of them, are making no contribution, economically or otherwise, to the support of the teenagers' children. The resulting deprivation and stress have a serious impact on development; the children score significantly less well on a variety of measures: health, learning ability, and emotional and behavioral stability (Dawson 1991).

Child care.   The critical need for quality child care during the developmental years has been documented repeatedly. Yet, decent, affordable child care continues to be in critically short supply for all but affluent families. Recently, a major study was conducted in a number of community settings, both center-based and family care-based. The child care was determined to be of such substandard quality that is was adversely affecting the infant's and children's development (Whitebrook, Phillips, and Howe 1994). What is worse, the negative effects of poor care multiply and become even more damaging at successively lower levels on the social-economic ladder.

Combatting poverty: We have known, for a long time, how to stop the costly and devastating effects of poverty on the development of infants and children. It was dramatically demonstrated in a study conducted 25 years ago called the Milwaukee Project. Two groups of mothers with low IQs, living in poverty, were assigned to either a control group or an experimental group. Mothers and infants in the control group received no special services. The experimental group received a variety of services: good nutrition, medical care, parent education, and stimulating infant and child care (Heber 1975). By the time the children in the experimental group were 4-years-old they were scoring significantly higher than the control group in developmental, intellectual, and language assessments. On an average, they were "exceeding the norms generally established by peer groups of the majority culture" (President's Commission on Mental Retardation, 1972). Follow up studies when the children were 9-year-olds indicated that the gains had held. Furthermore, and surprisingly, the entire family seemed to have profited from the program: brothers and sisters in the experimental group were scoring higher on standardized tests, mothers were more employable, and were earning substantially more money than the mothers in the control group (Heber and Garber 1975).

In the ensuing years there have been many studies taking off from Heber's pioneering work. Researchers such as Craig Ramey and his colleagues have demonstrated repeatedly that children enrolled in enriched programs gain significantly in IQ. These children also do better on achievement tests and are less likely to be held back in school. On the other hand, children in the control groups, those without an intervention program, continue to function in ways generally viewed as subnormal or retarded (Ramey, Lee, and Burchinal 1989). It also has become evident that even prenatally malnourished infants and infants with serious birth complications have benefited markedly through enrollment in stimulating infant and preschool programs, many having significantly higher IQs than similar infants reared at home by poorly educated mothers. (Ramey and Ramey 1992).

CLASSIFICATION OF DEVELOPMENTAL DISABILITIES

Should we label children according to their particular developmental disabilities? Should we categorize them in terms of their impairment: mental retardation, deafness, blindness, learning disability, emotional disturbance and so on? These questions have long been controversial. Those in favor of categorization argue that it is needed in order to get necessary information:

How many individuals have a particular problem? How widespread is it? Does it occur mostly in particular areas or among certain groups (urban, rural, immigrant, itinerant farm worker)? Is the problem increasing? Decreasing?

Disability of Students Age 6 through 21 Served School Year 1992–93	
Disability	Number
Specific learning disabilities	2,369,385
Speech or language impairments	1,000,154
Mental retardation	533,715
Serious emotional disturbance	402,668
Multiple disabilities	103,215
Hearing impairments	60,896
Orthopedic impairments	52,921
Other health impairments	66,054
Visual impairments	23,811
Autism	15,527
Deaf-blindness	1,425
Traumatic brain injury	3,903
All disabilities	4,633,674

Adapted from *16th Annual Report to Congress.*

How many teachers, clinicians, special facilities are needed?

What proportion of public money (**categorical funding**) is needed to provide, for example, necessary services such as braille and mobility training for those with limited vision?

Which individuals are eligible for Supplemental Social Security income and other legislated benefits?

Those opposed to labeling or categorizing argue that it can be harmful. The harm may be especially great where young children are concerned. The very young may get locked into categories that are developmentally unsuitable or put into programs that compound the child's delay.

Example: At 3½ years of age, Jodie was talking very little, seemed incapable of following simple directions, had few play skills. She scored low on an IQ test and was placed in a segregated preschool for mentally retarded children. It was not until age 7 that a severe hearing loss was discovered. Between 3½ and 7, crucial developmental years, Jodie functioned as a retarded child. Why? Because she had been labeled as retarded and consequently had *not* been identified as a candidate for deaf education services; she was not

receiving the stimulation needed to develop language and cognitive skills.

Current laws recognize the potential harm of prematurely classifying children under the age of 6. Categorical funding has been discontinued in the birth to age 6 part of the law. Instead, the more flexible concept, *developmental delay*, is used to cover all developmental problems.

Categorical Systems.   In spite of disagreements, categorizing does exist. Among other things, the system is used to allocate federal funding for educational services. The table at left, adapted from the 16th report to Congress lists how many 6- to 21-year-olds were served in each of 12 specific categories of impairment. Because we no longer categorize young children, the report gives numbers of children served in terms of age groups:

Birth through age 2: 138,493
Age 2 through age 5: 459,728

Even though the classification system no longer applies to children under the age of 6, everyone working with children of any age need to know something about each of the impairments. Here we will discuss the categories briefly with a little extra time given to the

Learning disabilities are difficult to define satisfactorily.

first four because they are the categories that continue to be misused and overused in many child care and early intervention programs. (In later units the types of impairments most common among young children will be discussed in terms of inclusion and intervention.)

Specific learning disabilities.   Specific learning disabilities (SLD) or learning disabilities (LD) have yet to be defined in any agreed upon way. As Mercer (1994) stated: *Given the respective definitions proposed by various organizations, committees and government agencies, it appears that the learning disabilities definition remains in a state of confusion* (p. 122).

In the school-age child, the label is often one of exclusion—what the child is: *not* mentally retarded, *not* hearing impaired or visually impaired, *not* having identifiable neurological problems such as cerebral palsy. A normal IQ is characteristic of most children with learning disabilities. Nevertheless, these children have problems learning to read, or to write, or to do arithmetic. Trouble with reading, which accounts for the majority of children with learning disabilities is referred to as *dyslexia. Dysgraphia* is the term sometimes used to describe problems with printing and writing. More than a hundred different labels have been assigned to children whose learning problems baffle clinicians and educators. The labels, it should be noted, do little to help children with their learning problems.

Speech and language impairments.   Speech and language problems account for the second largest category of educational disabilities among 6- to 21-year-olds. With young children it is difficult to clearly define what is and what is not a problem because so many factors are interacting:

rate of overall development
temperament or personality
being in a language-responsive environment with many
    opportunities to hear language and talk to others
cultural expectations
general health and well being

Also, as noted in Unit 4, there are a number of typical or *normal irregularities* that are common in the course of language development. These need not become problems unless the child is unduly pressured.

Speech and language problems often accompany other developmental disorders. Children with cerebral palsy may have serious speech problems as may children with hearing impairments and severe emotional disturbances. Whatever the cause, it is important that speech and language disorders receive attention as early as possible. Problems in this area can lead to serious disruptions in cognitive and social development.

Mental retardation.   It is unwise to label a young child as mentally retarded. Children change; they are evolving. The younger the child, the more likely it is that changes will occur. The range of "normal" intellectual functioning is enormous. Furthermore, a child's family circumstances may change, health problems may clear up, the child may enter an early intervention program. Any one of these has the potential of producing dramatic change in a child's cognitive skills. Recall the remarkable increases in the abilities of the children in the Milwaukee Project and in the many other studies during the ensuing years. In this text, therefore, mental retardation will not be treated as a separate and unique category. Instead, issues related to cognitive development and mental functioning will be addressed in the unit on cognitive and preacademic skills. Everyone working with children of any age must nevertheless be familiar with the formal definition of mental retardation. This definition has been revised once again by the American Association on Mental Retardation (AAMR 1992). The new definition reads:

> *Mental retardation* refers to substantial limitations in present functioning. It is characterized by significantly subaverage intellectual functioning, existing concurrently with related limitations in two or more of the following applicable adaptive skill areas: communication, self-care, home living, social skills, community use, self direction, health and safety, functional academics, leisure and work.

The AAMR manual tells us that the new definition of mental retardation is a description of an individual's present functioning rather than an inherent trait or permanent state of being: *Mental retardation is not something you have, like blue eyes or a bad heart. Nor is it something you are, like short or thin. It is not a medical disorder or a mental disorder. . . . Mental retardation reflects the "fit" between the capabilities of individuals and the structure and expectations of their environment.*

Elaborating further on this aspect of the definition the manual says:

Mental retardation is defined within the context of the environment in which the individual lives, learns, works, and plays. It exists when intellectual and adaptive limitations affect the individual's ability to cope with the ordinary challenges of everyday life in the community. The significance of these limitations is therefore relative to the individual's environment.

AAMR, recognizing that almost everyone will have trouble understanding the definition and the explanations offers a phrase-by-phrase break down along the following lines:

- *Mental retardation*: fundamental difficulty in learning and performing certain life skills; there must be substantial limitation in conceptual, practical, and social intelligence.
- *Significantly subaverage intellectual functioning*: IQ score of approximately 70 to 75 or below, based on one or more individually administered general intelligence tests. (It is recommended that these test scores, along with other available test scores and other pertinent information, be reviewed by a multidisciplinary team.)
- *Existing concurrently*; intellectual limitations and adaptive skill limitations occur together, at the same time in an individual's life.
- *With related limitations*: limited adaptive skills are more closely related to intellectual limitations than to cultural or linguistic diversity or sensory limitations (such as deafness or blindness).
- *In two or more of the following adaptive skill areas*: since intellectual functioning alone does not suffice as a diagnosis of mental retardation, there must be evidence of adaptive skill limitations.
- *Communication, self-care, home living, social skills, community use, self direction, health and safety, functional academics, leisure and work*: these are the skills essential to life functioning and must be referenced to the individual's chronological age.

- *Manifests before age 18*: the 18th birthday approximates the age when individuals in our society are expected to assume adult roles. (This age may vary from society to society.)

NOTE: The list of adaptive skills alone supports the earlier argument about the inappropriateness of labeling a young child as mentally retarded; all of the skills are either yet to be learned or are barely emerging during the infant, toddler, and preschool years.

The phrase-by-phrase explanations of the definition of mental retardation are almost as confusing as the definition itself. Nevertheless, this definition by the AAMR signals an important and much needed advancement in social and educational policy. It changes the way we view those who in earlier times might have been placed in an institution or assigned to classes for the mentally retarded. No longer can any individual be labeled as retarded solely on the basis of a low IQ score. Individuals who are functioning well in their home and in the community, regardless of their inability to read or write or pass IQ tests, are not to be labeled as mentally retarded.

Emotional disturbance.   Unlike mental retardation, emotional disturbance has no formally agreed upon definition. In many ways, its definition is the most controversial of the categories. Here is one example from proposed federal guidelines: the disability is characterized by behavioral or emotional response so different from appropriate age, ethnic and community norms, that the responses adversely affect educational performance, including academic, social, vocational, or personal skills. (Forness and Knitzer 1990.) Whatever the definition, emotional disturbance is a label that *should not be assigned to young children*. The reasons are similar to those given earlier for avoiding terms like mental retardation and learning disabilities with young children. Alternate terms for emotional disturbance (and more developmentally appropriate) might be behavior disorders or, better yet, behavior problems. These terms will be used interchangeably in this text. Even so, they are used with caution. Children's behavior during the early years is heavily influenced by child-rearing practices, cultural values, and expectations of the family and community.

Parents who are aggressive, for example, tend to have children who also behave aggressively (Hetherington and Martin 1979). Thus, the child's aggressiveness is perfectly "normal" in light of his or her upbringing.

The social emotional characteristics of young children also are highly influenced by particular stages of development. (In the past, early childhood educators and pediatricians used terms such as "The Terrible Twos" to describe the toddler's struggle for independence.) Behavior difficulties often arise out of the frustrations a young child experiences in trying to master basic developmental skills such as learning to feed, dress, and toilet one's self, learning what to fear and what not to fear, what is acceptable behavior and what is not.

In most cases, therefore, a child's behavior should be judged by what is developmentally appropriate for his or her particular age range and background. The majority of behavior problems occurring in early childhood do not carry over into adult life. There are exceptions: severe behavior disorders such as infantile autism or childhood schizophrenia. These psychoses and a variety of more common behavior disorders will be discussed in Unit 8.

Multiple disabilities. A number of children have more than one disability. It has been estimated that 20 to 50 percent of children with serious hearing deficits have additional problems. The same is true of children with cerebral palsy. Many of the syndromes are also characterized by several problems occurring together. It is not uncommon, for example, for a child with Down syndrome to have a heart defect, respiratory problems, a marked hearing loss, and hard-to-understand speech.

The number of children with multiple disabilities is rising. Possible reasons for the increase:

- Use of drugs and alcohol by increasing numbers of pregnant women. Equal amounts of alcohol (or other substances) may cause severe damage to one woman's unborn child, little damage to another's. Each woman's biochemical uniqueness determines what is excessive.
- Improved strategies for identification and treatment. For example, we can now do hearing and

vision screenings on children who were considered untestable a decade ago.
- Advanced medical practices now allow us to keep seriously damaged or very low-birth-weight babies alive. The tragedy is that we do not know how to cure many of the handicaps and disabilities these children are born with.

Hearing impairments. As defined by federal regulation, deafness is a hearing loss so severe that individuals cannot process spoken language, even with hearing aids or other forms of amplification. Hard-of-hearing refers to a loss that has a negative effect on a child's education, but not to the same degree as it does on children who are deaf. All hearing impairments have a negative effect on a young child's cognitive, social, and language development. The degree of developmental damage is determined by the severity of the hearing loss and the age at onset (when the hearing problem developed).

Deafness has an impact on every aspect of a child's development.

Generally speaking, the greater the loss, the greater the disabling effects; and, the earlier in life the loss, the greater the developmental damage. Because of the age factor, deafness and hearing impairments often are labeled according to when the damage occurred:

- *Congenital deafness*: The individual is deaf at birth and never had the benefits of normal hearing.
- *Adventitious deafness*: The individual is born with normal hearing but loses it through injury or disease. If the loss occurs after a child has acquired some language, the developmental problems tend to be less damaging.

Children who have even a short exposure to language before they lose their hearing do a great deal better in developing language skills than do children who were born deaf. Nevertheless, even a mild hearing loss can have negative effects on all aspects of development unless the child receives appropriate intervention services, preferably in an inclusive early education program.

Orthopedic impairments. Developmental problems that interfere with walking or other body movement are considered orthopedic or physical impairments. In many instances, orthopedic problems and neurological problems are closely related, one example being cerebral palsy. According to federal regulation, orthopedic impairments refer to:

Impairments caused by **congenital anomalies** and structural deformities such as club foot, absence of a limb, or paralysis,
Impairments caused by diseases such as polio,
Neurological and spinal cord damage resulting in problems such as paralysis of major muscles,
Impairments from other causes such as severely fractured bones, amputations, or burns.

It is commonly thought that neurological problems show up at birth. The opposite is often true. It may be weeks or months (even well into the first year) before the infant gives evidence of a neurological impairment. The problem may become noticeable only when certain of the very early **reflexive** (primitive) behaviors do not drop out on schedule and so interfere with the acquisition of new and more mature responses. For example, most newborns automatically grasp a finger placed in their hand. However, unless this primitive grasp reflex drops out between one and four months of age, infants will not be able to learn to release objects at will.

Health impairment.   Young children with severe health problems often have limited strength, vitality, and alertness. They also may experience pain and discomfort much of the time. A normal childhood may be nearly impossible because of frequent hospitalizations or intensive medical treatment.

Health disorders take many forms:

Heart problems (weak or damaged heart)
Leukemia (cancer of the bone marrow)
Asthma (disorder of the respiratory system)
Sickle-cell anemia (red blood cell malformation)
Hemophilia (a bleeding disorder)
Diabetes (faulty metabolism of sugar and starch)
Cystic fibrosis (lung and digestive problems)
Autism (sometimes considered a health problem, but also viewed as a pervasive developmental and behavioral disorder)

Vision impairments range from severe to mild.

Health disorders may be described as **chronic** or **acute** (although a chronic problem can go into an acute state). In either event, the child's overall development is under constant threat. True, health problems may not be the *cause* of other developmental disorders. Yet, they can create situations that lead to other problems.

> Example: A child who is physically weak, unable to run and jump and play with children of the same age, may be socially isolated. Brothers and sisters may resent having to play with the child instead of their own playmates. They also may resent that so much of the parents' attention and resources seem to be focused on the sick child. This may lead to the sick child feeling lonely, rejected, anxious, guilty, and even more isolated.

Visual impairments. As with other problems, there is no clear-cut definition of visual impairment. A legal definition is proposed by the National Society for the Prevention of Blindness:

- *Blind:* **Visual acuity** of 20/200 or less in the better eye with the best possible correction; or a much reduced field of vision (at its widest diameter, a visual arc of 20 degrees or less).
- *Partially sighted:* Visual acuity between 20/70 and 20/200 in the better eye with the best possible correction.

The American Foundation for the Blind offers an educational definition:

- *Blind:* Visual loss is severe enough that it is not possible to read print, requiring the child to be educated through the use of **braille** and other **tactile** and **auditory** materials.
- *Partially seeing:* **Residual vision** is sufficient to allow a child to read large print or possibly regular print under special conditions and to use other visual materials for educational purposes.

Total blindness, whether congenital or occurring after birth, is readily identified. The baby simply does not respond to people or objects within its range of vision. Less severe visual disorders may be more difficult to identify. Frequently the problem does not show up until it is time to learn to read and write. By this time the child may have developed a number of other problems in trying to compensate for the undiagnosed vision loss.

Combined deafness and blindness. Children who are described as having both deafness and blindness have a combination of vision and hearing problems so severe they require highly specialized intervention programs. Two such serious sensory deficits in combination usually result in a number of other problems in language, cognitive, and social development. Until the late 1960s education for children who were both deaf and blind was available only in private institutions. Consequently, children of affluent families were those most likely to be served. In 1968, the picture changed; federal legislation authorized the creation of eight model centers for educating children who had deafness and blindness. More recent legislation provides states with monies to develop their own programs for educating these very special children.

Autism. Autism is a disorder that includes emotional unresponsiveness and social-cognitive deficiencies. Until a few years ago autism was not generally viewed as a genetic or congenital condition. More recent research points to the conclusion that children are *born* with this disorder and that it shows up early— babies who do not cuddle or respond to affection. Autism does not come about because of unresponsive or unaffectionate parenting. "Whatever the specific origin, the evidence points to the conclusion that autism reflects different brain functions of some kind." (Bee 1992). Children with autism, in addition to their inability to relate to others, do not make eye contact, have delayed or strange language patters, tend to be resistant to change, and often engage in ritualistic behaviors or repetitive hand or body movements such as twirling or slapping their hands against their thighs.

For a fascinating account of parents' efforts on behalf of their autistic child see "Let Me Hear Your Voice: A Family's Triumph Over Autism" by Maurice (1993).

Traumatic brain injury. Injuries (either open- or closed-wound) to the head that cause tearing of the nerve fibers, bruising of the brain against the skull or bruising of the brain stem are now categorized separately as traumatic brain injury. The most common consequences as far as learning is concerned are:

- confusion in spatial orientation and directionality
- marked distractibility and short attention span
- problems in both short and long term memory
- impulsivity and sometimes, aggressiveness.

SUMMARY

Determining the cause of a developmental disability is a difficult process. The same is true of assigning a classification of exceptionality to a young child. Both issues, cause and classification, are subject to varying definitions, depending on professional perspective.

Biological and environmental factors, in combination, account for the preponderance of developmental problems. Biological factors include genetic disorders, diseases and infections that occur during pregnancy, and poor nutrition. Problems at the time of birth as well as diseases and infections following birth also may cause developmental damage. In young children, especially those raised in old and dilapidated housing, lead poisoning is a common problem. Poverty, in general, accounts for a large percentage of developmental problems, most of which are preventable with early intervention.

Classifying, or categorizing, children in terms of a particular disorder, is a common educational and administrative practice. Most child developmentalists argue against categorizing, especially for young children, because infants and children are changing so rapidly during the early years. Federal legislation supports this position, allowing states to use the blanket term *developmental delay*. Nevertheless, a classification system seems necessary from both the funding and the professional training standpoint.

STUDENT ACTIVITIES

1. Take a poll among the female members of your class to determine how many students are protected against Rubella. Find out where the inoculations are available as a public service in your community.
2. Discuss with your mother your own birth and that of your brothers and sisters to determine the kinds of problems, if any, that she or the infants experienced. (Feel free to carry out this activity with any woman that has given birth and is willing to discuss the issues with you.)
3. Study a copy of your state's system for funding the education of children with disabilities. Make a chart of the categories it uses with the number of students in each category. If preschool age children are included, indicate what percentage.
4. Serve as discussion leader: invite three or four other students to discuss with the class the issue of not labeling a young child as having learning disabilities, mental retardation, or emotional disturbance.
5. Make a list of the kinds of services available in your community for pregnant teenage girls; do the same for pregnant women with alcohol or drug related problems. With each service, indicate availability in terms of waiting list, beds available, and so on.

REVIEW QUESTIONS

A. *Short answer.*
   1. What is a congenital problem? Give an example.
   2. Define metabolic disorder. Give an example.
   3. What is meant by birth complications? Give an example.
   4. Most cases of mental retardation can be prevented. How?
   5. Why is the general term *developmental delay* preferable to the term *handicapped* when referring to children with disabilities?
   6. What is temperament and what effect can it have on a child's development. Give an example.
   7. What are the possible effects of lead poisoning on children?

8. How do a family's child-rearing practices influence a child's development? Give an example.
9. Explain why even a mild hearing loss may have a negative effect on a child's overall development.
10. What is the difference between a chronic and an acute health problem? Give an example of each.

B. *True or False. Choose the best answer.*

T F 1. Most developmental differences are caused by a combination of biological and environmental factors.
T F 2. Deafness may or may not be congenital.
T F 3. Biological insult is the term for unpleasant remarks made about a disabled person.
T F 4. Milk is removed from the diets of infants with PKU.
T F 5. Untreated maternal diabetes may result in death to the infant.
T F 6. Learning disabilities in school-age children may be associated with low birth weight.
T F 7. All young children with developmental problems should be assigned to a category.
T F 8. Speech and language disorders represent the fewest number of young children with developmental problems.

T F 9. Every individual with an IQ score below 70 on a standardized IQ test should be regarded as mentally retarded.
T F 10. A chronic health problem never becomes acute.

C. *Mix and Match.* Select the one *best* match from the items in column II and place that letter in the appropriate space in column I.

I	II
____ 1. classifying	A. poor diet
____ 2. mitosis	B. lack of oxygen
____ 3. amino acid	C. difficulty in printing
____ 4. rubella	D. Stanford-Binet
____ 5. autism	E. childhood psychosis
____ 6. anoxia	F. chromosome activity
____ 7. dysgraphia	G. club foot
____ 8. standardized IQ test	H. phenylalanine
____ 9. anemia	I. categorizing
____ 10. congenital anomaly	J. German measles

REFERENCES

American Association on Mental Retardation. (1992). *Mental Retardation: Definition, Classification, and Systems of Support* (9th ed.). Washington DC: Author.

Bee, H. (1992). *The Developing Child.* New York: Holt, Rinehart, and Winston.

Bellinger, D. (April, 1987). *Social class differences in the effects of in-utero exposure to lead.* Paper presented at the biennial meeting of the Society for Research in Child Development, Baltimore.

The Carnegie Task Force on Meeting the Needs of Young Children: Starting Points. (1994). New York: Author.

Crain, L. (1984). *Prenatal causes of atypical development.* Baltimore, MD: University Park Press.

Dawson, D.A. (1991). Family structure and children's health. *Vital and Health Statistics, 10:178.* (DHHS Pub. No. 91–505) Washington, DC: National Center for Health Statistics.

Earls, F. (1991). Panel on prevention of violence and violent injuries. Division of Injury Control, Center for Disease Control. Atlanta, Georgia.

Forness, S.R. and Knitzer, I. (1990). *A new proposed definition and terminology to replace "Serious Emotional Disturbance" in the Education of the Handicapped Act.* (Report of the Work Group on Definition. National Mental Health and Special Education Coalition): Alexandria, VA.

Heber, R., and Garber, H. (1975). The Milwaukee project: A study of the use of family intervention to prevent cultural-familial mental retardation. In B. Friedlander, G. Sterritt, and G. Kirk (Eds.), *Exceptional Infant,* 3. New York: Brunner/Mazel.

Hetherington, E.M., and Martin, B. Family interaction. (1979). In H.C. Quay and J.S. Werry (Eds.), *Psycho-pathological disorders of childhood.* New York: Wiley.

Hittleman, J., Parekh, A., and Glass, L. (April, 1987). *Developmental outcome of extremely low birth weight infants.* Paper presented at the biennial meeting of the Society for Research in Child Development, Baltimore.

Ho, H.Z., Glahn, T.J. and Ho, J.C. (1988). The fragile X syndrome. *Developmental Medicine and Child Neurology. 30,* 252–265.

Keith, L.G., MacGregor, S., Freidell, S., Rosner, M., Chasnoff, I.J., and Sciarra, J.J. (1989). Substance abuse in pregnant women: Recent experience at the perinatal center for chemical dependence of Northwestern Memorial Hospital. *Obstetrics and Gynecology 73,* 715–720.

Maurice, C. (1993). Let me hear your voice: A family's triumph over autism. New York: Fawcett Columbine.

Mercer, C.C. (1994). Learning disabilities. In Haring, N.G., McCormick, L., and Haring, T.G. *Exceptional children and youth: An introduction to special education*, (6th ed.). New York: Merrill.

McCall, R. (1979). The development of intellectual functioning in infancy and the prediction of later IQ. In J. Osofsky (Ed.), *Handbook of infant development*. New York: Wiley & Sons.

President's Commission on Mental Retardation. (1972). A proposed program for national action to combat mental retardation. Washington, DC: U.S. Government Printing Office.

Ramey, C.T., Lee, M.W., and Burchinal, M.R. (1989). Developmental plasticity and predictability: Consequences of ecological change. In M.H. Bornstein, N.A., and Krasnegor (Eds.), *Stability and continuity in mental development* 217–234. Hillsdale, NJ: Earlbaum.

Ramey, C.T. and Ramey, S.L. (1992). Effective early intervention. *Mental Retardation*, 30, 337–45.

Sixteenth Annual Report to the Congress on the Implementation of the Individuals with Disabilities Education. (1994). To assure the free appropriate education of all children with disabilities. Washington DC: U.S. Department of Education.

Streissguth, A.P., Barr, H.M., and Sampson, P.D. (1990). Moderate prenatal alcohol exposure: Effects on child IQ and learning problems at age 7 1/2 years. *Alcoholism: Clinical and Experimental Research, 14*, 662–669.

Whitebrook, M., Phillips, D.A., and Howes, C. (1994). Who cares? Child care teachers and the quality of care in America. In E. Galinsky, C. Howes, S. Kontos and M. Shinn. (Eds.), *The study of children in center, family, and relative-based child care*. New York. Families and Work Institute.

Wolraich, M.L. (1983). Encephalitis and meningitis. In J.A. Blackman (Ed.), *Medical aspects of developmental disabilities in children birth to three*. Iowa City: University of Iowa.

Zigler, E., and Hodapp, R.M. (1991). Behavioral functioning in individuals with mental retardation. *Annual Review of Psychology, 42*, 29–50.

Sensory Impairments: Vision and Hearing

OBJECTIVES

After studying this unit the student will be able to

- discuss hearing and vision problems and their impact on the development of young children.
- explain why a hearing loss, more than other sensory losses, interferes with early development.
- list three warning signs indicating an infant may have a hearing loss. For a child with language list seven or more signs of a possible hearing loss.
- outline the characteristics of an appropriate early intervention inclusion program for children who are blind or visually impaired.
- describe five strategies that teachers may use to facilitate learning in children with visual impairments in integrated preschool activities.

Everything that children learn about themselves and their world comes through their five senses—hearing, vision, touch, taste, and smell. In healthy newborns, the five senses are functioning from the very beginning, a notion contrary to earlier beliefs about the helplessly confused state of young infants. As Reisman (1987) puts it, "infants are born with some exquisitely tuned sensory abilities" (p. 65). From the moment of birth, every aspect of development depends on these systems being in good working order.

Infants and children with sensory impairments have a less easy time, developmentally. The most serious and most prevalent sensory problems are hearing and vision losses. Most of what infants and children are expected to learn is acquired through these two senses. A child who is both blind and deaf is at extreme developmental risk and requires highly specialized services.

The common belief is that it would be worse to be born blind than deaf. While both are serious, deafness has the potential for doing greater and more generalized developmental damage. Hearing loss almost always has a negative effect on language acquisition. This, in turn, has a negative effect on cognitive development. Cognitive learning, after the first year and a half of age, is tied closely to both receptive and expressive language. As noted in earlier units, the development of cognitive skills and language skills is nearly inseparable.

Children who are blind learn language with considerably less difficulty than children who are deaf (though certainly not as easily as normally developing children). Children who do not see can nevertheless benefit from the many incidental learning opportunities available every day. They hear casual conversations containing bits of information that add up to valuable learnings. They hear teachers' and parents' instructions and suggestions. All of this contributes to a greater potential for academic success. Because of the far reaching influence of language in forming and maintaining relationships, children who are blind also have more options for social learning than children who are deaf.

Infants and young children with severe hearing or vision problems require teachers who are trained to meet their special needs. Sometimes this is accomplished in a segregated setting, other times in a regular preschool. PL 99-457, it will be recalled, requires all children to be educated in the least restrictive environment to the degree that it meets their educational needs. Turnbull (1982) suggests that the relative restrictiveness of an intensive, highly specialized program may be necessary in the very early years, if the child is to have greater freedom in the long run. On the other hand, most early childhood educators argue that many of the developmental needs of children who have vision or hearing impairments are the same as for all children. These children, too, need the experiences that are available in a good preschool program. Merit can be found in both arguments. A combination of programs is a good solution for many children. There is no definitive answer, however, as to what is *best*. We do know one thing for sure—that the family and any other caregivers must be involved in the intervention procedures right from the start.

DEAFNESS AND HEARING IMPAIRMENTS

As described in Unit 5, children with hearing impairments may be classified in two ways, as deaf or as hard-of-hearing. Deafness refers to a hearing loss so severe that the individual cannot process spoken language even with hearing aids or other amplification devices. *Hard-of-hearing* refers to a lesser loss but one that nevertheless has a definite negative effect on social, cognitive, and language development.

Two other items from Unit 5 should be mentioned again. One has to do with severity: The greater the loss, the greater the interference with development. The second reminder relates to timing: The earlier in life the loss occurs, the greater the interference with development. Losses may be thought of as *prelingual*—occurring before speech and language has had a chance to develop; and *postlingual*—occurring after the onset of language. Lowenbraun and Thompson (1994) corroborate that children with a prelingual loss have greater difficulties in all areas of development throughout their growing up years. The most severe developmental damage occurs when a hearing loss is congenital, that is, the infant that is born deaf. Generally speaking, less overall damage is

sustained when the hearing loss occurs *after* the child has begun to learn language.

Types of Hearing Loss.   Hearing losses are categorized in various ways, through various kinds of assessments. To ensure valid results, screening and testing both should be done by audiologists who are specially trained to work with infants and young children. The results of hearing tests usually are plotted on what is called an audiogram (See Figures 6-1 and 6-2). A hearing loss is classified according to where the loss occurs:

- Problems in the outer or middle ear produce a **conductive hearing loss.**
- Problems in the inner ear (**cochlea** or auditory nerve) produce a *sensorineural* **hearing loss.**
- Problems in the **higher auditory cortex** produce central deafness.
- A *combined loss* is two or more of the above.

In most instances, a conductive hearing loss can be corrected or greatly reduced with appropriate medical treatment. A young child with chronic ear infections such as **otitis media** may suffer a hearing loss that comes and goes as the infection flares up and clears up, several times a year, perhaps. This is called an *intermittent* hearing loss. Once the infection is cleared up permanently, language is likely to improve.

Identifying an intermittent hearing loss is difficult. Many times the condition is missed entirely in routine screening tests; the child is hearing adequately and therefore responding appropriately at the time of testing. According to one clinician (Naremore 1979), more than half of the children who came through his clinic had some degree of undiagnosed hearing loss. These children had been diagnosed as having speech problems or had been categorized as learning disabled. Upon careful study of their health records, most of the children had histories of chronic otitis media. Yet the resulting hearing loss had *not been identified* in general screening procedures.

Unlike conductive hearing problems, sensorineural and central deafness do not respond readily to medical intervention. That picture is changing, however, with the coming of microsurgery and such things as

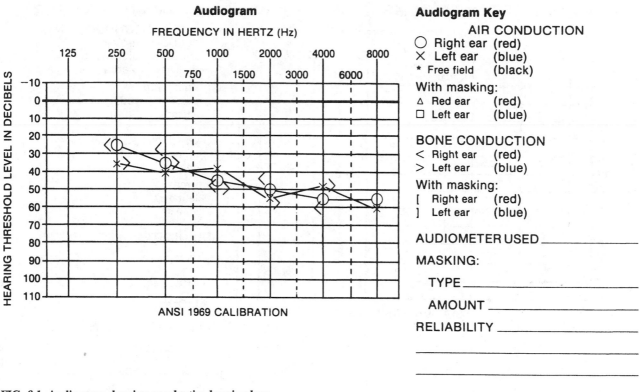

FIG. 6-1 Audiogram showing conductive hearing loss.

cochlear implant. Controversy continues to surround cochlear implants, however, especially the age the implant should be done. Lowenbraun and Thompson (1994) advise: Care should be taken to ensure that each child has sufficient practice with a hearing aid and auditory training prior to a decision being made about having the implant. (p. 410). For the time being, most young children with severe hearing losses are fitted with **amplification devices**, usually in the form of hearing aids. A child often wears a device in each ear.

Warning Signs. Soon after birth, most infants make a variety of responses to various noises. The whole body may move in a *startle* response, eyes may blink, or a rapid increase in sucking may occur. At about 4 months, infants begin to *localize*, that is, turn their head in the direction of sound. Over the next several months, they get better and better at localizing. Early

hearing is so good that infants can discriminate between voices and indicate preference for their mother's voice to that of a stranger's.

When infants do not make such responses, hearing loss is a definite possibility. On the other hand, all infants make so many random movements that the hearing impaired infant may appear to be all right. Furthermore, if the infant has some **residual hearing**, the loss may be most difficult to identify. That infant may be hearing just enough to respond appropriately *some of the time*, and so give the appearance of normalcy. Another complication is that even profoundly deaf infants babble, at least for awhile. Nevertheless, parents are usually the first to sense that *something is wrong*. Horton (1976) reported that the majority of the mothers of hearing impaired children that she studied had expressed concern before their child's first birthday. Even so, only in a few of these cases, had the physician pinpointed the problem.

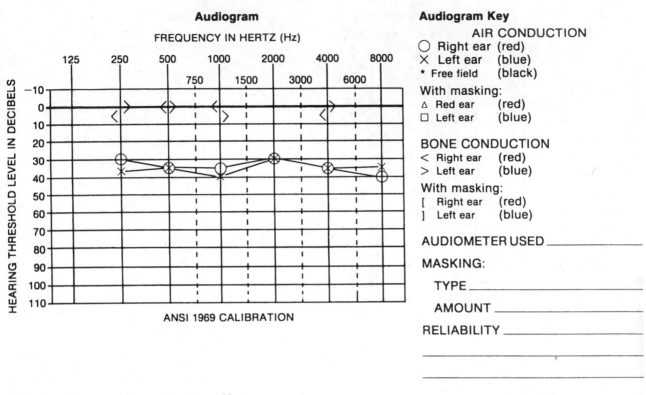

FIG. 6-2 Audiogram showing sensorineural loss.

Infant caregivers and early childhood teachers are in a strategic position for noting possible hearing problems or risk conditions. Persistent ear infections, discharge from the ears, or constant poking or banging at the ears often indicates a problem. Children with a conductive loss may drop certain initial consonants (the ones that are described as voiceless: p, h, s, f). They simply do not hear these sounds and so do not reproduce them. As for a sensorineural loss, a marked delay in speech and language development is a major warning sign.

With children who have acquired some language, teachers need to be alert to a child who

Does not respond when spoken to
Does not understand, or looks puzzled when addressed directly with a simple question or request
Cocks his or her head to one side, studies the speaker's face, or watches the speaker's mouth

Asks for frequent repetitions (huh? what?)
Turns one ear to the source of sound or speech
Seems overly shy, avoids children and teachers
Is inattentive
Makes inconsistent or irrelevant responses
Complains of ringing or buzzing in the ears
Has an articulation or voice problem
Speaks too loudly or too softly

When teachers become aware of a possible problem, the first step is to confer with parents about seeking clinical help.

The Impact of Hearing Loss.   *All hearing losses are serious.* (Cook, Tessier, and Klein 1992). The **cumulative effects** of a severe hearing loss on children's cognitive, social, and language development is clear. Many children with moderate to severe hearing losses are educationally retarded as much as 3 to 5 years. In addition,

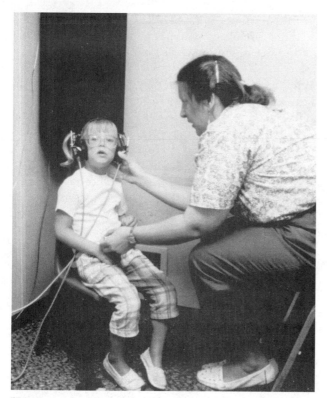

Hearing tests need to be done by audiologists trained to work with young children.

many have significant social and behavioral problems. As these children grow older, there is a tendency for them to fall even further behind due to the increasing complexity of school and community expectations.

Problems in later development may be related to restricted play opportunities during the early years. Play skills seem to develop quite normally up until about two years of age. At this point, hearing children begin to use words symbolically. They begin to attach words to play materials and activities. Major differences become evident, almost immediately, in the quality of play in hearing children as contrasted with children with hearing problems. Their play becomes more solitary and less imaginative (Gregory 1976).

Effect on language development.   The most serious and far reaching effect of a hearing problem is on early speech and language development. It appears that language acquisition may be tied to certain periods in a child's development (the *critical period* idea). According to this theory, a child who cannot take in sounds and verbal stimulation at certain points in development may never fully master language. In any event, inadequate auditory input during early development almost always leads to serious problems in language acquisition and in speech production. Another reason for faulty early language development may be lack of responsiveness from family and teachers. Unwittingly, they may fall into the habit of not talking to the child with hearing problems. It is easy to see how this happens. The child's range of responses are limited, thus providing inadequate feedback for family and friends. Consequently, the child's language skills become even more delayed.

Effect on cognitive development.   Once the typically developing child is beyond the sensorimotor stage, cognitive skills, as mentioned at the outset, become inseparably intertwined with language skills. In turn, language skills (including the ability to communicate thoughts) continue to be inseparably related to adequate hearing. Thus, children with hearing problems often do less well than hearing children when it comes to cognitive activities. As noted earlier, many children with severe hearing problems are several years behind educationally. Their educational retardation seldom is due to poor cognitive potential, however. Usually the cause is the inadequate auditory input; in other words, the child has been denied a major channel for cognitive development.

Effects on social development.   Children with hearing problems experience a high degree of social isolation. They begin to be left out of things, even within the family, at a very early age. True, the child may be in the room where a family activity is going on. Nevertheless, he or she often is ignored unintentionally, for a very simple reason: The child is not able to enter into the verbal give and take and so has no way of figuring out what is going on. Peterson (1987) points out that unless someone takes responsibility for helping the child understand everyday family and school events, the child is likely to remain a passive and silent observer (p. 197).

Even as they get older, may children with severe hearing deficits tend to be less mature socially. Often they have a low frustration **threshold**. This may be related to an earlier inability to make their preferences known. At times, these children also may seem to be uncaring, unaware of the needs and feelings of others. It is unlikely they are truly indifferent. More to the point is that they have not heard, and therefore, not learned the language of sympathizing, a language that most young children acquire almost spontaneously. Nevertheless, and for whatever reason, the research of Davis et al. (1986) indicates that many children with even mild to moderate hearing impairments have difficulty interacting with peers and establishing friendships.

Methods of Communication.   With the help of a trained teacher of the deaf, children with hearing impairments, even those with severe limitations, can be taught to speak and to understand speech. Many children learn lip reading, more accurately called speech reading. They quite literally learn to *read* what another individual is saying by watching face, mouth, tongue, and throat movements. Other forms of communication are available to hearing impaired children, too. McCormick and Schiefelbush (1990) describe the various systems as follows:

- *American Sign Language.* Ameslan (ASL) is the language of the majority of deaf people in the United States and Canada. It is a language with its own words and grammar.
- *Signed English.* This is a sign language that parallels the English language. For every word there is a sign. Word order is the same as spoken English.
- *Finger spelling.* This system is made up of an alphabet of 26 hand formed letters that correspond to the regular alphabet. One hand is held in front of the chest and the other hand spells out the words, letter by letter.
- *Total or simultaneous communication.* As the name implies, this is a system in which communication combines both speech and a sign system.
- *Informal systems.* Pantomime, gestures, and body movements are accompaniments to speech used naturally by most speakers. Amer-Ind, American

Indian Hand Talk (Skelly & Schinsky 1979) is a more formalized system that nevertheless is flexible and free of grammatical complications.

Which method?   A long-standing controversy has to do with which system to use in teaching language to a young child. Is there a *best* way? Should the child be held to oral communication exclusively, allowed to do no signing of any kind? Is a combination method, such as total communication the most effective? The total approach is favored by those who have studied families. It was found that the parents signed with each other and with their infants in ways characteristic of hearing parents talking to their very young children. Their children seemed to go through stages of language acquisition similar to those of normally developing children. Bee (1992) suggests:

> A combination of sign language and spoken language works well for the child and for the relationship between the child and the parent. Not only is the child exposed to a language at the normal time, but the child and parent can communicate with each other—something that is very difficult for a hearing parent who does not sign with a deaf child (p. 324).

There is good evidence that when emphasis is placed on oral language exclusively, children who are deaf have much more difficulty developing either speech or language than do children who are taught sign language, lip reading, and oral language at the same time. (Moores 1985).

The final word on the subject is likely to be that the decision about signing, or speaking, or combining the two must be made by the parents. The preschool teacher needs to accept the parents' decision and then work with them and an early childhood deaf education specialist to provide the child with the best learning environment possible.

Early Intervention with Children with Hearing Impairments.   The importance of early language stimulation and training for hearing impaired infants and young children cannot be overemphasized. Language deficiencies among older hearing impaired children may be the result of failure to begin language learning activities during the infant and toddler years.

The longer the delay in starting language intervention, the less likely it is the child will develop fully functional language skills. Without preventive measures, even a mild hearing loss can result in a permanent loss in language ability.

Guidelines for Teachers.   Throughout the years, preschool teachers have worked successfully with children with hearing impairments. Effective programming usually incorporates the skills of a specially trained early childhood deaf education consultant. The specialist assists both teachers and parents in providing an education tailored to a child's special hearing loss. Following are guidelines from these specialists.

1. Sit, kneel, or bend down to the child's level to talk. Look directly at the child. Children with hearing problems need to be talked to face to face.
2. Talk in a normal voice. Avoid a loud or strained voice and do not overenunciate. Overenunciation makes speech reading difficult.
3. Use gestures when appropriate, but avoid over-gesturing. Too many gestures interfere with the child's efforts to speech read.
4. Use brief, but complete, sentences when the child has reached that stage of language development. As with hearing children, **holophrastic** and **telegraphic** language belongs to particular stages of language development.
5. At group time, seat the child directly across from the teacher. This gives the child the best possible position for speech reading.
6. Face the light when talking to a child with a hearing problem. The light needs to be on the speaker's face, not the child's. Glaring light in the child's eyes interferes with bringing the speaker's face and mouth into full focus.
7. To get the child's attention, gently touch or tap a child on the shoulder or hand. Always be aware of the possibility of startling a person who does not hear and therefore may not see another person approaching.
8. When talking about something in the room, point to it, touch it, and hold it up. (If the teacher picks up the scissors and demonstrates

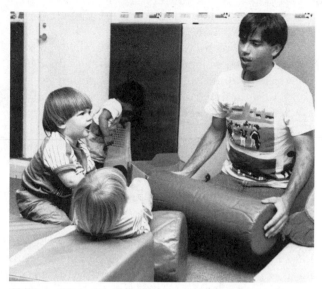

Children with hearing problems need to be talked to face-to-face.

the cutting task while giving the instructions, the child has a better chance of understanding what is expected.)
9. Include children with hearing impairments in all music activities. Provide many opportunities for them to participate by
   Putting their hands on various instruments so they may feel the vibrations
   Allowing them to play the instruments
   Having frequent rhythmic activities such as clapping, jumping, rolling, and twirling
   Pairing a normal hearing child with a hearing impaired child for various musical games
10. Involve all children, and especially those with hearing impairments in story time. Choose books with bright clear pictures that *tell* the story. Gesture when telling the story, and use facial expressions that give clues to the moods in the story.
11. Keep to a regular schedule of activities each day. To feel secure, young children, and especially children with hearing problems (who often do not pick up on environmental signals), need to know what comes next.

12. Some children with moderate to severe hearing loss make strange noises. They do not hear themselves but the noises often bother other children. Teachers must find subtle ways to help these children be quiet when necessary (perhaps gently putting a finger on the child's lips, and on the teacher's, in a "sssh" gesture).

13. In kindergarten or primary classrooms, avoid moving about the room or writing on the board while talking.

14. When a **manual interpreter** is present (unusual in an early childhood setting) allow the child and the interpreter to choose the most favorable seating.

Hearing Aids.   Electronic hearing aids are a great help, especially for individuals with a conductive hearing loss. A hearing aid has three basic parts: a microphone, an amplifier, and a receiver. Some of the larger devices are clipped into a shirt pocket or worn on a harness. With the coming of the transistor, most hearing aids are small and quite unnoticeable. Many can be inserted into the ear canal or placed on the bone directly behind the ear.

In spite of the great benefits of hearing aids, problems occur. The fact that a child is wearing a hearing aid does not guarantee the child is hearing. Teachers and parents need to be aware of possible minor breakdowns in the system, such as:

- *Improperly fitting or damaged earmold.* If the **earmold** does not fit properly, it can cause irritation and discomfort. The same holds true if the earmold becomes chipped or cracked. A cracked earmold also can make a squealing feedback sound which is disturbing.
- *Dead or feeble batteries.* Batteries die with amazing frequency. Teachers and parents know when batteries are dead because the child stops responding. However, batteries should be replaced well before they are dead so that children do not have to cope with periods of diminishing sound.
- *Worn cords.* The hearing aids fitted to young children often have cords. If the cord becomes worn or damaged, the hearing aid does not work. Cords are easy to replace and spares should always be on hand, both at home and at school.

- *Off and on switch.* Teachers must check regularly to make sure a child's hearing aid is turned on. Young children tend to turn the devices off, sometimes repeatedly. This happens most frequently when they are first learning to wear a hearing aid. Eventually, most children become accustomed to wearing the device and leave it turned on all the time. At this point, children can begin to check its working order for themselves. Nevertheless, adults should continue to spot check at least once a day.
- *Sore Ears.* The earmold should never be inserted into a sore, cracked, or infected ear. At the first sign of irritation the child should see a health care provider.

BLINDNESS AND VISION IMPAIRMENTS

Children with visual disabilities tend to be classified as *blind* or as having *residual* or *partial* vision. For educational purposes, the American Foundation for the Blind provides the following definitions:

- *Blind.* Visual loss is severe enough so that it is not possible to read print, requiring the child to be educated through the use of braille (a system of

A child may have residual or partial vision.

raised dots representing alphabet letters) and other materials using touch or sound.

- *Partially sighted.* Residual vision is sufficient to allow a child to read large print or possibly regular print under special conditions and to use other visual materials for educational purposes.

Total blindness is the inability to distinguish between light and dark. Few children are so drastically afflicted. Most have slight vision. Some can see the rough, general outlines of things, but no details. Others can distinguish light and dark or very bright colors. It should be noted that the usefulness of residual vision will be lost unless children are encouraged constantly to exercise whatever vision they have.

Types of Vision Problems. Vision problems vary as to cause, type, and intensity. Often they are grouped in terms of physiology, visual acuity, and muscular imbalances.

Physiology. Physical problems resulting in impaired vision are fairly common. These may develop prenatally, or the damage can occur at the time of birth or any time thereafter. The cause may be diseases such as maternal rubella, inherited disorders, injury, or drugs. Some medically prescribed drugs such as Acutane (used to treat acne) can produce toxic reactions in the fetus. Disorders that teachers are most likely to encounter include:

- *Cataracts.* A **progressive** clouding of the lens of one or both eyes.
- *Retrolental fibroplasia.* Formation of a kind of scar tissue behind the lens of one or both eyes; it is often caused by an overconcentration of oxygen administered to premature infants.
- *Glaucoma.* Gradual destruction of the optic nerve through a buildup of pressure caused by poor circulation of the fluids in the eye.

Visual acuity problems. Acuity problems usually are caused by *refractive errors.* Simply put, refraction is the bending of light rays. When there is a malformation of the eye or certain parts of it, refractive errors can occur. The most common refractive errors are:

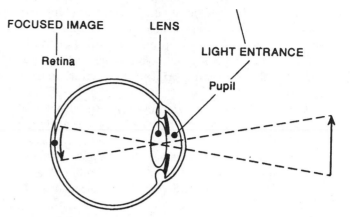

FIG. 6-3 Structure of the eye: refractory errors are common.

- *Astigmatism.* Blurred vision.
- *Hyperopia.* Farsightedness (close-up objects are seen less clearly).
- *Myopia.* Nearsightedness (far away objects are seen less clearly).

Muscular imbalances. When the major eye muscles are not working together, double vision as well as other problems may result. Common problems are:

- *Amblyopia.* A common term is *lazy eye.* In young children the brain may repress the image received from one eye, eventually destroying that eye's ability to function.
- *Strabismus.* Individuals with strabismus are sometimes referred to in uncomplimentary fashion as cross-eyed or wall-eyed. When this condition exists, the two eyes are unable to focus together on the same image.
- *Nystagmus.* Characterized by quick, jerky up-and-down or back-and-forth eye movements as the child tries to obtain a single image. These movements seriously interfere with the ability to see.

Identifying Vision Problems. Congenital blindness usually can be identified in the first year of life. It becomes obvious to parents that their infant does not look at them, or at objects they wave or hand to their child. Partial vision losses are more difficult to recognize. Often they go undetected until the child is in school. Even then, there are children with vision problems who are not identified until the third or fourth grade when the print in schoolbooks gets smaller, pictures are fewer, and the print becomes more densely packed.

On the other hand, many children with visual impairments are identified through routine screening tests in preschools and child care settings. The *Snellen Illiterate E* test is widely used for identifying visual acuity and muscle imbalance, beginning at about 2 1/2 years of age. The Denver Eye Screen Test is an instrument that can be used with even younger children (as young as 6 months). A major problem in trying to assess vision is that visually impaired children have no idea what they are supposed to be seeing. In other words, they really do not know that what they see is imperfect, different from what others are seeing. Parents and early childhood teachers often are the first to suspect possible vision problems in young children.

Warning signs.   The following list of warning signs, or alerts, is adapted from material published by The National Society to Prevent Blindness. The *alerts* are grouped according to children's behavior, appearance, or verbal complaints.

Rubs eyes excessively
Shuts or covers one eye; tilts head, thrusts it forward
Has difficulty doing work or playing games that require close use of the eyes.
Blinks excessively or becomes irritable when doing close work.
Unable to see distant things clearly
Squints, squeezes eyelids together, frowns
Crossed eyes or eyes each turn outward
Red rimmed, encrusted, or swollen eyelids
Inflamed, infected, or watery eyes
Recurring sties
Itchy, burning, or scratchy feeling eyes
Inability to see well
Dizziness, headaches, or nausea following close work
Blurred or double vision

If parents' and teachers' observations, or a vision screening suggest a problem, the next step is for parents to get medical assistance. The best qualified consultant is a

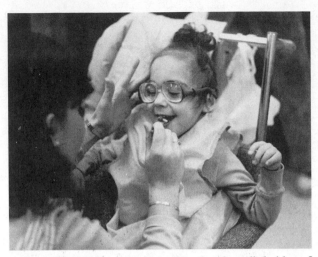

Children with early and severe vision loss have little idea of what they are supposed to be seeing.

pediatric ophthalmologist. The ophthalmologist may prescribe eyeglasses, medication, surgery, eye exercises, **occlusion** of one eye, or some combination of these.

Note of caution: if a screening test does not reveal a problem, but the symptoms continue, it is wise to refer a child for a medical workup anyway. Marotz (1983) explains that *false-positives* can occur. This means that a child with a vision problem (or any other kind of a problem) may pass the screening test. In the case of vision screening, there may have been unintended coaching by the examiner or the child may have peeked around the **occluder** during testing. Test results (of all kinds) always should be regarded with caution, especially when a teacher or parent has reason to believe that a child's behaviors indicate a potential problem.

Children, especially school-age children with weak residual vision, may be referred to a low vision clinic. The clinic can determine if the child will benefit from using magnifiers, telescopic lenses, specific electronic devices, or closed circuit greatly magnified television. As children advance in the elementary grades a number of other sophisticated reading and writing devices are available. Sacks and Rosen (1994) provide interesting descriptions of truly amazing vision-support devices.

Certain types of vision problems may be present even if a child's vision seemed to be adequate in a screening test.

The Impact of Vision Problems on Development. Poor vision has a negative impact on overall development. Obviously, the more severe the vision impairment, the greater the developmental damage or delay. Much of what a child learns comes from scanning the environment, then focusing and pondering what is going on. Learning comes too, from watching others, imitating them, and observing what follows. Poor vision affects a child's language development, large and small motor development and cognitive and social development. Why? Because the child's ability to interact with people, objects, and activities is seriously curtailed. For example, the child with vision problems may fail to recognize amusing events such as the kitten scampering about. Children with vision impairments may be oblivious to the consequences of their behavior (the spilled juice staining the bedspread). They may be unable to enter into new experiences because they have no visual sense of what is going on. A card game such as *Go Fish*, for example, cannot be understood just by listening to it being played.

It is likely that the inability to play freely is as great a hindrance to development as anything else. When sighted babies begin deliberately reaching for and playing with nearby objects, infants who are blind remain passive. They continue to hold their hands at shoulder height, a posture typical of very young children (Fewell 1983). Not able to be visually stimulated by seeing play activities, these babies play alone much of the time. In addition, they receive fewer invitations to play and so have fewer of the play challenges that sighted children exchange. Fewell and Kaminski (1988) make the following observation about children who are blind:

> The cognitive, social, language, and adaptive skills that are acquired and practiced in the play of children as they prepare for higher order skills cannot be expected to arise from these natural childhood experiences. The facilitation of play in blind children appears to be a challenge for parents and teachers (p. 152).

Effect on language development.   After the first few months of life, language acquisition depends on discovering and identifying objects and actions. This is difficult for children who cannot see the objects and the actions. They must depend almost entirely on what can be touched or heard which reduces their learning opportunities. Once the child with a vision impairment begins to understand how to explore objects and formulate ideas about them, language acquisition proceeds more rapidly. Nevertheless, it takes a child with a moderate to severe vision impairment at least a year longer to develop a full range of language skills. By school age, most are using language normally.

Effect on cognitive development.   Children who are blind and partially sighted generally lag behind in cognitive development and concept formation. Delays are more noticeable during the first three or four years of life. However, with adequate nurturing and early intervention, the child with a vision deficit (if there are no other disabilities), usually catches up by age 5 or 6.

Effect on motor development.   While a vision impairment is not the cause of delayed and imperfect motor development, it does exert a negative influence. The greater the vision loss, the greater the delays in reaching, crawling, and walking. In fact, a child with limited vision does not develop the ability to localize sound and move toward it until the end of the first year (Fraiberg 1977). Many children who are blind do not walk until they are 2 years old. Motor development is further delayed by the child's inability to learn skills related to judging distance, direction, body position, and an object's position in space. They often develop strange ways of walking and positioning themselves because they have no visual reference points or models.

Effect on social development.   Young children with vision problems often are unable to participate in the interactions that build good social skills and interpersonal relationships. They tend to be quiet and passive as infants. Parents, as noted earlier, must be helped to both stimulate and respond to their infant's developmentally different ways of interacting. Play skills, too, as mentioned above, develop more slowly in children who are visually impaired. Toys, for example, are used less creatively and play often is stereotyped because of the lack of visual models necessary to expanding the imagination.

Intervention Programs.   Early intervention programs serving infants and toddlers who are blind or visually impaired usually focus on the parent as teacher. For the first year, programs tend to be home-based. A teacher, trained in working with blind infants and their parents, visits the home on a regular basis. The teacher provides information about the effects of vision impairment on all aspects of development and coaches parents in special techniques for interacting with their infant. The teacher also is likely to provide instructional play materials, demonstrate teaching strategies, and help parents record their child's progress.

Intervention programs for older toddlers and preschoolers most often are center-based. The toddler program usually includes parents. They bring their children and stay to participate. Older preschool children are likely to stay at school without a parent. Even so, parents continue to be an integral part of their child's learning activities. The staff of an early childhood program in which there are children with severe vision impairments usually includes at least a part-time **orientation and mobility specialist**, a consulting developmental therapist, and the early childhood teacher.

Depending on the severity of the vision problem and the child's progress, many a child will transition from the segregated early childhood classroom to an inclusive classroom. Other children, needing further specialized training, may continue in the segregated setting part time. The remainder of the school day they participate in an inclusive room.

Most children with limited vision learn to function perfectly well in an adequately staffed preschool. Typically developing children are helpful. When teachers model appropriate ways to interact with a child with any kind of a developmental problem, children learn to do the same. They learn to call the child's name, or touch the child's shoulder to attract his or her attention. They learn to put things directly into a child's hands, naming each object at the moment. They learn to help the child get about by describing things specifically: "Here are the lockers. Jenny's locker is the second one. You can put her truck on the bottom shelf." However, assisting a classmate must never be a burden. Children who serve as helpers need to enjoy the job and feel special for being able to provide assistance.

Facilitating play in children with serious vision problems is a challenge for parents and teachers.

General Guidelines for Teachers.   A resource teacher or a specially trained consultant can help teachers arrange classroom and curriculum activities. This ensures good learning experiences throughout the program for the child with a vision impairment. The broad goal of early education for such children is to strengthen their intact sensory channels. Providing activities that require hearing, touch, taste and smell are basic to this goal.

The hardest part, for many adults, is not to overprotect a child who has little or no vision. Like all young children, they need to explore their environment if they are to learn. In the process, they may bump into a wall, fall down, get up, start out again, have another mishap, and another, and another. To make sure the child does not come to unnecessary harm, the classroom and play yard must be kept safe and orderly. Pathways need to be clear of strewn toys and misplaced equipment that the child with poor vision (and the teachers and other children) may trip over. Most important, vision impaired children need to continue to be helped with their mobility skills throughout the day. Learning to get about efficiently and safely on their own will be of prime importance throughout life.

Teachers must avoid the tendency to take over the rights of the child to learn self-defense and the rights of possession. One way is to refrain from speaking out prematurely on behalf of the child. On many occasions, however, the teacher may need to supply the words: "Melinda, say, 'No! My egg beater!' " Another time it may be necessary to tell the child that he or she is about to lose a turn. Example: "Marcie, Tammy has been waiting for a turn on that swing. She is next." "Tammy, tell Marcie, 'My turn.' " At this point, the teacher must be sure to follow through. It is important that the sighted child yield the swing, give back the egg beater, or respond to any other reasonable request from the child.

Working with Children with Visual Impairments. Determine the degree of residual vision; find out from the child's parents and the vision specialist what the child can see. Many visually impaired children see shadows, color, and large pictures or objects. Some children's **peripheral vision** may be their best vision,

Play spaces need to be kept free of strewn equipment and abandoned wheel toys.

thus a turned-away head does not necessarily signal inattention.

Make orientation and mobility skills a first teaching priority. Familiarize the child with the classroom layout and storage of materials. Whenever changes occur, be sure to reorient the child.

Put identifying material or subtle noise makers on the floor, doors, room dividers, and lockers. Examples:

A wind chime near the door to the play yard
Tile in the creative areas, carpeting in the blocks and
   large group area
Rough matting by doors to the outside
A patch of velveteen glued to the child's locker

Use specific words to tell the child what to do: "Put the book on the table" or "I'm sitting by the piano. Bring your shoes to me." Avoid nonspecific phrases such as "Come here," "Put it there," "Be careful."

Talk to the child about everything in the immediate environment. Give the names, over and over, for everyday objects such as ball, dog, cup, brush. Naming the object is not enough; to understand *watering can* for example, the child must hold one, feel what is inside, pour from it, handle it empty and filled with water.

Provide action words. Tell the child, many times over, what he or she is doing. "You are *running* in the grass." "You are *brushing* your teeth." "You are *drinking* juice."

Help the child to localize and sort out sounds. Describe the classroom sounds and tell where they are coming from: the guinea pig squeaking *by the window*; the faucet dripping *in the sink*; the fan whirring *up on the ceiling*. Help children learn to identify the sound of an eggbeater, the tick of a timer, the swishing of sandpaper blocks rubbing together. Play auditory guessing games. The teacher (or another child) can make the sound of one of several objects on a tray (tearing paper, closing a book, dropping a marble in a cup). The child with a vision problem locates the correct object(s) by touch. To make the game challenging for sighted children, too, the teacher can turn away from the children while making the sound, or can make the sound under a cloth or in a large box open only on the teacher's side.

Teach sounds that may signal danger in contrast to those that are simply frightening. The sound of the power mower in the playfield is something to stay away from. The drone of the vacuum cleaner signals something the child can help push. The fire alarm indicates STOP whatever is going on and stand by the door. The squeak of a chain warns to stay back because the swings are in motion.

Offer several opportunities each day to learn through smelling, touching, and tasting. Actual objects, rather than plastic replicas, are best for teaching. In a session on fruit, a real banana and orange should be used for feeling, cutting, peeling, smelling, tasting and comparing. Cooking experiences are good too, not just for children who are visually impaired, but for all children. Sorting activities also are important. Using something other than sight to tell the difference between shapes, sizes, textures, weight, and odors are but a few of the sorting and discrimination activities that provide valuable learning experiences for all children.

Provide many physical prompts. Demonstrations need to take the form of subtle physical assistance and hand-over-hand *put-throughs*. Always work from behind the child; gradually reduce assistance as the child masters the successive steps required to accomplish the task.

Provide left-to-right training. Informal practice in working from left to right is a skill all preschool children need in preparation for reading. Braille and other academic activities follow the same format. When using pegboards, for example, there can be teacher-initiated activities in which the child is encouraged to systematically fill the board by placing pegs in left-to-right and top-to-bottom progression.

Mannerism. Rhythmical, seemingly purposeless mannerisms may occur almost continuously with some children who are blind, especially when they are left too long on their own. They may rock back and forth for long periods, poke their eyes, flip their hands about in front of their face, or spin around and around. These movements may be accompanied by strange noises or high-pitched squeals. It is speculated that these behaviors develop because of reduced stimulation. Lacking vision, infants receive less motivation and challenge from their environment. In turn, they do not learn to explore their environment the way sighted infants do. It is almost as if the strange behaviors were the infants' efforts to create their own stimulation and so have something to respond to.

Whatever their causes, the strange behaviors can interfere with normal socializing. They make the child stand out as uncomfortably different. As teachers help children who have severe vision impairments learn appropriate play skills, the children will spend less of their developmentally valuable early learning time in unproductive spinning, poking, and twirling. Other children can be of help, too, especially with prompts from the teacher. Example: "Come Sarah, let's go and get Tammy and I'll pull you both in the wagon."

SUMMARY

Problems with hearing or vision greatly interfere with overall development. A severe hearing loss, however, has a more pervasive negative effect on development than a severe vision loss. Infants with sensory impairments need to be in an early intervention program that starts in the first months of life and includes their parents. These children need to be educated in the least restrictive environment. This may require a segregated setting, at least in the very early years, if the children are to receive the specialized education appropriate to their needs.

Hearing losses are classified in three ways: conductive hearing loss, sensorineural hearing loss, and problems originating in the higher auditory cortex. (Combined losses also occur.) The most devastating result of a severe hearing loss is interference with early speech and language development. Chronic ear infections, especially *otitis media* which may come and go, are responsible for problems with both hearing and language. Infants who do not startle or blink their eyes in response to loud noises, may have a hearing impairment. A hearing loss may be suspected in children who have acquired some language, if they ask for frequent repetitions or give a variety of other behavioral signs that they have difficulty hearing what is going on.

Specially trained teachers can teach speech as well as a variety of language systems including American Sign Language (ASL) to children with a hearing problem. However, the long-standing controversy continues: Should the child be taught to communicate *only* through speech? Or should the child be allowed to use all forms of communication? Regardless of the child's special program, early childhood teachers are important agents in facilitating language development and cognitive learning. Part of the teacher's responsibility is to check a young child's hearing aid each day to ensure it is working.

Children classified as educationally blind are those who do not have functional vision. For educational placement, partially sighted children are those who will be able to learn through specially presented printed or other visual materials. In the preschool child, identification of a vision problem may be difficult because screening tests cannot be relied on to identify all vision problems. Therefore, parents and teachers need to be alert to behavioral signs that a child may have a vision problem. If not identified and treated, poor vision has a negative impact on all areas of development.

Children with vision problems require more time, more practice, more verbal mediation, and more encouragement from adults. Early intervention programs serving infants and toddlers are usually home-based and focus on training parents as teachers. Young children, even those who are visually impaired, are readily accommodated in an early childhood classroom, if a specially trained consultant is available to assist the classroom teacher. It is important that teachers, and parents, restrain themselves from overprotecting the young child who needs to learn self-defense and the rights of possession in spite of a vision impairment.

STUDENT ACTIVITIES

1. Locate a person with a hearing or vision loss (friend, schoolmate, grandparent, parent). Talk with that person about the impact of the loss on every day life.
2. Invite several of the above persons to come to class and demonstrate the use of their amplification or magnification devices. If appropriate, ask if members of the class might try the devices.
3. Simulate greatly impaired vision by playing blindfold games in class such as moving about the classroom without mishap. Try moving toward one particular person based on that person's voice among several. Have several students blindfolded at one time and ask them to guess the source of sounds that you provide (closing a door, lowering a window shade, sharpening a pencil and so on.)
4. Prepare an identify-by-touch guessing game that sighted children and children with a vision problem could enjoy together. Try it out with your classmates and have them critique it. Alter your game to include appropriate recommendations. Now try the game out with young children.
5. Devise a game such as the one above but with a child with a hearing impairment in mind.

REVIEW QUESTIONS

A. *Lists.*
1. List four types of hearing loss.
2. List seven behaviors in a child who already has language that may indicate hearing loss.
3. List five ways that children who have a hearing impairment can learn to communicate.
4. List five ways a teacher can facilitate a child's understanding and speechreading.
5. List three things that can go wrong with a hearing aid.
6. List three common visual acuity problems.
7. List three muscular imbalance problems related to eye functioning.
8. List seven behaviors in young children that may indicate vision problems.
9. List the areas of development likely to be affected by blindness or impaired vision.
10. List five strategies for working with children with vision impairments.

B. *True or False. Choose the best answer.*

T F   1. Blindness, to a greater degree than deafness, interferes with early development.

T F   2. One identifying characteristic of hearing impaired infants is that they never babble.

T F   3. Poor cognitive abilities are the major cause of educational retardation in children with hearing impairments.

T F   4. Children who are deaf cannot participate in story time and always should be excused.

T F   5. False positives refer to children with vision or hearing problems who pass a screening test.

T F   6. Walking is more likely to be delayed in children with hearing impairments than in children with visual impairments.

T F   7. Opportunities to learn and practice mobility skills are essential curriculum activities for young children with vision impairments.

T F   8. Peripheral vision is of little use to individuals with vision problems.

T F   9. A wind chime placed near an open doorway may help to orient a child who is blind.

T F 10. Rocking, spinning around, poking the eyes are examples of self stimulating behaviors among some children with severe vision loss.

C. *Mix and Match.* Select the one *best* match from the items in column II and place that letter in the appropriate space in column I.

I	II
____ 1. otitis media	A. scar tissue formation
____ 2. amplification device	B. hearing aid
____ 3. cochlea	C. vision screening
____ 4. strabismus	D. blind at birth
____ 5. American Sign Language	E. children's eye doctor
____ 6. residual vision	F. crossed eyes
____ 7. retrolental fibroplasia	G. partial sight
____ 8. pediatric ophthalmologist	H. inner ear structure
____ 9. Snellen Illiterate E Test	I. intermittent hearing loss
____ 10. congenital blindness	J. ASL

REFERENCES

Bee, H. (1992). *The Developing Child.* New York: Harper Collins.

Cook, R.E., Tessier, A., and Klein, L.S. (1992). *Adapting early childhood curricula for children with special needs.* Columbus, OH: Merrill.

Davis, I., Elfenbein, I., Schum, R., and Bentler, R. (1986). Effects of mild and moderate hearing impairments on language, educational, and psychological behavior of children. *Journal of Speech and Hearing Disorders, 51,* 53–62.

Fewell, R.R. (1983). Working with sensorily impaired children. In S.G. Garwood (Ed.), *Educating young handicapped children.* Rockville, MD: Aspen Systems.

Fewell, R.R., and Kaminski, R. (1988). Play skills development and instruction for young children with handicaps. In S.L. Odom and M.B. Karnes (Eds.), *Early intervention for infants and children with handicaps.* Baltimore: Brooks.

Fraiberg, S. (1977). *Insights from the blind.* New York: Basic Books.

Gregory, H. (1976). *The deaf child and his family*. London: Allen & Unwin.

Horton, K.B. (1976). Early intervention for hearing impaired infants and young children. In T.D. Tjossem (Ed.), *Intervention strategies for high risk infants and young children*. Baltimore: University Park Press.

Lowenbraun, S. and Thompson, M.D. (1994). Hearing impairments. In N.G. Haring, L. McCormick, and T.G. Haring (Eds.), *Exceptional Children and Youth*. New York: Merrill.

Marotz, L.R. (1983). The influence of health, nutrition, and safety. In E.M. Goetz and K.E. Allen (Eds.), *Early childhood education: Special environmental, policy, and legal considerations*. Rockville, MD.: Aspen Systems.

McCormick, L. and Schiefelbusch, R.L. (1990). *Early language intervention*. Columbus: Merrill.

Moores, D.F. (1985). Early intervention programs for hearing impaired children: A longitudinal assessment. In K.E. Nelson (Ed.), *Children's Language, 5*, 159–196. Hillsdale, NJ: Erlbaum.

Naremore, R.J. (1979). Influences of hearing impairment on early language development. In D.G. Hanson and R.S. Ulvestad (Eds.), Otitis media and child development: Speech, language, and Education. *The Annals of Otology, Rhinology, and Laryngology, 88*, 54–63.

Peterson, N.L. (1987). *Early intervention for handicapped and at-risk children*. Denver: Love Publishing.

Reisman, J.E. (1987). Touch, motion, and proprioception. In P. Salapatek and L. Cohen (Eds.), *Handbook of infant perception: From sensation to perception, 1*, 265–304. Orlando, FL: Academic Press.

Rogers, S.J., and Puchalski, C.B. (1983). Social characteristics of visually impaired infants' play. *Topics in Early Childhood Special Education, 3(4)*, 54–56.

Sacks, S.Z. and Rosen, S. (1994). Visual impairment. In N.G. Haring, L. McCormick, and T.G. Haring (Eds.), *Exceptional Children and Youth*. New York: Merrill.

Skelly, M., and Schinsky, L. (1979). *Amer-Ind gestural code based on universal American Indian Hand Talk*. New York: Elsevier North Holland.

Turnbull, A.P. (1982). Preschool mainstreaming: A policy and implementation analysis. *Educational Evaluation and Policy Analysis, 4(3)*, 281–291.

Physical Disabilities and Health Problems

OBJECTIVES

After studying this unit the student will be able to

- define and give examples of physical disabilities and health impairments according to the Federal Register rulings.
- explain the general effects of physical disabilities and health impairments on overall development.
- describe the role of the early childhood teacher in working with children with physical disabilities and health impairments.
- discuss the implications of both obesity and undernourishment in young children in general, and in health impaired young children in particular.
- outline classroom emergency measures related to physical disabilities and health problems.

Physical activity and general good health are critical to early development. Infants and young children who eat well, sleep well, and move about freely are likely to acquire a well integrated range of cognitive, language, social, and physical skills. Problems with health and motor control, on the other hand, tend to interfere with everything a child tries to do or learn. Few have described the situation better than Caldwell (1973) in an early paper: "If he has any kind of motor dysfunction he cannot get up to find something better, or at least, cannot move himself to a situation where the environment might make a better match with his own developmental state." Young children are busy, active learners. A physical disability may impact overall development because it interferes with a child's ability to move about, explore, arrange and rearrange play materials, and seek out additional playthings and playmates.

Example: A 9-month-old tires of playing with familiar toys. She crawls to the bookcase and soon discovers the fun of taking books off the shelf. That infant has found a challenge for herself and a match for her rapidly developing motor skills. (Of course, pulling books off the shelf may be viewed as mischievous by parents or caregivers. If so, they need to *challenge themselves* to find new play materials that both challenge the child and meet their adult standards of appropriateness).

In this unit, the discussion will focus on the two broad categories of physiological problems.

Orthopedic impairment: relates to problems involving skeleton, joints, and muscles. Included are:

Missing limbs, clubfeet, congenital hip dislocations
Damage caused by diseases such as polio or bone tuberculosis
Neurological disorders such as cerebral palsy
Joint **contractures** caused by fractures, burns or amputations.

Health impairments: Defined generally as limited strength, vitality, or alertness due to chronic or acute health problems. Among them are:

Heart conditions   Epilepsy
Asthma   Leukemia

Sickle-cell anemia   Diabetes
Hemophilia   HIV/AIDS

Both categories represent somewhat artificial distinctions. Actual boundaries between physical disabilities and serious health impairments frequently overlap. Furthermore, neurological problems may complicate both. Orthopedic, health, and neurological dysfunction may all be present as in cerebral palsy, spina bifida, and other childhood conditions.

PHYSICAL DISABILITIES

Physical disability is a term that covers a range of problems. In general, it refers to any condition that interferes with the normal functioning of bones, joints, and muscles. The problems may be congenital (present at birth), such as cerebral palsy or hip dysplasia; or they may show up later as in the case of muscular dystrophy.

Cerebral Palsy.   Cerebral palsy (CP) has to do with "impairment of the coordination of muscle action with an inability to maintain normal postures and balance and to perform normal movements and skills" (Bobath and Bobath 1975, p. 29). CP is the most common source of physical disability among infants and young children. The basic cause of cerebral palsy is damage to the brain occurring before, during, or after the infant's birth. CP is a **nonprogressive** disorder resulting from oxygen deprivation (anoxia), injury, infection, hemorrhage (excessive bleeding), or malformation of the brain. Seldom can the exact cause be identified. The extent of the damage and its location determine how well the child will function. One way of classifying cerebral palsy is by type of **muscle tone**. Another is how the various parts of the body are affected. Often, however, CP is classified by both: type of muscle tone and affected body parts (e.g., spastic diplegia).

Classifications based on muscle tone: Spasticity.   Most children with cerebral palsy have abnormally high muscle tone. They are described as being hypertonic or spastic. Spasticity affects certain muscles more than others. When the muscles that flex a joint have a higher

muscle tone than the muscles that extend a joint, the constant flexion on the joint can cause a joint contracture to develop. When this occurs, the joint's range of motion is significantly decreased and the child's mobility is impaired. This can happen at any joint, but most frequently occurs in the hips, knees, ankles, elbows, and wrists.

Hypotonicity.   The hypotonic child is one who has too little muscle tone. The result is an inability to move about or maintain postural control (the rag doll syndrome). Infants of this type often are referred to as *floppy* babies. Many have difficulty with head control, and even simple movement requires great energy. This deprives them of learning experiences that most infants get from being held in an upright position and limits the quantity and quality of their interactions with the environment.

Athetosis.   Fluctuating or uneven muscle tone is called athetosis. Muscle control that goes from one extreme to the other (either too low or too high) is typical. Children with this condition tend to retain **primitive reflexes** past the normal time. This interferes with the development of **voluntary motor responses**. See Thurman and Widerstrom (1990) for an excellent discussion of primitive reflexes.

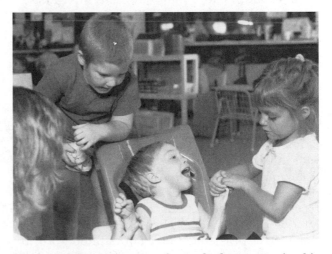

Hypertonicity causes muscles to lock, as seen in this child's clenched fist and grasp.

Ataxia. A lack of motor coordination, ataxia is characterized by poor balance and a lurching kind of walk. Fine motor coordination also is impaired. Children with ataxia may have great difficulty with fine motor activities such as feeding themselves, writing, cutting with scissors, and picking up small objects. Materials may get dropped or pushed off the table as a result of involuntary movements that the child cannot control.

Mixed. Approximately 30 percent of the children with CP have a mixture of spasticity and athetosis or ataxia.

Classifications based on body parts. A second way of classifying CP is according to the parts of the body that are affected. The following terms describe the location of the involvement:

- *Diplegia:* Involvement of all four extremities (legs and arms); in most cases, the legs are more severely affected.
- *Hemiplegia:* Only one side of the body is involved.
- *Paraplegia:* Involvement of the legs only.
- *Quadriplegia:* Involvement of both arms, both legs, trunk, and the muscles that provide head control.

The extent of motor impairment varies in children with CP. Some children have disabilities so severe they cannot hold their heads still or straighten their arms or legs. Others have control problems so slight as to be scarcely noticeable. Many children with cerebral palsy, like children with other developmental problems, fail to meet major motor milestones at expected times. A distinction must be made, however. Children with general developmental problems usually have delays in all areas. In contrast, children with cerebral palsy may have delayed motor skills (including speech), but *good cognitive and receptive language skills.*

Young children with cerebral palsy, especially those with mild to moderate involvement, usually benefit from an inclusive classroom experience. The success of the placement depends on the teachers and child receiving adequate assistance and support from the interdisciplinary team. A physical therapist or occupational therapist (sometimes both) should provide ongoing service whenever a child has a motor dysfunction (Washington, Schwartz and Swinth 1994).

Children with cerebral palsy often have excellent cognitive and receptive language abilities.

Spinal Cord Injuries. Spinal cord damage presents motor problems quite different from those associated with cerebral palsy. When the spinal cord is injured or severed, muscles below the point of damage become useless. Put simply, the muscles no longer receive messages from the brain. Alternately, sensations normally experienced below the point of injury no longer are transmitted back to the brain. It is important to note that the *brain itself is not affected.* However, because of interruption in **neural** communication between the brain and certain parts of the body, there is no sensation of where the limbs are or what is happening to them. A child may suffer serious burns, cuts, or broken bones without knowing it. Parents, teachers, and caregivers of young children must learn to be the *sensory monitors* for the child's nonfeeling extremities and trunk (Tyler and Chandler 1978). It should be noted that regeneration (repair or renewal) of the spinal cord is not possible with current medical technology.

The most familiar of the spinal cord injuries is spina bifida (**myelomeningocele** and **meningocele**). The damage comes from imperfect development of the spinal cord and spinal column during the first 30 days of fetal development. Children with spina bifida experience a number of problems in addition to paralysis of the affected limbs. Two are most common:

1. *Hydrocephalus.* Blockage of the circulation of the spinal fluid in the cranial (brain) cavity. If not corrected, usually through **shunting**, the fluid accumulates in the cavity, enlarging the head and damaging the brain.

2. *Incontinence* (lack of bladder and bowel control). A number of children with myelomeningocele are not able to receive messages from the urinary sphincter muscles. The result is the inability to hold or release urine. The same may be true of bowel activity. While this is a disability that is difficult to overcome, many children can be helped to learn techniques for managing their bowel and bladder needs independently. As the team assesses the child's developmental skills, adaptive behaviors, and emotional strengths, members can determine the child's readiness to learn toilet skills and other everyday tasks (Lozes 1988).

Muscular Dystrophy.   Progressive weakening of the muscles is the major characteristic of muscular dystrophy and related muscular disorders. There are several types of muscular dystrophy; each type involves specific muscle groups. The most common is Duchenne's disease, a sex-linked disorder that affects only boys. In Duchenne's disease progressive muscle weakness begins at the hips and shoulders and gradually moves out to the arms and legs. Hand skills often are retained, even when the limbs are severely impaired. One child, for example, was able to string small wooden beads in complicated patterns if the beads were placed in a basket in his lap. However, when he ran out of beads he was unable to lift his arms to get more beads from the nearby table. While still mobile, able to get around at all, a child with muscular dystrophy must be encouraged to move about the classroom frequently. Prevention of muscle contractures is a major goal of both therapy and classroom activities for these children. By 11 or 12 years of age children usually require a wheelchair in order to get around.

Osteogenesis Imperfecta.   *Brittle bones* is the common term for this congenital condition. The child's bones do not grow normally in length or thickness and they break easily. Joints, too, are involved and may show excessive range of motion as in children

Progressive weakening of the muscle structure characterizes several early childhood disabilities.

who can bend their thumb backwards to touch the wrist. Dwarfism, dental defects, and hearing problems also may be associated with this bone condition. Often, the child's hearing gets progressively worse, adding another dimension to teachers' planning. Generally, the child's cognitive skills are not affected, though a child may seem to be "behind" because of frequent hospitalizations and absences from school.

Osteomyelitis.   Infection of the bones is the simple definition of osteomyelitis. It can be crippling if not treated promptly and properly. Medication (antibiotics) as well as surgery are used to treat this condition in children.

Hip Dysplasia.   Also known as *congenital dislocation of the hip (CDH)*, this problem is the result of abnormal development of the hip joint. The head of the thigh bone (femur) may be out of the hip socket, or move in and out at random. Interestingly enough, the condition is found much more often in females than in males. The hip displacement is usually diagnosed soon after birth and treated nonsurgically. Without treatment, the child is not able to walk normally and often develops a waddling kind of gait.

Juvenile Rheumatoid Arthritis.   Arthritic conditions generally are associated with older people. However, young children also develop certain types of arthritis, especially juvenile rheumatoid arthritis. Chronic and painful inflammation of the joints and the tissue surrounding the joints is a major symptom. Sitting for long periods (though less painful for the child) causes further stiffening of the joints. Therefore, children with juvenile rheumatoid arthritis need both the freedom and the encouragement to move about a great deal, at home and at school. Symptoms often disappear by the time a child is 18 years old. The major goal of teachers is to help children keep their motor skills functional. Most children with juvenile rheumatoid arthritis are likely to be in total **remission** in ten years or less (Miller 1975).

Program Implications.   It is generally agreed that early and appropriate intervention has a positive effect on the acquisition of motor skills in young children with developmental problems. Children with physical disabilities, in spite of great individual differences, have basic classroom needs in common. These include:

The services of allied health professionals working as a team with classroom teachers

Adaptive equipment designed for each child's particular disability

Environmental adaptations to facilitate and support each child's learning efforts

Team effort.   The teachers' need for input from various health professionals in carrying out individualized early intervention programs has been discussed elsewhere in several contexts. A brief review, related to orthopedic and neurological problems, is presented here.

Good motor skills are critical to every aspect of a young child's development.

As noted repeatedly, good motor skills are critical to every aspect of children's development. The physical and occupational therapists trained to focus on early motor skills often are selected as case managers. The case manager works closely with parents, teachers, and other team members. For example, in drawing up an intervention program for a child with cerebral palsy, who also has a feeding problem, the physical and/or occupational therapist may call upon the nutritionist, the social worker, and perhaps the dentist to provide consultation or direct assistance. If a child also has a language or hearing problem the services of a speech therapist and audiologist would be enlisted. A psychologist is often asked to join the team to consult on a variety of issues including cognitive delays and behavior problems. The various disciplines, also may work or consult with the teacher (and parents) directly. At other times, the physical and/or occupational therapist may serve as a transdisciplinary agent who blends the various recommendations into intervention activities to be carried out in the child's everyday home and school environment.

The physical or occupational therapist needs to understand the goals of early childhood education and also needs to help teachers understand the goals of physical and occupational therapy. As therapists and teachers share the knowledge base of their respective professions, there is "shared implementation and integration of the child's daily therapy program into the everyday format of the classroom structure" (Mather and Weinstein 1988, p. 7).

The ways in which a child with physical disabilities is positioned and helped to move about, at home and at school is crucial to the child's development. Depending on the therapists' assessment, individual remediation activities are mapped out for each child. Never should the classroom teacher be expected to put a child through stressful exercises. Activities that are pleasant for both the child and the teacher (and often fun for other children as well) are the usual recommendations. *Under no circumstances do teachers initiate positioning exercises or remedial motor activities without specific guidance from a certified therapist.*

Adaptive Equipment.   The physical or occupational therapists also guide teachers in the use of special mobility devices, the working of **prostheses**, and the adaptation of regular play equipment. Some of the more common of these will be discussed below.

Mobility devices.   Braces, crutches, a walker, or a wheelchair are among the mobility devices prescribed for children who cannot move about easily. Young children with paraplegia may use a low, small-wheeled flat cart. They lie "tummy-down" on the cart and propel themselves from one activity to another by pushing with hands and arms. (One child referred to the device as his *crawlogator.*) Power wheelchairs are being prescribed more frequently for children as young as 2 years old. Even very young children can learn to control power chairs successfully, and can use them to achieve independent mobility within the classroom and school setting. For stand-up activities some children may use a prone-stander or standing-table.

Children with poor motor skills, even though they are able to walk, tend to fall more frequently than do other preschoolers. The falls are likely to distress adults more than they do the child. Usually, the child has become quite accustomed to falling down. Many disabled children are given training in how to fall as well as how to get themselves up again. The latter is especially important. Adults must restrain themselves from "rushing to the rescue," picking the child up before he or she has a chance to get up independently. Adults who restrain themselves save the child from being unnecessarily and additionally disabled through *learned helplessness.*

Children with poor balance and poor motor control sometimes can hold on to and push a piece of play equipment as a means of getting about. A doll carriage, stroller, toy shopping cart, or a large wooden box with a handlebar attached works well. If the box does not slide readily, wooden slats can be attached to the bottom. If the piece of equipment is too light, it can be loaded with bags of sand, thus providing a feeling of greater security. Never do teachers take the initiative in encouraging a child to walk. Neurological and medical factors first must be evaluated by a physician or other accredited specialist (Fallen and Umansky 1985).

Positioning devices.   Motor and neurological problems can be accompanied by muscular weakness that interferes with head and trunk control. Maintaining a sitting position becomes a problem, and so does grasping and hanging on to objects. The physical and/or occupational therapist can help teachers reduce the effects of motor problems by recommending or procuring

A child with paraplegia can get about on a "tummy board."

Adaptive equipment for a child lacking hand control and dexterity.

specially designed equipment such as **wedges, bolsters, and prone-boards.** *Cautionary note:* the inappropriate use of adaptive equipment can do *more harm* than good. It is essential that therapists help teachers both identify the purposes of each piece of equipment and understand its use with a particular disability and with a particular child. Therapists also must help teachers be aware of special precautions or situations that might arise while a child is using the equipment. Teachers can help therapists by describing classroom activities, and sharing with the therapist which activities are difficult for the child.

Adapting Materials. Ingenious teachers have adapted almost every ordinary preschool material to fit the needs of children with motor impairments. A sampling of ideas follows.

Manipulative materials. For children who must spend much of their time standing, or in a wheelchair, there are interesting materials that can be mounted on a board fastened to the wall. Wall displays allow children to grasp and manipulate objects they otherwise might not be able to manage. (The arrangements give a new dimension to materials for normally developing children too.) Items that can be mounted on a playboard include:

bolts, such as those used to lock doors
bicycle bells
light switches
old fashioned telephone dials
door knobs that turn
flannel boards or magnetic boards

Creative materials. For children with impaired fine motor skills, creative materials can be adapted in a variety of ways. Examples are mentioned below.

- Large crayons, chalk, or paintbrushes are available. Even these may be too small for some children to hang on to. If so, a section can be wrapped with layers of securely taped down plastic material enabling the child to get a firmer grip.
- Pencils, crayons, and colored pens can be pushed through a small sponge rubber ball. The child holds the ball to scribble and draw.
- Paper can be taped to the table. This prevents it sliding away when a child is coloring, painting, or pasting.
- Magic markers or thick-tipped felt pens can be provided for children with weak hand and wrist controls. They require less pressure than crayons but result in the rich bright colors that please children.
- Fingerpaint, potters' clay, and water play can be available more frequently. These materials require a minimum of fine motor control but make a major contribution in the improvement and strengthening of small muscle function.

Self-help devices. Many devices (available through special education catalogs) assist children in feeding, grooming, and dressing themselves. In addition, low-cost adaptations can be devised:

- Putting a small suction device (such as a bar soap holder) under a child's plate keeps it from sliding out of reach or off the table.
- Building up a spoon handle by taping a hair roller or piece of foam rubber in place gives the child better control of the spoon.
- For a child who cannot hold a spoon, a cuff can be made that keeps the spoon in the palm of the hand. The cuff is a wide strap which has a pocket

for the spoon and is fastened around the hand with a velcro closure.

- Velcro also can replace buttons and zippers and snaps. In many cases, the velcro can be put on over existing buttons and buttonholes.

Adaptations of the Classroom.   Alterations may be needed in the classroom and play yard if children with motor impairments are to have a safe and appropriate learning environment.

Wheelchair accommodation.   Space to maneuver a wheelchair in and out of activities and to turn it around is essential. Toileting areas must be clear so a child can wheel in and out of the bathroom easily, and pull up parallel to the toilet. Handrails mounted on the wall are needed so the child can learn to swing from the wheelchair onto the toilet seat. Ramps can be constructed to facilitate movement in and out of the building and the classroom.

Railings.   Attached in strategic places, indoors and out, railings help children with poor balance and faulty coordination move about more independently. Railings can serve other children, too, as exercise and ballet bars.

Floor coverings.   Carpeting, if it is well stretched and securely nailed down, is good for children with mobility problems. It also provides a warm and comfortable play surface for the many activities that all children engage in on the floor. When carpeting is not possible, crutches must have nonskid tips and shoes should have nonskid soles. Nonskid soles can be devised by gluing fine sandpaper, felt, or textured rubber onto the soles of a child's shoes.

Eye level materials.   It is helpful for teachers to ask, "How does the room appear at a child's level? Are there interesting things (such as the manipulative wall hanging discussed above) for all children to watch, touch, work with? What is available at eye level for a child on a scooter board, in a wheelchair, or one who gets about only by crawling?

Adaptive equipment enables children to participate in activities.

HEALTH PROBLEMS

It is not uncommon for children to experience a variety of health problems during infancy and early childhood. For the most part these are relatively mild and do not interfere appreciably with growth and development. On the other hand, there are children who are chronically ill and live every day with serious health problems. These present the child, parents, and teachers with ongoing problems that must be dealt with throughout the developmental years.

Asthma.   Asthma is among the most common, yet one of the most serious, of the childhood chronic diseases. During an attack the child has discomfort and tightness in the chest. Breathing becomes labored and may turn to wheezing as the individual tries to expel air that has become trapped in the lungs. Attacks may be brought on by certain foods, pollens, animal furs, temperature changes (particularly cold air), strenuous exercise, and respiratory infections.

Before the actual onset of an attack the child may begin to have a runny nose and then a dry hacking cough. During an attack breathing (wheezing) may become loud and labored. Lips and fingertips may take on a bluish look due to lack of oxygen. When a child begins to have an attack in the classroom the child should be encouraged to: (1) rest, relax and try to stay calm; (2) remain sitting in an upright position; and (3) sip warm water (avoid cold liquids).

Everyone working with children with special needs must know about emergency treatment. Many children have a medication, usually a medicated inhaler, that can be given to ease an attack and allow easier breathing. There should be no hesitation in calling

in **paramedics**, especially if the child's breathing becomes labored. A child can die from a combination of oxygen deprivation and exhaustion (Marotz 1995).

Cystic Fibrosis.   Among Caucasian children, cystic fibrosis is the most common of the inherited chronic diseases (in contrast to other racial groups where it occurs less frequently). The disease is incurable. Generally, the child has a life expectancy of 20 to 30 years, even with medical assistance. Cystic fibrosis is characterized by excessive mucus, a chronic cough, progressive lung damage, and the body's inability to absorb fats and proteins appropriately. Children have trouble gaining weight, in spite of an often excessive appetite. They also tend to have frequent, foul-smelling bowel movements and unusually salty perspiration.

The rate of deterioration varies from child to child: symptoms may be minimal in one 5-year-old, severe in another. In general, teachers should encourage physical activity as long as the child is reasonably well. Both the child and the family are likely to need considerable emotional support from teachers who also may be involved in helping the child with breathing exercises and aerosol therapy to loosen secretions.

Hemophilia.   Another inherited disorder is hemophilia, experienced only by males. (Mothers do not have the disease; they are the *carriers* or transmitters.) Hemophilia is a condition caused by a deficiency of certain clotting factors that result in the blood clotting too slowly or not at all.

> The chief danger is not bleeding to death from accidental injury . . . . It is internal bleeding that poses the greatest threat to life and health. Bleeding into the joints, especially knees, ankles, and elbows can cause severe and constant pain, and eventually permanent crippling. . . . Internal bleeding episodes, particularly in children, can be triggered by what seem to be trivial bumps, falls, and minor injuries. Often they occur without any known injury at all (Apgar and Beck 1973, p. 295).

Dr. Apgar goes on to advise that young children with hemophilia should be encouraged to be as active as possible without exposing them to unnecessary risks. "Active hemophiliacs in good physical condition

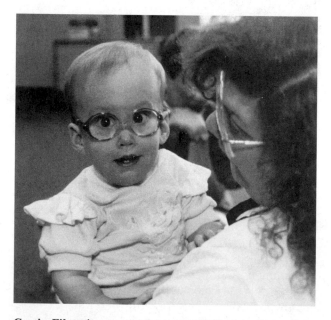

Cystic Fibrosis occurs almost exclusively among Caucasian children.

seem to have fewer episodes of bleeding than inactive youngsters with a similar degree of clotting deficiency. Sometimes, an increase in physical activity results in a decrease in bleeding." (p. 297) On the other hand, precautions must be taken whenever necessary. For example, some children may need to wear a helmet or have protective padding on knees and elbows to shield them from injury from falls common to all children. At the same time, teachers and parents must avoid treating the child as so special or so fragile that the child becomes excessively dependent or excessively concerned about personal health and well-being.

Leukemia.   Leukemia is one of several forms of cancer to be found among young children. It is a disease that destroys bone marrow through an overproduction of white blood cells. Viewed as a fatal disease up until a few years ago, **chemotherapy** has extended life expectancy by several years. Children with leukemia are usually pale, easily fatigued, and have difficulty maintaining their weight. In addition, they may have painful joints, bruise easily, and may have emotional problems due to both the disease and the stresses associated with treatment (Link 1982). For these children, focus should be on the qualitative aspects of life, not on the negative aspects of death. The teacher has a dual role:

1. Keeping track of the progress of the disease through frequent contacts with parents.
2. Encouraging and supporting the child in joining as much as possible in program activities.

Sickle-Cell Anemia.   Sickle-cell anemia, another genetically transmitted disease, is found almost entirely among Black children. Apgar and Beck (1973) suggest that in Africa the **genetic mutation** was probably an advantage—it offered protection against malaria (p. 128). In this country, countless generations later, this once useful sickle shaped red blood cell has led to a chronic health problem. Leaving out the technical aspects of the explanation, the problem stems from an abnormal formation of red blood cells. They become sickle-shaped and hook together. This interferes with their ability to carry sufficient oxygen, causing a blockage or *crisis* as it is called. The result is

Sickle-cell anemia occurs mostly among African American children.

severe pain in the abdomen, legs, and arms; swollen joints; fainting; and overall fatigue. There is no cure for the disorder.

A child with sickle cell anemia is particularly vulnerable to infection. The decision to enroll the child in an early childhood program is a delicate one that should be reached jointly by parents, physician, and staff (Kendrick, Kaufman and Messenger 1988). A child with a mild case of sickle cell anemia should continue to participate in regular preschool activities as long as she or he is well enough. Teachers can cooperate with parents and the physician in preventing a sickle cell crisis by helping the child avoid fatigue, stress, exposure to cold, and by making sure the child has adequate fluid intake.

Cardiac Disorders.   Heart disease is a common term for cardiac disorders. Many heart defects result in death during the infant's first year. Others can be surgically repaired, allowing the child to lead a normal life. Children with cardiac conditions who reach school age are less likely to have life-threatening problems (Myers 1975). Reasons for congenital heart problems range from genetic abnormalities to maternal alcoholism.

Children with heart disease may complain of shortness of breath. Physical activity may be more tiring than it is for other preschoolers. Some children experience *cyanosis*, a blueness of the skin due to poor oxygenation of the blood. The child with continuing heart problems should not be pressed to participate in activities that bring on excessive fatigue. Actually, most children with cardiac problems are fairly reliable monitors of their own exertion tolerance. Children who have had complete surgical correction should have no difficulty participating in all preschool activities. Teachers, parents, and health care providers, however, need to exchange information on a continuing basis. Together they can plan activity levels for home and school based on the current status of a child's condition.

Juvenile Diabetes Mellitus.   Also known as insulin-dependent diabetes or Type I diabetes, this form of diabetes is not often found in young children. Diabetes is a genetic disease, regarded as the most common of the inborn errors of metabolism. The problem arises because the pancreas (a gland located behind the stomach) fails to produce enough of a natural chemical called *insulin*. Insulin is required if the body is to **metabolize** glucose (a form of sugar). Without insulin, cells cannot use the glucose already in the bloodstream. The result is insufficient nourishment to carry on the body's functions. Children with diabetes must receive insulin on a regular basis (usually twice a day). However, adverse reactions to insulin are a constant threat. One such threat is *hypoglycemia*, excessively low levels of sugar circulating in the blood. Another is *hyperglycemia*, too much sugar circulating in the blood stream. Hypoglycemia can result in diabetic coma (unconsciousness).

Katz (1975) advises, *"If there is doubt, the situation should always be managed as a low sugar insulin reaction,* since the administration of sugar will cause no harm, while withholding sugar could have serious consequences" (p. 78). Teachers and caregivers will need to be involved in other ways, too:

- careful regulation of food intake
- monitoring the child's exercise and activity level
- observing the child for changes in behavior and signs of infection
- occasional urine testing.

It is important that teachers, parents, and health care providers be in partnership and communicate regularly. This ensures the best possible care for the child, with the fewest complications.

Seizure Disorders.   The terms *epilepsy*, *seizure*, and *convulsion* are used somewhat interchangeably to describe disturbances in the normal electrical discharges in the brain. What happens, in simple terms, is *bursts* of electrical energy. These result in reduced or total loss of consciousness. Uncontrolled muscular movements, ranging from brief twitching of the eyelids to massive shaking of the entire body accompany these bursts or episodes. The random motor movements have been categorized in various ways. Following is a classification teachers find useful:

1. *Febrile seizures* (the most common). They occur in 5 to 20 percent of children under the age of three. In general, the seizure is brought on by a high fever. Usually, it lasts less than 15 minutes and stops by itself. Rarely are these seizures harmful (Kendrick, Kaufman and Messenger 1988) nor do children who experience them develop epilepsy.
2. *Partial or psychomotor seizures* sometimes resemble a temper tantrum or an episode of bizarre behavior characterized by lip-smacking, repetitive arm and hand movements, or aimless running about. Though there is the appearance of consciousness, the child is usually unaware of behaving strangely (Jacobs 1983).
3. *Petit mal seizures* are those where there is momentary loss of consciousness. This may occur many times a day with some children. The lapses are so brief that they may go unnoticed even though there could be slight twitching of the eye lids, head, or hands. The child often is accused of *daydreaming*.
4. *Grand mal seizures* usually cause children to lose consciousness and fall to the floor with violently jerking muscles. They may stop breathing tem-

porarily, lose bowel or bladder control, and bubble saliva about the mouth.

A variety of medications are used to control seizures in children. The medication may have an adverse effect, especially in the beginning, causing the child to be drowsy or inattentive. An important role for teachers is to *observe* and *record* changes in the child's behavior. Behavioral observations assist the child's physician in altering medication or dosage as needed. In general, the anticonvulsant medications prescribed for a child are effective in preventing seizures. Rarely does the early childhood teacher encounter a grand mal seizure. However, it is important to know what to do should there be an episode. The following recommendations are adapted from material published by The Epilepsy Foundation of America:

1. Remain calm. Children will react the same way teachers do. The seizure itself is painless.
2. Do not try to restrain the child. Nothing can be done to stop a seizure once it has begun. It must run its course.
3. Clear the space around the child so that no injury from hard objects occurs and there is no interference with the child's movements.
4. *Do not try to force anything between the teeth.*
5. Loosen tight clothing, especially at the neck; turn the child's head to the side, wipe away discharge from the mouth and nose to aid breathing.
6. When the seizure is over allow the child to rest.
7. Generally it is not necessary to call for medical assistance unless the seizure lasts for more than ten minutes or is followed by another seizure. However, emergency medical help should always be summoned in the case of a first seizure (unless it is absolutely certain it is a febrile seizure). Many things can trigger seizures in young children: poisoning, infections, severe electrical jolts, and allergic reactions. If unsure about whether to call for medical help or not, it is always better to err on the safe side. (Marotz 1995).
8. The child's parents should always be informed of a seizure. Teachers and parents plan together how future seizures are best handled for that particular child.

The child with epilepsy should not be restricted from participating in the full program unless specific limitations are imposed by parents or physicians. A seizure episode can be turned into a learning experience for the children in the class. Teachers can explain in simple terms what a seizure is. They can assure children it is *not catching* and children need not fear for themselves or for the child who had the seizure. The Epilepsy Foundation goes on to suggest that it is important that teachers help children understand but *not pity* the child so that he or she remains "one of the gang."

Making sure the child receives the prescribed medication regularly and in the proper amounts is the best approach to preventing seizures. Teachers who are asked to administer medication must follow the guidelines described later in this unit. In concluding this section on epilepsy it seems important to reiterate two points. The first is a repeat of the cautionary note: *Never attempt to force anything between the child's upper and lower teeth.* This procedure, once thought necessary, was discontinued years ago. Children's teeth can be damaged and adult's fingers severely bitten. The second point that bears repeating is that *teachers remain calm.* In the interest of everyone, a teacher must not panic. Young children rarely become unduly alarmed about anything if their teachers do not appear anxious or upset. Children's anxieties over a seizure episode are reduced almost immediately if adults are confident and matter-of-fact about assuring them the child soon will be all right. In fact, the teacher's quiet care of the child having the seizure can be a valuable experience in human concern that is of benefit to all children.

AIDS (Acquired Immune Deficiency Syndrome). AIDS stands for Acquired Immune Deficiency Syndrome. It is a disease that leaves an individual open to contracting illnesses that a healthy **immune system** might otherwise overcome. It is caused by a human immunodeficiency virus (HIV). Individuals may be infected without knowing it and without showing symptoms of the infection. For example, there have been cases of AIDS being transmitted during routine blood transfusions to both adults and infants.

AIDS is transmitted primarily through sexual contact, blood-to-blood contact (as through shared hypodermic needles), or from an infected mother to her baby. It is estimated that one-third to one-half of the infants born to infected mothers will be infected. However, all infants of HIV infected mothers will test positive for the disease in the first year or so of life. Why? Because the infant is still operating on its mother's **antibody** system while its own is gearing up and getting ready to function.

There is no evidence of *casual* transmission by sitting near, living in the same household with, or playing with an individual with clinical AIDS (American Academy of Pediatrics 1990). According to Kendrick (1990) and the NAEYC Information Service (1991)

> HIV is not transmitted through urine, stool (diarrhea), vomitus, saliva (mouthing of toys and other objects), mucus, sweat, or other body fluid that does not contain blood. . . . All children with HIV infection or AIDS should be admitted to the program as long as their own health and developmental status allows them to benefit from the program (p. 270).

Typically, however, children who have AIDS are quite ill and unable to be in a child care program or preschool classroom. Also, children with AIDS are highly vulnerable to all of the many childhood infectious illnesses; enrollment in an early childhood group of any kind can be against their best interests. For those children who are well enough to be in a program, strict hygiene procedures are required of caregivers: thorough handwashing, wearing disposable gloves when dealing with bodily secretions, and cleaning caregiving surfaces with bleach and water solution. According to Best, Bigge, and Sirvis (1994):

> Because these precautions constitute good hygiene for anyone who requires physical care, their universal adoption allows protection for care providers while preserving the privacy of the student with AIDS (p. 314).

In an early childhood center, no individual (child or adult) should be attending or working in the program if they have open, oozing sores. Neither should they be in the program if there is any sign of bloody discharge accompanying diarrhea. This applies to everyone, those with and those without known HIV infection. The foregoing recommendations are in accord with medical, technical and legislative findings as reviewed by Dokecki, Baumeister and Kupstas (1989) and the NAEYC Information Service (1994). Information on AIDS/HIV is changing constantly; therefore it is essential that everyone working with infants, young children, and families keep abreast of current findings.

Obesity (Overweight).   While obesity is not necessarily a handicapping condition, it is a developmental disorder that effects between 15 and 20 percent of the children and youth in this country. Unchecked, obesity leads to significant long-term health problems as well as social and psychological problems. Overweight children often are teased by others and excluded from play activities. This leads to a poor self image, decreasing physical fitness, and fewer opportunities to build satisfying social relationships (Marotz, Rush and Gross 1993).

Fat babies do not necessarily become fat adults; substantial evidence exists, however, that overweight preschoolers are not likely to *outgrow* the problem. As weight increases, children move less vigorously and so continue to put on more weight. This further compounds both their physical and their psychological problems. The increase of obesity in children has risen dramatically in the past two decades. According to Brizee, Sophos and McLaughlin (1990), the increase is thought to be associated with reduced physical activity and increased consumption of convenience foods and fast foods, which tend to be high in fat. Certainly, genetics also play a part in a child's susceptibility to obesity. Nevertheless, the excessive weight itself is the result of two *controllable* factors:

- *Overeating*: The consumption of too many calories, or at least too many calories from the wrong kinds of food; often the overweight individual eats excessive amounts of food with poor nutritional content, popularly known as *junk food*.
- *Under exercising*: Lack of physical activity often is given as a major reason for obesity. It has been estimated that the prevalence of obesity in this country increases approximately 2 percent for each additional hour of television viewing, nationwide (*Harvard Education Letter* 1987).

All children, including those who are obese, need an adequate number of calories each day, but the calories need to come from the right kind of foods. "The best single rule for good nutrition is to offer a variety of nutritious foods while avoiding **empty calorie** snack items" (Wishon, Bower and Eller 1983, p. 24). Strangely enough, many children who are overweight are undernourished. The early childhood teacher can work closely with parents and nutritionist or health care provider to make sure a child with a weight problem is getting a daily intake of appropriate foods in appropriate amounts. Teachers also can focus parts of the early childhood curriculum on helping children understand the role of good nutrition and exercise in everyday life.

Some children with developmental problems require the concentrated supervision of a nutritionist or dietary specialist. Situations requiring intensive nutritional intervention vary. Sometimes patterns of excessive food intake may have been established unintentionally by parents and caregivers. By providing an

Children with developmental disabilities often need their food intake planned by a dietary specialist.

A well nourished child. (Normal weight gain depends upon offering good food, cutting out empty calories—junk food—and allowing children to eat only what they need.)

abundance of food, they may have thought to compensate for the many ordinary life experiences denied the child. Yet, the amount and kind of food offered may be in excess. Often the child's dietary needs are less than other children's needs, because of the child's related inactivity. Another example can be seen in certain syndromes such as **Prader-Willi**. The child engages in uncontrolled and obsessive food consumption. Refrigerators must be kept locked. Food cannot be left out in a pet's dish. Teachers must keep uneaten food, even leftovers on other children's plates, securely out of the way of the child.

Undernourishment. Consuming too few calories is as damaging to a growing child as consuming too many. Many physically impaired children burn far more calories each day than they are able to take in. One example is children with severe cerebral palsy. They use up tremendous amounts of energy on the unwelcome but constant and uncontrollable muscular reactions characteristic of their disability. Often these children are far below ideal body weight. The muscle impairment that burns so many calories also can lead to other nutritional problems. Some children have trouble holding food in their mouth, or with chewing and swallowing. Parents, teachers, and caregivers need specialized help in learning to provide easy-to-swallow foods that are high in nutritional value.

HEALTH PROBLEMS AND CLASSROOM PRACTICES

Early childhood teachers sometimes feel anxious, inadequate, even threatened when first asked to include a child with a serious health problem or a disabling physical condition in their class. However, teachers find that the more they work with children with special needs the more natural it seems. The NAEYC health manual (Kendrick, Kaufman, and Messenger 1988) advises teachers:

> Having good information is one of the best ways to feel confident and in control. When you know what to do—whether it is taking a temperature, performing CPR, or keeping a child relaxed during an asthma attack—both you and the child are going to profit from your knowledge. Lack of information often leads to panic in emergencies or improper care. You can provide the necessary care, remain calm, and maintain control (p. 20).

In addition to parents and the interdisciplinary team members who are involved in the child's inter-vention program, useful information for teachers comes from other sources. Most important are up-to-date health records on each child and complete knowledge about a child's medication program. Teachers also must be sure they know what they will do in both routine and emergency situations related to specific health problems among the children in the class. Every time a child with a health problem is to be enrolled, teachers must have a careful advance briefing by both the child's parents and a health care professional.

Health Records.   A complete and frequently updated health record must be maintained on every child in the group. It should contain the following essential information:

- Telephone numbers where parents and alternate emergency contacts can be reached at all times.
- Name of the child's regular health care provider or clinic with address and telephone numbers.
- Permission slips authorizing emergency health care and transportation, and the administration of prescribed medications.
- Child and family health history.
- Immunization information with dates.
- Results of medical assessment or physical and dental examinations and treatment.
- Results of special testing such as vision or hearing assessments.
- Dated reports, signed by the attending teacher, on all injuries or illnesses that occur while the child is in the classroom, play yard, or on a school sponsored excursion.
- Notations about allergies, special diets, treatment procedures, medications, prosthetic devices, or other health concerns.
- Notations on health related communications with parents and health care providers including referral recommendations and follow up.
- Ongoing records of medications given to the child while at school.

Administering Medication.   In many states, the law (or licensing agency) requires that medication of any kind, given in the early childhood center, must be

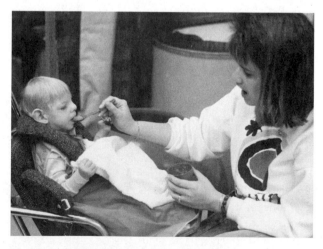

Feeding can be a long and difficult process.

done *only on written order from a physician.* Most states also require that the package or bottle containing the medication must be a child-resistant container and labeled with the following:

1. Child's name
2. Physician's name and phone number
3. Name of the medicine
4. How much is to be given to the child
5. Schedule for administering dosages

Teachers are not required to give medication (Kendrick, Kaufman and Messenger 1988). However, most teachers are willing to take on this responsibility if it enables the child to stay in the program. Staff members who dispense medication need to receive specific training in the procedure. Each time the medication is given, the time and date is to be recorded on the child's record sheet and initialed by the person who did the medicating. Medication must be kept in a *locked* cupboard or refrigerator, or *out of reach of all children.*

Emergency Considerations. All programs serving young children are required to have carefully laid out plans for emergency situations in general. (See Kendrick et al. 1988 for an excellent description of such plans.) When children with health problems and physical disabilities are enrolled, individual plans need to be formulated for each child. These include:

- Conferring with parents (or the child's doctor) to plan in advance for emergency health crisis
- Understanding the cause of a crisis and how often it is likely to occur
- Learning how a child may behave *before* as well as during and after a crisis
- Knowing what to do during and following the crisis and understanding when to call for additional help

Marotz, Cross and Rush (1993) recommend that all teachers, if they are expected to administer first aid to children, complete first aid and CPR training, preferably before they begin work. (p. 200)

Preventing a health crisis is important too. For example, it is well to prepare a list of classroom activities. Give this to the child's parents or physician and ask them to indicate activities that should be avoided or modified. In addition, the other children need to be prepared for a possible health crisis of classmates. Teachers can give simple explanations. They also can assure children that they (the teachers) will be able to take care of all of the children, not just the child having the problem.

SUMMARY

Physical problems in children include a wide range of impairments. Neurological involvement often accompanies the problems. The physical disabilities that teachers are most likely to encounter are described briefly in terms of characteristics, causes, program recommendations, and the responsibilities of teachers, including crisis management as needed.

Children with physical and other health problems are likely to benefit from being enrolled in an inclusive early childhood classroom. Interdisciplinary team members work with teachers in planning and implementing classroom activities; physical and occupational therapists are essential in cases of orthopedic involvement. A variety of other disciplines also play significant roles, depending on the nature of the child's problems.

Never do teachers initiate any kind of a therapeutic activity without specific instruction and supervision from a certified specialist. The specialist also learns from the early childhood educator how to accommodate therapeutic recommendations to the everyday activities and developmental principles of the classroom.

Regular classroom activities, materials, and equipment often can be adapted to meet the needs of children who are physically impaired. A major responsibility of teachers is to help children keep active and involved to the maximum extent possible. Teachers need to help children learn to do as much as possible for themselves so that their illness or disability does not take over their lives. Another responsibility of teachers is to prepare themselves to meet emergency situations. When teachers remain calm and quietly in charge, young children do not panic.

STUDENT ACTIVITIES

1. Divide into several groups of six or seven students. Select one person as a discussion leader and talk about disabilities or serious health problems that members have experienced firsthand or through living with a brother or sister, close relative, spouse, or friend who has a disability. Discuss common experiences and attitudes.
2. Work with three or four other students in preparing a manipulative board to mount on the wall. Expand on or take off on the ideas in the text. Be creative. Arrange for a tryout of the creation in one or more preschool classrooms.
3. Select a common preschool manipulative material and demonstrate ways it might be adapted so that a child with impaired fine motor skills could use it successfully.
4. Devise a game with balls, suitable for 4- and 5-year-olds, that would allow a child in a wheelchair to participate.
5. Select a possible crisis situation such as an asthma attack, insulin shock, or grand mal seizure. Describe what you would say to a group of 4- and 5-year-olds who had witnessed such an episode for the first time.

REVIEW QUESTIONS

A. *Define and give an example.*
   1. Contractures
   2. Chronic health condition
   3. Progressive disease
   4. Hydrocephalus
   5. Hip dysplasia
   6. Mobility device
   7. Adaptive equipment
   8. Diabetic coma
   9. Petit mal seizure
   10. Empty calories

B. *Multiple choice. Circle as many of the following statements that are correct.*
   1. Motor impairments can interfere with
      a. cognitive development.
      b. discovery learning.
      c. social interactions.
      d. none of the above.
   2. Muscle-related impairments include
      a. contractures.
      b. hypotonicity.
      c. genetic mutations.
      d. hypertonicity.
      e. recessive gene action.
   3. Congenital spinal cord damage
      a. is most likely to occur during the last 30 days of fetal development.
      b. may result in hydrocephalus.
      c. may require shunting.
      d. may interfere with bowel and bladder control.
   4. Prostheses include
      a. diet control.
      b. insulin injections.
      c. eye glasses or lenses.
      d. mechanical hands.
      e. leg and trunk braces.
   5. An asthma attack may be preceded by
      a. ravenous appetite.
      b. dry, hacking cough.
      c. loss of consciousness.
      d. runny nose.
      e. bluish look around the lips.
   6. Seizure disorders may be characterized as
      a. febrile.
      b. petit mal.
      c. grand mal.
      d. mixed.
   7. The school health records should include
      a. information as to whether children are born in or out of wedlock.
      b. information as to any jail records there are in the family or extended family.
      c. telephone and emergency numbers where parents can be reached at any time.
      d. signed permission slips authorizing emergency health care.
   8. Medication given at school must have
      a. child resistant lid or stopper.
      b. safe storage in a locked cupboard or refrigerator.
      c. the child's and the physician's name written on the label.
      d. a statement on the label guaranteeing teachers' immunity from legal liability.

C. *True or False. Choose the best answer.*

T F   1. Cerebral palsy is the least common source of physical disability among infants and young children.

T F   2. Muscle tone and muscle strength mean the same thing.

T F   3. Incontinence refers to lack of bladder and bowel control.

T F   4. All that teachers need is good common sense in using adaptive devices and positioning activities with children who have physical disabilities.

T F   5. Cystic fibrosis occurs most frequently among Black children while sickle cell anemia is most common among Caucasians.

T F   6. A young child with a history of cardiac disorder should never participate in outdoor large motor play.

T F   7. Consuming too few calories can be as damaging to a child as consuming too many.

T F   8. When excessive overweight "runs in a family" it cannot be controlled even with a change in eating and exercise patterns.

T F   9. A teacher who gives medications at school should record and initial the dosage.

T F   10. Teachers cannot be expected to handle health crises.

REFERENCES

American Academy of Pediatrics. (1990). Lack of transmission of human immunodeficiency virus from infected children to household contacts. *Pediatrics.* 85(2), 1115–1119.

Apgar, V.G., and Beck, J. (1973). *Is my baby alright?* New York: Trident Press.

Best, S.J., Bigge, J.L., and Sirvis, B.P. (1994). Physical and health impairments. In N.G. Haring, L. McCormick, and T.G. Haring (Eds.), *Exceptional children and youth: Sixth edition.* New York: Merrill.

Bobath, K., and Bobath, B. (1975). Cerebral palsy. In P. Pearson and C.E. Williams (Eds.), *Physical therapy services in developmental disabilities.* Springfield, IL: Charles C. Thomas.

Brizee, L.S., Sophos, C.M., and McLaughlin, J.F. (1990). Nutrition issues in developmental disabilities. *Infants and Young Children* 2:3, 10–22.

Caldwell, B.M. (1973). The importance of beginning early. In J. Jordan and R.F. Dailey (Eds.), *Not all little wagons are red.* Reston, VA: Council for Exceptional Children.

Coe, A.W. (1990). Cystic fibrosis: An introduction and the role of school personnel. *Education,* 110(2), 202–206.

Dokecki, P.R., Baumeister, A.A., and Kupstas, F.D. (1989). Biomedical and social aspects of pediatric AIDS. *Journal of Early Intervention.* 13:2, 99–112.

Fallen, N.H., and Umansky, W. (1985). *Young children with special needs.* Columbus: Merrill.

Fewell, R.R. (1988). Follow-up findings of a program for motor skill achievement. *Topics in Early Childhood Special Education,* 7:4, 64–70.

Grinker, J.A. (1981). Behavioral and metabolic factors in childhood obesity. In M. Lewis and L.A. Rosenblum (Eds.), *The uncommon child.* New York: Plenum.

Harvard Educational Letter (September 1986). Early intervention for handicapped babies. 2(5), 7.

Jacobs, I.B. (1983). Epilepsy. In G.H. Thompson, I.L. Rubin, and R.M. Bilenker (Eds.), *Comprehensive management of cerebral palsy.* New York: Grune & Stratton.

Katz, H.P. (1975). Important endocrine disorders of childhood. In R. Haslam and P. Valletutti (Eds.), *Medical problems in the classroom.* Baltimore: University Park Press.

Kendrick, A.S., Kaufman, R., and Messenger, K.P. (Eds.). (1988). *Healthy Young Children.* Washington, D.C.: National Association for the Education of Young Children. (Revision materials supplied by NAEYC Information Services, 1990.)

Link, M.P. (1982). Cancer in childhood. In E.E. Bleck and D.A. Nagel (Eds.), *Physically handicapped children: A medical atlas for children.* New York: Grune & Stratton.

Lozes, M.H. (1988). Bladder and bowel management for children with myelomeningocele. *Infants and Young Children.* 1:1, 42–62.

Marotz, L.R., Rush, J.M., and Cross, M.Z. (1993). *Health, safety, and nutrition for the young child.* Albany: Delmar.

Mather, J., and Weinstein, E. (1988). Teachers and therapists: Evolution of a partnership in early intervention. *Topics in early childhood special education.* 7:4 1–9.

Miller, J.J. III. (1975). Juvenile rheumatoid arthritis. In E.E. Bleck and D.A. Nagel (Eds.), *Physically handicapped children: A medical atlas for teachers.* New York: Grune and Stratton.

Myers, B.R. (1975). The child with chronic illness. In R. Haslam and P. Valletutti (Eds.), *Medical problems in the classroom.* Baltimore: University Park Press.

NAEYC Information Service. (1991). Washington, DC. Personal telephone query.

Thurman, S.K., and Widerstrom, A.H. (1990). *Infants and young children with special needs*. Baltimore: Brooks.

Tyler, N.B., and Chandler, L.S. (1978). The developmental therapists: The occupational therapist and the physical therapist. In K.E. Allen, V.A. Holm, and R.L. Schiefelbusch (Eds.), *Early Intervention—A Team Approach*. Baltimore: University Park Press.

Washington, K., Schwartz, I.S., and Swinth, Y. (1994). Physical and occupational therapists in naturalistic early childhood settings: Challenges and strategies for training. *Topics in Early Childhood Special Education, 14(3)*, 333–349.

Wishon, P.M., Bower, R., and Eller, B. (1983). Childhood obesity—Prevention and treatment. *Young Children*. November, 21–26.

Behavior and Learning Disorders

OBJECTIVES

After studying this unit the student will be able to

- put together a word picture that describes the behavioral characteristics of a child with autism.
- describe the behavioral characteristics of a child with ADHD and discuss different intervention options.
- describe eating and toileting problems sometimes associated with behavior disorders.
- provide a convincing argument against labeling or diagnosing a preschool child as learning disabled.
- list ten or more warning signs in a preschool child that suggest the potential for learning disabilities related to later reading, writing, and math skills.

Disorders associated with behavior and with learning have been linked to various developmental problems. The term *behavior disorders* is widely used to classify a variety of social and emotional disturbances ranging from mild to severe. "Deviations from age-appropriate behavior that significantly interferes with the child's own development or with the lives of others" is a definition offered by Spodek, Saracho, and Lee (1984). The term l*earning disorders* is often applied to children with normal IQs and reasonable adaptive functioning who nevertheless have difficulty learning to read, to write, or to do math.

A behavior or learning disorder may be a child's major or *primary* problem, or it may be a lesser or *secondary* problem. There are children who perform normally in all areas of development except for one or more inappropriate behavior patterns. In these cases, the behavior disorder is the primary problem. In contrast, there are children with readily identified disabilities who also demonstrate deviant behaviors. Children who are blind, for example, may develop ritualistic, seemingly nonfunctional behaviors. These can take up so much of the child's time that they interfere with the child acquiring developmentally appropriate skills.

The inability, or lack of opportunity, to learn appropriate behaviors or to understand routine expectations may be the cause of secondary behavior problems. The frustrations the child experiences in trying to perform normal developmental tasks and to engage in normal social exchanges is often a factor. Children with developmental problems tend to get little positive feedback from parents, caregivers, and teachers; yet their maladaptive behaviors such as head banging, shrill squealing, or eye-poking, draw a great deal of attention. Thus, the maladaptive behaviors come to predominate, making it even more difficult for these children to acquire necessary developmental skills.

When working with young children who present challenging or inappropriate behaviors, it is essential to keep in mind what is developmentally appropriate. Most four-year-olds do not follow all directions, challenge adults occasionally, and can go from laughter to tears in a few seconds. The term behavior disorder should be used with extreme caution when describing young children.

There is general agreement among most child developmentalists that preschool children (with few exceptions) *should not be labeled as emotionally disturbed.* Early development is characterized by constant change.

113

Therefore the label *emotionally disturbed* is premature, nonfunctional, and likely inaccurate. The issue is summed up neatly by Peterson (1987) who says, "How one judges deviance, normality, and hence pathology in a young child is highly influenced by social values and by the perspective of the individual who attempts to make the determination" (p. 272).

Peterson's advice should be kept in mind during the discussions that follow about the various behavior and learning disorders.

CONDUCT DISORDERS

The category, *conduct disorders*, according to the American Psychiatric Association (1987), refers to a number of antisocial behaviors such as excessive aggressiveness, fighting, bullying, irritability, lying, cheating, stealing, and chronic disobedience. Delinquency and truancy become common after early childhood. It appears that children with conduct disorders usually have had little social acceptance; often they were rejected by other children during their school years (Bates et al. 1991). Other factors associated with conduct disorders may be particular family behaviors and values such as ineffective discipline or patterns of reinforced aggressiveness within the family (Patterson, Capaldi and Bank 1991).

While conduct problems may be seen in preschool children it is unwise to refer to young children as having a conduct disorder. On the other hand, when aggressive and destructive behaviors threaten to become a young child's habitual way of responding to stress and frustration, intervention is imperative. The longer such behaviors dominate a child's social development, the more difficult they are to eliminate. These inappropriate behaviors become the norm for these children—the learned way to interact with others. Case histories of incorrigible juveniles make this tragically clear. Therefore, all of Unit 19 is devoted to the management of problem behaviors in young children.

Anxiety and Depression.   Young children are seldom diagnosed as having anxiety disorders or depression although there is an increasing incidence of such problems among preadolescents. The causes of these conditions are not clear. There is some evidence that children growing up with depressed parents are more likely to have bouts of anxiety and depression. This does not hold true for all children, however. In one study, more than 60 percent of the children of depressed parents showed no signs of the disorder. (Dodge 1990). Low self-esteem also seems to be associated with depression, especially among adolescents (Harter 1990).

It would be unwise, however, to completely dismiss the question of anxiety where young children are concerned. The possible precursors to such problems need to be recognized and dealt with. This is done in Unit 19 under the headings of separation anxiety, withdrawn and isolate behaviors, and overdependency. Throughout the entire text we also address the issue, directly and indirectly, in terms of building self-esteem in young children during the early years. Children with a firmly entrenched sense of their own worthwhileness seldom experience behavior disorders of consequence.

PERVASIVE DEVELOPMENTAL DISORDERS

Children with severe social-emotional problems often are classified as having a **pervasive developmental disorder**. The most commonly known conditions are *autism* and *childhood schizophrenia*. These are similar disorders whose major difference is time of onset; autism begins to emerge before a child turns three, schizophrenia in later childhood.

Autism.   One of the earliest signs of autism is resistance to being held or cuddled. The infant tends not to *mold* to the mother's (or caregiver's) body as most infants do. As toddlers and little children, autistic children treat other persons as *inanimate* (lifeless) objects. Rarely do these children make eye contact. Rituals to excess, and rigid requirements for sameness are typical: changing the position of a piece of furniture or offering a drink from an unfamiliar cup may trigger a violent tantrum. Self-stimulating behaviors such as spinning, rocking, head banging, or self-biting are common. A pediatric neurologist (Coleman 1989) rounds out the description as follows:

Strange hand motions or fixations are one aspect of behaviors referred to as autistic.

These children may line up objects or toys for hours on end. They love to look at spinning objects such as wheels of toy cars. . . . When they begin to walk they may walk on their toes. When they are excited they may flap their hands or make finger motions in front of their eyes. . . . Another bizarre behavior is their reaction to sensory stimuli. Many autistic children cover their ears to shut out vacuum cleaner sounds, the sounds of crying infants, or sometimes the most ordinary of sounds (p. 25).

The language of children with autism (some do not develop language) often is strange. A child may have beautifully clear speech with complex language, but it is so disorganized that it makes no sense. Another child may use language simply to express rote memorization. Many of these children can recite ever so many commercial jingles heard on television, but they have no communicative language. One 4-year-old knew all the words to every stanza of over 40 popular songs and folk ballads. That same child had no social language except for a few stereotyped, **echolalic** phrases. To add to the mysteries of autism, children

have been known to add, divide, and multiply complicated sets of numbers as rapidly as a calculator. (*Savant* was the name once popular for such individuals.) Others can read a newspaper, word for word, with expression; yet they understand not a word they read (Batshaw and Perret 1981).

The child who is severely autistic is not likely to be placed in an inclusive preschool until some degree of responsiveness has been achieved. Getting the child to that point usually depends on intensive treatment in a special program. When the breakthrough is accomplished, the child is likely to benefit from a regular preschool program. The following suggestions for teachers are adapted from Schor (1983):

When observing the child, always be alert to the possibility of an undetected hearing or vision loss (unrecognized problems are common because autistic children tend to be resistant to clinical testing).

Classroom focus should be on language and self-help skills along with an individualized and systematic program aimed at reducing inappropriate behaviors and facilitating interactions with others.

In communicating with these children:
- Keep the message simple and direct.
- Use objects and actions along with words (show the child the shoe and demonstrate pulling the lace through).
- Emphasize spoken language by having the child ask for something by name whenever possible.
- Give the child opportunities to interact with younger children who are at a more comparable level in language and social development.
- For behavior management programs use **tangible reinforcers** (small toys, stickers, music, favored foods if all else fails) and pair these with adult attention.
- Establish a predictable environment including teachers' language and behaviors, the daily schedule, and classroom furnishings and materials.

The suggestions continue, with emphasis shifted to the family: Support parents of children with autism in every way possible and work with other members of the interdisciplinary team to help parents find **respite care**. Another urgent need of parents is frequent assurance that the autism was *not* caused by a lack of love or caring on their part. Parents of children with autism often have been greatly wronged. Without valid evidence, it was implied that they (or, more often than not, the mother) were somehow responsible for their autistic child. According to Bee (1992), children are born with the disorder: "Whatever the specific origin, the evidence jointly points to the conclusion that autism reflects different brain functions of some kind" (p. 557). For a moving and fascinating true story of a family's efforts on behalf of their children with autism we recommend Catherine Maurice's book, *Let Me Hear Your Voice: A Family's Triumph over Autism* (1993).

Childhood Schizophrenia.   There is less scientific knowledge about childhood schizophrenia than there is about autism. The major characteristics include tantrums and repetitive or otherwise bizarre behaviors or postures. Other characteristics are rejection of and withdrawal from social contacts and unpredictable mood swings. The individual frequently is described as *cut off from reality* and given to hallucinations. Children with schizophrenia tend to be sickly and lacking in appealing physical features. This is in contrast to children with autism who typically are the picture of good health and described as exceptionally

good looking (beautiful is the word most commonly used). On the other hand, the child with schizophrenia usually displays normal language development though the language may be used for noncommunicative purposes. Many of these children talk to themselves in a private language that no one can decode. Finally, children with schizophrenia have been described as having more varied symptoms than autistic children and are more likely to have contact with other people (Rutter 1986).

The early childhood teacher seldom encounters children with schizophrenia because the onset of the condition comes after the preschool years. In the event that a child with these behaviors were to be enrolled in an early childhood program, many of the suggestions about working with autistic children apply.

Phobias.   Fears that result in excessive and unrealistic anxiety about everyday happenings are called *phobias*. The individual with a phobia may go into a panic reaction at encountering a feared object or event, or at the mere thought of encountering it. For example, there are individuals who take unrealistic measures such as climbing 20 flights of stairs to avoid riding an elevator; or they walk a mile out of the way, every day, rather than pass a well-fenced yard in which there is a small, securely tied dog that barks at passersby.

A certain amount of fear is normal. Fears are natural, adaptive mechanisms in young children and are built in for survival purposes. No child should be laughed at or shamed for his or her fears. By the same token, children's fears should not be allowed to get blown out of proportion. As with all developmental issues, it is a fine line between too much and too little attention. Normal fears can become unrealistically stressful if adults are overly attentive to the child's fearful responses. On the other hand, not enough attention can make the child feel insecure and rejected. These feelings can lead to other kinds of maladaptive behaviors and stressful reactions.

EATING AND ELIMINATION DISORDERS

Eating problems associated with particular disorders as well as over and underweight were described in Unit 7. Incontinence associated with spinal cord damage was also discussed. This section will look at several other eating and elimination disorders sometimes found among young children in group settings.

Pica.   The craving for nonfood substances is called *pica*. Early childhood teachers may encounter children who are constantly eating substances considered inedible: dirt, tar or grease, chalk, paper, or fingerpaint. Frequent consumption of nonedible materials is a health threat.

Many young children take little tastes of materials such as paste, playdough, or clay. This should not be confused with pica. However, it should be discouraged, with an explanation that it can cause stomach upset. If the child continues, the problem is usually solved by removing the material with the simple statement, "I can't let you play with the dough if you eat it." Children also may go on *food jags*. They insist on certain foods to the exclusion of all others. Except in extreme cases (or if too much pressure is put on the child to "eat right") the jag usually disappears in a reasonable time. There also is the occasional child who eats excessive amounts of a certain food. One 4-year-old was known to eat whole heads of lettuce, almost ravenously. Whenever a teacher is concerned about a child's eating habits, the parents and appropriate members of the interdisciplinary team should be consulted.

Soiling and Wetting.   It is not uncommon for early childhood teachers to encounter children who are not toilet trained, or are not reliable about getting themselves to the toilet in time. The same holds true for young children with developmental disabilities, many of whom may not be toilet trained when they reach preschool age. The reasons vary. Often it is conflict that results in a toilet training impasse between child and parents. In the early childhood program, where emotional involvement is at a minimum, toilet training usually can be accomplished quickly. Effective training guides are available including the well known *Toilet training in less than a day* by Azrin and Foxx (1971) and the Fredericks et al. (1975) program: *Toilet training the handicapped child*. It is the rare child, even one who is severely retarded, who cannot be taught to use the toilet.

Even though toilet trained, young children, with and without developmental disabilities, may have soil-

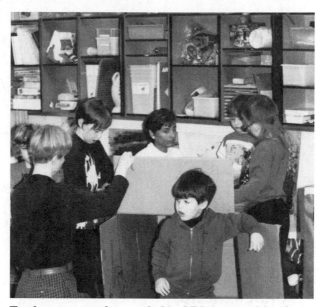

Teachers may need to remind a child engrossed in play to use the toilet.

ing or wetting episodes on occasion. They often give clues of an impending accident by jiggling or clutching themselves. What is needed is a quiet instruction from the teacher, *before* the accident occurs: "Run in and use the toilet. I'll save the swing until you get back." When a toilet accident does occur, a child should never be ridiculed or made to feel guilty. Even the most conscientious child can slip up. Clothing should be changed matter-of-factly and the soiled clothing rinsed out and put in a plastic bag. Every young child needs spare clothes at school, rotated from home if possible.

Chronic soiling or wetting sometimes occurs in an older preschool or primary-age child who has been reliably toilet-trained. Possible reasons:

- Persistent wetting, especially in girls, may be related to chronic urinary tract infection.
- A child may have a recurring, low-grade intestinal virus causing loose or runny bowels; children with diabetes may have failure of urine control at times.
- Some children are anxious about using a strange bathroom, or have been trained to greater privacy than is available at school.

Once in awhile, even when all physical disorders have been ruled out, the child continues to have problems. *Encopresis* (chronic soiling problem) and *enuresis* (chronic wetting problem) are the clinical names assigned to such conditions. Though there are a number of possible reasons, earlier difficulties associated with elimination or toilet training may have become intertwined with anxiety, fear, and other emotional reactions. These can result in a child's unpredictable and hard-to-control soiling or wetting accidents. Even in these cases, the clothes should be changed matter-of-factly, without reprimand or moralizing. Working together, teachers, parents, and the appropriate team member(s) can help a child with enuresis or encopresis gain reliable control.

ATTENTION DEFICIT HYPERACTIVITY DISORDER (ADHD)

What is ADHD? What are the symptoms? How is it different from hyperactivity? What can be done about it? Every day, these questions plague teachers and parents, clinicians and researchers. It seems we know so little and yet talk so much about this condition that characterizes some children, with and without developmental disabilities. Before getting into current notions about this complex behavior disorder a bit of history is needed to explain the lack of definitive answers.

History of ADHD.   The problem has been noted and studied for 50 years and more. It has undergone numerous name changes beginning with *brain injured* and *minimally brain damaged* (MBD). By the late 1960s there was concern about using medical terms for a condition characterized by behavior (excessive movement) rather than by identifiable physiological evidence. The term *hyperactivity* came into being. Many **psychopathologists**, however, felt it was not excessive activity that best described these children as much as their inability to pay attention. Therefore, in 1980 the American Psychiatric Association (APA) changed the name to ADD with two subcategories: ADD with hyperactivity and ADD without hyperactivity. Further disagreement among the association's members brought about the most recent name change—ADHD: some members believed that ADD could not exist without

hyperactivity; others insisted there were children with ADD who had no excessive motor activity. The compromise, in 1987, was the term *attention-deficit hyperactive disorder* (ADHD) accompanied by a list of behaviors intended to make it clear that hyperactivity did not necessarily coexist with ADHD.

Current attempt at defining ADHD.   Following is a list of symptoms adapted from the APA's 1987 diagnostic guidelines, describing the child with ADHD as one who:

1. Often fidgets or squirms about when seated.
2. Has difficulty staying seated when expected to do so.
3. Is easily distracted.
4. Has difficulty waiting for a turn.
5. Often calls out answers, even before the entire question has been asked.
6. Has trouble following through on instructions and directions (not due to noncompliance or lack of understanding).
7. Has difficulty staying with a task, at work and at play.
8. Shifts from one activity to another, seldom completing a task.
9. Seems unable to play quietly.
10. Talks excessively.
11. Frequently interrupts or intrudes.
12. Seldom listens attentively.
13. Is disorganized: loses assignments, pencils, toys.
14. Often seems unaware of consequences and so engages in potentially dangerous behavior such as crossing the street without looking for cars.

The American Psychiatric Association (1987) prefaces this list with the following statement:

In order to be considered as having ADHD, a child must exhibit eight or more of these behaviors at considerably greater frequency than observed for most other people of the same mental age. Further, the disturbance must have been ongoing for at least 6 months and must have begun before the age of 7. Incidence appears to be in the range of 3 percent to 5 percent of the population. Note that some of the behaviors are specific to hyperactivity, some to impulsivity, some to inattention (pp. 52–53).

Is it any wonder there is so much confusion in diagnosing these children? To complicate the matter further, many of the behaviors listed above also characterize young children who appear to be at risk for learning disabilities.

Causes of ADHD. Research has yet to reveal a specific cause of ADHD. Several hypotheses have been offered, one or two of which are backed up by fairly sound evidence. One is the possible role of genetic transmission. Bee (1992) reports a recent study in which one-fourth of the ADHD subjects had parents with a history of hyperactivity. Studies of twins also show possible genetic implications. Among identical twins, both are more likely to have hyperactivity which is not the case among fraternal twins. (Deutsch and Kinsbourne 1991). Researchers continue to work on the brain and its various functions, or misfunctions, to explain ADHD. A correlation has been found also between ADHD and a mother's smoking or drug and alcohol usage during pregnancy.

Intervention strategies. The most effective approaches to helping children diagnosed as having ADHD are medication and behavior management, often in combination. We will talk first about medication.

Medication. In assessing highly active children, it is argued that distinctions should be made between (1) the child whose high activity level is truly **organic**, and (2) the run-of-the-mill overly active child. The reason for making the distinction is that some children in the organic group may benefit from prescription drugs such as Ritalin or Dexedrine (but only if there is indisputable evidence of an organic disorder). However, the medication may have undesirable side effects, perhaps weight loss, insomnia, or increased blood pressure.

It should be noted that medication has been ineffective in treating one-quarter or more of children with ADHD. In addition, 4- and 5-year-olds do not show the improvement that older children do when on the drug. Younger children often experience an increase in behaviors such as clinging and withdrawing that could interfere with their social development. (Campbell 1985). Finally, even when there is improvement in activity level, the effects are short-term.

Medication brings no lasting benefit and can set up negative consequences for the child especially if parents and teachers inquire "Have you taken your medicine?" whenever the child is disruptive. According to Reeves (1990) this kind of question, associated directly with good and bad behavior, can instill the idea in the child that she or he really is not responsible for the behavior. As an aside, it is sometimes parents and teachers who come to rely on the medication; in other words, they may become "addicted" to having the child on medication because the child is much less troublesome when medicated.

Special Diets. Special diets should be viewed with skepticism. The controversial Feingold diet, for example, (introduced during the 1970s) linked artificial food coloring and food additives with hyperactivity. Dr. Feingold (1975) asserted that many children labeled as hyperactive would improve if synthetic colors, flavors, and natural **salicylates** were removed from their diets. Studies investigating his claims found no clinically significant differences between untreated groups of children and those on the diet (Conners 1980). True, no harm can come of feeding children foods that are nutritious and additive free. However, even if a curative diet is nutritious (and some are not), looking for a diet to cure a behavior disorder often results in ignoring basic problems that require quite different treatment (Worthington et al. 1978).

Behavior Management. Drugs and special diets do not teach; every intervention program must be accompanied by individually designed behavior management strategies. Landau and Mc Aninch (1993) point out that much of the feedback that children with ADHD get from parents and teachers and peers is in the form of complaints or reprimands; therefore, the use of rewards for appropriate behaviors (gradually removed as the child learns more acceptable behaviors), is particularly helpful. "Rewarding positive behaviors thus not only encourages the child to continue behaving well but also provides the child with desperately needed success, thereby building self-esteem (p. 55).

Behavioral procedures are discussed throughout the text with special emphasis on hyperactivity in Unit

19. The section that follows, on learning disabilities also applies, especially with children who are diagnosed as having ADHD without hyperactivity. However, the starting point always, regardless of the situation, is for teachers to examine the learning environment (Unit 14) to make sure an appropriate match exists between the environment and the child. To quote from Landau and Mc Aninch once again:

> children with ADHD benefit from the same environments that all children do; thus, designing classrooms appropriate for the child's development is an important step toward managing the behavior of a child with ADHD (p. 53).

Finally, it seems worthwhile to quote the *Young Children* Editor's note on the Landau and McAninch article: "Most children who are diagnosed by competent mental health professionals as having attention-deficit hyperactivity disorder, do; but as early childhood educators, we must always ensure that our classrooms are developmentally appropriate and that children are not being inappropriately labeled because our classroom is inappropriate" (p. 49).

LEARNING DISABILITIES

Children with learning disabilities have many characteristics in common, yet there are many differences among them, too. In varying degrees and in varying combinations, learning disorders are said to include:

Constant motion and purposeless activity
Poor perceptual motor skills
Low tolerance for frustration
Frequent mood swings
Poor coordination, both large and fine motor
Distractibility, short attention span
Poor auditory and visual memory
A variety of language deficits

It is obvious that learning disabilities encompass a wide range of disorders. Efforts at clinical classification are ongoing. Some text books discuss learning disabilities in conjunction with attention deficit disorders. In others, learning disabilities may be grouped

Fine motor control tends to be faulty in children suspected of having a future learning disability.

with cognitive disorders or impaired mental functioning. Other classifications are motor dysfunction and impaired motor planning. In this text, learning disabilities will be discussed in a separate category. The decision is based on the extensive overlap of learning disabilities with other disorders and developmental problems. Providing a separate discussion may serve to clarify some of the issues. Nevertheless, the overlaps remain confusingly evident in the sections that follow.

Learning Disabilities Defined.   *What is a learning disability?* Two answers come immediately to mind: the first, it is many things; the second, many other things it is not. The formal definition from PL 94-142 elaborates on this confusion by describing learning disabilities as:

> a disorder in one or more of the basic psychological processes involved in understanding or in using language, spoken or written, which may manifest itself in the imperfect ability to listen, think, speak, write, spell or do mathematical calculations. The term includes conditions such as perceptual handicaps, brain injury, minimum brain dysfunction, **dyslexia**, and developmental **aphasia**. The term does not include children who have learning problems which are primarily the result of visual, hearing, or motor handicaps, of mental retardation, of emotional disturbance, or of environmental, cultural, or economic disadvantage.

This definition often is referred to as either a definition by exclusion or as a *residual* diagnosis. It states clearly that a learning disability is *not* the result of:

Visual, hearing, or motor handicaps
Mental retardation
Emotional disturbance
Environmental, cultural, or economic disadvantage
Second language learning

Thus, we can say what a learning disability is *not*; what we cannot say is what it *is*. The confusion and indecision is not for lack of research. During the past 30 to 35 years, hundreds upon hundreds of studies have been conducted. Competent researchers in the field of psychology, neurology, education, and educational psychology have attempted to come up with definitive answers to the elusive question of how to define (and diagnose) learning disabilities. There is a sad kind of humor in Farnham-Diggory's statement (1986): "We are trying to find out what's wrong with children whom we won't be able to accurately identify until after we know what's wrong with them" (p. 155).

It is especially important to remember that students who are bilingual or learning English as a second language should not be categorized as having a learning disability. It is important to determine a child's competence in his or her home language, even if it is different than the language spoken at school.

The federal definition of learning disabilities raises several issues. Two of these may be especially relevant to early childhood education. One is the issue of the *disadvantaged*, the other, academic performance as a diagnostic measure.

Nondisadvantaged ruling. The legislative definition of learning disabilities automatically excludes children who are subject to environmental and economic disadvantage. Under the existing ruling, children from poverty sectors of our society are not eligible to participate in programs funded for remediation of learning disabilities. As a result, according to Thurman and Widerstrom (1990), "learning disabilities are restricted primarily to white, middle-class, mostly suburban children. Children from lower socioeconomic backgrounds do not quality for this label and tend to be labeled mentally retarded, with its more negative connotations" (p. 78). This issue may or may not create a problem at the preschool level. However, it is sure to have a negative impact, once a child gets into the primary grades.

Academic ruling. As described in the formal definition, learning disabilities are related primarily to academic performance: "the imperfect ability to listen, think, speak, read, write, spell, or do mathematical calculations." Because most early childhood educators consider it developmentally inappropriate for preschool age children to be spending their school hours in such pursuits, should young children ever be considered learning disabled? "No," seems to be the logical response; yet, not all teachers are comfortable with that, and for good reason. Many young children show maladaptive behaviors associated with learning disabilities in older children. They may be distractable, easily frustrated, excessively active, or poorly coordinated. These behaviors already are interfering with their everyday learning activities in a variety of ways. A number of early childhood educators believe it is in children's best interest to deal with these troubling behaviors during the preschool years, before they worsen and compound the child's problems.

Predicting learning disability. Is it possible that certain behaviors in a young child may be predictors of subsequent trouble with academic tasks? The answer seems to be "Yes," as long as it is understood that the judgment is based on *hunch* and educated guess work. Teachers of young children frequently spot a child whose behaviors appear to put him or her *at-risk* for learning disabilities and perhaps, later academic problems. Is it possible that these worrisome behaviors can be eliminated, or at least reduced, before they have a serious impact on later academic performance? Again, the answer seems to be "Yes." During the past several years, early identification of potential learning disabled young children has gained strong support. Child developmentalists, parents, and other disciplines such as medicine and psychology believe that many learning, social–emotional, and educational problems can be prevented or remediated if identification and intervention are provided before the child enters school.

Caution is necessary in identifying young children at potential risk for later learning disabilities. The first step is observation of the child in a number of activities. The next step is matching the observed performance to performance expectancies in all areas of development. It must be remembered that all young children are different, and all have much development yet to come. Another point is that young children often demonstrate marked differences or delays that are nevertheless within a normal range of development. These are some of the reasons for considering learning disabilities an inappropriate diagnosis for a young child. In most instances, it is more beneficial to the child to view early problems as developmental deviations calling for learning experiences that meet individual needs. Such a decision also is a more economical use of professional energy than trying to decide whether to pin (or not to pin) the label learning disabled on a child.

Prerequisite skills.   A cue in older preschool children that learning problems may lie ahead is a lack of what are sometimes called *readiness* or *prerequisite* skills. As described in Unit 11, these are skills thought to be necessary to academic success once the child enters grade school. However, simply waiting for the *unready* child to become *ready* rarely helps the child. Readiness comes through experience, learning, and the opportunity to practice and master developmental skills. What follows are examples of particular deviations or delays in various areas of development, thought to be related to potential learning disabilities.

Sensory-motor difficulties (gross motor).   Many developmentalists, with Piaget in the lead, theorize that early learning is sensory-motor based. Children that teachers express concern about (in terms of future academic performance) invariably show some kind of sensory-motor problems. In addition, they often show generalized delay in reaching basic motor milestones and exhibit one or more of the following characteristics:

- *Imperfect body control* resulting in poorly coordinated or jerky movements; trouble with running, throwing, catching, hopping, or kicking.

- *Poor balance* that may cause the child to fall off play equipment, fall down, fall into furnishings or other people. (Inability to walk a balance beam may be a symptom in a kindergarten or first grade child.)

- *Uncertain bilateral and cross-lateral movements* are often a sign of future problems with academic tasks. The child with a bilateral problem may not be able to use both arms in synchrony as children do when catching a ball or jumping off a wall. Or a child may not use opposite legs and arms in opposing harmony (cross-laterality) as seen in agile children climbing to the top of a jungle gym.

- *Inability to cross body midline* has long been viewed as a possible predictor of future academic difficulty. In such cases the child has trouble using the right hand to work on a task where any part of the task lies to the left of the midpoint of the child's body or vision. The same holds true of the left hand and the right-side focus. A common example is a child painting on a large piece of paper at the easel. The child transfers the brush from the right hand to the left when painting on the left half of the paper and back again, when painting on the right.

- *Faulty spatial orientation* interferes with children's ability to understand where they are in space, in relationship to their physical surroundings. For example, a child may walk into a wall; poor orientation interferes with the child perceiving the wall as

Imperfect perceptual motor skills are one characteristic of a possible learning disability.

being *right there*. Or the child may gear up for a mighty jump only to land with frightening force because the ground was much closer than the height the child had anticipated. Putting clothes on wrong-side-up or backward, or having difficulty going up and down stairs, also may indicate problems with spatial orientation.

Sensory-motor difficulties (fine motor).   Problems in buttoning, lacing, snapping, cutting, pasting, and stringing beads are characteristics of older preschool children thought to be at future academic risk. Often these children are unable to draw a straight line or copy simple shapes like a circle, cross or square. When they manage to draw a crude imitation, the circle is seldom closed, the corners on the square are rounded or irregular, and the cross is crossed far off center. Tasks of this kind and others, like cutting with scissors, are virtually impossible for these children to master without extensive training and practice.

Perseveration (repeating the same act over and over, seemingly endlessly) is typical of many children who seem likely to develop a future learning disorder. These children appear unable to stop what they are doing. A child may scrub back and forth, with the same crayon, or draw the same shape, minutes at a time, until stopped by a teacher or parent. Some children chant the same words or make the same hand gestures repeatedly until someone succeeds in diverting them to something else. Even when a change is accomplished, there may be carry over from the preceding activity. For example, the above mentioned child may have been moved into block play. Here the back and forth scrubbing continues on the floor, with the child using a block rather than a crayon to make the back and forth motions.

Cognitive disorders.   Trouble in organizing thoughts and processing information with logic is characteristic of many young children with potential learning disabilities. They tend to operate only in the *here and now* with little or no ability to deal with any kind of abstract thought or events. While concrete thinking is characteristic of young children, most older preschoolers are able to deal with a certain amount of abstraction. For example, it is the rare 4- or 5-year-old

who cannot relay a little information about the pet at home or the new swing set in their back yard.

Cognitively disorganized children also may have trouble carrying out simple directions or remembering what it was they were supposed to do, even while they are working on the task. Trouble in generalizing from one event to another is common, too. A rule about no running indoors may not generalize to no running in the classroom, or in the halls, or in the library, even though all are indoors within the same building. Especially frustrating for adults is that the same mistakes are made again and again, simply because there is no carryover from one event to the next.

Visual perception problems.   The ability to interpret what is seen is one definition of visual perception. A problem in visual perception has nothing to do with blindness or impaired vision. In other words, there is no physical problem. Instead, the problem lies with how the child's processing mechanism handles the information that comes in visually. Various aspects of perceptual motor skills were described in Unit 6; here the focus will be on other aspects related specifically to learning disabilities, where the problems take several forms.

- *Visual discrimination* is the ability to look at objects or pictures and note how they are alike and how they are different. Children with visual discrimination problems may have trouble sorting objects according to color, size, or shape. They may not be able to match lotto pictures, copy block designs, or tell the difference between the smiling and the frowning clown pictures. Often they can be seen trying to fit a large object into too small an opening or container.

- *Visual orientation* is related to spatial orientation. The child may recognize three-dimensional objects such as a head of lettuce, a cap, or a paintbrush but not recognize the same items in two-dimensional pictures. Another example of visual disorientation is recognizing objects in their normal or upright positions but failing to recognize them when they are turned over or lying sideways. One child insisted an overturned wooden armchair was a cage; the moment it was turned right-side-up, he labelled it as a chair. Even when the chair was turned over while he watched, he insisted it was a cage the moment it was turned on its side.

- *Visual memory* is remembering what was just seen, at least for a few seconds. Children with visual memory problems may not remember the name of the animal on their card, for example, even though the picture has been face down for only a moment. Or, in the familiar take-away game, they cannot recall what was removed even though there were only three or four articles on the tray when it was presented just a moment before.

- *Visual tracking* is skill in following objects visually. Children with tracking problems may have trouble keeping an eye on the ball, following the flight of a bird, buttoning buttons in order from top to bottom. Visual tracking is likely to be associated with reading skills in that reading requires systematic eye movements from left to right and top to bottom.

- *Visual motor integration* is a skill that can also be thought of as eye–hand coordination. Children with these kinds of problems may have trouble with almost every motor task that requires vision; fitting appropriately shaped pieces into a puzzle box, cutting on the line, drawing around a form, or tracing a simple shape. It is as if the child's hands cannot do what the eyes say needs to be done.

- *Auditory perception problems.* Many young children who seem to be candidates for future learning disabilities have trouble processing (making sense of) what they hear. Again, this is not a physical problem; deafness or being hard-of-hearing is not the cause of the child's problems. Basically, it is the inability to tell the difference between sounds; *hat* and *mat* may sound the same to these children; rhyming games are beyond them. Often, they cannot tell the difference between high and low musical tones, especially as the range lessens. Localization of sound is usually a problem, too. The child may have to look in two or three directions when trying to locate a whistler or a barking dog.

Language deviations. Children at-risk for learning disabilities frequently have trouble with receptive or expressive language, or both. Acquiring the more advanced grammatical forms and the ability to formulate organized sentences tends to come considerably later than for most children. While vocabulary is not necessarily more limited, trouble can arise, for example, when the child tries to call up a well-known word to describe a familiar concept. Carrying out directions that include common prepositions such as *in, on, under*, and *over* is often baffling. If the teacher says to put the block *on top of the box*, a child may look at the teacher questioningly while putting the object *in* the box. Many of these children have trouble repeating short sentences, rhymes and directions. In addition, they often have difficulty imitating sounds, gestures, body movements, facial expressions, and other forms of nonverbal communication.

Deficit social skills. Children who appear to have the potential for later learning disabilities tend to have more than their share of social problems. They may be bullying or aggressive, withdrawn, or overly dependent. Their behavior often confuses other children and so they have trouble making friends. When they do succeed in forming a friendship they tend to have difficulty keeping it. Sometimes the child puts too

Poor social skills often accompany learning problems.

many demands on the friend, or has such inadequate play skills that the friend loses interest. Also, their impulsiveness may cause them to say and do inappropriate things; they may not foresee the possibility of negative consequences such as hurt feelings or the unintentional destruction of a friend's favorite toy. When a child loses two or three friends (for reasons the child neither understands nor seems able to change) feelings of rejection are likely to follow. Rejection increases frustration, a sense of incompetence, and low self-esteem. These feelings, in turn, lead to a tendency to break into tears at the slightest provocation, to strike out, or to withdraw even more.

Program Considerations.   In concluding this section on possible learning disabilities in young children, one concept bears repeating: Characteristics associated with learning disabilities can be observed in all young children, at one time or another. Is there a preschool teacher anywhere who has not watched a child do a lovely painting only to see it overlayed from edge to edge and top to bottom with endless coats of paint? The teacher may mourn the loss of the painting (having mentally earmarked it for display at the parent meeting) but this once-in-awhile behavior is no cause for concern. As noted before, in connection with *all* developmental problems, it is a matter of degree: Are the behaviors happening excessively? Do they interfere with the child's development and general well being? Age, too, must be a consideration. It is always a warning sign when a problem behavior is extreme *and* persists significantly beyond appropriate age levels.

In working with children whose behaviors seem predictive of future learning disabilities, careful reexamination of the learning environment is essential (Unit 14). A thorough review of effective teaching strategies also is essential. These strategies have been described throughout the text in regard to various developmental issues. Many of the strategies have special relevance to working with preschool children who are at-risk for future school success. They include the following reminders:

- Be consistent in the use of positive reinforcement to increase behaviors that facilitate the child's development, thereby decreasing behaviors that interfere.
- Provide the child with encouragement and descriptive praise for each step forward, regardless of how small.
- Provide learning activities that support the child's home language and culture.
- Remember that every child has strengths, does good things; concentrate attention on these rather than on the child's weaknesses and misbehaviors.
- Use task analysis to teach whatever skills the child is having trouble with, whether learning to imitate, to focus attention, to say *NO* instead of hitting, or any other skill or behavior.
- Give directions one at a time and allow adequate time for the child to comply. Verify the child's understanding of the request; rehearse (walk the child through) the required response as often as necessary.
- Teach new concepts and skills in short sessions with concrete materials that allow a child to use several sensory modalities: seeing, hearing, and manipulating.
- Be patient. Children with learning problems may have to be told or shown many times in many

Provide lots of encouragement and rejoice in a child's strength.

different ways how to accomplish a simple task. Do not expect learning to generalize from one situation to another. Each situation seems new to the child.

- Help parents understand that their child is not being difficult or inattentive on purpose. Tell them of their child's accomplishments, no matter how small. To enhance the child's self-esteem, describe his or her accomplishments to the parent, in the presence of the child, whenever possible.

SUMMARY

Teachers of young children may encounter a number of problems related to anxiety. These include what is often referred to as *stranger anxiety*, as well as excessive dependency on adults or general withdrawal from social contacts. Other problems may be eating nonedible substances of which lead-based paint flakes are likely to pose the greatest risk. Mental retardation (even death) may follow excessive eating of this toxic substance. Soiling and wetting episodes that continue long past the expected age range for children to be reliably toilet trained may also be of concern.

Autism, schizophrenia, and phobias are sometimes classified as *pervasive developmental disorders*. Children with autism and phobias often are enrolled in an inclusive preschool; seldom, however, are early childhood teachers called upon to work with children diagnosed as schizophrenic. This disorder develops in later childhood or early youth. Children with autism are not likely to be enrolled in an inclusive preschool program until they have begun to respond to therapeutic treatment.

Learning disabilities are classified under a variety of headings, depending on the researcher's, the clinician's, or the teacher's theoretical background. In this text, the disorder was discussed as a separate classification in an effort to promote greater understanding. Confusion persists, nevertheless, due in part to the legislative definition which rules out poverty or other social disadvantage as a causative factor. Further confusion relates to the definition of learning disabilities as being specific to reading, writing, or math. For early childhood educators, this raises a number of questions. For example, is it ever appropriate to diagnose a preschool-age child as learning disabled? If not, what about the many behaviors (distractability, short attention span, visual perception problems, and many others) in some preschool children that resemble the behaviors of older children having serious problems with academic tasks? Is it not important to deal with these nonacademic behavior disorders in the early years, before they become greater problems that are likely to have a negative impact on subsequent academic learning? The answer seems to be *yes* and the question then becomes *How?* Strategies for teaching young children with all kinds of behavior disorders and potential learning disabilities are found throughout the unit as well as summarized at the end.

Throughout this unit runs a cautionary theme: behavior problems of every type are common among young children. Every child exhibits a number of them during the developmental years. It is only when problems begin to become excessive, to interfere with a child's developmental progress, that they are of great concern. Even then, to prematurely label or classify a young child who has so much development yet to come, often does the child a grave injustice. It is not how a child is classified, but how the child is cared for and taught, as an individual, that is the important issue in working with all kinds of behavior and learning problems in young children.

STUDENT ACTIVITIES

1. Observe an early childhood classroom for one hour. Make brief anecdotal notes related to episodes of children showing overdependency on adults, unrealistic fear, or avoidance of social contacts. Discuss these with the teacher to see if your recorded behaviors are characteristic of the children you observed.
2. At the close of the preceding observation, ask the teacher which child (or children) might be considered a potential candidate for academic learning disabilities. On a return observation, select one of these children. For 45 minutes, record every episode of behavior described in the text as possible forerunners of later academic problems. Take particular note of what seemed to trigger the behavior and what the teachers did immediately afterward.
3. Analyze the preceding record to see if there are recurring patterns or particular behaviors that interfere with learning that were repeated frequently. Assume you are the child's teacher. Draw up a set of guidelines that might be possible ways to work with the child.
4. Select any one of the visual perception problems described in the text. Design a learning activity for a one-to-one tutorial situation that would give a child practice in developing the skill, or in overcoming the deficit. Adapt the same activity to a classroom game format that would be fun for normally developing children while giving the impaired child opportunity to learn as part of the group.

REVIEW QUESTIONS

A. *Define the following terms:*
   1. Pica
   2. Enuresis
   3. Food jag
   4. Phobia
   5. Perseveration
   6. Echolalia
   7. Respite care
   8. Conduct disorder
   9. ADHD
   10. Pervasive developmental disorder

B. *True or False*
   T F   1. The onset of autism is before 36 months.
   T F   2. When a child has trouble separating from parents at the childcare center, parents should slip away as soon as a teacher can divert the child's attention.
   T F   3. Both too much and too little teacher attention can worsen a child's dependency problems.
   T F   4. Withdrawn children are less likely to be overlooked than acting-out children.
   T F   5. Most young children taste, even eat, nonfood substances at times.
   T F   6. Children with learning disabilities never come from economically disadvantaged homes.
   T F   7. Hallucinations often occur among individuals diagnosed as schizophrenic.
   T F   8. Speaking developmentally, learning disabilities and mental retardation mean essentially the same thing.
   T F   9. Auditory perception problems are identified by the degree of deafness.
   T F 10. Visual motor integration and eye-hand coordination mean essentially the same thing.

C. *Lists*
   1. List three questions a teacher might ask in deciding what observations to make of a child described as having social impairments.
   2. List four characteristics of autism in very young children.
   3. List six characteristics found among young children with possible learning disabilities.
   4. List four conditions that do not apply to children who are diagnosed as learning disabled.
   5. List five large motor problems found among children with sensory-motor difficulties.
   6. List three common language deviations that may indicate a learning disability.
   7. List seven tips for teachers who work with young children who appear to be at-risk for learning disabilities.

REFERENCES

Allen, K.E., and Goetz, E.M. (1982). *Early childhood education: Special problems, special solutions.* Rockville, MD: Aspen Systems.

Allen, K.E., and Hart, B. (1984). *The early years: Arrangements for learning.* Englewood Cliffs, NJ: Prentice Hall.

American Psychiatric Association. (1987). *Diagnostic and statistical manual of mental disorders.* Washington D.C.: American Psychiatric Association.

Azrin, N.H., and Foxx, R.M. (1971). *Toilet training in less than a day.* New York: Simon & Schuster.

Bates, J.E., Bales, K., Bennett, D.S., Ridge, B., and Brown, M.M. (1991). Origins of externalizing behavior problems at 8 years of age. In D.J. Peppler and K.H. Rubin (Eds.), *The development and treatment of childhood aggression*, 120. Hillsdale, NJ: Erlbaum.

Batshaw, M.L. and Perret, Y.M. (1981). *Children with handicaps: A medical primer.* Baltimore: Brookes.

Bee, H. (1992). *The developing child.* New York: Harper-Collins.

Campbell, S.B. (1985). Hyperactivity in preschoolers: Correlates and prognostic implications. *Clinical Psychology Review* 5, 405–428.

Coleman, M. (1989). Young children with autism or autistic-like behavior. *Infants and Young Children* 1:4, 22–31.

Conners, C.K. (1980). *Food additives and hyperactive children.* New York: Plenum Press.

Deutsch, C.K., and Kinsbourne, M. (1990). Genetics and biochemistry in attention deficit disorder. In M. Lewis and S.M. Miller (Eds.). *Handbook of developmental psychopathology.* 93–108. New York: Plenum.

Dodge, K.A. (1990). Developmental psychopathology in children of depressed mothers. *Developmental Psychology*, 26, 3–6.

Farnhan-Diggory, S. (1986). Time, now, for a little serious complexity. In S.J. Ceci (Ed.), *Handbook of cognitive, social, and neuropsychological aspects of learning disability.* Hillsdale, NJ: Erlbaum.

Feingold, B.F. (1975). *Why your child is hyperactive.* New York: Random House.

Fredericks, H.D., Baldwin, V.L., Grove, D.N., and Grove, W.G. (1975). *Toilet training the handicapped child.* Monmouth, OR: Instructional Development Corp.

Harter, S. (1990). Processes underlying adolescent self-concept formation. In R. Montemeyer, G.R. Adams, and T.P. Gullotta (Eds.), *From childhood to adolescence: A transition period?* 205–39. Newbury Park, CA: Sage.

Landau, S., and McAninch, C. (1993). Young children with attention deficits. *Young Children*, May, 49–58.

Maurice, C. (1993). *Let me hear your voice: A family's triumph over autism.* New York: Fawcetts Columbine.

Patterson, G.R., Capaldi, D., and Bank, L. (1991). An early starter model for predicting delinquency. In D.J. Peppler and K.H. Rubin (Eds.), *The development and treatment of childhood aggression* 139–168. Hillsdale, NJ: Erlbaum.

Peterson, N.L. (1987). *Early intervention for handicapped and at-risk children.* Denver: Love Publishing Co.

Reeves, R.R. (1990). ADHD: Facts and Fallacies. *Intervention in School and Clinic.* 26, 70–78.

Rutter, M. (1986). Infantile autism: Assessment, differential diagnosis and treatment. In D. Shaffer, A. Erhardt, and L. Greenhill (Eds.), *A clinical guide to child psychiatry.* New York: Free Press.

Schor, D.P. (1983). Autism. In J.A. Blackman (Ed.). *Medical aspects of developmental disabilities in children birth to three.* Iowa: University of Iowa.

Spodek, B., Saracho, O.N., and Lee, R.C. (1984). *Mainstreaming young children.* Belmont, CA: Wadsworth Publishing Co.

Thompson, R.A., and Lamb, M.E. (1982). Stranger sociality and its relationship to temperament and social experience during the second year of life. *Infant Behavior and Development*, 5, 227–28.

Thurman, S.K. and Widerstrom, A.H. (1990). *Infants and young children with special needs.* Baltimore: Brookes.

Worthington, B.S., Pipes, P.L., and Trahms, C.M. (1978). The pediatric nutritionist. In K.E. Allen, V.A. Holm, and R.L. Schiefelbusch (Eds.), *Early Intervention: A team approach.* Baltimore: University Park Press.

SECTION III
Planning for Inclusion

Unit 9

Partnership With Families

OBJECTIVES

After studying this unit the student will be able to

- define the concept of family uniqueness and explain how this concept affects teachers' practices in early childhood education.
- identify challenges that are common among families of children with developmental disabilities.
- outline the major requirements of the Individualized Family Service Plan (IFSP).
- define the concepts *enabling* and *empowering* as related to families of children with disabilities; explain the social significance of the concepts.
- list five or more ways for teachers to communicate with parents; discuss how the concept of cultural sensitivity affects the method teachers choose.
- draw up a format for holding a conference with the parents of a child with a serious behavior problem; include planning and follow-up.

Family involvement has long been a tradition in early childhood education. With the advent of intervention programs for young children with developmental disabilities, family involvement now is viewed as essential. Contrast this with earlier times when parents were advised, almost routinely, to institutionalize (sometimes at birth) a child with a disability.

Now there is a federal mandate to educate **all** children, and the majority of children with disabilities attend classes in public school buildings. These changes have come about because of changes in the way that society views people with disabilities and as a result of the hard work of parents and advocates for people with disabilities such as The Association for Retarded Citizens (ARC) and the United Cerebral Palsy.

The role of families in the planning, implementation, and evaluation of early childhood special educa-

tion programs has changed dramatically over the past 30 years as early intervention services have moved from a child-centered to a family-centered approach. Turnbull and Turnbull (1988) describe the shift:

> The pendulum has swung in many ways: from viewing parents as part of the problem to viewing them as a primary solution to the problem, from expecting passive roles to expecting active roles, from viewing families as a mother–child dyad to recognizing the presence and needs of all members, and from assigning generalized expectations from the professionals' perspective to allowing for individual priorities defined from each family's perspective (p. 21).

The swinging pendulum finally came to center on the two pieces of federal legislation described in Unit 3: PL 94–142 and PL 99–457. Both laws specifically

Family support is required by PL 99-457.

address family support as a legitimate requirement when providing intervention services for young children with disabilities. "The family dimension of the law emphasized the equal partnership role for parents and outlined certain responsibilities for parents for the purpose of enhancing services to children" (Bailey and Winston 1990). This unit will review the major mandates with special focus on the following issues:

Involvement of families in planning and implementing intervention services and educational programs for infants and young children with developmental problems

Rights and options of parents

Avoidance of professional intrusion into family affairs

Empowerment of the family

Service coordination and the family

Development of **culturally sensitive** early intervention services

As background, various aspects of family life will be touched on starting with the diversity of families in today's society. Having an infant with disabilities and its impact on parents and on family as a whole will be described. The rationale and justification for family involvement will follow, with emphasis on the family

as a system of interactive, reciprocal relationships. Strategies that early childhood teachers engage in when working with parents of children with disabilities will conclude the unit. Throughout primary caregivers will be referred to as parents.

FAMILY PATTERNS AND EXPECTATIONS

The makeup of families, and their expectations regarding the behavior of family members, varies from family to family and culture to culture. The emotional climate within families varies too. Often it is characterized by the way parents interact with each other and their children (not a one-way street, however, as we will see later in the unit).

What Is the Family? Today's families come in all shapes and sizes. Family members may be related by blood or marriage, or may be connected by a commitment to common goals and priorities. Families may be headed by a teenage mother, a single mother, a married couple, a gay or lesbian couple, a single father, an interracial couple, a grandmother providing primary care for children, or any combination of these or other variables. In addition to the parents' biological children, families may include adopted children, foster children, or other relatives who are living with the family. "Family is no longer a unitary concept that describes a specific set of characteristics. Rather, it has become a generic name for a group of individuals who are affiliated with one another" (Lynch and Hanson 1992, p. 288). Families are self-defined units whose members have made a commitment to share their lives.

As early childhood educators we have the privilege and challenge of working with a wide variety of families. The families may vary culturally, ethnically, racially, linguistically, socially, and economically. It is our responsibility to honor the personal choices and values of these families and to invite every family member to be a partner in the early intervention process.

Every family is different. Families may differ in the way they celebrate birthdays, spend leisure time, recognize accomplishment, negotiate conflict and express spirituality. The concept of **family uniqueness** recognizes that every family is a distinct collection of individuals who have come together to create a new whole. Although many families may share similar characteristics, it is important not to assume that these families share common beliefs and practices. For example, not all African–American families share common views on child rearing, or all Jewish families have the same priorities when it comes to early intervention goals, or all families headed by lesbian couples express their spirituality in similar ways. The concept of family uniqueness requires that practitioners learn how to work with families as individuals, how to communicate with families effectively, and how to develop cultural self-awareness to understand the ways our own beliefs influence our work (Harry 1992).

Many of the families with whom we work come from different cultures, speak different languages, and live in a different social environment than the staff members in our programs. These families may have different attitudes and beliefs about child rearing practices and early education. Our challenge as practitioners is to develop early intervention programs that are culturally sensitive and linguistically responsive to all of the children and families in the program (Gonzalez-Mena 1992). One step toward developing culturally sensitive programs is for practitioners to become more culturally competent. Lynch and Hanson (1992) recommend steps that early inter-

ventionists can take toward being more culturally competent.

- Learn more about the families in the community that you serve.
- Work with cultural mediators or guides from the family's culture to learn more about the culture; including interaction styles, child rearing practices, and cultural beliefs about disability.
- Learn words and forms of greetings in the family's language.
- Allow additional time to work with interpreters and be sure to find appropriate interpreters (for example older school-age, siblings are not appropriate interpreters for IEP meetings).
- Use forms of communication that are acceptable and meaningful to the family, for example if the family has limited English proficiency, notes home may not be an effective way to communicate.
- Recognize that the collaboration assumed in family-centered early intervention programs may not be comfortable for families from different cultures.

In addition to the cultural, ethnic, and linguistic diversity represented by the families in most early childhood programs, there are social factors that affect families and add to the diversity of family constellations found in programs. For example, divorce and remarriage continues to be a common occurrence. The majority of divorced men and women remarry. When children are involved, the arrangement is often referred to as **reconstituted** or **blended family**. It is not uncommon for *her* children, *his* children, and *their* children to be living under one roof. Additionally, children may talk about having two mommies or two daddies because of their relationships with their biological parents and their new stepparents by remarriage. Other children may talk about having two mommies or two daddies because their parents are lesbian or gay couples (Wickens 1993). Early childhood teachers must respect a child's family constellation and create a classroom culture that supports all types of diversity.

Another variation is the continuing increase in dual career families and of mothers of young children in the workforce. Babysitters (and nannies among the more affluent) often are viewed as a regular part of the child's family. Children also may grow up in extended families where combinations of parents, grandparents, aunts, uncles, and cousins live in the same household. Extended family arrangements also may include living with friends. More and more children attending early childhood program are homeless, or living in transitional housing or emergency shelters (Klein, Bittel, and Molnar 1993). These children are at increased risk for disabilities and pose special challenges for early childhood educators. Finally, children are the poorest Americans and are living in poverty in increasing numbers. These conditions can be stressful for parents and children, and early childhood teachers should take care to offer support and be sensitive of the situation.

Families of Children with Disabilities. Whatever the makeup of a family, those with children with disabilities will feel the impact on family life. Some families say they become more closely drawn together as they learn to adapt to a child's disability, and that the child's disability has enhanced the existing strengths of their family (Turnbull and Turnbull 1993). Others are less able to cope; still others are pulled apart. At one point it was thought that the divorce rate was greatly increased among families with a child with disabilities. Further studies (Wikler, Haack and Intagliate 1984) deny this; it appears that there are no differences in divorce rate when socioeconomic factors are held constant.

Although, when we talk about families, we usually mean parents, it is important to consider the needs of other family members in adapting to a child with disabilities. Often grandparents have a very difficult time accepting and understanding a child's disability (Meyer and Vadasy 1986). Although early childhood teachers may have limited contact with grandparents, they may serve as a support and resource for parents who are dealing with a difficult reaction from their parents or in-laws.

Another important group of family members that must be considered are siblings. Siblings will have a lifelong relationship with their brother or sister with a disability, and can benefit from special support and honest information about the disability. Meyer and

Grandparents often are major caregivers in a child's family.

Vadasy (1994) describe a program called Sibshops that provide siblings with opportunities for peer support. Sibshops allow school-aged siblings of children with disabilities to participate in recreational activities and share information and coping strategies to deal with the unusual concerns and special opportunities associated with having a sibling with a disability.

Family Abuse and the Child with Disabilities. Evidence does exist that children with disabilities tend to be the target of abuse in some families (National Center on Child Abuse and Neglect 1980). One explanation is that infants and young children with developmental disabilities, through no fault of their own, often behave in ways that upset their parents. For example, many infants who have impairments have high-pitched crying that seems to go on night and day. Such crying appears to jeopardize healthy parent–infant interactions (Frodi and Senchak 1990). Other infant behaviors can have adverse effects, too. Consider these examples:

Difficulty with feeding where the parent gets food into the child only after much time and effort and then, repeatedly, the child fails to keep it down; lack of responsiveness, as seen in sensory impaired infants, or low-birth-weight or very sick infants. In many instances, it is difficult to tell whether the child's disability and resulting behaviors led to parental abuse or if the abuse caused the child's disability.

Peterson (1987) described this dilemma: ". . . a normal child living in a stressful environment with an abuse-prone parent can become handicapped as a result of injury from abuse. On the other hand, a family with a handicapped child and without adequate support systems may incur enough stress to cause parents without abusive tendencies to abuse the child. In either case, awareness of the potential problem of child abuse is crucial for educators who deal with young handicapped children and their families (p. 424).

Adequate support systems are a key factor in ensuring the well-being of families of developmentally disabled children (Janko 1994). Support is often taken for granted when a family has regular income, comprehensive health insurance, adequate housing, and caring family and friends. Even so, additional support is usually required, and soon, when the newborn infant has serious developmental problems. Families do not plan to have a child with a disability. They expect a healthy infant who will grow slowly but surely into an independent and productive adult. From the start, parents of children with disabilities are faced with disappointments and adjustments. These will affect every member of the family and every aspect of the family's life together.

Family Adjustment.   Grief is the usual reaction when parents first realize they have an infant with a disability. (Even when an older youngster comes to be diagnosed as having a disabling condition, grieving is the normal response of most parents.) It is almost as if their child had died. In a way, it is so; the perfect baby or child that parents had planned for and expected will never be. In the process of grieving, parents may become angry, depressed, or overcome with unfounded guilt reactions. Or, they may deny that anything is wrong, regardless of the child's appearance or behavior. These reactions are normal and are expected. At the same time, parents need help in working through these feelings. They need to begin the process of adapting to the realities of caring for a child with a

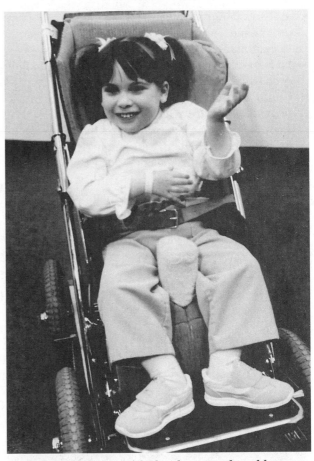

Families of children with developmental problems are called upon to make many adjustments.

disability. Almost immediately, they will have to begin to make urgent decisions and solve complicated problems affecting every member of the family. These might include:

- Expensive (and perhaps painful or life-threatening) medical treatment, surgery, hospitalization that may occur repeatedly and for extended periods
- Heavy expenses and financial burdens other than medical such as special foods and equipment
- Frightening and energy-draining crises, often recurring, as when the child stops breathing, turns blue, or has a major convulsion

- Transportation problems, babysitting needs for the other children, time away from jobs to get the child to consultation and treatment appointments
- Lack of affordable child care for families with children who have developmental disabilities
- Continuous day and night demands on parents to provide what are routine caregiving tasks (For example, it may take an hour or more, five to six times during a single day and night, to feed a child with a severe cleft palate condition)
- Constant fatigue, lack of sleep, little or no time to meet the needs of other family members

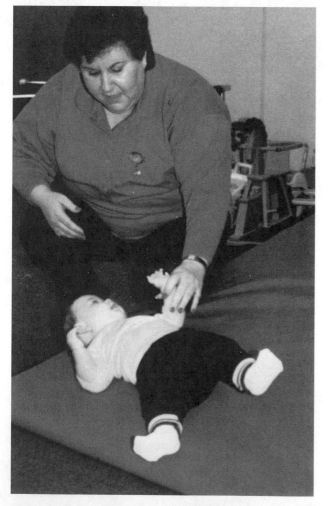

Truly effective early intervention includes parents.

- Little or no opportunity for recreational or leisure activities; difficulty (and additional expense) of locating babysitters who are both qualified and willing to care for a child with a disability, especially if the child has severe problems (medical or behavioral)
- Lack of **respite care** options
- Jealousy or feelings of rejection among brothers and sisters who may feel the special child gets *all* the family's attention and resources
- Marital problems arising from finances, fatigue, differences about management of the child's disability, feelings of rejection by husband (or wife) that they are being passed over in favor of the child
- Accessing early intervention services that are inclusive, community-based, family-centered, and meet all of the unique needs of the child with disabilities

When these problems are further compounded by social isolation and poverty, the subsequent development of a child with a disability as well as the growth and well-being of the rest of the family are doubly jeopardized.

Such problems suggest how nearly impossible it would be to provide effective intervention for a young child without including the child's family. It was Bronfenbrenner (1979) who convinced developmentalists of the range of environmental (and family) influences on a young child's development. The mother–child relationship, once thought to be the major determining factor, has proven to be but one of many. Innumerable strands of transactional relationships, both cultural and personal, are at work (Sameroff and Chandler 1975). They form the system, or *ecological niche*, into which the child is born and reared. A child's ability to cope or adapt depends on understanding his or her larger social system made up of family function, support of friends and community, and cultural beliefs.

INDIVIDUALIZED FAMILY SERVICE PLAN

The centrality of the family in providing effective early intervention services is formally recognized in PL 99–457 (the 1986 amendment to PL 94–142, the Education for All Handicapped Children Act, now called IDEA, the Individuals with Disabilities Education Act). The law broadened the services for children 3 to 5 years of age and developed a **discretionary program** (Part H) to provide services for children birth to 3 years old. Part H requires development of an Individualized Family Service Plan (IFSP) for each infant or toddler receiving early intervention services. The purpose of the IFSP is for family members and professionals to work together to identify priorities, resources, and concerns. Although similar to an Individualized Education Plan (IEP), the planning document used for children older than 3, an IFSP is a more interactive, dynamic, family-friendly document.

IFSP Requirements.   The purpose of the IFSP is to identify and organize resources to support families in rearing children who have developmental disabilities. Major stipulations include:

1. Help is to be provided in ways that meet the unique needs of each child and family.
2. The IFSP is to be an ongoing process that supports but *does not take the place* of parents' natural, caregiving roles.
3. A major function of the IFSP is to preserve the principle that infants and toddlers are best served within the family.

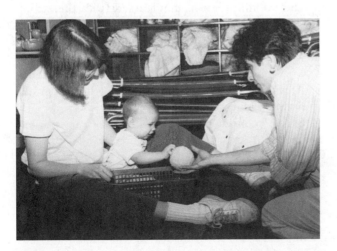

By law, the infant is to receive an interdisciplinary assessment.

4. Family-centered as well as child-centered services are to be provided through an interdisciplinary team approach.
5. Family members are to be essential participants on the team.
6. A service coordinator is to be appointed to manage services and keep the program moving.
7. Specific steps assuring a smooth transition to the next intervention program are to be described.

Identification of needs.   Once parental consent is obtained, each infant and toddler with special needs is to receive an interdisciplinary assessment (as prescribed in the IEP requirements of PL 94-142; see Unit 10). The purpose of the assessment is to identify the child's competencies and strengths, as well as areas of need. The assessment should look at **functional skills** and the child's ability to adapt to the environment. This process must be family-driven. That is, family members should be involved in every step of the assessment process. Family members are essential in identifying priorities and functional skills. Additionally, the assessment must be conducted in a culturally responsive manner (Barrera 1994). This includes conducting the assessment in the child's native language, that is the language that is spoken in the home; using assessment instruments that are appropriate for that language and culture; and interpreting the findings in a manner that takes cultural norms and practices into consideration.

The family is also asked to voluntarily participate in an interdisciplinary and interactive family assessment. The purpose of the family assessment is to identify the family's strengths and special needs as they relate to enhancing the development of their child. It is important to note that this is a voluntary activity. Family members are invited to be as actively involved as they wish; however, the family's degree of involvement does not affect the child's eligibility for necessary services.

Nonintrusiveness.   Constant care is needed to ensure that families are benefited, rather than weakened or demeaned, by participation in the IFSP process. The law does not give permission for any professional to intrude uninvited into a family's life or lifestyle. Family members are not to be prodded into discussing private or sensitive matters. Information gleaned from professional probing has little or no bearing on the child's problems. The out-of-family perception of a family's needs often misses the mark (Harry 1992). Instead, it is likely to represent the professionals' own biases and values. The entire IFSP process—developing, implementing, and evaluating—must be conducted in a culturally sensitive manner. Thus the law's emphasis on helping families to identify their own needs and to recognize their own abilities. Only when early intervention programs recognize and build on the diverse and unique strengths of each family will the IFSP concept fulfill its promise as a positive force in the lives of handicapped children and their families.

IFSP evaluation.   The IFSP is to be evaluated at least once a year. A review of the IFSP will be forwarded to the family every six months (more often on family request). The purpose of the evaluation and review is to appraise the progress made by the child and family toward the objectives spelled out in the IFSP. If progress is unsatisfactory, program revisions are in order.

Service coordination.   An interdisciplinary team approach to early intervention implies a number of individuals are dealing with the same child and family.

The appointment of the service coordinator and his or her duties are decided by the team.

PL 99-457 requires one particular person, designated as a service coordinator, to be in charge of each case. The service coordinator is often chosen because of professional expertise in relationship to the child's primary problem. The communication specialist might be the service coordinator when the main concern revolves around speech and hearing, the physical therapist when there are troublesome motor delays, and the nutritionist in **failure-to-thrive** cases. In addition to providing clinical skill, the service coordinator needs to be a sensitive listener, a child and family advocate, and a linkage agent (getting families linked to needed services).

The service coordinator is essential to team functioning and family support. Without a liaison or go-between, both the team and the family tend to become confused. There is duplication of efforts (the family may be put through three or four intake interviews, for example), intervention services lose continuity and coherence, and whole programs can fall into chaos and disintegration. Years ago, Meier (1976) described this fragmentation and scattering of services as the *Humpty Dumpty syndrome.*

Generally speaking, the duties of the service coordinator are decided by each team. Assigned tasks might include:

- Coordinating the individual child's assessments and identification of family needs with prescribed services
- Managing team and parent conferences
- Making sure that records are kept up-to-date, paper work gets done, appointments are made (and kept)
- Arranging the child's transition to other programs and providing follow-up services
- Serving continuously as a source of contact, interpretation, and support for the family.

Parents, to the maximum extent possible, are to have the opportunity to select their own service coordinator. In some instances, family choice cannot be an option and a service coordinator must be assigned. A family that feels its needs are not met adequately by the assigned service coordinator must be helped to find a more acceptable one.

Parents as service coordinators. Parents who wish to serve as their own service coordinators should be encouraged and supported in their efforts. The law requires that training be provided in how the system and how the network of back-up services operate (Bailey 1989). Gathering together the necessary resources and assistance should not add to the family's burdens. Instead, the family should reap positive benefits and become stronger and more capable through the process. Learning to take the responsibility for getting needed assistance is seen as one approach to reducing overdependency on the service system.

Program-to-program transition. PL 99-457 requires support for the child and family during transition from one program to another. The hallmark of effective early intervention is the child's graduation into a more advanced program—frequently that program is in a different setting. The transition between programs calls for a special kind of planning and support. The focus of Unit 11 is on planning and implementing transitions.

Enabling and Empowering Families. A major public concern about the Individualized Family Service Plan was that it would promote increased dependency on the early intervention system. It was feared that families would become less able to do for themselves. Out of this public concern grew the major philosophical thrust of the IFSP, the *enabling* and *empowering* of families. Deal, Dunst, and Trivette (1989) suggest the following definitions of the terms:

> Enabling families means creating opportunities for family members to become more competent and self-sustaining with respect to their abilities to mobilize their social networks to get needs met and attain goals.

> Empowering families means carrying out interventions in a manner in which family members acquire a sense of control over their own developmental course as a result of their own efforts to meet needs (p.33).

The intent of the enabling and empowering concepts is to strengthen families without taking away their ability to cope. The IFSP aims to support and build on those things the family already does well. Policymakers believe this can be accomplished by providing families with the information and skills that will enable them to try to solve their own problems and meet their own needs. The service coordinator plays the pivotal role in fostering and overseeing the empowerment of families. "Service coordination may be considered effective only to the extent that families become more capable, competent, and empowered as a result of the help-giving acts" (Dunst and Trivette 1989, p. 99).

THE PARENT–TEACHER PARTNERSHIP

Parents and teachers, necessarily, are partners in the business of children's learning. Parents, however, are the *senior partners*. They bear the ongoing and primary responsibility during the long years of a child's growth and development (many additional years when a child is developmentally disabled or delayed). Numerous research studies describe the benefits of active parent involvement in a child's early intervention program. Without it, children tended to regress or slip back once the program has ended (Simeonsson and Bailey 1990). Parent involvement has two major functions. One, it provides an ongoing reinforcement system that supports the efforts of the program while it is underway. Two, it tends to maintain and elaborate the child's gains after the program ends.

Parents and teachers are partners in children's learning.

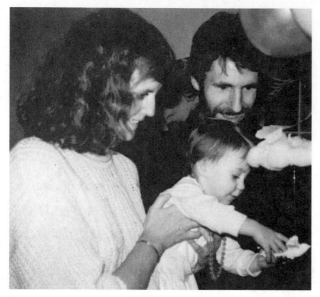

Parents are the major socializing agents.

Rationale for Parent Participation.   Many reasons can be given for encouraging parents' involvement in their child's early education and intervention program:

1. Parents are the major socializing agents for their child, transmitters of cultural values, beliefs, and traditions.
2. Parents know their child better than teachers or clinicians; thus, parents are a source of information available from no one else.
3. Family members can help the child transfer learnings from school to home and neighborhood; only a few hours a day are spent in school, many more hours are spent at home.
4. Consistency of adult expectations can be maintained. Young children become anxious when important adults do not agree on expectations. Confusion, even resistance, may result if, for example, teachers expect a child to put on his or her own coat while parents always do it for the child.
5. Pleasing parents is important to young children in that parents are the source of many pleasant and necessary reinforcers: food, warmth, comfort, outings, playthings, and all else.

6. Children with disabilities acquire developmental skills more quickly when parents learn to participate in home teaching.
7. Involvement in the early intervention program offers parents access to support from other parents and a better perspective on their own child's strengths and needs.

Degree of Participation.   The extent to which parents can be actively involved in their child's program depends on a number of factors:

Work schedule and job constraints
Additional young children at home who need care
Availability of transportation
Parental health (both physical and psychological)
Parental maturity and understanding of the child's needs
Attitudes toward school, teachers, and authority figures
Cultural and linguistic match with the program
Comfort level and perceived competence in the classroom

It is important to recognize that simply *maintaining a child's enrollment in a program is a form of parent involvement.* Lack of active participation does not imply disinterest in the child or the program. Instead, as noted by Barber et al. (1988), it may be a form of energy conservation:

> Family life with a child who has a disability is a marathon rather than a sprint. A crucial aspect of supporting families during the early years is to empower them with coping strategies that can help them to run the full course with their son or daughter and to avoid the trap of investing their energies heavily for a short period of time and then burning out (p. 197).

Communicating with Parents.   Teachers' approach to parents is the same as teachers' approach to children: respect and appreciation for individual differences in terms of culture, values, attitude, and learning style. When mutual understanding can be established between parents and teachers, children are more likely to experience a good learning environment. Two-way communication is the centerpiece of understanding. Talking with—rather than to—parents is the basis for effective communication. Teachers try simultaneously to share knowledge and obtain feedback. They also try to deal with parents' expressed and unexpressed concerns. Unexpressed concerns may be one of the biggest obstacles to communication. With some parents, it may be a long while, for example, before they are able to talk about their child's impairments, or even to recognize openly that a problem exists.

It is good to talk with the parents about how they would like to communicate with the teacher and the school staff. For example, do they prefer phone calls or notes home? If they prefer phone calls, is there a time that is most convenient and when will they have time to give the call their full attention? How often would parents like to hear from classroom staff? Teachers must work with the family to set up expectations for ongoing communication that meets the needs of the family and are sustainable by the staff. When considering how to communicate with the different families in an early childhood classroom, issues of culture, language, and literacy must be taken into consideration. For example, who in the family will be the primary contact? In most cases it is the mother, but this may not be acceptable or practical for some families. If the family is limited-English speaking, is there a member of the classroom staff, for example, a paraprofessional, who speaks their native language? Is it acceptable for this staff member to be their primary contact in the classroom?

Informal exchanges.   A tremendous amount of information can be exchanged during informal encounters. The quick conversations that occur in programs where parents pick up and deliver children are especially fruitful. To take full advantage of these, with as many parents as possible, arrival and departure time should be an extended period (20 to 30 minutes). One teacher is assigned specifically to these program periods. (See daily scheduling in Unit 14.) These brief exchanges often focus on specific issues such as the child's sleep patterns or relaying the physician's reasons for increasing a child's medication. *Mini*-progress reports also can be given; for example,

"Sissie can point to red, yellow, and blue now."
"Jane climbed to the top of the slide all by herself this afternoon."
"Michael hung up his jacket every day this week.

Appreciative comments such as the above, made by teachers to parents, in the presence of the child, are important. Parents come to realize that seemingly small events have developmental significance. Children learn that their accomplishments have merit; otherwise, why would the teacher pass the news on? And why would both of these important adults, parent and teacher, look so pleased? Appreciative comments have another function, too. They serve as models for parents. It helps them learn to put into words their own recognition and appreciation of the child's efforts. Furthermore, positive reporting, within earshot of other parents and children, contributes to both the parents' and child's self-esteem, because the evaluation was made publicly.

Because of its public nature, arrival and departure time are *not* used to discuss concerns about a child, or problems with behavior or learning. Never should these moments be used to talk about anything not suitable for the child to hear, or for other parents and children to hear. If a parent brings up a sensitive issue, the teacher listens and makes a quick note. As soon as possible the teacher promises to telephone the parent to talk it over or to arrange a conference. The teacher makes a point of asking for a specific time to make the call. This is to ensure the child is otherwise occupied. Any serious discussion between a parent and teacher seems to get blown out of proportion in a child's mind if it appears the adults are trying to keep the child from listening.

Parent observations.   Parents must be welcome at any time in all programs for young children. Since parents are the senior partners in their child's development, they have the right to see and question everything that goes on in the classroom. First-hand observations provide one of the best ways of providing indirect parent education. Watching their child interacting with other children and adults, with materials and activities, provides insights that can be obtained in no other way. Against a background of children with similar developmental levels, parents gain a better appreciation of their own child's skills and progress. Ideally, every parent observation is followed by at least a brief discussion with a teacher. If possible, the teacher should be the one who was in the activity area where the parent had observed for the longest period. When a conversation cannot take place on the spot, a follow up telephone call is important. The follow up conversation serves several purposes:

1. Teacher can answer questions a parent may have about what she or he observed; also, teachers can make necessary explanations: why certain play or group situations were handled as they were.
2. Teachers can help parents recognize the positive aspects of their own child's uniqueness and developmental progress.
3. Teachers can describe the appropriateness of individualized curriculum activities in enhancing the child's development and meeting the child's special needs.

Parent observations may be regularly scheduled events or impromptu and spur of the moment. As noted, brief, informal observations occur regularly as parents deliver and call for their children. When a formal observation is planned, it is well for teachers to

Parent observations may be scheduled or impromptu.

provide some type of structure. A clipboard and simple observation form works well. Parents are asked to note the child's activities, playmates, special interests, avoidances, if relevant. Focused observing helps parents note what actually is going on with their child. It is important that parents are made to feel welcome and comfortable in the classroom. Teachers can make a few small changes that may make parents and other visitors feel more welcome. Additionally, it is nice if teachers provide a place for the visitor to sit (preferably in an adult-sized chair) during the observation. Some parents like to visit frequently and like to be involved in classroom activities. Talk with parents beforehand and suggest ways that they can be involved in the classroom, for example, helping with art activities, reading books in the library corner, or working with children at the computer. Other parents like to visit frequently, but prefer to be less actively involved. Often these parents are pleased to help prepare materials needed in the classroom, such as cutting out figures or laminating materials. Talk with parents individually and determine strategies to make their visit to their child's classroom most pleasant and beneficial.

Telephone calls.   Telephone calls help to keep communication going between teachers and parents. When children are bussed and parents work, the telephone may become the chief means of maintaining contact. It is important to keep a log of telephone contacts that every staff member has with the family. These logs can be quite simple, but should note the date and length of the call and the subjects that were discussed. Telephone calls may be used for the same kinds of casual reporting as arrival and departure contacts. Many parents prefer that a convenient day and time of day be arranged in advance so they can plan to have a few minutes to talk freely. When teachers' calls become a regular event, most parents welcome them; a call from school no longer signals trouble. Usually, the focus is on routine matters such as the:

Outcome of a visit to the audiologist
Progress of an illness
Reason for an absence of several days

For children who are not picked up by their own parents, the teacher should telephone to report any unusual happening at school: torn or soiled clothing; a scrape, fall, or rash; or a child's refusal to eat. The teacher tries always to reach the parent *before* the child arrives home. This helps to avoid misunderstandings that tend to occur when messages are relayed from the bus driver or a parent driving the car pool. The advance call also forewarns of unpleasant surprises, difficult for some parents to deal with when caught off guard. Finally, the teacher's call, in advance of the child's arrival, protects the child. Young children often have difficulty explaining why something happened. They themselves may not understand it, may not perceive it accurately, may not have the appropriate words of explanation. If the teacher is first to reach the parent with potentially troublesome news, the parent can release anger or distress on the teacher, rather than the child. In addition, the call allows teachers to try to find out if parents consider it necessary to make changes in the program so as to reduce the likelihood of a recurrence of the incident.

Written notes. If immediate reporting and feedback is not an issue, written notes sent home with the child can be useful. Written notes describing the activities done during the week can be sent home at the end of each week as a nice way to keep parents involved in the classroom. They also help parents to ask their child specific questions about activities rather than broad questions about "What did you do in school today?" Once a relationship has been established between a teacher and parent, a written note often is preferred to a telephone call. Parents can read the note at a convenient time. They are saved the sometimes aggravating interruption of a call. The note may be a duplicated reminder of a meeting or an upcoming event. It may be a request, perhaps for additional clothing to be kept at school. It may be a report of an exciting breakthrough: "Lauren laced his shoes all by himself today." Parents appreciate a teacher's personalized recognition of their child, even in the form of a one-liner such as the report on lacing shoes. Notes of this kind give parents something specific and positive to talk about with their child. In addition, notes are one more ways for teachers to help parents recognize the developmental significance of a child's seemingly routine accomplishments.

The two way journal. Some centers take the brief written note idea a step further and set up a journal system. Parents and teachers both write in the journal. It travels back and forth, between school and home on a frequent basis. Once such a system becomes established, it seems a relatively effortless but rewarding system for keeping the communication lines open between home and school.

Audio and videotapes. For some families, written materials are not an effective way to communicate. For these families, an audiotape log may be very efficient. This type of system would have to be negotiated individually with a family. The family and the center would need to have a tape recorder on which they could listen to the tape and record a new message, then the tape would be carried back and forth between school and home. Many centers are now using videotapes to communicate with families. Videotapes are especially useful when trying to demonstrate a new program, or skill, or sign, that the child is learning. Again, this type of system needs to be negotiated individually with families to make sure that the family has easy access to a VCR and is comfortable having their child videotaped.

Newsletters. A newsletter, duplicated and sent home with children, is appreciated by most parents. The major reason for a newsletter is to describe the everyday events and learning activities that go on at school from spring vegetable planting to the installation of a child-friendly computer. A newsletter also can serve as a reminder about situations that involve all families such as colder weather and the need for warmer outdoor clothing. Newly enrolled children and families can be introduced in the newsletters. When the new child has a disability, emphasis can be on the many things the child can do: "Dorsey is learning to use her crutches outdoors but there are lots of things she doesn't need them for. She goes down the slide by herself and swings in the tire swings."

A newsletter must be written to fit the reading level of families receiving it. In many programs, newsletters need to be written in two or more languages. To ensure a simple and straightforward style, children can be involved in the writing. All children learn from talking about what to include in a newsletter. Many children have fun dictating parts of it. Teachers must be sure to read the finished newsletter to children before they carry it home. This enables children to talk with their parents about the contents and, perhaps, to prompt them to read the letter. In fact, a good rule for teachers is that they inform children of every communication with parents—telephone calls, notes, parent conferences. When a teacher says, "I called your father and told him how good you are at matching colors," the child realizes that good things truly are being reported.

Parent and Teacher Meetings.   Meeting together has been the traditional form of parent–teacher interaction. Usually held on the school premises, the meetings provide opportunities for parents to see their children's work, interact with teachers, and compare notes with other parents. An advantage of inclusive early education programs is that the parents of children with disabilities are included in the parent meetings for all parents. Often when children with disabilities attend segregated programs, parents are not invited to or do not feel comfortable attending PTA or other all-school functions.

Large group meetings.   Group meetings usually focus on issues of general interest such as aspects of child development or the early childhood curriculum. A recognized expert in a particular area may be invited to speak. Parent meetings that draw the best attendance tend to be those based on concerns of parents. Time for questions and open discussion is an important part of any parent–teacher get-together. An informal coffee hour often precedes or follows the discussion. Casual socializing helps parents and teachers, and parents and parents get to know each other better. An open-house hour sometimes precedes the group discussion. Parents visit their children's classroom where paintings, clay work, and woodworking projects can be on display. Toys, equipment, and teaching materials often are put out for parents to examine and manipulate. Many parents find they can talk more easily with teachers when they can focus on materials. For shy parents, looking at materials can be a special boon; it is something to talk about with other parents.

Parents and teachers can talk together informally about learning materials.

Parent support groups.   The purpose of support groups is to provide parents with an opportunity to talk to and learn from other parents. Usually parent support groups are for parents of children with disabilities. Teachers usually are not involved in the group, and often the groups are run through agencies other than early childhood centers. For example, Parent-to-Parent, a national support system for parents of children with disabilities, is usually housed in the local Association for Retarded Citizens (ARC). Teachers need to be familiar with the support services for parents in their area.

Parent conferences.   In addition to IEP planning, regular parent conferences should be scheduled two or three times a year, more often in some instances. Conferences can be helpful to parents or they can be threatening and intimidating. A positive note must be established at the outset. Parent conferencing requires a quiet place with comfortable seating. After greeting the parents cordially and exchanging social pleasantries, the teacher starts off by giving a brief progress report. The report should be interlaced with many examples of how the child is gaining (or has mastered) particular developmental skills. A recent parent observation can be a good takeoff point for the conference. Throughout, the teacher pauses frequently so parents have opportunities to comment, ask questions, and express their concerns. The conference closes with a brief summary of the discussion, a restatement of long- and short-term learning goals for the child, and restatement of the child's unique and valuable qualities.

In every parent conference, the focus must be on issues related to the child's development and learning. Teachers *do not* counsel parents on deeply personal concerns, regardless of the impact on the child. Teachers may, however, attempt to help the family find the appropriate resource.

Ethical issues are a concern of many teachers in their work with parents (Feeney and Sysco 1986). What should be done, for example, when a child has serious health problems that parents apparently do not recognize? Before going into such a conference, the teacher makes extensive observations and takes frequency counts, when appropriate, of the behavior in question. The teacher also consults with the other teachers. This ensures staff agreement that a serious problem exists and that it cannot be handled through rearrangement of particular aspects of the program. No matter how carefully the teacher sets a positive note at the outset of such a conference, nor how tactfully the teacher brings up the problem, parents will be threatened. Inevitably, they feel that whatever is *wrong* with their child is their fault (or is perceived by teachers as the parents' fault). At first mention of their child's shortcomings, parents feel alienated, defensive, sometimes angry. Little can be accomplished in that kind of emotional climate. Teachers, therefore, bring up major problems only when the child's present and future well-being is at stake and teachers cannot help the child without the parents' help.

It would be unconscionable for teachers not to bring up certain problems—suspected child abuse is one instance. (Remember, teachers are mandated by law to report suspected abuse and neglect to appro-

priate agencies such as Child Protective Services.) The teacher levels with the parents immediately. After brief greetings, the opening statements have to do with the frequency and seriousness of the injuries that have been observed and documented. However, if the child also acts worried, fearful, anxious, or withdrawn, the *teacher does not bring that up*. Parents may further abuse the child for behaving in a revealing way at school. From the parents' perspective, it may seem their child is getting them into deeper trouble. At no point does the teacher back down. The teacher states that a call will be made to the appropriate child protection agency immediately. In many instances, it is advisable for the teacher to hold this type of conference in the company of the school's director or nurse, or a member of the social service agency serving the community.

Even a conference such as this must end with a positive comment or two about the child (and relationship to parents if good times as well as bad times have been observed). In addition, there needs to be a brief summary statement and a commitment from teachers that they will work with the parents in every way possible. If it is a child with developmental disabilities, it is likely that a member of the interdisciplinary team will handle the situation. At the team and parent conference, the teacher often is the major source of supporting information.

Parent Feedback.   Most feedback from parents is obtained indirectly. Much of it comes from incidental comments during informal parent–teacher exchanges. Indirect feedback also may come from criticisms of the program made to another parent, but purposefully, within the teacher's hearing. Teachers cannot ignore such feedback. It must be noted and discussed with staff. Direct feedback from parents is often difficult to obtain. Many parents are afraid of alienating the staff who provide them with sorely needed child care or early intervention services. Other parents are intimidated by the teachers' expertise. Still others fear their comments or dissatisfactions will be considered trivial. Parents who do give direct feedback often are those who are chronically dissatisfied. They seem to be more interested in finding fault than in making constructive comments. While their comments may be frequent, they are likely to be the least helpful.

Questionnaires are one way of getting feedback. Parents' responses are most useful if questions relate to specific aspects of the program. In addition, questions should be designed so that parents can rate the *degree* of satisfaction on each item rather than having to give a *yes* or *no* answer. Suggestion boxes also can be helpful. Parents can make their comments anonymously if they are supplied with a form. They can fill it out at home and drop it in a box, unobserved. It is important to respond to all feedback from parents. The program's response may be noted in the newsletter, letters home, or on a bulletin board in a place that all parents will see. The best way to encourage parents to provide honest feedback is to be responsive to earlier feedback from them (Schwartz and Baer 1991).

Home Visits.   According to Powell (1989), "Home visiting programs represent an important strategy of parent-focused early education" (p. 97). Home visits have a long tradition of bridging the gap between school and home. Getting to know a family in its own setting enables teachers to work more effectively with children in the school setting. Home visits require teachers to behave differently than they do in their own classrooms. In a child's home, teachers are no longer the central figure—parents are. The teacher is a guest who needs to conform to the social and cultural ways of the family.

If there is more than one adult in the home who shares caregiving, ideally, home visits should be scheduled to involve all of them. If that is not possible on a regular basis, at least one visit should be conducted when all the caregivers can participate. Home visits are excellent opportunities to observe children's ability to function in their own environment and to observe the level of competence in functional skills. If a teacher is interested in a specific skill, teachers plan the home visit around a naturally occurring time for that skill to be used. For example, if the parents have many questions about feeding, it would be advantageous to schedule the visit around a meal time or snack time.

Much can be learned about the child's developmental opportunities from a home visit (Caldwell and Bradley 1978). For example:

- What types of materials are available for the child?
- Are there toys (or household items converted into play materials)?
- Are there books and crayons?
- How do the children who are not in a program spend their time?
- Is the home excessively neat or excessively disorganized?
- How do parents respond to their children? To a particular child? Are parents overly protective? Impatient with the child's shortcomings?

When home visits are scheduled on a regular basis, the visiting teacher usually brings learning materials. The teacher demonstrates use of the materials with the child. then the parent and child use the material together, with the teacher providing feedback. The visiting teacher also makes suggestions as to how the parent can extend and elaborate the activity during the period between visits. In some programs, parents are asked to make checks on a simple record sheet regarding various aspects of the child's progress.

Regardless of the approach, teachers always must remember the parents' role in their child's learning. Not only are parents the child's first teacher, they also are the child's most frequent teacher. With appropriate support, parents can make their home a significant learning environment for their children. Home is the place where all developmental skills can be practiced over and over, in a real-life setting, with those who have a personal stake in the child's development.

SUMMARY

The family, regardless of its makeup, is a young child's most important teacher. The family defines a child's culture and community; a major responsibility of a teacher is to respect cultural beliefs and practices. While early childhood teachers are partners in the teaching process, parents are always the senior partners. With children who have developmental disabilities, parents' involvement in their child's early intervention program is especially important. Involvement takes many forms. Simply keeping their child in the intervention program may be the only involvement some parents can manage.

An ecological approach to understanding early development was partly responsible for legislation authorizing the federally funded Individualized Family Service Plan. The IFSP is an interdisciplinary team effort that includes parents as team members. A service coordinator is appointed to keep the program organized and running. The emphasis is on helping families become stronger and more able through the IFSP process.

The teacher-parent partnership is fostered in a variety of ways. A relationship that will benefit children is based on open communication and teachers' respect of the range of individual differences among parents. Many of the most effective teacher-parent exchanges are brief and informal chats as when a parent delivers his or her child, or observes in the classroom. Telephone calls, written notes sent home with children, newsletters, and group meetings keep the lines open between teachers and parents. Formal conferences are another means of communicating with parents, as are home visits. Teachers also may seek parent feedback about the program itself through questionnaires and suggestion boxes.

STUDENT ACTIVITIES

1. Prepare a brief profile of three different family lifestyles found among your friends or extended family. Be specific about the caregiving arrangement for the infants and young children.
2. Select several classmates to role play parent–child pairs during a program's arrival time. Serving as teacher, initiate brief exchanges with the individual parents around a sleep problem, a child's new leg braces, a special painting a child has done, or a child's reluctance to play outdoors.
3. Prepare a one-page newsletter based on events that occurred in the classroom where you observe or practice teach.
4. Try to find a family with a child with a disability that you can talk with; if they are willing, ask them to tell you about any special expenses and caregiving arrangements they have had to deal with.
5. Select a partner to play the role of a parent who has a child with a disability. Demonstrate the kinds of nonintrusive questions you would ask to assist the family in identifying their needs and strengths.

REVIEW QUESTIONS

A. *Define and give an example.*
1. Extended family
2. Ecological niche
3. Nonintrusiveness (as related to PL 99-457)
4. Respite care
5. Service coordinator

B. *True or False. Choose the best answer.*

T F 1. Never, in this country, has it been recommended that newborns with disabilities be institutionalized.

T F 2. In today's society, family may be defined as two or more individuals who have made a commitment to share their lives.

T F 3. Divorce rate is lowest among families with a child with disabilities.

T F 4. The mother–child relationship is but one of several determining factors in a child's development.

T F 5. By law, the IFSP is to be evaluated every other month for child and family progress.

T F 6. Legally, parents cannot serve as service coordinator for their own IFSP.

T F 7. Every parent of a child who is developmentally disabled should be expected to volunteer in the classroom.

T F 8. Arrival and departure periods are a good time for teacher–parent discussions of children's problems.

T F 9. Impromptu parent observations should be discouraged.

T　F　10. Classroom newsletters may need to be written in two or more languages.

C. *Multiple Choice. Select all of the most appropriate answers in each group.*

1. Enabling families means
   a. taking care of all the details regarding the child's disability.
   b. carrying out interventions so that family members gain a sense of control.
   c. creating opportunities for families to become more competent and self-sufficient.
   d. communicating frequently with families.
   e. providing comprehensive service coordination.

2. In terms of child abuse, children with disabilities
   a. are never abused.
   b. are seldom abused.
   c. are more likely to be abused than normally developing children.
   d. may or may not have parents who were abused as children.
   e. may trigger parent abusiveness through no fault of their own.

3. Which of the following most accurately describes the situation of families with children with disabilities?
   a. freedom from financial strain.
   b. readily available and affordable child care.
   c. marital stability and family solidarity.
   d. frequent crises.
   e. constant fatigue.

4. The service coordinator's duties include
   a. playing detective and finding out what goes on in the family behind closed doors.
   b. reporting inappropriate family behaviors to the proper authorities.
   c. advising the family as to what is best for them and their child with a disability.
   d. keeping track of the operations of the interdisciplinary team.
   e. assisting the family in getting in touch with prescribed services.

5. It is good to involve parents in their child's early intervention program because
   a. parents have information about the child not available from anyone else.
   b. parents can help the child transfer skills from school to everyday life.
   c. parents and teachers can maintain consistent expectations for the child.
   d. parents gain access to support from other parents.
   e. only *a*, *b*, and *c* above.

6. To communicate effectively with parents, teachers are advised to
   a. talk with—rather than to—parents.
   b. share knowledge and get feedback from parents.
   c. work to alter parents' thinking if it reflects cultural or ethnic biases about children's learning.
   d. report children's accomplishments to their parents, in the child's presence, when possible.
   e. never bring up unpleasant problems associated with a child's development or behavior.

7. Parent conferences have a number of goals, some of which are
   a. to counsel parents on personal matters such as family finances and marital difficulties.
   b. to be sure the parent understands, from the beginning, that the teacher is a professional with solutions to whatever problems the parent may have.
   c. to allow parents ample opportunity to ask questions, *after* the teacher has made a full report.
   d. to close the conference with a review of the chid's problems and shortcomings.
   e. to offer assistance in helping a family find needed help such as an audiologist or a guidance clinic.

8. Teachers can get feedback on the parents' satisfaction with their child's program by
   a. attending to parents' conversations among themselves where the obvious intention is for the teacher to overhear it.
   b. providing anonymous questionnaires that parents can fill out at home.
   c. asking parents directly to list their complaints about the program.
   d. asking one parent who seems especially well satisfied to try to find out from other parents what their complaints are.
   e. always giving parents feedback on the feedback that other parents give about the program.

D. *Mix and Match. Select the best match for each item in column I from column II and place that letter in the appropriate space in column I.*

I	II
____ 1. blended family	A. part H, PL 99-457
____ 2. family interaction system	
____ 3. respite care	B. newsletter
____ 4. discretionary program	C. reconstituted family
____ 5. service coordinator	
____ 6. Humpty Dumpty syndrome	D. reciprocal interactions
____ 7. parent feedback	E. major socializing agents
____ 8. ethical issue	
____ 9. parents and family	F. relief caregiving
____ 10. classroom activities report	G. child abuse
	H. fragmented services
	I. questionnaire
	J. IFSP organizer

REFERENCES

Bailey, D. (1987). Collaborative goal setting with families: Resolving differences in values and priorities for service. *Topics in Early Childhood Special Education*, 7(2), 59–71.

Bailey, D. (1989). Case management in early intervention. *Journal of Early Intervention*, 13(2), 120–134.

Bailey, D.B., and Winton, P.J. (1990). Families of exceptional children. In N.G. Haring and L. McCormick (Eds.), *Exceptional Children and Youth*. Columbus: Merrill.

Barber, P.A., Turnbull, A.P., Behr, S.K., and Kerns, G.M. (1988). A family system's perspective on early childhood special education. In S.L. Odom and M.B. Karnes (Eds.), *Early intervention for infants and children with handicaps*. Baltimore: Brookes.

Barrera, I. (1994). Thoughts on the assessment of young children whose sociocultural background is unfamiliar to the assessor. *Zero to Three, 14(6)*, 9–13.

Bronfenbrenner, U. (1979). *The ecology of human development*. Cambridge, MA.: Harvard University Press.

Caldwell, B., and Bradley, R. (1978). *Home observation for measurement of the environment*. Little Rock: University of Arkansas.

Deal, A.G., Dunst, C.J., and Trivette, C.M. (1989). A flexible and functional approach to developing Individualized Family Service Plans. *Infants and Young Children*, 1 (4), 32–43.

Dunst, C.J. and Trivette, C.M. (1989). An enablement and empowerment perspective of case management. *Topics in Early Childhood Special Education*. 8:4 87–102.

Feeney, S. and Sysco, L. (1986). Professional ethics in early childhood education: Survey results. *Young Children*, 42 (1), 15–20.

Frodi, A. and Senchak, M. (1990). Verbal and behavioral responsiveness to the cries of atypical infants. *Child Development*, 61 (1), 76–84.

Gonzalez-Mena, J. (1992). Taking a culturally sensitive approach in infant-toddler programs. *Young Children, 47(2)*, 4–11.

Harry, B. (1992). *Cultural diversity, families, and the special education system*. New York: Teachers College Press.

Harry, B. (1992). Developing cultural self-awareness: The first step in values clarification for early interventionists. *Topics in Early Childhood Special Education, 12(4)*, 333–350.

Harry, B., Torguson, C., Katkavich and Guerrero, M. (1993). Crossing social class and cultural barriers in working with families. *Teaching Exceptional Children. 26*, 48–51.

Janko, S. (1994). *Vulnerable children, vulnerable lives*. New York: Teachers College Press.

Klein, T., Bittel, C., and Molnar, J. (1993). No place to call home: Supporting the needs of homeless children in the early childhood classroom. *Young Children 48(6)*, 22–31.

Lynch, E.W., and Hanson, M.J. (1992). *Developing cross-cultural competence: A guide for working with young children and their families*. Baltimore: Brookes.

Meier, J.H. (1976). *Developmental and Learning Disabilities*. Baltimore: University Park Press.

Meyer, D.J., and Vadasy, P.F. (1986). *Grandparent workshops: How to organize workshops for grandparents of children with handicaps*. Seattle: University of Washington Press.

Meyer, D.J., and Vadasy, P.F. (1994). *Sibshops: Workshops for siblings of children with special needs*. Baltimore: Brookes.

National Center on Child Abuse and Neglect. (1980). *Child abuse and developmental disabilities: Essays*. (DHEW Publication No. OHDS 79 30226). Washington, DC: U.S. Department of Health, Education, and Welfare.

Peterson, N.L. (1987). *Early Intervention for handicapped and at-risk children*. Denver: Love Publishing.

Powell, D.R. (1989). *Families and early childhood programs*. Washington, DC: National Association for the Education of Young Children.

Sameroff, A.J., and Chandler, M.J. (1975). Reproductive risk and the continuum of caretaking casualty. In F.D. Horowitz (Ed.) *Review of child development research*, 4, 187–244. Chicago: University of Chicago Press.

Schwartz, I.S., and Baer, D.M. (1991). Social validity assessments: Is current practice state of the art? *Journal of Applied Behavior Analysis, 24*, 189–204.

Simeonsson, R.J., and Bailey, D.B. (1990). Family dimensions in early intervention. In S.J. Meisels and J.P. Shonkoff (Eds.), *Handbook of Early Intervention* 428–444. New York: Cambridge University Press.

Turnbull, A.P., and Turnbull, H.R. (1993). Participatory research on cognitive coping: From concepts to research planning. In A.P. Turnbull, J.M. Patterson, S.K. Behr, D.L. Murphy, J.G. Marquis, and M.J. Blue-Banning (Eds.), *Cognitive coping, families, and disabilities* 1–14. Baltimore: Brookes.

Turnbull, A.P., and Turnbull, H.R. (1988). *Families, professionals, and exceptionality: A special partnership*. Columbus: Merrill.

Wickens, E. (1993). Penny's question: "I will have a child in my class with two Moms—What do you know about this? *Young Children, 48(3)*, 25–31.

Wikler, L., Haack, J., and Intagliata, J. (1984). Bearing the burden alone? Helping divorced mothers of children with developmental disabilities. In *Families with handicapped members: The family therapy collection*. Rockville, MD: Aspen Systems.

Identification and the IEP Process

OBJECTIVES

After studying this unit the student will be able to

- list the five steps in the assessment process.
- describe Child Find and the major steps in the identification of developmental problems.
- list and describe five observation techniques appropriate for use with young children.
- explain this statement: Scores obtained on IQ tests given to young children must be viewed with caution, even skepticism.
- discuss the role of the early childhood teacher in the identification of developmental problems and in the IEP process.
- summarize each of the major requirements of an IEP.

The identification of developmental problems is a responsibility of everyone associated with infants and young children and their families. It is intended that it be a responsibility of the federal government also, through the 1967 legislation entitled Early and Periodic Screening, Diagnosis, and Testing (Unit 3). One factor that led to the passage of this bill was the rapid increase in knowledge about the long-range impact of the early years on future development. A second factor was the shift from *cure* to *prevention* among professions working with young children. This was in contrast to the traditional medical emphasis on treatment of problems after they had developed.

Early identification of developmental problems allows for more effective intervention. It also helps in the prevention of secondary handicapping conditions through individualized programming and educational planning. The focus of this unit is on these two issues: early identification of developmental problems and the delivery of special services through the Individualized Education Plan (IEP).

ASSESSMENT OF YOUNG CHILDREN

In early childhood programs, assessment is a broad term that can include observing, gathering, and recording information. The type of assessment instruments used and data collected depend on the type of question that teachers are asking. Therefore, when conducting an assessment the first thing a teacher must do is know why it is important to collect the information. In other words, what are the questions that the staff are trying to answer?

Five interrelated steps have been identified in assessment of young children with special needs (Cohen and Spenciner 1994). These steps are described briefly below.

Step 1: Screening. The purpose is to identify children who need more thorough evaluation.

Step 2: Determining Eligibility. The purpose is to determine if a child has an identifiable disability and qualifies for special education services. This decision cannot be made on the basis of a single test. Assessment information from multiple domains and sources must be used to determine eligibility.

Step 3: Planning the Program. The purpose is to identify an appropriate program for a child and begin to plan what services will be delivered, how they will be delivered, and what skills and areas will be addressed.

Step 4: Monitoring Progress. The purpose is to determine how the child is progressing in the program. The information from these monitoring activities are used to modify the child's program.

Step 5: Evaluating the Program. The purpose is to make decisions about the effectiveness of the intervention program for individual children. Decisions can be made about specific activities, specific modifications, or the entire program.

Assessment information can be collected in many different ways, including observation (Schweinhart 1993), collecting work samples (Meisels 1993), **portfolios, standardized tests**, and checklists. Often, however, when teachers hear the word assessment, they think about standardized instruments that have been developed to collect a specific type of information. Three common types of tests used in assessment are **criterion-referenced tests**, **norm-referenced tests**, and IQ tests.

Criterion-referenced tests. Some screening instruments are criterion-referenced; that is, a child's performance on each task is compared to preselected standards (*criterion*). A child's performance is *not* compared to the performance of other children. Criterion-referenced test items might ask, for example, Can the child lace and tie his or her own shoes? Walk seven consecutive steps on a balance beam? Match five shapes and colors in one minute?

Norm-referenced tests. With norm-referenced tests the question becomes: How well does the child do, *compared to other children the same age*, on tasks such as counting pennies? Naming letters of the alphabet? Stacking 6 one-inch cubes? Norm-referenced tests provide standardized information intended to relate to children's abilities at various ages. In other words, the norm-referenced test provides scales that compare the performance of one child to the averaged performance of other children of approximately the same age. It must be recognized, however, that these tests tend to be less than reliable with young children (Cohen and Spenciner 1994).

IQ tests. Most intelligence tests (IQ tests) are norm-referenced. Tests such as the Weschler Intelligence Scale for Children (WISC) and the Stanford-Binet Intelligence Scales are sometimes given to young children. The avowed purpose is to attempt to determine:

How much a child knows
How well the child solves problems
How quickly a child can perform a variety of mental tasks

The scores from IQ tests must be viewed with caution, even skepticism (Neisworth and Bagnato 1992). A number of factors may lead to poor performance on an IQ test (or any other test, for that matter). The child may be tired, hungry, or unwell at the time. The child may be anxious about the unfamiliar testing situation and the unfamiliar person giving the test. The child also may be answering in ways appropriate to his or her own language or culture but inappropriate in terms of standardized test responses (recall the earlier discussion on cultural differences). Furthermore, some children are hampered by an unidentified developmental problem. A partial vision or hearing loss, for example, can interfere with a child's ability to respond appropriately; thus, the child's IQ score falsely indicates a retarded range of mental functioning.

IQ scores of infants and young children *do not predict future intellectual performance*. In fact, they are not even good at assessing a young child's current intellectual capabilities. The major problem with IQ scores is that they do not account for the child's learning opportunities (or lack of learning opportunities). Neither do they reflect the quality of the learning experiences a child may have had. The use of a single test score to determine a child's intellectual competence must always be challenged. In fact, *more than one instrument should be used in any screening program to ensure a valid picture of the child's development*. As Perrone (1990) points out:

Teachers and parents have been told that tests have meaning, that they point out what children know and understand, that they can help give direction to instruction. The tests *don't* match the promise. Their contribution to the education of young children is virtually nil (p. 13).

The teacher's role in assessment in an inclusive early childhood setting will be primarily in helping to identify children for early identification and collecting data that will be used in the development and evaluation of the IEP. The rest of this unit addresses those two issues.

THE PROCESS OF EARLY IDENTIFICATION

Early identification of developmental problems can take place any time from a few weeks after conception to age 18. These years are formally recognized as the *developmental period* of the human lifespan. Early identification of problems is not limited to the first 5 to 8 years of life, however. A child may be perfectly healthy up to age 12 or 15, then show first-time symptoms of a developmental disability (**juvenile rheumatoid arthritis**, for example). The older child is as much in need of *early identification* of the emerging problem as is a 2-year-old showing first-time symptoms of any kind. In both cases, early identification can lead to prompt treatment. Prompt treatment can reduce the severity of the problem and prevent it from affecting other areas of development.

All young children should be screened.

Case Finding.   Case finding is the process of locating children in need of special services. Developmental problems often go undetected because many children and their families have inadequate health care or are without health care of any kind. To deal with this situation a federal program entitled Child Find was established in the 1960s.

Child Find.   Effective Child Find depends on widespread publicity. Announcements of Child Find roundups should be simply written and free of clinical **jargon.** They should be written in as many languages as are spoken in the community and posted in churches, synagogues, and other religious institutions as well as in laundromats, supermarkets, child care and community centers and in shelters for homeless families. The publicity should emphasize that developmental problems often are hard to recognize; that *all* young children should be screened to locate problems that may not be obvious in everyday contacts with the child. Child Find programs also must be easy to get to. Many families (often those most in need of such services) depend on public transportation.

Screening.   Screening, that is, the identification of developmental problems (or potential problems), is the major purpose of Child Find. The goal is to provide easily administered, low-cost testing for as many children as possible. Children with obvious disabilities should not be put through the screening procedures. They and their families need to be referred directly to the appropriate health care or social service agency.

Screening tests describe a child's level of performance, but *only at that point in time* (Allen and Marotz 1994). Comprehensive screening evaluates the child's current abilities, deviations, delays, and impairments in all areas of development. If problem areas are identified during routine developmental screening, clinical diagnosis is indicated. Several points should be emphasized:

1. Accurate results can be achieved only with **reliable and valid tests** developed specifically for use with young children. There is a scarcity of such tests. In the absence of valid instruments, testing is of no value (NAEYC 1988, p. 12).

2. Results from screening tests do not constitute a diagnosis; they should never be used as a basis for planning an intervention program.

3. *Follow-through is essential.* "Identifying children with potential problems is only the first step; encouraging families to seek further assessment for their child is the next" (Hanson and Lynch 1989, p. 95).

Parents as partners in screening. Parents have a wealth of firsthand knowledge about their children. They know what their child can and cannot do in everyday life. Often, they are the first to suspect a problem, even if unable to clearly specify its nature. It is estimated that 65 to 75 percent of the hearing problems in young children were noted first by their parents. The parents knew *something* was wrong. They did not necessarily recognize it as a hearing loss but they did report to the health care provider that their child acted *strange* or "talked funny."

A hearing loss, as well as a number of other subtle problems, may not show up during a routine medical checkup. When a problem cannon be pinpointed by the clinician, parents sometimes are led to believe that nothing is wrong with their child. Often they are advised to go home and relax, to get over being so anxious. Ignoring parents' observations is not in the child's best interests, however. Nor is it a good way to begin or build a constructive relationship with the family. Neglecting a problem in its early stages may result in a long-range negative impact on development.

Cultural, ethnic and linguistic differences. Family customs, beliefs, and language influence a child's performance on screening tests (Banks 1994). A child's responses may be scored as *wrong* even when they are *right* according to the family values. The result may be an invalid (false) evaluation, suggesting that there is reason to be concerned about the child's development, when none exists. These unjust procedures became dismayingly apparent in the early days of special education reform, and continue to be apparent in the over representation of minority students in special education. This type of inappropriate assessment leads to inaccurate diagnosis and labeling and often results in children who "were doing fine until they went to school" (Harry 1992, p. 61). These children often function perfectly well in their own environment and in their own language, but have few skills and little background for functioning in schools designed to accommodate only the majority culture.

To avoid such errors, safeguards must be built into the screening and assessment process (Barrera 1994). These include:

- Assessment must be conducted in the child's native language
- Assessment instruments that are designed for use in the native language must be used. Simply translating a test that was written in English and standardized on English speaking students is *never* appropriate.
- Assessment should be conducted and interpreted by a "culture-language mediator" (a person who is fluent in both the native and majority language and culture).
- Multiple forms of information should be collected including work samples and child observations.
- Test items and procedures should be designed to measure a child's known strengths as well as document any perceived weaknesses.

Types of screening instruments. Early childhood screening takes many forms. Most screening instruments that are currently used attempt to assess all developmental areas. There are some very specialized screenings, such as the Apgar that is used only immediately after birth to assess the infant's need for medical attention. Other screening tests assess sensory functions, such as the Snellen Eye Chart for vision, and pure tone audiometry for hearing.

When selecting a multi-domain screening test, some issues to consider are the **sensitivity** and **specificity** of the tests. Sensitivity refers to the ability of a test to correctly identify children who have a disability; and specificity refers to the ability of not referring children who do not have a disability. Some of the more commonly used screening instruments include the DIAL-R (Developmental Indicators for the Assessment of Learning–Revised) and the Denver II. Both of these screening instruments rely on teachers and parents as informants. The advantage is obvious—

Several screening tests are available for assessing older infants as well as newborns.

these are the adults who know the child best. (A list of screening and other early childhood assessment tools is provided in Appendix A.)

Teachers also play a major role in screening for giftedness among young children. No single test identifies the young and gifted child. Several measures must be used. IQ scores, level of motivation and creativity (which is difficult to define and measure) may be useful when backed up by a teachers' observations and knowledge of a child.

Who does the screening?   Screening programs may be conducted by professionals or **paraprofessionals**. Regardless of who is doing the screening, training in test procedures is important. Some screening tests—certain hearing tests or medical tests—should be administered only by members of that discipline. Other tests such as the Denver II or the Snellen Illiterate E test can be administered by a variety of individuals trained to use the instrument. Community screening programs generally are conducted by teams whose members are skilled in administering a number of tests. (For an excellent analysis and listing of

screening and assessment instruments see Thurman and Widerstrom 1990.)

In many communities, teachers of young children assist in conducting mass screening programs sometimes called *roundups*. Even if not a member of a roundup team, early childhood teachers and infant caregiver/teachers are key figures in the early identification process. It is essential that they take responsibility for recognizing warning signs that a developmental problem exists or may develop.

Limitations of screening.   Screening is an important process in the early identification of development problems in children. As consumers of screening tests, however, teachers must be cautious when interpreting the data from a screening. First, remember that a screening is only a "snapshot" of a child in time. Also, this snapshot is often taken in a strange place, when the child is surrounded by new people, tired, hungry, and being asked to do a number of activities that may be unfamiliar and seem silly (Hills 1993). Therefore the picture of child competence (or incompetence) that begins to develop during the screening may not be representative of the child's behavior at school, home, child care, or any other setting. As a member of a screening team, a teacher can

Early childhood educators play a major role in screening for giftedness.

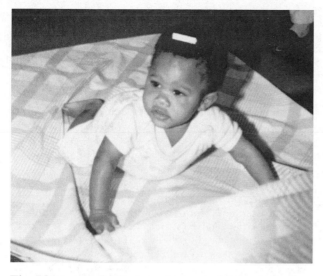

The IQ scores of infants and young children are often invalid; furthermore, they do not predict later intellectual performance.

be aware of how surroundings, familiarity of the examiner, and the physical state of the child can influence the results of a screening and attempt to optimize the setting in which screenings are conducted.

TEACHERS' ROLE IN EARLY IDENTIFICATION

The teachers' role is critical in the identification of developmental problems in infants and young children. It is teachers' recorded observations of children in many situations, over time, that provides a valid picture of each child's skills, capabilities, and special needs.

Teachers' Qualifications.   Teachers have special qualifications and opportunities for identifying children with developmental problems or potential problems. They have knowledge of early development. They understand the regularities and irregularities typical of early development which enable them to recognize developmental deviations. Teachers also have had special training that allows them to provide infants and young children with sound developmental

activities that bring out the best in each child during the assessment process.

Teachers are further advantaged in that they see children in a natural environment. In the classroom, a child is likely to be comfortable and spontaneous. Furthermore, teachers can observe children of similar age and interests and so judge each child's development in the context of a broad display of normalcy. Teachers also have extended periods of time and many situations and activities in which to observe children. Contrast this with clinicians such as the doctor, the audiologist, the psychologist who usually see the child only on brief and tightly scheduled visits in clinical settings. At these times the child may be ill at ease and behaving quite differently than in a familiar home or school environment.

The teacher as observer.   Observation, according to Irwin and Bushnell (1980) is "both a scientific tool and an everyday skill of value to teachers and parents. . . ."(p. 62). The search for developmental problems always begins with systematic observation of children as they work and play in the preschool or child care center. An NAEYC position paper (1988) stresses that teachers' "assessment of young children should rely heavily on the results of their observations" (p. 13).

Observers must be *objective*—that is, they write down only what a child actually does and says. Subjective recording, by contrast, occurs when teachers put their own interpretations on children's behavior. Note the differences in the following statements:

- *Objective:* Susie smiled and laughed frequently through the morning; she cried only once.
- *Subjective:* Susie was happy and carefree today.
- *Objective:* Mark stamped his feet and screamed "No" each time he was asked to change activities.
- *Subjective:* Mark gets angry all the time.

Systematic observations.   Most teachers are used to observing children; few, however, record their observations in an organized way. Systematically recorded observations are the key to effective identification of developmental problems. Each observation should start with these four parts:

1. Child's name or initials (confidentiality of information is essential).
2. Date and time of day.
3. Setting (and in some situations, names or number of children and teachers present).
4. Name or initials of the observer.

Teachers' observations take many forms. The questions teachers need to have answered determine the observation strategy they will select. In most cases, it is preferable if more than one person observes the child, especially if there is hint of a serious problem. When two people agree they are seeing the same thing, personal bias and misinterpretation of a child's behavior is reduced.

Types of Observations.   Discussed below are a sampling of the many kinds of observation tools that are useful in working with young children. (For a comprehensive overview of observation strategies, see Beatty 1990; Irwin and Bushnell 1980).

Checklists.   Checklists are a quick and effective way of collecting systematic information on one or many children. Teachers, aides, parents, volunteers, and children themselves can record on checklists. Many young children recognize their own name when printed in large letters. If teachers need to know, for example, which 4- and 5-year-olds are using particular learning centers, they can post a list of children's names close by. Most children can make a mark by their name as they enter; the teacher can do if for those who cannot. At the end of the day (or week) teachers know which children are using which centers, which children are doing a great deal of coming and going (useful information in planning individual programs). Checklists can be as simple as the one just mentioned or they can be designed to give much more information as in the Teacher Observation Form and Checklist (Figure 10-1). Most useful are checklists that teachers themselves design to answer their own questions about children and the program.

Frequency counts.   An effective way of making a recorded observation is simply keeping track of how often something happens. Teachers who are concerned about a particular behavior need to know how often it takes place: Excessively? Infrequently? Only under certain circumstance? Every time the behavior occurs, a tally mark is made on a piece of paper posted on the wall or carried in teachers' pockets. Over a period of several days the tally marks can provide significant information as to *whether* a given behavior is actually a problem as well as *how much* of a problem it is.

> Example: One teacher was concerned about John's safety because of what she thought were his frequent attempts to climb over the fence during outdoor play. The other teacher thought it seldom happened. An actual frequency count showed the fence-climbing attempts occurred four or five times each play period. Teachers now could agree there was a problem. They assessed the play yard and realized there was not much for John to climb on. They began to set up climbing activities several days a week. John's fence-climbing dropped to one or no episodes per day. On days when no climbing activities were set up, John's fence-climbing was again high. The frequency counts gave teachers clues to the extent of the problem as well as to their success in reducing the unsafe behavior.

Duration measures.   A duration measure indicates how long an event or a behavior lasts. This type of observation, like frequency counts, provides significant information that nevertheless is easy to collect. By simply noting a start and stop time on a child's activities, teachers can gauge such things as span of attention, how much time a child spends in either appropriate or maladaptive behaviors, or under what circumstances a behavior (thumbsucking, perhaps) is most likely to continue.

> Example: Teachers were concerned about Lanny's poor attention span. They decided to find out how many minutes at a time he spent at various activities. Several days' observations indicated he spent many minutes (15 to 20) with hands-on activities (painting, block-building, puzzles). In contrast, he had a short attention span—only a minute or two—for activities that required listening (music, stories, conversation). These duration measures were invaluable as teachers planned Lanny's program, conferenced with his parents, and participated in the team meetings.

Anecdotal notes.   These are brief observations, each recorded individually on three-by-five cards or another

Teacher Observation Form and Checklist
For Identifying Children Who
May Require Additional Services

Child's Name: _____ Birth Date: _____

Date: _____ Recording Teacher's Name: _____

LANGUAGE	YES	NO	SOMETIMES
Does the child:			
1. use two- and three-word phrases to ask for what he wants?			
2. use complete sentences to tell you what happened?			
*3. when asked to describe something, use at least two or more sentences to talk about it?			
4. ask questions?			
5. seem to have difficulty following directions?			
6. respond to questions with appropriate answers?			
7. seem to talk too softly or too loudly?			
8. Are you able to understand the child?			

PREACADEMICS	YES	NO	SOMETIMES
Does the child:			
9. seem to take at least twice as long as the other children to learn preacademic concepts?			
10. seem to take the time needed by other children to learn preacademic concepts?			
11. have difficulty attending to group activities for more than five minutes at a time?			
12. appear extremely shy in group activities; for instance, not volunteering answers or answering questions when asked, even though you think the child knows the answers?			

MOTOR	YES	NO	SOMETIMES
Does the child:			
13. continuously switch a crayon back and forth from one hand to the other when coloring?			
14. appear clumsy or shaky when using one or both hands?			
15. when coloring with a crayon, appear to tense the hand not being used (for instance, clench it into a fist)?			

* Question applies if child is four years or older.

Fig. 10–1 Teachers Observation Form and Checklist.

MOTOR (continued)	YES	NO	SOMETIMES
16. when walking or running, appear to move one side of the body differently from the other side? For instance, does the child seem to have better control of the leg and arm on one side than on the other?			
17. lean or tilt to one side when walking or running?			
18. seem to fear or not be able to use stairs, climbing equipment or tricycles?			
19. stumble often or appear awkward when moving about?			
*20. appear capable of dressing self except for tying shoes?			

SOCIAL	YES	NO	SOMETIMES
Does the child:			
21. engage in more than two disruptive behaviors a day (tantrums, fighting, screaming, etc.)?			
22. appear withdrawn from the outside world (fiddling with pieces of string, staring into space, rocking)?			
23. play alone and seldom talk to other children?			
24. spend most of the time trying to get attention from adults?			
25. have toileting problems (wet or soiled) once a week or more often?			

VISUAL OR HEARING	YES	NO	SOMETIMES
Does the child:			
26. appear to have eye movements that are jerky or uncoordinated?			

27. seem to have difficulty seeing objects? For instance, does the child:
    tilt head to look at things?
    hold objects close to eyes?
    squint?
    show sensitivity to bright lights?
    have uncontrolled eye-rolling?
    complain that eyes hurt?			

28. appear awkward in tasks requiring eye-hand coordination such as pegs, puzzles, coloring, etc.?			

29. seem to have difficulty hearing? For instance, does the child:
    consistently favor one ear by turning the same side of the head in the direction of the sound?
    ignore, confuse, or not follow directions?
    pull on ears or rub ears frequently, or complain of earaches?
    complain of head noises or dizziness?
    have a very high, very low, or monotonous tone of voice?			

* Question applies if child is four years or older.

Fig. 10-1 (continued)

GENERAL HEALTH	YES	NO	SOMETIMES
Does the child:			
30. seem to have an excessive number of colds?			
31. have frequent absences because of illness?			
32. have eyes that water?			

33.   have frequent discharge from:
         eyes?
         ears?
         nose?			

34. have sores on body or head?			

35.   have periods of unusual movements (such as eye blinking) or "blank
         spells" which seem to appear and disappear without relationship to the
         social situation?			

36. have hives or rashes? wheeze?			
37. have a persistent cough?			
38. seem to be excessively thirsty? seem to be excessively hungry?			

39.   Have you noticed any of the following conditions:
         constant fatigue?
         irritability?
         restlessness?
         tenseness?
         feverish cheeks or forehead?			

40. Is the child overweight?			
41. Is the child physically or mentally lethargic?			
42. Has the child lost noticeable weight without being on a diet?			

Fig. 10–1 (continued)

format that is convenient for the classroom staff. The reason for the small size paper is to ensure brevity. Anecdotal notes are recorded on each child in each area of development at regular intervals.

Looking back on three months of motor notes, teachers could see how helpful the physical therapist had been. The techniques she demonstrated when working with Joey helped teachers to help Joey to improve his motor skills. Furthermore, in looking over social notes during the same period, it appeared Joey was most likely to get on the climbing frames if other children were there, too. Cognitive notes indicated he

had learned most of the names of the children he climbed with and often counted how many children were on the climber. The composite picture, made up of these brief anecdotal notes, is one of a child making steady progress within and across developmental areas.

Running records.   These are narrative recordings — attempts to write down everything that a child says and does for a period of time. Taken periodically, a well-rounded picture can be obtained of each child's overall behavior and development. Running records are a useful form of observation; they also are the

---

Child: Joey   Observer M.J.
Play yard   1/12/95

MOTOR DEVELOPMENT

Joey climbed up eight rungs of the climbing
tower. On each rung he started with his left foot
and brought his right foot up next to it before
going on to the next rung. With each step up he
grasped the bar directly above with the alternate
hand (left foot, right hand). In coming down he
reversed the pattern.

Fig. 10–2 Example of a motor note.

most time consuming. Unlike other written observations, teachers rarely can take a running record while
teaching. However, a teacher can be released from
direct work with children for an occasional 20 or 30
minutes to take a running record. Volunteers often
are willing to relieve teachers for this purpose or take
running records themselves. When there is a child
that teachers are especially concerned about, volunteers' observations can be of great value.

Logs, journals, and diaries.   Records of this kind are
similar to the running record but less comprehensive.
Written accounts may be kept in a loose leaf notebook
with a section for each child. (Some teachers prefer a
separate folder for each child; the important point is
to find a format that is convenient and easy to use.)
Notes are jotted down during class time or immediately after children leave for the day. The jottings may be
general notes about a child, or focused notes on some
aspect of the child's behavior. For example, teachers
may need to know more about a child's outdoor activities before planning an individualized program to
increase play skills: Who does Angelo play with? Does
he play on the climbing equipment? Ride the wheel
toys? Build with outdoor blocks? Is he accepted into
the play of other children? What other children? Are
some play periods better than others? Why? The
answers to these questions (or any others teachers

may have about any child) provide clues for program
planning.

Time sampling.   Time sampling has to do with periodic
and momentary observations to determine the presence or absence of a behavior: Is Leeanne engaged
most of the time with play materials? Does Marty
engage mostly in solitary, parallel, associative or cooperative play? In some sampling, teachers look at the
child in question at regular intervals. Usually it is only
a brief glance, perhaps once every two minutes, or five
minutes, or fifteen minutes. On the other hand they
may take a quick look only two or three times a day, at
certain periods such as circle time. With each glance,
if the behavior is occurring, the teacher makes a mark
on a tally sheet. It may turn out that Leeanne, for
example, was engaged with materials only three out of
the fifteen samples. Might this be an indication that
she needs different materials? Or help in extending
her span of attention? As for Marty, he was playing
alone in 5 percent of the samples in associative play
about 40 percent, in cooperative play in the remaining samples—a nice balance for an almost 5-year-old.

Language samples.   As noted in Unit 5, speech and
language problems account for a major portion of

**Observation notes may focus on some particular aspect
of a child's behavior.**

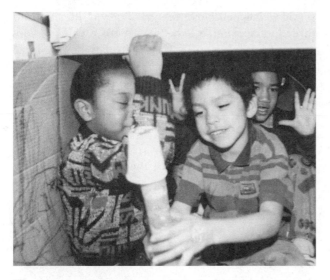

The observer writes down, phonetically, whatever words or sounds the child utters.

developmental problems. Before treatment can begin, the current level of a child's skills first must be assessed. A good place to get information about a child's language is in the classroom. Here the child is doing what comes naturally, with familiar things to talk about and familiar people to talk with. Language samples are verbatim recordings (word for word or sound for sound) of exactly what the child says or what sounds the child makes. If the child says "du gul," it is written "du gul" (phonetically) even if the observer knows the child is referring to "the girl." If the child is squealing "Eeeeee" and pointing to the juice, "Eeeeee," is what the observer writes down, not "Billy wanted juice." It is important for the observer to note the pointing along with the vocalization to show that Billy was able to communicate his need.

Early Identification: Cautionary Notes for Teachers. Teachers' observations are of indisputable value in identifying developmental problems. Nevertheless, the information must be used with care, even caution. It may do a 3- or 4-year-old more harm than good to attach too much importance to a developmentally "normal" speech irregularity such as a lisp or mild stammering. Excessive concern, or pressure, on prob-

lems of this type can be as damaging as failing to recognize a problem. It must be remembered, too, that some behaviors may not be what they appear to be. A child may seem to be hyperactive—constantly jumping up, pushing ahead of other children, grabbing the book the teacher is reading from. These behaviors actually may be the child's efforts to bring things into closer eye or ear range because of a vision or hearing deficit.

Teachers avoid making diagnoses. Diagnosis implies decision-making based on clinical expertise in interpreting **symptoms**. A proper diagnosis requires specialized expertise, often from several disciplines, to identify even fairly common problems. Examples from teachers' classroom experiences are plentiful, as in the following case:

Charles was a nine-year-old with delayed language skills. He had several inappropriate behaviors, including (but only on some days) crying and whining while hitting himself about the cheeks. Charles's parents had been told the behaviors were signs of emotional disturbance. Teachers, however, observed times when there was no self-hitting and crying. They suggested the parents get another opinion. The ultimate clinical diagnosis was abscessed back teeth with pain that flared up intermittently. Charles's "emotionally disturbed" behaviors ceased once the teeth were treated.

Teachers avoid labels. As emphasized in Unit 5, labeling a young child as retarded, hyperactive, or emotionally disturbed can have disastrous effects. The intervention program tends to focus narrowly on what the label implies while overlooking the child's skills and strengths. Lost is the healthier individual that might have emerged if the stereotyping label never had been hung on the child. Such a loss very nearly occurred in a case study reported by Allen and Goetz (1982).

Maria was labeled early in life as retarded. Near her fourth birthday she was placed in a preschool program where little was expected of her as a *retarded child*. However, a volunteer observed Maria's many problem-solving skills with materials and equipment. Intrigued by the volunteer's observations, the head teacher took several running records. These showed the same kinds of high level cognitive behaviors.

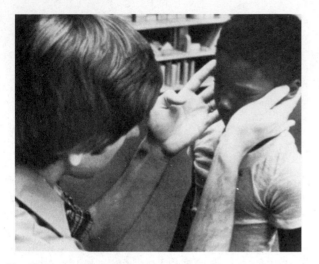

Teachers do not diagnose: a proper diagnosis requires clinical expertise.

Consultation with Maria's mother revealed that both she and Maria had been severely abused by the father before he left permanently two years earlier. The mother revealed further that she, too, had often suspected that Maria "wasn't all dumb." The staff helped Maria's mother arrange for a comprehensive reassessment by a child study team. Following the assessment, program changes (systematically reinforcing use of language and social interactions with children and teachers) were immediately put into effect. Within a year Maria was indistinguishable from any other child in the group in terms of mental functioning.

Teachers avoid raising parents' anxiety. Most parents know their child has a problem even though they may be reluctant to admit it. The teacher's role is to help parents see their child more realistically without raising their anxiety unduly. Teacher report what the child *can do*, as well as what the child cannot do. This helps parents become better attuned to their child. It also provides an opening for teachers to help parents recognize the need to seek professional help to build the child's strengths. (Work with families is discussed in Unit 9.)

Teachers assist in making referrals. Child Find and early identification procedures are to ensure that children with developmental problems are referred for special

services. Nevertheless, teachers never refer a child directly, regardless of the severity of a child's problems. The teacher's role is to help parents recognize the need for treatment. The next step is linking the family to the needed services. This is accomplished readily if the program is served by a child study team. If not, the teacher may have to play a more active role. Marotz, Cross, and Rush (1993) suggest: "a teacher who is familiar with local services, such as hospitals, clinics, health departments, medical specialists, private and public service agencies, and various sources of funding can be helpful to parents in obtaining the comprehensive medical care and assistance the child needs" (p. 72).

Making careful judgments. Deciding if a behavior is appropriate is sometimes difficult. The most important considerations, as noted earlier, are the ways of the child's family and community. Often these are quite different from what the teacher is used to. Therefore, it is important to ask the question: *Does the behavior interfere with the child's willingness to engage in a wide range of learning experiences and social activities that are included in the developmental curriculum?* If the answer is "No" then it is not likely that teachers need to be overly concerned.

Carefully kept records and staff consultation are part of determining each child's developmental needs.

Remembering that each child is different. It must be remembered, too, that no two children of the same age develop exactly alike (Unit 4). To expect uniformity is contrary to basic developmental principles. On the other hand, a nonintervention policy of expecting children to "grow out" of a developmental difference that has the potential for causing trouble also is dangerous. A "wait-and-see" attitude may condemn some children to unnecessary delays in treatment. The delay may lead to **cumulative deficits** that become increasingly difficult to overcome over the months and years.

Frequency. Many times, it is not the type of behavior but the amount that is of concern. Almost all inappropriate behaviors are seen in children (and even in adults) at one time or another. Every young child cries, whines, sulks, clings, disobeys, and talks back. Rarely are these behaviors considered unusual, let alone harmful. They are a normal, even desirable aspect of the developmental process because they indicate a full range of emotional responses. Seldom are they cause for alarm unless:

a behavior occurs excessively; (children who frequently hit, bite, or kick others)

a behavior is used constantly or exclusively in place of more developmentally appropriate responses (children who seem always to whine and cry for what they want instead of asking)

a behavior interferes with significant learning experiences (hiding in a cubby much of the day, thereby withdrawing from classroom activities)

Environmental factors. Situations outside the child often are responsible for the frequent occurrence of a problem behavior. One clue that indicates the likelihood of an environmental cause is when a behavior occurs to excess under some conditions but not under other conditions. In these instances, it is probable that the environment, not the child, is at fault. Consider the following examples:

A 4-year-old's inability to share may be caused by a shortage of attractive materials or equipment rather than selfishness.

The inability of a 7-year-old to *cut on the lines* may be due to faulty scissors.

The unresponsiveness of an infant may change when the infant is offered appropriate activities.

INDIVIDUALIZED EDUCATION PLANS (IEP)

The individualized education plan (IEP) is a kind of blueprint for providing early intervention services. Teachers are essential throughout the IEP process; in the assessment of children; in the adaptation and modification of classroom activities to implement the individualized program; and in the evaluation process. Linkage between classroom practice and the treatment recommendations of the child study team is forged by teachers. Furthermore, the ongoing evaluation of the appropriateness of each child's daily program is largely dependent on the teacher. In other words, teachers are central to the entire IEP process.

The IEP Team. The IEP is developed by a child study team made up of professionals from various disciplines. The child's parent or parents (or **surrogates**) and the child's teacher must be included in the IEP deliberations. The type of team and the disciplines involved are varied. Several models for child study teams have emerged in the past few years.

- *Multidisciplinary*—professionals working independently of each other in a kind of *parallel play* format; each discipline is viewed as important but taking responsibility only for his or her own area of clinical expertise.
- *Interdisciplinary*—professionals working together to identify priorities and develop goals; professionals will coordinate and collaborate across disciplines and incorporate skills from other disciplines into their own practice. All disciplines will provide services in the most natural and least restrictive setting—usually the classroom. (The term interdisciplinary will be used in this text.)
- *Transdisciplinary*—professionals teaching each other through continuous staff development; joint team functioning; role release and role substitution; determining role definition (who does what) around the characteristics of each child and family;

relying on each other to build on the range of strengths found among different types of child development experts.

Requirements of the IEP.   The IEP is to be based on developmentally valid, nondiscriminatory assessment information. Program and placement decisions are to be formulated from information from multiple sources: test scores, observation in situations in which the child is comfortable and at ease, input from significant persons in the child's life (parents, grandparents, teachers, out-of-home caregivers).

The completed IEP includes statements about:

The child's present levels of performance and skills developed

Long-term (annual) goals for the child and short-term objectives that will accomplish the long-term goals

Specific services to be provided and starting dates

Accountability (evaluation) to determine if objectives are being met

Where and when inclusive programs will be provided

These requirements will be discussed one by one. (Transition plans, required by PL 99-457 will be discussed in Unit 11.)

Assessment.   Prior to writing an IEP, a child's developmental skills must be assessed. As described earlier, this is an information gathering process. It is not, however, a one time operation; instead, it should be

---

Child's Name: Tyrone S.   Age: 4 yrs, 2 mo
Center City Public School District
September 17, 1994

Present Level of Functioning
    Social development: Tyrone does not play with other children. He never approaches another child and runs away every time a child approaches him.

Annual Goals
    Tyrone will learn to play cooperatively with other children.

Short-Term Objectives
    Tyrone will play next to other children during highly preferred activities (for example, sandbox, sensory table, finger painting) for two 10 minute periods each day.

Special Services
    School district will provide transportation to and from community preschool placement and school district will pay Tyrone's tuition for a half day program at the Learning Center Community Preschool.
    Speech therapist will visit the preschool once a week to work with Tyrone and meet with the teacher.
    Behavior management program coordinated by classroom teacher and **itinerent special education teacher**.

Beginning and Duration of Services
    Tyrone will begin attending the Learning Center on October 5. Other services will be in place by October 12. Placement and services will be re-evaluated by April 5, 1995.

Evaluation
    Tyrone will be reassessed on the Preschool Profile in March. A graph will be kept showing the amount of time Tyrone spent playing next to children each day.

Fig. 10–3 Example of an individualized program.

an ongoing process throughout the year so that a child's progress can be tracked and programs adjusted as needed. Ongoing assessment provides a comprehensive description—a developmental profile—of a child at particular points in time.

Depending on the results of earlier screening tests, specific disciplines (audiologist, nutritionist, physical therapist, and others) do specialized assessments. The early childhood teacher is responsible for collecting general information and often provides the "glue" for putting together the overall developmental picture of the child. As noted earlier, it is the teacher, working with a child every day, who is especially suited to assessing children's strengths and needs. Observing children's play in the classroom gives teachers valuable information about a child's developmental skills and the effectiveness of intervention strategies. *NOTE:* It is necessary to watch a child over several days and several play episodes. Consecutive observations ensure that what is observed is representative of the child's everyday behaviors (Bailey and Wolery 1989).

Numerous assessment instruments have been developed over the past 30 years. (Appendix A provides a partial list of assessment tools.) In addition, there are developmental profile forms that many teachers of young children find even more useful. NAEYC publishes one such profile designed especially for infant and toddler caregivers (Lally et al. 1986). The developmental profile offered in this text (Appendix B) has been used extensively by teachers for ongoing assessments of children, birth to age 6. A separate chart or profile is kept on each child. Periodic observations are made of each child in several areas: gross and fine motor, preacademics, self-help, music, art, and stories, social and play behaviors, receptive and expressive language.

The itemized skills on the chart are but examples of behaviors characteristic of broad, general skills. A child may show an achievement in various ways. For example, an item in the 0 to 12 months preacademic square reads: "Puts blocks in, takes blocks out of container." The basic skill is picking up and releasing an object within a prescribed space. An infant who can pick up a cookie, drop it in a cup, and then take it out, should receive a passing score.

Highlight pens of several colors allow a quick reading of each child's status in all developmental areas. Items that the child passes in the initial assessment are lined through in one color; a different color is used for each subsequent assessment. Skills that a child does not have are left unmarked. Inconsistent successes—responses that a child displays infrequently or *sometimes*—are especially important. They should not be lined through, but flagged, perhaps with an asterisk. These *sometimes* responses often indicate appropriate starting points for a specific intervention program.

The profile is updated periodically on the basis of observations and notes made by teachers as they work with children. The updating usually reveals that each child has acquired some of the flagged *sometimes* skills. Skills that were left unmarked in an earlier assessment often become a newly marked set of *sometimes* skills. What the teaching staff has on hand at all times is a current, visual profile of each child—word pictures of overall functioning in relationship to developmental expectations for children of like ages.

Prerequisite skills.   Necessary sequence of skills show up clearly on the preschool profile as does the interrelatedness of developmental areas. Mastering a skill in a particular area of development often depends upon specific achievements in other areas. For example, a child cannot perform certain self-care tasks such as buttoning and unbuttoning until the **pincer grasp** is well established. Developmental deficits also show up clearly. Deficits may accumulate because of unrecognized relationships among developmental areas. By keeping a child's profile up-to-date, a deficiency in one area may be pinpointed and so explain problems in other areas. Language disabilities, for example, often lead to poor play relationships because of the inability to adequately express ideas and preferences. Poor verbal skills also may delay cognitive development or have a negative effect on intellectual performance because inadequate language interferes with formulating and expressing thoughts.

Long-term or annual goals.   The IEP must include written statements specifying expected learning outcomes for each child each school year. Annual goals are usually presented as broad general statements about what can be expected of the child. Example: Erin will learn

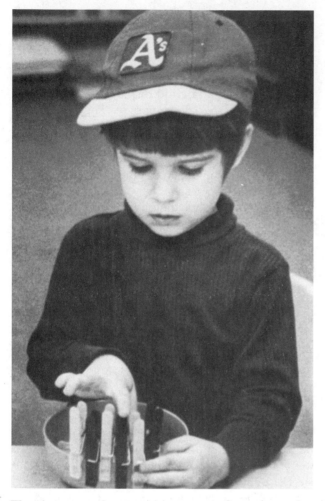

The pincer grasp is prerequisite to many fine motor tasks.

enjoyment of life. Example: Melinda was a bright and lively child born with severely malformed hands. Even as an infant, it was obvious she had a talent and love for music and rhythm. While long-term goals for this child must include learning to use a **prosthesis** on each hand (a major priority), her musical development is important, too. At least one goal related to music should be written into Melinda's IEP.

Short-term objectives.   Every IEP must include lists of short-term objectives. These are *mini-programs*, step-by-step learning that enables the child to achieve the designated long-term goals. Short-term objectives usually focus on skills or behaviors that can be measured (counted or timed) and acquired withing a few weeks or months. The measurements give objective evidence of a child's progress. Learning to wear and become adept at using her prostheses might be a long-term goal for the child mentioned above. Exactly how this is to be accomplished, and how it is to be measured is spelled out in the short-term objectives. Enhancing the child's musical talents might also be worked into the goal and objectives.

> Example: Each day, for 15 minutes or more, Melinda and a teacher will work together at the piano picking out single-note tunes while Melinda is learning to wear her prostheses.

The amount of time spent playing the piano and the number of tunes learned might be the measurable aspect of these objectives. Furthermore, learning to play tunes on the piano is likely to be reinforcing for Melinda in her efforts at wearing her prostheses.

According to Evans and Kiely (1980) short-term objectives include answers to the following questions: Who? What? When and Where? How well?

WHO will be engaged in acquiring the behavior?
WHAT specifically is the behavior?
WHEN and WHERE is the behavior to be exhibited?
HOW WELL is the behavior to be perfected?

Following are two examples of short-term instructional objectives in the Evans and Kiely format:

to: (1) be more independent; (2) get along with other children; (3) use nonaggressive ways to get what she wants.

Long-term goals center on priorities essential to the child's overall development. These sometimes are referred to as functional goals (Notari-Syverson and Shuster 1995). For every child, the number and kind of goals will vary. Never, though should goals for a child be so numerous or so complex as to overwhelm the child and family. Furthermore, self-sufficiency goals, as important as they are, should not rule out goals that help to improve the child's self-esteem and

EXAMPLE I

Goal: Acquiring balance.
Short-term objective: learning to hop.

WHO   John B.
WHAT   will hop on either foot
WHEN and WHERE   during free play time
HOW WELL   five consecutive hops on each
                  foot

EXAMPLE II

Goal: Increasing span of attention.
Short-term objective: Increasing sitting and decreasing talking out of turn during a story time.

WHO   Becky S.
WHAT   will sit quietly and not talk out
                  of turn
WHEN and WHERE   classroom story time
HOW WELL   for 10 minutes on five
                  consecutive days.

In the first example the measurement was a frequency count: how *many* times John could hop on one foot in a given period. In the second example, a duration measure was used: how *long* a time Becky could go without talking out of turn. (How objectives such as these are reached is discussed in Units 15 and 17.)

Graphing (transferring the measures to a chart) brings progress into focus. John's graph indicates it was the nineteenth day (the thirteenth day of intervention) before he hopped 5 times on the left foot within the allotted time. According to Becky's graph, she was quiet only one or two minutes of the story period at first. Not until day 15 of intervention did she reach the short-term objective of staying for 10 minutes without talking. This she continued for the next five days, thus meeting criterion.

Displaying children's progress in graphic form requires minimal effort on the part of the teacher, yet the benefits are many. For reasons not fully understood, each child's progress seems to be greater when teachers keep updated graphs (Fuchs and Fuchs 1986). It may be that behavior changes, even when slow, appear more clearly on a graph. The visual display also may help both teacher and child be more

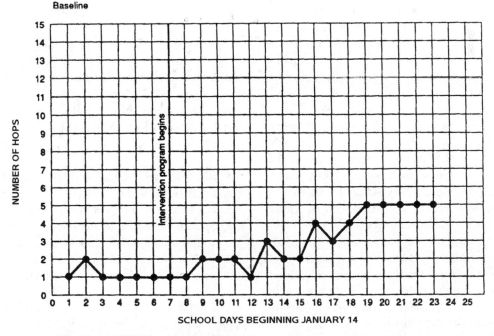

Fig. 10-4 John's hopping program.

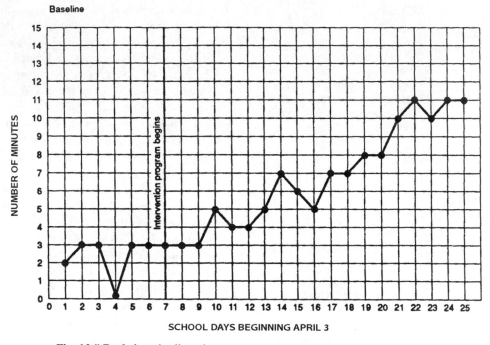

Fig. 10-5 Becky's quiet listening program.

aware of progress and so feel more successful. Success always leads to increased motivation. Lack of progress also is readily apparent on a graph. In such cases the program can be changed promptly so as to improve the child's performance and decrease frustration for teacher and child.

Specific services to be provided. A statement of the specific intervention services, supports, and equipment to be provided for each child must be included in every IEP. In addition to a list of what services will be provided, an IEP should contain a description of how services will be provided. This is especially important with the movement toward **activity-based intervention** (Bricker and Cripe 1992). Activity-based or naturalistic intervention embeds the specialized instruction required by the child into the ongoing activities in an early childhood classroom. For example, rather than removing a child from the classroom, the physical therapist will join the class during outdoor playtime and work with John on his hopping. In another example, the speech therapist might conduct a cooking activity during the free choice time where she can address the language objectives of many children at once. This type of naturalistic intervention has been demonstrated to be more effective than **pull-out** types of therapy services (Noonan and McCormick 1993). Depending on the individual needs of a specific child, the specific services section of an IEP might contain requirements for:

- Bi-weekly in-class sessions with a speech therapist or physical therapist (or both).
- Bus service to and from preschool.
- Special educational support services provided by an **itinerant special education teacher**.
- Monthly consultations by a behavior specialist to assist in behavior management issues.

Projected dates for services. Projected starting and stopping dates are to be specified for each service prescribed for a child.

Example: Amanda will receive orientation and mobility training at her home two afternoons a week and at school one morning a week from October 1, until the end of the semester when it will be determined if training is to continue.

Two reasons are given for the time line mandate. One is to ensure that no child is left waiting indefinitely for services essential to his or her progress. The second is to prevent special services from being terminated prematurely. A reasonable length of time must be allowed for accomplishing the objectives and goals stated in the child's IEP.

Evaluation (statement of accountability). At least once a year each child's program must be evaluated to see if objectives are being met. Evaluations are to be based on specifically described procedures such as test scores and written observations. In actual practice, evaluations should be conducted more often. As mentioned earlier, an in-place system of ongoing assessments simplifies the procedure. The Preschool Profile, for example, provides both ongoing assessment and program evaluation. Every item on the profile describes a specific child behavior; its presence or absence can be noted by a teacher. Graphs also provide program accountability. By using the preschool profile to periodically assess a child and by keeping graphs of a child's progress, a convincing evaluation process is always in operation.

SUMMARY

Case finding and the identification of developmental problems can take place any time after the first few weeks of conception. The earlier a problem is identified, the more likely it is that it can be treated effectively and that associated problems can be prevented. To this end, federally funded mass screening programs referred to as Child Find are regular events in most communities. All young children (except those with obvious disabling conditions) should be screened, because many problems are subtle and difficult to recognize.

Many kinds of screening instruments are available. Some are geared to overall development, some to specialized areas such as hearing and vision, some to particular ages or developmental domains. Whatever the test, it must be given in the child's first language with scrupulous regard for the customs of the child's family and the child's physical and psychological state. More than one instrument must be used in the assessment process. Even then, the results of many tests must be viewed with extreme caution, especially IQ tests. Most early childhood educators view standardized IQ tests as being of little value when working with young children.

Teachers are major agents in the early identification process. Direct observation is a teacher's best tool in determining a child's developmental status and the suitability of specific classroom activities for the group and for the individual children. Observation forms and checklists, especially those that teachers devise themselves, help teachers answer questions about children's behavior and classroom practices. Teachers must always use their information with care and in the best interests of the child and family.

The individualized educational plan (IEP) is a major and logical outcome of early identification and assessment procedures. A child's teacher and parent(s) are a required part of IEP planning along with members of the interdisciplinary child study team. The IEP must be in written form. It is to be based on nondiscriminatory tests and observations and is to specify long-term goals and short-term objectives. Services that will be provided and their start and stop dates will be specified. Finally, the IEP must describe the accountability component: how the effectiveness of the IEP will be measured.

STUDENT ACTIVITIES

1. Arrange a sheet of paper so that you can take a frequency count on how often a teacher initiates a conversation with children. While observing during free play, select one particular teacher and tally how many times that teacher initiates conversation with children. Do the same on another day with a different teacher. Compare the observations.

2. Select a partner. Each of you, independently of the other, take a half-hour running record of the same child. Compare your observations to see if you were seeing the same things. Critique each other's running records for objectivity.

3. Write to three school districts in your state and ask for copies of their IEP forms. Compare and contrast these with the IEP requirements as given in the text.

4. Make a copy of the Preschool Profile. Observe the same child for 30 to 45 minutes on three different days. Draw a horizontal line through the chart, indicating the child's age. Using a highlight pen, color through the skills that you see the child engage in during your observations. (The skills may be on either side of the line.) When finished with the above activity show the Profile to the child's teacher. Ask the teacher to discuss with you how well your profile assesses the observed child.

5. Plot the following data points on graph paper. (You can draw your own grid with pencil and ruler.)
   Number of times Leslie spoke to teachers:

9/27	3
9/28	11
9/29	4
10/2	0
10/3	0
10/4	7
10/5	8
10/6	8
10/9	1
10/10	2
10/12	10

REVIEW QUESTIONS

A. Briefly answer the following questions;
   1. What is Child Find?
   2. What is the purpose of screening programs?
   3. Who does diagnosis?
   4. What is the value of a chart like the Preschool Profile?
   5. What is the difference between a norm-referenced and a criterion-referenced test?
   6. What is the referral process?
   7. Who develops the IEP?
   8. Define long-term IEP goals and short-term objectives.
   9. Why graph behavioral data?
   10. What is meant by a *statement of accountability* as related to the IEP?

B. Circle the *three best* answers in each of the following.
   1. Early identification of developmental problems can take place
      a. before birth.
      b. during or immediately following birth.
      c. any time between 0 and 18 years.
      d. not after the early childhood years (9 to 18).
   2. Child Find is a screening process that
      a. should include all young children except those with an obvious disability.
      b. is only for children at high risk for developmental problems.
      c. can be conducted by professionals and paraprofessionals.
      d. should result in referrals for children in need of special services.
   3. The result of screening tests
      a. are good predictors of children's future development.
      b. are not to be used for planning curriculum.
      c. may or may not be valid.
      d. should always be backed up with family information and direct observations.
   4. IQ tests
      a. can be discriminatory assessment instruments.
      b. are of little value when working with young children, according to a NAEYC positions paper.
      c. do not take into account a child's learning opportunities.
      d. always provide a valid assessment of children's intellectual ability because they are standardized on large numbers of children.
   5. Three common models for child study teams are
      a. interdisciplinary
      b. multidisciplinary
      c. supradisciplinary
      d. transdisciplinary

6. An IEP for each developmentally disabled child
   a. is required by law.
   b. may or may not be in writing, depending on the school district's policy.
   c. is based on interdisciplinary assessment and diagnosis.
   d. includes parents (or surrogates) in the planning stage.
7. The IEP must contain specific statements describing
   a. the services that will be provided.
   b. when the services will commence.
   c. reasons why certain prescribed services will not be provided.
   d. special equipment or prostheses needed.
8. Examples of long-term goals are
   a. Jay will learn to read with comprehension.
   b. Marty will learn to groom herself properly.
   c. Craig will become more friendly and outgoing.
   d. Sarah will learn to brush her teeth.
9. A short-term objective is written in terms of
   a. who is to be acquiring a particular skill?
   b. why is that person to learn that skill?
   c. what, specifically, is the skill?
   d. how well is the skill to be mastered?
10. An up-to-date Preschool Profile provides
   a. a *word picture* of a child's current development.
   b. an ongoing assessment across developmental areas and ages.
   c. evidenced of possible deficits or delays.
   d. an artist's sketch of each child at year's end.

C. True of False.
   T F 1. Child Find is the federal government's all-out effort to locate missing and kidnapped children.
   T F 2. Screening tests provide a trustworthy diagnosis of a developmental problem.
   T F 3. Parents tend to be overly anxious so it is well to pay little attention to their complaints about their young children.
   T F 4. IQ scores are not good predictors of a young child's future mental functioning.
   T F 5. Situations outside the child may be responsible for a child's poor performance.
   T F 6. Almost all inappropriate behaviors are seen in all children at one time or another.
   T F 7. *Nerdeje was cross and out-of-sorts all day long.* This is an example of a subjective statement about a child.
   T F 8. Duration measures are concerned with how often something happens.
   T F 9. Anecdotal notes are brief and focused on a particular area of development.
   T F 10. A major responsibility of teachers is to refer children to the appropriate clinicians for needed services.

REFERENCES

Allen, K.E., and Goetz, E.M. (1982). *Early childhood education: Special problems, special solutions.* Rockville, MD: Aspen Systems.

Allen, K.E., and Marotz, L.R. (1994). *Developmental profiles: Prebirth through eight.* Albany: Delmar.

Bailey, D.B., and Wolery, M. (1989). *Assessing infants and preschoolers with handicaps.* Columbus: Merrill.

Banks, J.A. (1994). *An introduction to multicultural education.* Boston, MA: Allyn & Bacon.

Barrera, I. (1994). Thoughts on the assessment of young children whose sociocultural background is unfamiliar to the assessor. *Zero to Three, 14(6),* 9–13.

Beatty, J.J. (1990). *Observing Development of the Young Child.* Columbus: Merrill.

Bergan, J.R., and Feld, J.K. (1993). Developmental assessment: New directions. *Young Children, 48(5),* 41–47.

Bricker, D., and Cripe, J. (1992). *An activity-based approach to early intervention.* Baltimore: Brookes.

Cohen, L.G., and Spenciner, L.J. (1994). *Assessment of young children.* New York: Longman.

Evans, D., and Kiely, J. (1980). *Educational Training for Head Start.* Mimeographed.

Fuchs, L.S., and Fuchs, D. (1986). Effects of systematic formative evaluation: A meta-analysis. *Exceptional Children, 53,* 199–208.

Greenspan, S.I., and Meisels, S.J. (1994). Toward a vision for developmental assessment of infants and young children. *Zero to Three, 14(6),* 1–8.

Hanson, M.J., and Lynch, E.W. (1989). *Early Intervention.* Austin, TX: PRO-ED.

Harry, B. (1992). *Cultural diversity, families, and the special education system.* New York: Teachers College Press.

Hills, T.W. (1993). Assessment in context—teachers and children at work. *Young Children, 48(5),* 20–28.

Irwin, D.M., and Bushnell, M.M. (1980). *Observational strategies for child study.* New York: Holt, Rinehart and Winston.

Keefe, C.H. (1995). Portfolios: Mirrors of learning. *Teaching Exceptional Children, 27(2),* 66–67.

Lally, J.R., Provence, S., Szanton, E., and Weissbourd, B. (1986). Developmentally appropriate care for children from birth to age 3. In S. Bradekamp (Ed.) (1987). *Developmentally appropriate practice in early childhood programs serving children from birth through age 8.* Washington, D.C.: National Association for the Education of Young Children, 17–33.

Lynch, E.W., and Hanson, M.J. (1992). *Developing cross-cultural competence.* Baltimore, MD: Brookes.

Marotz, L., Cross, M., and Rush, J. (1993). *Health, safety, and nutrition for the young child.* Albany: Delmar.

Meisels, S.J. (1993). Remaking classroom assessment with the work sampling system. *Young Children, 48(5),* 34–40.

Meisels, S.J. (1985). *Developmental screening in early childhood: A guide.* Washington, D.C.: NAEYC.

NAEYC (1988). Position statement on standardized testing of young children 3 through 8 years of age. *Young Children,* 43, 3.

Neisworth, J.T., and Bagnato, S.J. (1992). The case against intelligence testing in early intervention. *Topics in Early Childhood Special Education, 12,* 1–20.

Noonan, M.J., and McCormick, L. (1993). *Early intervention in natural environments: Methods and procedures.* Pacific Grove, CA: Brooks/Cole.

Notari-Syverson, A., and Shuster, S.L. (1995). Putting real-life skills into IEP/IFSPs for infants and young children. *Teaching Exceptional Children, 27(2),* 29–32.

Perrone, V. (1990). How did we get here? In C. Kamii (Ed.), *Achievement testing in the early grades: The games grown-ups play.* Washington, D.C.: National Association for the Education of Young Children.

Schweinhart, L.J. (1993). Observing young children in action: The key to early childhood assessment. *Young Children, 48(5),* 29–33.

Thurman, S.K., and Widerstrom, A.H. (1990). *Infants and young children with special needs.* Baltimore: Brookes.

Planning Transitions to Support Inclusion

SUSAN FOWLER* AND ROBIN HAZEL**

OBJECTIVES

After studying this unit the student will be able to

- identify two major goals of an early childhood transition program.
- identify possible accommodations to be made by children, families, and service providers during the transition process.
- describe a transition planning format that includes program and personnel responsibilities.
- discuss ways to ease a child into a new program.
- suggest support services that could assist a child in adjusting to a new classroom.

The need for planning to assist young children as they enter preschool from early intervention services is recognized in PL 99-457 (Unit 3). In fact, the Individualized Family Service Plan (IFSP) should contain a plan for the child's and family's transition to preschool. Planning also is needed to assist young children as they move from one early childhood program to another and as they enter kindergarten. Although not required by law, it is also considered best practice to develop a transition plan as a component of the IEP, when children are moving from preschool to kindergarten or from a special education program to an inclusive program. To develop and implement effective transition plans, early childhood educators will need to develop specific skills and procedures for facilitating both the child's and the family's transition to the next program.

As children and families move from one type of program to another, be it a new preschool or kindergarten program, they encounter new faces, new environments, and new procedures. Planning these transitions is critical. It is, however, an often neglected component of early intervention programming. It is especially important for children who are moving into inclusive environments. Children with special needs may require more attention and planning and take somewhat longer to adjust than their peers. They may evidence separation problems from their parents during the first week or two in their new school if this is their first group experience away from home (Haymes, Fowler and Cooper 1994). Entry into a new program may require accommodations on the part of the service providers, the family and the child (Rice and O'Brien 1990). The child may need to play and work more independently. The family may need to alter their before-school child care arrangements to fit the schedule of the new program. The preschool teacher may need to redesign circle time to accommodate a new child with a vision problem.

If the child fails to make the necessary accommodations, or if the accommodations are made but do not

---

*Susan A. Fowler, Ph.D. Professor and Chairperson of the Special Education Department at the University of Illinois at Champagne-Urbana.

**Robin Hazel is Coordinator of Northeast Kansas Education Service Center's Parents as Teachers Program.

last, the result is an unsuccessful placement. The consequence is yet another transition; the implications are that either the individuals who were involved have failed, or the educational system has failed (Johnson et al. 1986). Thus, planning both the changes required by the transition and ways of maintaining the changes are critical factors in ensuring a successful transition.

TRANSITION GOALS

The purpose of transition planning is to lay out a process that enables a family and child to make a comfortable and positive change from one program to another. Ideally, the process produces a minimum of disruption in family routines while maintaining the child's academic and social progress. The following is an example of the accommodations required of a child, a family, and a teacher during one transition program:

Abby, born with spina bifida, had gotten about in a wheelchair most of her life. Psychological assessments indicated average to above-average intelligence. She had been in a private, special education preschool and child care center since infancy. Both parents worked full time. As Abby neared her fourth birthday, her parents decided she was ready to attend a regular preschool. Four months later, at the start of the school year, Abby was enrolled in a community preschool in the morning while continuing her special class placement in the afternoon.

The new program was different in a number of ways from the special education preschool program. It had more group activities and less individualized attention. Abby's parents were concerned about her ability to pay attention and participate actively in large group experiences. The dual placement also meant that they, the parents, had to rearrange their daily schedules so they could transport Abby from the morning program to the afternoon program. They realized that some days they would need to ask a friend or relative to provide midday transportation.

The community preschool teachers had concerns too. They redesigned some of the materials and activities so that Abby would be able to participate during the first critical days of the transition. The teachers wondered, though, if they would have the time or energy to continue to adapt materials and learning experiences. They wondered, too, if they could consistently include Abby in large motor activities, given the demands on teachers' time made by a group of active 4-year-olds.

The transition process requires systematic planning.

The success of the transition into the community preschool ultimately would be measured by the extent to which Abby, her family, and her teacher were able to sustain the many accommodations required of them. It is the *sustainability* of the accommodations that determine the success of a transition (Rice and O'Brien 1990).

TRANSITIONS IN PERSPECTIVE

The transition process requires systematic planning and evaluating. It also requires ongoing modification to keep it in tune with the needs of individual children, their families, and the service providers who are involved (Hains, Rosenkoetter and Fowler 1991). The perspectives of all must be considered in identifying the accommodations needed. A particular mother, for example, may believe that *she* should be consulted about every aspect of *her* child's education; that *she* should be the one to make the decisions about *her* child's transition to another program. In the same family, the father may believe it is best to leave such decisions to the teachers. The professionals involved in the transition may have ideas quite different from either parent's about the decision-making process and who should decide what. Awareness of these several perspectives is critical to the child's movement between programs.

Child's perspective.   Children change programs based on their developmental progress or because they reach an age in which they become eligible for the next program. For instance, children typically leave infant and toddler services and enter preschool services following their third birthday and most children start kindergarten if they are age 5 by the start of the school year. A change in the program or services provided within a program may also be initiated based on clinical evidence. For example, an updated diagnosis or a change in diagnostic findings may be the reason for a transition. Another factor may be that the child has acquired new and functionally significant skills. Whatever the reason, the child's ability to adapt to the next program is the central issue in determining the success of the transition. (Fowler 1982; Rosenkeotter, Hains and Fowler 1994).

The accommodations required of a child during a transition will depend on the individual child and the *sending* and *receiving* programs. The child will need to make new friends, generalize old skills to new situations, and learn unfamiliar routines while attempting to explore a new environment. Children often have difficulty transferring even well-established skills to new situations. What looks like a similar set of expec-

A child may have problems transferring well-established skills to new situations.

tations to professionals may not look at all the same to a child who has learned to respond to distinct cues or events that are not present in the new program. A child, for example, may be used to only one teacher or one particular type of instruction. That child may do well in a tightly structured, individualized program but have difficulty in a loosely structured program. Therefore, as professionals and parents prepare a child for a transition they need to ask: What will be different for the child? What skills does the child already have that will be useful in the new setting? What skills does the child need to learn before a transition is attempted?

A child's strengths and developmental differences or delays should be identified before the transition plan is developed. What accommodations will be easy for the child? Which will be difficult? To answer these questions each child must be assessed in terms of:

His or her current skills

The conditions under which the child demonstrates particular skills (Does the child do them at home but not at school, or vice versa?)

The skills the receiving program expects the child to have before entering the program.

Family's Perspective.   To ensure success, transition planning for a child must include the family. The formal transition plan developed for children when they move from earlier intervention services to preschool services require that the family be provided with information and training regarding the transition process and information regarding their legal rights. It is the best practice to provide the same information to families whose child is entering kindergarten or changing preschool programs. Transition plans may include ways in which the family will prepare for the change in programs (e.g., visiting potential programs, participating in meetings and staffings) as well as ways in which the family may help their child to prepare for the new program.

Because stress often is associated with change, transitions can be difficult for families (Turnbull, Summers and Brotherson 1986). A family must adjust to differences between programs by adapting to new schedules, finding new services, and accepting new responsibilities. Families may have to educate new school personnel about their child's special needs. They may be expected to set new goals for their child. They may need to adjust to fewer contacts with their child's teacher. Plans for the family component in a child's transition will vary, depending on the family's identified priorities and needs, nature of the child's disabilities, the culture of the family, and other family characteristics and beliefs.

Family characteristics.   Who makes up the family? Families should be free to define who its members are and may include extended members of the family in their constellation as well as close friends. Is the child the first child in the family to receive special services or to enter preschool or kindergarten? How many other children are in the family? What is the relationship of the extended family? What are the roles of the family members: wage earner? unemployed? decision-maker? caregiver? housekeeper?

Nature of the child's disability.   What effect does the child's disability have on his or her ability to participate in family activities? Does the child's disability interfere with family members' activities and needs? Cause financial, emotional, and physical strain on the family as a whole? Or only on particular family members? Does the child's problems pull the family together, make it stronger, as family members try to meet the needs of the disabled child?

Culture of the family.   What is the first language of the family? If it is not English, then all written information about the transition and the programs into which the child may transition should be made available to the family in their first language. Likewise, if a family is not fluent in English, an interpreter should be available for all meetings and discussions about the child's change in programs so that the family can be fully informed of the process and their options. Other important questions include: What is the family's cultural/ethnic background? Is there a match between the family's culture and the program that the child is entering? To what extent does the curriculum support the culture of the family by providing a sense of continuity between home and school with regard to cultur-

al values and practices? Is there respect for the child's first language and planning to address language differences between home and school? What are the family's beliefs and value systems? To what extent does the family's culture influence their interactions with service providers and their role as decision makers? Some families may regard questions as a sign of disrespect and defer to the decisions of service providers, as the experts, based on their culture and belief that the providers are the only experts. Service providers who understand or recognize the potential influence that culture and language may play in the family's involvement in their child's transition, will be better able to support the family in identifying their priorities.

Family beliefs.   Do family members talk about their feelings and fears? Do they focus only on the present (or past, or future)? Do they deal only with *the facts* of the situation? What appears to be the self-image of various family members? What seems to be *their* view of their lives compared to the lives of others? Do they face life with a sense of humor, a sense of resignation, a sense of getting even, a sense of hope? (Hazel, Barber, Roberts, Behr, Helmstetter and Guess 1980).

Developing successful transition activities depends on recognizing the diversity that each family brings to the planning process. Each family has its own misgivings. Each family has to decide, on their own, priorities and accommodations that they are willing and *able* to make.

Family Priorities and Needs.   Families may have strong preferences or priorities regarding the services that their child receives or the program that they enter. For instance, many working parents will need full-day child care. To meet this need they may prefer a program where the child can be enrolled all day and have special services delivered within the program by a consultant or itinerant service provider. Other families may be comfortable enrolling their child in more than one program in order to match their full-day child care needs. Some families may list as a priority that the child be served in an inclusive program, others may prefer one designed specifically for children with special education needs. Some families may request that their child with special needs be enrolled in the same school as their other children. Families must have an opportunity to discuss their family priorities and needs regarding new services or programs for their child, or service providers will run the risk of recommending a program that will conflict with the needs of the child's family and that ultimately may fail, if families are unable to ensure consistent attendance by their child.

In general, families are concerned about:

What services will be available in the next setting, and how can they obtain these services?
How will their child adjust to the new program, both socially and academically?
How will the new teacher adjust to their child, and vice versa?
What changes in daily routines will be required?

Families need adequate time to address these questions if they are to make logical decisions about their level of involvement in the transition planning. Some families choose to let professionals make the decisions, others want to make the decisions themselves; most families fall somewhere in between. According to Johnson et al. (1989), parents should be given the opportunity to:

Communicate their preferred role in the decision-making process.
Exchange information with the staff about their child.
Help select learning goals for their child.
Help in identifying potential placements.
Help make decisions based on their child's needs and the resources available.
Participate in forming a relationship with the staff of the new program.

Program Perspectives.   From the service provider's perspective, transitions from one program to another may reflect a number of changes: who receives services, what services they receive, how and when services are delivered, and by whom they are delivered (Fowler and Ostrosky 1994). In the transition process, one program or provider becomes the sender and the other becomes the receiver. To ensure that children

and families move smoothly from sender to receiver, without a gap in services and without unnecessary duplication of assessments and services, a plan is needed. Children and families should not have to wait for services that they need and the services in the new program should build upon the services that the child and family received previously, reflecting the child's developmental progress. It may be helpful for agencies who send and/or receive many children each year to also develop an interagency agreement with each other. The agreement should specify the roles and responsibilities of the sending and receiving programs to ensure good planning and communication between programs and their staffs (Rosenkoetter et al. 1994).

Communication and coordination between sending and receiving programs: To what extent do the two agencies communicate in advance of a child's transition and engage in collaborative planning? Public Law 99-457 requires that sending and receiving agencies jointly plan the transition of 3-year-old children from the earlier intervention services to preschool services. At least 90 days before the child's third birthday, the sending agency must begin the process of planning. A critical component of the planning is notifying the potential receiving programs well in advance of the child's third birthdate that 1) the child may be eligible for continued services at the preschool level; 2) identifying what assessments are needed to determine eligibility; 3) specifying who will conduct these assessments; 4) identifying program and service options for the child and family; and 5) calling a meeting to plan for services at the preschool level. Coordination is also necessary to ensure that families provide consent for the release of information to the new program and that records are transmitted in a timely manner. To ensure coordination and collaboration, sending and receiving programs may develop informal or formal agreements, depending on the complexity of the transition process and the number of children involved each year in transition.

Formal transition planning is not required for children moving from preschool to kindergarten. However, it is important for staff to meet and plan collaboratively with the family for this shift in services.

The greatest barrier to transition planning often appears to be lack of time. Staff involved in transitions must have time in their schedules for communicating with the other program and with the family. It is helpful to have formal lines of communication between agencies. It is also helpful to have clear lines of communication within each agency. Information may need to be shared among staff involved in delivering special services so that they can plan together. This again takes a commitment of time.

Agencies may need to develop a clear timetable of transition events (e.g., meetings, report writing, evaluations) to ensure that those involved know what is expected and when it is expected. Along with the timetable, they must identify time within a daily schedule for staff to address the transition events.

TRANSITION PLANNING

Planning is the key to successful transition for child, family, and teachers. As noted earlier, the accommodations required of everyone during a transition tend to be stressful. Careful planning reduces stress by putting the focus on specific issues related to the child's and the family's needs and preferences. When parents and professionals work as partners in developing a plan acceptable to all, it is likely that everyone will be more comfortable about what they are to do.

Successful transition planning should be an ongoing and integral part of every child's program. Transition planning should begin early in a child's enrollment in the original program and extend as long as needed into to new placement (Fowler and Titus 1993). Planning an individualized transition requires ongoing commitment. Time must be built into the regular school schedule for staff and parent meetings, for visits to the sending and receiving programs, and for exchange of child and program information. Ten basic steps (described in the following pages) are identified as central to the transition planning process. The steps are written from the perspective of the sending program; however they can be adapted to meet the needs of the receiving program as well.

Step 1: Coordinating the Transition. When several people work together to plan a child's transition, it is essential to appoint one person to coordinate efforts and take responsibility for getting things done. The

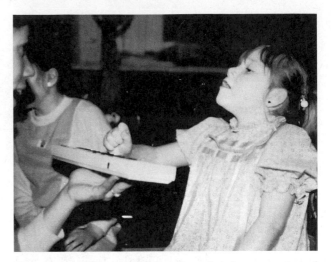

Learning goals for a child are formulated as parents and teachers exchange information.

transition coordinator may be the director of a program, a teacher, another member of the staff, or the service coordinator for the IFSP (Unit 10). An interdisciplinary team, for example, may rotate the coordinator position among its members, depending on the child's and the family's special needs. A major responsibility of the transition coordinator is to be familiar with:

His or her own program's transition procedures
The transition procedures of both the sending and the receiving programs
The resources, placement, and service options available in the community

Step 2: Visiting Alternative Programs. Early childhood professionals within the community need to be familiar with each other's programs. Familiarity creates understanding and cooperation. Learning about the specific expectations of a program or classroom helps the current teacher and the family decide if the child:

Will benefit from learning new routines or skills
Will require support in the receiving program or other accommodations in order to participate fully

Story reading expectations vary from teacher to teacher and program to program.

The transition coordinator (or individual teachers) should visit the programs where their children are most likely to be enrolled. If possible, visits should extend through a full session. Only by sitting in on a program in its entirety can the observer become familiar with the schedule in action, the range and tempo of activities, and the teaching style.

Visits can be arranged by calling the school. An increasing number of schools have an early childhood or kindergarten specialist whose job it is to arrange meetings to discuss a program-to-program transition. The program director or school principal also should be included as they can best describe the services available in their program or school district.

While observing, the coordinator should make written notes focused on similarities and differences between the programs. Differences that seem likely to create problems for the child should be underscored. Observation notes often are arranged under the following headings:

1. Environment—the physical arrangement of the classroom, the number of teachers and aides, and the daily schedule.
2. Behavior—what children and teachers do and how they interact.
3. Classroom activities—the learning opportunities provided for the children.

Step 3: Meetings within the Sending Program staff. After the coordinator has visited several programs, staff should meet and discuss the information obtained from the visits. Attention should be directed toward the differences between the programs—for example,

> The coordinator has observed five kindergartens in the area. Many former preschool children were enrolled in these programs. Most of the kindergarten teachers used a *learning centers* approach. Each day the children were divided into four groups. Each group was assigned one learning center at a time. The children were expected to stay and work at the assigned center for 15 minutes. Then they were rotated as a group to the next center. By the end of the session, each child had been at each center. Two adults supervised the four centers.
>
> In the preschool the children also had three or four activities from which to choose. They were not required to spend a certain amount of time in any one activity, nor did they have to visit all of the activities. The children were not grouped in the preschool; a child could change from one activity to another at any time. An adult was available in each activity.

Several obvious differences existed between the preschool and the kindergarten. The kindergarten children were expected to be more independent, have a longer attention span, and greater involvement in the program activities. Children transferring from a less structured preschool to this kindergarten might have difficulty making the necessary accommodations. The staff would need to discuss how the differences between the programs would affect a particular child's transition.

Minor differences are not likely to cause problems. When major differences exist, however, changes must be made. The receiving and sending programs (or both) need to adjust their way of doing things in order to ease the child's transition. A team effort is necessary if these changes are to be made, and made successfully. Differences will remain, of course. It is important for programs to assess whether their expectations are appropriate for the developmental level of the children whom they serve and to make adjustments when necessary. The goal is to prepare all children for a successful entry into their new program.

TEACHING STAFF
1. How many teachers, aides and volunteers work in the classroom?
2. How many children are in the classroom?
3. Do the numbers of adults and children in the program differ from the child's current program?

PHYSICAL ARRANGEMENT
1. Is the physical arrangement of the program different from the child's current program?
2. Do children at group time sit on individual mats or on a group rug?
3. Do children work at tables or at desks?
4. Are play and work areas integrated or separated?
5. Is the bathroom next to the classroom, down a hall, elsewhere?

DAILY SCHEDULE
1. Is the program in session longer than the child's current program?
2. To what extent are learning activities integrated with play or separated into specific time blocks?
3. How many minutes do children spend:
   a. in a large group setting (singing, sharing, listening to stories, having snacks)?
   b. in small groups?
   c. engaging in preacademic and fine motor activities?
   d. in free play activities?
   e. in recess and large motor activities?
   f. moving from one scheduled activity to another (for example, going to recess, waiting to be called from a large group to a small group)?

BEHAVIOR
1. Do children play or work in groups with minimal adult supervision?
2. If the classroom has learning centers, do the children choose their activity? Or, does the teacher send children to activities?
3. Are the children praised frequently for appropriate social behavior? For working? For finishing work?

SELF-HELP
1. What self-help skills do most of the children have (for example, dressing for outdoors, shoe tying, independent toileting)?

PREACADEMICS
1. How do children learn:
   a. in large or small groups?
   b. do the children respond to questions as a group or on an individual basis? And, how are questions from children answered?
   c. are children grouped according to their ability?
2. Are academics taught (for example, are the children learning the alphabet and numbers, phonics, simple addition)?
3. What skills do most entering children have? (Ask the teacher at the end of the visit.)

Fig. 11–1 Sample classroom assessment.

Step 4: Family and Staff Meetings.   Family and staff should begin a serious discussion about the child's transition several months before the child changes programs. Federal law requires that planning for the transition from early intervention services to preschool begin at least three months before a child's birthday. This is to ensure that entry to preschool is smooth and services are not interrupted. Some states require a six month planning period. Likewise, several months of planning may be needed when children change preschool programs and when children move from preschool to kindergarten. This gives the family time to learn about program options and an opportunity to prepare their child and themselves for the change.

Transition planning may occur during the IEP and IFSP meeting or may require a separate meeting. It will be important to identify and include goals for transition in the IEP or IFSP. To ensure that sending and receiving programs are working together on behalf of the child, it is helpful to have a representative of the receiving program participate in a planning meeting.

This meeting also is the time to help the family identify how much time they can devote to being involved, what they are able to do to prepare for the transition, and the issues they want to address. Figure 11.3 provides specific suggestions as to the kinds of information families like to have regarding their child's transition. Specific ideas on how a family might help prepare their child for transition can be found in Figure 11.4. A major task of the transition coordinator is to help the family determine the level of involvement best for them.

It is helpful for the sending program to develop a written report summarizing the child's progress, as identified by staff observations and current evaluations, current goals, and suggestions for future goals. Before sharing this information and any other records about the child, staff from the sending program must obtain written consent from the parents. Parents have the right to review their child's records and to request that certain information not be shared. After obtaining **informed parent consent**, the written report may be shared with the receiving program.

Step 5: Sending Program—Preparing the Child.
Classrooms within programs vary greatly in their physical arrangements, the structure of learning activities, and the style of the teacher. To the best of their ability, teachers will want to prepare the child for the next environment, especially if it is quite different from the current one. For example, a child leaving a traditional preschool and entering a regimented classroom would be sure to benefit from learning some of the specific skills needed in the next classroom.

Once the transition goals have been identified, the sending program can devise activities for working toward those goals. The specific activities will depend on the skills needed for the next program. Generally, the sending program can incorporate the following ideas into their current program:

- Gradually give children more responsibility for their personal and classroom possessions.
- Teach children to ask for attention in nondisruptive ways (raising their hands, for example).
- Help children learn to follow directions given to the group in general.
- Teach children to care for their toileting needs as independently as possible and to recognize the symbols designating boys' and girls' toilet facilities.
- Gradually reduce the number of prompts from teachers to children during all kinds of tasks.
- Gradually increase the amount of time children work and play independently, without teachers' involvement.
- Teach children to line up and move in lines, if this is the practice in the new setting.
- Help children learn to complete one task before starting another.
- Teach children to recognize their printed name and to claim ownership of materials and possessions.
- Teach children to follow classroom routines and change of activity patterns (as much as possible, introduce routines of the new program).
- Vary the length of activities.
- Vary the amount of help provided during and between tasks.
- Vary the type and number of instructions given to children.

Many receiving programs will expect children to be able to raise their hands when wanting the teacher's attention.

Summary Report On:

Birthdate:

Address:

Enrollment Dates:

From:

Referral:

Classroom behavior:

Cognitive and speech/language skills:

Skills currently being worked on:

Future task suggestions and specific problems:

Social skills:

Motor skills:

Self-care skills:

Preferred activities:

Problem behaviors and ways to deal with them:

Current impressions—child's strengths and
  weaknesses:

Other services to contact for information:

Fig. 11-2 Summary report.

This list suggests information that families often like
to have regarding their child's transition:

- Readiness skills that will help the child in the
  new program.
- General differences between the current program and the potential program(s)
- Changes that may affect the child and family,
  such as daily schedule or transportation, and
  how best to prepare for the differences
- Legal rights about testing, records, and the
  child's educational program
- The kinds of child and family information that
  will be shared with the next program
- The ways in which staff from both programs will
  be involved in the transition process
- Additional assessments and evaluations that may
  need to be required

Fig. 11-3 Transition information for parents.

Activities that help to prepare children as they make
the transition from one program to another:

- Talk with the child about the impending
  changes
- Provide opportunities for the child to make new
  friends
- Teach the child to care for personal belongings
- Teach the child to share toys and materials
- Teach the child to use toys and equipment
  appropriately
- Help the child acquire as many self-care skills
  and as much independence as possible
- Encourage the child to ask for help when
  needed
- Allow the child to practice working and playing
  independently
- Teach the child to follow directions
- Read with the child more frequently, encourag-
  ing increased attention and involvement in the
  stories
- Help the child learn his or her full name,
  address, and phone number, if appropriate
- Take the child to visit the new program and the
  new teacher
- Talk with the child about rules and activities in
  the new program

So all may remember which transition goals were
selected, include the goals in the child's IEP or IFSP

Fig. 11-4 Preparation of the Child.

- Teach everyday safety rules such as crossing the street.
- Role play meeting new children and ways of making new friends.

Step 6: Placement Staffing—Selecting the Next Program and Services. Several meetings may be necessary to determine appropriate services and programs for a child. It is important that the transition coordinator, the teacher, and any other professionals who worked with the child attend these meetings. Likewise, representatives from the receiving program also must be at this meeting to assist in making decisions regarding the child's future services and program. Representatives may include a transition coordinator, a member of the program's special service staff, and a teacher representing the classroom program. The family must also be present and be encouraged to invite others involved with the child (a grandmother, perhaps, who frequently provides care for the child). Ideally, those from the receiving program would have observed the child in the current program prior to the placement meeting.

The group as a whole should discuss the child's overall performance and future needs. Information prepared by the sending teacher and the family regarding the child's abilities and progress toward transition goals should be circulated. This information provides the format for the discussion of what services the child needs and the potential sources of such services. There must be ample opportunity to ask questions, request further information, and receive clarification of particular issues. The discussion and decision about services and placement should be driven by the child's identified needs. If the child has an IEP, then the individualized education plan which identifies the child's needs and appropriate services needed to meet the needs should form the foundation of the discussion. Before determining a placement, family and staff from both programs should identify the special and related services that the child will need, including transportation. The frequency and duration of these services need to be discussed and specified. The frequency and duration of special services should match the child's needs and not a program's schedule. In other words, programs

should not specify in advance that all children receive 60 minutes of speech therapy; the duration of services should be determined by each child's needs.

Once these decisions have been made, the discussion may then focus on where the services should be delivered. When thinking about an appropriate placement, it is important to consider the principle of least restrictive environment (LRE), which states that children should be education to the maximum extent possible with other children who do not have disabilities. For younger children, the principle of LRE addresses the natural environment—where the child would be, if the child did not have a disability. Natural environments for infants, toddlers and young preschool aged children may include the home and child care settings. For school aged settings, the least restrictive environment may be the regular classroom. The opportunities for the child to be included in activities with typically developing children should be discussed. When thinking about the next program, be it preschool, daycare, or kindergarten, it is important to consider:

ratio of teachers to children
availability of classroom aides or assistants
medical or other clinical personnel available
staff's prior experience with children with special
    needs
enrollment procedures (and for private programs,
    waiting lists)
entry dates to the new program
readiness requirements, if any
location of program and time required to transport
    the child
location of program with respect to the programs
    attended by the child's siblings and neighborhood
    peers
accessibility

Once potential placements have been identified, it may be appropriate for family members and staff to visit the programs before reaching a decision. It may also be important to discuss the ways in which special services will be delivered within the programs they are considering.

At times, there may not be a choice where the child attends school. In some rural communities, only one

The transition coordinator and the child's teacher are but two of the key people at the placement staffing.

child care center may be available for preschool aged children, or only one kindergarten. In other instances, the school district may offer only one preschool program. In these cases, it is important to discuss the special education and related services that are available and to determine how these are delivered to ensure that the child's individualized education program will be fulfilled.

Once the appropriate placement has been determined, the parents, transition coordinator, and the teacher should meet with the new teacher, principal or program director, and the special service staff that will be involved with the child during and after the transition. The purpose of this meeting should be to review the child's current performance and special needs as well as future goals. Arrangements also should be made for the receiving teacher to visit the sending program and for the child and parents to visit the new program.

Step 7: Transfer of Records. Transferring a child's records can become a major problem. Sometimes the right records are not sent, do not reach the appropriate person, or do not get read. A clearly defined process for transferring records needs to be made between the transition coordinators and agreed upon by both programs' administrators. Written procedures for transferring records assure that the right records

are sent to the right persons in a timely manner. *Parental approval must be obtained before sending records of any kind to another person or program.* Parents must be informed about the records to be sent, who they will be sent to, and when they will be sent. Parents also must have the opportunity to examine all records before they are transferred. The following questions can serve as a guide when planning the transfer of records.

- What method does each program use when getting parental consent for transfer of records?
- To what extent do the sending and receiving programs use the same types of records?
- What information collected by the sending program does the receiving program need?
- When and how will additional information be obtained?
- Who is responsible for sending the records?
- Who in the receiving program will accept and be responsible for the records?
- When and how will the records be sent?

Step 8: Child and Family Visit the New Program. A visit to the new program by the child and parents should be planned as early as possible so they can see what the new program is like. The transition coordinator can make the appointment. The visit should include a tour of the building, time to explore the classroom, and time for the child to play in the play yard. It is of great value if the new teacher can arrange to spend a few minutes with the child and family. This kind of informal visit helps both the child and the

Scheduling time in advance for the child to explore an unfamiliar play yard is important.

family experience the new program and possibly reduce anxieties about the impending change. *The initial visit is not the time for parents or teachers to discuss the child's specific needs or problems.* A meeting without the child must be scheduled when such issues are to be discussed.

Step 9: Moving into the New Program.   For some children, a full session in the new setting may be too much at first. Scheduling arrangements should vary, depending on each child. Program flexibility is critical when young children, with or without developmental problems, are starting a new program. Following are three suggestions for children who are not ready to start out independently or with a full session:

1. The child might attend the new program for only one hour a day for the first week or so; the time then can be extended; how quickly it is extended depends on how quickly the child adjusts.
2. The sending teacher, transition coordinator, or parent might accompany the child for the first few days. As the child becomes comfortable in the new classroom, adult support gradually can be withdrawn.
3. The child might continue to attend the old program part time while starting to attend the new program the rest of the time.

With systematic planning and cooperation among staff and family, the new experience can be made comfortable for all children as they make the transition from one program to another. The following ideas are directed to teachers in the receiving program so they can help to make transitions easier on children.

* Talk about the new program with the children, how they (the children) are growing up, how the new program is different and even a little scary perhaps, but that it will be fun too.
* Initially, provide additional time for free play so children can become familiar with one another.
* Give simple, one- and two-step instructions; gradually get children used to longer and more complex instructions.

* Vary the duration and type of activities more frequently at first.
* Vary the amount of teacher help during academic tasks, but always be available for a child who needs help.
* Throughout the transition period, review classroom rules and routines each day (more often for some children).
* Assign experienced children as *buddies* for new children.

Step 10: Support Services.   During the first weeks, even months, of a new program the child may need extra assistance. This may be in the form of support services offered by the transition coordinator, the previous teacher, or the special service staff. Many receiving teachers welcome such offers; others must be encouraged to use them. Four services that might be available to the receiving teacher are described below.

Staff communication.   It may be helpful for the receiving teacher to talk with the transition coordinator or the child's former teacher during the first weeks of school. These staff members are familiar with the child's special needs and know what worked in the child's prior program. They can suggest solutions based on their past experience and help problem-solve with the new teacher.

Talking about a concern often leads to a solution.

Sometimes the coordinator can provide the best help by simply listening quietly to a teacher describe his or her program day. Talking about a problem often leads to a solution. These meetings also can provide opportunities for teachers to express their feelings—both the frustrations and pleasures of working with a special child.

Teacher–family communication.   The child's family is a prime resource. Regular contact between the teacher and parents allows sharing of a child's progress, opportunities to express concerns, and identification of solutions.

Sharing materials and activity ideas.   Transitions can be eased if the new classroom offers experiences familiar to the child. The sending program might lend a favorite learning or play material to the receiving program. Something familiar to use or hang onto tends to promote a child's sense of security. With familiar objects and activities readily available during the first few weeks of the transition, the classroom, teachers, and classmates seem less strange.

In-Class Support.   Providing an aide or volunteer for short periods several times a week often helps both the receiving teacher and the child during the transition period. The aide can supplement the regular teaching activities in the classroom (especially useful when a child needs intensive instruction or supervision during the adjustment period, however long that may be). An aide can work individually with the specific child, or work with a small group that includes the child. Support may be provided by regular classroom aides, or though volunteers, such as a parent volunteer. In some instances, older students in a school may be available to volunteer in the classroom, given appropriate supervision.

SUMMARY

For children with special needs and their families, a successful transition from one program to another is critical to the child's long-range progress. PL 99-457 formalized the importance of transition services with the directive that they be a component of the Individualized Family Service Plan (IFSP). The number and type of accommodations made by children, families, and service providers during periods of transition, and the sustainability of these accommodations, are critical factors in a successful transition. A procedure that calls for a minimum number of disruptions for the child, the family, and the teacher, yet sustains the child's progress, is the goal of transition planning.

The various perspectives of child, family, and professionals must be considered if the accommodations that each must make are to be successful. To increase the likelihood of successful transfers from one program to another, systematic transition planning should be a component of all early childhood programs. Planning should begin within a few weeks of a child's enrollment and continue throughout the year and into the next program for as long as necessary. Transition planning requires a number of steps. As a starting point, two representatives—one each from the sending program and the receiving program—are appointed to serve as transition coordinators. The coordinators are responsible for visiting other programs and becoming acquainted with classroom practices and staff. The coordinators need to learn the expectations of the other programs and how they differ from their own. Next the coordinators work with their own classroom staff to help to minimize the differences between programs for the child who will be in transition.

Parents need to be consulted frequently throughout the transition process. They are to be informed of the program's transition procedures, helped to identify transition-related goals for the child, and share in discussing where the child is to be placed in the new program. The parents and transition coordinators discuss how to make the transition and together write a specific transition plan. The plan should meet with the approval of everyone—parents, administrators, and teachers. At the time the child is actually transferred, careful pacing is required. Moving through changes too rapidly tends to be upsetting for any young child, and especially for a young child with developmental problems. One recommendation is that the child's time in the new program be increased gradually.

As the child enters the new program, the receiving teacher needs to know what support services are available if needed (and wanted). Possibilities for support services include consultations with the staff from the sending program, from special service staff members in the current program, and from the family. There also may be loans of materials from the sending program and supplementary teaching in the form of volunteer and aide services. It is the rare child, even one with serious disabilities, who cannot be helped to succeed in a carefully selected new program. Changing from one program to another can and should be a positive experience for child, family, and teachers. What is required is careful, individualized planning.

STUDENT ACTIVITIES

1. Obtain permission to observe an entire preschool session; answer the questions on the classroom assessment form.
2. Obtain permission to observe an entire public school kindergarten session; answer the questions on the classroom assessment form.
3. Compare your preschool and kindergarten assessments. List similarities and differences.
4. Write a summary report on a child who will soon be entering preschool or kindergarten. Include what you believe the student's strengths and needs are regarding transition. Ask a preschool or kindergarten teacher to read your report and comment on how helpful such a report would be.
5. Interview the family of a child with special needs. Ask them to describe the issues they faced during their child's transition.

REVIEW QUESTIONS

A. *Lists.*
  1. List three general goals of transition planning.
  2. List three accommodations a child may have to make when moving to a new program.
  3. List four family characteristics that often affect the transition process.
  4. List four concerns that many families have, related to transitions.
  5. List three responsibilities of the transition coordinator that relate specifically to classroom programs.
  6. List three types of individuals who should be involved in planning a child's transition.
  7. List four support services that might be offered as children with disabilities move into kindergarten.

B. *True or False. Choose the best answer.*
  T F   1. Transition planning includes identification of accommodations that need to be made by the child, family, and service providers.
  T F   2. The amount of disruption during a transition is not likely to affect a child's social or academic progress.
  T F   3. The child's success in the new classroom is the sole responsibility of the receiving program.
  T F   4. The transition coordinator should be familiar with service and placement options throughout the community.

  T F   5. When major differences exist between the sending and receiving programs, it is up to the family to resolve the differences.
  T F   6. Environmental, behavioral, and learning activities should be noted when observing potential placements.
  T F   7. The family is the one to decide its own level of involvement in transition plans.
  T F   8. The transfer of a child's records is seldom a transition problem.
  T F   9. Parents should not visit the new classroom until their child's adjustment is accomplished.
  T F   10. Aides or volunteers may be especially useful when a child in transition needs intensive supervision or instruction.

C. *Multiple Choice. Select the one best answer from the choices offered to complete each statement.*
  1. No amount of transition planning can avoid
     a. a great deal of family disruption.
     b. marked loss of academic and social progress for the child.
     c. many negative experiences for both the sending and the receiving teachers.
     d. a certain number of accommodations required of child, family, and teachers.

2. Transition planning should *not* necessarily be concerned with
   a. the child's strengths and needs.
   b. the family's strengths and needs.
   c. the coordinator's needs.
   d. the coordinator's skill as related to the child's and family's needs.
3. When observing a program during transition planning the observer should *not* be concerned with
   a. the physical environment.
   b. interactions between children and teacher.
   c. how well teachers are dressed.
   d. the learning activities children are engaged in.
4. If teaching methods differ greatly between the sending and receiving programs
   a. each program should strive to make their program indistinguishable from the other.

b. the sending program can ignore the differences.
   c. it is up to the receiving program to bring their teacher methods into compliance with the sending program.
   d. both programs should consider accommodations they might make to facilitate the child's transition.
5. A family visit to the child's new program
   a. should be scheduled as far in advance of the actual change as can be managed.
   b. should not take place until after the child has adapted to the new setting.
   c. is the time for an in-depth discussion of the child's behavior problems.
   d. is not necessary.

REFERENCES

Fowler, S.A. (1982). Transition for preschool to kindergarten for children with special needs. In K.E. Allen and E.M. Goetz (Eds.), *Early childhood education: Special problems, special solutions.* Rockville, MD: Aspen.

Fowler, S.A., Hains, A.H., and Rosenkoetter, S.E. (1989). The transition between early intervention and preschool: Administrative and policy issues. *Topics in Early Childhood Special Education, 9(4),* 55–65.

Fowler, S.A., Schwartz, I., and Atwater, J. (1991). Perspectives on the transition from preschool to kindergarten for children with disabilities and their families. *Exceptional Children, 57,* 136–145.

Fowler, S.A., and Titus, P.F. (1993). Handling transitions. In P.J. Beckman and G.B. Boyce (Eds.), *Deciphering the system: A guide for families of young children with disabilities.* Brookline, MA: Brookline Books.

Fowler, S.A., and Ostrosky, M.M. (1994). Transitions to and from preschool in early childhood special education. In P.L. Safford (Ed.), *Yearbook in Early Childhood Education.* New York: Teachers College Press.

Haines, A.H., Rosenkoetter, S.E., Kottwitz, E., and Fowler, S.A. (1985). Paper presented at the CEC/DEC National Early Childhood Conference —Children with Special Needs in Denver, CO, October 1985.

Hains, A.H., Rosenkeotter, S.E., and Fowler, S.A. (1991). Transition planning with families in early intervention programs. *Infants and Young Children, 3,* 38-47.

Hanline, J.F. (1988). Making the transition to preschool: Identification of parent needs. *Journal of the Division for Early Childhood, 12(2),* 98–107.

Hazel, R.A., Barber, P.A., Roberts, S., Behr, S.K., Helmstetter, E., and Guess, P. (1986). *A community approach to an integrated system for children with special needs.* Baltimore: Brookes.

Johnson, B.K., McGonigel, M.S., and Kaufmann, R.K. (1989). *Guidelines and recommended practices for the individualized family service plan.* Chapel Hill: National Early Childhood Technical Assistance System and Washington, D.C.: Association for the Care of Children's Health.

Johnson, T.E., Chandler, L.K., Kerns, G.M., and Fowler, S.A. (1986). What are parents saying about family involvement in transitions? A retrospective transition interview. *Journal of the Division for Early Childhood, 11(1),* 10-17.

Rice, M.L., and O'Brien, M. (1990). Transitions: Times of change and accommodation. *Topics in Early Childhood, 9(4),* 1–14.

Rosenkoetter, S.E., Hains, A.H., and Fowler, S.A. (1994). *Bridging early services for children with special needs and their families: A practical guide to transition planning.* Baltimore, MD: Brooks.

Turnbull, A., Summers, J., and Brotherson, M. (1986). Family life cycle, theoretical and empirical implications and future directions for families with mentally retarded members. In J. Gallagher and P. Vietze (Eds.), *Families of handicapped persons: Research, programs and policy issues.* Baltimore: Brookes.

Unit 12

Preparing Teachers for Inclusive Programs

OBJECTIVES

After studying this unit the student will be able to

- describe the knowledge and training needed to work with children with developmental disabilities in inclusive early childhood programs.
- define developmentally appropriate learning experiences and justify the statement that all young children—typically developing, developmentally disabled, and gifted—need such experiences.
- discuss three or more characteristics of early educational programs for children with special needs.
- compare *contingent stimulation, teachable moments, teaching on the fly,* and *incidental teaching*; identify a developmental principle they have in common and the significance to children's learning.
- list ten or more characteristics found among effective teachers of young children with developmental disabilities and early childhood teachers in general.

Teachers are the most significant and central element in early childhood classrooms. Program quality is determined by teachers' skills in managing the learning environment. Quality is further determined by teachers' personal attitudes about children and themselves and by their philosophical beliefs on how children learn. In an inclusive classroom the need for quality teaching is critical. The developmental diversity among children calls for skilled and sensitive teachers who will respond to children's special needs with a range of individualized programs. At the same time, inclusive classrooms call for teachers who recognize that young children with developmental disabilities are more like normally developing children than they are different from them.

All children need learning activities geared to their levels of development and interests. Normally developing children need such experiences; gifted children need them; children with developmental delays and disabilities need them. Effective early childhood teachers use the developmental approach as the basis for every aspect of their teaching. They recognize that

all children have basic needs and all children have special needs. They recognize further that special needs cannot be met unless basic developmental needs also are met.

It is this philosophy that led to the decision to make this section of the text separate and distinct. It focuses on those general teaching skills and general developmental and behavioral principles that apply to *all* young children and all early childhood teachers. A later section (Section 4), with its several units, is given over to the special teaching strategies needed to work with particular developmental disabilities. The point to be emphasized is this: *if children with developmental problems are to benefit from special approaches, learning activities must take place within a developmental framework.* In other words, teachers make particular adaptations as will be described in Section 4; these adaptations are then grafted on to each child's individualized developmental program.

This unit will focus on a brief review of basic developmental principles of greatest significance in early childhood education. These principles (touched on in Unit 4) apply to every type of program: full day child care, Head Start, half-day preschool, infant and toddler programs, and inclusive classrooms. The principles apply, also, to every type of child—developmentally disabled, normally developing, and gifted.

TEACHER TRAINING AND RETRAINING

An early childhood program that offers inclusive experiences for children with developmental problems is both challenging and rewarding. Teachers encounter the richest and widest range of developmental likenesses and differences among children. Skilled teachers enjoy this diversity once they are convinced of the underlying developmental similarities among children of varying ability levels.

The children in an inclusive classroom most likely reflect the ethnic, racial, linguistic, and cultural diversity of their community. Additionally, every child comes from a family who have their own traditions, beliefs, and life ways. "Life ways consist of a family's cultural customs, courtesies, beliefs, values, practices, manner of interacting, roles relationships, language,

Skilled teachers enjoy the diversity found in working with children of varying abilities.

rituals, and expected behaviors" (Luera 1993, p. 2). This diversity adds both richness and challenge to an early childhood program. The richness comes from the opportunities children, families, and teachers have to learn from and about each other. The challenge comes in creating learning experiences and environments that are culturally sensitive to all the children in the classroom.

Children attending an inclusive early childhood program may also vary greatly in their abilities and needs. Most of the children will be typically developing. Some of the children may have physical disabilities, health impairments, or sensory impairments, but may be developing normally in the cognitive domain. Other children may have language delays and cognitive delays, but may be developing normally in the motor domain. A few children may have multiple or severe disabilities.

No one professional can meet the needs of all the diverse learners in an inclusive early childhood program. Teachers in an inclusive classroom are members of a team of professionals that work together to meet the needs of all the children in the classroom. Each member of the team brings specialized knowledge to planning and implementing an appropriate educational program for a child with special needs (professional who make up the team are described in Unit 2). Teamwork is especially important in providing the systematic and specialized instruction that is necessary to meet the needs of children with challenging behavior or severe disabilities. The expertise that the early childhood educator brings to the team is how to create a classroom environment and learning activities that are fun, motivating, safe, interesting, responsive, and supportive.

The challenge for teachers is to work with the team to make the adaptations that accommodate the developmental needs of the range of children in the classroom. Program adaptation is not a new or unusual task for early childhood teachers. Adjusting curriculum and teaching strategies to individual differences and developmental variations has long been the heart of early childhood education. The full implications of the challenge for teachers is to make adaptations that accommodate the developmental needs of the children. The major requirement for working with young children who are developmentally different is the knowledge and expertise that comes from working with young children in general. In the early days of inclusive programs, Jenny Klein (1977), a prominent figure in the training of early childhood teachers, summed it up this way:

> any teacher who really understands the young child can work with the handicapped. By utilizing and building on knowledge of young children and child development, teachers are able to sort out things that are related to handicaps and behaviors that are related to other aspects of the child's development.

More recently, the Association of Teacher Educators (ATE), the Division of Early Childhood (DEC), and the National Association for the Education of Young Children (NAEYC) developed a joint position statement discussing training for professionals working with young children with special needs. These organizations agree that the most effective educational programs for young children with developmental disabilities are delivered within the context of high quality programs serving typically developing young children. The statement identifies

six philosophical assumptions about what constitutes effective early education:

- The uniqueness of early childhood as a developmental phase,
- The significant role of families in early childhood development and early education and intervention,
- The role of developmentally and individually appropriate teaching practices,
- The preference for service delivery in inclusive settings,
- The importance of culturally competent professional actions, and
- The importance of collaborative interpersonal and interprofessional actions.

This statement is a result of the efforts of NAEYC and DEC working together to integrate the principles of developmentally appropriate practice and recommended practices in early childhood special education to meet the needs of all young children in inclusive programs. A document outlining guidelines for developmentally appropriate practice (DAP) for young children was published by NAEYC in 1987

"Any teacher who really understands the young child can work with children with special needs."

(Bredekamp 1987). Developmentally appropriate practice consists of two dimensions: age appropriateness and individual appropriateness. Although this document had a tremendous impact on early childhood education, many educators questioned the appropriateness of the guidelines in meeting the needs of children who are culturally diverse or who have special learning needs. As Wolery, Strain and Bailey (1992) note, children with disabilities have needs that are different than those of typically developing children. The collaborative efforts of NAEYC and DEC have been successful in creating training guidelines and training materials (Wolery and Wilbers 1994) that integrate the richness of the developmentally appropriate practice guidelines and the systematic nature of the recommended practices for early childhood special education (DEC Task Force 1993). These materials will benefit all young children by improving the quality of services and the ability of teachers to meet the needs of *all* children in their programs.

Teachers' Concerns.   At the mention of inclusion, many early childhood teachers are concerned about having to work, unassisted, with children with challenging behaviors or severe disabilities. The concern is understandable, but should not occur. As discussed above, children with disabilities should not be included without appropriate supports. These supports may be related services such as occupational therapy, physical therapy or speech therapy, instructional assistance from an early childhood special education teacher, or extra assistance in the classroom such as an aide. Remember, *the law requires that an appropriate educational program be provided for every child;* and an appropriate program is one that meets the unique and varied needs of the individual child in the least restrictive environment possible.

Coordinated teaching.   Some children with special needs may have dual placements. That is, the child may spend the morning at a parent co-op program and the afternoon at a Head Start program. Other children may spend time in an inclusive early childhood program, but receive related therapy at home. Still other children will have different multiple placements that combine preschool, child care, and therapy

Children can be provided various kinds of mainstream experiences.

services. Regardless of the specific placements, it is important that all the staff working with the child and family in different placements be in contact and work together to provide a coordinated and consistent program. In addition to the benefits for the child with disabilities, working with itinerant early childhood special education teachers or physical, occupational and speech therapists can help the early childhood teacher better meet the needs of all children. The director of one inclusive child care program describes the benefits to children with and without disabilities.

> An average of one hundred families are enrolled at one time in our program. About 45 of the children have handicapping conditions that range from mild to severe. The rest of the children are developing normally. Reactions to the Center's mainstream model are favorable. The waiting list for enrollments for normally developing children is nine months. An interesting note has to do with children's developmental progress (both the handicapped children and the non handicapped children). Over a three-year period, children in both populations progressed at rates better than had been predicted. In fact, normally developing children progressed at a rate that was considerably greater than what is usually expected (Gil 1987).

Supplemental Training.   To provide effectively for children with developmental disabilities, teachers do not need extensive retraining. What teachers do need is additional knowledge about specific developmental disabilities as each child with a particular problem is about to be enrolled. Teachers also need on-the-job experience with special children, but always with help from support staff and the parents of each child with special needs. The kinds of information offered in this text provide a useful and comprehensive starting point. Additional training options also are available:

- All states have a designated lead agency for implementation of PL 99-457. These agencies provide community-based inservice training for professionals working with young children.
- Most states have regional and local chapters of NAEYC that provide annual conferences and other educational programs.
- Two year colleges and vocational/technical schools often are the sources of early childhood and special child teacher-training programs.
- Nationwide, Head Start provides training for their staff on how to include children with disabilities.
- Many local, state, and regional child care organizations now offer training on how to include children with disabilities in child care programs.
- Workshops and seminars sponsored by agencies like United Cerebral Palsy and the ARC are available in many communities.

Agencies and service organizations that focus on specific developmental problems can recommend or provide films, articles, books and other kinds of information. (Appendix C offers lists of agencies and organizations.) These materials describe the disabilities and the problems that confront the child and family. If a visually impaired child, for example, is to be included, it is imperative that teachers begin immediately to find out about blindness and how it affects early development. The American Association for the Blind or any of several other organizations focusing on visual impairment will provide helpful materials. To be truly effective, such materials are best used as background for information provided by the family. Parents are the best source of information about their children and their children's disabilities. No amount of special course work or special training can take the place of the information that parents have to offer about their child.

THE APPLIED DEVELOPMENTAL APPROACH

A Child Is a Child.   It is true that early childhood teachers do not need extensive special education training to teach in an inclusive early childhood setting. They do, however, need a particular mind set: seeing each child as a child, rather than as a stutterer or a behavior problem or a Down syndrome child. By viewing every child as first a child, teachers come to realize that many troublesome behaviors are not related necessarily to a child's disability. Blaming a child's tantrums or excessive shyness or aggressiveness on his or her disability is commonplace, but seldom justifiable. More accurate and certainly more helpful to the child is to view problem behaviors from the developmental perspective: as developmental commonalities or developmental irregularities or cultural diversities that are seen in all children to a greater or lesser degree. Children's speech is a prime example. Individual children speak differently just as communities speak differently. Consider the vast range of differences in the way the English language is used in vari-

A child is first of all a child.

ous parts of this country; obviously, there is no one *right* usage of the language. Difference, therefore, does not necessarily mean a developmental disorder.

Review of Developmental Principles and Practices. Teachers who work with children with developmental problems need, first and foremost, a thorough foundation in normal growth and development. It is nearly impossible to recognize or evaluate developmental deviations without an understanding of the range and variations of behaviors and skill levels found among both normal and special populations.

Developmental sequences.   Noting sequences of development rather than chronological age is a key factor in working with young children. Effective teachers operate on the principle that it is more useful to know that a child is moving steadily forward than to know that the child is above or below the so-called norm.

> Example: A 39-month-old child with a central nervous system disorder (CNS) is just beginning to pull up to a standing position. The child's teachers are predicting that she soon will be walking and are planning her program accordingly. How can the teachers be so confident? Easy; they know this child has passed, in order (though late), each of the preceding large motor milestones.

Interrelationships among developmental areas.   Understanding the interrelatedness of developmental areas is important, too. Recognizing that each area of development effects and is effected by every other area, is essential when teaching young children.

> Example: A developmentally delayed 4$\frac{1}{2}$-year-old had refused solid foods throughout his life. Clinical findings indicated that the prolonged soft diet, requiring little chewing, had contributed to poorly developed muscle tone, hence poorly controlled movement of the mouth and tongue. One result was almost unintelligible speech that in turn played a part in delayed cognitive and social development. Teachers and clinicians agreed that the child needed help in acquiring speech, social, and cognitive skills. They also agreed that even with treatment it was unlikely there would be much improvement in any of the developmental problems unless the child learned to eat solid foods. That probably would not happen until parents could be helped to get their child on an appropriate diet.

Developmental inconsistencies.   As noted again and again, development is an irregular process, even among normally developing children. A period of rapid development often is followed by an unsettled period known as a time of **disequilibrium**. During such periods, children seem to be developmentally disorganized: calm and capable one moment, screamingly frustrated (and frustrating) the next. Some children may even regress, appear to go backward for awhile.

> Example: a 3-year-old with a 9-month-old sister competing for attention may revert to babyish ways. He tantrums for no apparent reason, loses bladder control that seemed to be well-established, demands a bedtime bottle that had been given up months before. Teachers can help parents understand that their child is continuing to progress well in every other aspect of development; therefore it is unlikely that the current problems will persist. It may be agreed that there is no need for a clinical assessment on the child for the time being; that the situation is likely to be but a temporary regression to infantile behaviors. It is further agreed that both parents and teachers will continue to observe the child carefully in the event the situation does not right itself within a reasonable period.

Transactional aspects of development.   Continuous interplay goes on between children and their environment. The process is referred to as the transactional aspect of development. The concept recognizes the young child as a dynamic individual who is affected by, and has an effect upon, almost everyone and everything that he or she comes in contact with (Horowitz 1987). Learning of some kind is going on in every child every waking moment of every day. These learnings can be both positive and negative; they are the consequence of direct and indirect or unintended teaching. It is easy for teachers to recognize their role in promoting intentional learnings: they set up appropriate curriculum activities, respond to children positively, allow children to explore and experiment. Seldom, however, are teachers aware of inappropriate learnings that may be promoted, unintentionally. For example, the experience of a single wagon or a single puzzle for a large group of 3- and 4-year-olds may teach more about shoving and pushing, or waiting endlessly, or doing without than the fine and gross motor skills the materials were intended to promote.

An overview of a case study (Allen and Goetz 1982), focused on efforts to help a child extend his attention span, is given below. The situation illustrates how an undesirable behavior may be learned because of teachers' well-intentioned efforts in combination with the transactional nature of teacher–child interactions.

> James was a five-year-old who seldom stayed with an activity more than a moment or two. Teachers were constantly intercepting him, trying to settle him down, get him interested in something. As the weeks went by James continued to flit, more than ever, it seemed. What was he learning from the teachers' efforts? Certainly not to focus his attention, which was their goal. Instead, he was learning, at some unrecognized level, that flitting about was a sure way to get the teacher attention he needed and could not seem to get in any other way. Unfortunately, this constant flitting maintained a short attention span which interfered with James acquiring other essential learnings.

Fascinating accounts of this transactional process are found in research studies with both normal and developmentally disabled infants. One example is Fraiberg's (1974) comments on unsettling transactions between blind infants and their mothers. The infant's inability to see its mother's face interferes with its ability to respond to her smiles. The unresponsiveness often is perceived by the mother as rejection. Without her realizing it, her behavior changes: She smiles less and less because her infant provides her with less delight. Both mother and baby, through no fault of their own, promote mutual unresponsiveness. This come at a critical developmental period when both need to be engaging in the reciprocally reinforcing behaviors that lead to a strong parent– child attachment.

Negative examples were cited because of a general tendency for adults to overlook or underappreciate their everyday responses to children. Many of these responses carry the unsuspected potential for inappropriate learnings emerging from routine transactions between children and adults. It must be remembered that children are learning *something*, for better or worse, from every environmental encounter. On the other hand, adult–child transactions have an equally powerful potential for promoting healthy development.

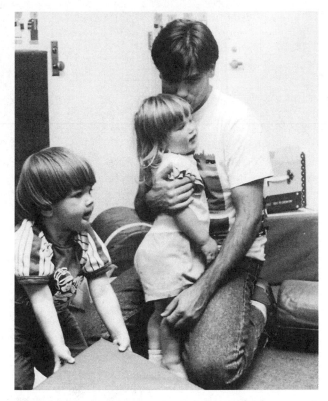

Adult-child transactions have powerful potential for promoting healthy development.

Contingent stimulation.   Closely related to transactional processes is the principle of contingent stimulation. In the context of child development, *contingent* implies a kind of dependency or conditioning in which new learnings come about because of the responses of another. With young children, in particular, it refers to the ways in which parents and other significant adults respond to cues from the child. Adults who react to an infant's cooing, gurgling, and babbling stimulate the infant's continuing efforts to communicate. Contingent simulation is readily observable in the simple give-and-take games that both parents and their babies initiate and take such delight in: peek-a-boo, pat-a-cake, chase-and-hide, toss-the-toy out of the crib. When adults make their responses at least partially contingent on what the infant or child says and does, specific developmental benefits result:

Language development is earlier and better.
Cognitive development is accelerated and richer.
Self-esteem is much more evident.
Attachments are more secure.

In the early 1970s, Burton White was already reporting similar benefits in his study of mother–child interactions. He was interested in discovering why some normally developing infants seemed to be more competent than other normally developing infants. For several years he observed mother and infant pairs from every socioeconomic level. He concluded that it was not the *amount* of time that a mother spent with her infant, it was *when* she gave her attention. Mothers of competent children, he noted, seldom spent ten, even five minutes at a time responding to their children. What they did to was to provide a great deal of *teaching on the fly*, brief moments when they were totally focused on their child. These spontaneous mini-teaching episodes were usually in response to (contingent on) contacts initiated by the children (White 1975).

Infants and young children show readiness for new learning in many ways throughout the day.

Readiness to learn.   The concept of readiness is receiving increased attention and visibility due to current educational reform movements. At the head of this movement is Goals 2000: Educate American Act, President Clinton's educational reform act. The first goal is: "By the year 2000, all children in America will start school ready to learn." In this context, readiness is viewed as a **multi-dimensional, holistic** concept incorporating the physical, emotional, social, motor, and cognitive well being and development of the child (Boyer 1991). This concept is helpful in thinking about the multiple influences on a child's life and the effects they have on schooling. Readiness to learn is facilitated by a high quality early childhood program, but what happens during the school day is only a part of what affects a child's readiness to learn.

Teachable moments.   Teachable moments are those naturally occurring opportunities when a child is most likely to learn a new skill. Teachable moments are a combination of genetic and environmental factors: *maturation, motivation,* and *opportunity*. When these three come together a child is often ready to learn a new skill and teachable moments are likely to occur. Consider the following two examples.

> An infant reaches for the spoon while being fed, a cue that he or she is *ready*, that is, mature enough and has acquired the necessary perceptual–motor skills, to reach for and hold a spoon (though not always right side up). The reaching also indicates readiness to begin to explore the difficult business of self-feeding. What is needed now is opportunity. Opportunity tends to come in the form of a patient adult who is willing, for many meals straight-running, to scrub the floor, the high chair, and the child after every meal.

> Toddlers often get to the point where they hold their wet diapers away from their bodies, or they demand to be changed, or they step out of their wet diapers by themselves. These children, ranging anywhere from 15 to 40 months of age, are giving clear cues that they are moving toward the idea of learning to use the toilet.

The concepts of readiness and teachable moments are easily translated into classroom practice by observant teachers tuned to developmental difference among children. Every day, in many ways, every child shows interest in working at new learnings.

Examples: A 2-year-old trying to put on a shoe, heel-to-toe.

The 3-year-old struggling to make an upside-down coat stay on the hook.

The 4-year-old asking, "Where did the ice go?"

The 5-year-old trying to balance a teetering block structure.

In each case, based on knowledge of the individual children, the teacher makes decisions about how to use the moment to a child's best advantage.

Incidental Teaching.   Incidental teacher (first described by Hart and Risley 1982) provides a well-organized format for making the best possible use of teachable moments. In many ways, incidental teaching is similar to contingent stimulation and White's notions about mothers who teach "on the fly." All three depend on child-initiated contacts. An incidental teaching episode, however, is *always* initiated by the child. The child approaches the teacher asking for help, materials, or information. Because the contact is child initiated, the teacher knows the child is interested and therefore likely to be receptive to a brief learning activity about whatever it is that prompted the contact.

Incidental teaching represents the systematic application of principles compatible with both a developmental and a behavioral approach to early learning (Warren and Kaiser 1988). From the developmental point of view, the approach exemplifies:

Meeting a child where his or her interests lie

Responding in a way that matches the child's skill level

Introducing the bit of novelty that provides challenge for the child.

From the behavioral perspective, incidental teaching is a combination of the shaping, prompting, and reinforcement procedures central to effective teaching. (Reinforcement procedures, including shaping and prompting, will be discussed in Unit 13.) In spite of being child-initiated, every incidental teaching episode occurs in a planned environment, one that teachers have arranged to make good use of children's contacts. Effective incidental teaching depends on teachers' efforts at:

- Providing an interesting classroom environment where children can be busy, active, and inquiring.
- Selecting appropriate objectives for each child that match his or her skill levels and interests.
- Answering a child's initiation with a request for an expanded or more sophisticated response that is related to one of the child's IEP objectives (for example, if a child who is working on learning to use color words points to the truck and says, "truck," the teacher may respond by saying, "which truck?").
- Responding to the child with whatever is most appropriate in terms of his or her initial contact.

These practices are illustrated in the following example having to do with a child with muscular dysfunction. One of the IEP objectives for Andre was to increase his ability to reach.

Teachers observed Andre over several days and identified a number of his play preferences. On the physical therapist's recommendation, the preferred materials were put in full view but out of reach. Whenever Andre asked for, or otherwise indicated interest in a toy or material, a teacher held it out to him slightly out of reach, but close enough so he could get it with a little effort. When he got his hands on the object his efforts were applauded: "You *reached* for the truck and now you are going to play with it." As Andre's reach improved, teachers gradually increased the distance. Later, to facilitate the development of overhead reaching, teachers held things just a bit above Andre's eye level. This, too, they increased gradually.

Further discussion of incidental teaching will be postponed until Section 4 (Units 15 and 16). At that time, specific use of the procedures with developmental problems such as language and social, will be described.

Characteristics of Effective Teachers.   In addition to a thorough knowledge of child development, other traits characterize effective teachers in an inclusive setting. True, teaching styles and interactions with children reflect a teacher's own unique personality; nevertheless good teachers seem to have a number of characteristics in common. These are described below.

Enthusiasm.   Teachers of young children need unlimited enthusiasm for children's progress and accomplishments, great and small. This is especially important for children with developmental disabilities; they may learn at a slower rate and in smaller steps than do normally developing children. Thus, they tend to experience less sense of accomplishment and fewer feelings of success, both of which are spurs to learning. However, every child is quick to *catch* enthusiasm for almost any activity from a patient, skillful teacher who rejoices with the child over each step or partial step forward.

Enthusiasm is a reciprocal or mutually supportive process: The teacher's enthusiasm stems from the child's accomplishments, small as they sometimes are. The child's accomplishments, in turn, depend on the teacher's skills and enthusiasm in promoting the child's learning. It is imperative, therefore, that teachers of young children know how to carry out *task analyses*, the process of sequencing developmental tasks into small, **incremental steps**. Small-step successes give both child and teachers many opportunities to enthuse together about their work. (Task analysis is based on behavioral procedures and will be discussed in Unit 13.)

Teachers must have unlimited enthusiasm.

Consistency.   The effective teacher is consistent and can be depended on to provide a predictable and stable environment. All children need to know *what comes next* in classroom routines. They need to know what the limits are in terms of their own behaviors. Most importantly, they need to know teachers will not behave unreasonably; for example, allowing children to climb up the front side of the slide one day and the next day banning the same children from play on the same slide for doing exactly the same thing. Consistency is especially important for children with behavior problems or those functioning at a lower intellectual level. These children tend to have even more trouble coping with uncertainty and unexpected changes.

In addition to expectations being consistent, expectations also need to be communicated in ways that all children can understand. The teacher then can be confident about holding to expectations, knowing they are developmentally and individually realistic and understood by all. Consistency provides children with security, an especially important factor for children with developmental problems. Children who feel secure tend to be more self-confident. They learn to make sound judgments when they are sure of what is expected of them and know things will remain the same unless teachers give fair warning.

Consistency does not rule out change. Children change throughout their developmental years. Teachers' expectations also must change. What remains consistent is the developmental appropriateness of the changing expectations and the teachers' care in communicating the changes to the children. Consistency, however, must never be confused with rigidity or inflexibility. An inflexible teacher is not an effective teacher.

Flexibility.   The ability to be flexible, to improvise, to adapt an activity to individual or group needs at any given moment is a hallmark of effective teaching. A flexible teacher knows when to cut an activity short if it turns out to be too difficult or if it fails to hold children's interest. The opposite also is true: A flexible teacher knows how and when to extend and elaborate an activity that has developed into an especially absorbing and worthwhile experience for one or more children. *Flexibility does not rule out consistency.*

Truly effective teachers are a blend of consistency and flexibility. They are good judges of when to *bend the rules*. They know when to overlook a minor transgression as when a child is trying to handle a frustration or work through any other kind of learning experience like in the following examples:

Jana's physical attacks on children were frequent. Never had she been heard to *tell* anyone what she wanted; instead, she hit, grabbed, or shoved. One day, however, she stunned teachers by shrieking, "Get out, you stupid!" The rudely shouted command and name calling was directed at an approaching child who obviously meant no harm. The teacher, though regretting the verbal assault on a well-intentioned child, ignored the inappropriateness of Jana's response. Instead, the teacher supported Jana for *talking*, not *hitting*. This was done in the presence of the other child, to promote the child's understanding that Jana was learning to replace hitting with talking.

The teacher's flexibility indicated responsiveness to the most urgent priority for Jana as well as to the child who had been rebuffed. It let the child know classroom expectations were operating in spite of occasional exceptions. As for the unacceptable verbal behavior, even should it accelerate for awhile, teachers were not unduly concerned. When verbal requests dependably replaced physical assaults, a new goal, polite requesting, could be written into Jana's IEP.

The second example focuses on a gifted 5-year-old and a blockbuilding activity.

The classroom rule was that block structures could be built only as high as the builder's head. Toward the end of the school year, a capable 5-year-old had discovered a balancing principle that enabled her to build the tower she was working on higher and higher. At one point she stood on a stool to continue building. (Technically, when standing on the stool, the blocks were not as high as the child's head.) The teacher's decision to be flexible about the height of the block structure was based on the purposefulness of the child's experimentation. The teacher's continuing presence conveyed consistency about classroom rules: that one child may not endanger another.

Trustworthiness.   The more that children can trust the consistency of teachers' expectations, the more trustworthy children themselves become; hence, the more

Teachers need to be flexible, allow children to improvise and initiate.

flexible teachers can be. Teachers who respect children and their need to develop **autonomy** can give children even greater freedom to explore and experiment with their own behavior. The consistent teacher knows that children know what is expected of them. The teacher knows, too, that children usually can be trusted to stop themselves before a situation gets dangerously out of bounds. Consistency on the part of the teacher allows mutual trust to flourish as the school year progresses. DeVries and Kohlberg (1990) summarize these ideas more formally within a Piagetian context:

> In a relationship of cooperation characterized by mutual respect, the adult minimizes his authority in relationship to the child and gives him as much opportunity as possible governing his own behavior on the basis of his interests and judgments. By exercising his ability to govern his own beliefs and actions the child gradually constructs internally coherent knowledge, morality, and personality (p.37).

Setting limits.   If children are to have a safe and healthy learning environment, teachers must set limits. Everyone needs limits, and especially young children who are trying so hard to learn the many things expected of them. Limits, in the form of classroom rules,

The more that children can trust teachers' consistency, the more autonomous they can be.

allow children to relax, know that they can depend on someone else to make some of the decisions. Rules, in general, should be limited to health and safety issues and stated positively as much as possible. Whatever rules there are *must be enforced.* Therefore, the number of rules should be kept to a minimum because enforcing rules is not a productive role for teachers. Teachers need to be interacting with children positively rather than policing them. On the other hand, teachers must have firmly in mind what cannot be allowed. A typical set of rules, designed to clearly govern teachers' decisions about situations in which children must be redirected, might include the following:

1. Children are not allowed to push other children when in high places.
2. Children are not to hit other children (always a controversial rule; each group of teachers and parents must determine what is unacceptable hitting and what is acceptable self-defense).
3. Children may not throw sand, toys, books, or other hard objects.
4. Teachers' cupboards (hopefully out of children's reach) are to be opened only by teachers.
5. Children are not to leave the classroom or playyard without a teacher or other authorized adult.

The rules that adults agree on often are stated in terms of what *cannot be allowed* to avoid misunderstandings among teachers. When guiding children, rules are translated into positive statements:

"The sand stays in the sandbox."
"Books are to read and look at."
"Those are the teachers' cupboards; children's cupboards are down here."

Only when a child fails to heed a reminder or redirection, need teachers give negative and emphatic commands: "Kelly, I can't let you throw sand." Rules apply to every child in the group. "No sand throwing," means *No sand throwing.* This includes children with developmental delays and limited cognitive abilities. There can be no double standards. Doubles standards do the special child a disservice by not helping him or her learn acceptable behavior. Furthermore, double

At times, teachers need to make specific statements: "I cannot let you kick your ball into the sandbox when children are playing there."

standards can lead to resentment and dislike of the erring child among children who try to abide by the rules. Fortunately, there is no need for double standards. Every child can learn to abide by the few and necessary safety rules required in a classroom.

On many occasions, children truly do not understand what is expected of them from teachers' efforts at positive redirection. This often is true of children new to a program, of very young children, or children with developmental delays. When a teacher advises "The sand stays in the sandbox," many a young child

continues to throw sand about, while carefully keeping it within the boundaries of the sandbox. Clearly, the child is not getting the message the teacher had intended; neither are the other sand players receiving the protection they deserve. They are just as endangered as if the child continued to throw sand up and out. In these instances specific statements of rules and expectations may be more appropriate right from the start. Clear and indisputable limits offer security to children who may not understand the subtleties of verbal redirection, may not be able to stop themselves, and may not know when to stop.

Facilitating and supporting children's efforts.   Though teachers must set limits and hold to them, their major role is that of facilitator, a person who makes things happen. A facilitative teacher recognizes that experience, not teachers, are the best instructors for young children. Therefore, the facilitative teacher:

- Provides a range of interesting and appropriate materials and activities
- Presents these in ways that are attractive and conducive to children's learning
- Offers the right amount and kind of assistance (not too much, but never refusing to assist)
- Is aware of what the next step is for each child on each developmental task
- Responds to children with ample feedback as to the effectiveness of each child's efforts

Facilitation and support, in just the right degree, is especially important during children's play. As Gordon and Brown (1996) point out, it can be difficult for teachers to decide when to join children at plan and when to remain outside the activity. The important question is whether their presence will support what is happening or whether it will inhibit the play. In an inclusive classroom, teachers tend to find it appropriate to join in more frequently, but as unobtrusively as possible. Low-keyed teacher participation can go a long way toward fostering play relationships between children with and without disabilities, especially when the teacher quietly fades in and out, depending on the progress of the activity.

Actualizer and integrator. Supporting a child with special needs in an inclusive early childhood program includes environmental arrangement, curricular adaptation, and systematic use of teaching strategies to help the child be as effective as possible with interactions with the environment. The amount and type of support that a child needs is dynamic and changes according to the activity, materials, and other factors including the child's state. For example, is the child tired or extremely motivated? Effective teachers provide the right type and amount of support to the child without being intrusive or fostering over dependence.

Example: The teacher is reading one of the children's favorite books, "Brown Bear, Brown Bear." The children's favorite part is that they get to tell the teacher what the bear sees. Anthony, who is nonverbal, especially loves this activity since his teacher made him picture symbols of all the different characters in the story. Now, Anthony responds quickly and happily along with his classmates.

Teachers in an inclusive setting are *actualizers* and *integrators* of individualized intervention programs prescribed by the various disciplines. They translate clinical recommendations into interesting preschool activities that can be carried out in the classroom in ways that benefit all children.

Example: The speech therapist was working with a 5-year-old on beginning B, M, and P sounds. At the small group breakfast table the teacher improvised a riddle game based on the therapist's objectives. The teacher described and gave the beginning sounds of various foods the children had encountered over the year. Children supplied the words or labels. The cues for the child in speech therapy had to do with such things as bananas, milk and pears; butter, muffins, and plums. Everyone at the table participated and learned from the game and had fun with it. No one was the wiser (including the special child) that speech therapy was going on.

Classroom activities of this kind actualize and integrate the therapy sessions; in other words, they provide a bridge that allows the child to practice, **generalize**, and **consolidate** what is learned in therapy sessions to **functional**, everyday life situations.

The foregoing discussion of the attitudes and attributes of effective teachers in an inclusive early child-

hood program is by no means complete. Teachers also need to know how to:

- integrate behavioral and developmental principles when teaching young children.
- work with parents and members of other disciplines.
- arrange and present materials and equipment.
- schedule the daily program to provide children with an appropriate balance of child-initiated and teacher-structured learning experiences.

The remaining units in this text elaborate on these and many more of the skills needed to be an effective teacher of young children.

SUMMARY

In an inclusive classroom the need for quality teaching and appropriate learning experiences is critical. Children with developmental disabilities are especially in need of learning experiences presented by teachers who adapt developmental programs to children's special needs. Teachers work in the classroom with a team to meet the needs of children with disabilities.

Early childhood teachers in an inclusive classroom do not need extensive retraining or a degree in special education. Knowledge about particular disabilities is available, as needed, through various training programs, organizations, resource centers, and the parents of children with particular developmental disabilities. What teachers in an inclusive preschool or child care setting need most is extensive knowledge and experience in working with young children in general. To this end, the unit briefly reviewed significant developmental principles and practices: developmental sequences, the interrelatedness of developmental areas, inconsistencies in development, the transactional aspects of the developmental process, and contingent stimulation.

Special mention was made of readiness, teaching on-the-fly and incidental teaching. Incidental teaching is an effective approach to teaching all children; it is especially effective when working with children with developmental problems, Because an incidental teaching episode is child-initiated it signals a teacher that the child is *ready* and interested in learning whatever it is that he or she has contacted the teacher about. The teacher's responsibility is to be *ready* to take advantage of this teachable moment. Other characteristics of effective teachers in an inclusive early childhood program include enthusiasm, consistency, flexibility, trustworthiness, limiting children as necessary, and actualizing and integrating therapy-prescribed activities into the regular classroom program.

STUDENT ACTIVITIES

1. Locate and record the names and locations of several agencies in your community that provide resources for children with disabilities and their families. Select one and report on the kinds of materials they have available for teachers and for parents. Obtain samples, if possible.
2. Talk with teachers in an inclusive preschool or child care center about children with developmental disabilities and their families. Record their comments, concerns, and general attitudes about the children and their parents.
3. Observe a preschool session. Count the number of child-to-teacher contacts. Briefly describe those the teacher turned into a teaching on-the-fly or incidental teaching episode.
4. Locate a program that serves children with severe disabilities. While observing, list the special equipment and services provided for the children.
5. Make up an example of each of the following classroom situations:
   1. A teacher being consistent about a rule.
   2. A teacher being flexible about a routine.
   3. A teacher being both consistent and flexible about the same rule or routine.

REVIEW

A. *Define and give an example.*
   1. Developmental diversity
   2. Developmentally appropriate practice
   3. Generalized learning
   4. Applied developmental approach to early education
   5. Disequilibrium
   6. Readiness to learn
   7. The facilitative teacher
   8. Functional situation
   9. Incidental teaching

B. *True or False. Choose the best answer.*
   T F   1. The life ways of a family have no influence on classroom practice.
   T F   2. The Association of Teacher Educators, the Division of Early Childhood, and the National Association for the Education of Young Children have extremely different positions on how teachers of young children and young children with disabilities should be trained.
   T F   3. The Education 2000 goals cite readiness as a national priority.
   T F   4. All early childhood teachers who teach in an inclusive program must have a degree in special education.

   T F   5. Parents are not a reliable source of information about their child's disability.
   T F   6. The tantrums of a child with a disability are not necessarily related to the child's disability.
   T F   7. Crawling, pulling-to-stand, and then walking are part of a developmental sequence.
   T F   8. An example of the transactional aspects of development is an infant and mother who almost always return each other's smiles.
   T F   9. The more consistent a teacher is the more likely it is that children can be given greater freedom in managing their own behavior.
   T F 10. Punishing a child for going up the slide the wrong way is an example of facilitative teaching.

C. *Write a short essay in response to the following question:*
   If extensive retraining is not required to teach in an inclusive preschool or child care classroom what do teachers need to do to ensure that children with developmental disabilities have a good learning experience?

REFERENCES

Allen, K.E., and Goetz, E.M. (1982). *Early childhood education: Special problems, special solutions.* Rockville, MD: Aspen Systems.

Boyer, E.L. (1991). *Ready to learn: A mandate for the nation.* Princeton, NJ: Carnegie Foundation for the Advancement of Teaching.

Bredekamp, S. (Ed.) (1987). Developmentally appropriate practice in early childhood programs serving children from birth through age 8. Washington, D.C.: National Association for the Education of Young Children.

DEC Task Force on Recommended Practices (1993). *DEC recommended practices: Indicators of quality programs for infants and young children with special needs and their families.* Reston, VA: Council for Exceptional Children.

DeVries, R., and Kohlberg, L. (1990). *Constructivist early education: Overview and comparison with other programs.* Washington, D.C.: National Association for the Education of Young Children.

Fraiberg, S. (1974). Blind infants and their mothers: An examination of the sign system. In M. Lewis and L.A. Rosenblum (Eds.), *The effect of the infant on its caregiver.* New York: Wiley.

Gil, L.L. (1987). Report: Project Outreach: *A model for mainstreaming handicapped infants, toddlers, and preschoolers in generic programs.* Mimeographed. Northwest Child Development Center. Seattle, WA.

Gordon, A.M., and Browne, K.W. (1996). *Beginnings and beyond. Foundations in early childhood education.* Albany: Delmar.

Hart, B.M., and Risley, T.R. (1982). How to use incidental teaching. Austin, TX: PRO-ED.

Horowitz, F.D. (1987). *Exploring developmental theories: Toward a structural/behavioral model of development.* Hillsdale, NJ: Erlbaum.

Klein, J. (1977). Head Start services to the handicapped—Mainstreaming the preschooler. *Head Start Newsletter,* 9(8).

Luera, M. (1993). Honoring family uniqueness. In S.M. Rehberg (Ed.), *Starting point: A series of definition papers,* 1–9. Olympia, WA: Office of the Superintendent of Public Instruction.

Warren, S.F., and Kaiser, A.P. (1988). Research in early language intervention. In S.L. Odom and M.B. Karnes (Eds.), *Early intervention for infants and children with handicaps.* Baltimore: Brookes.

White, B.L. (1975). *The first three years of life.* Englewood Cliffs, NJ: Prentice Hall.

Wolery, M., Strain, P.S., and Bailey, D. (1992). Reaching potentials of children with special needs. In S. Bredekamp and T. Rosegrant (Eds.), *Reaching potentials: Appropriate curriculum and assessment for young children,* Washington DC: National Association for the Education of Young Children.

Wolery, M., and Wilbers, J.S. (Eds.) (1994). *Including children with special needs in early childhood programs.* Washington, D.C.: National Association for the Education of Young Children.

SPECIAL FOCUS
Talking with Children about Death and Dying

WENDIE BRAMWELL*

INTRODUCTION AND BACKGROUND

Early childhood education programs provide young children the opportunity to acquire skills that help them find their way through the ups and downs of growing up. Early childhood educators provide foundations for helping children learn to communicate with one another, for expressing their feelings, and for acquiring the art of compromise when disagreeing. Even so, one critical area is invariably overlooked in early childhood teacher-training programs: Death. It is a topic that causes many of us to look away, to redirect the conversation, or to answer with short, uncomfortable comments. We have been raised to avoid talking openly about death and dying because it is painful and personal. Yet, by keeping too great a distance from the topic of death we are ignoring an important part of living for ourselves and for our children.

As educators, many of us avoid dealing with the topic of death by convincing ourselves that children are too young to understand its complexities. Some of us may assume that children are immune or should be sheltered from the pain and grief associated with loss. But how can we ignore a topic of such vital importance? How many children in our classrooms experienced the death of a family member, friend, or pet during the school year? Have we not overheard conversations about shootings and violence from our very young children? Has a child in our school not died sometime during the school year? Has a teacher or staff member died? Seldom is there a school year when children are not confronted with at least one of these circumstances.

It is becoming increasingly important to understand responses to death as we move toward inclusion in early

childhood programs, especially as we include children with more severe medical problems. Children with special needs and their families have a higher risk of confronting death and dying due to accidents, frequent hospitalizations, medical complications, and fragile health conditions (Kudrajavcev, Schoenberg, Kurland, and Groover 1983). As classrooms welcome all children, teachers and staff must expand their own understanding and appreciation for life as well as for death.

ESTABLISHING GROUNDWORK

It may be difficult for early childhood educators to know where to begin in offering guidance to young children on the topic of death and dying, subjects that have preoccupied philosophers and theologians for thousands of years. Yet, we must begin somewhere. A two-pronged approach may work: understanding the developmental levels of children's comprehension of death, and understanding our own feelings and views about death.

DEVELOPMENTAL CONSIDERATIONS

Understanding the developmental context of a child's notion of death is an easier task than examining our own values and beliefs. With a sweep of the hand, children are often dismissed from family discussions and arrangements dealing with death. Sometimes this may be appropriate yet it excludes children from a process that can help their understanding and healing. How can we know what will be best for a child? We can begin by listening carefully to children to gain insights into their thoughts. The 6-year-old who exclaims that he will "cling to the couch if death comes" has a very different concept of death from the 9-year-old who matter-of-factly answers that death means "You have had your life."

Interpreting what children say will be more meaningful if we understand the developmental stages of

Wendie Bramwell is an early childhood educator and currently works on an early intervention training project at the University of Washington and as an instructor of early childhood special education classes at Bellevue Community College.

children's concepts of death. Current evidence acknowledges that even children under the age of 5 do understand death on some level. Kubler-Ross (1981) reports that her 4-year-old child buried a dog in the fall. Suddenly the child said, "This is really not so sad. Next spring when your tulips come up, he'll come up again and play with me." This 4-year-old's notion that things do not remain dead is reinforced over and over in children's stories. Snow White and Sleeping Beauty arise from the dead by being kissed. Tinkerbell is clapped back to life and the Beast is revived because of Beauty's pure love.

Allen Mendelson, in the *Young and Special* (1982) video series entitled "Let's Not Even Talk About It," describes the reaction of children in his class to the death of Bryan, their 4-year-old classmate. "Death is not finite for most 4-year-olds and that would come out over a period of days; 'Bryan's not here again today.' And it was my job to say, 'Right. And Bryan will never be here again because he died.' The reality took awhile for different children. 'Oh, he's not at school today, he's dead, but maybe he will be here tomorrow.'"

Between 5 and 7 years of age, children begin to understand the permanence of death but may think of it as a person, a "deathman," who will come and remove them bodily from their environment. This varies greatly from culture to culture but there is evidence that many children of this age fear that death has a form that can take them away.

Consistent with their sense of invincibility, young children talk about eluding death. They assert that they can run, hide, stomp or destroy whatever form death might take. They also rationalize their safety from death. When a 7-year-old classmate died in a drowning accident after slipping into the lake from an icy deck, children were overheard saying things like, "I don't have a deck" or "I don't even know where the lake is" or "My shoes are the kind that don't slip."

By middle childhood most children can grasp the four subconcepts of death as outlined by Essa and Murray (1994): finality, inevitability, cessation of bodily functions, and causality. Although cognitively understanding what has happened, children of this age may feel guilty or responsible for what has happened. They may be anxious about their future. In the book *How It Feels When a Parent Dies*, Jill Krements

(1981) reports the words of a 9-year-old whose father has died. "I was worried that my mother might have to go back to work and there would be somebody new picking me up from school every day." When 8-year-old Stephen learned that his father had died in a plane crash, the first thing he asked his mom was if he "could keep Skippy and Shadow, our dog and cat, and could we keep our house." Thoughts such as these make the needs of the older child far different from those of the younger child who simply doesn't understand what it means to die.

Beyond the developmental context of death there are other important factors that influence children's understanding. Children who are critically ill or who have experienced a death close to them at a young age have an earlier and deeper understanding than their same age peers (Kubler-Ross 1983). Clearly, cultural and religious influences also greatly affect a child's perception of death and its significance. For example, each year families in Mexico celebrate the "Night of the Dead (La Noche de Muertos). Families clean gravestones, prepare favorite dishes of deceased family members and set up a vigil for spirits who will return for this particular evening. Shops are filled with humorous, whimsical skeletal figures participating in mundane daily activities. Greg Palmer, in *Death: The Trip of a Lifetime* (1993), interviews the Lucas family in Mexico about the celebration of death. Mrs. Lucas explains, "The Night of the Dead is good for families. It gives us a reason to talk about death with our children so they are used to it before it happens to one of us. They are not afraid of it. And they get a feeling for the family, too. That it's not just the living, it's still my mother and my husband's brother and the baby they did not know."

INTROSPECTION

If young children have an imperfect understanding of death, do we then conclude that adults have a "perfect" understanding? No. Even though most adults understand death on a conceptual level, each successive experience with death contributes to a deeper understanding, even appreciation for death. Death, like every part of living, is a topic about which adults continue to increase their understanding throughout their lifetime.

Essa and Murray (1994) report, "Adults who explore and give thought to their own feelings about death find it easier to help children understand and cope with death." Teachers have been taught to turn to books, offer handouts or bring in experts when a need arises for new information, but death requires more introspection than most other topics. If we look at our own early experiences with death we can begin to understand what has shaped our current beliefs. We need to recognize what was comforting, what was missing in terms of comfort and explanations, what contributed most to fears or what contributed most to being able to cope. These remembrances will help us take the first step toward helping children.

Adults who have the opportunity to talk about death often will reveal what is important to know and understand about children. One adult student vividly remembered her first kindergarten friend. They held hands, played together at recess, and shared lunch. Her friend stopped coming to school and no explanation was ever offered for her absence. It was only much later that she learned the child had died. The sense of loss and confusion still permeated her telling of this incident. Friendship, throughout her life, always felt risky because her first experience had been so distressing. Another adult who lost someone she loved through a violent crime remembers being criticized for talking about the event with a detachment that her listeners associated with indifference. She explained that the only way she could talk about the event was to remove herself emotionally because it was too painful to live through the feelings each time.

All too often, we do not talk about death until someone close to us dies. Grief intermingles with unresolved feelings about deaths in the past and the task of supporting children becomes diluted with our own turbulent feelings. If we are to offer the very best guidance to children, we must first understand our own feelings and memories by talking with others. With insights gained from such experiences, we might more easily grasp the importance of clear and accurate information for children. We also may have a deeper understanding of the child who appears to be able to shrug off the death of a loved one as though it were "no big deal."

GRIEF AND MOURNING

Rituals associated with death have taken many forms throughout the ages and across cultures but their purpose remains the same: to acknowledge death and the accompanying feelings and to provide the bereaved with a community in which they can express and share their grief. Children often create their own rituals when a pet dies. Beloved objects are placed with the pet before burial, a choice site in the yard is selected and often tiny pebbles or flowers mark the site, in imitation of the adult rituals. If we look carefully at these gestures we begin to understand that children are seeking the same sense of closure that adults seek from rituals. When we exclude children from ceremonies associated with dying we are creating what Doka (1989) calls "disenfranchised grievers"—children who are discouraged or even prevented from displaying their grief.

Adults need to create opportunities for children to express their thoughts and feelings. Sometimes this happens in traditional religious observances where friends and family gather together to honor and remember the deceased. At other times families may prefer to create their own rituals that allow children the chance to talk about death as this family did:

The oak piano bench was draped with a lace table cloth. Carefully arranged on it were a rose, a candle, a precious stone, a crocheted granny square and a photo. The bench was pulled close to two couches that faced one another. Sitting on the couch were five children ages 7 to 14 who had been brought together to commemorate their grandmother who had died after a long illness. Other family members and a grief counselor were also assembled in the dim light, talking about memories and thoughts and listening to one another. There were awkward but poignant silences but gradually the children started to talk. There was an outpouring of sadness and guilt and unexpected associations. The pets who had died in previous years were discussed in detail. There was some anger about the perceived expectation to cry and be sad. There was guilt that the expected tears did not readily flow. There were sweet memories of shared moments and there was a great sense of emptiness at the loss.

Grief manifests itself in unique ways for both adults and children. Adults who sanction, encourage and respect the ways in which children express loss are helping to move children out of the category of "disenfranchised grievers." The stages of grief that Kubler-Ross (1969) has identified (denial, anger, bargaining, depression, and acceptance) describe many of the feelings that cycle through one's grieving experience. Yet there are behaviors that come out of grieving that seem so disconnected from the experience of loss that it is hard to recognize them as grief-related. Some children act out in angry, violent ways saying hurtful and hateful things about the people closest to them. Some have disruptions in their sleeping and eating habits. Others have a difficult time in school focusing and remembering. As parents, and as teachers of young children, we need to accept these feelings and try to understand them. We can best accomplish this by becoming more introspective about our own feelings about death. The more aware we are of our own feelings, the better prepared we will be to respond to children's expressions of grief.

GRIEF AND FAMILIES OF CHILDREN WITH DISABILITIES

As our awareness of the different stages and manifestations of grief increases, so will the realization that events other than a death can send us into a grief cycle. Loss of many kinds, a separation or divorce, a move or a job change are a few of the life events that may evoke a grieving response. Ken Moses (1987) suggests that parents of children with disabilities experience a grieving process that is strikingly similar to that of people who experience a death. Working with groups of parents, Moses saw anxiety, anger, denial, guilt, depression, and fear expressed over and over again. Gradually he came to understand that the par-

ents were grieving the *loss of the dream* of what their child was to have been for them.

> "Disability shatters the dreams, fantasies, illusions, and projections into the future that parents generate as part of their struggle to accomplish basic life missions. Parents of impaired children grieve for the loss of dreams that are key to the meaning of their existence, to their sense of being. Recovering from such a loss depends on one's ability to separate from the lost dream and to generate new, more attainable dreams."

Families who are dealing with the kind of loss associated with a child with disabilities have complex and often conflicting feelings that surface and resurface throughout the years. As early childhood educators, we will find ourselves listening and responding to this type of grief as our centers and classrooms become inclusive. If we listen and respond to their needs, we will recognize dynamics that affect all family members. For example, brothers and sisters of children with disabilities are often misunderstood or overlooked as families meet the needs of their child with disabilities. While the parents adjust to the challenges of a special needs child, siblings often feel the child is receiving a disproportionate amount of attention. We can understand why guilt and depression, even anger, are not uncommon feelings under these circumstances.

Children and adults who have experienced a death and families with children who have disabilities are connected by their common experience of loss. We connect best with others when we share similar meaningful experiences. Although confronting the issues of loss can be painful, failing to do so can be isolating and ultimately self defeating. By exploring the topic of death and dying teachers of young children can achieve a deeper understanding of an important part of children's lives.

REFERENCES

Doka, K.J. (1989). *Disenfranchised Grief.* Lexington, MA: Lexington Books.

Essa, E.L., and Murray, D.I. (1994). Young children's understanding and experience with death. *Young Children, 49*(4), 74–81.

Evans, P.M., and Alberman, E. (1991). Certified cause of death in children and young adults with cerebral palsy. *Archives of Disease in Children, 66*(3), 325–329.

Eyman, R.K., Grossman, H.J., Chaney, R.H., and Call, T.L. (1990). The life expectancy of profoundly handicapped people with mental retardation. The *New England Journal of Medicine.* 323:584–589.

Krementz, J. (1981). *How it feels when a parent dies.* New York: Knopf.

Kudrajavcev, T., Schoenberg, B.S., Kurland, L.T., and Groover, R. (1983). Cerebral palsy—trends in incidence and changes in concurrent neonatal mortality: Rochester, MN, 1950–1976. *Neurology, 33*(11), 1433–1438.

Kubler-Ross, E. (1981). *Living with Death and Dying.* New York: Macmillan.

Kubler-Ross., E. (1969). *On Death and Dying,* New York: Macmillan.

Kubler-Ross, E. (1983). *On Children and Death,* New York: Macmillan.

Mendelson, A. (1982). *Young and Special,* a Video Based inservice for Mainstreaming Preschool Children, "Let's Not Even Talk About It." Circle Pines, MN: American Guidance Service.

Moses, K. (1987). "The Impact of Childhood Disability: The Parents Struggle." *WAYS.*

Palmer, G. (1993). *Death: The Trip of a Lifetime.* New York: Harper Collins.

Implementing Inclusive Early Childhood Programs

The Developmental-Behavioral Approach

OBJECTIVES

After studying this unit the student will be able to

- describe three early education practices that are a blend of developmental and behavioral principles.
- define positive reinforcement and describe how skilled teachers use it in teaching young children.
- explain the relationship between developmentally appropriate expectations and the behavioral approach to working with young children.
- define punishment and offer a convincing argument against its use with children.
- explain task analysis and its importance in working with children in general and with children with developmental problems in particular.

From earliest infancy, healthy development goes hand in hand with a nurturing and responsive environment to produce ongoing behavior changes in children. Behavior changes are critical—they are the only assurance that developmental progress is taking place. In early childhood programs the children's changing behaviors also are an index of the quality of the program and the effectiveness of the teaching practices. Consider the following examples:

Last month Susie refused to try any of the wheel toys; today she pedaled a tricycle independently for five minutes.

Yesterday Joy counted only to seven pushes as the teacher was pushing her on the swing. This morning she counted ten pushes in succession.

Today Bart built a bridge with blocks for the first time.

In these particular cases the accomplishment represented one of the short-term objectives written into each child's IEP. At the same time the accomplishment represented behavior changes indicating developmental progress. Once again: *it is not possible to have healthy development without ongoing changes in behavior.* Developmental/behavioral changes range from the simple to the complex. They come about because of physical growth, maturation, experience, observational learning (modeling), and practice. The changes are orderly. They take place in accordance with specifiable *laws* of behavior and predictable biological sequences.

Basic developmental principles have been discussed specifically in Unit 4 and elsewhere throughout the text. This unit will provide a brief analysis of behavioral principles, especially those that have particular relevance for teachers of young children. The major focus is on reinforcement procedures, with emphasis on positive social responsiveness from teachers and other significant adults. Punishment will also be discussed, not because it is recommended practice but because of its widespread and inappropriate use. Many adults fail to recognize the ineffectiveness of punishment; others seem to be unaware of alternate ways of managing children. In this unit, positive reinforcement practices are emphasized as the first and preferred approach to effective discipline.

Step-by-step learning (task analysis) and learning through modeling (imitation) are additional principles that play a major role in early childhood teaching and learning. The discussion of these topics includes the timing of teacher's attention, the role of praise, and the inappropriateness of competitiveness in presenting early learning experiences. The unit starts with a brief overview of the gradual merging of developmental theory and reinforcement/behavioral principles in early childhood education.

DEVELOPMENTAL AND BEHAVIORAL PRINCIPLES: A BLEND

Effective early childhood teachers rely on *both* developmental and behavioral principles when deciding how and what to teach children. They know that the best measure of the effectiveness of their teaching is change in children's behavior. The examples of behavior changes in Susie, Joy, and Bart demonstrate the results of facilitating each child's learning by combining the two principles. In each instance, behavioral objectives (new skills to be learned) had been selected on the basis of each child's individual learning needs and the teacher's knowledge of development. Decisions also had been made about preparing the environment to assist each child in learning the new skills through play activities. Bricker and Cripe (1992) refer to these procedures as an activities-based approach in writings on early intervention.

Historical Influences. A developmental-behavioral approach to teaching has been evolving for 40 years

Children learn new and important skills through play activities.

and more. Mid-century, developmentalists were in the majority. Researchers such as Gesell et al. (1940) and Erikson (1950) believed that development was very nearly independent of experience, a natural *unfolding* of innate or inborn abilities. The role of teachers (and parents) was neither to unduly restrict nor to push the child. Then came theorists like Hunt (1961) who argued that development was *not* independent of external influences. Rather, it was controlled to some unknown extent by environmental experiences. Hunt had been greatly influenced by Piaget (1952) who theorized that changes in a child's thinking (cognitive structure) were direct results of a child's exploration of the environment. Hunt went one step further. He suggested that learning depended on a good *match* between the child and the experiences available to the child.

The problem of the match. In early childhood education the *problem of the match* became a central issue. Teachers were trained to provide play materials and learning opportunities that attracted and held children's attention. At the same time the materials were to include new and intriguing elements. These were to be just a bit beyond the child's current skill level. Providing exactly the right *match* was the way to produce pleasure and continuing eagerness (motivation) to learn. There was no need for teachers or parents to push or prod the child. The *joy of learning*, often referred to as *intrinsic motivation*, would take over. Children would seek out additional learning of their own accord, simply because they wanted to.

Learning from success.   The role of environmental influences also was central to the developmental ideas of Bijou (1959). He believed the results (*consequences*) of a child's behavior were the crucial element. According to Bijou, children tend to learn whatever brings feelings of success and positive outcome. They avoid behaviors that result in failure or negative consequences. Teachers were trained to present tasks step-by-small-step, and to build in positive feedback as the child moved through the steps. The result: a learning environment in which children had frequent success and were motivated to learn more.

Environmental arrangements.   Arranging the learning environment to help a child take a next step in skill development is a long established and fundamental principal in early childhood education. Following are three examples from different periods in the history of early childhood education.

Friedrich Froebel (1782–1852). Hailed as the founder of the kindergarten movement, Froebel is likely to have been the first to propose that early learning experiences be broken down into their smallest components. Froebel also argued that young children need hands-on experiences: materials to enjoy, examine, and manipulate.

Maria Montessori (1870–1952).This gifted physician was a champion of the educational potentials of disabled and developmentally delayed children. She spent her life demonstrating systematic and sequential learning activities based on what she called **didactic materials**. Many of these materials, as well as her ideas about a prepared environment, are central to today's early education practices.

John Dewey (1859–1952). Father of the *progressive education* movement is the title often given to Dewey. He,

Montessori advocated didactic materials and planned environment.

too, put major emphasis on the learning environment, especially as represented by the teacher who was to respond, support, and guide children's exploration of everyday materials.

In each of these approaches to early education, the route to sound learning reflects a developmental and behavioral blend that includes:

1. A prepared learning environment matched to children's current skill levels.
2. Materials and activities sequenced in small enough segments to provide both success and challenge.
3. Emphasis on learning through play and active involvement with appropriate materials.
4. Responsive teachers who serve as guides and facilitators rather than instructors.

BEHAVIOR PRINCIPLES AND PRACTICES

Misinformation, faulty implementation, and abuse of behavioral practices has led to a "knee jerk" reaction in many early childhood educators whenever the behavioral approach is mentioned according to Wolery (1994) who goes on to say: "The behavioral perspective, although often seen as stressing the impact of the environment, in fact proposes that learning occurs from dynamic interactions between children and their environment" (p. 98). And on the next page: "Particularly beneficial are those child-environment interactions that are initiated and directed by children and in which they are highly engaged.

As this text has pointed out through each edition, the behavioral approach to early intervention consists of arranging the environment and implementing teaching strategies in ways that enhance children's learning opportunities. While the approach is important in working with all kinds of children it is particularly important in facilitating learning among children with developmental delays, deficits, and deviations.

All Children Are Teachable.   In an inclusive classroom, the most significant and useful behavioral principle for teachers is one that bears repeated emphasis: *All children are teachable.* Every child can learn. Some children learn faster than others. Some children learn more than others. Some children learn some things easily, other things only with great effort. Some children learn from one kind of teaching, others from a different method. But all children can learn. This well established concept is documented by several decades of behavioral research. Bijou and Cole (1975) summarize:

> Traditionally, an individual who did not learn what was presented was considered incapable, indifferent, unmotivated, or lacking. The behavioral view on the other hand is if the student does not learn, something is lacking in the teaching situation (p. 3).

To make the *teachability* of all children a day-by-day reality, teachers need to understand and practice basic behavioral principles. In the inclusive classroom the procedures are especially important. Each child can be provided a responsive learning environment matched to his or her developmental level and special interests. Gifted children can be provided with learning opportunities that neither push nor hold them back, but instead, foster their unique interests and talents. Children with developmental problems , though some may learn more slowly or with greater effort, are provided a responsive and reinforcing learning environment matched to *their* developmental skill levels. The essence of the behavioral approach is to start

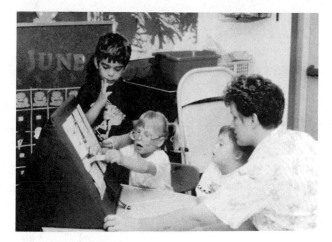

Start with what the child can do.

where the child is, developmentally, and build from there.

Children who have severe impairments may have few behaviors to build on. Skilled observers, however, are able to pick up on subtle cues that indicate a child's possible interest and awareness (Beckman et al. 1986). For example, a child's eyes may widen as the caregiver approaches the crib even though the child cannot raise or turn his or her head in the caregiver's direction. In some instances, teachers, parents, and caregivers themselves, may have to decide the starting point. An example might be a child with multiple disabilities who displays few behaviors of any kind. Simply getting the child to look in a given direction may be a first priority. Even to accomplish this, a teacher often has to structure the environment to evoke (trigger) an attending response from the child: the sight or fragrance of a favorite food or the sound of a loud bell—whatever will attract the child's attention and give the teacher a behavior to respond to and expand on.

Reinforcement Procedures.   Reinforcement procedures come from research related to **operant conditioning**, **behavior modification**, and **learning theory**. Volumes of studies demonstrate that behavior is triggered by antecedent events (something that precedes, such as hunger pangs or a particular sound) and then increases or decreases according to its consequences (**reinforcers**). The principles can be put into a simple ABC format:

A: *Antecedent* events (that which precedes or comes before a behavior).
B: *Behavior* (responses of the individual).
C: *Consequences* (that which follows a behavior).

A and C are environmental events, planned or unplanned, that both precede and follow a behavior. Example:

A.	B.	C.
Mother opening a bag of cookies	Child, watching: "I want cookie"	Mother hands child cookie

The child' request (B) was triggered by seeing mother opening a package of cookies (A). It is likely the child will ask for a cookie every time mother opens a package because the request resulted in a cookie (C). Unwanted behaviors often are reinforced through these same procedures, always in operation, but often unrecognized. In the cookie example, the mother may have said (C): No cookie until after lunch. This may have set off clamoring and whining (B) in the child. Mother may refuse several times but with each refusal the whining gets more insistent and finally she gives the child a cookie. (Sound familiar?) The child is likely to learn from this and similar exchanges that asking does not always pay off but insistent whining does. The moral of this story: if mother was going to allow a cookie she should have done it on the first request, rather than having the child learn that whin-

Antecedents are what the teacher does before expecting the child to respond: the selection and presentation of materials and activities. Photo Credit: Mary Levin

ing, which drives mother up the wall, usually pays off and so will be repeated whenever the child is crossed.

If specific learnings, B, are to occur (or not occur as in the case of inappropriate behaviors) then A and C must be decided on and systematically arranged. In simple terms, A is what teachers do *before* they would have a child respond. This includes the selection, arrangement, and presentation of activities and materials (and playmates in some instances). C is what teachers do immediately following a child's response, such things as providing or withholding reinforcers (the next topic to be discussed). Whatever adults do in A and C (or fail to do) effects the child's behavior and learning (Allen 1974).

Reinforcement takes three forms: *positive, negative,* and *neutral*. Reinforcement, as we will see, may also be both positive and *intrinsic*. In this text, the focus will be mainly on positive reinforcement because of its value in working with young children. First, however, the other forms of reinforcement will be overviewed briefly.

Intrinsic reinforcement: a sense of pleasure, satisfaction, and self-esteem.

Negative reinforcement.   The strengthening of a behavior by the removal of an unpleasant consequence is the definition of negative reinforcement. Negative reinforcement is a confusing concept that has been explained in a variety of ways. Bee (1992) gives one of the more easily understood definitions:

> Negative reinforcement occurs when something *unpleasant* is stopped. Suppose your child is whining and whining at you to be picked up. What happens? He stops whining. So your picking up behavior has been *negatively reinforced* by the cessation (stopping) of the child's whining and you will be *more* likely to pick him up the next time he whines. At the same time, his whining has been *positively reinforced* by your attention and picking up, so he will be more likely to whine on other occasions.

Learning the definition of negative reinforcement is of greater technical value than usefulness in the classroom. One point must be made, however: negative reinforcement is not the same as punishment which will be discussed later.

Neutral reinforcement.   Consequences that are neither pleasant nor unpleasant is the simplest definition of neutral reinforcement. The term refers to aspects of the environment that are just there, taken for granted: the air we breathe, the ground we walk on, the constant traffic noise outside the window or the hum of the refrigerator in the corner. Only when a change occurs do these events lose (or assume) their neutral status and become positive or negative reinforcers. For example, the familiar drinking fountain on the playground provided positive reinforcement in that thirsty children could drink. When it became damaged and was not repaired, it soon became a neutral item. It no longer signaled children that a reinforcer was available in the form of water to drink when thirsty.

Intrinsic reinforcement.   Feelings of pleasure and personal satisfaction describe intrinsic reinforcement. It comes from working on or accomplishing a task, discovering something new, solving a problem. For poor readers, who have to work hard at figuring out words (let alone meaning) there is little or no intrinsic reinforcement: reading is taxing, something to be avoided. In young children the same holds true whether it is tricycle riding, block building, or working with puzzles.

Positive reinforcement. In technical terms, positive reinforcement is something that follows a response and results in the increase of that particular response. In simpler terms, a positive reinforcer is a pleasant consequence; therefore it has a high probability of increasing whatever behavior preceded it. For example, Carla always asks her father rather than her mother for certain privileges. Why? She has learned that her father is likely to grant (reinforce) her request, her mother to deny it.

Money is a pleasant reinforcer for most adults. Adults continue to work week after week or month after month because they get paid regularly. With this kind of reinforcement (regular paychecks) men and women keep working, some beyond retirement age, many at jobs they do not particularly like. Young children usually are not interested in money; nevertheless, they do have a wide range of reinforcers such as:

Preferred foods and drinks
Toys, play, and other favorite activities
The attention of certain adults

Different children like different things. A reinforcer for one child may be of little value to another. Candy is a good example: It is generally assumed that all children like candy. Not true; a number of children do not like candy (or is it that they have taken to heart their parents' counsel that it is not good for them?).

Adult social reinforcements. One reinforcer that is both powerful and universally appealing to young children of every culture is *adult social reinforcement.* Adult social reinforcement is made up of the attention of significant adults: parents, teachers, grandparents and other family members, and nurturing caregivers. Generally, adult attention is readily available and potentially plentiful. Years of research provides conclusive evidence that adult attention is likely to increase those behaviors which it immediately and consistently follows. The opposite also is true: When adult attention is consistently and immediately with-

held or withdrawn, the behavior decreases. The following excerpt from a case study points up the appropriate and systematic use of teachers' attention in helping a child acquire a needed behavior—improved span of attention.

> Concern's about James's lack of attention span led teachers to make a series of observations. It was obvious that James was getting a great deal of attention from teachers, yet there was no increase in his attention span. Teacher agreed, therefore, to focus their attention on James *only* on those moments, no matter how brief, that he was engaged with a material or activity. They agreed, further, not to interact with him just as he was leaving an activity nor when he was flitting about. That is, they refrained from doing what they usually did at those times which, was to attempt to steer the child into an activity. Teachers consistently held to this plan as to when they would provide attention and when they would withhold it. James's span of attention soon began to increase.

For a complete discussion of the practices used with James and with many other children whose behaviors were of concern to teachers, see Allen and Goetz (1982). Those studies (and the studies of many other researchers) demonstrate how powerful teachers are as sources of reinforcement for young children. Best of all, the studies indicate how simple reinforcement procedures bring out the best in each child—all that has to be done is what good teachers do so well: responding to children in encouraging and positive ways and providing materials and activities matched to children's interests and skill levels. Following are brief descriptions of everyday teacher behaviors that serve as powerful reinforcers for almost any young child:

- *Verbal responsiveness*—relevant comments, interested questions, answers to children's questions, exclamations of approval such as "Great!".
- Descriptive praise that focuses on some aspect of what the child is accomplishing: "Paula, you laced your shoes all by yourself!" (NOTE: In addition to the terms *descriptive praise, encouragement* and *effective praise* also are terms in common usage. For a discussion of these forms of adult attention see Hitz and Driscoll (1989) and Allen and Hart (1984).

- *Physical proximity*—quietly standing or sitting close to a child and showing genuine interest by watching, nodding, smiling or listening.
- *Physical contact*—touching, hugging, holding a child's hand, tussling, rocking or otherwise physically comforting a child. (Teachers must note and discuss the occasional child who avoids or shrinks from adults' touch.)
- *Physical assistance*—providing support on the climbing frame, pushing a swing, helping a child achieve balance on a walking beam.
- *Providing things that children want*—play materials, activities, mini-excursions such as a ride in the elevator or crossing the road to watch a carpenter, a favorite snack, and reading a story.

Withdrawing or Withholding Reinforcers.   Another form of adult social reinforcement, less pleasant to practice, is taking away (withdrawing or withholding) something that is important to a child—a favorite toy, activity, playmate, or the attention of an important adult. Withholding reinforcement is used when an inappropriate behavior is not decreasing, in spite of teachers' efforts. (Recall the staff's first efforts to redirect James, with the resulting increase in flitting about?) Though punishment itself will not be discussed until later, withdrawing/withholding reinforcement, in one sense, is a form of punishment. It has less damaging side effects than physical or verbal punishment, however. It is also more effective. Equally important, it cuts down on the emotional conflict between adult and child that so often accompanies other forms of punishment. In early childhood settings, withholding attention and other reinforcers can be accomplished in several ways.

1. Teachers may ignore an incident, act as if they do not see the undesirable behavior (as long as the child is not endangering self or others). Ignoring can be accomplished by a teacher turning away for the moment, as all teachers do, a dozen times a day, to focus on another child or activity.
2. Teachers may remove materials or equipment if a child continues to misuse them.
3. Teachers may remove the child from play with other children or from an activity.

Though it will be stressed again and again, let it be said here as well, that in a well-arranged and developmentally appropriate early learning environment, the need for any kind of negative procedure is rare. Hence the rationale for including in this text the entire next unit on environmental arrangements and the consequent positive effect on children's behavior.

Incompatible Behaviors.   Incompatible behaviors are two or more responses that cannot occur together: An inappropriate behavior cannot occur at the same time an appropriate behavior is occurring. For example, it

Whatever significant adults do (or do not do) affects a child's behavior.

is impossible for children to walk and run at the same time. Therefore, if the rule is *no running in the classroom* teachers turn their attention to children who are remembering to walk. The child who runs, after a first reminder, receives no further teacher attention until the running stops. Other examples: listening is incompatible with talking out; making a neutral comment is incompatible with teasing; waiting for the cookie basket to be passed is incompatible with snatching cookies. In other words, whenever a child is not being inappropriate, he or she is engaging in some kind of appropriate behavior (even if it is only standing and watching for a moment). This gives teachers the opportunity to respond to something appropriate rather than wasting their time and emotional energy on inappropriate behaviors.

Withholding attention from maladaptive or inappropriate behaviors need not (and should not) result in a child getting less adult attention. Misbehaving children tend to be attention seekers; ignoring their inappropriate behaviors often results in more varied and even greater inappropriateness as they increase their efforts to get attention. The strategy is for teachers to attend to other, more appropriate (or at least, less objectionable) behaviors the child engages in. The best behaviors for teachers to attend to are those that are incompatible with the inappropriate behavior. James, once again, will be the example.

> James's constant flitting about the classroom prevented him from focusing on any one activity. In other words, flitting and focusing are incompatible behaviors. Teachers therefore gave up attending to his flitting and instead paid attention to those moments, brief as they might be, when he became engaged in an activity. The teacher in charge of the activity provided interest and support as long as James was engaged. When he left, that teacher and the others immediately turned their attention elsewhere, until such time as he lingered again, even briefly, with another activity. As noted earlier, James's attention span soon began to show marked improvement.

Catch the child being good.   Florence Harris, a remarkable teacher of young children (as well as a teacher-trainer and researcher) used to counsel teachers and parents: "Catch the child being good" (Harris, Wolf and Baer 1964). She urged adults to freely and spontaneously respond to (reinforce) the many appropriate things that children do all day long. Harris's counsel is significant in that it is almost impossible for a child to be good and bad at the same time; appropriate behaviors, therefore, have the potential of *crowding out* inappropriate behaviors. The strategy is to focus very little of the attention the child receives on what teachers have agreed are inappropriate acts. The same amount of attention should be directed instead, to almost anything else the child does. Adults need spend no additional time on the child. They simply spend the time in ways that are more effective and certainly more pleasant for teachers and children.

Catching a child being good is contrary to what usually happens, however. Adults tend to remain fairly neutral until a child does something the adult considers inappropriate. *Then* the child is likely to get a great deal of attention, but of a punishing kind which will do little to eliminate the unacceptable behavior. *Catch the child being good* is the essence of **preventive discipline** to be discussed in greater detail in Unit 14.

Punishment.   Punishment, by its common definition, consists of those adult behaviors that most children find unpleasant—scolding, nagging yelling, ridiculing, criticizing, isolating, slapping, shaking, spanking. As noted earlier, punishing children is not an effective way of managing them. True, punishment often stops an undesirable behavior at the moment. However, it usually is a short-lived victory for the adult and one that tends to backfire. Yelling at children is an example. Most children will stop, for the time being, whatever they are doing that is causing them to be yelled at. That behavior, however, is almost sure to return, again and again, under various circumstances.

Side effects of punishment.   Punishment has undesirable side effects. In the yelling example, the behavior the adult does not like is stopped at the time. This reinforces the adult for yelling at the child. Result? The adult yells at the child all the more. (This, by the way, is an example of *negative reinforcement*). In addition, the adult, according to Bee (1992), is modeling yelling, literally teaching inappropriate yelling behavior to the child:

Children who are yelled at yell back on other occasions. So, to a considerable degree, you get back what you give (p. 499).

The same holds true of spanking or other forms of physical punishment. Some children who are spanked frequently, or otherwise physically punished, become highly aggressive (Bandura 1973). Other children react very differently. Some behave as though they were tightly coiled springs. They often behave well at home or school but once out from under adults' eyes they seem to explode into a range of forbidden behaviors. Still other children appear troubled, turn inward, hold back, become passive. It is as if they fear that *whatever* they do will result in ridicule, criticism or some form of physical punishment. In general, punishment leads to loss of self-confidence and self-esteem. Frequently punished children (either verbally or physically punished) seldom feel good about themselves or their world. Such feelings have a negative effect on all aspects of their development.

Stopping a Harmful Behavior. All children must be stopped, on occasion. A child who is endangering self or others, or causing serious disruptions at home or in the classroom must be controlled. For many children, a reminder or a mild verbal reprimand is enough. This is especially effective in classrooms (and homes) where preventive discipline is practiced, where children receive adequate amounts of positive attention for the good things they do all day long. When a mild rebuke does not work, a sharply sounded "No!" or "Stop!" may be needed, followed by a *short* and *specific* statement of the potentially harmful act. The statement must be delivered directly to the child at eye level: "NO!" Janie, I *can't* let you push Tammy off the tricycle." When none of this works, which seldom need happen, the child may have to be removed, briefly, as described below.

Withdrawing the child. *Sit and watch.* Sit and watch is a mild form of time-out used with children who seem to have a hard time understanding expectations. The procedure calls for children to sit briefly (not more than a minute or two) at the edge of an activity and watch the appropriate play of other children. Two learnings are available. One is helping children learn,

at their level of understanding, the consequences of repeatedly overstepping the limits. The second is the opportunity to observe appropriate play of other children. The goal (as it should be with all forms of discipline) is to help children become self-managing.

Children often realize they have made a mistake in self-management the moment they are asked to sit and watch. To help the child remember, the teacher asks the child to say what the appropriate alternative is, perhaps, "Keep the sand in the sandbox." If a child does not remember, the teacher states the expectation and then has the child repeat it. Children who are significantly lacking in self-management skills may have to be removed from play several times in a row. Each time, the teacher removes the child matter-of-factly, without scolding or chiding, and the child is helped to restate the appropriate behavior.

Time-out. The extreme form of withdrawing reinforcement is time-out. Time-out means removing the children from all reinforcement including teacher attention, other children, materials, and equipment. Let it be stressed at the outset: *time-out should be used only as a last resort.* It should be reserved for seriously inappropriate behaviors that recur—behaviors that teachers have not been able to deal with by ignoring

It is in the classroom, *not in time-out*, that teachers help children learn appropriate way of behaving.

their inappropriate aspects and instead, responding to whatever might be appropriate about the situation.

On those occasions when time-out has to be used, the time-out period should be short. Never should it exceed three minutes; one minute is usually enough. If the child is making a disturbance in time-out, the one-to-three minute release rule still applies, beginning when a child has quieted down. An important reminder: Children do not learn *what to do* in time-out; they only learn *what not to do*. If children are to learn how to work and play with each other and with materials, they need to be involved (Schickedanz et al. 1982). It is in the classroom, *not in time-out*, that teachers can help children learn appropriate ways of responding. Good teachers seldom need to use time-out or any other punishment procedure when preventive discipline is the practice and all children receive adequate amounts of positive attention. It must be remembered, however, that what is an *adequate amount* of positive attention will vary from child to child, depending on individual differences.

A few final words about punishment: On those occasions (hopefully infrequent) when punishment cannot be avoided, it should come early in the sequence of misbehavior and at the mildest level possible (Patterson 1975). In talking about parent–child relationships (but equally applicable to teacher–child relationships), it is important to immediately take the toy from the child who has ignored the reminder about not banging it on her sister or the television. Bee (1992) puts it this way:

> Consistently withholding small privileges will "work," especially if the parent is also warm, clear about the rules, and consistent. It is far less effective if the parent waits until the screams have reached a piercing level or until the fourth time a teenager has gone off without saying where she's gone—and *then* weigh in with yelling and strong punishment (p. 449).

STEP-BY-STEP LEARNING

Step-by-step learning (task analysis) is a major teaching strategy to be used with all children. It has proven particularly useful when teaching children with developmental problems. The process consists of reinforcing *successive approximations* (a series of small steps) toward learning a complex behavior. In analyzing any kind of a task—tying shoes, counting bears, printing letters, defending possessions, making friends—the first requirement is to break the task down into steps that are small and logical. They also must be in sequence, progressing from the known, simple, and easy to the more difficult and complex. The smaller the steps the better. Small steps provide frequent opportunities for success. Many small steps, and therefore many small successes, help the child avoid unnecessary frustrations. Too many frustrations are defeating to young learners, and even more defeating for children with developmental problems.

Observation and Task Analysis.   To analyze a task, early childhood teachers often find it helpful to first watch a young child perform the task, especially a child who has only recently mastered a particular skill. The child's motor coordination and general approach to the problem is likely to be more finely sequenced and developmentally appropriate than those of an older child or an adult performing the same task. When adapting a procedure to an individual child, the starting point is determined by observing that child. The rule is to start where the child is, with what the child *can do*. This provides a successful experience at the start. It also enables the teacher to make positive comments immediately, thus getting the new learning off to a good start.

It is true that the first step may be far removed from what is seen as the end behavior. Many times it is nothing more than a child standing and watching an activity that has been targeted as a developmentally necessary skill for that child. This, however, is but a first step to learning a more complex skill.

Prompting, Cueing, and Fading.   Step-by-step learning often needs to be accompanied by, and reinforced with, physical and verbal assistance referred to as *prompting* and *cueing*. Prompts and cues help all children, and especially children with developmental problems, acquire a skill they may be having trouble with. *Fading* is the process of gradually and systematically reducing assistance (the prompting and cueing) as much and as soon as possible without interfering with the child's progress. The goal is for the child to learn to perform the task as independently as is feasible. To illustrate the procedures, learning to hang up a coat is described below.

> The teacher accompanies the child to the cubby or locker and gives verbal cues: "Here is your locker. Here is the hook for your coat."
>
> The teacher explains and demonstrates: "This is the loop that keeps your coat on the hook. It goes over the hook like this."
>
> Taking the coat off the hook but holding it open, the teacher prompts: "Can you find the loop?"
>
> When the child finds it, the teacher says, "Right. Now you can put your finger in just like I did."
>
> Teacher: "Now, slip it over the hook." If the child cannot yet coordinate the necessary movements, the teacher guides the child's hand (a manual prompt).
>
> After a few tries the teacher is able to withdraw physical assistance the instant before the loop goes over the hook and so can say to the child, "Look at that! *You* hung up your coat. Good for you!"

In this example, physical assistance was gradually reduced while verbal prompts and cues and positive comments were continued. As the child got better at the task, verbal help was also reduced, but only as the child had nearly accomplished each step. Some tasks and some children need even smaller, more specific steps and special kinds of assistance. *Manual prompting* is a common form of special assistance leading to skill mastery. It consists of positioning the adult's hand around the child's and actually putting the child through the motions. Once the child has the *feel* of the movements, manual prompting gradually is reduced.

Teachers must guard against overwhelming children with directions when helping them learn a complex task. Directions, like rules, should be kept to a minimum. They should be given only if the teacher is prepared to help the child carry through with additional prompting, cueing, and physical assistance. As with rules, directions are most effective when worded briefly, specifically, and positively. It is more informative and helpful to say, "Hold tight with both hands," than it is to say, "Be careful. Don't fall." The latter statements provide children with no information about what they should be doing. The primary goal is to encourage children's independence, especially in a child with developmental impairments. Therefore, teachers provide just enough assistance to ensure the

child's success but not so much as to promote overdependence., Adults most effectively promote children's independence by *waiting*, allowing children adequate time to figure out what they are going to do next, and how they will do it. This is in contrast to what happens all too often: The adult says "Put on your sock." Many a young child is still trying to figure out which is the open end of the sock when the adult grabs it and expertly puts it on the child's foot. What message does this convey to the child?

Amount and Timing of Reinforcement.   How much reinforcement is *enough*? The answer varies from child to child and task to task. Almost continuous reinforcement (feedback) may be needed when a child is beginning to learn something new. *Every time* the new behavior occurs (or an approximation to the new behavior), the adult tries to respond in some way. At times, smiling and nodding may be all a teacher can take time for. In all instances, adult attention is gradually reduced as the child becomes more able. The goal, always, is that the child's success (intrinsic motivation) takes over, keeping the child eager to continue learning. To accomplish this, a balance must be achieved: not so much adult attention that the child becomes dependent, but enough so learning continues until the skill is well established and intrinsically reinforcing.

Praise.   Praise, because it is so central to children's learning, will be discussed in several places in this text. It is mentioned here because of its relationship to step-by-step learning. Praise statements, like prompts and cues, need to be specific. It is of little value, in terms of children's learning, to make statements such as "Good boy," "Good work," "That's nice," "What a pretty picture." In contrast, *descriptive praise* (saying what it is that is good) gives the child specific feedback, always an aid to further learning. When the teacher says, "You're putting all the *red* blocks on the *red* squares. Good for you," the child knows exactly what it is that he or she is doing well. Such information is useful to the child in learning the rest of the color-matching task. Furthermore, the focus is on the child's efforts, rather than strictly on outcome or product.

Rarely if ever should teachers make statements such as, "*I* like the way you tied your shoes" (or patted the

Descriptive praise: "You got your coat off *all by yourself!*"

baby, or shared a cookie, or any of the other good things children learn to do). Contrast the statement about shoe-tying with this one: "Risa, you tied both shoes all by yourself! That makes you feel good, doesn't it?" The first statement implies that a child should be working to please others and needs to depend on external sources as a measure of personal worth. The second praise statement recognizes the accomplishment in a way that encourages the child to feel good about him- or herself. A child's confidence, self-esteem, and love of learning are thus nurtured.

LEARNING BY IMITATION

Many kinds of learning take place without direct reinforcement from anyone or anything outside the child. Children watch and then imitate; that is, they model their behavior after others. The involvement and self-feedback the child experiences (intrinsic motivation)leads to learning. Specific labels for this kind of learning are *observational learning* or *modeling* (Bandura 1977).

Children learn both appropriate and inappropriate behaviors by watching what is modeled on television,

in the classroom or neighborhood, by parents and family members. Teachers of young children are powerful models for classroom behavior. For example, teachers who believe that children should not sit on tables should not sit on tables themselves. Teachers who believe children should not yell at them should not yell at children. "Do as I say but not as I do" cannot be the rule.

The skills spontaneously modeled by older or more skilled children serve as motivation for other children. Young children are eager to learn. It is almost inevitable they will try things they see more mature children doing. To facilitate imitation learning in less skilled children, teachers can provide descriptive praise or feedback to the more skilled child: "Marilee, you are getting down, all by yourself, one foot and one hand at a time." An approving statement of this kind serves several purposes.

1. Marilee is encouraged to appreciate her own individuality and to value her own skills and capabilities.
2. An indirect lesson is provided for children within hearing distance who may not yet have achieved Marilee's level of climbing skills.
3. The teacher's words, "slowly and carefully, one foot and one hand at a time" are clues to what they might try, in their own way, as they work at becoming proficient climbers.

NOTE: Young children with disabilities do not always engage in spontaneous imitation. In these instances, specific training has proven effective. Peck and his colleagues (1978) conducted a study with three young children with Down syndrome. During free play, the teacher put the three children in close proximity to other children who were modeling an appropriate play behavior and said: "See how (model's name) is stacking the blocks. Now you do it." If the child imitated the peer model, the teacher praised and patted or hugged the child. If there was no imitation, the teacher physically put the child through the action and then praised: "You are stacking blocks, too. Good for you." Significantly, the effects of such training generalized to situations when the teacher was not present.

Not all children know how to imitate, however. Many children with special needs require specific instruction; in other words, they must first learn *how* to imitate before they can learn *through* imitation. In these instances, teachers need to provide specific kinds of assistance as described in Unit 17.

Competition Is Inappropriate. Descriptive statements, such as those about Marilee's climbing, carry no implications that any one child is better than another. Promoting competition among young children establishes an uneasy learning environment. Children cannot appreciate the process of learning, or their own uniqueness, if adults imply they should try to be better than someone else. The only competition that enhances development is when a child's progress is approvingly measured against that child's own earlier performance (Brophy 1981). Example: "You are really learning colors. Now you know all the color names on this new card, too."

The foregoing is a much abbreviated sketch of learning through modeling. The practice will be further examined in subsequent sections where the focus will be on teaching particular skills.

SUMMARY

Developmental concepts and behavioral principles have become blended into well-articulated early childhood teaching practices. The effectiveness of an early education program is demonstrated by changes in children's behavior. To have healthy development, ongoing changes in behavior must occur. The blend of developmental and behavioral principles and practices is good for all children and particularly important in inclusive programs where the range and skill levels among children is extensive. The blend of practices demonstrates that all children are teachable; if a child is not learning, the blame is on the program, not the child.

In the behavior perspective, systematic reinforcement procedures, if imposed on a developmentally appropriate structure, account for children's learning (or failure to learn). The principles can be put into an ABC format: A stands for what happens first (that which precedes the child's behavior); B stands for the child's behavior; C stands for consequences, or reinforcement (that which follows the behavior). Reinforcements (consequences) are negative, neutral, and positive.

Positive reinforcement is the teacher's best tool. It is readily available through teachers' assistance, genuine interest, and positive reactions to each child and each child's activities. Positive reinforcement also resides in the interesting and appropriate materials and activities provided by teachers.

In some instances, reinforcers must be withheld or withdrawn so a child does not get attention for behaviors that are detrimental to his or her development. When teachers must withhold reinforcement for an inappropriate behavior, it is important they double their efforts to give the child positive attention for useful behaviors incompatible with the inappropriate behavior. By so doing, inappropriate behaviors are likely to be *crowded out* by more appropriate ones. Withdrawing attention may mean, in some extreme cases, withdrawing the child. This is referred to as time-out with a milder version being labeled sit-and-watch. Time-out is used in those infrequent situations where systematic positive practices have failed to produce necessary behavior changes. Periods of withdrawing the child from play must be brief, not more than a minute or two. A child does not learn appropriate skills when isolated.

Punishment is the least desirable and least effective of all forms of child management. Though the punished behavior may stop for the moment, it usually returns again and again. Frequent punishment has many undesirable effects, including heightened aggressiveness and diminishing self-esteem

Other educational practices related to reinforcement procedures include task analysis and learning through observation (modeling). Task analysis is the process of breaking a learning task into small sequential steps for those children who need special help in the form of reduced frustration and more frequent successes. Step-by-step learning is further facilitated with prompting and cueing that is reduced gradually as the child learns the task. Children also learn by watching others, by modeling their behavior on that of a more skilled child. In every kind of learning situation, teachers provide encouragement and descriptive praise to the degree that is appropriate for individual children. Never, however, do teachers promote competition; competitiveness among children has no place in early childhood education.

STUDENT ACTIVITIES

1. Observe for one hour in an early childhood classroom. Write down every example of adult social reinforcement that you see and hear.
2. Imagine a child engrossed in painting at the easel or at a table. List ten positive statements you might make that recognizes the child's worth and efforts.
3. Discuss with several of your classmates how they felt as little children when they were punished and what they feel might be the long term effects, if any.
4. For several days, watch an older child brush his or her teeth. Do a task analysis of the activity starting with the child's approach to the basin.
5. Talk with the parents of a preschool child. Ask what behaviors, both positive and negative, they feel their child may have learned through imitation or modeling from family, television, or at school. (If you have a preschool child of your own, examine your own reactions.)

REVIEW QUESTIONS

A. *Lists.*
   1. List four early education practices common to both developmental and behavioral theory.
   2. List three possible sources of intrinsic reinforcement.
   3. List five types of teacher behaviors that are likely to be positively reinforcing for most young children.
   4. List five pairs of behaviors that are incompatible with each other.
   5. List three possible negative effects of frequent punishment on young children.

B. *True or False. Choose the best answer.*
   T F   1. Healthy development cannot occur without ongoing behavior change.
   T F   2. Punishment is the least effective way of helping children learn appropriate behavior.
   T F   3. According to behaviorists, children learn the behaviors that result in positive consequences.

   T F   4. According to learning theory, when learning is not taking place, it is the program and not the child that is at fault.
   T F   5. Negative reinforcement and punishment mean the same thing in behavioral terms.
   T F   6. Candy, chewing gum, and ice cream are positive reinforcers for all children.
   T F   7. To decrease an overly active child's *flightiness*, teachers redirect the child the moment he or she leaves an activity.
   T F   8. Children do not learn what *to do* in time-out, only what not to do.
   T F   9. Adults who yell at children to stop yelling may be teaching children to yell when displeased or upset.
   T F   10. Teachers can do an effective task analysis by watching an accomplished child perform the task.

REFERENCES

Allen, K.E. (1974). Behavior modification principles. In J.C. Cull and R.E. Hardy. (Eds.) *Behavior Modification in Rehabilitation Settings.* Springfield IL: Thomas.

Allen, K.E., and Goetz, E.M. (1982). *Early childhood education: Special problems, special solutions.* Rockville, MD: Aspens Systems.

Allen, K.E., and Hart, B. (1984). *The early years: Arrangements for learning.* Englewood Cliffs, NJ: Prentice-Hall.

Bandura, A. (1973). *Aggression: A social learning analysis.* Englewood Cliffs, NJ: Prentice-Hall.

Bandura, A. (1977). *Social learning theory.* Englewood Cliffs, NJ: Prentice-Hall.

Beckman, P.J., Robinson, C.C., Jackson, B., and Rosenberg, S.A. (1986). Translating developmental findings into teaching strategies for young handicapped children. *Journal of the Division for Early Childhood,* 10:1, 45–52.

Bee, H. (1992). *The Developing Child.* New York: Harper and Row.

Bijou, S.W. (1959). Learning in children. *Monographs of the Society for Research in Child Development,* 24.

Bijou, S.W., and Cole, B.W. (1975). *The feasibility of providing effective educational programs for the severely and profoundly retarded. Educating the 24-hour retarded child.* Paper presented at National Association for Retarded Citizens. New Orleans.

Bricker, D., and Cripe, J.J.W. (1992). *An activity-based approach to early intervention.* Baltimore: Brookes.

Brophy, J.E. (1981). Teacher praise: A functional analysis. *Review of Educational Research,* 51(1), 5–32.

Dewey, J. (1950). *Experience and Education.* New York: Macmillan.

Erikson, E.H. (1950). *Childhood and Society,* New York: Norton.

Froebel, F.W. (1911). *The Education of Man.* W.N. Hailmann (Trans.). New York: Appleton.

Gesell, A., Halverson, H.M., Thompson, H., Ilg, F.L., Castner, B.M., Ames, L.B., and Amatruda, C.S. (1940). *The first five years of life: A guide to the study of the preschool child.* New York: Harper and Row.

Harris, F.R., Wolf, M.M., and Baer, D.M. (1964). Effects of adult social reinforcement on child behavior. *Young Children,* 1, 8–17.

Hitz, R., and Driscoll, A. (1989). Praise or encouragement? New insights into praise: Implications for early childhood teachers. *Young Children,* 43, 6–13.

Hunt, J. McV. (1961). *Intelligence and Experience.* New York: Ronald Press.

McEvoy, M.A., Odom, S.L., and McConnell, S.R. Peer social competence interventions for young children with disabilities. In S. Odom, S. McConnell, and M. McEvoy (Eds.), *Social competence of young children with disabilities: Issues and strategies for intervention.* Baltimore: Brookes.

Patterson, G.R. (1975). *Families. Applications of social learning to family life.* Champaign, IL: Research Press.

Peck, C.A., Appolloni, T., Cooke, T.P., and Raver, S. (1978). Teaching retarded preschool children to imitate non-handicapped children, training and generalized effects. *Journal of Special Education,* 12, 195–207.

Piaget, J. (1952). *The origins of intelligence in children.* New York: International Universities Press.

Montessori, M. (1912). *The Montessori method: Scientific pedagogy as applied to child education in "Children's Houses."* A.E. George (Trans.). New York: Frederick A. Stokes.

Schickedanz, J.A., Schickedanz, D.I., and Forsyth, P.D. (1982). *Toward Understanding Children.* Boston: Little, Brown.

Wolery, M. (1994). Designing inclusive environments for children with special needs. In M. Wolery and J. Wilburs (Eds.), *Including children with special needs in early childhood programs.* Washington, D.C.: NAEYC.

Arranging the Learning Environment

OBJECTIVES

After studying this unit the student will be able to

- explain how classroom and play yard arrangements and the daily schedule influence children's learning.
- define preventive discipline, explain the procedure and its special merits in working with children with developmental problems.
- list seven or more ways that teachers can increase the safety of indoor and outdoor learning areas for children with disabilities.
- discuss the major issues in planning a program schedule for children in an inclusive setting.
- describe smooth transitions and the learnings available to children during transitions.

The learning environments provided by early childhood programs will influence, even determine, the development of countless numbers of children. Those environments also will determine how effectively teachers will teach and the kinds of messages children will get about themselves and others. According to Harms (1989):

The environment that adults create for children is a powerful tool for teaching. Through the way we structure children's surroundings, we communicate our values, provide guidance about how children are to behave in the environment, and influence the quality of their learning. Teachers of young children need to become aware of the constant influence the environment has on the children in their care (p. 232).

THE INCLUSIVE ENVIRONMENT

In an inclusive classroom, environmental arrangements assume special importance because of the range of abilities among children.

Teachers who arrange play spaces and activities, both indoors and out of doors, so that children with special needs can be included easily and naturally, convey a powerful message about human values: *all types of children can play together and have fun.* Having fun together is likely to be the best avenue to genuine integration. Wolfensberger, best known for his concept of *normalization* (1972), recommends bringing as few pieces of special equipment as possible into the classroom because they brand children as too different. True, many children with developmental disabilities cannot function without certain types of special equipment. Wolfensberger argues these should be only what is essential to enabling the child to enter into classroom activities.

Therapeutic equipment is available, however, that is fun for all children: huge medicine balls, tumble tubs, balance beams, portable stair climbing apparatus, trampolines, and the like. (Specialized equipment and specific environmental adaptations have been discussed in Section II under the various disability headings.)

Teachers must always keep in mind that children are first and foremost children. Their basic needs are essentially no different from those of all children, just more pronounced. For example:

Loud and distracting noises are difficult for most children; for hearing impaired children such noise may be intolerable.

Moving about safely, in an environment free of clutter, slippery floors, or rumpled rugs, contributes to the safety and security of every child; for children with

Teachers arrange play space and activities so that children with disabilities can be included easily and naturally.

limited vision or physical problems, an environment free of obstacles protects against serious injury.

Minimizing clutter and confusion enhances the ability of all young children to concentrate on the tasks at hand; for children with attention or learning disorders, reducing distractions may be the best way to promote learning.

Regardless of special problems, a well planned learning environment is necessary to meeting developmental needs. It is unacceptable to provide one kind of environment for normally developing children and a different kind for children with special needs. As Olds (1979) points out:

> Wheelchairs, braces, crutches, and caregivers can support a body as it grows, but they cannot provide sustenance for eyes, ear, hands, brains and muscles that become limp, useless, and restless with passivity and disuse. [Those who] prevent the special needs child from experiencing the activity and risk-taking essential for normal development, simply retard and prejudice a disabled child's chances for a positive developmental outcome (p. 94).

Teachers also need to use guidance procedures (discipline) that will reduce prejudice and promote positive outcomes in children with developmental problems. Helping these children learn to behave appropriately reduces the behavioral differences that often set them apart. The most efficient way to accomplish this is by arranging the learning environment in ways that prompt acceptable behavior in all children. Such arrangements are one aspect of preventive discipline, discussed next.

PREVENTIVE DISCIPLINE

What do environmental arrangements have to do with discipline? Everything! Well-arranged classrooms and play yards are a major factor in the discipline of all children. Discipline is most effective when it is based on anticipation. Through their observations of children and their knowledge of child development, teachers can anticipate potential trouble spots and deal with them *before* they occur. In other words, adults prevent mishap, hence the term *preventive discipline* (Harris and Allen 1966).

An environment free of clutter is essential for all children's safety, and especially so for children with developmental problems.

Preventive discipline depends on what teachers do and say to forestall trouble. In a way, this entire unit on arranging the learning environment is about discipline. By placing the drying rack next to the easel, for example, teachers help children avoid the many problems (and tension-provoking reminders) associated with carrying a dripping painting across an area. By providing a parking place for wheel toys (instead of letting children abandon them mid-road) teachers help children avoid injuring others or getting into angry exchanges as to which child really *owns* a piece of equipment. The point to be underscored is this: *environmental arrangements are a major determinant of children's behavior and of children's learning.* Preventive discipline accomplishes the following:

1. It communicates to children how to behave and then facilitates children's efforts.
2. It makes it easy for children to learn the vast number of behaviors and skills necessary to growing up confident and competent in a world that expects so much of young children and the adults who care for them.
3. It helps children avoid unnecessary and ego-deflating errors that squander children's time and self-esteem.

4. It assures a positive environment in which teachers enjoy teaching and children of different developmental levels enjoy learning together.

ARRANGEMENTS FOR LEARNING

Early learning environments are as varied as the programs they represent and the buildings that house them. Facilities range from multimillion dollar child care centers (all too few), to storefronts, church or home basements, public school classrooms, or semi-renovated warehouses. The setting, even the newest or most lavish, does not guarantee quality learning experiences however. The physical plant may contribute to quality, but it does not ensure it. As Gordon and Browne (1996) point out, the *environment* is more than a plant; it is the physical and human qualities that combine to create a space in which children and adults work and play together.

Setting up and maintaining an effective early learning environment puts teachers' knowledge of child development to the test. Classroom and play yard arrangements must be sensitive to developmental sequences and individual differences. Teachers must know what to do when one child is experiencing learning difficulties, another is not making developmental progress, a third is hampered by behavior problems. Teachers must recognize that the first move is to step back and take a look, observe the child in the context of the daily program. Necessary changes in the environment then can be made. Almost always, *it is the environment that needs fixing, not the child.*

Types of Learning. The first step in planning an inclusive early learning environment is specifying the kinds of learning that will be offered. Most programs plan three broad types of experiences: learning through self-help routines, through teacher-structured activities, and through discovery learning periods. Each of these will be discussed in terms of physical arrangements.

Self-help or independence. These are skills related to socially prescribed routines such as toileting, dressing, eating, cleaning up, doing one's share. Learning to perform these tasks is tied closely to the child's emerging sense of independence and competence. During toddlerhood and the early preschool years, teachers systematically guide children through each step of each routine until the various skills become *automatic.* Children with developmental problems often need additional help from teachers in learning basic self-help skills. Much of the help can be provided indirectly: by arranging the environment so that all types of children can work and play together throughout the program day. This social blend assures a variety of good models, children who already have mastered many developmental tasks Unit 7).

Other environmental arrangements that promote independence among children with special needs are appropriately sized furnishings and accessories. Hooks, wash basing, toilets, and drinking facilities that can be reached and child-operated allow children to help themselves. Children with impairments can learn to take care of their own special needs through various environmental arrangements. Examples:

The child who is in a later stage of toilet training can be given a pre-set timer that will go off as a reminder to get to the bathroom.

The learning environment can be arranged so that children of every skill level can work and play together.

Everything in the classroom should be in good working order.

A prearranged comfortable and secure place to go to remove leg braces as needed frees a child of having to wait for an available adult.

Teaching a child how to adjust the volume on his or her hearing aid reduces the amount of time the child is uncomfortable or not "tuned-in."

Having everything in the classroom and play yard in good working order reduces frustration and increases children's initiative and independence.

The latter point is especially important. Few situations make a special child (or anyone else, for that matter) feel more incompetent than a doorknob that spins aimlessly, a faucet that will not turn off, a drawer that will not open. The experiences are especially devastating for children with developmental disabilities—they have to do more than their share of coping as it is. When something cannot be made to work, children often do not realize it is the equipment and not themselves that is at fault. To the special child it may seem yet one more unsuccessful attempt to accomplish an everyday task. *Induced incompetence* is a term used to describe the effects of poorly functioning equipment on children with developmental disabilities.

Toilet Facilities.   Learning to toilet themselves is a developmental goal for most children during the early years. A first consideration is that toilets are of appropriate size and height. Another consideration is adequate space for maneuvering crutches, a walker, or pulling a wheelchair parallel with the toilet. A handrail is needed so the child may steady him- or herself. A hollow block or small footstool may be provided for a child's feet to rest on, thereby reducing insecurity and fear of falling off the toilet. (Special adaptations for teaching toileting to children with developmental disabilities will be discussed in Unit 18.)

In programs for toddlers, or any program where some children are still needing help with toilet training, teachers need to be immediately available to the children's bathroom. For preschoolers who have become fairly trustworthy in handling their toileting needs, it is well if the bathroom is accessible to all activity areas. Accessibility from the outdoor play area is especially important so that children can get to the bathroom in a hurry as they often need to do. School-age children can be expected to use a bathroom out of sight of teachers, even down the hall. A teacher, nevertheless, needs to be available near the door where children leave and return.

Locker Areas.   The locker area, or cubbies, in nursery school language, should be as near as possible to the outdoor exit and the bathroom. This location helps children learn to keep track of coats and mittens as

Each child needs his or her own cubby.

they come in to use the toilet facility. If there are no distractors en route, many children can be responsible for toileting themselves during outside play. This arrangement may put the lockers at some distance from the door through which children arrive and depart for home. However, it need not be a problem if the traffic lane from entry door to lockers is free of obstacles and clutter.

Sleeping Area.   The sleeping area in all-day programs must be carefully planned and free of distractors. If a separate nap room is not available, a nap area can be partitioned off with low barriers. A rug, or some other kind of clearly indicated space, should be near the entrance to the nap area. This space should be out of visual range of the lunch area where other children and teachers are likely to be finishing up and clearing away. It is in this particular spot that children remove their shoes and relax before entering the nap area. Another consideration is location of storage for cots and bedding. Teachers' time and energy is too valuable to be spent fetching and carrying; it should be reserved for helping children learn the routines related to moving into a relaxing rest time.

Teacher-structured activities.   Teacher-structured activities (also referred to as large and small group activities and one-on-one tutorials or instruction periods) are interspersed throughout the program day. The teacher's intent is to impart knowledge and skills that children need but cannot learn solely from a self-guided exploration of the environment. Stories, songs, fingerplays, care of materials, control of paint drips (if the child so indicates), gentleness with animals, names of objects, and concept information are but a few of the content areas that might comprise a teacher-structured activity. These activities may be formally planned learning experiences or they may arise spontaneously out of a child's immediate interest or need. (See incidental teaching in Unit 12).

Children with developmental problems sometimes need more (but perhaps shorter) teacher-structured activities. They also may need teacher-structured activities related to skills that other children seem to acquire spontaneously. Pointing at objects might be an example: Most children need no help in learning

Teacher-structured activities are interspersed throughout the program day.

to point; usually they have to be taught *not to point*. Children with perceptual–motor problems or cognitive limitations often need direct instruction in learning to point.

In arranging the location for formal, teacher-structured activities such as preacademic tasks, stories, music and rhythms, a first consideration is ease of transitions to and from other activities. Children change activities more readily if teacher-structured activities can be approached from all other areas. Furthermore, seeing that an attractive activity is starting up often serves as a cue. Children still in the process of restoring a play area may be prompted to finish up quickly and get to an activity such as stories. Placing large group activities in easy access of all other activity areas is of help to teachers, too. The teacher conducting the group activity can be subtle when sending a child with shorter attention span to a teacher in another activity area. Disruption of the group experience is avoided for the children still involved.

Discovery learning.   Freeplay, child-initiated activities, and free choice periods are other names for discovery learning. These are uninterrupted blocks of time, in a

well-planned play environment, both indoors and outdoors, that are fundamental to early learning. It is through play that children discover their world and themselves. Play allows children to apply their own ideas as well as the learning they have acquired in teacher-structured activities. At every developmental stage, children need opportunities to play and to have access to play materials. Some children, especially those with particular types of developmental problems, do not play of their own accord, or even know how to play; they must be helped to learn play skills, (Teaching children to play will be discussed in Unit 15).

Very young children and some children with developmental problems do not always benefit from *large* blocks of unstructured time. They may spend too much of their developmentally valuable time unengaged or inappropriately engaged, because of their limited skills or short span of attention. For these children, brief teacher-structured activities are easily interspersed during discovery learning periods. Learning to point, mentioned earlier, will be used as an example:

> Baillie needed to learn to point. During a free play period, the teacher in the immediate area noticed Baillie standing about, seeming not to know what to do with herself. The teacher took her companionably by the hand, and said, "Let's go pointing" (an improvised game Baillie enjoyed). While keeping her eye on the other children, the teacher walked around the area with Baillie for a minute or so, having her point to well known objects. The teacher then helped Baillie point to what she would like to do next and followed up by having the teacher in that area help her settle in.

Discovery learning areas work well when they radiate around the location of teacher-structured activities. Where these activity centers are placed is determined by furniture, storage, and the clean-up requirements of each area. Tables that are used for lunch and for preacademics are likely to determine where puzzles and other fine motor materials are to be used during alternate periods. A large rug in the manipulative area often is suitable for group activities such as music and rhythms. Transitions from small-group to large-group activities can be eased by placing individual carpet squares on the rug in a circle or semicircle (as place markers for individual children) at the start of the transition.

Each material has its own distinct space.

The block area needs to be clearly separate from the rug and manipulative areas. Ideally, it is a large open space, free of furniture or equipment except for shelves with materials related to block play. The shelves and a floor marker such as tape, a painted line, or a piece of very low-pile tightly stretched carpeting (glued or tacked down) marks off the block play area. If a housekeeping center is offered it usually is set into a corner with another set of low shelves serving as third side dividers. Partially enclosed in this way, the housekeeping area is distinct from other areas. In some classrooms, two sets of low, open shelves can be placed back to back. One set faces the manipulative area, the other opens onto housekeeping play, thereby conserving space while clearly marking two distinct areas.

A sink in the classroom usually determines where children will use paints, clay, and other wet materials. If there is no classroom sink, the creative area should be placed as near the bathroom as possible. It is well to have a tub of water and paper towels always available in the creative area. Children then can remove the excess of fingerpaint or clay before moving into the bathroom. Even more important is placement of the creative area well away from traffic lanes between activity areas. This forestalls dripping materials and children's dripping products being carried into other areas. NOTE: This is a prime example of preventive discipline through environmental arrangements.

Teachers' selection and grouping of materials indicates clearly how each area is to be used. Children, and especially very young children and children with developmental delays, should not be given mixed signals. For example, children are likely to think it must be all right to color in the library books if crayons are left on the book shelves. In contrast, the examples that follow offer environmental signals dictating appropriate behaviors.

The block area contains only those items related to block play. Accessory items to be incorporated into block play (cars, trucks, doll house furniture, zoo animals) are grouped, rotated regularly, and displayed in the same area, on shelves separate from but adjacent to the block storage shelves.

Manipulative materials are displayed only in the manipulative area. Each material is given a distinct place with related parts grouped together (hammer, individual tins of nails, and hammering board; pegs and peg boards; large, *unstrung* wooden beads and rigid tipped string). The display tells the child what to expect of the material and how to use it. Never is a broken or incomplete set of play materials put out for children. (It is better to have no puzzles than those with even one missing piece.)

In the creative area the availability of easel painting is made visually distinct by the large easel paper, paint containers and brushes, aprons, and drying rack, all grouped together. These are separate from groupings of crayons and paper, scissors, and collage materials that also are displayed, distinct each from the other, on the shelves, with their several parts grouped.

PLANNING EARLY LEARNING ENVIRONMENTS

Cutting across all aspects of environmental planning are certain basic principles. These include safety, visibility, ease of movement, versatility of equipment, activity concentration, teachers' availability, and structured flexibility.

Safety. Safety in all types of preschool classrooms and play yards is a major consideration for two reason:

preventing accidents and injuries and fostering independence. Independence comes about only in a safe and secure environment where children know that adults can be depended on to protect them from harm and from harming themselves. Teachers make sure that area rugs have nonskid backing or are glued or tacked down. A skidding rug is a hazard for all children and teachers, and is especially hazardous for children who are blind or physically impaired. Teachers also make sure that material and equipment is nontoxic, free of cracks and splinters, and in good working order. It is frustrating for any child to try to steer a wheel toy that has a bent axle; for a child with limited motor skills it may lead to a serious accident. This can frighten the child from further efforts to join in outdoor play. If the accident involved other children, avoidance of the child may follow. The children who were hurt (and their parents) usually do not understand it was the equipment, not the child with the disability that was at fault.

Order and organization.   Clutter and disorganization are incompatible with safety. Teachers must make sure that *everything has a place and*, when not in use, *everything is in its place.* A child with seriously limited vision needs to know that the dough, cookie cutters, and rolling pins (with no potentially hurtful objects mixed in) are always to be found, for example, in the lower left corner of the housekeeping cupboards. Logical arrangements contribute to the child's independence; they enable the child to put materials away when finished with them, a responsibility of every child. The ongoing restoration of play areas is especially important in inclusive classrooms. The child mentioned above needs to be confident that a rolling pin that rolled off the table earlier will not be left there for him or her to fall over later.

Teachers who routinely help children restore play areas after each use provide valuable lessons in common courtesy as well as regard for the physical safety of the children with impairments. By the same token, regard for others also must be the concern of the child who uses special equipment. A child needs to learn how to position his or her crutches when they are not in use so they do not fall about, endangering others. A child who uses a wheelchair only part of the time must learn to park it in an agreed upon place, not abandon it haphazardly.

Matching children and equipment.   A critical aspect of safety has to do with matching equipment and materials to the skill levels of the children in the group. Wheel toys, all oversized, for example, pose a safety hazard for younger, smaller children. They also are a hazard for children with special needs who may not be able to exercise good judgment in selecting suitable equipment. In many instances, the poor judgment is simply lack of experience. Children with developmental problems often have been overprotected by well meaning adults concerned that they not hurt themselves. All children if they are to develop independence must learn to take risks. Learning to take risks, however, can be accomplished only where children are protected from becoming frightened or seriously harmed.

Safe outdoor environments.   Outdoor play, in a safe and carefully arranged play yard, is an essential aspect of a quality program for young children. It is here that children practice physical skills such as running, jumping, ducking, pumping, climbing, and kicking. They learn to throw, catch, and bat and combine these skills into games. The out-of-doors also provides opportunities for children to learn voice and tone modulations; shouting, chanting, whistling, imitating a siren, all without causing discomfort to others.

Outdoor equipment needs to be simple yet versatile.

Outdoor equipment needs to be simple yet versatile. It should include ladders, planks, jumping boards, and simple climbing frames. There should be walking boards of various widths placed at different heights and combined with small portable climbing frames, ladders, and gangplanks with side rails. Equipment of this type can be arranged and rearranged to meet the needs of children with delayed motor skills as well as advanced children. The arrangement in the outdoor classroom can be elaborate and simple at the same time. Children just beginning to try out their gross motor coordination can be as well served as daring children in need of constant challenge. According to Frost (1986), "The best playgrounds are never finished."

Visibility. A major function of early childhood education is encouraging children to explore and experiment with materials and equipment. This means that children are going to be taking risks as they try out new skills; therefore, every child needs to be visible to teachers at all times. Some of children's experiments will work, others will not but all provide teachers with opportunities to teach. A 6-year-old who decides to try jumping off a swing-in-motion, for example, presents a teaching opportunity. A teacher may make suggestions concerning speed and a jumping-off point suitable for a first attempt. Also, the teacher is alerted, ready to catch the child who does not heed suggestions or whose timing goes awry.

Visibility is especially critical in working with children with developmental problems who cannot always gauge their own limitations. At the first indication that a child is about to attempt something dangerously beyond his or her capabilities the observant teacher can intervene immediately. The child's efforts can be redirected to provide encouragement for continued work on the skill, but in ways more suited to the child's skill level.

Ease of Movement. Children and teachers need to be able to move about freely. Movement is enhanced when traffic lanes are unobstructed and are adequate for maneuvering trucks and doll carriages or wheelchairs and crutches. Traffic lanes, free of obstructions and unpleasant *surprises* (unmopped puddles of water on the floor, an abandoned doll carriage, an upturned rug edge) are critical, especially for children with limited vision. Ease of movement within interest centers is important, too. Crowded activity areas, where children's movements are restricted, inevitably lead to conflict and aggression. Problems are prevented by providing several attractive interest centers. Small groups, of varying developmental levels, then have space to play together, or side-by-side.

Activity Concentration. Visual emphasis on the activity appropriate to each area is essential if children are to learn self-management skills. This principle was discussed in considerable detail in a preceding section on discovery learning. Here it will be touched on, but briefly, to underscore how central the practice is to the arrangement of early learning environments. Locker location again provides the example: Not only should lockers be immediately visible and close to children as they enter the room, they also should be the *only thing available* at that point. In other words, the locker area contains only lockers. To include toys would suggest to children that play with those toys in that area was appropriate. But, toy play would interfere with effective use of the locker area for teaching relevant social and self-help skills, The same holds true for all other activity areas. (Remember the earlier crayon/library book example?)

Teachers' Availability. Teachers who are readily available are the key to a safe and comfortable early learning environment. Young children are learning *something*, each of their waking moments. Teachers, therefore, must be where they are most needed throughout the program day to facilitate learning. When children can move independently between activities, undistracted by inappropriate or unsafe activities, teachers can teach rather than police. A teacher often can bridge two areas, being available to children both in the locker area and in an adjacent discovery learning area.

Structured Flexibility. To meet the range of developmental levels found within a group of young children, the learning environment must be well structured. At the same time it must be flexible and adaptable. A structured environment, where rules and expectations are consistent, provides a secure yet freeing framework: Children can explore and test limits and teachers can react spontaneously to the infinite variations in children's learning.

Systematic advance planning and logical revision of arrangements are essential to both program structure and program flexibility. Both are based on teachers' periodic assessments of their programs. A widely used assessment instrument is the Early Childhood Environment Rating Scale (ECERS) (Harms and Clifford 1983). It is designed to give an overall picture of space, materials, activities, daily schedule, and supervision. Another instrument, the Preschool Assessment of the Classroom Environment (PACE) (McWilliam and Dunst 1985) also is useful, having been tested in inclusive classrooms. (For additional environmental evaluation tools see Appendix A.)

Much more could be said about arranging appropriate learning environments for young children. Softness (Prescott, Jones and Kritchevsky 1972), aesthetics (beauty), privacy, lighting variations, built-in lofts, and display of children's work—these are some of the additional dimensions that teachers need to be aware of.

SCHEDULING

In the inclusive classroom, learning opportunities based on appropriate arrangements of space, material, and equipment are further enhanced by an organized schedule. Systematically structured transitions between program activities also are critical. Teachers need to know where each is to be, and what each is to be doing, at each point in the program. As with arrangements for the physical environment, scheduling decisions are based on type of program. The number of hours children spend in the setting, their age and ability range, and the ratio of adults to children are major considerations. Full-day programs have quite different constraints on both schedule and organization than do half-day programs.

In this unit, specific types of schedules will not be described. The focus, instead, will be on principles related to scheduling. However, to illustrate application of the principles, a sample schedule, based on a half-day program is included. This is followed by discussion of transitions.

Principles Related to Scheduling.   Specific principles must be addressed when planning daily, weekly, seasonal, and year-long activity schedules for both children and teachers. Foremost among scheduling factors are individual differences between children and their changing skill levels over time.

Accommodating individual differences.   To determine the sequence of activities, teachers must be sensitive to individual differences between children and their special needs and preferences. Teachers strive to maintain a global outlook of the day, or the room, and the opportunities for learning. This view varies throughout the year as teachers get to know children better and as children become more skilled. The length and type of classroom activities and amount of outdoor time often is different from fall to spring and spring to summer. In the fall, for example, children

Structure promotes freedom.

may need longer active play periods out of doors as they adapt to new children, new adults, and a group experience. In the spring, the time spent in small groups and independent activities may be much extended. By spring, many children will have a longer attention span and increased self-management skills. A summer schedule, in most climates, should provide more outdoor time. Easel painting and work with clay, for example, takes on entirely different dimensions out in the fresh air. Basic activities, moved out of the classroom and onto outdoor tables, give teachers and children a refreshing change of pace.

Varying activity levels. Periods of high physical activity should alternate with periods of quiet activities. Most children are subject to a kind of energy *spill-over* from active play periods. Therefore, learning experiences that require children's concentration should not be scheduled immediately following vigorous free play. A way around this is to insert a brief "cooling down" period. One way to do this is by spacing books at regular intervals on the circle area where a large group activity will be held. (Books should always be available to children, even during free play periods. If children are taught proper care of books from the start, their misuse during this transition activity is unlikely.) As children gather by ones and twos, they look at books until most of the children have assembled and the teacher-structured activity begins.

Ensuring orderly sequences. Activities need to follow an orderly and predictable sequence. Most young children have trouble accepting any departure from what they are used to. Change in routines may be even more difficult for very young children and children with developmental problems. Children with autistic-type behaviors or attention disorders frequently become overly attached to the daily schedule. Commonplace routines become rituals that must be held constant; the unexpected may drive the child into a frenzy. Even so, all children (and most adults) feel more secure, knowing what comes next. According to Read, Gardner and Mahler (1986):

> A fixed sequence to parts of the program gives a child confidence in himself because he knows what to expect. He can predict the order of the day. The order need not be rigid; it should be flexible. It should also be modified from time to time, for a trip or special event. Flexibility can be predictable, too (p. 87).

Giving advance notice. Children do not give up on activities easily; teachers, therefore, should give warning well in advance of an activity change. Several minutes before a transition, the teacher advises: "Soon it will be time to put away the blocks and get ready for snack." It comes as no shock, when the teacher announces a few minutes later, "Time to get the blocks on the shelf; I'll help you get started." Ample time must be allowed for children to finish each activity and accomplish each routine. All children need the satisfaction that comes with task completion. Very young children and those who move slowly or with difficult need additional time. Therefore, activities and transitions are scheduled so that all children can move at their own pace, whether fast or slow. It is demeaning a child's efforts, even insulting, to carry a child who could walk from snack to music, given enough time.

Application of Scheduling Principles. Schedules vary; they are based on type of program, number of teachers, and number and type of children. Never should one early childhood program be ruled by another program's schedule. Neither should it be ruled by the hands of the clock. It is *sequence of activities* and *allocations of ample time* for children's learning needs and interests that are the critical elements. Actual number of minutes spent in stories or transitions or snack is irrelevant. The schedule of activities outlined below, and the accompanying clock times, are suggestions only. (In full-day child care settings early morning, late afternoon, meal, and naptimes all require extra special planning.) In the following sample of a daily schedule, the comments in each time slot and program activity suggest the potential learnings and relationships inherent in each activity.

Sample Daily Schedule. *8:30 a.m. to 9:15 a.m. Arrival.* The ideal arrangement is one in which a teacher receives children over an extended period of time. This allows the teacher to provide a brief health check, give personal greetings, and engage in a short

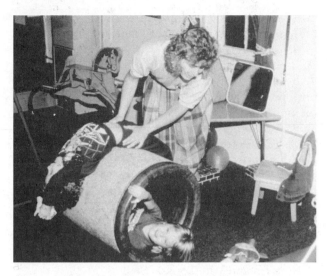

Give warning well in advance of an activity change.

conversation with each child and adult. As the parent leaves, the child can be given assistance in learning independence skills as needed—using nose tissues, storing belongings, turning coat sleeves right side out. Once the routine is accomplished, the receiving teacher can plan with the child which discovery area he or she will work in first.

Arrival time is also good for letting a child know that the teacher has perhaps planned something special with that child in mind. Or, it may be that the teacher has set a requested material aside for the child's use, or has remembered to look up the answer to a questions the child and teacher had pondered the preceding day. Daily exchanges such as those assure children they are coming into a stable and caring environment where teachers see them, hear them, and respond to their individual needs and preferences.

8:30 a.m. to 9:45 a.m. Discovery learning.   The amount to time each child spends in the first discovery learning period will vary, depending on time of arrival. Children who arrive early often are ready to be among the first to start the transition to the next activity. Many programs find that this first period works well as an outdoor period: Children and teachers are saved one transition requiring undressing and dress-

ing for outdoor play. Whether indoors or out, teachers have arranged, before children's arrival, a variety of play and work options. To promote large motor activities, for example, mazes and obstacle courses, simple or complex, are set up to accommodate children in a wheel chair, or on a "tummy board" (one child called it his *crawlagator!*). Such activities are fun for all, not just the child with motor problems.

9:45 a.m. to 10:00 a.m. Transition.   Restoring, or cleaning up activity areas, by children with teachers' help, is a major focus of transitions. Play materials are put back on shelves or in containers, wheel toys are parked, dress-up clothes are hung up or folded away. All children can help. A child with cerebral palsy can hold a container for other children to put Legos into. This is important: shared cleanup activities promote a sense of *belonging*. Shared cleanup also provides a way for children to learn to respect materials and equipment. They also learn to take pleasure in leaving an attractive environment for other children to enjoy. As children finish their part of the clean up they move at their own pace into self-help routines such as removing outdoor clothes, toileting, hand washing, and nose care. A mid-program snack usually follows.

10:00 a.m. to 10:20 a.m. Snack and small group interaction.   Adults and children *eat together* in small groups. Small groupings, with participating adults, provide children needed assistance as they practice finger or spoon feeding, pouring, drinking, using utensils. Snack time is a good time for teachers to model everyday social skills. It also gives children unpressured opportunities to practice the courtesies that society requires of all: passing, sharing, polite requesting, and acknowledging.

Conversation, too, provides important opportunities for learning during snack time. All children can be helped to participate. Even children with minimal language skills can join in with gestures and vocalizations. Though conversational activities appear to be spontaneous, many teachers find they need to come prepared with conversation *starters* or with specific concepts that children can be helped to develop as they talk together. A teacher who starts a conversation with "Guess what I saw on my way to school this morn-

In self-care routines, children should be allowed to move at their own pace.

ing" is sure to elicit at least one response that other children can be helped to build on.

10:20 a.m. to 10:50 a.m. Preacademic activities. During this period, focus is on learning opportunities that enhance children's perceptual motor skills, their speech and language skills, and their basic cognitive and problem-solving skills. Many early childhood programs have responded to public pressure "by emphasizing academic skill development with paper-and-pencil activities that are developmentally inappropriate with young children" (Bredekamp 1987, p. 1). More appropriate are classifying and categorizing activities and language and concept-building games and experiences.

Major goals of the preacademic period (Unit 17) are that children begin to develop task-orientation skills (focusing on the job at hand) and a lengthening span of attention. These two skills, basic to all learning, can be acquired only if the preacademic activities are interesting and matched to each child's current skill levels. Children with behavior and attention disorders or cognitive delays are in special need of activities related to task orientation and attention span. Like all other children, they, too, can develop these skills when provided with enjoyable tasks.

10:50 a.m. to 11:00 a.m. Transition. Children and teachers restore the preacademic work areas. Children needing help are toileted; others use the toilet as needed.

11:00 a.m. to 11:35 a.m. Discovery learning. In this second discovery learning period the emphasis often is on individual or child-selected small group art experiences, computer activities, simple crafts, and exploration of various interest centers. Over the course of the week, teachers try to involve all children in work with one or more of the creative materials that are set out each day. The following are examples of materials that might be offered, two or three per session:

Easel or finger painting, mural painting, and occasional specialty painting activities (see Mayesky, Neuman and Wlodkowski 1989).
Crayons, chalk, "magic markers"
Potters' clay
Paste, paper, collage materials
Wood glueing, stitchery, **mobiles** and **stabiles**

All children, even those with severe disabilities, can learn to use these materials; some will need more prompting from the teacher, especially in the beginning. "Multiply handicapped children *can* learn to work with purpose, with an end product in view. They discover that hands are tools for making objects. The sense of achievement is a giant step toward a form of independence" (Schattner 1971).

11:35 to 12 noon. Music, rhythms, stories, departure. As children finish their discovery learning activities they gradually move into a large group activity. The first part of this period can be a time for finger plays, songs, chants, and rhythmic activities such as jumping, rolling, and tiptoeing to music. Children with the shortest span of attention for large group activities are drawn off first to a small group story. This process continues until two or three story groups are in progress and all children are engaged in a teacher-conducted story activity. As stories end, children and teachers talk about what went on at school that day and what to look forward to on the next day of school, or over the weekend. In many settings, music, stories, and departure time can be conducted outdoors when the weather is fair.

11:50 a.m. to 12 noon. Departure. Children leave the story groups, a few at a time, to go to their lockers. Children with developmental disabilities may need extra time or assistance. These children are intermixed in this staggered process so that the teacher's assistance can be divided effectively. As children put their wraps on, they greet the person who picks them up and say goodbye to the teacher who is supervising departures. The remaining two or three children return to a story location or use crayons at a nearby table for the few minutes before they are picked up.

Scheduled time for teachers. Teachers need scheduled times to carry out their own responsibilities and to have planned breaks during each session. Such time is not a luxury; it is essential. When children are present, teacher's focus must be on teaching, *not* on preparing materials, *not* on cleaning up, *not* on discussing children's learning needs. A block of paid preparation time is scheduled before children arrive. Paints are mixed, teacher-structured activities are set up and positioned for use, the play yard is arranged. At the end of the session, teachers again need time for a final cleanup of each play area.

Scheduled time for frequent even though brief, staff meetings is also important. This can be most difficult to arrange in full-day programs, but it can be done. Here teachers discuss the events of immediate concern and the needs of individual children. Even the best of teachers are significantly less effective if they do not have scheduled, uninterrupted times to talk together about children's needs, staff–child relationships, and alterations in the physical setting or daily schedule. Failure to recognize the need for paid staff time for planning and preparation may well be one aspect of the current child care staffing crisis described by Daniel (1990).

TRANSITIONS

Transitions in which children and teachers are busy but interacting comfortably, are the hallmark of a quality program. A smooth transition appears effortless. The effortlessness is deceptive, however. It is the result of considerable planning, knowledge about each child, and attention to a multitude of details. Transitions should be used for teaching and for help-

ing children learn about their own capabilities (Sainato and Carta 1992). At no time should children be waiting about idly or in enforced silence.

The underlying principle of smooth transitions is that each child moves individually, at his or her own pace, from one activity to the next. The individual differences among children provides the gradual movement between activities for the group as a whole. Different children, because they use materials with different levels of involvement, will finish cleanup at different times. The different learning needs of children in different preacademic activities prompt teachers to hold children for different lengths of time. Arrangements such as these are ideal for all children—for very young children, for children with developmental disabilities, and for typically developing and gifted children.

Effective transitions require planning for children and adults. Teachers must know who is supervising what areas and activities. Effective transitions, like all quality programming, require an adequate ratio of teachers to children. This is especially true in inclusive programs where the ratio of teacher to children must be increased as the number of children with developmental disabilities increases. NAEYC supports this position in the following statements:

Children's time should never be wasted in idle waiting or standing about.

Implementation of developmentally appropriate early childhood programs requires limiting the size of the group and providing sufficient numbers of adults to provide individualized and age-appropriate care and education (1985).

Even the most well-qualified teacher cannot individualize instruction and adequately supervise too large a group of young children. . . . Younger children require much smaller groups. Group size, and thus ratio of children to adults, should increase gradually through the primary grades (Bredekamp 1987).

SUMMARY

The arrangement of early childhood environments determine how well children learn and how well teachers teach. For children with developmental disabilities, an inclusive learning environment is the most suitable, with adaptations made for special needs. A well arranged learning environment communicates to children what it is that they can do in any given area. Children are less likely to transgress or behave inappropriately in a planned and well-structured environment; hence the term *preventive discipline* for this kind of indirect guidance.

The environment is planned in terms of types of learning that goes on throughout the program day: self-care skills, teacher-structured activities, and discovery learning. Teachers arrange the activity areas that support the various kinds of learning in terms of six basic principles: safety, visibility, ease of movement, activity concentration, teachers' availability, and structured flexibility. Periodic assessment of all aspects of the environment is critical to advancing each child's development.

A daily schedule based on children's individual needs and differences furthers the benefits of the well arranged classroom and play yard. Each segment of the daily schedule (in planned and predictable sequence) provides valuable opportunities for teaching and learning throughout the program day. Children are given advance notice when activity changes are scheduled; children with various learning impairments often need extra advance warning and special help in dealing with departures from established routines. Regularly scheduled staff meetings, brief though they may be, allow teachers to teach more effectively.

Transitions are designed to enable children, from the most delayed to the most advanced, to move at their own pace between program activities. Transitions characterized by idle waiting about or enforced quiet are developmentally inappropriate and detrimental to children's learning and self-esteem.

STUDENT ACTIVITIES

1. Observe a discovery learning period (indoors or out of doors). Was there evidence of preventive discipline in terms of environmental arrangements? Describe. Were there other ways the environment might have been altered to provide more effective discipline? Describe.
2. Observe a preschool classroom and draw a rough sketch of the floor plan; indicate location of furnishings, activity areas, doors and windows. Which areas will accommodate a child in a wheelchair or walker? Which will not? Resketch the floor plan showing possible modifications that might better accommodate these children.
3. Select any five activity areas in an early childhood program for 3- and 4-year-olds (music, easel painting, water play to suggest a few). With three or four other students working with you as a teaching team, draw a basic plan for presenting these activities. Now decide, among you, what changes might be introduced into each structure to better serve both gifted children and children with special needs.
4. Observe three different self-help routines in a child care center. Describe the strengths and weaknesses of each for working with children with developmental problems according to the guidelines discussed in this unit.
5. Draw up a daily schedule for a group of twenty 4- and 5-year-olds who are in all-day child care. Assuming three or four of these children have impaired motor skills and somewhat limited cognitive skills indicate special schedule adaptations that might be needed.

REVIEW QUESTIONS

A. Briefly define and give examples of each of the following concepts as they relate specifically to environmental arrangements and scheduling of activities in early childhood inclusive programs.
   1. Safety
   2. Orderliness
   3. Visibility
   4. Ease of movement
   5. Activity concentration
   6. Area restoration
   7. Structured flexibility
   8. Varied activity levels
   9. Activity sequences
   10. Advance notice

B. True or false. Choose the best answer.
   T F   1. When a child is not progressing it may be the environment rather than the child that needs fixing.
   T F   2. Teachers should not allow any child with a hearing impairment to try to reset his or her hearing aid.
   T F   3. Every young child benefits from long, uninterrupted periods of free play.
   T F   4. Selection and grouping of materials communicates to children how they are to be used.
   T F   5. Discovery learning areas are rich in materials that promote exploration.
   T F   6. The bathroom contains materials relevant only to toileting routines.
   T F   7. A child using crutches should not have to be concerned about the crutches being a potential safety hazard for others.
   T F   8. The length and type of classroom activities may vary, depending on time of year and children's progress.
   T F   9. Classroom activities should *always* start on time or within a minute or two of the time posted on the daily schedule.
   T F   10. Young children should line up and wait without talking for the teacher's signal to move to the next activity.

C. Select the *least suitable* answer in each of the following groups of statements.
   1. The early childhood environment exerts a powerful influence on children's
      a. behavior
      b. genetic background
      c. value system
      d. cognitive development
      e. willingness to explore

2. Children with developmental problems
   a. should not participate in active group games because of the safety factor.
   b. need as normalized an environment as possible.
   c. may use special equipment that is fun for others.
   d. may find clutter and disorganization especially difficult to deal with.
   e. need environmental arrangements similar to those of other children.

3. Preventive discipline
   a. depends on what teachers do and say before trouble starts.
   b. reduces inappropriate use of learning materials.
   c. reduces the need for overly frequent directions and redirections from teachers.
   d. does not work with children with developmental problems.
   e. creates a more positive learning environment for children and teachers.

4. Teacher-structured activities
   a. are designed to foster learnings that children may not get through free play.
   b. can be formal or spontaneous.
   c. may focus on certain social skills.
   d. should consist of work book ditto sheets that children can take home.
   e. may need to be shorter for children with attention and learning deficits.

5. A safe early childhood environment
   a. is well organized and free of clutter.
   b. provides materials and equipment in good repair and in good working order.
   c. promotes greater independence in children of every developmental level.
   d. matches materials and equipment to children's ability levels.
   e. depends on keeping children with disabilities indoors to avoid injury from other children's use of swings or wheel toys.

6. The daily schedule should include
   a. balance between teacher-structured and child-initiated activities.
   b. balance of active and quiet activities.
   c. active play followed *immediately* by quiet, tightly structured activities.
   d. predictable sequences of activities.
   e. ample notice for children to finish up an activity and restore the area.

7. At arrival time the receiving teacher
   a. discusses children's wrongdoings of the preceding day with each parent.
   b. greets each child and each adult personally.
   c. helps the child plan what to do first.
   d. shares special information or material with a child.
   e. does a brief health check of each child.
8. During snack times, teachers
   a. promote conversation among children.
   b. take a much-needed break.
   c. teach self-help skills related to eating.
   d. model socially acceptable table manners.
   e. sit and eat with a small group of children.
9. Regularly scheduled staff meetings
   a. are a luxury; nice but not necessary.

    b. should occur, ideally, everyday at a time when children are not present.
    c. provide an opportunity to talk about children's needs and program adaptations.
    d. allow teachers to focus on teaching during the hours the children are in school.
    e. foster staff cooperation and relationships.
10. Smooth transitions between activities are
   a. effortless.
   b. the product of careful planning.
   c. characterized by children moving at their own pace.
   d. made easier for teachers and children when the teacher/child ratio is appropriate to the age level of the group.
   e. predictable and based on established routines.

REFERENCES

Bredekamp, S. (1987). *Developmentally appropriate practice in early childhood programs serving children birth through age 8.* Washington, D.C.: National Association for the Education of Young Children.

Daniel, J. (1990). Child care: An endangered industry. *Young Children.* Washington, 45:4, 23–26.

Davidson, J. (1980). Wasted time: The ignored dilemma. *Young Children,* 35, 13–21.

Frost, J.L. (1986). Planning and using children's playgrounds. In J.S. McKee, (Ed.). *Play: Working partner of growth.* Wheaton, MD: Association for Childhood Education International.

Gordon, A.M., and Browne, K.W. (1996). *Beginnings and beyond—Foundations in early childhood education* (4th ed.). Albany, NY: Delmar.

Harms, T. (1989). Creating environments for growing and learning. In Gordon, A.M., and Browne, K.W. *Beginnings and beyond. Foundations in early childhood education* (2nd ed.). Albany, NY: Delmar.

Harms, T., and Clifford, R.M. (1983). *Early childhood environment rating scale.* New York: Teachers College Press.

Harris, F.R., and Allen, K.E. (1966). Under six: Children in preschool. *KCTS Television Series and Viewers Guide.* Seattle: University of Washington.

Mayesky, M., Neuman, D., Wlodkowski, R.J. (1989). *Creative activities for young children.* Albany, NY: Delmar.

McWilliam, R.A., and Dunst, C.J. (1985). *Preschool assessment of the classroom environment.* Unpublished rating scale. Family, Infant, and Preschool Program. Morganton, NC: Western Carolina Center.

NAEYC (1985). *Guidelines for early education programs in associate degree granting institutions.* Washington, D.C.: National Association for the Education of Young Children.

Olds, A.R. (1979). In S.J. Meisels (Ed.). *Special education and development.* Baltimore: University Park Press.

Prescott, E., Jones E., and Kritchevsky, S. (1972). *Day care as a child rearing environment.* Washington, D.C.: National Association for the Education of Young Children.

Read, K.H., Gardner, P., and Mahler, B. (1986). *Early childhood programs: A laboratory for human relations.* New York: Holt, Rinehart, and Winston.

Sainato, D.M., and Carta, J.J. (1992). Classroom influences on the development of social competence in young children with disabilities. In S.L. Odom, S.R. McConnell, and M.A. McEvoy (Eds.). *Social competence of young children with disabilities: Issues and strategies for intervention.* Baltimore: Brookes.

Schattner, R. (1971). *An early childhood curriculum for multiply handicapped children.* New York: John Day.

Wolfensberger, W. (1972). *The principle of normalization in human services.* Toronto: National Institute on Mental Retardation.

Facilitating Social Development

OBJECTIVES

After studying this unit the student will be able to

- define this statement: *The degree to which parents and caregivers respond appropriately to an infant's cues may be a major factor in determining that child's social development.*
- define *social skills* and explain their importance in the overall development of young children, especially children with developmental problems.
- outline the steps or phases that infants and children go through in acquiring social skills; explain the importance of this knowledge to teachers in an inclusive setting.
- describe the possible impact of a serious hearing loss or vision problem on early social development.
- list at least ten ways a teacher can help children with special needs learn appropriate play and social skills.

Social development depends on each individual acquiring the many behaviors that help people live together in a family and in a society. These skills must be learned by all children; those with developmental differences, those who are developing normally, and those described as gifted. How well social skills are learned depends on the quality of the interpersonal relationships in the child's everyday life. Only through interacting with others, can infants and young children learn the social skills (as well as the accompanying language and intellectual skills) necessary for healthy development. Only through interacting with others can young children get the necessary feedback about their social competence.

Interpersonal relationships are reciprocal; that is, there is mutual responding or *turn-taking*. During the early months and years, social interactions depend on the child's ability to give and receive social messages. Children with developmental problems may fail to respond to social signals, or they may give too few appropriate signals. Either situation reduces feedback and may lead to negative responses; both situations will interfere with emerging social development. It is not unusual for the social delays in children with disabilities to become greater than the problems associated with their primary disability (Bailey and Wolery 1989).

No child, simply because he or she has a developmental disability, should be excused from learning acceptable social skills. Normally developing children seem to acquire social skills spontaneously, or with only brief episodes of informal coaching. Children with developmental problems often need systematic help; appropriate social behaviors may have to be taught directly, over a considerable period of time. How teachers help young, atypical children acquire such a **repertoire** is the focus of this unit. First, however, social skills will be examined from a developmental perspective.

SOCIAL SKILLS AND OVERALL DEVELOPMENT

Though discussed as an independent topic, social skills are never truly separate from other areas of development. Each influences all others. The following example, typical of social activities of normally developing 4-year-olds, illustrates the close interrelatedness of skills.

John ran to Aaron who was sitting on the edge of the sandbox filling cake tins with sand.

Social skills reflect children's skill levels in various areas of development.

John: "Let's decorate cakes. Here's some decorations," (pouring small plastic rings into Aaron's cupped hands).

Aaron: "Too many," (handing a few back) "That's plenty."

John smiled at Aaron and began alternating rings around the edge of his sand cake while singing "Now a blue one, now a yellow one."

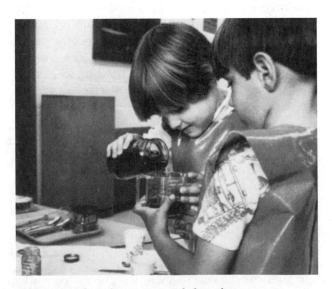

Taking turns is an important early learning.

Aaron stuck twigs in his sand cake and pulled a ring down over the top of each twig. Then he sang Happy Birthday several times, each time naming a different classmate.

A number of developmental skills can be identified in this play interaction. Both large and small motor skills are evident: running, pouring, catching, picking, and placing. Cognitive skills include math concepts of *some*, *too many*, and *plenty*, as well as color recognition, naming colors, and understanding such concepts as *decorate* and *alternate* (now a blue, now a yellow). Memory was obvious, too, with Aaron singing Happy Birthday and recalling several classmates' names. Both children demonstrated good communication skills in the form of verbal exchanges, listening to each other, and smiling.

These developmental skills were in addition to and blended with high level social skills such as:

Each child initiating his own ideas
Following suggestions from each other
Sharing materials
Role playing (cake decorators)

The above exchange shows the developmental complexities that work *for* some children but *against* others. In the John and Aaron episode, each child was helping the other to learn, each was spontaneously reinforcing the other for a variety of skills and responses. *Spontaneous* peer reinforcement may not always happen for children with developmental disabilities; instead, their poorly developed play skills often lead to rejection. A negative cycle is set in motion: a continuing lack of skills shuts out further opportunities to learn; lack of learning opportunities results in little positive feedback. The combination sometimes sets up emotional reactions which may cause as much developmental interference as the disability itself. It is important, therefore, that young children with (and without) developmental problems be helped to earn *appropriate* social skills.

APPROPRIATE SOCIAL SKILLS: WHAT ARE THEY?

One definition of appropriate social skills is that they are *prescribed* ways of behaving; they are *expectations* of particular groups as to how group members will conduct themselves in private and in public. Prescriptions for what is socially appropriate vary from community to community and society to society. Variations exist even within the tight circle of home, preschool, and neighborhood. But, confusing choices often result, especially for young children as in the following examples:

Five-year-old Doug had learned he could get almost anything he wanted from his parents and teenage brothers by trantrumming. The same behavior in the neighborhood and preschool did not pay off. Children taunted, "Crybaby, crybaby," and ran off, leaving him shrieking.

Rebecca painted with obvious enjoyment during the first week of school. One day she began to cry, pointing to a small paint smudge on her sleeve. The teacher assured her it would wash out and that the apron protected most of her dress. Rebecca would not return to the easel, even on subsequent days. What emerged were confusing social expectations between home and school: Teachers had assured Rebecca it was all right if paint got on her clothing; at home, she was scolded if her "good school clothes got all dirty."

Lynn spent much of her time playing in the streets with older, aggressive children. There she learned to hit, run, dodge, grab, and kick, the *social skills* necessary to that particular street setting. In the preschool, these same behaviors were considered socially unacceptable. Lynn had to learn to restrain the aggressive behaviors at school but to keep them ever ready when playing in the street.

These examples described by teachers are from real life. They point out how difficult it is to specify what is appropriate. In each instance, children were exhibiting social skills relevant to given situations in their lives. Yet, they also were receiving contradictory signals about the inappropriateness of those same behaviors in another context. Most children learn to deal with such contradictions. They find ways to adapt their behavior to the expectations of various situations (a social skill necessary for all of us at every life stage). Such adaptations tend to be more difficult for children with developmental problems. They are likely to have trouble learning to discriminate when a behavior is appropriate and when it is inappropriate. Trying to understand, for example, why it is all right to brush one's hair over the bathroom sink but not over the kitchen sink is not easy.

Rather than attempting to define a term like social skills it may be of greater value to list their various aspects. The major social skills to be learned during the early years relate to getting along with others:

• Interacting with children and adults, in a variety of ways, at home and away from home
• Trusting and enjoying known adults outside the immediate family
• Recognizing and protesting inappropriate advances from known or unknown adults within or outside the family
• Attending to self-care needs at home and in public places with consideration for others
• Sometimes initiating play ideas with children, other times, following other children's lead

Children need to be able to trust and enjoy adults outside the immediate family.

- Participating in group activities through listening, taking turns, and contributing to group effort
- Sometimes putting aside individual needs and interests so the needs and interests of the group may be met
- Working and playing independently as well as cooperatively; learning to be alone without feeling isolated or rejected
- Using language as the powerful social tool that it is for persuading, defending, reasoning, explaining, solving problems, and getting needs and preferences attended to

ACQUIRING SOCIAL SKILLS

Social skills are learned behaviors. Children's learning of a full range of social skills—the socializing process—cannot be forced or hurried. Learning such skills is a major occupation of the developing child. Refinement of previously learned social skills and the learning of new ones is ongoing throughout the life span.

Temperament and Emotions. The development of social skills, as noted earlier, is influenced by home, school, and community expectations and by the interpersonal relations withing these environments. A child's emotional reactions, or more precisely, **temperament**, also exert influence. Thomas and Chess (1977) described three types of infants: *easy, difficult,* and *slow to warm-up.*

Easy babies tend to be lively but not excessively so; they are fairly calm in their reactions to the unexpected and are open to new experiences such as trying out unfamiliar foods. They tend to be regular in their eating and sleeping habits. In general, they are happy and contented.

Difficult babies are likely to be irritable, easily upset, vigorously resistant to the unfamiliar. They cry more frequently and they cry in a way that grates on parents' and caregivers' ears (and nerves). Biological rhythms (eating, sleeping and elimination patterns) are difficult to regulate; the child is often labeled as *spoiled.*

Slow-to-warm-up infants show few intense reactions, either positive or negative. They seldom are outright resistant to new experiences but neither are they

A child's temperament influences social development.

eager to sample the unknown. For example, instead of fighting off a new food, they may simply not swallow it. They store it in one cheek or let it quietly slide out of their mouth. *Passive-resistant* is a term used to describe this type of behavior.

These personality or temperament traits may have genetic linkage. However, this is difficult to demonstrate and also relatively unimportant. What is important is that babies respond differently to what may be similar circumstances (as when they are in the same infant care program). These personal behavior patterns appear to persist into childhood, affecting how others respond to a child. Parents and caregivers play a role in the persistence of personality traits. Behaviors that one caregiver reacts to as a difficult temperament might not be perceived as at all difficult by another caregiver. One caregiver might describe a child as distractible, impulsive, and hard to manage while another might perceive the same child as an eager, active, happy-go-lucky runabout.

Granted that every child's social responses are influenced by temperament, the fact remains that all social behaviors are learned. They can be seen and heard and sometimes felt, as when one child pats or strikes another. Social skills are observable ways of behaving. Like all behaviors, they can be eliminated, strengthened, or modified. This is true even of those responses labeled *emotional.* Think about it. Is it not through their behaviors that we know children's emotional state? If they are feeling good about themselves? Sympathetic toward others? Hostile? Generous? Fearful? Picture the following:

Three children jumping on a jumping board, smiling and talking

Two children laughing while they divide cookies

A 5-year-old running from a snarling dog

Two children walking together with arms entwined

Such behaviors provide specific clues to which children are feeling happy, frightened, loving. They provide clues, also, to how well the children's social skills are developing. Each of the responses were *learned* through social interactions with the child's physical and interpersonal environment. By carefully observing children's behaviors (facial expressions, body posture, gestures, verbalizations) emotions can be recognized and dealt with in ways that strengthen both emotional development and social skills.

Social Reinforcement.   The development of appropriate social skills depends almost entirely on the amount and type of social responsiveness available to a young child. All children need opportunities to interact with others in a give-and-take fashion. Most newborns *come equipped* with social behaviors that attract and hold the attention of significant adults. In the typical situation, the baby cries and someone comes and provides comfort. The baby is soothed and stops crying. The caregiver is pleased. This puts in motion a reciprocal system that is socially and mutually reinforcing for both infant and adult. Even the newborn is highly skilled at taking turns. Bee (1992) puts it this way:

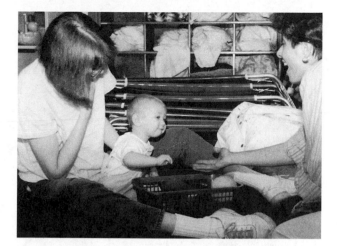

Infants and young children need give-and-take interactions.

As early as the first days of life, the baby sucks in a "burst-pause" fashion. He sucks for awhile, pauses, sucks for awhile, pauses, and so on. Mother enters into this "conversation," too, often by jiggling the baby during the pauses. The conversation looks like this, suck, pause, jiggle, pause, suck, pause, jiggle, pause. The rhythm of the interaction is really very much like a conversation and seems to underlie many of the social encounters among people of all ages. The fascinating thing is that this rhythm, this turn-taking, can be seen in an infant one day old (p. 98).

Adult responsiveness.   Social reinforcement, in the form of adult responsiveness, is a crucial factor in determining a child's social development. Following is a pertinent excerpt from a 1980 U.S. government pamphlet, Infant Care:

When your baby first smiles, you pay attention to him and smile back. When he smiles again, you smile back and pay attention to him again, talk to him and cuddle him. He soon learns that when he smiles good things happen to him, so he learns to do a lot of smiling when you are around. In just the same way, when you pay attention to his first cooing and gurgling sounds, your smile, your voice, and your fondling reward him. He coos and gurgles more and more frequently. The same holds true for all kinds of social behaviors in the infant and young child. When you respond to something your child does by giving atten-

Infants soon learn that smiling makes good things happen.

tion, a smile, a kind word, or by fondling or joy, your baby will do that thing more and more frequently. If you ignore it, it will happen less and less (p. 11).

Contingent stimulation.   The process of adult reinforcement is sometimes referred to as *contingent stimulation*. The degree to which parents, caregivers, and family members respond appropriately to the infant's cues is a major factor in determining a child's development. As noted in Unit 12, when there is at least partially contingent stimulation (responding) from significant adults, infants and young children develop better. They have earlier language, more advanced cognitive abilities, greater self-esteem, and more durable attachments.

Impact of Developmental Problems.   A potentially responsive early environment cannot *guarantee* a child will develop necessary and appropriate social skills. Through no fault of parents or caregivers, children with developmental problems often are deprived of

stimulation and reinforcement because of their own limitations. Consider these examples:

An infant who is deaf cannot hear the crooning, loving sounds that its mother makes during bathing, dressing, and feeding routines. Thus, the infant does not make the lively responses typical of an infant with normal hearing. The infant's lack of responsiveness reduces mother's efforts to interact. To further compound the situation, an infant's hearing loss often goes undetected during the developmentally crucial early months. Not realizing her infant has an impairment, mother may take the infant's lack of interest in her conversation as rejection; unwittingly she may respond less positively to the child as well as less often. Social reciprocity, the give-and-take of the system, goes awry. This puts the child's social development as well as cognitive and language development at risk.

Infants who are blind also are at high risk for poorly developed social skills. According to Fraiberg (1974), they do not engage in the **mutual gaze** interactions that appear to be crucial to the attachment process between parent and child. Mothers of babies who are blind often report they feel rejected when their infants do not look at them. Interestingly enough, Fraiberg noted that 4-week-old babies who are blind did begin to smile just as the sighted babies did. But then, something happened. At about two months, when sighted babies were smiling with increasing delight at their mother's face, the babies with the visual impairment were smiling less frequently and more tentatively. Gradually, the mothers in Fraiberg's studies on infant blindness seemed to withdraw psychologically from their babies, even though they continued to give physical care.

These examples do not imply that infants and children with special needs cannot learn appropriate social skills. Quite the contrary: they can and do. With the help of relevant members of the interdisciplinary team, parents learn to recognize alternate kinds of signaling and responding behaviors. An infant that is blind, for example, may begin to thrash about at the sound of mother's approaching footsteps. Mother comes to value this response in the same way she would value a welcoming smile from a sighted infant. Another example: The infant who is deaf may *snuggle in* when picked up. Mother learns to respond by stroking the child rhythmically; better yet, by stroking *and* singing or crooning. Though the baby does not hear the singing it usually gives pleasure to the mother.

Singing also may transmit subtle vibrations from the mother's chest or throat that further stimulates the infant's responsiveness.

Overstimulation and overresponding may also interfere with an infant's ability to make use of a responsive environment. Overstimulation often occurs among fragile infants; those who are premature or very low birth weight. They are easily overloaded with (what for them is) too many signals coming in from the environment. Their underdeveloped nervous systems simply cannot handle the *rush* and so the infant *shuts down*, withdraws, may become rigid, even rejecting of loving pats and cuddling. In a sense, the infant is "unavailable to its environment, becoming unable to obtain information or give feedback, causing the parents and other caregivers to feel less competent and effective" (Bennet 1990, p. 36). The opposite is true of the overresponding infant. In some instances, an infant with a central nervous system disorder (CNS), for example, may have an involuntary, but rigid arm extension when attempting to turn its head into nursing position. The infant's strong-arming may be perceived by the parent or caregiver as rejection or obstinacy, a reaction that interferes with establishing a warm relationship (Taft 1981).

These illustrations point out once again, the need to identify a developmental problem as early in infancy as possible. Early identification, followed by interdisciplinary intervention for infant and family, is a key factor in preventing other problems (insecure attachment, for example) that invariably compound the impaired child's original problem.

Social Skills in Sequence.   In inclusive programs, teachers will encounter children who are functioning at many levels of social competence. To work effectively with these children, some of whom will have developmental problems and others who will not, teachers must have a thorough understanding of the sequence of social development during the early years.

During the first year of life, infants' social responding is directed to parents, brothers and sisters, grandparents, and to frequent and regular caregivers. If all goes well, strong **affective** bonds are established between the infant and significant individuals in the infant's life. Somewhere in the middle of this period a

child may begin to show **separation protest** and then, fear of strangers. The stranger anxiety may last until 18 months or so. Generally speaking, this shyness disappears of its own accord if the child is not unduly pressured. During this reluctant period, infants appear to be somewhat interested in outsiders and to have moments of responsiveness to strangers. From the safety of the grocery cart or the pack on father's back, many babies will smile at a smiling stranger. From the security of a high chair in the restaurant infants often follow each other with their eyes. They even laugh at each other's antics. Hammering on the high chair tray or throwing spoons to the floor appears to be a hilarious and mutually enjoyable pastime for a pair of infants, total strangers though they may be.

Role of early learning programs.   Infant, toddler, and preschool programs play a crucial role in the development of appropriate social skills. Opportunities to learn social skills are available in the varied activities that teachers present and the ways teachers present them during self-help routines. Toddlers, for example, need opportunities to gain the skills required to be a member of a group. Therefore, a group story time is scheduled, but it involves only brief periods of sitting, in a loosely structured group. The toddlers are allowed to participate spontaneously and are free to

Early intervention programs offer many types of social experiences for infants and young children.

Older children need to begin to function in a more structured group on some occasions.

chime in with their own comments and exclamations, relevant or otherwise.

Older preschool children, on the other hand, need to begin to learn how to identify with a group: sitting in somewhat the same ways as the others and following directions given to the group. At the same time they need to learn how to function as individuals within a group by making contributions of general interest and by practicing ways of interrupting tactfully. School-aged children, who have learned group membership skills, need help with finding ways to organize and influence group activities. They also need to learn ways of responding in positive ways to the ideas and suggestions of others, both when agreeing and disagreeing. These patterns in the development of social skills can be guidelines as teachers work with all types of children in the inclusive setting.

Play.   Through play, young children become interested in each other. At first, they do not see each other as personalities or playmates. A fellow 18-month-old, for example, is something to be pushed or poked, prodded or ignored. It is not unusual to see one toddler shove a doll buggy directly into another toddler. It is as if the first child regards the other as just one more obstacle to be gotten out of the way. When the second child falls down and cries the first child may look surprised, appearing not to connect the pushing down and the crying.

A next step in the development of early social skills comes out of interest in the same materials. Often this leads to shrieks of "Mine!" as each child tries to hang on to the same toy. Following is an amusing example of evolving social skills and use of the same play materials:

> Two boys, just under 2 years of age were in the housekeeping area. One child was busily taking cups and plates from the cupboard and putting them on the table. The other child was just as busy, taking them off the table and returning them to the cupboard. It took several alternating trips back and forth before either noticed they were at cross purposes. The discovery led to mutual fury and clamor: "Mine! Mine! Mine!", almost in unison.

A next stage continues to focus on materials and equipment rather than on other children. There is, however, some independent *interacting* on common projects such as raking leaves, heaping them into piles, hauling them off in separate wagons. At this stage young children also begin to run, jump, climb, and ride wheel toys in small packs. These spontaneous groupings seem to be based on common activities rather than friendship. Then comes a cooperative stage: children actually play together and engage fairly regularly in a give-and-take of materials and ideas.

Cooperative play leads into the next higher order of social skills, that of forming more or less durable friendships. Other children now are valued both as personalities and as companions in play. Friends are preferred playmates and are first on the birthday invitation list. Friends are also to quarrel with, to make up with, and to threaten *not* to invite to your birthday party.

Teaching children to play.   Play often has been described as the *breath of life* to children. It is also the major avenue for early learnings of every kind. Even in infancy, most children seem to play spontaneously and apparently effortlessly. In play-oriented early childhood programs, children appear to be self-propelled as they move through the curriculum. They learn new skills and practice them in the course of self-initiated play activities. They participate in group activities and join eagerly in teacher-initiated play opportunities. Almost every skill that children master is mastered through play.

Such may not be the case for children with developmental disabilities. The play of children with a hearing impairment is less social and more solitary. However, children with severe hearing loss, even those with serious language deficits, have been reported as having imaginary playmates (Mogford 1977). As for children with severe vision impairments, Rogers and Puchalski (1984) report significant delays in their symbolic play (make believe, pretend, using one object to represent another, as when a doll blanket becomes a magic cape). Children with autistic behaviors or limited cognitive skills also tend to be lacking in symbolic play skills. Developmental problems of this kind may lead to inappropriate use of materials such as hammering the cookie cutters with the rolling pin or breaking the crayons into pieces.

Children with developmental disabilities often have fewer play skills. They may hang back, not knowing how to get into other children's play; or try to gain entry in inappropriate ways, for example, crashing a truck into housekeeping play, which leads to rejection. It is essential, therefore, that children who do not know how to play be taught. Teaching children to play may seem contrary to tradition. Yet, no child should be deprived of this powerful avenue for learning and the many enjoyable experiences that come with it. Strategies for teaching play include:

1. Physically guiding the child to a play activity and helping him or her to settle in.
2. Orienting the child toward the material or equipment and handing material to the child to establish physical contact.
3. Putting a clothespin (or some other object) in the child's hand, for example, and moving the hand so it is directly above a container.
4. Verbalizing to the child what he or she is doing: "You have a clothespin in your hand. You can drop it in the can."
5. Rejoicing over the smallest accomplishments: "Look at that!" (or "Did you *hear* that"!) *You* dropped the clothespin in the can." (In the beginning it does not matter that the child is involved only because the teacher's hand is around the child's hand, manually shaping the child's response.)

Children with disabilities sometimes need to be taught how to play.

6. Arranging for the child to be near other children in a given activity thereby enabling the teacher to point out and describe what other children are doing and so begin to promote imitation.
7. Gradually helping other children join in activities, once the child has acquired a semblance of a play skill (two children might drop clothespins into the same can).
8. Providing social reinforcement for the play: "It looks like *you two* are going to fill that can full of clothespins."
9. Moving the child slowly but steadily toward group play by building small groups of two, then three, *nonthreatening* children who participate with the child with the developmental problems in simple play activities such as tossing bean bags into a box.

As a child with special needs begins to play more spontaneously, teachers continue their assistance, but in less directive fashion. For example, when helping a group of children decide where to play after music time, the teacher reviews the options for each child. The child with the developmental problem is helped

Arranging for a child to work or play near another child facilitates social development.

learn to be explicit about what they are doing in certain situations. For example, it can be disconcerting for a child who cannot see to have materials moved from the rehearsed location. Yet, telling the other children not to touch his or her materials may cast a negative shadow on the special child. Instead, children can be taught the simple social skill, the courtesy (due to all children) of stating what they are doing whenever they use or change another person's materials: "Kelly, I need some of your paste. I'm going to move it over here (guiding Kelly's hand) so we can share, okay?"

Gentle insistence. Not all children with developmental problems are eager to play, nor do they want to be taught to play; they may even avoid play materials and would-be playmates. These are the children who sometimes need to be gently pushed (perhaps pressured a bit) just to get them to try a play activity that teachers know will be of developmental benefit to them.

to choose *after* several other children have made their choices. Because the child has heard the choices reviewed several time and has heard several children choosing, making a choice becomes easier. It is helpful, too, for the teacher to pair the special child with another child who has chosen the same activity. This provides a good model for the less-skilled child in both locating the activity and in getting off to a good start.

Activities must be planned carefully so that children with developmental problems can experience maximum success. When a child with severe vision loss is participating in an art activity, the teacher might describe and physically help the child locate materials by guiding his or her hand:

> Here is the big circle to paste the little circles on. The little circles are here in the basket. Here is the paste, by your right hand. The sponge to wipe your fingers on is next to it. Corliss is working across the table from you (promoting the activity's social aspect).

Along with helping the child with developmental problems, teachers also need to help all children

Example: Jolene was a somewhat solitary 3-year-old with cerebral palsy. An instructional objective written into her IEP by the interdisciplinary team was that Jolene learn to ride a tricycle. The physical therapist adapted a tricycle by adding a trunk support and stirrups. Jolene, however, would not get on. Teachers' coaxing intensified her resistance until just the sight of the tricycle set her to crying. The teachers were ready to give up. Not the physical therapist, who impressed on them the therapeutic value of tricycle riding for this particular child. The therapist maintained that this preschool *treatment* would promote more general development, as well as motor coordination, than any number of clinic sessions.

After talking it over with Jolene's parents, a plan was agreed on: one teacher would lift Jolene onto the tricycle and support (and comfort) her while the therapist put Jolene's feet in the stirrups and pulled the vehicle from the front. This they did, with Jolene crying louder and louder at first. The teacher continued to support her physically and to comfort her while the therapist moved the tricycle gently forward, talking quietly to her and describing what was going on. Gradually, Jolene quieted.

Within a few days she stopped resisting the riding sessions. Furthermore, and much to the teachers' relief, she appeared to be enjoying the sessions. Six weeks later, Jolene was riding her specially fitted tricycle independently, in the company of other children. Giving in to Jolene's anxieties (as well as the teachers') would have been to deprive Jolene of learning a play skill central to both her mobility *and* her social development.

Incidental Social Learning.   As in the above instance there are times when it is not only appropriate but even urgent to teach play skills directly. Most of the time, however, teachers can promote social interactions fairly easily by being alert to what goes on naturally among children. More frequently than realized, brief, positive interactions are occurring between children with and without developmental disabilities: smiling, handing materials, moving aside, helping to pick up the pieces of a dropped puzzle, and so on. Teachers can quietly remark these commonplace interactions: "Martin, when you held the door open for Corey it was easy for him to get his wheelchair through. See how he is smiling at you?" When the teacher makes similar comments to Corey, both children are introduced to a next level of socialization. The result may be interaction between the two.

Children's concern or anxiety about another child's disability also offer opportunities for incidental social learning. A teacher may notice a child looking obliquely at the patch over another child's eye; or witness one child's reluctance to hold another child's malformed hand; or overhear a child expressing fear about *catching* the paralysis of the wheelchair-bound child. The children's concerns are genuine, not to be shushed or ignored. They provide opportunities for teachers to promote social learning and interactions. Often the teacher and the child with the disability can respond together. Using the eye patch case as an example, the teacher might first acknowledge the one child's concern and then help the second child explain. If the child with the eye problem is not at that verbal stage the teacher can explain and ask for the child's corroboration. "The doctor put the patch on one eye so your other eye can learn to see better, right?" The explanation can be expanded further, depending on the interest and comfort level of both children. Always the teacher works in reassurances for the concerned child, that the disability is not catching, that there are many, many things the other child

can do. Often the two children can be gotten into a joint activity at that point.

A child's first tentative steps toward joining a play situation is another form of incidental social learning that teachers need to note and reinforce. The child who stands and watches may be nearly ready to interact. A teacher might watch with the child for a moment or two at a time, while commenting on the activity: "It looks like Bart is making cookies and Cami's making a pie." Another time, sensing the child's readiness, the teacher might help the child actually get into play: "Matt is bringing more cookie cutters for everyone to use." The teacher also can prompt the other children directly or indirectly.

Example: Josh, a child with Down syndrome, had a drum in his hand but was standing apart from a small group of children who were experimenting with rhythm instruments. Teacher: "It sounds like you need a drummer in your band." (pause) Teacher: "You could ask Josh. He has a drum." If Josh joined in, the teacher could then provide reinforcement to all, as a group: "What a good band! Mary and Meg and John and Josh and Karen, your music really sounds good." (It is well not to make specific mention of the children having invited Josh into the group; this could make Josh stand out unnecessarily as so different as to need special treatment.)

Incidental social learning can be expanded even further thorough play activities already in progress. Teachers need to reinforce the interaction, but subtly, to avoid distracting either child. Depending on the situation the teacher might:

Move closer, kneel down, watch with interest, but avoid eye contact to keep from interrupting the children's mutual focus.

Smile and nod if either child turns toward the teacher (but keeping the teacher's focus on the activity, not the child with special needs).

Bring additional materials to extend the play, placing it close to the activity (with or without comment, depending on the situation).

Make encouraging comments that further promote joint effort: "Missy and Sam, you are building a long, long road. It looks like it's going to go all the way to the gate!"

Keep the children's focus on each other, not on the teacher.

Frequent episodes of social interaction among children with and without disabilities characterizes quality inclusion programs. Such intermixing is most likely to occur, says Wolery (1994), "when children with special needs are in small groups, when competent peers are in the group, when the group includes mixed ages, and when teachers encourage and support exchanges and imitation" (p. 115).

Affection or friendship training.   Teachers can promote positive social interactions between children with disabilities and those without impairments through *affection* or *friendship* training (McEvoy, Twardosz and Bishop 1990). These researchers suggest that group games, songs, and rhythmic activities can be adapted to promote interaction. In such activities as the *Hokey Pokey, If You're Happy and You Know It,* or *The Farmer in the Dell* teachers can readily change the words to promote both physical and verbal exchanges as when the farmer *hugs* the wife (Brown, Raglund and Bishop 1989, published a manual that describes how to adapt typical songs and games to promote social interactions.)

Twardosz and her colleagues (1983) offer three reasons to explain the effectiveness of the affection procedure in promoting social interactions between typical and atypical children. One is the pairing of two children of differing abilities in a pleasurable experience. A second has to do with desensitization—children getting used to each other and so less wary of differences. And the third, children are given opportunities to practice affectionate behaviors in a nonthreatening and supportive situation.

Sharing and Turn Taking.   Sharing and taking turns is the foundation for mutually satisfying play between children. Yet, these skills are the most difficult to learn. Why? Because they involve *giving up something,* and giving up anything is contrary to the young child's perfectly normal, **egocentric** view of the world. "MINE! MINE! MINE!" is the clarion call of every healthy child at one stage of development (at least in our society). With adult support, patience, and many unpressured opportunities to learn, most children, eventually, cooperate when a teacher says:, "Mary, two more turns around the driveway and then it is Sara's turn." The teacher can say this in many different ways to each child, over the weeks and months: "Sara, watch. Mary is going around the driveway two more times; then it will be your turn. Let's count." or, "Mary, Sara waited a long, long time for the tricycle you were riding, so she gets a long turn, too. I'll call you when she's through."

Gradually reducing the amount of available material is another way to teach sharing. As always, it is the teacher who makes it happen. Conflict among children is avoided when the teacher plans such a step carefully, monitors the situation, and helps children work it through.

Examples: A teacher might put out fewer but larger portions of play dough to encourage children to divide their dough with latecomers to the activity. With a teacher's help, some children (certainly not all) will be able to break off a part of their dough; when two or three children do this, the newcomer has an adequate amount to work with. The teacher then can reinforce the acts of sharing. A spin-off is that children who did the sharing have provided good models for the children not yet able to share.

Several individual baskets of colored wooden cubes might be poured into one larger basket. The children must then share common but plentiful material. Again, the teacher must be there to teach, partly by assuring the children there is plenty for all. If one child is accused of taking more than his or her share the teacher might suggest that each child take no more than five cubes at a time (thus teaching counting, concurrently).

A child who has great difficulty sharing may be put in charge of a plentiful but uncontested material, perhaps *tickets* for snacks, or for a *train ride* (chairs lined up), or tickets, *just because.* The tickets may be nothing more than a quantity of small squares of colored paper, irresistible, nonetheless, to most young children. As the child passes out the tickets the teacher can comment what a good job he or she is doing of *giving away* tickets, but remarking also: "You have a lot left."

Always, it is the teacher's job to promote and respond to friendly interactions between children, thereby making spontaneous sharing somewhat easier. When two children decide to work a puzzle together, the teacher might reinforce the friendly interaction by sitting down briefly and watching the children work. When two children are using a wagon together, the teacher spends some time pulling them around. Teachers also can point up situations that involve friendly interactions: "Martha and Jay, you really have a long train now that you have hitched all your cars together." In addition, teachers help children wait for a turn or a material by offering alternates until the preferred material is available.

Self assertion.   The problem may be the reverse with some children. They may give up too easily or fail to defend themselves or their possessions. All children need to learn to stand up for their rights. It is especially important that teachers find ways to help children with disabilities fend for themselves; otherwise some may resort to trading on their handicaps to get what they want ("You shouldn't take my doll because I can't walk as good as you"). Following is an example of how a teacher might help a child with severely limited vision assert her rights.

Five-year-old Lisa, blind since birth, was playing with an interlocking floor train. Bart took one of her cars.

Lisa, touching her train, realized a car was missing. She began to rock back and forth, whining and poking at her eyes. The teacher said, "Lisa, Bart has your car. Tell him to give it back." The teacher turned to Bart: "That car is Lisa's. Be sure to hand it back when she asks you for it." By not retrieving the car, the teacher helped both children: Lisa, to learn about the rights of possession; Bart to recognize that all children have rights that are to be respected.

Materials and Equipment.   The materials and equipment available to children greatly influences their learning of social skills. Paints, crayons, and scissors, for example, are most commonly used in nonsocial but constructive play activities (Rubin and Howe 1985). Materials that have proven to be good socializers include:

Housekeeping and dress-up play
Mural painting or collage pasting (several children working on the same long paper)
Unit blocks and large hollow blocks
Trucks, cars, and airplanes
Lotto and other simple board games
Musical instruments

When small groups gather there should be sufficient material to go around, thus inviting each child's participation. It is well, also, to have some duplicate material. A child with a developmental problem then has the opportunity to use the same material as another child and so to learn appropriate usage through imitation. On the other hand, too much or too many different materials tends to promote solitary play. Example: A wheel toy for every child defeats a major goal of most programs: that of promoting sharing and turn-taking. A practical ratio is about one wheel toy to every three or four children; all kinds of inventive doubling-up games and cooperative ventures can be the result, such as wagon and tricycle trains.

Imitation and Modeling.   Young children learn many behaviors and skills by watching other children and imitating what they do. Providing children with developmental problems with models for appropriate behaviors, especially social behaviors, is a major argument in favor of inclusions. It must be stressed, however, that

Children learn by watching.

including children does not automatically lead to their learning appropriate play behaviors and social skills, From the start of the inclusion movement it has been apparent that spontaneous social interactions between children, with and without developmental problems, occurs infrequently (Allen, Haring and Hayden 1970). Teachers play a central role in promoting the interactions. They *make it happen* by:

Arranging the environment to ensure interactions between disabled and nondisabled children

Reinforcing children, in general, for playing together

Reinforcing children with developmental problems when they imitate appropriate behaviors.

Each of these practices are discussed in detail in various sections of the text. Here let it be stressed that if children with special needs are to learn from children who are developing typically, they must be involved in a wide range of play activities. Once again: *Teachers make it happen.* Teachers set up activities designed specifically to facilitate play interactions, often through small group experiences. Such activities include:

Pasting projects (collage) where children perhaps decorate a big carton for storing sand toys

A giant size pegboard with children taking turns putting in pegs from their own baskets

A big picture book to look at together, each child pointing to a preselected character when it appears (more verbal children can tell what their character is doing)

TEACHER-STRUCTURED PEER INTERACTIONS

At times, teachers decide which children will play together in which activities. This ensures the inclusion of a child with disabilities in an activity with children best suited to that child's skill levels. The grouping can be done on the basis of mutual interests, temperament, or abilities. Wagon trains, mentioned earlier (several wagons and tricycles hitched together in separate pairs) can be introduced. This game (and many others that teachers can devise) allows a child who cannot walk the excitement of being involved—being towed in a wagon also occupied, perhaps, by a normally developing child. The child with the disability is an integral part of a spirited outdoor social activity. A rocking boat also promotes closeness and interaction as children synchronize their efforts to make it rock. A note of caution: children who are just beginning to interact with other children usually should not be paired with overly rambunctious children.

Discovery learning periods are especially good times for promoting social learning through imitation and modeling. Teachers need to provide several interest centers and several attractive activities where interaction is almost automatic: the water table, the dough table, a simple cooking experience. Easily conducted science and math experiences promote interactions, too, as when a few children go into the yard together to pick up leaves to sort by size, type or color. The key issue is that *interactions occur and are pleasurable* for both the normally developing children and children with developmental problems. "Play experiences that are fun and enjoyable are likely to lead to a happier and more satisfying peer relationship" (Li 1983).

Peer tutoring and peer mediating. Peer mediated strategies take a variety of forms, yet all have certain elements in common, according to Wolery (1994):

Typically developing children are taught specific ways of engaging less competent children in social interactions.

The mediating children are taught to keep trying to engage the less competent children in social interactions.

Children with special needs and the other children have ongoing opportunities to play together and practice skills together.

Teachers provide children with support and reinforcement for working and playing together.

As discussed in Unit 1, children who are developing in typical fashion may also occasionally act as teachers for children with disabilities. Sometimes these episodes occur spontaneously as when:

* One child helps another to rearrange and separate his or her fingers when putting on mittens.
* A child indicates which cube goes where when two children happen to be involved in sorting color cubes for storage.
* Another child at the table shows the child pouring from a pitcher how to steady it with the other hand so as to pour slowly and avoid the juice overflowing the cup.

Teachers also can plan child-teaching-child events. Such peer teaching episodes are appropriate to any part of the program:

* At music two similar instruments might be provided with a hearing child designated to help the child with deafness to recognize when and with what force to join in.
* During preacademics the teacher could have two children work together, asking the sighted child to help the child who is visually impaired learn to put the wooden shapes into a form board.
* During discovery learning a teacher might ask a child with language limitations to show a child wearing a prosthesis how to make a tunnel, "just like yours."

In every instance, teachers pair children carefully to ensure an appropriate match of skills and temperament. It is important that the child with a disability and the other child enjoy and benefit from the interaction. Never should either child feel burdened; never should either child's learning opportunities in any other area be curtailed. Carefully managed, peer tutoring is of benefit to both children. The child with developmental problems has the opportunity to learn through play from someone who is a master at play, another child. The child-models practice and refine their own developing social skills and learn a new and higher order social skill, that of teaching or imparting knowledge. Hartup (1983) suggests even greater gains: That the tutor gains in self-esteem because of the increased status that comes with being teacher. The tutor also gains in sensitivity in that a certain amount of nurturing is required when teaching a less able peer. Furthermore, it appears that child/tutors undergo positive behavioral and attitudinal changes toward the children with disabilities who are being tutored (Franca et al. 1990).

Fair play. Children who are developing typically also are good models for the simple everyday, *fair play* behaviors expected of children in an early childhood program. Appropriate use of materials and equipment is one example. All children need to learn to use community property responsibly. No child can be allowed to paint on the walls, crash a tricycle repeatedly, deface books, or waste materials. It is especially important for children with developmental problems to learn respect for materials and equipment, and to learn it in the company of other children, whenever possible. Otherwise, they may be viewed as unwanted playmates, disrupters of play activities, someone to be disliked or avoided. Let it be stressed, once again, that classroom rules (whatever they may be) apply to all children. There can be no double standards. To allow any child to repeatedly and unduly disturb or distress other children does the disturbing child a grave injustice, and exclusion from play activities. Exclusion from activities and play models closes the major avenue a teacher has for helping children learn appropriate social skills.

SUMMARY

Children with developmental delays and disabilities, like all young children, need to learn how to get along with others. To do this, they must learn appropriate social skills. Such learning may be more difficult for children with developmental problems. Like all other skills, social skills are dependent on every other area of development, one or more of which may be impaired in some children. Notwithstanding, children of all developmental levels can and do master basic social skills as prescribed by their respective families, schools, and communities.

Even though affected by each child's temperament, all social skills are learned behaviors. They depend largely on reciprocal responsiveness between the child and significant adults, starting within the first hours and days of life. However, children with certain developmental disabilities may not be able to engage in the give-and-take typical of normally developing children. For them, the entire socialization process may go awry unless special help is provided for them and their family by relevant members of the child study team. Enrollment in an inclusive early childhood program can help to advance social skill learnings for children with developmental problems.

Play is a major medium in early learning, especially in learning social skills. Not all children know how to play; some may even be reluctant to try. In such instances, the children should be taught, using firm but gentle insistence if needed. This ensures that all children have both the fun and the incidental learning opportunities that are available only in play.

Learning social skills through imitating and modeling after normally developing children is a major argument for inclusive classrooms. For modeling to take place, children with disabilities and those without must interact, which they tend not to do spontaneously; teachers must make it happen. Teachers promote interactions among all types of children by arranging both the physical and the social environment. They also encourage peer tutoring, sometimes planned in advance, more often incidental in occurrence. Both the normally developing child and the child with developmental problems can benefit from peer tutoring and various kinds of peer mediation.

STUDENT ACTIVITIES

1. Observe in a child care center that has a wide age range, from toddlers to kindergarten age children, if possible. Record anecdotal notes (Unit 10), on three different children at three different age levels, displaying three different but developmentally appropriate social skills; during your observation, note any inappropriate play you see. Explain why you consider it inappropriate.

2. Visit a preschool, public school, or child care center that includes children with developmental disabilities. Observe one of the children who has a disability for 30 minutes. Record the social skills the child displays; analyze your observations and list the social skills you feel the child lacks in terms of his or her age and developmental level.

3. While making either of the above observations, list the indoor and outdoor play materials and equipment that

seem to promote the most and the best cooperative play. Note in particular if children with developmental problems are using the equipment. If not, try to decide why not.

4. Work with another student or two as a teaching team and make plans as to the kinds of activities or materials you might present to promote sharing among 3-year-olds, some of whom have a developmental delay.

5. Assume you are working with a 4-year-old with a cognitive delay and few play skills. You feel it is important that this child learn to play with blocks. How might you go about teaching block play to this child? Be specific. Select a classmate to be the child and demonstrate your teaching strategies in class. How might you include another child to help in teaching block play? Demonstrate.

REVIEW QUESTIONS

A. *Lists.*
1. List three developmental areas that are related to and support the acquisition of social skills.
2. List five skills that both define and are a part of learning to get along with others.
3. List three types of infant temperament according to Thomas and Chess (1977).
4. List five types of materials that are most likely to promote social development in young children, both normal and atypical.
5. List five steps a teacher might take in helping a child with a developmental delay learn play skills.

B. *True or False. Choose the best answer.*
   T F   1. The development of social skills and motor skills is unrelated.
   T F   2. Children may need to behave differently at school than they do at home.
   T F   3. The environment has little or no impact on a child's social skills learning.
   T F   4. One can judge fairly accurately how a child is feeling about a situation by observing his or her behavior.
   T F   5. Adult responsiveness is a critical element in children's social development.
   T F   6. Because play is *natural* in childhood, it is developmentally inappropriate to try to teach any child to play.

   T F   7. Normally developing children should be taught never to touch the play materials of a child who cannot see.
   T F   8. It can be good for both a normally developing child and a child with a disability to talk together about the disability.
   T F   9. Standing and watching other children's play is never a legitimate use of a child's time, especially if the child is already experiencing a developmental delay.
   T F 10. An inclusion classroom automatically ensures that children with developmental problems will learn appropriate social skills through modeling the behavior of children who are developing typically.

C. *Define briefly each term.*
   1. reciprocal (in terms of social development)
   2. peer mediation
   3. temperament
   4. contingent stimulation
   5. mutual gaze
   6. symbolic play
   7. incidental learning
   8. modeling
   9. peer tutoring
   10. egocentric viewpoint

REFERENCES

Allen, K.E., Haring, N.G., and Hayden, A.H. (1970). *Building social skills in the preschool child.* Film: Media Services, Child Development and Mental Retardation Center, University of Washington, Seattle.

Bailey, D.B., and Wolery, M. (1989). *Assessing infants and preschoolers with handicaps.* Columbus, OH: Merrill.

Bee, H. (1992). *The Developing Child.* New York: Harper and Row.

Bennett, F.C. (1990). Recent advances in developmental intervention for biologically vulnerable infants. *Infants and Young Children,* 3(1), 33–40.

Brown, W.H., Raglund, E.U., and Bishop, N. (1989). *A socialization curriculum for preschool programs that integrate children with handicaps.* Nashville, TN: Vanderbilt University.

Fraiberg, S. (1974). Blind infants and their mothers: An examination of the sign system. In M.L. Lewis and L.A. Rosenblum (Eds.), *The effect of the infant on its caregiver.* New York: Wiley.

Franca, V.M., Kerr, M.M., Reitz, A.L., and Lambert, D. (1990). Peer tutoring among behaviorally disordered students: Academic and social benefits to the tutor and tutee. *Education and Treatment of Children,* 13:2. 109–128.

Hartup, W.W. (1983). Peer relations. In P.H. Mussen and E.M. Hetherington (Eds.), *Carmichael's manual of child psychology* (4th ed.). New York: Wiley & Sons.

Infant Care. (1980). U.S. Department of Health and Human Services. DHHS Publication No. (OHDS) 80–30015. Washington, D.C.: U.S. Government Printing Office.

Li, A.K.F. (1983). Pleasurable aspects of play in enhancing young handicapped children's relationships with parents and peers. *Journal of the Division for Early Childhood,* 7, 87–92.

McEvoy, M.A., Twardosz, S. and Bishop, N. (1990). Affection activities: Procedures for encouraging young children with handicaps to interact with their peers. *Education and Treatment of Children,* 13, 297–73.

Mogford, K. (1977). The play of handicapped children. In B. Tizard and D. Harvey (Eds.), *Biology of play*. Philadelphia: Lippincott.

Odom, S.L., and McEvoy, M.A. (1988). Integration of young children with handicaps and normally developing children. In S.L. Odom, and M.B. Karnes (Eds.), *Early intervention for infants and children with handicaps*. Baltimore: Brookes.

Peck, C., Appoloni, T., Cook, T., and Raver, S. (1978). Teaching retarded preschoolers to imitate the free play behaviors of nonretarded classmates: Trained and generalization effects. *Journal of Special Education*, 12, 195–207.

Rogers, S.J., and Puchalski, C.B. (1984). Development of symbolic play in visually impaired infants. *Topics in Early Childhood Special Education*, 3, 57–643.

Rubin, K.H., and Howe, N. (1985). Toys and play behaviors: An overview. *Topics in Early Childhood Special Education*, 5:3, 1–9.

Taft, LT. (1981). Intervention program for infants with cerebral palsy: A clinician's view. In C.C. Brown (Ed.), *Infants at risk. Assessment and intervention, An update for health-care professionals and parents.* (no place of publication given) Johnson and Johnson.

Thomas, A., and Chess, S. (1977). *Temperament and development.* New York: Bruner/Mazel.

Twardosz, S., Norquist, V.M., Simon, R., and Botkin, D. (1983). The effect of group affection activities on the interaction of socially isolated children. *Analysis and Intervention in Developmental Disabilities*, 13, 311–338.

Wachs, T.D., and Gruen, G.E. (1982). *Early experience and human development.* New York: Plenum.

Wolery, M. (1994). Designing inclusive environments for young children with special needs. In M. Wolery and J.S. Wilbers (Eds.). *Including children with special needs in early childhood programs.* Washington, D.C.: National Association for the Education of Young Children.

Facilitating Speech, Language and Communication Development

OBJECTIVES

After studying this unit the student will be able to

- define *language* and explain how it develops according to the several theories described in the unit.
- outline the major steps in language development, the order of their development, and give examples of each.
- explain the difference between receptive and expressive language and discuss the developmental significance of each.
- list eight ways that teachers can help children with special needs expand their language and communication skills.
- discuss dysfluency among young children and describe appropriate responses from teachers and parents.

Learning their native language is a complex developmental task, yet most children accomplish it easily. In fact, children seem to have fewer problems learning language than researchers do defining it. Language can be defined as a complicated symbol system. Symbols can be thought of as *signals*: words, signs, gestures, and body movements that either stand for something else or represent ideas. Another way to define language is by its three interrelated processes: communication, speech, and language.

Communication is the exchange of thoughts and ideas, feelings, emotions, likes and dislikes. While speech is a major form of communication, there are other forms:

Gestures and body language. These may be used alone or with speech. Holding up a hand with fingers upright and palm facing another individual almost universally indicates "Stop." To make the command doubly emphatic, the action may accompany the spoken word. Touching conveys messages such as irritation or caring as when an adult grabs a child's arm forcibly, or gently brushes the hair out of a child's eyes.

Printed words. Books, letters, and directives allow communication without speech or one-to-one contact. The same can be said of art forms such as music, dance, paintings, and the like which also are powerful forms of communication.

Speech is the *sounds* of a language, the ability to communicate verbally. Speech depends on articulation, the ability to produce sounds distinctly and correctly.

Language, as noted above, is a *code* or *symbol* system that enables individuals to express ideas and communicate them to others who use the same code. The code of every language is based on informally transmitted *rules* about grammar (syntax) and word meaning (semantics).

In spite of its complexity, most children acquire language with relative ease. One psychologist has suggested it would be virtually impossible to prevent normally developing children from learning to talk (Flavell 1985, p. 248). Another opinion, sometimes lamented by parents and early childhood teachers, is that once children begin to talk, there is no stopping them.

Communicating with others is the essential purpose of language. It functions as both a social and a cognitive activity. Allen and Hart (1984) describe the interrelationship: Language serves as a social skill for interacting with others, for expressing needs and ideas, and for getting help, opinions, and the cooperation of others. It serves also as a cognitive skill for understanding, inquiring, and telling about oneself and one's world.

LANGUAGE ACQUISITION

Several theories propose to explain how children acquire language. These will be touched on briefly as background for the remainder of the unit.

Imitation and Reinforcement.   Children learn from imitating the speech and language habits of others. In turn, they receive feedback (reinforcement). There is agreement that imitation and reinforcement play an indisputable role in language acquisition. Yet these processes cannot account for the tremendous variation and creativity in a young child's language. Children's choice of words and their sentence construction often bear no resemblance to anything any adult would say.

The research on *motherese* is cited as both evidence and partial explanation of the role of imitation and reinforcement on early language development. *Motherese* is defined as certain patterns of speech found in virtually all adults who care for young children. Adults, especially mothers, and even older brothers and sisters, tend to simplify and slow their speech when talking to the very young (Snow and Ferguson 1977). They speak in higher pitched voices, use short and grammatically simple sentences, repeat words and phrases. It is not that parents have figured out that talking this way is the best way to teach language. Experience has shown them it is the best way to get their children to understand them. It also appears to be the best way to keep a youngster's attention.

Maturation or Innateness Explanation.   According to this theory, language unfolds or emerges as a part of the developmental process. The child is viewed as having a kind of built-in mechanism that makes language learning an almost automatic process. This approach

Language acquisition depends upon a combination of factors, including the ability to imitate.

does not take into account the child's emerging cognitive skills. Most developmentalists believe that cognition cannot be left out of a language acquisition explanation; it figures too prominently in what children have to say.

Cognitive Explanation.   The child's language, from this point of view, *may* start with some kind of a built-in mechanism. However, the process is far from automatic, as implied in the preceding explanation. It is closely tied to the child's cognitive skills: Increasing cognitive structures are what enable children to bring increasing order and precision to their language.

Integrated Explanation.   Language acquisition most likely is a combination of the above explanations. Kuczaj (1982) is credited with combining the explanations into a three-part format:

1. The maturationally determined mechanism for learning language.
2. The *input*, or quality and timing of the child's early language experiences.
3. The use the child makes of input; the strategies the child devises for processing spoken language and then reproducing it.

Bee (1992) suggests, "For psychologists and linguists, the child's rapid and skillful acquisition of language has remained an enduring puzzle" (p. 296).

Regardless of differences of opinion, it appears that healthy newborns arrive with a potential for language. They come equipped to learn to talk and the environment teaches them how. There is no dispute that language skills are developed through participation in language activities. Early language activities, for the most part, are informal and spontaneous. They occur during daily routines, casual play, and impromptu social exchanges. Such interactions, *in the everyday world*, are the main ingredients of language development. When language is not developing properly, the child is put at great developmental risk. Failure to acquire normal language can be a developmental disaster. The educational and social consequences may persist for years to come (Warren and Kaiser 1989).

SEQUENCES IN LANGUAGE ACQUISITION

Language acquisition, like all areas of development, is a sequential process. It follows a step-by-step pattern from early primitive sounds and movements to the complex language and fluent speech characteristic of native speakers.

Prelingual Communication.   Language development begins in early infancy, long before the first words appear. Known as the preverbal, or more accurately, *prelingual* stage, the infant's language is characterized by body movements, facial grimaces, and vocalizations. During this period, the foundation of communicative language is established. The earliest efforts take the form of crying, then cooing, then babbling.

Crying.   Healthy newborns spend most of their time sleeping. When they are awake, crying is a major form

Language development begins long before the infant's first words.

of communication. It is infants' most reliable way of ensuring their needs are met. Infant cries vary. Many parents seem to distinguish one cry from another and become skilled at anticipating hunger, discomfort, or their infant's need for company.

Cooing.   By two months or age most infants are cooing, that is, making a string of single vowel sounds such as "eeeeeeeeee" or "aaaaaaaaaa." Characteristically, the sounds indicate well-being or pleasure. Cooing increases as parents and caregivers respond with smiles and similar sounds. These early *conversations* between infant and parent seem to promote the infant's awareness of turn-taking as a way of interacting vocally with others.

Babbling.   About 6 months of age, infants begin to combine consonant and vowel sounds. These they repeat over and over: bu bu bu bu, gu gu gu gu, da da da da, ma ma ma ma. Ma ma ma and da da da are purely coincidental in spite of parents' jubilation that their infant is now calling them "by name." It is no wonder, however, that da da and ma ma become shaped so rapidly. Babbling, like all other aspects of language is readily affected by adult attention. In a classic study conducted many years ago, Rheingold and her colleagues (1959) demonstrated that when adults smiled at the babbling baby, patted its tummy, or responded with similar sounds, the babbling increased.

Self-echoing. Infants who have been babbling for awhile begin to sound as if they were having conversations with themselves. They repeat a sound several times, pause as though listening to what they had to say, then repeat the sound again. This sequence makes it appear that infants are echoing their own sounds, hence the occasional use of the term *echolalia* (Rathus 1988). (It should be noted that the term echolalia is more commonly used in describing the speech patterns of children diagnosed as having autism.)

Intonation. During the latter part of the echo period, a new characteristic appears. Infants' vocalizations begin to be marked by *intonation*, that is, rising and falling variations in pitch that resemble adults' speech. "Learning the tune before the words" is the way Bates et al. (1987 p. 299) describe this period.

First Words and Sentences. Every aspect of early language development is exciting. Major accomplishments for the child are making first words and then sentences. Once these are mastered, language development progresses with giant strides.

Vocabulary. As babbling increases, first "words" begin to emerge. Parents often miss out on these first words because they are hard to recognize. In the beginning, infants tend to vary the sounds. They appear to be unsure, at first, which combination of vowels and consonants to settle on when referring to a particular object or action. After the milestone of the first recognizable word, somewhere around the first birthday, new words follow slowly. Months go by before there is a real burst in vocabulary growth. The sequence goes like this:

> During the three or four months following the first words, the child may acquire less than a dozen new words.

> A rapid increase in vocabulary, up to about 50 words, often comes between 14 and 18 months.

> Between 18 months and the second birthday, a normally developing child is likely to have learned between 250 and 300 words.

> After the age of 2, children acquire hundreds of new words a year.

> At age 6, many children have a vocabulary of 14,000 words.

Receptive and expressive vocabulary. From the very beginning, all of us have two types of language: receptive and expressive. Receptive refers to words and concepts a child understands (inner language). Expressive refers to the words the child uses to communicate verbally.

Receptive Language. Throughout life we understand more words than we use when speaking. By the end of the fifth year, the typical child, as noted above, knows approximately 14,000 words. However, that same child is likely to have many fewer words (2,500) in his or her expressive vocabulary. Receptive language always *precedes* expressive language. Before speaking its first words, it is obvious an infant understand much of what is said. Most infants squeal with delight when a parent says, "Let's go bye-bye"; or a caregiver says, "Time for applesauce" (if that happens to be a favorite food of the moment). Later, good receptive skills are demonstrated when a toddler runs to her grandfather as he calls out, "Where's my favorite little girl?"

Expressive Language. Words and sentences that an individual speaks (or signs, for those who are deaf) come under the heading of *expressive* language. Gestures, grimaces, body movements, written words, and various art forms are included under the same heading. Expressive language takes two forms:

1. Initiative—the individual starts a communicative interaction with another
2. Responsive—the individual answers or behaves in some way in response to another's verbal initiation

Both initiating and responsive language skills are essential to effective communication. Simple check-

	No	Yes	Some-times
Does the child respond:			
to your voice by looking?			
to "What do you want?" by pointing?			
to "Give me the _____;" or "Find the _____" when there are no gestural cues?			
when there are gestural cues?			
to "Do you want it?" by nodding?			
with words?			
to "What do you want?" with words?			
to "Tell me about" with sentences?			
to "What is it for?" with phrases or sentences?			
to commands to get two different objects?			
to directions for two different actions?			
to questions with four- to five-word sentences?			

Fig. 16-1 Child's expressive response behaviors.

lists are important assessment tools. They can be thought of as *probes* or mini-tests. When the answer to a question is *yes*, a teacher has evidence of the child's progress. *No* indicates the need for follow-up to see if a problem exists. *Sometimes* suggest an emerging skill that is likely to benefit from specially focused learning activities.

Early Sentences.   Children's progress in putting words together to form sentences is as rapid as vocabulary growth during the early years. Learning to combine words in a particular order pays off; it enables the child to convey more complex thoughts. This

aspect of language acquisition is known as the development of syntax. It has several stages beginning with holophrastic.

Holophrastic language.   (*Whole phrase* is an easy way to remember the meaning of the term holophrastic.) At this stage, the child uses a single word to convey an entire thought. The intended meaning, however, is as unmistakable as a compete sentence. Holophrases always occur in reference to something the child sees or hears (or smells, tastes, or touches). In other words, what the child is experiencing supplies an environ-

	No	Yes	Some-times
Does the child initiate by:			
making sounds in combinations?			
making "talking sounds" to get attention?			
using inflectional patterns to ask questions?			
pointing to items he wants?			
asking for items by name?			
talking in phrases that sound like words?			
telling you what he sees in two- and three-word phrases?			
telling you what happened?			
telling you where something is?			
"telling about," using adjectives?			
asking why?			
"telling about," combining sentences with *and*?			
asking how?			

Fig. 16-2 Child's expressive initiating behaviors.

mental context for the intended meaning. The child's intonation or voice inflection also contributes to meaning as do gestures such as pointing or looking up. The single word "Doggie," depending on context, infection, and gesture, can be readily understood to mean:

"I want to play with this dog" (while toddling after the dog).
"See the dog" (while pointing to a dog).
"Where did the dog go?" (while looking outside).
"Is that a dog?" (while pulling the fur on a stuffed animal).

During this period the child may use the same word for several objects or events. For example, *doggie* may mean *all* furry four-legged creatures; *bye bye* often means both the absence of someone as well as someone leaving. Later in this unit other kinds of overgeneralizations will be discussed.

Telegraphic speech.   Toward the end of the second year, the child begins to speak in simple two word sentences. These sentences convey meaning even though many words are left out. Hence the term *telegraphic,* because of the similarity to the way telegrams were written. Few parents or caregivers mistake the intent of the telegraphic statements or demands. Following are several such *sentences,* recorded on a 2-year-old:

Mama's purse?
Daddy bye-bye.
Baby hungry.
All done!

These abbreviated two word phrases are an important milestone in language acquisition. They indicate that the child is learning the word order (syntax or grammar) of the language. Without appropriate word order, words cannot convey meaning, especially as sentences get longer. The following example has all of the correct words for a reasonable request: "Can door you the so come open will up I?" Without conventional word order it is going to take awhile to figure out what the child wants!

The Development of Language Complexity.   Between 2 and 5 years of age, language acquisition pro-

As children learn syntax, they are better able to make sentences and convey more complex ideas.

gresses rapidly in normally developing children. Children learn to:

Use all of the *wh* questions—*Who? Where? What? When?* and the seemingly never ending, *Why?*

Transform positives to negatives—*can/cannot, will/won't, is/isn't.*

Change verb forms, as required, to convey particular meanings: *run/ran*; I *will* go/I *went*; It is *raining*/It *has rained.*

Classify objects or animals—at first all dogs were just "dog." Now this dog is a collie-type of dog while the other one is a poodle-type of dog.

Indicate "more than one" through the use of plurals: boy/boys, kitty/kitties, lots of toys.

Convey ownership: mine!, hers, our, theirs, Daddy's.

(See Allen and Marotz (1994) for more detailed age-by-age analysis.)

Overregularizations.   The years of rapid language development are characterized by several kinds of errors. Developmentally, these should be thought of as misconstructions, rather than as errors. They repre-sent children's *best efforts* to apply the complex rules of the language to the situation at hand. Often the mis-constructions occur because children are trying to regularize the irregular, this leads to *overregularization.* Many children will say *digged* instead of *dug* for awhile. When they say *digged*, they are relying on an earlier learning that called for adding *ed* to a verb to indicate action in the past. These children, as yet, have no understanding of such things as irregular verbs. In a sense, *digged* is right. The child is applying the rule correctly. They are wrong only in not having learned when *not* to apply it.

Young children also mix up and overgeneralize var-ious forms of plurals. They may say feets instead of feet, mouses or mices rather than mice, gooses rather than geese. According to Rathus (1988) such *errors* aid rather than hinder language learning:

overregularization does represent an advance in the develop-ment of syntax. Overregularization stems from accurate knowledge of grammatical rules—not from faulty lan-guage acquisition. In another year or two, mouses will become boringly transformed into mice, and Mommy will no longer have sitted down (p. 277).

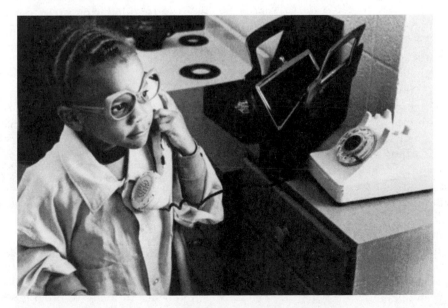

Between two and five years of age, language learning is rapid.

When such *errors* occur, the adult, without emphasis or comment, simply uses the correct form—"Yes, the mice ran away." The child should not be criticized or corrected directly. Neither should children be made to feel self-conscious or cute, regardless of how charming or amusing an adult may find the misconstructions. Unless undue attention is focused on the situation, these perfectly normal irregularities will self-correct in good time.

By the end of the fifth year, the development of syntax is nearly complete. Most children will be adept at concocting compound and complex sentences and will have a minimum of 2,500 words in their expressive vocabulary. Furthermore, they will continue to add new words throughout their lives.

Teachers can expect 5- and 6-year-olds to understand most of what is said to them, but only *if they have the vocabulary*. Adequate vocabulary depends on a child having been raised in an adequate language environment. Some children are not so privileged. For example, a child who knows color names may fail to perform a color-matching task. Why? Because the word *match* (or the concept *match* in a task-related context) is not in the child's vocabulary. A teacher, several times a day, may have to teach the vocabulary related to given tasks. Failure to do so may result in some children being unable to catch on to what is expected of them and to be labeled slow or dull.

Nonverbal Communication.   Children's efforts to communicate nonverbally are important. Adults need to be aware of what children do, as well as what they say. This is especially important with children who have language problems or delays. A child who shrugs, scowls, smiles, flinches, or looks off into space is communicating. Teachers (and parents) should try to respond to such efforts as often as possible. A responsive language environment is crucial to the development of communication skills.

Augmentative communication systems.   Some children with severe disabilities do not acquire speech easily; others use some words but have such poor articulation that their speech is largely unintelligible. For these children, an augmentative system uses gestures, signs, symbols, or pictures. These systems can be relatively simple, using only a few gestures; or they can be complex, using a **voice synthesizer** connected to a computer. In most cases an augmentative communication system is developed and introduced by the speech therapist using input from the family and teacher.

For preschool children, most augmentative systems use either sign language (Zeece and Wolda 1995) or a picture/symbol exchange (Bondy and Frost 1994). When selecting an augmentative communication system, the issue of intelligibility is important: Will the people in the child's environment be able to understand and communicate with the child using the system? Many young children with severe disabilities do not have the fine motor skills necessary to use sign language effectively. For these children, a picture or symbol based system may be a better choice. When introducing an augmentative communication system, it is important to choose signs or symbols that are functional for the student and occur frequently in the child's environment (Reichle et al. 1992). This will provide many opportunities for the child to practice the sign or symbol throughout the day. Children using augmentative communication systems should be encouraged to use their systems in all different environments and activities including snack time, on the playground, during circle time activities, and during free play. Using the system across activities will promote generalization and improve communication skills.

Signing

Signing is a natural part of communication in an early childhood setting. Short expressive gestures, songs, and fingerplays have been used successfully with young children for years. Think about the hand gestures used with such nursery classics as "The Eensie Weensie Spider," "Head, Shoulders, Knees, and Toes," or even "Old McDonald Had a Farm" (Zeece and Wolda 1995, p. 4).

Signing is a natural part of communicating in an early childhood setting. Teachers and children have always clarified what they were saying by using signs at specific moments. In inclusive programs, a simple sign system whose complexity can be geared up or down, offers a tremendous boost to language and communication development for all children. Signing is both functional and fun for children who are preverbal or nonverbal, learning a second language, gifted and in need of ongoing challenge, or shy about speaking up. Signing also is successful with children with cognitive and behavioral disorders.

The sign language that Zeece and Wolda refer to in their article is SEE2, *Signing Exact English* (the numeral 2 sets this system apart from another system with the same initials: Signing Essential English). According to the authors, teachers can teach beginning signing with very little training if they are willing to learn along with the children. They offer the following guidelines for teachers:

> Observe the classroom to see what signs are already being used and build on these. Well known nursery rhymes and songs are recommended as a good starting point.

> Introduce a sign in the context of activities that interest children, at their level of understanding, with adaptations made for individual differences and a child's willingness and ability to participate.

> Move slowly and incrementally, pick favorite, familiar activities that both teacher and children enjoy. By watching adults who enjoy signing, children learn that signing serves a valuable and useful function.

> Speak and act naturally when signing; avoid speaking louder than usual or using exaggerated speech. Natural speech patterns convey that this is an accepted, everyday way of communicating.

Zeece and Wolda conclude their insightful and informative paper by pointing out that signing can be an exciting and valuable component in inclusive early childhood programs. "Differences are not only accepted, they are fostered" (p. 8). NOTE: At the end of this excellent article the authors provide a comprehensive list of resources for those interested in exploring signing in early childhood education.

WHAT TEACHERS DO

Teachers have a major role in facilitating language development in infants and young children. The bedrock foundation for building children's language and communication skills, according to Schwartz et al. (1993) is the social communicative context of the environment. This means that in the inclusive classroom teachers will engineer a social context where people are sensitive to children's attempts to interact with others and where the physical environment and the people in it make communication easy and enjoyable for children. In this context, teachers and children become partners who share responsibility for selecting and maintaining communicative interaction. It is an environment arranged to prompt both children's language and an appropriate degree of teacher-responsiveness (not too much and not too little).

Arranging a Language-Learning Environment.   To promote language development, teachers arrange the learning environment so that every child has many opportunities to talk. Teachers also make sure there is plenty to talk about. Activities are arranged so that both materials and teachers are responsive to children's language efforts. The basics of arranging an effective early learning environment are covered in Unit 14. Teachers' skills and attitudes are discussed in Unit 12. Concepts specific to language acquisition are reviewed here.

Teachers' Expectations.   The environment should be consciously arranged so children are both expected to

Teachers make sure there is plenty for children to talk about.

communicate and have reasons for communicating. Using language then becomes an unpressured yet integral part of all classroom activities. Teachers also provide a relaxed atmosphere in which children are allowed plenty of time to say what they want to say. Highly verbal children are helped to learn to listen, so that less assertive or less verbal children have a chance to talk also.

Teachers themselves work at being good listeners and alert responders. They answer children in ways that indicate they are interested and wanting to hear more. One of the ways that teachers convey interest is by responding with *open-end* questions. They avoid questions that can be answered *yes* or *no,* or have only one right answer. When a child says, "We went to Grandma's yesterday," the teacher might reply, "And what did you do at Grandma's?" Contrast that response from the teacher with: "Did you have a good time?"

While teachers need to be good responders, it is important they not talk too much. Rarely can children maintain interest in long and wordy responses. Nor can they remain interested in a response that tangents off to fit the adult's perception of where the conversation should go. Children learn language by engaging in language, not by standing around while adults talk at them. *Teachers do not need practice in talking,* children do. In an effective early learning program. talking is going on all of the time, but it is children who are doing most of the talking. Teachers are serving as facilitators, sometimes prompting, sometimes questioning, sometimes reflecting a child's thoughts back to the child (a sure signal to the child that the teacher is really listening).

The role of questions.   Questions, asked or answered, are an important part of language acquisition. A child who turns away without responding when someone says "Hi, how are you today?" quite effectively ends the exchange. Rieke, Lynch and Soltman (1977) point out that if this happens frequently, teachers, family, and playmates may quit trying to communicate. The child loses out on two important sources of learning:

1. The language play and practice that facilitates language acquisition.
2. The necessary information that most children get through everyday verbal exchanges.

Teachers ask questions *only* if they expect (and are willing to wait for) answers. If an answer is not forthcoming the child is helped to formulate one. It may be a simple verbalization or gesture originated by the child, or a response modeled after one the teacher provides. In any event, the child is expected to respond. Children, both normally developing and those with developmental problems, soon fall quite naturally into the routine of responding, if teachers' expectations are realistic and consistent.

It cannot be overemphasized that teachers should not talk at children excessively; on the other hand, they do need to be responsive when children initiate interactions. Several years ago the first author and a colleague conducted a study of children's efforts to communicate (Allen and Ruggles 1980). In the several free play situations that were studied, 65 percent of children's questions and adult-directed comments got no adult response on the child's first attempt. Some children gave up, didn't try again, at that particular time. Others kept trying, getting louder and more insistent. When a teacher finally did respond, it was often impatiently, or with a reprimand about the child's insistence. In either event, both teaching and learning opportunities were lost. (This issue will be discussed further under *incidental teaching.*)

Activities.   Children need to have many things to talk about. They need novel materials to ask questions about. They need excursions, preferably simple ones such as a visit to the house under construction across the street, to practice verbal recall. They need easily managed picture books that enable them to "read" the story. They need songs and rhymes, chants, and play with words. They also need active play for prompting language of every kind. For children in need of special help with language skills, Kaczmarek (1982) emphasizes the importance of materials and equipment that require physical activity:

> Gross and fine motor activities can be pleasant and powerfully reinforcing contexts for systematic language/communication intervention. Manipulating materials in fine motor activities and exercising large muscles in gross motor activities are frequent favorites of many handicapped and nonhandicapped children, . . . since the language required in such activities is

appropriate to the activity, linking the two is apt to aid in rapid skill acquisitions (p. 22).

Direct Assistance.   Many children with developmental problems require direct and specific assistance from teachers in order to develop independent language and communication skill. Direct assistance is used to augment, not replace, the rich and responsive communication context that is the tenor of a quality inclusion program. Schwartz et al. (1993) offer a hierarchy of direct teaching strategies:

Choice-making: the teacher presents two options and asks the child to make a choice.

Mand-model: The teacher directs a request to the child.

Topic continuation: The teacher follows the child's conversational lead.

Time-delay: The teacher blocks access to the desired material or activity while looking at the child expectantly.

Incidental teaching: The teacher waits for a child to initiate and then responds immediately in a way to prompt a response from the child.

The authors point out that the degree of support to be given will vary across and within children. It also will vary according to the child's developmental needs, the familiarity of the task, the familiarity of the child's communicative partner, and the child's motivation at the moment. Here we will examine only one of the strategies, incidental teaching.

Incidental teaching.   Hart and Risley (1982) demonstrated conclusively that incidental teaching is an effective strategy for improving language. Their research focused on both normally developing children and children with developmental delays. Incidental teaching is defined as a child-initiated interaction between an adult and an individual child. Usually the child is engaged in free play or some other child-initiated activity. He or she may be seeking information, assistance, materials, feedback, or reassurance. This means the adult can make use of a naturally occurring reinforcer to promote a brief but immediate learning episode. Furthermore, the teaching

opportunity is perfectly matched to the individual child's learning requirement of the moment: The child is initiating the *lesson* based on an interest and a need. The essential feature in incidental teaching is that *the child initiates the contact.* The more frequently a child contacts a teacher, the more opportunities there are for teachers to teach and for the child to learn. It is important, therefore, that each child make frequent contacts. To ensure such frequency, teachers need to be:

Readily available and eager to foster learning according to each child's individual skill level

Interested in what the child is offering or inquiring about; prompt and positive in making a response (the response may be verbal, it may be giving physical assistance, or giving additional materials and equipment)

Conscious of keeping the contact brief and focused on the child's expressed interest

Sure the contacts are pleasant, even fun, for both the child and the teacher

During an incidental teaching episode the teacher never tells a child "No, that's wrong," never criticizes, reprimands, drills, or lectures. The whole point of incidental teaching is to have the child find the encounters so pleasant, so rewarding that he or she will return to the teacher again and again for more teaching and more learning.

Incidental teaching—an example: Emily, a 4-year-old with a language delay, held a paint apron up to the teacher. The teacher knelt down, smiled, and waited, giving Emily time to make a request. Emily remained silent. After a moment the teacher said, "Emily what do you need?" (The teacher did not anticipate Emily's need by putting the apron on for her.) When Emily did not answer, the teacher asked, "Emily, do you want help with your apron?" Emily nodded. "Tell me 'apron'," prompted teacher. Emily made a sound somewhat similar to apron and the teacher said, "Yes, *apron.* Here, let me put it over your head. Now, I'll *tie* it." The teacher's last sentence modeled *tie*, the next word that would be expected once Emily had learned to say *apron.*

Had Emily not said *apron,* the teacher would have put the apron on and tied it anyway. The teacher also would have described the procedure in simple language as above. Never should a child be scolded, nagged, or coaxed. If teachers introduce pressure into incidental teaching opportunities, many children stop making the contacts. Some do without. Others turn to communicating their needs less appropriately through whining, crying, or sulking. Children who are most in need of the highly individualized help that makes incidental teaching so effective are usually the first to be put off at any sign of pressure.

SPEECH IRREGULARITIES

Speech irregularities, or dysfluencies, are perfectly normal. Most children, 80 percent or more, will show some kind of dysfluency during the early years. These need not be viewed as worrisome. For a time, the ability to formulate thoughts and ideas is greater than the child's ability to pronounce words correctly or to get the words organized into sentences that make sense. The irregularities that early childhood teachers are most likely to encounter will be discussed briefly.

Articulation Errors.   Articulation refers to the production of speech sounds. Perfectly normal articulation errors are likely to occur as young children work

Articulation refers to the production of speech sounds.

at mastering the complex sounds that make up everyday speech. Misarticulations usually are classified as omissions, substitutions, additions, or distortions.

- *Omissions.* Sounds are left out, often at the beginning or end of words: "That's my agon (wagon)," "Here's the boom (broom)."
- *Substitutions.* Interchanging sounds such as b and v: "Put the balentines on the vack seat," or replacing one sound with another: "wabbit" for "rabbit."
- *Additions.* Inserting sounds not part of a word: "warsh" (wash) or "Notta now" (Not now).
- *Distortions.* Deviations in speech sounds usually occur because of tongue misplacement or missing teeth as is the case with many 6-year-olds: "schwim" for "swim" or "tink" for "think."

Lisping.   Rarely is lisping (pronouncing *s* as *th*) a worrisome problem in preschool children. Seldom does it persist. Exceptions may be those few cases where the child's lisp has been showcased by adults who think it is cute. If lisping should continue beyond the primary grades, parents are usually encouraged to seek consultation.

Dysfluency.   Stuttering is a common word for dysfluency or fluency disorders. Cluttering is another term also used to label a fluency problem. (Both terms are losing favor among developmentalists and speech and language clinicians.) *Dysfluency* better describes children's excessive repetition of particular sounds or words, noticeable hesitations between words, extra sounds, or the undue prolonging of a sound. Such speech irregularities are common, even normal. To label a young child as a *stutterer* is unwise, in part because of the self-fulfilling consequences discussed in Unit 5. Most children outgrow their dysfluency (Prins 1983). For those few who do not, it may be that too much attention was focused on the dysfluency during the child's early years.

Guidelines.   A developmentally common speech irregularity seldom needs to turn into a major problem. Teachers and parents can help to forestall such a consequence by practicing preventive *do's* and *don'ts*.

Teachers and children should have fun with language activities.

What adults can do:

1. Make sure the child is getting good nutrition, adequate rest and many more hours of active play than viewing television each day.
2. Provide comfort, care, and support; reduce tensions as much as possible, (difficult, but not impossible even in this hurried world).
3. Have fun with the child and with language; inject humor, simple rhyming activities and simple riddles into everyday routines.
4. Discipline with calmness, firmness, and consistency; avoid harshness, ridicule, or teasing.
5. Offer activities where the child can be successful, develop self-esteem.

What adults should not do:

1. Do not correct or nag the child; avoid saying, "Slow down," "Take it easy," "Think before you speak."
2. Do not call attention to dysfluencies directly or indirectly; the child becomes all the more tense when an adult focuses intently with exaggerated patience, a forced smile, or a rigid body, waiting for the child to "get it out."
3. Do not interrupt a child or act hurried; young children need plenty of time when trying to put their ideas into spoken language.

4. Do not compare a child's speech with another child's, especially if the comparison is unfavorable to either.
5. Never attempt to change a child's handedness. It is little more than myth that hand dominance and speech disorders are related.

These suggestions are well summarized by what one group of speech and language specialists call *benevolent neglect* (Rieke et al. 1977). Benevolent neglect is based on accepting common errors. To correct a child unnecessarily undermines the child's confidence as a speaker. If children are to improve their language skills, they must keep talking. Children who fear they will be criticized each time they speak will speak less and less. Rieke and her colleagues offer adults an important rule: *Never force a child to repeat anything that you have understood* (p. 43).

Referral.   The importance of not overreacting to perfectly normal speech and language irregularities cannot be overemphasized. On the other hand, if a genuine problem exists, it needs to be identified as early as possible and an intervention program put into effect immediately. The early childhood teacher may be the first to perceive a problem. (See Unit 10, the teacher's role in early identification.) Whenever a teacher is in doubt as to whether a child has an actual problem, parents should be counseled (and assisted, if need be) to seek help. Parents often have the feeling that *something* may be wrong. On the other hand parents can become so accustomed to their child's speech that they do not realize how poor it actually is. Speech, language, and hearing (audiology) clinicians who specialize in young children provide the most reliable testing and consultation.

Early warning signs.   Knowledge of normal development and skills in observing children help teachers to recognize early signs of a possible problem. The Speech-Language-Hearing Division of Kansas University Affiliated Facility at Lawrence, Kansas, offers the following suggestions about what to look for and when to counsel parents to seek help. Consultation is indicated if a child:

Is a year late in acquiring any speech and language skill

Is not aware of sounds or noise

Is not talking by 2 years of age

Leaves off beginning consonants after 3 years of age

Uses markedly faulty sentence structure after 5 years of age

Uses mostly vowel sounds in speech

Is noticeably nonfluent after 6 years of age

Regularly uses a voice which is monotone, too loud or too soft, too high or too low for the child's age and sex

Sounds as if he or she were *talking through the nose,* or has a cold when none exists.

Has frequent ear infections *and* signs of possible delay

Intervention.   Young children with speech and language problems need an individualized intervention program. For best results the early childhood teacher and the therapist work together in designing, implementing, and evaluating the intervention. The speech therapist may work with the child directly in the classroom or may remove the child from the classroom for short individual sessions. It is becoming commonplace for the therapist to move with the child in the classroom, using the ongoing activities as the context for specialized instruction (Kaiser, Yoder and Keetz, 1992). If the teacher and the therapist decide that the child would benefit from **pull out** therapy sessions, these sessions are short, (usually a half-hour or less) once or twice a week.

Treatment may be largely ineffective unless therapy activities are coordinated with classroom and home activities. This allows practice throughout the day in situations that can be both fun and rewarding for the child. Therapists can promote classroom cooperation by informing teachers regularly about what goes on: the particular skills the therapist is working on and the progress the child is making. Therapists also can demonstrate specific strategies for the natural setting where the usefulness of language is obvious to the child.

The foregoing does not imply that teachers are expected to become language specialists. They can, however, readily learn simple procedures for facilitating individual children's speech and language devel-

opment. An example might be working on getting a child to make the initial "b" sound. As a demonstration for the teacher, the therapist helps the child make the sound. The teacher and child practice several times in the presence of the therapist. The teacher then works with the child whenever an opportunity presents itself. The teacher uses incidental teaching strategies and the child learns quickly because making the "b" sound always is related to something the child wants or is interested in.

BILINGUALISM AND ENGLISH AS A SECOND LANGUAGE

Many communities have concentrations of families who speak little or no English. These may be families who are recent newcomers to the United States from many places around the world. They also may be minority cultures as Spanish-speaking families in some parts of the United States or French-speaking families in parts of Canada where the language of the schools and government is English.

While English as a second language (ESL) is common in our schools and child care centers, research offers no consensus on the "right" way to teacher non-English speaking children. Increasing numbers of programs, however have a teacher, aide, or parent assistant who speaks both English and the alternate language. This person serves not only as translator but also as interpreter of community customs. Cook, Tessier, and Klein (1992) give this example:

> One difference often noticed is the degree to which different languages expect or avoid eye contact. Teachers who do not understand social differences may accuse the Indian or Puerto Rican child of not paying attention when he or she is avoiding eye contact to show respect (p. 248).

Everything in this unit about facilitating language acquisition applies to helping children acquire a second language. The importance of not pressuring, reprimanding, or correcting a child's efforts needs to be underscored. At the same time, teachers must expect children to talk, both in their own language and in the language they are learning, as much or as little as they are able.

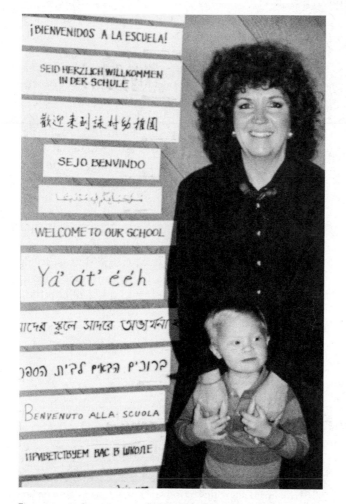

Languages from around the world are found in today's schools and child care centers.

For young children, drill and direct instruction is counterproductive. In the first author's years of working with children from other countries, incidental teaching has proven to be the gentlest and most effective approach. A young child learns how to get what he or she wants (powerful motivation) through language interactions with an adult who can be trusted to accept whatever responses the child can make.

Neither developmental damage or serious delay comes from learning a second (or third) language during the preschool years. There is evidence that bilingual children may be advanced in cognitive development compared to children who speak only one language (Hakuta and Diaz 1985). It is true that bilingual children may have a temporarily lower IQ score. This seems to occur only while they are learning the second language (Bee 1992). The many differences these children must accommodate, not only language but social customs and expectations as well, might account for the temporary regression. One has only to think for a moment about how difficult it must be for a child to be thrust into a culture where teachers do not even know how to say his or her name properly! This is especially true of children from Southeast Asian countries whose names and manner of addressing others is so very different. Yet, so much of an individual's self-esteem is centered on being addressed appropriately. It is critical, according to Morrow (1989), that teachers learn how to use both the child and the parents' names. This serves as a positive way to establish, from the start, an effective home–school relationship. See Bunce (1990) for an excellent overview of approaches to facilitating language and literacy in children who are bilingual and bicultural.

Pronouncing a child's name correctly is important to the child and to the family.

A final note on bilingual or non-English speaking children (as well as English speaking children with a dialect): Teachers need to discriminate between language delays or deficiencies and language differences.

SUMMARY

Learning to speak and use the native language is probably the most complex of the developmental tasks mastered by infants and young children. Explaining how children do it has been the subject of thousands of research studies as well as major, and often conflicting, theoretical formulations. In spite of disagreements about how children accomplish this difficult task, most children do, and with little apparent effort,. Without specific instruction, children move through the developmental sequences in speech and language acquisition, from crying, cooing, and jabbering to producing complex sentences and many-syllabled words in their first five or six years. Speech and language irregularities come and go, and appear to be self-correcting unless the child is pressured.

A number of young children have problems speaking or learning the language; some children have trouble with both. Problems may range from developmentally normal delays and dysfluencies to serious problems requiring the services of a speech and language specialist. An undiagnosed hearing loss is always a possibility and needs to be ruled out first in diagnosing a language delay or impairment in a young child. A stimulating classroom environment with interesting materials and activities, coupled with incidental teaching, has proven effective in enhancing the speech and language skills of all children at all levels of language development.

Teachers' knowledge of normal development and their skill in observing children is essential to identify children with language problems. It is important that teachers discriminate between language that is developmentally delayed or deviant and language that is culturally different. An increasing number of children in our schools are bilingual, even trilingual. These children, in an appropriate learning environment, experience no serious disruption in language or cognitive development.

STUDENT ACTIVITIES

1. Listen to a child between 3 and 6 years of age. Record 25 spontaneous language samples in the child's home or classroom. (Review language sampling techniques in Unit 10.) Decide if the child's language is developing normally, is accelerated, or delayed. Substantiate your decision.
2. Write down or taperecord at least 15 verbal responses of adults while they are caring for a child or children between 1 and 3 years of age. Is there evidence of motherese? Specify which responses.
3. Select a partner to play a 3-year-old who approaches you, the teacher, with a sweater in hand. The child asks,

"My sweater?" You want to increase this child's language skills in general. Demonstrate ways to do this by using incidental teaching strategies.
4. Work in small groups of four or five. Appoint a recorder. Generate as many ways as possible, including nonverbal, to let a child know you are interested in his or her new shoes and want to hear more about them.
5. Select a partner to act as the parent of a 3-year-old who says to you, the teacher, "I'm really concerned. Ryan has been stuttering the last two weeks." Counsel this parent.

REVIEW QUESTIONS

A. *Short Answer.*
1. Explain the difference between speech and language.
2. What is *motherese?*
3. What is the difference between receptive and expressive language?
4. Give five examples of nonverbal communication.
5. List four types of articulation errors.
6. Define *benevolent neglect* as related to speech and language development.
7. List five indications that a child should be referred for speech and language assessment.
8. What is the effect of bilingualism on a young child's cognitive development?

B. *True or False. Choose the best answer.*
T F   1. Language may or may not involve speech.
T F   2. Newborns have no means of communicating.
T F   3. Echolalia is a worrisome problem in speech and language development.
T F   4. By first grade, the typical child may have a receptive vocabulary of 14,000 words.
T F   5. Holophrastic language originated in India.
T F   6. A young child should always be corrected for overregularizing verb forms.
T F   7. In an incidental teaching episode, it is always the child who initiates the event.
T F   8. The term dysfluency is preferred to the terms stuttering and cluttering.
T F   9. Teachers should not try to carry out speech and language intervention activities in the classroom.
T F   10. There is one preferred way to teach ESL.

C. *Rearrange in appropriate sequence (from earliest to most complex) normal language development.*
1. telegraphic speech
2. grammatical overregularizations
3. crying
4. vocal intonation
5. holophrastic speech
6. echolalia
7. complex sentences
8. babbling
9. first words
10. cooing

REFERENCES

Allen, K.E., and Hart, B. (1984). *The early years: Arrangements for learning.* Englewood Cliffs, NJ: Prentice-Hall.

Allen, K.E., & Marotz, L.R. (1992). *Developmental profiles: Prebirth to Eight.* Albany, NY. Delmar.

Allen, K.E., and Ruggles, T. (1980). Analysis of teacher–child interaction patterns in the preschool setting. Paper presented at the Alice H. Hayden Conference, Seattle, WA.

Bates, E., O'Connell, B., and Shore, C. (1987). Language and communication in infancy. In J.D. Osofsky (Ed.), *Handbook of infant development* (2nd ed.). NY: Wiley.

Bee, H. *The developing child.* (1992). NY: Harper and Row.

Bondy, A., and Frost, L. (1994). The picture exchange communication system. *Focus on Autistic Behavior, 9(3),* 1–19.

Bunce, B.H. (1990). Bilingual/bicultural children in education. In L. McCormick and R.L. Schiefelbusch (Eds.). *Early Language Intervention,* Columbus: Merrill.

Cook, R.E., Tessier, A., and Klein, L.S. (1992). Adapting early childhood curriculum for children with special needs. Columbus: Merrill.

Flavell, J.H. (1985). *Cognitive development* (2nd ed.) Englewood Cliffs, NJ: Prentice-Hall.

Hakuta, K., and Diaz, R.M. (1985). The relationship between degree of bilingualism and cognitive ability. In K.E. Nelson (Ed.), *Children's Language.* Hillsdale, NJ: Erlbaum.

Hart, B., and Risley, T. (1982). *How to use incidental teaching for elaborating language.* Lawrence, KS: H & H Enterprises.

Kaczmarek, L.A. (1982). Motor activities: A context for language/communication intervention. *Journal of the Division for Early Childhood.* 6, 21–36.

Kaiser, A.P., Yoder, P., and Keetz, A. (1992). Evaluating milieu teaching. In S.F. Warren and J. Reichle (Eds.), *Causes and Effects in Communication and Language Intervention,* 9–47. Baltimore: Brookes.

Kuczaj, S.A. II (1982). On the nature of syntactic development. In S.A. Kuczaj II (Ed.), *Language development: Syntax and Semantics. I.* Hillsdale, NJ: Erlbaum.

Lansky, B. (1986). *Baby Talk.* Deep Haven, MN: Meadowbrook.

Morrow, R.D. (1989). What's in a name? *Young Children,* 44(6), 20–33.

McCormick, L. and Schiefelbusch, R.L. (1990). Early language development. Columbus: Merrill.

Owens, R.E. Jr. (1984). *Language Development.* Columbus: Merrill.

Prins, D. (1983). *Treatment of stuttering in early childhood: Methods and issues.* San Diego: College-Hill Press.

Rathus, S.A. (1988). *Understanding child development.* New York: Holt, Rinehart, and Winston, Inc..

Reichle, J., Mirenda, P., Locke, P., Piche, L., and Johnson, S. (1992). Beginning augmentative communication systems. In S.F. Warren and J. Reichle (Eds.), *Causes and effects in communication and language intervention,* 131–156. Baltimore: Brookes.

Rheingold, H.L., Gewirtz, J.L., and Ross, H.W. (1959). Social conditioning of vocalizations in the infant. *Journal of Comparative and Physiological Psychology,* 52, 68–73.

Rieke, J.A., Lynch, L.L., Soltman, S.L. (1977). *Teaching strategies for language development.* New York: Grune and Stratton.

Schwartz, I.S., McBride, B., Pepler, L., Grant, S., and Carta, J.J. (1993). *A classroom-based curriculum for facilitating communicative independence in young children with special needs.* Paper presented at the Division of Early Childhood Conference, San Diego, December, 1993.

Snow, C.E., and Ferguson, C.A. (1977). *Talking to Children.* Cambridge, England: Cambridge University Press.

Speech, language, hearing development in preschoolers. Prepared by the Speech-Language-Hearing Division of Kansas University Affiliated Facility at Lawrence, KS (no date).

Warren, S.F., and Kaiser, A.P. (1988). Research in early language intervention. In L.S. Odom, and M.B. Karnes (Eds.), *Early Intervention for Infants and Children with Handicaps.* Baltimore: Brookes.

Zeece, P.D., and Wolda, M.K. (1995). Let me see what you say; let me see what you feel! *Teaching Exceptional Children.* 27(2), 4–10.

Facilitating Preacademic and Cognitive Learnings

OBJECTIVES

After studying this unit the student will be able to

- make a case against prescribed paper-and-pencil tasks in preschool programs; describe instead the learning activities that should be emphasized.

- suggest five or more ways that teachers can help young children with developmental problems learn to focus their attention on preacademic activities.

- discuss readiness in terms of both maturation and learning theories. Explain the implications of both for children with developmental problems.

- Describe seven basic preacademic skills needed by children with and without developmental problems.

- Demonstrate three or more ways that teachers can help children, including those who are developmentally impaired, become involved in preacademic group activities.

Both academic and preacademic are terms viewed with skepticism among many early childhood educators. The resistance arises from concern that their use might put a stamp of approval on a "pushed-down" elementary curriculum for young children. Terms such as cognitive or sensory-motor activities or intellectual experiences often are used as alternates. The term *emerging literacy* also is enjoying popularity.

EMERGING LITERACY

The majority of children in this country learn to read and write and do simple math between 5 and 8 years of age. The *norm*, or generally accepted time, for beginning such teaching is somewhere around the sixth birthday, in what we call first grade. This seems to be the age, in most literate cultures, when youngsters can best deal with such tasks. This assumes, however, that earlier and necessary learnings have taken place—that there have been adequate opportunities for the foundations of literacy to emerge.

Emerging literacy involves many and diverse skills that lead up to children becoming successful in reading,

writing and other academic expectations. The process of becoming literate begins in early infancy and continues throughout the developmental years. It is a combination of cognitive and social processes. Primarily, it is exposure to activities and people who read and write and use language in a variety of ways, thus ingraining such values in the child from infancy on.

Interest in emerging literacy has been growing, in part, because of concern over the enormous number of Americans who are **functionally illiterate**. There also is growing concern over the increasing number of children who start school without the early experiences and communication skills that enable them to understand and participate in an academic curriculum. These issues, along with many others, are addressed in this unit on facilitating cognitive and preacademic development.

As mentioned earlier, there is resistance to using terms like academic and preacademic in conjunction with programs for young children. However, a growing number of preschool teachers and administrators welcome at least one of the terms—*preacademics*. They see it as more descriptive, when properly defined, of the many types of learning activities that both characterize the well-rounded preschool program and are relevant to young children's ongoing learning experiences. Nevertheless, the issue is far from resolved.

IDENTITY CRISIS

Identity crisis in the field of early childhood education is the way Wolery and Brookfield-Norman (1988) refer to the differing viewpoints mentioned in the introduction. They point out that terms such as *preoperational* and *readiness* are commonly used to described the cognitive skills and abilities of children who are no longer infants, but are not yet reading, writing and doing arithmetic (p. 109). Though called preoperational or readiness skills, these skills in a very real sense, are preacademic skills—the skills most necessary for young children to acquire during the preschool years if later they are to engage in formal academic activities.

The term preacademics has become an issue, in part, because of a growing demand for more structured academic instruction in early childhood programs. Many parents, striving for what they perceive as best for their children, believe that early, formal instruction in reading, writing, and math will help their children succeed in school. Preschools and child care centers are pressured to demonstrate that children are doing more than playing, that they are learning "something worthwhile." The pressure has led to many early childhood programs emphasizing paper-and-pencil

Children need years of play with real objects.

tasks and workbook exercises. Such activities, however, represent an inappropriate and ineffectual teaching format for the majority of young children. They are also contrary to philosophical beliefs about appropriate early learning experiences. As Bredekamp (1987) points out:

> Children need years of play with real objects and events before they are able to understand the meaning of symbols such as letters and numbers. . . . Throughout early childhood, children's concepts and language gradually develop to enable them to understand more abstract and symbolic information.

BANNING PREACADEMICS: ILL-ADVISED?

Certainly, the foregoing is true; it is especially true for children with highly literate families that seem automatically to provide day-long opportunities for the development of their children's concepts and language. But what about infants and very young children whose family situations cannot provide them with the kinds of stimulation and learning opportunities that support concept and language development? Schickedanz et al. (1990), in a well-reasoned and timely article, asks if the movement to "ban academics in preschools" is not ill-advised in that it further delays those children who need it most? (p. 12). These children are denied opportunities to get the same kind of intellectual underpinnings that the majority of children get as a part of everyday family life. "For children who do not get academic learning at home, academically stimulating preschools are an opportunity equalizer" (Schickedanz et al. 1990).

These authors suggest further: "Preschoolers *are* ready for academic content—lots of it," and draw on their research for evidence. They offer a long list of academic-type activities that a young, middle-class child is likely to engage in almost daily with family members, usually the mother. Their conclusion is that it is the teaching methods, not academics per se, that is the preschool problem; that academic skills learning *can be imbedded* in experiences that are appropriate for young children. In other words, academic learning is not an either/or situation. We can provide young children with both: Bredekamp's "years of play with real objects and events" *and* academic kinds of learning experiences within the context of playful and appropriate activities that "preserve childhood" (to borrow a phrase from Greenberg 1990).

In truth, by whatever name—cognitive, language, sensory motor, intellectual, academic, or preacademic (the term used in this unit)—such activities are an integral part of most early childhood programs. However, to say it once again: *Never should the learning experiences be presented in the form of work books, ditto sheets, prescribed paper-and-pencil tasks, and* **rote memorization**. Such activities are not appropriate to any preacademic curriculum or to any child, regardless of developmental level. The focus, always, must be enjoyable activities that promote children's effective use of language, their emerging abilities to formulate concepts, and their interest in and curiosity about the world around them.

PREACADEMIC EXPERIENCES

Preacademic skills, including those related to concept development, can be observed from infancy on, even in children with developmental disabilities.

Example: A 9-month-old infant with a serious hearing impairment reached for the therapist's earring. The therapist took it off. The baby then grasped the therapist's chin and turned her head so he could see and then reach for the other earring. It seems obvious this infant already was exploring rudimentary math concepts of *twos* and *pairs* as well as the spatial concept of symmetry and balance.

Children with disabilities may place anywhere along the developmental continuum in preacademic skills. A child who has severe motor disabilities may be advanced in preacademic learnings. Obviously the hearing impaired infant mentioned above was off to a good start in understanding math concepts. How well this infant's lead would be maintained depends on the intervention services and learning opportunities available to him.

Many children with developmental disabilities never realize their cognitive potential; others excel far beyond their typically developing peers. This unit, therefore, will not approach preacademic learning for children with disabilities (or the gifted) as being somehow different

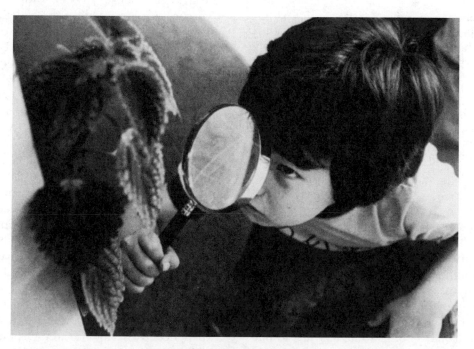

Children need to find out about things that interest them.

from preacademic learnings for all other children. Instead, the emphasis will be on *starting where the child is* and working from there, step-by-step. Subsequent units on specific disorders will describe adaptations that can be imposed on the basic principles described here.

In most early childhood programs, a daily preacademic period is the rule, rather than the exception. The teacher's role in these relatively structured periods should be to first set the scene and then follow the children's lead. Based on those leads, teachers then guide children into needed learnings. Always, teachers respond to children's interest, questions, and readiness for further information. Most importantly, the teacher guides and prompts children to *use* skills and information they already have.

Direct Teaching.   During preacademic activities the teacher is likely to engage in a limited amount of direct teaching. Teachers may suggest to children what to do and say. Whenever possible, however, they combine direct teaching with an indirect and facilitative approach.

> Example: A child asked, "What's that?" pointing to a picture of a little-known animal. The teacher engaged in direct teaching by reading the caption, *okapi*. (It would have been unrealistic to expect the child to "discover" the name of this exotic animal.) After reading the name, the teacher immediately asked the child to name it, too. The teacher then reinforced the correctness of the child's response: "That's right; it is an okapi." The child (and the other children) still seemed interested and so the teacher took advantage of this teaching opportunity. He opened another book with pictures of familiar jungle animals and helped the children find a somewhat similar animal (a giraffe) and discover the likenesses and differences between it and the okapi.

Preacademic tasks often are presented in structured settings at specified periods. They also should occur informally throughout the program day. A combination of the structured and the informal seems best suited to young children as long as *major emphasis is on the informal*. Example: A child with limited cognitive skills is trying to count buttons while learning to button his coat. A responsive teacher makes a game of it,

teaching the two skills together. This is done, informally, in the context of an activity that has meaning for the child. In such an approach, preacademic learnings often go unlabeled and unrecognized as "real learning" or "real school work." Thus, the work–play argument persists in spite of decades of research indicating that children's work and play are inseparable.

Early Learning: Eagerness and Anticipation. Children are born ready and eager to learn. Preserving and promoting this eagerness has long been a goal of early education. Rather than to drill and instruct, the role of the preschool teacher is to help children observe, ask, and find out more about things that interest them. Therefore, children of all developmental levels, from the most delayed to the most gifted, need activities that support awareness, curiosity, and the urge to question. Activities that involve sensory experiences—touching, seeing, hearing, tasting, and smelling—are essential. In other words, children need a learning environment where they are free to experience materials and activities through their senses in their own way and at their own pace. Children with sensory deficits need such experiences, too, if their eagerness to learn is to be preserved. However, they often need teachers' help in learning to used their undamaged senses to the best possible advantage.

As Katz and Chard (1989) put it, "Children's minds should be engaged in ways that deepen their understanding of their own experiences." At the same time, preschool teachers can advance *indirectly* but significantly, children's anticipation of learning to read, write, and do math (in other words, their emerging literacy). Teachers do this by writing out a child's questions, reading the question back to the child, helping the child find the answer or make a measurement. They help children keep a log by writing down what each child dictates about observed changes (a plant's growth perhaps). With these kinds of preacademic activities, most children, when they reach the primary grades, are ready and eager to learn to read about, tell about, write about (even measure) their experiences. It is, however, the responsibility of early childhood teachers to make convincing arguments on behalf of these important preacademic practices. Teachers must *sell* parents, administrators, and policymakers who may be pushing for work books and other paper-and-pencil tasks (Wolery and Bredekamp 1994).

Valuing Today's Learning.   An important goal in Preacademic planning is recognizing that *today's* living and learning is an important dimension in overall development. Enjoyable and challenging preacademic activities contribute to an everyday sense of well-being and accomplishment. The immediate developmental value of these activities is not to be questioned, even though they contribute to long-term, school-related accomplishments, Everything that is recommended for infants and young children—good nutrition, quality child care, medical attention—has the same dual purpose: To foster everyday well-being *and* long-term development.

Expecting children to engage in activities that do not relate to their interests or developmental level can snuff out a child's eagerness to learn. Children seldom enjoy or master tasks that are a poor developmental match (Hunt 1961). True, countless numbers of children survive the mismatch during their early years and go on to function adequately during their school years. Other children, and especially those with developmental problems, may feel immense frustration resulting in:

A poor opinion of themselves and their ability to
   learn;
A dislike of school, school work, and teachers;
School-related avoidance behaviors (crying, acting
   out, daydreaming, chronic stomach aches).

PREACADEMIC SKILLS

Preacademic skills are a mix of many skills from every area of development—cognitive, social, language, and fine motor. While the concept of readiness is a major issue in discussing young children and preacademic skills, the child from infancy on gives evidence of being ready for certain kinds of preacademic learnings.

Readiness and Preacademic Activities.   Since preacademic skills are a mix of many developmental skills, each skill could be labeled a *readiness skill.* Some readiness skills are directly related to future academic performance, others are indirectly related (large motor skills for example). A readiness skill might be described as the underlying behavior a child needs to learn or to perform particular tasks. Traditionally, readiness has been perceived in two different ways:

1. *Readiness as maturation.* In the traditional sense, readiness consists of built-in patterns of physiological changes. These account for the development of progressively more complex skills. This theoretical position led to the "ages and stages" approach to describing children's development. It also led to the notion that children should be allowed to "unfold" each at his or her own pace.

2. *Readiness as learning.* This theory attributes changes in children's skills to experience and the step-by-step mastery of developmental tasks. Example: if an infant has learned to recognize food, find its own mouth (put finger food and other objects into it), and hold a spoon right side up most of the time, that child is likely *ready* to begin the more complex behavior of spoon feeding. In other words, children are ready to learn a new and more complex skill when they can perform and synchronize the necessary though less difficult skills that precede the more complex skill.

From the *unfolding* (maturation) point of view, it is assumed children will learn what they need to learn simply by growing up in a safe, nurturing environment. Thus, when a child shows developmental irregularities or delays, the cause often is cited as immaturity: "The child is not ready. Let's wait and see." This puts many a child "on hold" during a critical developmental period and proves disastrous for young children who are at biological or environmental risk. The result may be further delay in development and a worsening of the child's problem. Often that is the case with infants with an undiagnosed hearing problem, whose language and cognitive skills become extensively but unnecessarily impaired.

The learning approach emphasizes that experience is critical; children must have opportunities to learn.

All readiness skills can be taught.

Many home and community environments do not (or cannot) support essential early learning experiences. In such settings, children may have little opportunity to master the necessary readiness skills that seem to come so *naturally* to most children. Learning theory also demonstrates that all developmental tasks and all readiness skills can be taught through a sequencing or task-analysis approach. These teaching strategies have proven especially useful in working with young children with developmental problems who often have difficulty acquiring readiness skills on their own. The teacher's task is to identify missing skills in each child and then teach them, step-by-step. Readiness skills likely to be missing include:

Adequate attention span
Ability to imitate
Perceptual motor efficiency
Fine motor controls (eye–hand–wrist coordination)
Ability to formulate concepts
Short-term and long-term memory
Ability to follow instructions

Each of these skill areas as well as specific prereading, prewriting, and premath skills will be discussed separately, though, in reality, they are inseparable. Preacademic skills are intertwined with each other and with

all other areas of development. This interrelatedness is the essence of the *whole child* concept of development. Example: When children are recalling their trip to the zoo, all skills come into play, even overlap, as the teacher helps children discuss and act out what they saw, heard, and did. This interrelatedness of developmental skills also makes a convincing argument against an academic, subject matter approach in the education of young children.

Paying Attention.   *Attention span,* the length of time an individual is able to concentrate on an activity or event, is critical to all learning. The ability to simultaneously *tune in* on certain aspects of the environment and *shut out* others is essential. When working a puzzle, a child needs to be able to focus on the frame board and the puzzle pieces while ignoring other children's play activities. As stressed in Unit 14, children's ability (or inability) to focus their attention depends largely on classroom arrangements.

Example: Jeri, a typically developing 3-year-old, picked up and put down puzzle pieces from several puzzles that were mixed and scattered about the table. She looked at the puzzle frames, put the pieces down, wandered around took a much-too-difficult puzzle off the shelf, dumped it out, looked at it briefly, tried to take a completed puzzle away from another child, left the area.

In this instance, Jeri's "short" attention span, at least for puzzle work, can be related directly to a poorly arranged environment. A child cannot be successful (or even interested) when materials are overly difficult or haphazardly presented. Many children have the potential for longer periods of attention. Yet, like Jeri, they do not stay with activities if the materials are in disarray, a poor developmental match, or uninteresting.

It is true that attractiveness of materials and the ways in which they are presented are important factors in determining children's concentration. Even so, there are children who have trouble becoming involved on their own, regardless of the attractiveness of the setting. They need help from teachers in getting started. Once their attention is engaged, however, they too learn to focus. Bailey and Wolery (1984), suggest several ways that teachers can help children of all developmental levels focus their attention:

- Provide materials that are appealing and colorful, can be manipulated, and have built-in feedback such as a jack-in-the-box.
- Offer participation as a privilege rather than a responsibility: children who finish putting blocks away *get* to come to stories.

- Give children an immediate role: "Julie has the punch to punch the train tickets."
- Instruct or prompt an activity: "I'll help you start a fence at this end. Where shall I put my first block?"
- Identify children's preferences for materials; preferred materials result in longer engagement.

Further strategies for increasing children's engagement with learning activities will be discussed in Unit 19 in the section on overly active children and attention deficit disorders.

Imitation and Modeling. As noted in several other units, the ability to *imitate* is essential to all learning. When trying to learn a new skill such as driving a car, jumping rope, pronouncing a new word, the first step, usually, is to try to model the behavior that was observed. This process (observing and modeling) is repeated until the learner is satisfied with his or her performance, or decides to abandon the effort. Most infants and young children imitate spontaneously. They do not have to be taught, but they do need good models and opportunities to practice. The many peek-a-boo games, finger plays, action songs, chants, and rhyming games found in most cultures probably

The ability to imitate is essential to all learning.

were devised (unintentionally) to motivate imitation in infants. Such activities, popular in most preschool programs, are there for the same reason.

A distinction should be made between *learning through imitation* and *learning to imitate*. Children who do not imitate spontaneously must be taught, if they are to learn other developmental skills. However, the inability to imitate often goes unrecognized and so becomes the cause of continuing learning difficulties. When a child with developmental problems is enrolled in a group, an informal assessment of imitation skills should be a priority. (A simplified version of a game such as Simon Says can tell a teacher a great deal abut a child's ability to imitate.) If imitation skills are lacking, initial teaching priorities should be concentrated in that area. Bailey and Wolery (1984) make the following suggestions for teaching children to imitate:

- Imitate the child. Imitating the child's vocalizations and gestures often stimulates the child and also reinforces the child's further efforts.
- Provide models appropriate for the child's level of development; if a child at 7 years of age is functioning more like a 3-year-old, then behaviors typical of the younger age should be the starting models, with special concentration on those behaviors the child already has.
- Provide whatever assistance is needed to help the child learn to imitate. Placing a mirror in front of the child, for example, allows the child to judge the accuracy of his or her imitations.
- If necessary, be directive in teaching the child to imitate. Physically put the child through an imitative response. (The teacher might say, "Marla, point to the circle," while stretching out the child's index finger and placing it on the "point-to" object. An encouraging and descriptive comment follows: Marla, look at that! You're *pointing* to the circle!")
- Make imitating a rewarding and playful experience; learning to imitate should be fun.
- Provide positive feedback and encouragement for approximations (first efforts) to an imitative response. When a child finally points to an object, even though it may not be the one requested, respond positively: "You're *pointing* to a blue truck. Good for you. Now let's find the red one and you can point to it, too.

Perceptual Motor Skills.   Perceptual motor skills are made up of two closely related processes. One has to do with understanding sensory messages: what is seen, heard, touched, tasted or smelled. The second is the translation of the messages into appropriate actions. Generally, more than one sense is involved in a response; this is referred to as sensory integration. Following are three examples of perceptual motor skills coupled with sensory integration.

1. A 2-year-old stops her play and turns at the sound of an engine. She looks up, moves her eyes back and forth, and then points to an airplane. This child is exhibiting integrated visual (seeing) and auditory (hearing) skills resulting in appropriately matched motor responses of turning, scanning, and pointing.
2. A 4-year-old picks up a bar of cocoa butter, smells it, bites off a corner, and then spits it out while making a wry face. The child is expressing appropriate smell and taste perceptions and responding with relevant perceptual motor responses: the cocoa butter smelled like candy, and she took a bite. It tasted more like soap than candy however, so she spit it out while making a face indicating an unpleasant taste.

Every preschool activity requires perceptual motor skills in one form or another; here the skills are stacking, bridging, and balancing.

3. A 5-year-old, during group time, reaches into the *mystery bag* and verbally identifies unseen objects by touch.

Every preschool activity involves various forms of perceptual motor activity. Outdoors there is climbing, jumping, riding wheel toys, watching a caterpillar creep, and splashing in puddles,. Indoors there is block building, play with table toys, painting, working with clay, coloring, cutting, and pasting. Music, stories, and dramatic play provide opportunities to rhyme, pantomime, and pretend. Such play activities help young children, regardless of their activities, practice the perceptual motor skills essential to everyday living.

Children with impaired perceptual motor skills often receive incomplete or distorted sensory messages. In some instances, children have become nearly immobilized because they are so distrustful of moving about. Example: Children with impaired depth perception are sometimes hurt and badly frightened by stepping off into unanticipated space. Thus, children with sensory problems need special activities, adapted materials, and additional support in using their intact senses. Some of these adaptations were described in Unit 14 on environmental arrangements; others will be described later in this unit and in subsequent units on specified disabilities.

Fine Motor Skills.   Fine motor skills include eye-hand coordination and efficient use of the fingers, hands, and wrists. These skills are closely related to perceptual motor skills. Both are essential in learning self-care skills (Unit 18) as well as learning to use all kinds of tools; paint brushes, hammers, crayons, and eventually pencils for printing and then writing. Practice in fine motor control is provided by preschool activities such as:

Water play—pouring, squeezing, measuring
Block building—stacking, bridging, balancing, putting away
Creative arts—painting, stitchery, hammering, wood working, clay, cutting, pasting, crayoning
Housekeeping—dressing dolls, pouring "tea," stirring "soup," and setting the table

Manipulative materials, sometimes referred to as *table toys*, are especially good for promoting perceptual motor skills. Among the most useful are:

Wooden beads and strings with metal tips
Puzzles and parquetry blocks
Picture dominoes and lotto games
Nesting and stacking cups, kitty-in-the-keg, form boxes
Pegs and peg boards, hammer and nail sets
Montessori graduated cylinders and color boards

When appropriately matched to children's skill levels, manipulative materials ensure practice sessions that are informal and fun for all children. They also can be used successfully by children with developmental disabilities because they are so readily adaptable. The following examples demonstrate how manipulative materials can be adapted or specially presented:

Offer only the largest size wooden beads with a stiff wire hanger on which to string them; a straightened coat hanger, ends wrapped with tape, works well.

Select puzzles with few pieces and each piece a recognizable object.

When a child has mastered the simple puzzles but the next ones seem too complex, teachers need to be inventive. For example, several of the inside pieces of more difficult puzzles can be taped down from underneath with a strip of Scotch tape doubled back on itself. These pieces remain in the frame when the child turns the puzzle out. Less is required of the child; fewer pieces have to be replaced to complete the task and the job is simplified because finding the fit for border pieces is usually easier. In addition, the task gradually can be made more difficult by taping down fewer and fewer puzzle pieces. The advantage to this procedure is that each time the child completes the task there is always the reward of seeing the completed puzzle. (The foregoing example, by the way, is an excellent illustration of a teacher's creative efforts at task analysis.) As an aside, the strategy might be altered in centers that teach children to take puzzle pieces out one-by-one. Instead of turning the puzzle over, the teacher might be the one to remove the free pieces and then let the child with the disability reassemble the puzzle.

Present only four or five of the largest nesting cups. Put them out in a straight line, in order. Hand them to the child, one-by-one, to ensure successful nesting from the outset. Then let the child begin to pick up the cups, but continue to present them in order. Gradually randomize the order of presentation, but revert to fewer cups, temporarily. As the child becomes proficient, cups can be added, one at a time. (For a child who has a more severe impairment, every other cup might first be presented to maximize size differences; the drawback is that the child does not get the quality of sensory feedback that is achieved when the cups are nested in precise order.)

Concept Formation.   Concepts and concept formation are difficult terms to define without becoming overly technical. For the purpose of this text, concepts will be defined as *internal images* or ideas (mental activities) that organize thinking. Concepts enable us to make sense out of our world. By continuously formulating new concepts, young children impose order on all of the many things they must learn during the early years. A number of subskills related to concept formation are described below in an effort to clarify the process.

Discrimination.   Concept development depends on the ability to *discriminate,* that is, to perceive likenesses and differences among related objects and events. Put even more simply, it is the ability to "tell things apart"; to specify "same or different"; to match objects, sounds, and ideas in terms of one or more attributes (characteristics). Opportunities to practice making

both simple and complex discriminations are found throughout the preschool day. Examples:

- At music time the teacher introduces a song asking who is wearing sandals? Boots? Running shoes? Blue socks? Striped socks? No socks?
- A variety of sorting tasks are available such as putting the yellow pegs in one compartment, the blue pegs in another.
- Unit blocks are replaced according to the size and shape drawn on the shelf.
- During a preacademic period, a patterned string of wooden beads may be presented for children to copy—a small round blue bead, a big square red bead, a long green bead—repeated several times. This task is complex in that the beads vary on three dimensions, shape, size, and color. It should be noted, too, that the fine motor and perceptual motor skills are demanding, as well. It might be that a child could make the necessary discriminations but not have the fine motor skills for stringing the beads. This is an instance where the teacher would need to make an adaptation in materials, perhaps providing a wire rather than a string for the child to thread the beads onto.

Discrimination tasks can be adapted to fit any developmental level. For gifted children the bead stringing task can be made more complex by introducing number concepts as well as color, space, and shape: repeats of three small round blue beads, two large square red beads, one long green bead. Or, it can be made very simple for a child with a developmental delay: a square red bead alternating with a square blue bead; or simpler yet, having the child select and string only large blue beads (with only large red beads in the basket as distracters). Adaptations for individual differences are unlimited.

Classification.   The process of imposing order on objects and events is another major characteristic of concept formation. This skill is sometimes described as the ability to classify; that is, to form *categories.* In other words, children learn that cats, dogs, and squirrels have certain characteristics in common: fur, four legs, a tail, and so on. On the basis of these shared

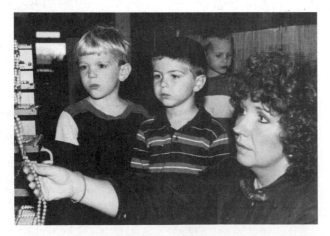

Concept development depends upon the ability to perceive likenesses and differences.

attributes, the creatures all fall into the category of *animal.* Each category is subject to further breakdown, as the child's experiences broaden. "Dog" becomes a category by itself when the child learns to discriminate among different kinds of dogs—Poodles, Collies, Airedales. Learning to classify, like learning to discriminate, can be taught.

Seriation. *Seriation* is the process of arranging objects and events along orderly and related dimensions (a prerequisite skill is the ability to make fine discriminations.) Everyday examples include:

Tall, middle-sized, shortest; and eventually, "These tall
   ones are taller than those tall ones"
First, last, next-to-last
Happy, sad, "saddest one of all"

Seriation experiences, like those in the above list, help children learn to make comparisons about quantities, time and space, and affect (feelings). Learning to tell about what happened in the order of occurrence is another seriation skill that many older preschoolers begin to master.

> Example, "Yesterday we went to Grandma's. We got to play in the attic. Then we had dinner but first Grandma made us wash our hands and face 'cause we got so dirty. After dinner Grandpa read to us and then it was time to go home and I slept in the car."

Many preschool activities lend themselves to seriation practice and to endless adaptations for children with limited abilities. For example, children can retell a story that has just been read, or teachers can ask, "What comes next?" when reading a familiar story. Sequenced picture cards (commercial or teacher-made) also are useful. The cards tell a story when arranged in proper order: The first card may show a child digging a hole in the ground, the second shows planting a seed and the third, pulling up a carrot. For more advanced children, the series can be longer and more complex, including pictures related to watering, weeding, and sprouting. For the very limited child, the teacher might use just two pictures, a child climbing up on a stool and then jumping down. At first, the

teacher and child can alternate placing the cards, with the teacher stating what comes *first* and what happens *next.*

Spatial and temporal relationships.   Learning how objects and events are related to space, to time, and to the child is another aspect of concept formation. Spatial and temporal (time) concepts include:

On, in, under
In front of, behind, next to
In between, in the middle, second from the end
Yesterday, today, tomorrow
Soon, afterwhile, later, not yet

Many children seem to learn such concepts automatically. However there are children, with and without developmental problems, who need direct instruction. Spatial and temporal concepts are best taught as children themselves are moving about in space and time. For example, each child must learn to recognize his or her body-occupying space in relationship to the body-space of others. This may not come easily and certainly it does not come early. Toddlers, as mentioned in Unit 4, may "plough through" other toddlers as if they did not exist.

Active play is especially good for developing spatial awareness. Outdoors, a teacher might comment, "Tim, you climbed *so high.* You are *on top of* the ladder box." If the child is having difficulty forming spatial concepts, the teacher should do an immediate follow-up: "Where are you Tim?" and wait for the child to respond. If the child does not respond, the teacher models the words, "High. On top." and when the child repeats the statement the teacher corroborates: "That's right, Tim. You are *high;* you are *on top.*"

Learning to understand *time,* is difficult for most children. "Yesterday is eons away and tomorrow can be expected at any minute" (Cook et al. 1987, p. 187). As with spatial concepts, time concepts are best learned in relationship to play and everyday activities. Short and more immediate time intervals are better understood in the beginning:

"Time to come in *after* you run around the track two
   more times."

Active play is especially helpful in children's development of spatial awareness.

"Snack comes when we finish this story."
"We will get back in time for lunch."

Memory.   The ability to remember what previously has been experienced and learned is a skill necessary to all new learning. Two kinds of memory are required: long-term and short-term (being able to remember what took place awhile back as well as what happened in the immediate past). Tasks requiring rote memorization are inappropriate for young children and of limited value for any age child. Activities that encourage children to practice remembering within their everyday work and play activities are the kind that foster learning. Such activities might include:

Conversational questions *of interest to the child* (with
    teacher prompts, after a suitable pause):
    What did you have for breakfast . . . (orange juice?
        cereal? anything else?)

Where does your kitten sleep? . . . (in a basket?)
What was the caterpillar doing on the leaf? . . .
    (crawling? chewing on the leaf?)
Remembering each others names and teachers' names,
    and using these names appropriately.
Remembering where materials are stored so as to get
    them out and put them away properly.
Telling what object (or objects) has been removed in
    games such as "cover the tray."
Story and picture reading activities as mentioned
    under seriation.
Leaving the bathroom in prescribed order for the
    next children who will be using it.

For children with cognitive, neurological, or related problems the teacher often begins memory training by telling the child what comes next: "The paper towel goes in the basket." The teacher follows up immediately: "Where does the paper towel go?" (The child only has to remember long enough to repeat the information (or comply). A child's memory system may be activated more slowly if he or she is delayed; therefore it is important to give adequate time to respond. In teaching towel disposal, for example, the teacher, must be allow time for the child's memory to become charged and produce action.

Following Instructions.   The ability to follow instructions and carry out requests is important. Children

A memory activity: putting materials away in their designated places.

with developmental problems often have trouble with such tasks. Whenever a child has repeated difficulty teachers ask themselves:

1. Does the child hear (or see) well enough to know what is expected?
2. Does the child have the necessary vocabulary to understand the request?
3. Does the child understand the concepts (understand *match* when the teacher says, "Match circles of the same color")?
4. Is the child able to imitate the behaviors expected, as when the teacher demonstrates how to fold a paper in half?
5. Are the instructions too complicated or given too rapidly?

Three- and four-step directions, spoken in rapid sequence, are more than most young children can manage. It is true that a few older preschoolers might be able to carry through on: "Would you be so good as to go to the sink and wet a sponge—I think there's one under the sink or in the bathroom—and then wipe up all that messy paint on the floor and halfway up the table legs?" Many others would be completely lost. A few might try to carry out the last step in the direction (the only thing they remember) by rubbing at the paint on the table leg with their hand perhaps.

The younger the child in age, experience, or developmental level, the simpler directions should be. *It is important that teachers take nothing for granted about what children understand.* For very young children and for children with developmental problems, directions should be given one at a time. The process works best when a teacher gets down to a child's eye level and speaks directly to the child. Language needs to be clear and free of unnecessary words or explanations as in the following example (based on the confusing and complex set of directions quoted above):

> "Marty, We're going to have to get this paint wiped up. Would you go to the sink (enough of a pause to let the child start moving toward the sink) and find a sponge?"
>
> When the child has sponge in hand, the teacher gives the next direction: "Now wet the sponge."
>
> If the teacher wants to make sure the child does not cross the room dripping water all the way, an

intermediate instruction should be given: "Squeeze the water out of it."

Some children might not know what the teacher expects, so the teacher says, "Like this," pantomiming how to squeeze a sponge. "Now let's go over and wipe up the paint on the floor." When that is accomplished, the teacher can draw the child's attention to the paint on the table legs.

Most children, unless they have a severe impairment, can learn to follow instructions if they are allowed to begin with one-step directions like those in the example. When the child has mastered one-step directions, it is logical to move to two- and then perhaps three-step directions, In an inclusion setting it is a good idea to pair a child with a developmental disability with a child that is developing typically: "Judi and John, will you get the chalk and the small chalkboards and put them on the big round table?"

Prereading, Prewriting and Premath Skills.   Other preacademic skills are more closely associated with reading, writing and math. These include:

- "Reading" a series of pictures on a page from left to right and top to bottom. (Many picture books and board games are set up to promote this kind of prereading, visual organization.)
- Pencil or crayon activities that begin to show some degree of eye-hand control (scribbling large swirling circles upon circles; making marks children often describe as *writing*; great effort and occasional success at writing their own name).
- Free style cutting with scissors. (Some children spontaneously try to "cut on the line.")
- Counting a row of objects from left to right (or top-to-bottom as in coat buttoning) by touching each in turn (one-to-one correspondence).
- Grouping objects in sets of two, three, or four.
- Identifying groups of objects as the same, more, or less.
- Understanding that different but similar sounds are not the same. (Numerous songs, fingerplays, poems, and teacher-improvised games contribute to this learning.)

None of these tasks are simple. They require at least minimal competence in the underlying skills discussed earlier in the unit. However, all preacademic skills can be taught. All can be sequenced to facilitate children's learning, including children with developmental disabilities. Learning to cut on the lines will be used as an illustration:

Julio was a 7-year-old with uncertain fine motor skills. Using a pair of specially designed scissors that allowed him to put his hand over Julio's, the teacher helped Julio learn to hold the scissors and then to "cut" the air with them. Next, the teacher prepared strips of paper about 3/4-inch wide with heavy lines drawn across them at one-inch intervals. The teacher held up a strip and instructed Julio to open his scissors. The teacher then inserted the strip between the scissor blades, in contact with one of the black lines, and said, "Cut." It was a simple matter for Julio to close the scissors. Success was immediate and evident: a cleanly cut piece of paper came off with each contact. To add interest to the task, the teacher soon switched to strips of brightly colored paper, feeling that Julio would not now be distracted from his cutting task by the variations in color. Julio's cuttings were put in an envelope to either take home or play with or paste into a "picture" at school.

PLANNING AND PRESENTING PREACADEMICS

A successful preacademic program depends on careful planning, whether the learnings are informal and incidental, teacher initiated and conducted at group time, or at assigned table work. How the materials are presented and how children are grouped also determines the success of the learning activities.

Grouping Children.   A preschool class of 15 to 20 children is best divided into three or four small groups for teacher-structured preacademic activities. The number of teachers, aides, and volunteers that are available usually determines the number of groups. Group size can be increased as children become more skilled and more experienced. The closer children get to their kindergarten year, the greater is the need to have opportunities to work in larger groups. Younger children and children with developmental disabilities continue to need smaller group experiences so teachers can direct help to specific delays and deficits.

Children often are grouped according to age and experience at the time of entry. After children's skills have been assessed, they can be regrouped according to abilities, interests, or special talents. Each child's group placement needs to be reviewed every three or four months. (See use of the Preschool Profile, Unit 10.) Reassessment is especially important for children in the middle ability range. Reorganization of these children's programs often is overlooked because teachers tend to concentrate on the brighter children and on the slower children. A child's social development also may be a factor in deciding on preacademic group placement. A shy child with high-level preacademic skills might be placed with children less skilled. This provides the shy child with opportunities to practice both preacademic and social skills in a low-keyed, noncompetitive situation. It also allows the shy but academically competent child opportunities to tutor other children which increases the child's self-confidence and sense of worth (Katz and Chard 1989). Social interactions are easier when they grow out of a child's competencies.

Arranging Preacademic Group Activities.   An overall goal for preacademics is to help children be interested, comfortable, and appropriately challenged. To ensure that children do participate actively in preacademic activities, the following arrangements are suggested. These are especially important with children who are delayed, overly active, or have trouble staying on task.

Short periods.   Start with short preacademic periods: three, four, or five minutes in the beginning. Gradually lengthen the time children are expected to stay. One of the first restructuring of group membership may be based on children's span of attention. Activities should always be concluded *before* children lose interest.

Familiar materials and activities.   Start with materials that children enjoy and are familiar with (the *problem of the match* once again): crayons, simple puzzles and manipulative materials, pictures of everyday objects to talk about, match, and group. Such materials allow most children to feel comfortable and competent, right from the start.

Clearly define each child's work space.

Individual work space.   Clearly identify each child's work space at the table or on the floor to promote independent work habits and respect for the personal space of others. Except for writing or drawing tasks, a 15 by 18 inch piece of felt makes a good individualized work area. The felt rectangle clearly identifies a child's space; it also reduces noise, and prevents materials from sliding around. Plastic food trays from the grocery store and vinyl placemats also can be used to define individual work spaces.

Individual setups.   Manipulative materials, collage materials, matching tasks, and many other types of materials are best presented in individual setups. Small shallow baskets or discarded produce or meat trays work well. Such an arrangement reduces the tendency that many young children, or children with behavior disorders have of grabbing and hoarding materials. It also reduces conflict while children are learning to work in relatively confined spaces.

Name cards.   Work spaces should be clearly labeled with each child's name on a card lettered neatly in large print script characteristic of the local primary grades. The name cards should stand up in holders that teachers can arrange according to current grouping plans. A name may be printed in glue and sanded while wet in order to give it a raised texture for a child with a visual impairment.

Preferred materials and activities.   Noting what materials and activities are preferred by which children is important. These can be presented several days in a row to firm up the child's comfort and competence. Preferred materials also are useful as takeoff points for increasing the complexity of a learning task, as a reinforcer, and as a motivator: "Jolene, after you finish matching the circles you can work the train puzzle."

Changing tasks.   If a child is inattentive or frustrated the teacher needs to observe the child in the context of the learning situation. Without fail, the problem resides not in the child but in the learning environment. Changes need to be made in the materials or activities so they more closely match the child's interests and ability level. Always it is well to have additional materials immediately at hand to present as alternates, or to offer to children who finish early.

Advance preparation.   Before children arrive, all materials for preacademic groups should be assembled and handy to where each group will meet. Once children are engaged, it is important their attention not be distracted by a teacher having to go in search of additional materials. Teacher's absence, even for a moment, while rummaging through a drawer on the other side the room, may prompt inappropriate behavior in children, making it difficult to get the activities back on track.

Transition activities.   From the start, children should be introduced to the idea of self-directed transition activities or *holding activities.* These are materials that children can work with independently while waiting for group activities to begin. Transition/holding materials are open-ended materials (no particular starting and stopping points) such as crayons, wooden beads to string, form boards and boxes, books to look at. They require little teacher supervision or assistance. Just before the planned activities are to begin, the teacher gives warning that it soon will be time to put aside the transition materials. Putting them aside

Teachers make everything ready before children arrive.

is just one more routine like all of the others that underpin the program day. All children, including children with developmental problems, can and should learn classroom routines. Occasionally, a child is truly reluctant to relinquish a transition activity; the teacher helps the child put the material aside, often with the promise that the child can go back to it during the next discovery learning period. (*The material then must be held aside for the child and the promise must be honored.*)

Moving about.   Young children cannot be expected to sit still, except briefly. To expect long periods of sitting still and being quiet is guaranteed to lead to behavior problems. All but the shortest preacademic periods need to include tasks where moving about is built into the task or is made legitimate by the teacher who encourages children to:

Go and get, or return materials: a magnifying glass, perhaps, to determine details on an insect.
Play "find the . . . " game: moving about the room to find something *round* or *red* or *growing*.

Include activities that make it legitimate for children to get up and move about during preacademic periods.

Stand and clap or jump or spin around the number of times the teacher indicates.

Walk around the table to observe or help another child.

Enjoying Preacademics.   Preacademic activities should be enjoyable for children and for teachers. When preacademic sessions are fun, children will be eager to participate. Eagerness to learn invariably promotes successful learning. Successful child learning is enjoyable for teachers: it represents a teacher's success as a teacher. With that kind of reward (motivation) teachers tend to put more and more of themselves into their teaching. The result? Their teaching gets ever better and their enjoyment increases proportionately. A positive and mutually reinforcing system is activated for both children and teachers.

SUMMARY

Preacademics is a term that is defined variously among early childhood educators. In this text it refers to a range of informal, cognitive, language, and perceptual motor tasks that are a part of most early childhood programs. Preacademics does not include drills and workbooks or paper-and-pencil tasks that some policymakers argue are the ways to enhance a child's future school success. It is true that appropriate preacademic experiences do contribute to future school learning, but that is a secondary, although important function. Promoting children's day-by-day integration of developmental skills and fostering their eagerness to learn is the major value of preacademic activities throughout the early years.

Preacademic skills are sometimes equated with readiness skills; both can be taught if they do not come about in due course through normal developmental processes. In other words, a child's short attention span or inability to imitate or follow instructions is not ascribed to immaturity. Instead of a "wait-and-see" approach, the specific skills are taught, step-by-step, thereby avoiding further and additionally damaging developmental delay. In addition to attention span, imitation skills, and following instructions, other specific preacademic skills include perceptual motor skills, memory, and the ability to formulate concepts. Certain prereading, prewriting, and premath skills may also be subsumed under preacademics; but these are child-initiated, not teacher directed "seat work" activities.

Small group activities, based on a variety of preacademic learning opportunities, are offered in most early childhood programs. When attractively arranged and appropriately presented, most children, including children with developmental problems, enjoy such activities, especially if teachers help them to acquire whatever prerequisite skills they may lack. The most important aspect of all preacademic activities is that they should be enjoyable to both children and teachers. Enjoyment leads to success and success leads to further enjoyment in learning and in teaching.

STUDENT ACTIVITIES

1. Observe a preschool or child care program during a preacademic period. Describe the kinds of activities that were offered, amount of time spent in various activities, level of children's engagement and enjoyment. If the program does not have a structured preacademic period, describe activities that might qualify as preacademic.

2. Observe one particular child in a group, preferably a child with a developmental disability or delay. Describe the kinds of adaptations that teachers made to enhance this child's preacademic learnings. If you saw no such adaptations, suggest what might have been done.

3. Select three of the manipulative materials listed (or materials of your own choosing). Demonstrate for the class ways the materials might be presented or adapted to match the skills of a gifted child and a child with delayed cognitive development.

4. Observe a teacher for twenty minutes. Write down everything the teacher does that relates to facilitating children's preacademic learnings (based on the ways that preacademic activities are defined in this unit).

5. Work with two other students. Hold a simulated teachers' meeting in which the major concern is children's lack of interest in the preacademics sessions. Discuss the problem in terms of rearrangement of materials, activities, and grouping of children, with special consideration for children who show overall developmental delay.

REVIEW QUESTIONS

A. *Lists*

1. List five ways that teachers can help children get started or become interested in preacademic materials.
2. List three ways a teacher can help a child begin to learn to imitate.
3. List seven types of manipulative materials that promote perceptual motor skills.
4. List two spatial and two temporal relationships.
5. List five possible reasons that might explain repeated failure to follow directions.

B. *True or False. Choose the best answer.*

T F 1. Preacademic tasks are always presented during teacher-structured activity periods at a particular time in the program.

T F 2. Work and play activities should be clearly separate in early education programs.

T F 3. Teacher-directed paper-and-pencil tasks are a good match for the perceptual-motor abilities of 3- and 4-year-olds.

T F 4. Attention span may be influenced by the way learning materials are presented.

T F 5. In terms of readiness, learning theory emphasizes the importance of children's experiences and opportunities to learn.

T F 6. All children imitate others spontaneously.

T F 7. Sensory integration refers to a classroom in which some children have hearing problems, others have vision problems.

T F 8. Painting, stitchery, and hammering require both perceptual motor and find motor skills.

T F 9. Concept formation includes discrimination, classification, and seriation.

T F 10. Group size for preacademics is partly dependent on children's skill levels and experience.

C. *Multiple Choice: Circle the* one *best phrase to complete each statement.*

1. The most appropriate reason for offering preacademic activities in the preschool is
   a. teaching children to print.
   b. teaching children to memorize and recite poems.
   c. instilling eagerness to learn.

2. Readiness skills
   a. cannot be taught.
   b. can be taught.
   c. never emerge spontaneously in young children.

3. A child's span of attention often depends on
   a. teacher's firmness in insisting the child sit down and pay attention.
   b. sex of the child.
   c. attractiveness of learning materials.

4. Teaching children to imitate
   a. often leads to cheating in school
   b. is a developmental skill that does not need to be taught.
   c. is a developmental skill that sometimes requires direct teaching.

5. A common reason that young children have trouble following directions is because
   a. they do not have an attention span.
   b. they are stubborn and willful.
   c. they often are given directions too lengthy and complex.

6. An appropriate prereading task for 4-year-olds:
   a. circling words that are the same on a ditto sheet.
   b. "reading" picture books in left-to-right and top-to-bottom progression.
   c. sounding out pairs of printed words and telling which ones rhyme.

7. In grouping children for preacademics
   a. children's age and experience is a factor.
   b. bright children always should be grouped together.
   c. group membership should remain constant.

8. A child's favorite materials
   a. should have no bearing on a teacher's choice of academic tasks for that child.
   b. should be offered only when the child has done something that pleases the teacher.
   c. are a good taking off point for a teacher when presenting a new task to a child.

9. Preacademic group times
   a. should be at least 20 to 30 minutes in length for 3- and 4-year-olds.
   b. should consist of activities that keep children working independently and quietly seated.
   c. should offer activities that allow children to move about as they need.

10. Transition or holding activities
    a. require a great deal of teacher supervision.
    b. are materials that can be easily put aside.
    c. are similar to rewards and are to used only when all children are finally sitting quietly.

REFERENCES

Bailey, D.B., and Wolery, M (1984). *Teaching infants and preschoolers with handicaps.* Columbus: Merrill.

Black, J.K., and Puckett, M.B. (1986). Informing others about developmentally appropriate practice. In S. Bredekamp (Ed.). *Developmentally appropriate practice in early childhood programs serving children from birth to 8.* Washington, D.C.: National Association for the Education of Young Children.

Bredekamp, S. (Ed.) (1987). *Developmentally appropriate practice in early childhood programs serving children from birth through age 8.* Washington, D.C.: National Association for the Education of Young Children.

Cook, R.E., Tessier, A. and Armbruster, V.B. (1987). *Adapting early childhood curricula for children with special needs.* Columbus: Merrill.

Greenberg, P. (1990). Why not academic preschools? *Young Children,* 45(2), 70–80.

Hunt, J. McV. (1961). *Intelligence and Experience.* New York: Ronald Press.

Katz, L.G., and Chard, S. (1989). *The Project Approach.* Norwood, NJ: Ablex.

Schickedanz, J., Chay, S., Gopin, P., Sheng, L., Song, S., and Wild, N. (1990). Preschoolers and academics: Some thoughts. *Young Children,* 46(1), 4–13.

Wolery, M.R., and Brookfield-Norman, J. (1988). (Pre)academic instruction for handicapped preschool children. In S.L. Odom and M.B. Karnes, (Eds.). *Early intervention for Infants and Children with Handicaps.* Baltimore: Brookes.

Facilitating Self-Care and Independence Skills

OBJECTIVES

After studying this unit the student will be able to

- explain why it is important that all children, including those with disabilities, learn self-care skills.
- describe five ways a teacher can help young children learn self-care skills.
- discuss the concept of helpful and not-so-helpful "kindness" when assisting young children in their efforts to achieve independence.
- select a common self-care skill such as bathing and list its component parts, or subskills. Select any one of the subskills and list its component parts.
- demonstrate forward and reverse chaining in teaching a self-care skill such as tooth brushing or hand washing.

A major goal of inclusive early childhood programs is balance: *ensuring that children do things on their own (without help) and ensuring that they are not left out because they cannot do something* (Wolery 1994, p. 154). Two basic principles guide quality programs, according to Wolery: 1) the principle of independence—that children be encouraged and allowed to do as much as possible for themselves in learning environments designed to support their endeavors; and 2) the principle of participation—that children with special needs be a part of all activities and that adaptations be made to encourage a child's participation to the maximum extent possible. While these two principles apply to all early childhood curriculum areas, they are especially relevant in helping children with special needs acquire the self-care or self-help skills that are the focus of this unit. These skills, when adequately learned, enable individuals to manage personal needs and to *adapt* their behaviors to social expectations.

The specific skills and adaptive behaviors that children need to learn are determined by the culture in which they live. Though patterns differ, all cultures prescribe ways of eating, toileting, dressing, behaving sexually, and keeping public places orderly.

An individual's competence in self-care and adaptive skills may be the distinguishing factor between those who are considered mentally retarded and those who are not. Recall the AAMR definition of mental retardation (Unit 5)? It says that regardless of IQ scores, an individual is not to be considered mentally retarded if he or she displays adequate personal independence, social responsibility, and has the functional skills for daily living based on his or her age and the expectations of the culture.

Skills in these areas are generally assessed through checklists, developmental profiles, and the professional judgment of teachers and clinicians. Expectations vary according to age level. In infancy and early childhood, the expected behaviors are those commonly associated with typical developmental processes. The primary methods for assessing a child's self-care and independence skills is through direct observation using sequential lists of developmental milestones; and through interviews with parents (Noonan and McCormick 1993).

SELF-CARE SKILLS AND THE CURRICULUM

Competence in self-care leads to greater independence. Therefore, helping young children develop a full range of self-care skills is a major curriculum goal in early childhood programs. The goal holds for all children, and perhaps, especially for children with developmental problems who need to learn to live as independently as possible with their disability, and in spite of it. The more proficient they become in caring for their personal needs, the less likely that they will be placed in segregated classes (Spodek, Saracho and Lee 1984, p. 229).

Self-care skills are learned behaviors. This means they can be taught. Traditionally, the family had major responsibility for teaching self-care skills. Early childhood programs provided backup assistance. As infants and children are enrolled at ever younger ages in all-day child care programs, the pattern is reversing. Early childhood teachers often have the major responsibility for initiating self-care training. In addition, and especially for children with developmental problems, schools are assuming increasing responsibility. This trend can be attributed to:

Increasing numbers of children with special needs in the mainstream of education.

Legislation requiring that all children have an individualized and appropriate education.

Improved teaching strategies derived from behavioral principles.

Early childhood programs can be a comfortable place for children to learn self-care skills. Teachers are trained to help children carry out these tasks. It is an established part of the teachers' job and time commitment. For many parents, already overburdened with responsibilities and stresses, teaching self-care skills may be just one more frustrating and time consuming task among many. If their child is developmentally disabled, the burdens may be overwhelming. Furthermore, the resistance and stress often associated with teaching certain self-care skills (toileting, for example) can lead to emotional conflict between parent and child. It is almost as if the parent's own self-esteem is damaged if the child is not acquiring the socially approved self-care skills. Teachers do not have that kind of personal involvement in the child's performance. They do not feel a need to push for early performance. Instead, whether a child has a disability or not, most preschool teachers know that time and effort is saved by slowing the pace and expecting less when teaching any new skill.

Even when parents assume the major responsibility for teaching self-care skills, early childhood educators often find themselves involved. Frequently they are asked by the child study team to play a supporting role. This is good for children, parents, and teachers. Parents must be involved if children are to have ample opportunities to practice the self-care skills that occur most frequently and most naturally in the home setting. Support for parents during their child's train-

Early childhood teachers are trained to help children learn self-help skills.

	Dressing	**Feeding**	**Toileting and Washing**	**General**
2 to 3 years (24 to 36 months)	Can take clothes off to put on other articles of clothing but tires easily and gives up. Generally cooperative when helped.	Can use a fork but still prefers spoon or fingers. Will feed self food that is liked. Drinks from glass.	Verbalizes toilet needs in advance. Retention span for urination lengthening—can "hold" longer.	Can open some doors with easy latches or low knobs. Goes up and down stairs, mark time fashion, usually holding rail. Can push chair or stool around to climb on and get what is wanted.
3 to 4 years (36 to 48 months)	Undresses self rapidly and well. Can put on most articles of clothing and can do some unbuttoning and zipping depending upon the size and place of buttons or zipper. Can put clothes away in drawers or hang them up given right height hooks.	Usually eats with fork; can spread with knife. Can pour from pitcher into glass with few mishaps. Enjoys eating with family but may dawdle endlessly.	May insist on washing self in tub but does it imperfectly. Very few toilet accidents. Often wakes at night and asks to be taken to toilet.	Can tell own age, sex, and first and last name. Can follow 2- and 3-step directions. Able to separate from parent—to stay at preschool by self.
4 to 5 years (48 to 60 months)	Laces shoes; some children learning to tie. Dresses and undresses with little or no assistance especially if clothes are laid out. May dawdle excessively over dressing. Can tell front from back but may still have trouble getting some garments on just right.	Uses knife, fork, and spoon appropriately; often needs help with "tough" meat. Likes to make own breakfast and lunches (dry cereal, peanut butter sandwiches, etc.)	Can bathe and dry self, at least partially. Can put self through entire toileting and hand washing and drying. May forget sometimes.	Plays in the neighborhood and comes home when called, most of the time. Can put play materials away but usually needs reminding. Can do many household chores: set table, empty trash, feed pets. May "forget" some steps.
5 to 6 years (60 to 72 months)	Ties own shoes. Can manage almost any article of clothing. Can assist younger brother or sister in getting dressed.	Can use all eating utensils well but often messy because always in a hurry to get back to play. Uses appropriate table manners but tends to forget.	Bathes and dries self with minimal supervision—usually does not wash own hair, but may help. Totally self-sufficient in toilet routine.	Can go to school by self. Can be trusted with small sums of money and a small list at the neighborhood store. Can make own bed, put soiled clothes in hamper. Learning to distinguish left from right.

Fig. 18-1 Examples of self-help skills for various age groupings.

ing results in a higher level and higher quality of self-care skills in the children. Teachers must remember, though, that parents and the needs of the family must be considered when deciding which self-care skills are to be taught. If a child's incessant activity causes more family stress than does lack of toilet training, it is likely the family will view the activity problem as having the higher priority. It is important, therefore that teachers (even though they and the child study team might view toilet training of first importance) consider both the child's needs and the family's priorities. This may mean setting the expectations of the program aside for awhile.

In any event, for many children today, and for many more young children in the foreseeable future, teachers are and will be the major source of self-care learning. Thus, teachers become a significant factor in children's development: even more so in the development of children with disabilities. Bailey and Wolery (1984) describe the benefits:

> Teachers who do so (teach self-care skills) not only increase children's ability to care for themselves, allowing them to function independently, but also decrease the number of behaviors that point out the differences between handicapped and typical children. For example, a child who is 6 years old and does not feed herself is more obviously different from typical children than the 6-year-old handicapped child who does (p. 334).

Integrating Self-Care Skills.   Eating, dressing, toileting, and care of the classroom and play yard are significant program areas in the early childhood curriculum. As Wolery (1994) points out, "The best instruction occurs in context; that is, when the skill is needed by the child" (p. 158). Self-care activities occur throughout the program day. They take up a significant share of both teachers' and children's time and energies and so require systematic planning.

Interrelatedness of self-care learnings.   Opportunities for learning self-care skills need to be integrated with every other part of the curriculum. Mealtimes, for instance, can be arranged to promote a variety of curriculum goals in addition to those directly associated with eating.

Examples: If conversation during meals is acceptable in the culture, several small tables may be set up to promote child-child and child-teacher conversations at these times.

Preacademic as well as self-care learnings can be carried out at mealtimes as teachers and children informally discuss names, colors and textures of foods, their origin, and nutritional value.

Mealtimes provide opportunities for the **generalization** of cognitive skills presented in preacademic activities. Knowledge about the concept *green*, for example, can be extended by drawing attention to foods such as peas, broccoli, and lettuce; or by asking children to think of other foods that are green.

Perceptual motor skills can be practiced—lifting and pouring from a pitcher, filling a glass to a certain level, cleaning up spills, presenting the pitcher, handle first, to the adjacent child.

Spilling and mopping up are both a part of self-help mastery.

Self-care routines such as eating provide a variety of opportunities for learning. One might be learning about sequence: what comes before and after eating; and learning to estimate: how much food to take relative to one's own hunger or the amount of food available. The ability to estimate, it might be added, is a learning necessary for all young children. How important it is, for example, that a child be able to estimate how long it is safe to wait before going to the bathroom!

Opportunities to practice language are plentiful during self-care routines. There are opportunities to learn the names and function for the objects and actions that are a part of everyday lives: clothing, furnishings, working parts of equipment such as toilets that flush and sinks that drain. Learning to comprehend and follow directions given by the teacher is another language skill that can be practiced during self-care routines. Still another is the opportunity for verbal expressiveness as when children are encouraged to state their preferences, seek help, or explain to another child how to hang up a coat. In addition, self-care activities provide occasions for children to learn language that is somewhat abstract (not supported by the activity at hand). During the arrival routine, a child telling the teacher about what happened to Grandmother's dog is an example of this important kind of activity.

Individualizing Self-care Programs.   Effective self-care programs allow children to participate individually. Young children, as noted repeatedly, operate at different levels of motor, social, and cognitive ability. They need differing amounts of time and assistance in completing self-care tasks. Some children, with or without special needs, learn self-care skills early and with ease; others have varying degrees of difficulty. Inconsistent levels of competency may exist within the same child. Depending on the skill, a child may master some self-care skills well in advance of the normally expected time, others much later. Example: Melissa was a bright and healthy child. At 34 months she still wore diapers during the day because of fairly frequent wetting incidents, yet she did not require diapers at night. For some indiscernible reason she had had a dry bed from an unusually early age—shortly before her second birthday.

Building independence.   The preschool years are the prime time for children to learn self-care skills. Children are striving for independence during these years. They are eager to help themselves. They work hard at it if adults allow them to operate at their own pace. They constantly watch and attempt to imitate the self-care efforts of older children and adults. Furthermore, they are willing, in fact, insist on, practicing, practicing, practicing. Think about older babies learning to walk. They take a few steps, fall down, get up, take a few more steps, fall down, over and over again. Once the falling down period is past, they are even more insistent about practicing their walking. It seems for awhile, as if every waking moment is given over to the task. A toddler's perseverance and physical energy seems never-ending, as in these familiar examples:

> The discovery of how to unlace shoes leads to the child, for days straight-running, taking the laces out of his or her shoes 12 to 15 times a day.
> The perseverance of a 2-year-old in pushing, pulling, tugging, shoving, dragging a kitchen chair over to the kitchen sink. Why? To get a drink of water, "all by myself."
> The 3-year-old's struggle, twisting, and turning in a mighty effort to get an undershirt on without help. The shirt, of course, may end up inside out or back-to-front, but that is all right. Learning that shirts have a right and wrong way of being worn comes later and requires much finer discrimination skills than the child possesses at this point.

Building in success.   All children need to experience the joy and self-esteem that comes from mastering self-care skills. Pride in accomplishment can be seen on the face of a 2-year-old who finally gets the chair in position to get that drink of water. It can be heard in the gleeful shout of the 3-year-old: "I got my shirt on all by myself"; or the quiet pleasure of the 5-year-old who finally learns to tie shoes (never mind the lopsided bow or the dangling laces). It can also be seen in the self-importance of the 6-year-old who learns to make peanut butter sandwiches, not only for himself, but for his little sister. Such experiences help children feel successful and in better control of their lives.

Though children with severe impairments may sometimes be the exception, most children with devel-

Being able to feed oneself enhances early autonomy and self-esteem.

Let the Child Do It. "ME DO IT! ME DO IT!" What parent or teacher has not heard that refrain from a red-faced, frustrated, struggling 3-year-old? The urge to do for oneself is strong in typically developing young children. Though not expressed as aggressively, perhaps, the urge also is there in children with developmental problems. At least it most likely was there at some point in the child's developmental history. The efforts of children with special needs to do for themselves often goes unrecognized. Adults tend not to expect children with disabilities to even try to learn self-care skills. Also, the earliest strivings for independence may have been snuffed out by well-meaning family members and caregivers who could not bear to watch the child struggle. In many instances, children become further disabled, "crippled by kindness" as the saying goes.

opmental disabilities can learn self-care skills. Like typically developing children, they, too, feel good about themselves simply by getting the shirt on, inside out or backwards. Not all children with disabilities are able to verbalize their accomplishment. They may not be able to say, "Look what I did!", but their facial expressions leave little doubt as to their feelings of satisfaction.

It is true that getting about in a wheelchair or with a walker is bothersome. Such disabilities need not prevent independence, however. What does interfere with independence is *not* being taught how to manage routine matters such as toileting, dressing, and eating. Having to ask for help over and over, every day, is the real burden. It is troublesome, both for the person with the impairments and for those who must stop what they are doing (often reluctantly) to give help. Constantly having to seek help gets to be embarrassing, especially during adolescence.

SELF-CARE SKILLS AND THE TEACHER

As noted earlier, teaching self-care skills is an integral part of the early childhood program. As with all other curriculum areas, specific principles and guidelines determine when and how teachers facilitate such learnings.

Jeff's wheelchair increases his options and his independence.

How Much Assistance?   Not all adults know how to help a child with developmental disabilities (or those *without* developmental problems, for that matter.) Misplaced kindness leads many adults to take over. They do too much for children. They do things for, and to, a child that the child could do, given enough time and space. What happens when a teacher or parent steps in and expertly zips up the zipper the child has been working on so intently? Or reties the shoe the child has just tied with so much effort? Or whips off the wrong-side-out sweater the child is crowing about having gotten on "all by myself"? A negative message is conveyed. It is as if the adult were saying, "You aren't good enough," "Can't you do anything right?" Such *assistance* often sets up patterns of conflict between adult and child; or it may have the opposite result. The child learns to be passive, sitting or standing about, while the adult does more and more

Adults sometimes must hold themselves back, literally, allowing the child to find the way.

for the child. This can lead to *learned helplessness*, another way a child can become overly and unnecessarily dependent.

In early childhood programs such adult "helping" may be the result of understaffing. Teachers may have too many children to look after. They feel they cannot take the time to let a child make repeated efforts to fasten his or her jacket while other children are waiting to go outdoors. More frequently, however, such "helping" comes from teachers' lack of confidence in their own skills. It is common among inexperienced teachers who do not know what to do in many situations. They, themselves, feel helpless. By doing things *for* the child the teacher feels busy and needed, more competent, more successful. It is not only the inexperienced who feel obligated to help, however. Many adults feel uncomfortable, hard-hearted if they let a child struggle.

To prevent *learned helplessness*, even the kindest and most well-meaning assistance must not be pressed on a child unnecessarily. Kindness to children with developmental disabilities lies in finding ways to help them help themselves.

- Kindness is guiding a child's arm and hand so he can reach all the way down into his wrong-side-out coat sleeve. It is demonstrating how to grasp the edge of the cuff. It is helping the child learn that he *can* pull the cuff through, discovering that *he* can make a coat sleeve come right-side out.
- Kindness is putting a rubber suction cup under the plate of a child with cerebral palsy so the plate stays in place while he works at feeding himself.
- Kindness, in the case of a 6-year-old just learning to walk with crutches, is laying her clothes out within easy reach. When everything she needs for dressing herself is at her fingertips, she manages on her own.

Another aspect of kindly assistance is to provide ample encouragement and positive feedback to children who are trying to take care of their own needs. The best way to do this is to tell children exactly what it is they are doing right (descriptive praise). Children need encouragement in the form of immediate feedback when they are successful, or getting closer to a success-

Learned helplessness is prevented by letting children do as much as possible for themselves.

ful performance. They need to now, too, that their efforts are appreciated. Children thrive when a teacher says:

"You poured your milk nice and slow. Not a drop got on the table!"
"Look at you! You've already buttoned three buttons. Only two to go."
"You remembered *again* today to rinse the soap off your hands and to turn the water off. You are getting good at washing your hands all by yourself."

At the same time, kindness is *not* expecting children to do what they are not yet able to do, or to perform tasks that are too complex for their developmental level. No child learns efficiently when overly frustrated or confronted with frequent failure. Teachers, therefore, must know when to help, how to help, and how much to help.

When to Help. Knowing when to help depends on several teaching skills discussed earlier. Among these are an understanding of developmental sequences, "readiness," and the interrelatedness of developmental areas. Consider the following:

Because a 2-year-old managed to get a chair to the sink to get a drink of water does not mean the child

can turn the water on. Large motor skills (in this instance, shoving a chair into place) generally precede find motor skills (here, the eye–hand–wrist control needed to turn on the water). The adult needs to anticipate the possible outcome of the less than fully developed fine motor skills. Assistance, if needed, should be offered *before* the child becomes overly frustrated at not being able to get a drink. After all, great effort went into getting the chair in place.

Many children, at an early age, are able to grasp a spoon and get it to the mouth. That is no guarantee, however, that a filled spoon will remain right-side-up and so deliver the food into the mouth. Usually, adult help is needed at this point so the child can learn to keep the spoon upright, loaded, *and* on target.

Least intrusive assistance. Assistance should be given as subtly as possible to preserve children's pride in their own efforts. In the first example above, the adult might loosen the faucet just to the point where the child can make the water flow. In the second, a teacher might quietly place a hand around the child's hand after the spoon has been loaded, then remove the helping hand as the spoon enters the mouth. This unobtrusive assistance gives the child a sense of accomplishment while learning a difficult task.

Excessive demands. Occasionally, there is a child who gives up without trying, who makes excessive demands for adult assistance. It is likely that such a child is in need of extra attention. Teachers must find ways to give the needed attention; at the same time, they must avoid giving in to excessive demands. The alternative is to watch for times when the child is doing a task independently and then give warm and positive attention: "You remembered where you left your cap! Looks like you're all ready to go outdoors. Do you want to help me take the new balls out?"

When children can't. It is true that children need to be encouraged to do for themselves as much as possible; nevertheless, teachers must make exceptions. A child may ask for help with a task long since mastered. Children, too, have their "off" days. Like adults, they become tired, upset, feel unwell. All children can be expected to be dependent at times. They need to know that it is alright to ask for help, to say, "This is too hard. I can't do it by myself." A child should *never* be ridiculed or belittled for asked for help, no matter how simple the task. Children who have been helped to feel competent most of the time will ask for assistance only when they truly feel, at the moment, that the task is too much for them to do by themselves. In such situations, it is important that help be given immediately, in just the right amount. The adult should never take over. Instead, the adult helps the child find a way to resolve the impasse as in the coat sleeve example cited earlier. Always, though, the child should feel there is more help available if the problem is not solved on the first attempt or even on the second or third.

Game-like Assistance. One way to keep a child involved and successful in a self-care situation is to create a game-like atmosphere. The exchange that follows is focused on Robert, born with cerebral palsy. He had recently passed his sixth birthday and was finishing up his third year in an inclusive early childhood program. Throughout the sequence, the teacher can be seen giving just the right amount of appropriately timed assistance and feedback in order to keep Robert involved. Interactions between the teacher and the child are followed by interpretive comments.

I

Robert put his foot in an unlaced shoe in the teacher's lap.
Teacher: "Hi, Robert, what do you need?"
Robert pointed to his shoe.
Teacher: "Tell me what you need."
Robert: "Tie my shoes."
Children need practice using language. The teacher, therefore, required Robert to ask for what he needed. In working with children with no language, or more delayed language the teacher likely would have settled for one word, or even the simple gesture of raising the foot and pointing to the untied shoe. In the latter case, the teacher might respond, while tying the shoe, "You are showing me that your shoe needs tying." Because Robert had the ability to verbalize his need, he was asked to do so.

II

Teacher: "Alright, but first you need to lace them."
The teacher began to sequence the task for Robert by reminding him the shoe first had to be laced. A subsequent time, the teacher might ask Robert to tell what needed to be

done before the shoe could be tied. Learning to state the order in which a complex task is to be accomplished is a skill step that gives the child experience in thinking through ordered sequencing for all tasks. Note that the teacher did not require Robert to stop and say "Please." The teacher chose to focus his efforts on the self-care task itself rather than on social niceties.

III

Robert: "No, you lace them. I don't know how." As he said this he kept his eyes on two favorite playmates who seemed to be about ready to start the transition of coating up for outdoor play.
With Robert's refusal to lace his shoes, the teacher reassessed the situation. It was immediately obvious that Robert did not want to be left behind when his friends went out to play. Yet the teacher knew they would be gone, long before Robert, with his less well developed find motor skills, could lace his shoes by himself. What to do?

IV

Teacher (smiling): "Robert, you are kidding me. Every day I see you lacing your shoes, But sit down here on the floor and I will help you."
The teacher knew Robert could lace his shoes and felt it was not good for him to get away with saying he was not able to do it. On the other hand, his eagerness to be ready to play with his friends was important, too. The teacher decided, therefore, to make a joke out of telling him she knew he could tie his own shoes, but to give him assistance, nevertheless.

V

Robert sat on the floor. The teacher inserted the tip of one lace partly through an eyelet, while instructing: "Robert, you pull it through."
Having Robert sit on the floor gave him a firm base and the necessary balance for lacing the shoe. The teacher did the part of the job that would have given Robert the most difficulty, getting the lace started into the eyelet. The tasks the teacher held Robert to could be done quickly and with immediate success, thus giving promise that the shoe was much closer to being laced.

VI

As Robert pulled the first lace through, the teacher said, "Great! You got that one through. Now hand me the other lace." The lacing continued in this fashion until only the top pair of holes was left.

With each step, the teacher gave Robert encouragement, positive feedback, and a cue for the next step in the sequence ("Now hand me the other lace").

VII

Teacher: "I bet you can do the last two by yourself. Here, I'll hand *you* the laces this time."
Robert: "I know which ones. I can do it."

With the job so close to being finished, the teacher sensed it would not be difficult for Robert to finish it up. Hence, the friendly challenge to Robert to take the responsibility.

VIII

Teacher: "Look at that, Robert. All done! You finished the lacing all by yourself. Here, let me tie your shoes and you will be all ready to play." The teacher then called to Robert's friends: "Robert's ready to go out, too. Wait while he gets his coat on, okay?"

Because task completion is important to children's learning, the teacher gave specific praise, "Robert, you finished the lacing all by yourself." Then the teacher made sure Robert's efforts really paid off—having his friends wait for him. Also, no suggestion was made that Robert work on shoe tying, even though it was a task on his IEP. That would be saved for another time. Instead, the teacher tied the shoes quickly so there would be no further delay.

Robert was a child who had made good progress in acquiring self-care skills in spite of his disabilities. Other children with developmental problems may have learned to do much less for themselves. Many cannot put on their own coat. They cannot feed themselves or take care of their own toilet needs. Some children cannot ask for what they need. In these cases, the teacher's job is more demanding. Teaching children with more severe disabilities requires ongoing assistance and support from relevant members of the child study team. The specifics of such assistance must be written into the IEP and the IFSP and faithfully implemented by the school district.

Task Analysis.   Self-care skills can be taught in different ways. The Hawaii Preparing for Integrated Preschool (PIP) Curriculum (Noonan et al. 1991) identifies several complex self-care skills and their component parts. PIP suggests the following strategies for teaching such skills in context; that is, in inclusive settings during related play activities:

- Demonstrate the skill for the child.
- Encourage the child to join in an activity involving the skill.
- Physically assist or guide the child if necessary.
- Provide the child with practice opportunities.
- Reinforce the child's efforts to use the skill.

If one approach is unsuccessful, another should be tried, and then another, if need be. Teaching a child to put on a coat, for example, can be accomplished in several ways. The usual way (often the most difficult for young children) is to have the child reach behind and put in one arm at a time. Another way is to place the coat on the floor or on a table, with the child facing the opened-out coat. The child puts both arms into the sleeves and tosses the coat over the head. A third way is to place the opened coat on a chair. Because this coating-up procedure seems to work best for young children, it will be described step-by-step.

1. Place the coat on a child-sized chair. Arrange it so it looks as if a child had slipped out of it while sitting on the chair.
2. Have the child sit on the chair (on the coat).
3. Point to one of the armholes and ask the child to look at the armhole.
4. Guide the child's arm into the armhole.
5. Give positive, specific feedback and then a cue as to what comes next: "There! You have one arm in. Now let's look at the other armhole."
6. Repeat for the other sleeve.
7. The child, at this point, may spontaneously *shrug* the coat over the shoulders. If not, the teacher moves the child's arms up and forward to make it happen.

Maturation and Learning: Toilet Training as an Example.   As noted at the outset, all self-care skills are learned. It follows, then, that all self-care skills can be taught. Starting on toilet training too early dooms the child and the adult to failure. Success depends, in part, on physiological maturity, especially of the **sphincter muscles**.

Toilet training, once thought to be totally dependent on maturation, can be task analyzed and taught in its component parts. With some children, each part,

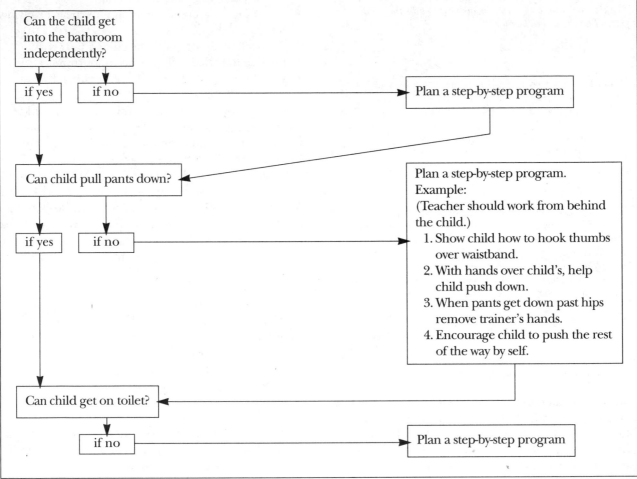

Fig. 18-2 Toileting sequence.

in turn, may need to be task-analyzed and taught step-by-step. Ordinary toilet training includes 12 to 15 steps. It starts with getting into the bathroom, pulling the pants down, getting up onto the toilet. It concludes with getting off the toilet, pulling clothes up, and flushing. What could be more simple? Yet, for many young children with and without developmental problems, one or more of the steps may present great difficulty. Even the seemingly simple task of getting on and off the toilet may need to be broken down into smaller steps. For sure, using toilet tissue effectively is a challenge for all young children!

Step-by-Step Planning.   In teaching any self-care skill the teacher must know exactly where each child is in that particular skill sequence. This can be accomplished by asking a simple question about each step: Can the child do it? If yes, the teacher proceeds to the next step: if no, the teacher figures out the substeps appropriate for that child at that point in the sequence.

Toilet training programs.   Commercial toilet training programs have been developed for children with disabilities (Azrin and Foxx 1971; Fredericks et al. 1975; Snell 1978). Basically, the programs involve the same procedures discussed here, with even greater emphasis on small steps. The programs also provide information on toilet training **nonambulatory** children and those with other special problems. (Children who are on seizure medication, for example, must not be given quantities of liquids.)

Chaining.   Many self-care tasks can be thought of as chains of individual responses. Toileting, shoe lacing, feeding oneself—all are examples of a skill composed of a set of smaller behaviors chained together and organized into what seems to be a single skill. When adapting the chaining concept to teaching self-care skills, the child is helped to learn one response, one link of the skill chain at a time. Once the child is performing the first component in the chain, the next step, or link, is introduced. Single components of the chain are added one by one until the child can perform all of them, in order, from start to finish. Step-by-step learning can be made easier if the child can see the entire chain being performed.

On many tasks, forward chaining and reverse (backward) chaining are equally successful. The choice depends on the particular task and level of skill the child displays. In *forward chaining*, the teacher helps the child learn the first step in the chain, then the second, and so on. In *reverse chaining*, instruction begins with the last step and progresses backwards to the first component.

The child in the zipping activity that follows has fairly well developed fine motor skills; the teacher, therefore, has broken the task into only six component parts. The steps are suitable for teaching the task with either a forward or a reverse chaining approach. Throughout, the teacher will demonstrate or provide manual prompts as needed.

Step 1. Using both hands, the bottom front edges of the coat are brought together at the bottom.

Step 2. The zipper pin is inserted into the housing.

Step 3. The zipper pin is seated in the housing by pushing up and down with opposing movements of each hand.

Step 4. The tab on the zipper is grasped between thumb and forefinger.

Step 5. The bottom of the coat at the zipper housing is held with one hand while the zipper tab is pulled to the top with the hand holding the zipper tab.

Step 6. The zipper tab is pushed down firmly into locked position.

In reverse chaining, the child first masters step six, then five, and so on, back to step one. The advantage of backward chaining is that the child always is reinforced by task completion, even in the first lesson. Accomplishing the last step sends a motivating message to the child, that the time has come to get on to something more interesting. At some point, the chain becomes one integrated skill that scarcely needs thinking about.

Special Considerations.   In the zipping task (and in many other dressing and self-care tasks) it is most effective if the adult works from behind the child. This ensures that the teacher is performing the hand and finger movements in the same way that the child will be expected to reproduce them. Young children do not have well-developed spatial orientation nor do they have a concept of reversibility. Teachers' demonstrations, therefore must be conducted from the child's perspective. For this reason and others, the use of lacing, buttoning, and zipping boards for children to practice on has been questioned. It is confusing for many children to try to reverse and transfer the motions learned in practice sessions to their own bodies. Cook, Tessier and Klein (1992) report that some teachers have been most ingenious in overcoming this problem. They attach the formboards to a pillow on which they have sewn elastic loops that are slipped over the child's arms, up to the shoulders. This holds the pillow at the upper torso position, allowing children comfortable practice sessions.

A word about the importance of suitable clothing when learning self-care skills: Children who are being toilet trained need underpants (and outer pants) with elastic at the top so they can be pulled down easily. Children who are learning to dress themselves can learn more readily if their clothing has big, sturdy zippers that work, large buttons and unrestricted buttonholes, and simple fastenings on belts and overalls. When children are having prolonged difficulty in learning to dress themselves, temporarily providing clothing a size or two too big is sometimes a help. Teachers never presume to tell parents how to dress their children, yet parents often welcome suggestions that help their children learn more easily.

Programs Fail, Not Children.   A mandate for all teachers is to exercise additional ingenuity whenever a child seems unable to learn a task that seems matched to his or her developmental level and prerequisite skills. If a child is not learning, it is the fault of the program, not the child. The teacher must change the sequence, the size of the steps, the motivation (reinforcers) or the task itself until the child succeeds. Teachers must have faith that all children in an inclusive early childhood program can learn an adequate range of self-care skills.

SUMMARY

The terms self-care, independence, self-help skills, and adaptive behavior can be used interchangeably to mean taking care of one's personal needs in socially acceptable ways. Traditionally, families had the major responsibility for teaching self-care skills to children; in recent years, early childhood teachers are involved. Opportunities for learning and practicing self-care skills should be integrated with every part of the curriculum. Throughout the day, children need to experi-

ence the independence, the pleasure, and the glow of self-esteem that comes from mastering self-care skills.

A child's disabilities need not prevent the learning of self-care skills. Adult helpfulness and genuine kindness is helping children learn ways to do for themselves. Children trying to master a self-care skill need feedback as to what it is they are doing right. Knowing when and how to help depends on teachers' knowledge of developmental sequences and "readiness," and the interrelatedness of developmental areas. Many skills, once thought to be totally dependent on maturation, can and should be taught, especially to children with developmental problems.

Teaching self-care skills can be done in a lighthearted, game-like fashion using a variety of approaches. If one method does not work another should be tried (and another, if need be). Specific step-by-step planning, that is task analysis, is necessary to teach self-care skills effectively. Most self-care tasks can be thought of as chains of many smaller responses. Self-care skills can be taught through forward chaining or reverse chaining. The major advantage of reverse chaining is that the child always has the satisfaction of completing the task, even in the first teaching episode. It must be remembered that programs fail, not children. When teachers exercise ingenuity, children are likely to succeed.

STUDENT ACTIVITIES

1. Observe an inclusive preschool or child care center during arrival or departure time, a toileting period, or a meal or snack time. List 10 or more self-care skills and adaptive behaviors you see children engage in.
2. When next you wash your hair, take note of what you do. When finished, write down what you did, step-by-step, starting with the decision to wash your hair and ending with it arranged as you always wear it.
3. Select one of the major steps in the toileting sequence (or any other self-care skill) and analyze it into its com-

ponent parts. Write a six- to ten-step program for teaching that subskill to a 4-year-old who has a serious hearing loss but no other impairments.
4. Ask a fellow student to role play a child who cannot tie a shoe. Teach the task to the "child."
5. Assume that *learning to count five or more objects* is written into the IEP of a 4-year-old. Give examples of how teachers might integrate this learning task with several self-care routines.

REVIEW QUESTIONS

A. *Short Answer.*

1. Today early childhood teachers rather than parents often are the ones to train young children in self-care skills. Why?
2. The text states that self-care skills should be integrated with all parts of the curriculum. Explain.
3. What is meant by "crippling a child with kindness"?
4. How much help and what kind should be given to a child who is trying to learn a self-care skill?
5. What is the role of maturation in toilet training?
6. What is chaining and what is the difference between forward and backward chaining?
7. It is suggested that buttoning, zipping, and lacing boards may not be appropriate for a young child trying to learn those skills? Why not?
8. What is the rationale for a teacher or parent working from behind a child when teaching zipping, buttoning, or putting on boots?

B. *True or False. Choose the best answer.*

T F 1. Programs for learning self-care skills should be kept separate from other parts of the early childhood curriculum.

T F 2. Learning self-care skills is related to both maturation and opportunities to learn.

T F 3. Children with special needs are always delayed in learning self-care skills.

T F 4. Mastering self-care skills tends to lead to increased self-esteem in young children.

T F 5. *Learned helplessness* is a way of describing unnecessary dependency.

T F 6. Once a child masters a particular self-care skill, he or she has no reason to need or expect further help.

T F 7. Helping a child learn self-care skills is serious business; never should teachers treat it as a game.

T F 8. The ability to toilet oneself depends on both maturation and learning.

T F 9. Depending on the task, both forward and backward chaining can lead to mastery.

T F 10. If a child is not learning, the fault is likely to be in the program, not the child.

C. *Multiple Choice. Circle the letter representing the* one *best answer in each of the following.*

1. According to AAMR, adaptive behaviors include all but which one of the following?
   a. personal independence.
   b. proficiency in basic math and reading.
   c. a sense of social responsibility.
   d. functional self-care skills for everyday living.

2. Learning self-care skills
   a. is totally dependent on maturation.
   b. is somewhat dependent on maturation.
   c. is impossible for most handicapped children.
   d. should always be done in the child's home.

3. Mastering self-care skills does *not* require
   a. adequate perceptual motor development.
   b. the ability to learn through imitation.
   c. freedom from developmental delay or disability.
   d. opportunity to practice.

4. Children with developmental delays
   a. are seldom successful in acquiring basic self-care skills.
   b. have a right to expect teachers and parents and classmates to wait on them.
   c. can never receive too much help.
   d. should be expected to do as much for themselves as they are able.

5. How and when to help a child struggling to button her coat depends on all but which one of the following teaching skills?
   a. knowledge of growth and development.
   b. ability to sequence self-care skills.
   c. skill in adapting the task to the learner.
   d. realizing that a handicapped child should never have to struggle or be frustrated.

6. Successful toilet training depends on
   a. starting before the first birthday.
   b. maturation of the abdominal muscle.
   c. maturation of the sphincter muscles.
   d. the child's ability to say when he or she needs to use the toilet.

7. Which of the following words do *not* relate to behavioral chaining?
   a. forward
   b. backward
   c. fencing
   d. linking

8. If a child in an early childhood program is not responding to the toilet training program
   a. give up; some children are untrainable.
   b. don't let the child play outdoors until she learns to stay dry.
   c. advise parents to keep her home until they teach her to use the toilet.
   d. alter the program or change programs.

REFERENCES

Atwater J.B., Orth-Lopes, L., Elliott, M., Carta, J.C., and Schwartz, I.S. (1994). Completing the circle: Planning and implementing transitions to other programs. In M. Wolery and J.S. Wilbur (Eds.). *Including children with special needs in early childhood programs*. Washington, D.C.: National Association for the Education of Young Children.

Azrin, N.H., and Foxx, R.M. (1971). *Toilet training in less than a day*. New York: Simon and Schuster.

Bailey, D.B., and Wolery, M. (1984). *Teaching infants and preschoolers with handicaps*. Columbus, OH: Merrill.

Cook, R.E., Tessier, A., Klein, M.D. (1992). Adapting early childhood curricula for children with special needs. Columbus, OH: Merrill.

Foxx, R.M., and Azrin, N.H. (1973). *Toilet training the retarded: A rapid program for day and nighttime independent toileting*. Champaign, IL: Research Press.

Fredericks, H.D., Balwin, V.L., Grove, D.N., and Moore, W.G. (1975). *Toilet training the handicapped child*. Monmouth, OR: Instructional Development Corp.

Noonan, M.J., and McCormick, L. (1993). *Early intervention in natural environments*. Pacific Grove, CA: Brooks/Cole.

Noonan, M.J., Yamashita, L., Graham, M.A., and Nakamoto, D. (1991). *Hawaii Preparing for Integrated Preschool (PIP) Curriculum*. Source: Preschool Preparation and Transition Outreach Project, University of Hawaii at Manoa, Department of Special Education, Honolulu, Hawaii 96822.

Snell, M.E. (Ed.), (1978). *Systematic instruction of the moderately and severely handicapped*. Columbus, OH: Merrill.

Spodek, B., Saracho, O.N., and Lee, C.L., (1984). *Mainstreaming young children*. Belmont, CA: Wadsworth.

Worley, M. (1994). Implementing instruction for young children with special needs in early childhood classrooms. In M. Wolery and J.S. Wilbur (Eds.) *Including children with special needs in early childhood programs*. Washington, D.C.: National Association for the Education of Young Children.

Managing Problem Behaviors

OBJECTIVES

After studying this unit the student will be able to

- describe developmentally normal behavior problems. Explain the factors that determine that a behavior problem require special attention.

- discuss the use and misuse of the term hyperactivity and the role of medication and diet in dealing with the problem. Suggest alternatives.

- list eight positive strategies for preventing (and reducing) behavior problems in the preschool classroom.

- present a plan for managing a newly enrolled 4-year-old who is still hitting and kicking children at the end of the fourth week.

- identify the most important points to be made in counseling a parent who is concerned that her 3-year-old has trouble sharing.

It would be difficult to find a child who has not been accused of being a behavior problem by somebody at some time. All young children engage in maladaptive and inappropriate behaviors, at least once in awhile. It is one way that children learn the difference between appropriate ways of behaving. It is how they learn what to do (and not to do) where and when.

Developmentally Normal Deviations. At what point is an inappropriate behavior a problem behavior? There is no easy answer because so many factors influence a child's development. The range of individual differences among children further complicate matters.

Nevertheless, it is unlikely that there is a typically developing child who has never had a tantrum or an irrational fear, who has not balked at being separated from a parent, a pacifier, a security blanket, or a favorite stuffed animal. Rarer still are children who are never moody or withdrawn, aggressive or antisocial, argumentative or oppositional. It is typical of young children to retreat or respond negatively or aggressively to situations that are new, frightening, or beyond their understanding. A stranger, replacing a long-time favorite caregiver may trigger a run of problem behav-

iors. The reactions usually are temporary (assuming the new caregiver is a good one). The untoward behaviors disappear once the child gains understanding and confidence about the new situations. A child also may exhibit unusual behaviors when overly tired, hungry, or coming down with an illness. These are not likely to become fixed patterns of behavior unless they are the only way a child can be sure of getting adult attention.

Temperament. Behaviors viewed as inappropriate may be a reflection of the child's basic personality. Some children seem to be born with a temperament that makes them easy to manage, others with a temperament that makes them more difficult. An interesting aspect of this proposition is what Thomas and Chess (1986) call *goodness of fit*. These authors suggest that it is not the child's temperament itself that determines behavioral outcome. Instead, it is how the child's personality characteristics match the demands of the environment, especially the expectations of parents and caregivers. Consider, for example, a child who is active, independent, constantly curious, into everything. This child may be seen as troublesome, a behavior problem, and a candidate for frequent punishment by overworked parents who hold high standards for order and routine. On the other hand, energetic, adventuresome parents might view this active, into-everything child as highly desirable. They might go out of their way to reinforce, nurture, and respect the child's efforts at exploration and experimentation.

Young children who have been prematurely labeled as mentally retarded or emotionally disturbed often exhibit behavior problems. A common reaction is for adults to excuse these behaviors, explaining that the child "can't help it" or "doesn't know any better." Making such excuses is neither fair to the child nor is it sensible. All young children, regardless of their developmental level, can be helped to learn basic social requirements. Early childhood programs that fail to provide such learning opportunities do these children a serious injustice. Other children will come to dislike and reject them. This may result in further increase in the child's acting out or lead to excesses of aggression or withdrawal.

Thumb sucking seldom need be considered a problem unless it seriously interferes with a child's participation in learning activities.

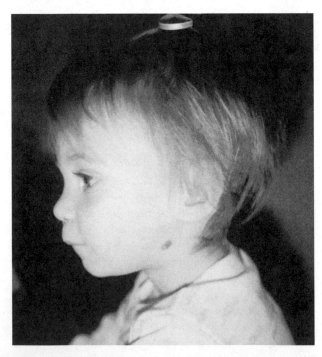

A child's temperament partly determines behavioral outcome.

When Is a Behavior a Problem?   Occasional episodes of maladaptive behaviors are seldom cause for concern. Only when a behavior or a pattern of behaviors becomes excessive is it a problem. This raises the question: How much is *too much*? For classroom purposes, it is useful to define excessive behavior as that which interferes seriously with a child's (or other children's) ability to engage in normal everyday activities. Consider the following examples:

A 4-year-old who has a brief tantrum once or twice a month is not likely to be a worry. The 4-year-old who trantrums several times every day, over minor frustrations, is cause for concern.

Thumb sucking is seldom a problem except for the occasional child whose thumb sucking is so continuous that the child seldom engages in activities that require two hands.

Biting others is a fairly common, but unacceptable behavior, even among toddlers. In the interest of safety, the biting has to be controlled, but the toddler seldom is viewed as having a serious behavior disorder. On the other hand, a 5- or 6-year-old who bites others, even infrequently, is of concern.

The remainder of this unit is about behavior problems. The focus in on troublesome behaviors that teachers are most likely to encounter among toddlers and young children, with and without developmental problems. Each of the behaviors that will be discussed can range from occasional to very nearly constant in terms of their occurrence and intensity. The urgent message in this unit is for teachers to help children avoid or overcome these problems so they do not become fixed during the developmental years.

Hyperactive Label: Misused and Overused. For years, the term *hyperactivity* has been misused and overused, especially where young children are concerned. Typically, children in preschool and early primary classrooms show a broad range of activity levels. Some seem to be on the move continuously. Teachers often feel as if these children *never* settle into any activity for any length of time. Yet, few are of medical concern because of organic problems. Only 1 to 3 percent of the children labeled hyperactive are truly hyperactive in the clinical sense (Trites and Laprade 1983). A child who can stay with any activity for several minutes at a time is not clinically hyperactive. As one pediatrician explains it: A child who passes the "TV test" (sits in front of the television set and attends to a favorite program) is *not* hyperactive. The child may be difficult to entertain, not interested in typical learning tasks, or perhaps worried and unhappy, but not hyperactive in the medical sense (Holm 1978, p. 162).

Even in cases of known organic involvement, the hyperactive *behaviors* must be dealt with as maladaptive behaviors, regardless of other treatment procedures. Hyperactivity in young children places them at great risk for accidents because they do not anticipate the consequences of their actions. Also, adults become more frustrated by excessively active, impulsive children who must be watched constantly. "The

behavior itself is problematic and will require training and reinforcement of more desired behavior patterns" (Peterson 1987, p. 239).

Reducing Hyperactivity. Systematic classroom observation usually reveals one or more activities that engage even the most overly active child for 3 to 20 minutes at a time, several times a week. Such observations are important. They give teachers a place to start a positive behavior management program designed to increase the child's span of attention. Even brief focus on an activity, any activity, sends a signal to teachers; *Now is the time to give attention*, while the child is engaged. This is in contrast to what teachers (and parents) usually do:

Attempting to stop the child, with a suggestion: "You need to finish the puzzle."

Making an effort to involve the child in another activity—"There's room for you at blocks."

Trying to find out "what's wrong"—"You don't like it when paint gets on your hands?"

A series of research studies (Allen and Goetz 1982) indicates that even the most well-intentioned responses from adults, given when the overly active child is on the move, increases the child's "flitting." (Remember the anecdotes about James [Unit 13]) When teachers do not attend to flitting, it decreases markedly. The studies demonstrate that teachers need to keep an eye out for those moments when the child is engaged in an activity. It is then that they go to the child with a relevant comment, interested watching, or a gentle challenge: "I bet you can fill that pail full of sand, all the way to the tip. I'll watch while you do it." Few children can resist staying with a task when so challenged by an interested and responsive adult.

A child's span of attention often can be extended by calling attention to unexplored aspects of the activity or by asking questions. While supervising the water table the teacher might ask, "What do you think would happen if we put a little yellow food coloring in the blue water?" An overly active child's stick-to-itiveness may also be enhanced by offering additional but related materials: "Here are some new cookie cutters to use with the dough when you get it all rolled out." Or, "The big doll looks like it needs a bath, too." The key is to always offer the ideas and materials *while the child is still engaged* in the activity—*before* the child has lost interest and leaves.

Overly active children, when they look as if they are getting ready to quit an activity, can be helped to plan where they will play next. Noting that a child is about to leave an area, the teacher can say, "Let's decide where you want to play next." If the child seems unable to make the decision, the teacher offers choices: "There is room for you in the block corner or at the water table." Once a choice has been made it is well for the teacher to accompany the child to the area. If there is a teacher in the block area, for example, the first teacher can say something like, "Julie has come to work with blocks. Will you help her get started?" Otherwise, the accompanying teacher helps the child get involved.

To further reduce overactivity in young children, the following ideas have proven useful in all types of early childhood programs and inclusion classrooms.

- Observe the child in various activities over several days. If observations indicate that a child's attention begins to wander after five or six minutes of music time, plan to end that child's participation as it gets toward the five minute mark. A second teacher can quietly draw the child away and provide another activity before the child wearies of music. The child can be given crayons or a puzzle, or might assist the teacher setting up snack tables. It is important that a special activity *not be offered* if the child has already disrupted the music group.
- Keep the classroom and play yard neat and orderly. Do not have too many materials out at one time. Have children restore (tidy up) each play area before they leave it. A disorderly environment encourages disorderly behavior, especially with overly active children.
- Alternate active and quiet experiences, large and small groups, teacher-initiated activities with child-initiated activities. (Review Unit 14 on environmental arrangements for guidelines to helping all young children focus more effectively on curriculum activities.) Extended free play periods can be especially difficult for overly active children. Amount of free play time and play choices usually need to be limited.

An orderly environment promotes orderly behavior in children.

When working with an overly active child, teachers also need to review various aspects of their program at regular intervals:

Are the classroom activities interesting, attractive, and lively? In other words, are they fun and are they challenging?
Are the activities a good match to the child's skill levels?
Is the child getting attention when focusing on an activity, even for a moment or two, rather than for flitting about?

Working toward positive answers to these questions is essential in reducing hyperactivity and in maintaining a quality program for all children. Furthermore, when behavior management strategies and knowledge of what is developmentally appropriate are laced together with care and concern for the child's well-being, hyperactivity inevitably lessens. This three-pronged approach works effectively also with children who display a variety of other behavior problems.

Aggressiveness.   Aggressiveness, like so many other terms we apply to children, is difficult to define. What is considered aggressive by one group of people, one parent, or one teacher may seem unnoteworthy to another group, another parent, another member of the teaching team.

Conflict and ethical issues.   Aggressive behavior, according to Caldwell (1988) is a typically American problem. In other words, our society, our way of life, seems to both spawn and reinforce aggressiveness. Any child displaying continuing aggressiveness creates conflict among teachers, among parents, and among children. Often it spreads into conflict between teachers and parents, with children caught in the middle. Ethical issues are always at stake. Take the case study of 4-year-old Eric, presented to readers of *Young Children* by the NAEYC Ethics Commission (Feeney 1988): Eric was described as a large and extremely active child who often frightened and hurt other children. His parents felt his behaviors were typical for boys his age. Other parents were complaining about Eric. The teachers were stressed and tired, their patience was wearing thin. In readers' responses to the case study, Feeney (1988) reported that conflict prevailed:

> Values that conflict in this case are the needs of the group (for safety and serenity) versus the needs of the individual (to be responded to appropriately, to express anger and frustration). Also in conflict are the family's need for a program for their child and the teachers' need for an environment that fosters mental and physical health (p. 48).

Two major principles were inferred from the responses: one, children's safety must be the teachers' highest priority; two, the rights of every child in the classroom should take precedence over the needs of the individual child, especially when his behavior hurts others.

There was conflict as to whether the child should be banned from the classroom. Caldwell, in her comments, suggested it is probably a tactical error to insist the child leave the group until "his behavior improves." No matter what the underlying causes, some of the elicitors of the outbursts are sure to be found in the group experience, so Eric will eventually have to work things out in that setting (p. 50). The authors of this text agree, while recognizing at the same time that reducing aggressive behavior and maintaining the child in the group is not easy. However it can be done, and done safely. Furthermore, problems need not become so out-of-hand as Eric's if the unacceptable behaviors are dealt with at the outset, before they reach crisis proportions.

Managing aggressiveness.   An individualized program based on behavioral procedures is imperative in situations where aggressive behaviors are truly troublesome. Always, *the behavior management program is in addition to and concurrent with teachers' best efforts at understanding the child's current feelings.* It is in addition to finding legitimate ways for the child to "blow off steam." It is in addition to working with parents to help alleviate the child's stress, frustration, anxieties, or lack of self-esteem. The child who kicks, hits, and knocks children about, either physically or verbally, invariably needs more adult attention. However, the attention never should be given at the moment the child is hurting another child. At a different time, the teacher encourages the child to talk about the situation, the angry feelings, and what he or she might do "next time." They might even rehearse alternate and more acceptable responses.

Young children often behave aggressively because they feel left out or do not know acceptable ways of getting into play. Many children with developmental delays lack the play skills or the verbal niceties that make them desirable playmates. The teachers' responsibility is twofold: one, take the initiative in helping the child acquire the necessary play and social skills (review Unit 15 for teaching strategies); two, watch for approximations to more appropriate play and interact with the child pleasantly at those times. (Review Unit 13 on behavioral practices.)

When a child with a history of excessive aggression hurts another child, the teacher turns full attention to the child who has been hurt or attacked. *The child who did the hurting receives no adult attention at that time.* It is never necessary for the teacher to explain how much it hurts another child to be hit or pushed down. The child who behaves aggressively has been given that information innumerable times. Furthermore, the behavior of the hurting child conveys the message eloquently. Should the teacher feel explanations about not hurting other children are needed, it should be done at another time, as noted earlier. Such discussions are suited to a small group—objective conversations with the offending child present, and hopefully participating.

A child who is frequently and severely aggressive may need to be removed from the group temporarily for each aggressive episode. This step is taken when other forms of working with the child are not having the needed effect. No child can be allowed to hurt other children repeatedly. When more positive methods have failed, time-out (Unit 13) is a nonaggressive way to help a child learn that he or she absolutely cannot attack other children. The use of time-out is a decision to be made jointly with teachers, a consultant from the interdisciplinary team, and the child's parents. State regulations also need to be reviewed. If agreed upon, the child is shown the time-out space and procedures explained: specifically, when and why the child will be removed. From then on, the child is removed from classroom contacts as a consequence of every aggression against another child. It is best if a second teacher removes the child to the time-out space; the original teacher then can comfort and calm the child who has been hurt.

Moving a child into time-out should be done with a minimum of adult attention. The teacher accompanies the procedure with a firm "**NO**" followed by a brief, but equally firm statement, "I cannot let you hurt children." No other attention is given to the child at that time. One, two, or three minutes later, depending on the situation (but never more than five minutes, even in the most distressing cases) the teacher goes to the child with a matter-of-fact statement, "Let's try again. Where would you like to play?" When returning the child to play the teacher does not lecture, moralize, or try to extract promises from the child "to be good." What does seem to work is making a suggestion regarding a next activity: "There's room for you at the water table. I'll help you get started." A successful start is often the key to a successful play experience, especially if a teacher checks in frequently with favorable and interested comments.

Disruptive and Destructive Behaviors.   Every early childhood classroom, at one time or another, has a child who seems bent on upsetting the program. These children interfere with teacher-directed activities and with other children's projects. Music periods are interrupted by the child making inappropriate noises, faces, and comments, or running aimlessly about the room. Books are tossed around recklessly and toys are unnecessarily damaged. The child tram-

ples other children's sand structures, topples their block towers, wets their clothes and hair at the water table. The list of possible misdeeds is long. What early childhood teacher has not seen them all?

Need for attention.   Children who behave in these ways have learned it as a sure way of getting adult attention. These are children who often have low self-esteem and stresses in their life. Like the overly active child, they are greatly in need of large amounts of attention from important adults. These children often appear to feel that when they are being good they are ignored (which is often the case); and when they misbehave they get immediate attention (which, too, is often the case). Young children are seven times more likely to get teachers' attention when they are behaving inappropriately than when they are behaving well (Strain et al. 1983). Therefore, the refrain that has been heard, and will be heard, again and again in this unit and elsewhere in this text is *give attention to children when they are behaving appropriately.*

The dilemma is that teachers and parents usually feel the child is getting a great deal of attention, even a disproportionate amount compared to other children. This is likely to be true; adults *are* giving large amounts of time-consuming attention, but squandering it on the very behaviors that are bothering them. They also are spending large amounts of unproductive time correcting the havoc created by the child. *Half as much of that time directed toward the child when not misbehaving would go twice as far toward producing a more constructive environment.* Remember Harris's advice, "Catch the child being good"? Efforts to discuss this with parents or teachers often leads to the assertion that the child "never does anything right (or good)." This, of course, is not true of any child. The first step, as always, is for adults to make several observations of the child. Invariably, they are amazed at how much of the time the child is appropriate; and how rarely appropriate behavior draws adult attention (Allen and Goetz, 1982).

Mastering routines.   Many of the techniques for helping the overly active child apply to children with disruptive behaviors. Always, underlying causes must be studied; part of the cause may be stresses of one kind or another. Or it may be much simpler. Many disruptive children have never understood or mastered classroom routines and expectations. They need to be *walked through* routines, one step at a time. At the easel a child may need to be shown, and then asked to practice, returning each paintbrush to its own color paint pot. A first step may be for the teacher to remove all paint containers but two. This makes it easy for the child to do it "right." It also allows the teacher to give specific, descriptive feedback: "Great! You remembered to put the red paint brush back in the red paint pot." Lengthy verbalizations must be avoided, or the important message will get lost. Expectations can be discussed in small group sessions, when necessary. As the child paints, the teacher makes appreciative comments, when appropriate, about the brightness of the colors or how beautifully the child combined red and blue *on the paper* to make another lovely color.

Redirection. Behaviors that damage equipment or other children's learning experiences cannot be allowed. With most young children, simple, positive redirection is best. Statements such as, "Paint on the *paper*." "Walk *around* Mark and Judi's launching pad" "Tricycles stay *on the path*" are all that is required. Other children, especially those with a history of disruptive behavior, may pay little heed to subtle redirection. When the child ignores redirection, what is needed is a clear and firm statement about limits as well as expectations: "I cannot let you paint on the walls. The paint brushes stay at the easel." If the child persists, either the material or the child is removed, depending on the situation.

Time-out. Before resorting to time-out for disruptive behavior, teachers must have done everything possible to modify both the classroom environment and their own responses as outlined in the section on the overly active child. Only then do teachers consider the temporary use of time-out to break the pattern of disruptiveness and to assure the child that teachers follow through when they say, "I can't let you. . . ." Spodek, Saracho and Lee (1984) warn, rightfully, of the danger of teachers overusing time-out as a management strategy (p. 141). Always, time-out is reserved for serious situations. It provides *temporary relief* from

an uncontrollable problem and helps the child learn to respond to more desirable guidance procedures such as redirection.

Noncompliance. Refusing to do what an adult asks, or ignoring an adult request, is a frequent and typical behavior among young children. Seldom is this a serious problem unless it becomes a habitual way of responding to adults. In those instances the child often is labeled *noncompliant* or *oppositional.* Following are three episodes, recorded in less than an hour, characteristic of one 4-year-old's habitual noncompliance:

> Father: "Michael, hang up your coat."
> Michael: "No, you do it."
> Father: "Alright, but you pick it up off the floor and hand it to me."
> Michael: "You pick it up." Michael started playing with a truck in the cubby next to his. Father hung up the coat, said good bye, and left.

> Teacher: "Michael, let's pick up the blocks." Michael ran to his locker and sat in it, looking at a book he had brought from home.

> Teacher: "Michael, it's time to come in."
> Michael: "Not coming in," while continuing his climb to the top of the climber.

The first steps in dealing with noncompliance (or any other problem behavior) is collecting specific information through several systematic observations and then consultation with parents and appropriate team members. It must be determined that the child does not have a hearing loss or a problem with receptive language. Innumerable children with these kinds of undiagnosed problems have been labeled noncompliant or disobedient (and have received unjust punishments as a consequence). Others have had damaging labels of mentally retarded or emotionally disturbed attached to them because they failed to do as they were told. The injustice is that it is nearly impossible for such children to follow directions without special intervention.

Prevention strategies. Oppositional children frazzle teachers' and parents' patience. However, most noncompliance (as well as other behavior problems) can

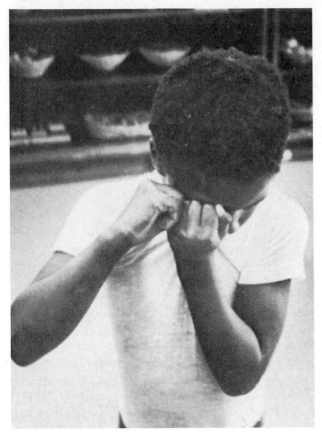

An undetected developmental problem may be the cause of a child's seeming noncompliance.

be reduced to manageable proportions thorough *preventive discipline* (Unit 14). Basic to this form of discipline is systematic observation of the child to determine what triggers the inappropriate responses. Once trouble spots are identified, teachers can plan ways to handle the situations *before* a problem develops. The essence of the strategy is to determine what is it about the environment, including adults' behavior, that prompts a child's resistance.

Considerable space was devoted to preventive discipline in Unit 14. That information should be reviewed whenever planning for and dealing with children who are oppositional. A number of related strategies also are effective with all kinds of behavior problems, great and small, and with all kinds of children with and without developmental disabilities.

- Give advance warning. Give children ample warning before bringing an activity to an end, especially a play activity. Provide a clue as to what comes next: "Soon it will be time to come in and get ready for snack." To the child who always resists coming indoors: "Sara, you can be the *last* one in today." The offer, however, is made before the child has lined up her oppositional arguments.

- Reduce overload. Check frequently to make sure the child is not overloaded with directions, expectations, and picky rules (Unit 12). Even a compliant child may develop some noncompliance if overwhelmed with rules and instructions.

- Make requests and give directions clearly and briefly. Adults tend to say things like: "We're going in to get washed for snack so don't forget to hang up your coat when you take it off but first put your truck in the shed and shut the door." (This was an actual word-for-word recording of a teacher's verbalization in a child care classroom.) Such a jumble of directions is confusing to any child, and sets up even greater opposition in a noncompliant child. The way to help a child through such a routine is to give advance warning about going indoors. When the time comes, give directions one or two at a time in the order they are to be carried out; in this case, parking the truck and then shutting the shed door. (To review giving instruction to young children see the more detailed discussion in Unit 17.)

- Provide choices. All children, and particularly noncompliant children, need opportunities to make choices as often as possible:

Do you want to sit here with Miss Bobbie? Or over there with Mr. Paul?
Would you like to put the cups *or* the napkins on the table?
Who are you going to ask to help you decorate the window?
It's a warm day. You can decide if you want to wear your sweater outdoors.

Choosing and making decisions helps a child develop a sense of responsibility and independence. It also reduces the child's feelings that he or she is always being told what to do.

When giving instructions, look at and speak directly to the child.

- Beware of choices that are not choices. Adults must be careful of the choices they offer young children. Whenever a choice is offered, the adult must be prepared to honor it. The teacher does not ask, "Would you like to park your wagon and come in for music?" unless it is alright for the child to stay outdoors and play with the wagon during music. The child has been offered an option that the teacher had no intention of honoring. What follows is argument, confusion, or a power struggle depending on the child. The more appropriate approach, once the earlier warning has been given, is for the teacher to say, "Time to come indoors for music. You can park your wagon by the door or in the shed."
- Focus the child's attention. Teachers can reduce confusion for all young children by making sure the child is paying attention before giving instructions. To ensure the child's attention:

Precede every request by speaking the child's name: "Gail, the pegs go in the basket."
Get down to the child's level (the half-kneel, an almost automatic posture among preschool teachers, works well).

Look into the child's face and speak directly to the child. Check the child's understanding by getting verification: "Where does the puzzle go?"
Demonstrate, as needed, and hold a rehearsal: "Jon, turn the pages like this. Now you try it."

- Allow time to comply. An instruction should not be repeated until the child has had ample time to comply. Too often teachers give the instruction a second time (even a third) while the child is gearing up, getting ready to comply to the initial request. When enough time has been given and it becomes obvious the child is not going to comply, the direction should be offered a second time. The teacher's voice quietly conveys the expectation that the child surely will do it this time. Never does the teacher coax or nag, bribe or offer a reward. Following the second request, if no compliance after a reasonable period, the teacher turns away to do whatever else needs doing. The child does not go on to another activity, however, until the coat is picked up, the book is put away, or whatever was the request. (See the example below.)
- Practice consistency and firmness. Teachers need to be matter-of-fact, firm, and consistent when

giving directions to children who are noncompliant. They also must be quietly confident of their own authority. If a teacher says, "Raoul, you may go to the woodworking table as soon as your blocks are picked up," then Raoul must do just that—pick up the blocks before going to woodworking. The teacher in the block area alerts the other teachers that Raoul has a job to do in the block corner before he can play elsewhere. If other children are busy putting blocks away, the teacher pushes a fair share aside for Raoul to take care of. At this point, the contingency can be restated clearly and simply: "Raoul, this is your share of the blocks to put away. You can go to woodworking as soon as your finish." In many cases, the teacher offers to help the child: "As soon as you get started, I will help you put the blocks away."

- Make sound judgments. Because consistency is important, teachers must not set a requirement they may not be able to carry out. In the Raoul example, it would be unwise to tell the child he could not go home until the blocks were picked up, especially if he were in a carpool or being bussed. Drivers cannot spare that kind of time. In such instances, the teacher provides an option: "Raoul, the driver will be here in a few minutes. How about getting your blocks picked up before he comes?" If the child says "No" or ignores the request, the teacher accepts it. The teacher's authority is not undermined, and an argument was avoided that the teacher could not have won.

Temper trantrums. Young children who have frequent, full blown temper tantrums require special help. The advice often given is for adults to ignore the tantrum. While that is good advice, it may prove nearly impossible to carry out. Parents report, repeatedly that they tried ignoring their child's tantrums and "it didn't work." The reason it did not work is because most adults give in long before the child gives in.

A child with a history of tantrums that are suddenly ignored may go to even greater extremes—having tantrums of even greater fury and duration. As a tantrum becomes more violent, the adults trying to ignore the tantrum get increasingly anxious; finally they can no longer restrain their concern for the child. They provide attention in one way or another. As this pattern is repeated, the tantrums become worse.

The child learns two damaging lessons from such experiences: one, that it takes ever greater and more prolonged fury to break down the adults' defenses; two, the defenses invariably do break down and the adult eventually will provide some kind of attention. This leads to deepening trouble for both the child and the adults. Therefore, while ignoring tantrums is the surest way of ridding the child of such behavior, most adults need help and support in carrying out such a program. Any one of several professionals on the interdisciplinary team are qualified to work with parents and teachers in managing a child's tantrums.

Management of trantrums. Difficult as it may be, tantrums can be handled at school. It takes careful planning among teachers, parents, and a psychologist, nurse, or other member of the developmental team. It is best if one teacher is designated to handle the tantrum and is coached and supported by the specialist. At the start of the tantrum the child needs to be removed to a separate place where injury is not likely to occur. Always, the child is shown the space in advance and given an explanation of its purpose. The teacher withholds all attention while the child is having the tantrum. However, the teacher (or another adult) stays close by but does not make eye contact or appear to be watching the child. When the tantrum stops the teacher waits a moment and then returns the child to a play activity with no lecturing or moralizing. Tantrums first get worse, but then disappear within a week or less if adults can be totally consistent in carrying out the procedures (Allen and Goetz 1982).

Lesser tantrums often are handled by the teachers in the classroom. These, too, are likely to accelerate briefly when attention is first withheld. Again, it is well if one teacher is designated to manage the tantrum to provide consistency of procedures. The other teacher(s) focuses on the rest of the children who may become uneasy as the tantrum accelerates. A special story or game or record can be presented to keep the children occupied and diverted. Sometimes children can be taken on a walk around the building or to the gym or library while the tantrum is going on. Always the children are assured that the tantrumming child will be all right and is being well cared for by the other teacher.

Teachers and parents must recognize that tantrums are always an indication that the child is experiencing stress, anxiety, frustration, or other upset. Underlying causes must be sought, and the preschool or child care program studied for changes that might be made to help the child. In the meantime, and along with the other efforts, tantrums must be brought under control. Otherwise, the tantrums themselves prevent the child from benefiting from the changes being made on his or her behalf.

Separation Problems.   It is quite normal for infants and young children to be both fearful of strangers and unwilling to separate from a parent or major caregiver. The behavior tends to peak between 12 and 15 months of age and then to lessen gradually. No consistent relationship has been found between the number of caregivers a child has had and the intensity of a child's protests over separation. In other words, a child who has had multiple caregivers is no less anxious about strangers than a child cared for by a very few caregivers (Thompson and Lamb 1982). In families where there is general instability, children may be especially fearful of strangers and have trouble separating, throughout the preschool years and beyond.

Entering preschool or a child care center for the first time can be intimidating for children. Young children with developmental problems may experience even more anxiety. They are likely to have had fewer play experiences away from home. They often have been the focus of intensive adult care and concern that is inappropriate in a school situation; separation anxieties are common. In general, they need not become a major problem if the first days of school are carefully planned by teachers and parents. (See Allen and Hart 1984, p. 181–99, for a detailed description of appropriate procedures.)

In a few instances, a child and parent may have prolonged and severe separation problems. At the least hint the parent may leave, the child embarks on a full-blown tantrum. The severe reactions may have come about because the parent, after agreeing to stay, had tried to slip away without saying good bye. In these cases, teachers must involve parents in a plan to help the child learn to separate. Discussions of the problem should take place away from the classroom and out of the child's earshot. The situation can only worsen if the child is further burdened with the parents' and teachers' concerns. The focus of the separation program is on the parents' gradual withdrawal, usually over several days. The amount of time required depends on the child and the severity of the problem. Throughout the parent's separation efforts, teachers encourage and appreciate the child's participation and active use of materials. Gradually, teacher support replaces parent support.

The occasional child, who actually likes coming to the program, may use protest as a way to keep parents at school. Such children engage in every activity and play happily as long as the parent stays. As soon as the parent tries to leave, the child puts on a scene. These parents often complain about the child's behavior. Yet, after saying good bye they tend to pause and look back, as if waiting for the child to begin a tantrum. (Maybe it is the parent who is having a separation problem?) In these cases the teacher may have to assist the lingering parent in leaving swiftly with only a brief and matter-of-fact good bye. The child almost always settles back into play after a token protest.

Overdependency.   The early childhood teacher may be the target of a child's efforts to get extraordinary amounts of attention. Sometimes this is the child who had separation problems, but not always. The overly dependent child may cling to a particular teacher, hang on to the teacher's clothing, shadow the teacher's every move. Complaining, whining, and tattling may be accompanying problems. Working with a child like this requires teachers to walk a fine line between giving too much and too little attention. Too much is likely to increase the dependency; too little may lead the child to feeling rejected, even distrustful.

To receive full benefit from the program, a child must be helped to relate to all teacher and eventually to children. Once the child is familiar with the program and the routines, the *weaning* process can begin. It is not a question of reducing the amount of attention; it is one of making decisions as to *when* to give the attention in order to help rather than hinder the child's progress. Consider the following examples:

The teacher watches for those moments when the child is not clinging and immediately gives attention: "It looks like you are enjoying the book. Let's read the pictures. What do you suppose is going to happen to the kitten?"

When a child is pulling at teacher's clothing or person, the teacher resists the impulse to react or respond. Hard to do, yes; but it is to the eventual benefit of both child and teacher. As always, *preventive measures are best*: as the child approaches, the teacher can reach out and put an arm around the child or take the child's hand *before* the clinging or clutching starts.

Teachers support the child in taking personal responsibility, beginning with nonthreatening situations: "If you want to play in the rocking boat I'll go with you while you talk to Sherri. If you ask, I know she'll stop rocking so you can get in."

Finding ways to get the child to allow other teachers to respond to his or her needs is another step in solving the problem. The teacher chooses those times when the child really wants something, as when one teacher says to another: "Miss Jane, Charles wants the red truck. Will you get it out for him?" or to the child, "I can't read your book because I have to set up fingerpainting. Let's ask Mr. John to read it to you."

The occasional teacher finds it flattering to be singled out for undivided devotion and unintentionally reinforces the child's dependent behaviors. In these instances, both child and teacher need the help of other staff members.

Overly dependent, anxious children may also complain of headaches, stomachaches, or nearly invisible cuts and scrapes. Though the hurt is real to the child, it also has become a sure way of getting focused attention from an important adult. Most young children can be expected to have this kind of complaint on occasion. When the complaints go on, day after day, it is cause for concern. The first step is to check with parents to make sure there are no physical problems. Classroom procedures then become the same as for other problem behaviors: minimum attention to the aches and scrapes, additional attention when the child is actively engaged in play activities. This helps the child to focus on the fun times at school.

Withdrawal.   Some children seem to be alone most of the time. They turn away when other children approach. In structured, large group activities they may be there in body but are remote, *not there* in spirit.

Teachers seldom express the degree of concern over these children that they do with children who act out. The behaviors of the withdrawn child are easily overlooked; those of the disruptive child seldom go unnoticed. Yet the child may be in greater developmental jeopardy than the child who acts out.

Withdrawal problems and their causes can be so complex as to require clinical treatment and a therapeutic classroom. The children that teachers encounter in early childhood programs are likely to have less serious problems with less obscure origins. The cause may be a recent upheaval at home such as a parent leaving or a serious illness in the family. It may be a change of neighborhood where the new children's ways seem strange, even frightening or bullying. It may be the first venture of an only child, or a child with a developmental disability, into a play setting with other children. These children may have been overprotected unwittingly, in the parents' efforts to keep them from getting hurt or catching a childhood disease. Then, there is shyness, pure and simple. All children experience shyness off and on; in some, shyness becomes a habit of long standing. Whatever the cause, teachers usually can help these children become more involved.

Careful observation, as always, is the first step. Specific questions need asking:

- Does the child engage in particular activities when playing alone?
- Are there materials and equipment that the child appears to enjoy or prefer?
- Does the child spend time watching certain children or certain activities more than others?
- Is the child likely to leave an activity if certain children approach? Does the child avoid these children consistently?
- Are some children less threatening for the child to sit next to in group activities? To play next to in parallel play situations?

When a child's preferences (and avoidances) have been noted, plans can be made to reduce the child's isolation. *Start small* is always the motto. Following are three examples of first approximations to social interactions for Jeanine, a child whose isolate behaviors were of concern:

On several occasions the teacher had observed Jeanine watching housekeeping play with apparent interest. The teacher arranged that he and the child together deliver additional materials to the activities in progress. Teacher: "Jeanine and I have brought more birthday candles. We'll put some of them on the cake, too, okay?"

Jeanine seemed fascinated by the rocking boat. A quiet but friendly child asked the teacher for another ride. The teacher responded, "Yes, Jon, but let's give Jeanine a ride, too. Here Jeanine, you sit across from Jon." Another time a third child is invited, who also is seated across from Jeanine. Then a fourth who sits *next to* Jeanine. In each of these early steps the teacher selected quieter, less rambunctious children to share the ride.

Jeanine was watching two children working with peg boards. Teacher: "Jeanine, I'll put a peg board down here for you. (The teacher placed the peg board at the end of the small table, near, but not between the other children.) All three of you can reach the basket of pegs." Having Jeanine take pegs out of a common basket was a step forward from the week before. At that time, the teacher had seated her near the other children but had given her a small basket of pegs of her own.

Occasionally, a shy child will focus almost exclusively on one or more of the adults in the program. Overdependency does not seem to be the problem; it is as if some children prefer the company of adults. They find ways to always sit next to the teacher. They linger during transitions to help the teacher clean up. They engage the teacher in long, one-to-one conversations. This may be pleasant for the teacher, but it does not promote the kind of social development that comes with learning to interact with other children. The teacher's job becomes one of consciously involving another child or two in the conversation or the cleanup operation. If no other children are about, the teacher responds to the child pleasantly but briefly; then moves to an area where there are other children. Usually the shy child follows. This increases the teacher's chances to involve other children.

Inability to Share.   It is questionable that the inability to share and take turns is serious enough to include it in a discussion of behavior problems. Many of today's children, in group care since infancy, learn to share early and readily. However, the issue continues to be

of concern to many early childhood teachers. Sharing and taking turns are learned behaviors. It is suggested that developmentally, the **egocentric** young child needs to establish a sense of *mine* before accommodating to the concept of *thine*. For many young children, the learning does not come easily. Suggestions for helping all types of young children learn to comply with these social expectations are outlined below.

- Plentiful materials is one key to helping young children learn to share. In all early childhood programs, there should be duplicates of the most popular materials. Large sets (Lego, for example) can be divided into two or three smaller sets. These are distributed among individual baskets or boxes enabling several children to have their *very own*. A nice side effect is that spontaneous trading of particular pieces often emerges.
- Interest centers need to be attractive and located in various parts of the classroom and play yard. With several attractive set ups, children do not need to stand around waiting. The teacher can advise, "You could play at the water table or the woodworking bench for awhile. I'll call you when there is room on the bouncing board." The teacher must remember to alert the child when space becomes available. By

Many of today's children learn to share early and easily.

that time, the child may not want to change activities, but the teacher's part of the bargain has been kept.

- A game-like atmosphere can help children learn to wait and take turns. The teacher might use a kitchen timer and advise: "When the timer bell rings it is Bart's turn"; or, "It will be Bart's turn with the big rolling pin when the timer goes off." Older preschool children can look at the clock with the teacher and understand, "When the big hand gets to 5 it will be your turn" or "There's no room at blocks right now but you can go there first, right after music." Children and teachers can also count turns: "Josh, you can have two more turns around the track. Then it will be Susie's turn. She has waited a long time. . . . Susie, you and I will count."

Children must be stopped when they knock other children off of equipment because they want a turn, or when they use force to get or keep the toys they want. As with other forms of aggression the teacher states the case clearly and firmly: "I cannot let you take Maria's doll" or "I cannot let you knock Jerry off the swing." At the same time, the teacher helps the other child hang on to a possession by encouraging specific verbalizations such as "Tell Nonie, 'That's my doll. Give it back'" or "You can't have the swing 'til I'm through." At that point, the teacher makes sure the doll is returned or the place on the swing is recovered. If necessary, the teacher physically assists in the return.

SUMMARY

The focus of this unit was on a variety of behavior problems found in young children. One of the most common of these is the *grab bag* classification, hyperactivity. Most young children, probably less than 1 to 3 percent, are truly hyperactive in a clinical or organic (brain damage) sense. Seldom is the level of activity reduced effectively through medication or special diet alone; a systematic behavior management program is also necessary.

The remainder of the unit was given over to behavior problems sometimes described as "acting out" behaviors. Many of these behaviors are perfectly normal. They tend to be *trial-and-error* responses, a part of children's efforts at learning to discriminate between acceptable and unacceptable ways of responding to the expectations of their own home, school, and community. Seldom are acting out behaviors cause for serious concern unless they become excessive to the point of threatening the child's well-being or the rights and safety of others.

Most behavior problems can be managed through careful arrangement of the environment—materials, activities, space, routines, expectations, and adult attention, especially when adult attention is focused on all of the good things each child does, each day. When a child's behavior causes damage or injury, the child must be stopped; it is unethical to do otherwise. In extreme cases, where the child has not responded to careful rearrangement of the environment, temporary use of time-out may be needed. Brief time-out periods always are used in conjunction with other procedures, including acceptance and understanding of the child's stresses and special attention to the child's appropriate behaviors.

STUDENT ACTIVITIES

1. Wear a watch and observe an early childhood program during an entire free play period (30 to 45 minutes). Consult with the teacher first to identify which child might be considered overly active. During the first half of your observations, record the types of activities the child engaged in and the amount of time spent in each (also record time spent wandering about). Make the same recordings on a normally active child for the second half of the observation. Compare the observations and try to analyze the differences or similarities in the two children.

2. Select two or three fellow students and form a classroom teaching staff whose concern is a 4-year-old overly aggressive child. Work together to formulate a guidance plan for this child. Prioritize the steps in your plan beginning with the steps you will take before undertaking direct intervention with the child.

3. Select a partner; one of you play the role of teacher, the other, a noncompliant child. Demonstrate several ways the teacher might work with this child to obtain compliance *before* the child balks at a request. Reverse roles and play out several ways of helping a child share a wagon.
4. Separate a sheet of paper into five columns. Head each column with terms commonly used to describe children's acting-out behaviors: aggressive, destructive, disruptive, noncompliant, tantrum. Observe during a free-play period and put a mark in the appropriate column each time one of the behaviors occur. Circle the mark if a teacher responds in any way. Figure out the ratio of teacher responses to child behaviors. Analyze to see if certain behaviors draw more teacher attention than others.

REVIEW QUESTIONS

A. *Short Answer.*
1. Describe the timing of teachers' attention in working with an overly active child.
2. What are the basic components of an intervention plan to help a child who is overly aggressive?
3. What can teachers do to help prevent noncompliance in young children?
4. Extensive research indicates that ignoring tantrums gets rid of them. The problem is that this advice often backfires. Why?
5. How can teachers reduce a child's overdependency?
6. What is meant by preventive discipline?

B. *Multiple Choice. Circle the one* least *appropriate phrase for completing each of the following statements.*
1. Psychologically healthy 5-year-olds
   a. may sometimes balk at parents' leaving.
   b. have irrational fears sometimes.
   c. have temper tantrums on occasion.
   d. often bite other children when frustrated.
   e. can be argumentative and oppositional.
2. *Goodness of fit* (Thomas and Chess 1985) includes such factors as the
   a. child's temperament.
   b. child's energy level.
   c. adults' expectations.
   d. adults' frustration threshold.
   e. adults' sensitivity to the fit of child's shoes.
3. Which of the following is cause for serious adult concern?
   a. the 18-month-old who pushes the doll carriage into other toddlers.
   b. the 2-year-old who refuses to share his toys or cookies.
   c. the 3-year-old who refuses to pick up her blocks two days in a row.
   d. the 5-year-old who bites other children once or twice a month.
   e. the 6-year-old who often is slow about coming in from outdoor play.
4. A child's aggressiveness may be due to:
   a. stress.
   b. anxiety.

c. heredity.
d. frustration.
e. low self-esteem.
5. When one child repeatedly hits or pushes other children, teachers should
   a. explain immediately, each time, that it hurts children to be hit or pushed.
   b. comfort the child who was hurt and ignore the aggressing child.
   c. be on the alert to give the child attention for nonaggressive interactions.
   d. at times other than stress occasions, teach and rehearse with the child ways to cope without hitting.
   e. plan together and with parents, strategies for handling the behavior.
6. Use time-out
   a. as seldom as possible.
   b. only after consistently more positive efforts have failed.
   c. at the first sign of noncompliance.
   d. at that point when staff, parents, and consultants agree there is no alternative.
   e. for very brief periods, usually from one to no more than three minutes at a time.
7. A child's noncompliance may result from
   a. too much pressure and too many rules.
   b. hearing loss or poor receptive language.
   c. not being given enough choices.
   d. just plain orneriness or general dislike of adults.
   e. not being given sufficient time to comply.
8. A temper tantrum
   a. is best ignored, but may become worse, at first.
   b. may be nearly impossible to ignore, especially when it gets more violent.
   c. should not be ignored unless the adult is prepared to ignore until the end.
   d. is a learned behavior and so responds to reinforcement.
   e. is an emotional behavior and does not respond to reinforcement.

C. *True or False. Choose the best answer.*

T F 1. Children who are cognitively delayed cannot help being aggressive and destructive.

T F 2. Thumb sucking is inappropriate and is a sign of potential developmental disorder.

T F 3. Children's safety must be a teacher's highest priority, according to Feeney's (1988) NAEYC ethics report.

T F 4. Children who disrupt classroom activities are usually in need of attention: therefore teachers should never withhold their attention from these children.

T F 5. Every child, even the unruly has "good" behaviors that adults can respond to.

T F 6. Many behavior problems can be managed through particular rearrangements of materials, activities, schedule, and adult attention.

T F 7. The term hyperactivity is often misapplied.

T F 8. Sharing and taking turns are learned behaviors.

REFERENCES

American Psychiatric Association. (1980). Diagnostic and statistical manual of mental disorders (3rd ed.). Washington, D.C.: American Psychiatric Association.

Allen, K.E., and Goetz, E.M. (1982). *Early childhood education: Special problems, special solutions.* Rockville, MD: Aspen Systems.

Allen, K.E., and Hart, B. (1984). *The early years: Arrangements for learning.* Englewood Cliffs, N.J.: Prentice Hall.

Bee, H. (1992). *The Developing Child.* New York: Harper & Row.

Caldwell, B.M. (1988). Ethic's commission member's comment. *Young Children,* 43:2, 50.

Conners, C.K. (1980). *Food additives and hyperactive children.* New York: Plenum.

Cook, R.E., Tessier, A., and Armbruster, V.B. (1987). Adapting early childhood curricula for children with special needs. Columbus, OH: Merrill.

Feeney, S. (1988). Ethic case studies: The aggressive child. *Young Children,* 43:2, 48–51.

Feingold, B.F. (1975). *Why your child is hyperactive.* New York: Random House.

Holm, V.A. (1978). The pediatrician with an interest in child development. In K.E. Allen, V.A. Holm, and R.L. Schiefelbusch (Eds.). *Early interventions: A team approach.* Baltimore: University Park Press.

McNellis, K.L. (1987). In search of the attentional deficit. In S.J. Ceci (Ed.), *Handbook of cognitive, social, and neuopsychological aspects of learning disabilities,* 2. Hillsdale, NJ: Erlbaum.

Peterson, N.L. (1987). *Early intervention for handicapped and at-risk children.* Denver: Love Publishing.

Spodek, B., Saracho, O.N., and Lee, R.C., (1984). *Mainstreaming young children.* Belmont, CA: Wadsworth.

Strain, P.S., Lambert, D.L., Kerr, M.M., Stagg, V., and Lenker, D. (1983). Naturalistic assessment of children's compliance to teachers' requests and consequences for compliance. *Journal of Applied Behavior Analysis,* 16, 2143–49.

Thomas, A., and Chess, S. (1986). The New York longitudinal study: From infancy to early adult life. In R. Plomin and J. Dunn (Eds.), *The study of the temperament: Changes, continuities, and challenges.* Hillsdale, NJ: Erlbaum.

Thompson, R.A., and Lamb, M.E., (1982). Stranger sociality and its relationship to temperament and social experience during the second year of life. *Infant Behavior and Development,* 5, 227–28.

Trites, R.L., and Laprade, K. (1983). Evidence for an independent syndrome of hyperactivity. *Journal of Child Psychology and Psychology,* 24, 573–86.

Worthington, B.S., Pipes, P.L., and Trahms, C.M. (1978). The pediatric nutritionist. In K.E. Allen, V.A. Holm, and R.L. Schiefelbusch (Eds.), *Early Intervention: A team approach.* Baltimore: University Park Press.

Looking Ahead:
Inclusion in the Nineties

MARY A. McEVOY* AND CHRISTINA SHERAN**

LOOKING AHEAD: INCLUSION IN THE NINETIES

It is with great joy that we announce the birth of our son, Jamie. He was born at 6:00 P.M. on Sunday, October 8—weighing in at 7 pounds and measuring 21 inches. He is a beautiful baby who we welcome into this world and into a large group of wonderful family and friends who have expressed their love and support in many ways. As you may know, young Jamie has already faced some difficult challenges. He was born with heart defects as well as Down syndrome. Nevertheless, he has inspired us with his courage and determination to survive. He has helped us understand a deeper meaning of love.

Recently we received this birth announcement. We have thought a lot about little Jamie since we heard of his birth. There have been happy thoughts, focusing on the joy that the birth of a baby brings, about how much there is to teach little Jamie and about the very special relationship that he has already developed with his family.

We also have thought a lot about the challenges that Jamie and his family will face. Perhaps one of the

highest hurdles will be the barrier to inclusion that will present itself when Jamie reaches an age where his needs for peer interaction become important. What will Jamie face? What does this term "inclusion" mean . . . and how will Jamie and his family achieve it?

The chapters in this book have provided an excellent overview of the current trends and issues related to preschool inclusion. Whether the issues are concerned with public policy, diversity, planning and program development, or implementation of inclusive practices, the field of early intervention has embraced "inclusion" and has continually addressed the critical issues and barriers affecting successful implementation of this important process.

For a number of years there has been a significant amount of research and program development, which has investigated the issue of preschool inclusion. In fact, since the early 1970s, a number of federally and locally funded projects have demonstrated that children can and do learn in inclusive settings (e.g., Alpert and McEvoy 1988; Fowler 1992; Strain, Guralnick, Smith, and Wolery 1994). Despite this, there remains a discrepancy between what the research tells us about inclusion and what is occurring in practice across the country. For example, administrative barriers, theoretical and conceptual differences between early childhood education, and differing perceptions of inclusion have impacted the widespread effectiveness of inclusive practices (Odom and McEvoy 1990).

As we look ahead to what preschool will be like for Jamie when he is 3 or 4 years old, we can identify at least three major issues related to inclusion that are receiving increasing attention at both the research and practice level. These include a focus on the social ecology of inclusion, an emphasis on inclusive communities, and

* Mary A. McEvoy, Ph.D. is a Professor in Early Childhood Special Education and Director of the Center for Early Education and Development at the University of Minnesota.

** Christina Sheran, M.S. is a speech-language pathologist and is currently a doctoral student in Early Childhood Special Education at the University of Minnesota.

Preparation of this chapter was supported, in part, by Grant #HO24D40006 from the US Department of Education. The authors wish to thank Judy Bartlett for her technical assistance on an earlier draft of this chapter.

the continuing identification and alleviation of administrative and programmatic barriers to inclusion. These areas are being investigated currently under the auspices of three federally funded projects. What follows is a brief description of each of these projects and how they are impacting the way that we think about and implement inclusive practices.

THE SOCIAL ECOLOGY OF INCLUSION

The United States Department of Education, Early Education Programs for Children with Disabilities, recently funded an Early Childhood Research Institute on Inclusion (ECRII). For the next five years, a consortium of investigators from Vanderbilt University, Washington State University–Vancouver, University of Maryland, and San Franciso State University will conduct a line of research that will identify barriers to inclusion, design strategies for overcoming these barriers, and examine the effect of these strategies. The work of this institute will focus on an in-depth program of research that will broaden our view of inclusion to include family and early interventionists' perceptions of inclusion, a definition of community inclusion, and social policy. In addition, particular attention will be given to the ways that families' cultural context affects inclusive program practices.

The implications for this research are significant. Unless we begin to identify and evaluate inclusion from a multiple systems level perspective we may be unable to affect meaningful change. For example, investigators from ECRII will be assessing how different stakeholders (e.g., parents, early interventionists, and administrators) define inclusion and how theses different definitions of inclusion are enacted by stakeholders in the system. In fact, there may actually be multiple "definitions" of inclusion within a single system . . . definitions that are impacted by differing perceptions, a child's abilities, and other variables. These different definitions and perceptions may work at cross purposes in supporting inclusion. However, it is possible that differing definitions actually enhance the social ecology of inclusion. In his classic book *The Future of Children*, Nick Hobbs (1975) provided a framework for inclusion that is still relevant today:

In schools that are most responsive to individual differences in abilities, interests, and learning styles of children, the mainstream is actually many streams. Sometimes as many streams as there are individual children, sometimes several streams as groups are formed for special purpose, sometimes one stream only as concerns of all coverage. We see no advantage in dumping children in an undifferentiated mainstream; but we see great advantages to all children, exceptional children included, in an education program modulated to the needs of individual children, singly, in small groups, or all together. Such a flexible arrangement may result in functional separations of exceptional children from time to time, but the governing principal would apply to all children; school programs should be responsive to the learning requirements of individual children and groupings should serve this end (p. 179).

Our goals for the nineties should incorporate Hobb's (1975) idea of inclusion so that we can be responsive to the different needs of children, families, and community providers. The work of ECRII, using an ecological systems conceptual framework, will assist us greatly in identifying these numerous "streams" of inclusion.

A FOCUS ON INCLUSIVE COMMUNITIES

As the United States becomes more culturally diverse, schools must prepare children to function effectively in a challenging and changing world. Thus, it appears critical that we move forward with an agenda of full inclusion within a child's greater community. A primary goal of education should be to bring individuals together to facilitate a deeper understanding of the diversity in our society and the importance of acceptance. A significant amount of research has shown that social interactions between young children with and without disabilities can be enhanced in inclusive preschool settings (see McEvoy, Odom, and McConnell 1992). However, we must begin to assure that these interactions are also reinforced in community settings outside of classroom hours. Abery (1991) has noted that unless children with and without disabilities participate in similar community experiences outside of the classroom, social relationships developed in school will remain, at best, on an acquaintanceship level.

Investigators on a second USDE project, directed by Susan Fowler (1993) at the University of Illinois at Urbana–Champaign, are looking at ways to facilitate inclusion in community settings. With a particular focus on creating environments that support communication and social interactions of young children, the FACTS/LRE Project outlines ways that parents and community providers can work collaboratively to facilitate the inclusion of young children. The Project emphasizes the transition of young children from infant care programs to community programs such as Head Start, nursery schools, and private daycare facilities, all of which may have very different needs related to inclusion.

Children bring a number of differences to any setting. Some children may be shy, may represent different cultural, ethnic, geographic or socio-economic differences, may have disabilities, or may have be at-risk for disabilities. The FACTS/LRE Project provides assistance to early interventionists to meet the needs of *all* children in inclusive community-based programs, not just children with disabilities (Venn et al. 1994).

ADMINISTRATIVE AND PROGRAMMATIC BARRIERS TO INCLUSION

The Research Institute on Preschool Mainstreaming (RIPM), funded by OSEP (1989–94), was directed by researchers form Allegheny Singer Research Institute, St. Peters Child Development Centers, Inc., and the University of Washington–Seattle. One of the primary foci of this research institute was the identification of administrative and programmatic barriers to preschool inclusion. Through policy analysis and interviews with key participants (early interventionists, parents, and administrators), Smith and Rose (1993) identified a number of policy issues and attitudinal barriers that prevent the provision of inclusive services to children and families. These include written regulations, standards, and statutes (e.g., program and personnel standards; fiscal, eligibility, transportation, and coordination policies) that are enacted at the local, state, and federal level. A significant conclusion of their research was that successful inclusive programs depend strongly on an administrative and professional commitment to integration.

A major strength of this research was not only the identification of barriers, but the provision of solutions to overcome them. In their *Administrators Policy Handbook on Preschool Mainstreaming*, Smith and Rose (1993) provide strategies for changing attitudinal and policy barriers. These include, among many other solutions, developing and implementing a standard compliance monitoring program to be used by all public programs, including Head Start, community-based preschool programs, and private programs. In addition, Smith and Rose suggest that administrators work collaboratively to develop policies and practices that stress interagency, interdisciplinary, and collaborative arrangements to assure that administrative issues are not the primary barrier to inclusive opportunities for all children.

SUMMARY

We are happy to report that little Jamie's parents are already promoting inclusion for him. He shops in a community grocery store with his father, he participates in early childhood family education programs with his mother, and he recently attended his first Minnesota Gophers hockey game. We hope that for Jamie and his family that his first experience with segregation does not co-occur with his enrollment in an early education program. The programmatic impact of the three projects highlighted above are significant. These projects, as well as numerous other efforts across the country, are enhancing and expanding the way that we think about and implement inclusive opportunities for young children like Jamie.

REFERENCES

Abery, B. (1991). Promoting social inclusion beyond the School Community. *IMPACT*, University of Minnesota, 4(3), 16–17.

Alpert, C. and McEvoy, M.A. (1988). The Peabody Least Restrictive Environment Project: Final Report. Unpublished Manuscript, Vanderbilt University, Nashville, Tennessee.

Fowler, S.A. (1993). *FACTS/LRE*. Family and Child Transitions into Least Restrictive Environments. Urbana-Champaign: University of Illinois.

Hobbs, N.A. (1975). *The future of children*. San Francisco: Jossey-Bass.

McEvoy, M.A., Odom, S.L., and McConnell, S.R. (1992). Peer social competence intervention for young children with disabilities. In S. Odom, S. McConnell, and M. McEvoy (Eds.), *Social Competence of Young Children with Disabilities: Issues and Strategies for Intervention*. 113–133. Baltimore: Brookes.

Odom, S.L. (1994). Early Childhood Research Institute on Inclusion. Vanderbilt University: Nashville, Tennessee.

Odom, S.L. and McEvoy, M.A. (1990). Mainstreaming at the preschool level. *Topics in Early Childhood Special Education*, 10(2), 48–61.

Smith, B.J. and Rose, D.F. (1994, August). Preschool integration: Recommendations for school administrtors. Paper presented at the First Annual Research Forum on Preschool Inclusion. Washington, DC.

Smith, B.J. and Rose, D.F. (1993). *Administrators Policy Handbook for Preschool Mainstreaming*. Cambridge: Brookline Books.

Strain, P.S., Guralnick, M.J., Smith, B.J., and Wolery, M. (1994). Research Institute on Preschool Mainstreaming. Paper presented at the First Annual Research Forum on Preschool Inclusion. Washington, DC.

Venn, M.L., Fink, D.B., Hadden, S., and Fowler, S.A. (1994). Facilitating inclusion in community settings: Creating environments that support the communication and social interactions of young children. *FACTS/LRE Project*, Urbana-Champaign: University of Illinois.

Glossary

Activity-based intervention: a method of providing early intervention services in which teaching opportunities are embedded in the regularly scheduled classroom activities.

Acute: the sudden onset of an illness; usually of short duration; a chronic problem may have acute episodes periodically.

Adaptive: the ability to meet the expectations of the community for common behaviors such as self-care skills and basic social skills such as knocking before entering through a closed door.

Advocacy group: individuals who band together to work for a particular cause; the Council for Exceptional Children works toward a free and appropriate education for all children with disabilities.

Affective: refers to feelings or emotions.

Amino acid(s): one of the chief components of proteins; they are obtained from the individual's diet or are *manufactured* by living cells.

Amniocentesis: a medical test for genetic abnormalities that can be done about the 16th week of pregnancy (gestation).

Anemia: a reduced number of red blood cells usually resulting from inadequate nutrition; often characterized by listlessness and lack of color; often treated with iron supplements.

Anomaly: an irregular feature. In early childhood special education, this often refers to a physical anomaly, that is an irregular physical feature such as a child who is born with missing fingers or a misshapen arm.

Antibody: a substance, manufactured either by the body or artificially, to help the body fight diseases of various kinds.

Aphasia: the imperfect ability to express oneself, or to comprehend spoken or written language; usually due to damage or disease in the language area of the cortex.

Attachment process: building positive and trusting bonds between individuals, usually infant and parents or major caregiver; closeness and affectionate interacting.

Attentional deficits (or ADD/ADHD): short attention span, distractability, and heightened levels of movement and physical activity.

Atypical development: any aspect of a child's physical or psychological makeup that is different from what is generally accepted as normal to early childhood.

Audiologist: a specially certified professional who focuses on hearing testing and hearing impairments.

Auditory: what is experienced through hearing.

Augmentative communication system: A communication system that is used to supplement a child's verbal language. The system may be sign language, picture symbols, or a sophisticated computer system such as a voice synthesizer.

Autonomy: self-directing, acting and reacting independently; the ability and willingness to make choices and decisions.

Behavior modification: a system by which particular environmental events are systematically arranged to produce specified behavior changes.

Best practices: recommended strategies that are agreed upon by members of a profession, or are developed by a professional organization (such as NAEYC).

Braille: a system of writing for the blind that uses patterns of raised dots *read* by the fingers.

Cardiac problems: those that involve the heart in terms of physical damage or poor functioning.

Case law: how courts interpret and implement laws. Much of the legal support for inclusion has come through case law.

Categorical funding: public or private money being assigned on the basis of particular types of handicaps or disabilities.

Cerebral palsy: a condition caused by injury to certain parts of the brain; usually results in paralysis and uncontrollable muscle movement in particular parts of the body.

Chemotherapy: the use of chemicals in the treatment of diseases, often cancer of various kinds.

Chorionic villus sampling (CVS): a test for genetic abnormalities. It can be done between the ninth and eleventh week of gestation; this procedure is often preferred because it can be conducted earlier than amniocentesis.

Chromosomal disorder: a vast number of developmental problems that come about at the moment of conception when the genetic information from each parent is merged and mapped out.

Chronic: term for a health problem of long duration and frequent recurrence.

Cochlea: a bony, snail-shaped structure in the inner ear that allows hearing to occur.

Cochlear implant: a device, surgically placed by opening the mastoid structure of the skull, that allows electrical impulses (sound) to be carried directly to the brain.

Compensatory education: educational programs (such as Head Start) that are designed for children who are disadvantaged. The purpose of these programs is provide these children with some of the opportunities (social, educational, medical) that most children enjoy.

Conductive hearing loss: refers to problems in the mechanical transmission of sounds through the outer or middle inner ear.

Congenital anomaly: a developmental difference present at birth; it is not necessarily of genetic origin.

Consolidate: this term refers, in children, to bringing together several new developmental learnings and applying them, as a *package*, to everyday living.

Contingency-type games: might be thought of as "if/then" interactions: as in peek-a-boo when the caregiver drapes a towel over her face and then baby lifts it and looks under, and both laugh.

Contractures: a permanent tightening of muscles and joints.

Control group: a group of individuals in an experiment who do not receive the treatment being tested.

Criterion-referenced assessment instruments: assessment instruments that describe a child's developmental level and progress according to performance on a prescribed set of skills, tasks, activities, and curriculum items.

Culturally sensitive: classroom activities, materials, and curricula that respect and acknowledge the different ethnicities that are represented in the classroom and community.

Cumulative deficits: an adding on or layering on of developmental problems; an undiagnosed hearing loss can result in an accumulation of additional problems (language, cognitive, and social).

Cumulative effect: an adding on or accumulation of consequences.

Custodial: in reference to infant caregiving, means protecting the child from harm and providing only for the child's biological need, rather than focusing, as well, on nurturing the infant and promoting his or her social, personal, and cognitive well-being.

Deficit curriculum model: focuses on a child's disabilities and delays, tries to remediate (cure) what is wrong with the child; in contrast, the developmental model builds on a child's strengths and works through the problems within a developmentally integrated curriculum.

Developmental continuum: the range of skills or behaviors among children in any one area of development—from no ball-throwing skill to spinning out a hard ball overhand; the child who can play catch probably is somewhere in the middle on that continuum.

Developmental predeterminism: proclaiming in advance how a child is going to turn out by making predictions based on both racial and family genetics without regard for culture and experience.

Developmental therapist: a merging of the roles of pediatric physical therapists and occupational therapists to promote understanding of the interrelatedness of the motor and the sensory systems and the viewpoint that the head, trunk, and extremities function as a unit, not as separate systems.

Didactic materials: manipulative materials in which the child's errors and successes are self-evident; the material and not the teacher provides the information. Montessori was the originator of many such materials.

Discretionary legislation: implementing (fulfilling) a law is up to decisions made by the individual state or local agency.

Discretionary program: implies choice or option; Part H. of PL 99-457 is a discretionary program: states can decide for themselves whether they will provide services for handicapped infants and toddlers and their families.

Disequilibrium: out of balance or out of harmony; a way of describing a child who seems to be experiencing temporary developmental irregularities.

Dyad: a pair of individuals whose relationship has social significance such as husband and wife or mother and child.

Dysfluency: hesitations, repetitions, omitted or extra sounds in speech patterns.

Dyslexia: an impaired ability to read; may also refer to an inability to understand what is read.

Earmold: that part of an amplification device (hearing aid) that is fitted to the individual's ear.

Echolalic: describes an individual whose language is characterized by meaningless repetition of words and sentences used intelligently by others; a condition often associated with autism and schizophrenia.

Egocentric: in reference to young children, it implies a restricted view of the world; from one perspective only, the child's own.

Empirical: information that is based on observation or experiment.

Empty calories: refers to foods in which there is high calorie content and low nutritional value; most foods with high sugar content are packed with empty (nonnutritive) calories.

Enabling environment: an environment, it can be classroom or home, that supports a child's optimal development. An enabling environment can support development through the activities provided, the structure provided, adult behavior, or many other types of support.

Enzymes: complex proteins that produce specific biological-chemical reactions in the body.

Ethnicities: groups of people who share a common racial, national, religious, linguistic, or cultural heritage. Most early education programs are made up of children representing many different ethnicities and require that teachers plan activities and use materials that are sensitive and relevant for children from diverse backgrounds.

Exceptional children: a term coined at the 1930 White House Conference on Handicapped Individuals to refer to all children who were different from normally developing children.

Failure-to-thrive: refers to under-sized infants whose bodies, for various reasons (organic, genetic, or environmental) either do not receive or cannot utilize the nurturance necessary for proper growth and development.

Family uniqueness: family uniqueness recognizes that every family is different. This perspective encourages teachers to honor and respect the unique characteristics of every family, rather than making generalizations about a family because of ethnicity or culture.

Fragile X syndrome: a chromosomal abnormality associated with mental retardation. This syndrome affects more males than females and the behavioral characteristics often resemble autism.

Functional: when referring to children's learning, functional refers to the child acquiring skills that are useful in everyday living.

Functionally illiterate: a person is functionally illiterate if they do not have adequate reading and writing skills to complete day-to-day tasks such as reading a bus schedule, reading notices from their child's school, completing a job application, or completing a registration form for their child to attend school.

Generalization: the spread of a learned response from the training situation to everyday, real life situations.

Generalize: when describing children's learning, to generalize is to apply what has been learned in one situation to a variety of other related situations.

Genetic mutation: a relatively permanent alteration in the chromosomal materials that control inherited characteristics.

Higher auditory cortex: that section of the gray matter of the brain that processes sound.

Holistic: a view of development that emphasizes the importance of the whole child and the interrelatedness of developmental domains.

Hydrocephalus: (overly simplified, *head filled with water*) the result of undrained fluids which leads to enlarged head and ultimate deterioration of the brain.

IDEA: The Individual with Disabilities Education Act. Federal law (PL 101-476) is the reauthorization of the original law (PL 94-142) that describes the types of educational services that must be provided to students from birth through 21 who have disabilities.

Immune system: that aspect of body functioning responsible for warding off diseases.

Incremental steps: each new step adds something to the preceding steps in a regular order; often a very small increase.

Individualized education plan (IEP): an educational plan that is mandated for every student with a disability (ages 3–21) by PL 94-142. The IEP is the blueprint for the services the child receives and a new IEP must be developed every year. It describes the child's current level of functioning and includes short- and long-term goals and objectives. All IEPs must be approved by the parents.

Individualized family service plan (IFSP): similar to an IEP, the IFSP describes services for very young children with disabilities (0–3) and their families. The IFSP is mandated by PL 99-457. The IFSP is written collaboratively with parents and describes the child's current strengths and needs. The IFSP describes what services will be provided and the major expected outcomes. Plans for the transition at age 3 are also included in the IFSP.

Informed parental consent: parent permission for a program, assessment, or specific activity (such as video taping) that is given after parents have been given information about different choices, possible risks, and benefits.

Interdisciplinary: refers to several different professions working together on a common problem; they share information and exchange roles, depending on the case.

In utero: means unborn; literally, in the uterus.

Irreversible developmental damage: one from which there is no recovery such as a missing arm or a child with Down syndrome; the irreversibility of the problem does not mean the individual cannot find ways of living life more normally.

Itinerant special education teacher: a special education teacher who works as a consultant with the teachers or directly with children with disabilities in a community-based early childhood program such as a child care or Head Start program. The itinerant teacher works with teachers from the community program and the family to write, implement, and evaluate the IEP or IFSP.

Jargon: refers to specialized language from a particular profession that is not easily understood by the ordinary person. When a medical person refers to an URI many people do not realize the topic often is the common cold.

Juvenile rheumatoid arthritis: a disorder that involves the joints: stiffness, swelling, and limited motion; may be accompanied by inflammation of the eyes which can have serious consequences.

Landmark legislation: a turning point or an entirely new approach to public policy. The Education for All Handicapped Children Act is considered landmark legislation because of provisions never before written into any law on behalf of the handicapped.

Learning theory: emphasizes the dominant role of environment and reinforcing experiences in all learning; *Social learning theory* adds other dimensions: that learning also occurs through observing and imitating and individuals can generate their own satisfactions (intrinsic reinforcement).

Least restrictive environment (LRE): children with disabilities must be educated alongside their typically developing peers to the greatest extent possible. The most normalized environment in which the needs of a child with disabilities can be met appropriately is called the least restrictive environment. LRE is also a principle that guides many placement decisions of children with special needs.

Linguists: individuals who specialize in languages, often being themselves proficient in several languages.

Manual interpreter: an individual who translates spoken language into sign language for those who are deaf.

Manual prompt: positioning the teacher's hand around the learner's and actually putting the learner through the motions.

Meningocele: similar to the *myelomeningocele* except that the protusion contains only the covering of the spinal cord and usually causes little or no neurological impairment.

Metabolize: the chemical process within living cells by which energy is manufactured so that the body can carry out its many functions.

Mieosis: the process of cell division that produces germ cells in which only one member of each chromosome pair is passed on to the new cell.

Mitosis: the process of cell division for all cells except germ cells.

Mobiles: an art form made up of balanced lengths of wire (or string) to which bits of various materials are attached so that air currents move them about when they are hung up.

Multidisciplinary: members of various disciplines working independently but exchanging their findings about a case; each concentrates on his or her own discipline.

Muscle tone: the interaction between the central nervous system and motor activity; it does not mean the same thing as muscle strength. Without muscle tone there is no voluntary movement.

Mutual gaze: the steady looking at each other's face that goes on between intact neonates and their mother or primary caregiver.

Myelomeningocele: a congenital protrusion of the spinal cord through the vertebrae; paralysis of the lower trunk and legs is often the result.

Neonatal: the first four weeks following birth.

Neonatal intensive care unit (NICU): the nursery in a hospital that treats newborn infants who are critically ill.

Neural: the nerves and nervous system.

Neurological: nerves and the nervous system in general.

Nonambulatory: the inability to move oneself about, usually the inability to walk.

Normalization: the care and education of people with disabilities should be as culturally normal as possible with services provided in regular community facilities rather than in segregated schools and institutions.

Norm-referenced assessments: assessment instruments that compare a child's developmental level to a normative sample of same-age peers.

Nonprogressive: in terms of diseases or other health problems, a condition that does not get worse; it stays "as is."

Obesity: an excess of body fat; considerably overweight for age and body build.

Occlusion: to obstruct; as used here, to prevent vision. *Occluder* would be the object the examiner used to prevent the child from seeing (usually one eye at a time).

Operant conditioning (also called instrumental conditioning): a type of learning that results from the consequences of a person's behavior; operating intentionally on some aspect of the environment to produce change.

Organic: within the individual's own body or neurological system.

Orientation and mobility specialist: a therapist who teaches vision impaired individuals awareness of their position in the environment and of significant objects within the environment (orientation) as well as how to move safely and efficiently (mobility) by utilizing their remaining senses including any useful vision.

Orthopedic: the bones and joints; a broken hip would be considered an orthopedic problem.

Paramedics: individuals who handle emergency medical situations. They have some medical training, but are not doctors.

Paraprofessional: a trained person who assists a certified professional as an aide.

Parent surrogate: someone appointed to act in place of someone else, a substitute parent.

Pathologist: a certified professional who focuses on diseases or impairments; a speech pathologist specializes in speech-related problems.

Pediatric ophthalmologist: a physician who specializes in diseases and malfunctioning of the eyes during the developmental years.

People first terminology: use of language in referring to people with disabilities that speaks of the person first and then the disability. For example, you would say "a child with autism" rather than "an autistic child." This type of language emphasizes abilities rather than limitations.

Peripheral vision: that degree of vision available at the outer edges of the eyes.

Pertussis: the clinical name for whooping cough.

Pervasive developmental disorder: a serious emotional disturbance that affects a child's social-emotional development. Behavioral characteristics are similar to autism.

Pincer grasp: the ability to pick up a small object using the forefinger and thumb (a developmental skill that does not come in until the latter part of the infant's first year).

Portfolio: a carefully selected collection of a child's work that is used to document growth and development.

Prader-Willi syndrome: a genetic disorder characterized by obesity, short stature, disorders in sexual development, as well as a tendency to behavioral and cognitive disabilities.

Prerequisite skills: skills which must be acquired before a next higher level skill can be attempted. Children must be able to stand before they can walk and be able to walk before they can run.

Preventive discipline: child management procedure for arranging the environment in ways that reduce the occurrence of maladaptive behaviors and increase the occurrence of appropriate behaviors.

Primitive reflexes: the responses the infant is born with: such behaviors as grasping, stepping, rooting, and sucking. Most of these drop out around 4 months of age and are replaced by similar but voluntary behaviors as in the sucking response.

Progressive: in terms of health, a condition that gets steadily better (or worse).

Proprietary: private, benefiting an owner.

Prosthesis: an artificial device replacing a body part (for example, a leg) that is damaged at birth or later removed.

Psychopathology: mental disorders as viewed from a psychological perspective.

Pull-out services: a model of delivering specialized support services such as physical therapy or speech therapy in which the child is removed from the classroom and taken to a special therapy setting. This model of service delivery is no longer recommended unless there are special circumstances that require that the child be removed from the classroom (for example, the physical therapy requires that a piece of the child's clothing be removed).

Pulmonary: refers to the lungs and respiratory (breathing) system.

Punishment: technically, it is the presentation of an aversive event, or the removal of a positive event contingent upon a response that decreases the probability of its occurrence.

Reciprocal relationships: where each member gives and receives in response to the giving and receiving of the other.

Reflexive: an involuntary body reaction to specific kinds of stimulation (a tap on the knee produces the knee jerk). Infants are born with a number of reflexes that should drop out as the nervous system matures.

Reinforcement: a general term for a consequence, an event, or procedure that increases or maintains the behavior it follows; pay checks are reinforcement for working.

Reinforcers: increase the behaviors which they follow; however, reinforcers are specific to individuals: candy is a reinforcer for many children but for many it is not.

Reliable and valid tests: **Reliable** relates to consistency: how accurate, dependable, and predictable a test is. **Valid** refers to tests that measure what they say they are measuring. For example, a low score on a verbal IQ test for a child with an undiagnosed hearing impairment is not likely to be valid. The test actually is not measuring the child's intelligence, though it purports to be doing so; instead it is a measure of how well the child's faulty hearing allows for interpretation of the questions.

Remission: in reference to health problems, temporary or permanent relief from the problem.

Repertoire: in describing behavior, it is the sum total and range of an individual's skills.

Residual hearing: refers to whatever degree of hearing is left to a person who is deaf or hearing impaired.

Residual vision: whatever remaining vision after disease or damage to the person's visual system.

Respiratory distress syndrome (RDS): a problem commonly found among premature infants because of the immature development of their lungs; may also occur in about one percent of full-term infants during the first days of life.

Respite care: temporary caregiving so that regular caregivers (usually the mother) gets some relief and time away from the sick or disabled individual.

Responsive environment: an environment that supports a child's efforts to explore and discover through interactions with other individuals, play materials, and activities.

Rote memorization: memorizing things without understanding them; being able to recite something that has little or no meaning for the one who memorizes it.

Salicylates: chemical compounds commonly known as salts of various kinds.

Secondary prevention: Secondary prevention refers to the early identification of handicapping conditions (or potentially handicapping conditions) and providing appropriate intervention services before the condition worsens or effects other areas of development (causes a *second layer* of problems).

Sensitivity: the ability of a screening test to identify correctly children with disabilities, and refer these children for further evaluation.

Sensorimotor: Piaget's term for the first major stage of cognitive development from birth to about 18 months when the infant moves from reflexive to voluntary behavior.

Sensorineural hearing loss: a malfunctioning of the cochlea or auditory nerve.

Sensory impairments: an impairment that affects the ability to sense the environment through a specific sensory modality such as hearing or vision. Some sensory impairments affect multiple senses.

Sensory system: any one of several ways individuals receive information or input from their environment; the most familiar sensory systems are vision, hearing, tasting, smelling, and touching or feeling.

Separation protest: the fussing or displeasure that an infant displays between 8 and 12 months (approximately) when mother or principle caregiver tries to leave.

Shunting: a process for implanting a tube (shunt) into the brain to allow proper circulation and drainage of fluids within the skull.

Signing: nonoral communication systems such as finger spelling or ASL (American Sign Language in which fingers, hands, arms, and upper torso are used to communicate ideas).

Socially deviant: refers to behavior that is atypical, different from the social norm; behavior not expected in a given situation; inappropriate or maladaptive behaviors.

Social ecology: the complex relationships between a child and the different people, places, and organizations in his/her life. For example, the relationship between a child's parents and his child care providers influences his social ecology.

Specificity: the ability of a screening test to identify correctly children who do not have a disability and not refer these children for further evaluation.

Sphincter muscles: those muscles that determine bowel and bladder control (the retention and release of urine and fecal material).

Stabile: similar to mobiles, stabiles are designed to be stationary.

Standardized norms: norms based on a large number of averaged scores of similar age children on the same test items. For example, the average 17-month-old can build a tower of 3 cubes.

Standardized tests: assessment instruments include precise instructions for administration and scoring. Most standardized tests are norm-referenced. That is, they compare a child's progress and development to a sample of other children the same age.

Stigmata (stigma): an identifying mark or characteristic: a diagnostic sign of a disease or disability.

Surrogate: a person appointed to act for another person, to serve in their stead; surrogate parents serve as substitute parents.

Symptom: a sign or indication there may be a problem. (Sneezing and a runny nose often are symptoms of an allergy problem.)

Tactile: what is learned or perceived through touch.

Tangible reinforcers: material things that the individual likes; in children, favorite foods and drinks, toys, stickers and so on (older children usually like money).

Temperament: an individual's psychological makeup or personality traits.

Therapeutic: treatment of a disease or disability.

Threshold: the physical or psychological point at which an individual begins to respond to certain kinds of stimulation.

Toxemia: toxins (poisons) in the system that lead to medical problems, such as poorly functioning kidneys or high blood pressure in pregnant women.

Transactional relationships: the understanding that children and adults influence each other in their ongoing relationships and that both child and adult learn from these interactions. Future interactions are influenced by earlier interactions.

Transdisciplinary team: a team that shares the responsibilities for assessment, program planning, implementation, and evaluation across members. Team members from different disciplines share discipline-specific roles, information, and expertise.

Visual acuity: how well an individual is able to see; keenness of vision.

Voice synthesizer: a computer than can produce spoken words. This type of assistive technology is often used by people with severe communication disabilities.

Voluntary motor responses: those that the individual controls as when the involuntary or primitive sucking reflex gives way to an infant deciding when and if she or he will suck.

Wedges, bolsters, and prone boards: therapeutic positioning devices used by physical (developmental) therapists in treating individuals with impaired motor skills.

Selected List of Screening Tools and Assessment Instruments for Use with Infants and Young Children

The first section describes screening instruments that are designed to identify possible developmental problems. The second section describes norm-referenced instruments that are designed to determine eligibility for special education services. The final section describes criterion-referenced instruments that can be used for program planning and evaluation.

SCREENING INSTRUMENTS

AGS Early Screening Profiles
(Harrison, et al. 1990)

This screening instrument is designed to be used to identify potential delays and disabilities in children between the ages of two years and six years, eleven months. This screening instrument uses both direct testing of the target child and parent and teacher questionnaires. This screening instrument has seven components: cognitive/language profile, motor profile, articulation survey, self-help/social profile, home survey, health history survey, and the behavior survey.

Battelle Developmental Screening Test
(Newborg, Stock, Wnek, Guidubaldi, & Sviniski, 1988)

This 96-item screening instrument consists of a subset of items from the Battelle Developmental Inventory. It is designed to identify children from birth to eight years old who may have developmental disabilities. The BDI Screening Test assesses children in five domains: personal-social, motor, adaptive, communication, and cognitive.

Denver II
(Frankenburg & Dodds, 1990)

This instrument is a revision of the Denver Developmental Screening Test (1975). This screening tool is designed to be used with children birth through six and is designed to identify potential delays in four areas: fine motor adaptive, language, gross motor, and personal-social. This screening instrument is often used by pediatricians and their staff.

Developmental Indicators for the Assessment of Learning - Revised (DIAL-R)
(Mardell-Czudnowski & Goldenberg, 1990)

This screening tool is designed to identify potential delays in children two to six years old. Children are screened individually in the areas of motor, communication, and concepts. Administration of each area can be completed by different test operators, or the entire assessment can be administered by one operator. This screening instrument is often used in Head Start classrooms.

NORM-REFERENCED INSTRUMENTS

Battelle Developmental Inventory
(Newborg, Stock, & Wnek, 1988)

This instrument includes both a screening and a full multi-domain battery for children from birth through eight. Test items are grouped into the following domains: personal-social, adaptive, motor, cognitive, and communication. The BDI utilizes direct testing, interviewing, and observation to collect assessment information. This instrument can be used to determine eligibility for special education services.

Bayley Scales of Infant Development II
(Bayley, 1993)

This instrument includes norms for children from 1 to 42 months, and is one of the most widely used norm-referenced assessments with very young children. This instrument is divided into three scales: mental, motor, and behavior. This test can be used to identify very young children with developmental disabilities, however, research indicates that an infant's scores on the test do not predict later IQ performance reliably.

Scales of Independent Behavior
(Bruiniks, et al., 1984)

The purpose of this norm-referenced instrument is to measure adaptive (e.g., self-care skills) and problem behaviors of children and young adults (norms are provided from birth through 18 years). Information is collected by interviewing a key informant (e.g., parent or teacher).

Test of Early Language Development - 2 (TELD-2)
(Hresko, Reid, & Hammill, 1991)

This instrument is designed to assess expressive and receptive language skills in children between the ages of 2 and 8. This instrument can be used to determine eligibility for special education, determine a child's strengths and weaknesses in the area of communication, and document a child's progress.

CRITERION-REFERENCED INSTRUMENTS

Assessment, Evaluation, and Programming System (AEPS)
(Bricker, 1992)

This curriculum-based instrument is designed for children birth to three (a version for children 3–6 is currently being developed). The AEPS is a linked system, integrating assessment, program planning, implementation, and evaluation. This system includes a criterion-referenced assessment for children, family reporting forms, a curriculum, planning documents, and child progress monitoring forms. The AEPS includes assessment and curriculum information for six domains: fine motor, gross motor, adaptive, cognitive, social-communication, and social.

Brigance Diagnostic Inventory of Early Development - Revised
(Brigance, 1991)

This instrument can be used to assess children from birth to seven in 11 developmental domains: social-emotional, fine motor, preambulatory, gross motor, adaptive, speech and language, general knowledge and comprehension, reading readiness, basic reading, writing, and math. This test is developed to assist teachers in program planning rather than determining a child's eligibility or diagnostic category.

Hawaii Early Learning Profile (HELP)
(Furuno et al., 1988)

This profile, based on a *developmental milestones* model for all areas of development include tasks and skills suitable for children from birth to three. Many interdisciplinary teams find this profile useful in identifying problems and prescribing intervention strategies. The HELP profile provides an easy to read chart of developmental milestones for each developmental domain. Many professionals find these charts helpful in communicating with families and child care providers.

Early Learning Accomplishment Profile (ELAP)
(Glover, Preminger, & Sanford, 1978)

This assessment instrument is designed to assist in program planning for children from birth to 36 months. The following domains are represented in the assessment: gross motor, fine motor, cognitive, language, adaptive, and social-emotional. This instrument is designed to be administered by a teacher in a classroom or child care setting.

Preschool Profile

	Gross Motor Skills	Fine Motor Skills	Preacademic Skills	Self-Help Skills	Music/Art/Story Skills	Social Skills and Play Skills	Understanding Language	Oral Language
0–12 months	Sits without support. Crawls. Pulls self to standing and stands unaided. Walks with aid. Rolls a ball in imitation of adult.	Reaches, grasps, puts object in mouth. Picks things up with thumb and one finger (pincer grasp). Transfers object from one hand to other hand. Drops and picks up toy.	Looks directly at adult's face. Tracks objects (follows them smoothly with eyes). Imitates gestures: e.g., pat-a-cake, peek-a-boo, bye-bye. Puts block in, takes block out of container. Finds block hidden under cup.	Feeds self cracker: munching, not sucking. Holds cup with two hands, drinks with assistance. Holds out arms and legs while being dressed.	Fixes gaze on pictures in book.	Smiles spontaneously. Responds differentially to strangers and familiar persons. Pays attention to own name. Responds to 'no.' Copies simple actions of others.	Looks at people who talk to him. Responds differentially to variety of sounds: e.g., phone, vacuum, closing doors, etc. Responds to simple directions accompanied by gestures: e.g., *come, give, get.*	Makes different vowel sounds. Makes different consonant-vowel combinations. Vocalizes to the person who has talked to him. Uses intonation patterns that sound like phrases; e.g., intonations that sound like scolding, asking, telling.
12–24 months	Walks alone. Walks backward. Picks up object without falling. Pulls toy. Seats self in child's chair. Walks up and down stairs with aid.	Builds tower of 3 cubes. Puts 4 rings on stick. Places 5 pegs in pegboard. Turns pages 2 or 3 at a time. Scribbles.	Follows one direction involving familiar actions and objects: e.g., *Show me (toy). Give me (body part). Get a (familiar object).* Completes 3 piece formboard. Matches similar objects.	Uses spoon, spilling little. Drinks from cup, one hand, unassisted. Chews food. Removes garment. Zips, unzips large zipper. Indicates toilet needs.	Moves to music. Looks at pictures in book, patting, pointing to, or naming objects or people. Paints with whole arm movement, shifts hands, makes strokes.	Recognizes self in mirror or picture. Refers to self by name. Plays by self, initiates own play activities. Imitates adult behaviors in play. Plays with water and sand. Loads, carries, dumps. Helps put things away.	Responds to specific words by showing what was named: e.g., toys, family members, clothing, body parts. Responds to simple directions given without gestures: e.g., *go, sit, find, run, walk.*	Asks for items by name. Answers *What's that?* with name of object. Tells about objects or experiences with words used together (2-3 words): e.g., *more juice.*
24–36 months	Runs forward well. Jumps in place, two feet together. Stands on one foot, with aid. Walks on tiptoe. Kicks ball forward. Throws ball, without direction.	Strings 4 large beads. Turns pages singly. Snips with scissors. Holds crayon with thumb and fingers, not fist. Uses one hand consistently in most activities. Imitates circular, vertical, horizontal strokes.	Matches shapes. Stacks 5 rings on peg, in order. Demonstrates number concepts to 2 (i.e., selects set of 1 or 2; can tell how many, 1 or 2).	Uses spoon, no spilling. Gets drink unassisted. Uses straw. Opens door by turning handle. Puts on/takes off coat. Washes/dries hands with assistance.	Participates in simple group activity: e.g., sings, claps, dances. Chooses picture books, points to fine detail, enjoys repetition. Paints with some wrist action, makes dots, lines, circular strokes. Rolls, pounds, squeezes, pulls clay material.	Plays near other children. Watches other children, joins briefly in their play. Defends own possessions. Engages in domestic play. Symbolically uses objects, self in play. Builds with blocks in simple lines.	Responds to *put it in* and *put it on.* Responds by selecting correct item: big vs. little objects; one vs. one more object. Identifies objects by their use: e.g., *Show me what mother cooks on by showing stove, or Show me what you wear on your feet* by showing shoe.	Asks questions. Answers *Where is it?* with prepositional phrases: e.g., *in the box, on the table.* Answers *What do you do with a ball?* e.g., throw, catch. Tells about something with functional sentences which carry meaning; e.g., *me go store or me hungry now.*

341

	Gross Motor Skills	Fine Motor Skills	Preacademic Skills	Self-help Skills	Music/Art/Story Skills	Social Skills and Play Skills	Understanding Language	Oral Language
36–48 months	Runs around obstacles. Walks on a line. Balances on one foot 5 seconds. Hops on one foot. Pushes, pulls, steers wheeled toys. Rides (i.e., steers and pedals) trike. Uses slide without assistance. Jumps over 15 cm. (6") high object, landing on both feet together. Throws ball with direction. Catches ball bounced to him.	Builds tower of 9 cubes. Drives nails and pegs. Copies circle. Imitates cross.	Matches 6 colors. Makes tower of 5 blocks, graduated in size. Does 7 piece puzzle. Counts to 5, in imitation of adults. Demonstrates number concept to 3.	Pours well from pitcher. Spreads substances with knife. Buttons/unbuttons large buttons. Washes hands unassisted. Cleans nose when reminded. Uses toilet independently. Follows classroom routine with minimum teacher assistance. Knows own sex. Knows own age. Knows own last name.	Knows phrases of songs. Listens to short simple stories (5 minutes). Painting: names own picture, not always recognizable; demands variety of color. Draws head of person and one other part. Manipulates clay materials: e.g., rolls balls, snakes, cookies, etc.	Joins in play with other children; begins to interact. Shares toys, takes turns with assistance. Begins dramatic play, acting out whole scenes; e.g., traveling, playing house, pretending to be animals.	Responds to *put it beside and put it under.* Responds to commands involving 2 objects: e.g., *Give me the ball and the shoe.* Responds to commands involving 2 actions: e.g., *Give me the cup and put the shoe on the floor.* Responds by selecting correct item: e.g., hard vs. soft objects. Responds to *walk fast by increased pace, and to walk slowly by decreased pace.*	Answers *Which one do you want?* by naming it. Answers *if ...what what & when* questions: e.g., *If you had a penny, what would you do? What do you do when you're hungry?* Answers questions about function: e.g., *What are books for?* Asks for or tells about with grammatically correct sentences: e.g., *Can I go to the store? I want a big cookie.*
48–60 months	Walks backward heel-toe. Jumps forward 10 times, without falling. Walks up/down stairs alone, alternating feet. Turns somersault.	Cuts on a line continuously. Copies cross. Copies square. Prints a few capital letters.	Points to, names 6 basic colors. Points to, names 3 shapes. Matches related common objects: e.g., shoe, sock, foot; apple, orange, banana. Demonstrates number concept to 4 or 5.	Cuts food with a knife; e.g., sandwich, celery. Knows own city/street. Follows instructions given to group.	Sings entire songs. Recites nursery rhyme. "Reads" from pictures (i.e., tells story). Recognizes story and retells simple facts. Painting: makes and names recognizable pictures. Draws a person with 2–6 parts.	Plays and interacts with other children. Dramatic play: closer to reality; attention to detail, time and space. Plays dress-up. Builds complex structures with blocks.	Responds by showing penny-nickel-dime. Responds to command involving 3 actions: e.g., *Give me the cup, put the shoe on the floor, and hold the pencil in your hand.* Above items are selected from *The Sequenced Inventory of Communication Development*, University of Washington Press, University of Washington, 1975	Asks how questions. Answers verbally to *Hi* and *How are you?* Tells about something using past tense and future tense. Tells about something using conjunctions to string words and phrases together: e.g., *I have a cat and a dog and a fish.*
60–72 months	Runs lightly on toes. Walks a balance beam. Can cover 2 meters (6'6"), hopping. Skips. Jumps rope. Skates.	Cuts out simple shapes. Copies triangle. Traces diamond. Copies first name. Prints numerals 1–5. Colors within lines. Has adult grasp of pencil. Has handedness well established (i.e., child is left or right handed).	Sorts objects on one dimension: i.e., by size or by color or by shape. Does 15 piece puzzle. Copies block design. Names some letters. Names some numerals. Names penny, nickel, dime, quarter. Counts by rote to 10. Can tell what number comes next.	Dresses self completely. Learns to distinguish left from right. Ties bow. Brushes teeth unassisted. Crosses street safely. Relates clock time to daily schedule.	Recognizes rhyme. Acts out stories. Draws a person with head, trunk, legs, arms, and features. Pastes and glues appropriately. Models objects with clay.	Chooses own friend(s). Plays simple table games. Plays competitive games. Engages in cooperative play with other children involving group decisions, role assignments, fair play. Uses construction toys to make things: e.g., house of legos, car of rig-a-jig.	See preacademic skills.	Child will have acquired basic grammatical structures including plurals, verb tenses and conjunctions. Following this developmental ability, the child practices with increasingly complex descriptions and conversations.

This profile is a working draft only and was prepared by the Communication Disorders Specialists Linda Lynch, Jane Rieke, Sue Soltman, and Teachers Donna Hardman and Mary O'Conor: The Communication Program was funded initially as a part of the Model Preschool Center for Handicapped Children by Grant No. OEG-072-5371 U.S. Office of Education, Program Development Branch, BEH., Washington, D.C. at the Experimental Education Unit (WJ-10) of the College of Education and Child Development and Mental Retardation Center, University of Washington, Seattle, WA

Preschool Profile (continued)

Sources of Information, Support, and Training Material for Teachers and Parents of Children with Developmental Disabilities

PROFESSIONAL ORGANIZATIONS

(*Note:* The memberships of most of these organizations include professionals, family members, and students)

Alexander Graham Bell Association for the Deaf
3417 Volta Pl., NW
Washington, DC 20007
(202) 337-5520

American Council for the Blind (ACB)
1010 Vermont Ave., NW
Suite 1010
Washington, DC 20005
(800) 424-8666

American Cleft Palate Foundation
331 Salk Hall
University of Pittsburgh
Pittsburgh, PA 15261
(412) 681-9620

American Association on Mental Retardation (AAMR)
1719 Kalorama Rd., NW
Washington, DC 20009-2683
(202) 387-1968

American Speech-Language-Hearing Association
  (ASHA)
10801 Rockville Pike
Rockville, MD 20852-3279
(800) 638-8255

Association for the Care of Children's Health
7919 Woodmont Ave., Suite 300
Bethesda, MD 20814
(301) 654-6549

Autism Society of America
234 Newcombe St., SE
Washington, DC
(202) 561-8527

Council for Exceptional Children (CEC)
   Division for Early Childhood (DEC)
1920 Association Dr.
Reston, VA 22091
(703) 620-3660

Epilepsy Foundations of America
4351 Garden City Dr.
Landover, MD 20785
(800) EFA-1000

March of Dimes Birth Defects Foundation
1275 Mamoroneck Ave.
White Plains, NY 10603
(914) 428-7100

Muscular Dystrophy Association
810 Seventh Ave.
New York, NY 10019
(212) 586-0808

National Association for the Deaf
814 Thayer Ave.
Silver Spring, MD 20910
(301) 587-1788

National Association for the Education of Young
    Children (NAEYC)
1834 Connecticut Ave., NW
Washington, DC 20009-5786
(202) 232-8777

National Association for Sickle Cell Disease, Inc.
4221 Wilshire Blvd., Suite 360
Los Angeles, CA 90010
(800) 421-8453

National Association for the Visually Handicapped
22 West 21st St., 6th Floor
New York, NY 10010
(212) 889-3141

National Down Syndrome Society
141 Fifth Ave.
New York, NY 10010
(800) 221-4602

National Easter Seal Society
2023 West Ogden Ave.
Chicago, IL 60612
(312) 243-8400

National Federation of the Blind
1800 Johnson St.
Baltimore, MD 21230
(301) 659-9314

National Head Injury Foundation
PO Box 567
Framingham, MA 01701
(617) 679-7473

Spina Bifida Association of America
343 South Dearborn St.
Room 310
Chicago, IL 60604
(800) 621-3141

The Association for Persons with Severe Handicaps
    (TASH)
29 W. Susquehanna Ave., #210
Baltimore, MD 21204
(410) 828-8274

United Cerebral Palsy Association
66 East 34th St.
New York, NY 10016
(212) 481-6300

FAMILY ORGANIZATIONS

Association for Retarded Citizens of the U.S. (ARC)
[formerly National Association for Retarded Citizens-
    NARC]
2501 Ave J.
Arlington, TX 11357
(800) 433-5255
(This association has many active local chapters)

Children with Attention Deficit Disorder (CHADD)
1859 North Pine Island Rd., #185
Plantation, FL 33322
(305) 384-6869
(This association has many active local chapters)

Parents helping Parents
47 Maro Dr.
San Jose, CA 95127
(408) 272-4774

Parent to Parent
301 W. Franklin St., Room 1608
Virginia Commonwealth University
Box 3020
Richmond, VA 23284-3020
(804) 225-3875
(This association has many active local chapters)

Sibling Support Project
Children's Hospital and Medical Center
PO Box 5371, CL-09
Seattle, WA 98105-0371
(206) 368-4911

SOURCES FOR INFORMATION AND OTHER RESOURCES

Clearinghouse on Students with Disabilities
Office of Special Education and Rehabilitative Services
Department of Education
Switzer Building, Room 3119-S
Washington, DC 20202
(202) 245-0080

National Center for Clinical Infant Programs
2000 14th St., N., # 380
Arlington, VA 22201-2500
(703) 528-4300

National Information Center for Handicapped
    Children and Youth (NICHCY)
PO Box 1492
Washington, DC 20013
(703) 522-0870

National Institute on Child Health and Human
    Development
9000 Rockville Pike
Building 31, Room 2A32
Bethesda, MD 20205
(301) 496-4143

Becoming Aware of Baby and You: Examples of Ways to Interact with Your Baby[a]

MONTHS OF AGE	MOTOR	COGNITIVE	LANGUAGE	PERSONAL/ SOCIAL	PERCEPTUAL (ESSENTIAL EXPERIENCES)[b]
Birth to 3 months	Lay on side or stomach, often nuzzle, cuddle, stroke baby gently Rhythmically rock in rocking chair Slowly move object in 180º arc for baby to follow with eyes Hold in different positions: head lifted to shoulder, face forward or to side	Expose to soft toys and musical toys Place rattle in hand—gently pull, change from hand to hand Carry baby with you, preferably in front carrier	Look at and establish eye contact when talking with baby Smile, talk, and sing to baby Smile, talk, and sing in direct response to baby's sounds, movements, and cries—from different places in room Encourage sucking and tongue activity Imitate baby's sounds	Respond to needs when baby cries Hold baby, especially when feeding Respond with animated expressions to your baby Smile at your baby Play with and enjoy your baby	Assist baby in staying calm and interested in his/her surroundings—internal regulation
3–6 months	Massage baby, rubbing arms, legs, and body with lotion Gently bounce on knee (while supporting upper body) Hold in standing position Anticipate that baby will soon be rolling—tummy to back and back to tummy—crawling and sitting Place on blanket with freedom to roll	Provide different views from crib Put bells on booties Put patterned sheet on bed Provide objects to be picked up and reached for—with both arms Provide mirror so baby can look at reflection Attach toy to string for baby to pull	Talk about occurrences as you take baby outside, to store, etc. Play music and recordings of nursery rhymes Imitate baby's sounds Encourage child to locate sound source with eyes and to imitate your sounds Provide soft dolls and animal toys to elicit vocalizations	Respond to baby's smiles, coos, and gurgles Respect baby's attitudes toward strangers Respond as consistently as able to attention seeking behavior	Assist baby in making a rich, deeply multi-sensory investment in the animate world—attachment

MONTHS OF AGE	MOTOR	COGNITIVE	LANGUAGE	PERSONAL/ SOCIAL	PERCEPTUAL (ESSENTIAL EXPERIENCES)[b]
6–9 months	Provide small items to be picked up with "swipe" motion Allow baby to crawl (avoid walkers when appropriate) Assist child as attempts to sit up (place pillows so child isn't hurt by fall) Offer toys barely beyond hands to encourage reaching	Position baby so able to watch you Provide mirror for baby to see self and others Provide mouthable (chewable, suckable) objects to manipulate and explore, passing hand to hand	Call baby by name Imitate baby's da-da, ma-ma, and ba-ba Wave bye-bye, play pat-a-cake Sing nursery rhymes with accompanying simple actions aimed at involving baby Use gestures and hand signals and accompanying words	Support baby's efforts at independence (e.g., let hold spoon) Offer small amounts of liquid from a spoon in preparation for drinking from a cup Provide small pieces of soft finger foods for self-feeding Explore the house—together Label and talk about body parts	Assist your baby to achieve purposeful "communications" and differentiated responses to the world
9–12 months	Explore space moving around, under, and over furniture Let baby "unwrap" items (use paper or cloth, be sure paper doesn't go in mouth) Roll a ball to baby, retrieve and repeat "Baby safe" surroundings for crawling and standing child Be ready to catch child as she pulls self to standing, stands momentarily, and walks holding to furniture, etc.	Place toys in container baby can dump and refill Play "cause and effect" games, tailoring your response to baby Hide toys or ticking clock and help baby find (baby can watch as you hide the object!) Clap hands together, bang toys together—together! Push buttons with one finger	Talk with baby in front of a mirror and acknowledge yourselves Read books and tell baby simple stories When child offers you an object—accept, comment upon, and give it back Respond to speech sounds Introduce "no-no" consistently	Enjoy and admire your baby's "antics" (e.g., wearing basket or empty box as hat!) Play "where's baby?" hiding behind furniture Let baby try to feed self, hold cup, wash with cloth or sponge Use baby's name when giving simple commands, directions or requests Refer to self as "ma-ma" or "da-da"	Assist your baby to initiate complex, organized assertive, innovative, integrated behavioral and emotional patterns
12–15 months	When someone is available to watch, let child crawl up and down stairs Crumple paper into balls and throw Lift child up to touch toys that are high and out of reach Provide opportunities to shovel sand and empty into bucket Take short "walks" together	Provide photos or pictures of familiar events you and your baby are engaging in Provide "toy" or real (when safe) objects to use to imitate your actions (telephone, broom, etc.) Introduce water and sand play when you can supervise	Provide words for actions When child is trying to do something new, provide models and verbal directions Play games where you enact action words Try to understand baby's feelings and say words for those feelings; express your feelings with words	Plan plenty of time for undressing and make it easy Make clean-up time a game—gradually expect more and more cooperation Help child to express feelings in socially acceptable ways Provide small amounts of liquid in a small cup Provide safe bits of finger foods for self-feeding	

MONTHS OF AGE	MOTOR	COGNITIVE	LANGUAGE	PERSONAL/ SOCIAL	PERCEPTUAL (ESSENTIAL EXPERIENCES)[b]
			Record words baby uses Attempt to interpret baby's gestures (shaking head for "no-no" and holding out arms to be picked up)		

[a] Adapted from Irving Preschool Educational and Diagnostic Center, 1982.
[b] For further information, see Greenspan & Porges, 1984.

Index